The Journals and Miscellaneous Notebooks

of

RALPH WALDO EMERSON

❧ GENERAL EDITORS ☙

WILLIAM H. GILMAN   ALFRED R. FERGUSON

MERRELL R. DAVIS

MERTON M. SEALTS, JR.   HARRISON HAYFORD

The Journals and
Miscellaneous Notebooks
of
RALPH WALDO EMERSON

VOLUME IV

1832–1834

EDITED BY

ALFRED R. FERGUSON

THE BELKNAP PRESS

OF HARVARD UNIVERSITY PRESS

Cambridge, Massachusetts

1 9 6 4

Preface

Though the editor of this volume can hardly hope to discharge his full obligation to individuals, institutions, and foundations by acknowledgment alone, the incantatory process of naming may serve as a partial expression of gratitude.

The Ralph Waldo Emerson Association has continued to provide regular grants-in-aid which have been indispensable to the progress of the edition. The Association generously added a supplemental grant for research on this volume and, in the person of its treasurer, Mr. David Emerson, has been unfailingly helpful.

The Fred L. Emerson Foundation has provided a substantial grant-in-aid. Ohio Wesleyan University supplied a sabbatical leave as well as grants for travel and for summer research.

For active assistance in typing, research, or proofreading, the editor wishes to express his gratitude to Miss Millicent Kalaf, who typed the bulk of the text, and her predecessor, Mrs. Linda Gallasch. His thanks are also due to Mrs. John A. Leermakers, Ralph Harry Orth, Roy Ward, Roland Boecklin, and Mrs. Alfred R. Ferguson.

Professor William A. Jackson, Director of the Houghton Library, has shown unflagging kindness; Mr. William Bond and Miss Carolyn Jakeman, also of the Houghton Library, have offered not only constant encouragement but wise advice and technical aid. Mr. Robert H. Haynes and Mr. Foster Palmer have courteously made the resources of Widener Library available. For various courtesies the editor is indebted to Professor Wallace Williams, Mrs. Edith W. Gregg, the Concord Antiquarian Society, and the staffs of Houghton, Widener, Lamont, the University of Rochester, and Ohio Wesleyan University libraries.

Unless otherwise noted translations of quotations from Latin and Greek are from the Loeb Classical Library and are reprinted by permission of the Harvard University Press and the Loeb Classical Library.

The editor designated on the title page of this volume has been responsible for its preparation; the surviving General Editors have actively contributed in various ways.

A.R.F.   M.M.S.
W.H.G.   H.H.

Contents

FOREWORD TO VOLUME IV

The Journals: 1832–1834   ix
Chronology   xvii
Symbols and Abbreviations   xx

PART ONE

THE TEXTS OF THE JOURNALS

Q   3
Sicily   102
Italy   134
Italy and France   163
Scotland and England   209
Sea 1833   236
A   249
Maine   388

PART TWO

THE TEXTS OF THE MISCELLANEOUS NOTEBOOKS

France and England   395
Pocket Diary 2   420
Composition   427

Appendix   441
Textual Notes   445
Index   447

vii

Illustrations

Following page 298

Plate I   *Journal Q, page 38*

Plate II   *Sicily, page 14*

Plate III   *Sea 1833, page 3*

Plate IV   *Journal A, page 100*

Foreword to Volume IV

One pattern of Emerson's life from the spring of 1832 through the end of 1834 may be metaphorically described by the first and last entries in the journals of the period. On March 10, 1832, Emerson began a new journal, entitled Q, almost exactly three years after his ordination to the ministry in his father's church, the Second Church on Hanover Street in Boston. During his three years in the ministry he had written a great many notes for and first drafts of sermons in his journals. Now in his new journal he began by jotting down some ideas on the follies of gluttony, the dangers of unrestrained appetite, and the need for Christian temperance. Out of these notes he framed his 147th sermon, a somewhat conventional discourse on temperance which he delivered to his congregation on March 18.

Perhaps because, as he himself was fond of noting, "truth is a circle," he recurred to the subject of temperance in his final entry in Journal A on December 29, 1834. In this entry, however, he was making no notes for a sermon; his notes would now be used either in a lecture or, recording as they did his deepest convictions on the primacy of the soul, possibly in a first draft of an essay. "Excite the soul, & the weather & the town & your condition in the world all disappear, the world itself loses its solidity, nothing remains but the soul & the Divine Presence in which it lives," he wrote. His interest in temperance had obviously shifted from how to be good to the relationship of a virtue to the permanent moral laws of the universe. After he recalled Aristotle's distinction between temperance as a means and temperance as an end, he concluded his notes by reminding himself that this virtue, like all others, "becomes dowdy in a sermon." The circle from one sort of temperance to another was complete, but within the enclosing lines Emerson's thought had veered.

No longer was he writing out his thoughts as raw material for a sermon. During these years he had left the pulpit of his fathers to preach from more secular platforms. He had turned his back on the Unitarian ministry to become a spokesman for all America, to minister to "all who would live in the spirit." By the end of 1834 he had begun to lecture in such buildings as those which housed the Mechanics Institution, the Boston Society for the Diffusion of Useful Knowledge, or the Lyceum lecture series. In his final entry for 1834 he set down in his journal his own hard-won awareness of a transformation: ". . . when a man speaks from a deeper conviction than any party faith, . . . when he declares the simple truth he finds his relationship to the Calvinist or Methodist or Infidel at once changed. . . ."

That his relation to his own party faith, to the Unitarianism in which he had begun his ministry, would change, seems predictable to the reader of his journals. For some years his comments had been increasingly unorthodox and his criticism of the established church sharper. Insistence upon the genuine man, upon the soul, upon the laws of compensation, upon the God within, upon self-reliance as a form of God-reliance, had accompanied an increasing distaste for the forms and the ceremonies of worship. The question of immortality, made immediate by the death of his wife, had led him to ponder upon what he called the conversion of "the fragility of man into the Eternity of God." In the spring of 1832 his concern for the ceremonies connected with the Lord's Supper brought his doubts to a peak and led him to meditate upon such heterodox avenues to truth as Swedenborgianism with its symbolic vision, Quakerism with its distaste for form, and Zoroastrianism whose primeval allegories he read in French as poetry and in whose oddities he saw embodied an inward, spiritual truth. "Do we not," he asked, "seem nearer to divine truth in these fictions than in less pretending prose?" On January 10, 1832, three months before the record of this volume begins, he had noted his growing dissatisfaction with the ministry: "It is the worse part of the man, I sometimes think, that is the minister." On April 29 he wrote, "You may give the law or take it. Let a man set down his foot & say, 'this or that thing I can't & won't do.' " On May 22 he copied from *The Edinburgh Review* a remark from an English critic and clergyman, "There are propositions contained in our liturgy & articles which no man of common sense among us believes." On June 2 during a week of "moral excitement" he sent a letter to his church suggesting that he be freed from celebrating the Lord's Supper. To his journal he confided: "I have sometimes thought that in order to be a good minister it was necessary to leave the ministry. The profession is antiquated. In an altered age, we worship in the dead forms of our forefathers."

Throughout much of June and July the Second Church was conveniently closed for repairs, leaving its minister free to await the response of his parishioners in the quiet of the White Mountains of New Hampshire. Significantly he had fled to the hills before in the moment of crisis after the death of Ellen. In the mountains he felt that "the pinions of thought should be strong and one should see the errors of men from a calmer height of love & wisdom." Certainly among the errors of men were their outmoded ceremonies. On July 15 he recorded the "hour of decision"; he determined to preach no more if he must be bound by form. Perhaps his congregation would understand that, as he noted, "Religion in the mind is not credulity & in the practice is not form. It is a life. . . . It is to love, it is to serve, it is to think, it is to be humble." Yet if his church could not accept his ministry under its altered terms, he would resign. "I cannot," he wrote, "go habitually to an institution which they esteem holiest with indifference & dislike." Instead of being related to ceremony or institution, religion, he felt, rested on the single man and his infinitude; it depended upon the soul within, the "divine inmate." Emerson set down his decision firmly: "Let the soul speak & all this drivelling & ↑these↓ toys are thrown aside & man listens like a child."

As he listened to the commands of his soul in the White Mountains he was already a priest unfrocked, although his resignation was not irrevocably accepted by the Second Church until October 28 after much further exploration of possible means of reconciliation. Doffing the decent black of the pastor, he was free to choose the gown of the lecturer and teacher, of the thinker not confined within the limits of an institution or a tradition. Heeding his inner voices he had abandoned the professional career that stretched invitingly before him; he had adopted the advice which he set down in his journals in verse during the final month of his connection with the church: "I will not

xi

live out of me/ I will not see with others' eyes/ . . . I would be free."

But free for what? During this time, Emerson had no fixed direction in mind. He could — and did — write bravely about the need for the genuine man and record lovingly William Sewel's stories concerning George Fox, the thoroughly consistent man who said "What I am in words, I am the same in life." At the moment, however, Emerson had no plans for his own future and he was suffering under constant debilitating illness that sapped his strength and hope. True, as he wrote in the summer, "A stomach ache will make a man as contemptible as a palsy. . . . Still the truth is not injured." Yet to suffer under diarrhoea made him, as he noted, as weak as a reed.

During the fall of 1832 he underwent not only the final throes of separation from his church but one relapse after another in his health. He was, his brother Charles wrote in a letter of November 27, "sick again — very much dispirited — & talking of the South, the West Indies & other projects." His plans, as his brother reported them a week later, were still not precise: "He will probably go away this winter & by sea, but where he knows not. . . ." He himself wrote a month before Christmas of the projects that danced like sugar plums through his imagination — "of action, literature, philosophy," of a magazine that might bring fame and fortune. But early in December when his illness worsened, he decided suddenly to board the brig *Jasper*, sailing for the warmer climate of the Mediterranean. On Christmas day, like Melville's hero on the *Pequod*, he plunged "like fate into the lone Atlantic" to recapture health and purpose in a European *Wanderjahr*.

The record of Emerson's ten months of travel which makes up a large part of this volume is unusually detailed and personal. His earlier journals had been primarily accounts of thought rather than of experience. But from the moment of his sailing for Malta on Christmas, 1832, until his return to New York on October 7, 1833, he kept what is actually a diary with daily entries accounting for what he had seen, done, spent, as well as thought. The fullness of his record came, no doubt, in part from his awareness of the strange and new in Europe, or more precisely of the strange and old. He was obviously, as he remarked, keeping a very full journal as a substitute for the letters he found too little time to write. Moreover, to supply his family with a proper narrative, he kept his record with unusual care, writing out entries and then later revising them, often by expanding an original pencil entry with a substitute version over it in ink. In part his record is full because, as he complained, he had little time or opportunity to read during his travels.

These diaries present his reaction to tradition and to the ancient world as he saw it and not as he read about it. Often he found the past admirable, whistling with delight at the curiosities of La Valetta after his miserable delay of two weeks in Maltese quarantine. The beauty of the churches there led him to wish for similar ornamentation and charm in the bare edifices of New England. But often, like Samuel Clemens later, he breathed out vivid Americanisms (see plate 3 from Journal Sicily), especially before the squalid misery of the beggars. Against any threat of the past to the individual soul he stood firm. "Here's for the plain old Adam, the simple genuine Self against the whole world," he wrote in Naples.

Rebel against the lure of the past though he often was, he fell under the spell, sometimes very unwillingly, of Europe — of the power of Michelangelo and the massive grandeur of St. Peter's; of Florence where the towers rose near the Bello Sguardo "richly out of the smoky light on the broad green plain"; of Milan from whose cathedral he saw "one of the grandest views on earth." Yet he had come to Europe really to see men, not things, and here he was often disappointed. As he wrote after six months in Europe:

Thus shall I write memoirs? A man who was no courtier but loved men went to Rome & there lived with boys. He came to France & in Paris lives alone & in Paris seldom speaks. If he do not see Carlyle in Edinburgh he may go to America with out saying anything in earnest except to Cranch & to Landor.

As his remark indicates, he had enjoyed Landor at Fiesole even though the Englishman had undervalued Socrates and overpraised Southey. His meeting with Carlyle, whose "Germanick" writings he had been fascinated by for over a year, was of even higher joy, though it occurred at Craigenputtock rather than in Edinburgh. In England he saw Wordsworth and Coleridge, both interesting though neither as complete as he had dreamed him. And lonely as Paris was he saw Oliver Wendell Holmes there and dined on the Fourth of July with Lafayette "& nearly one hundred Americans." As a thinker he was most impressed, perhaps, by his brush with science at the Jardin des Plantes when he suddenly felt an occult relation with the very scorpions, was "moved by strange sympathies," and made up his mind to "be a naturalist." Then he realized, perhaps with some help from Goethe through Carlyle, that Nature tells all her secrets once. His first task as lecturer would be to repeat the secrets as he learned them.

When he returned to America in the fall of 1833 Emerson was still without any firm prospects. Fortunately he had been assured a small but steady income from the estate of his wife Ellen, whose death had so clouded the closing years of his ministry; and during his travel he had recovered his health, delicate though it always remained. He was, however, a man without a profession, and all his warm dreams of founding a magazine or making a career as a writer seemed moonshine. Yet within four days after disembarking in New York he had accepted an invitation which would point him toward a new career: he agreed to give the introductory lecture to the Natural History Society of Boston at the Masonic Temple on November 5. As in his earlier journals notes for sermons dotted the pages, from now on his record would be the source for lectures and later for essays. As he wrote in the first pages of his new journal in early December, 1833, "This Book is my Savings Bank. I grow richer because I have somewhere to deposit my earnings." He was still to add to his income for some years by desultory preaching in supply to this or that church (often in parishes already far gone toward Swedenborgianism or verging on the tenets of the Quakers), but when he spoke somewhat generally upon the "Uses of Natural History," he was marking out a new seed field for his ideas to take root in. He himself during these months finally settled down in Concord in the old Manse with his mother and his Ripley grandfather. Though he was soon to move within Concord to the Coolidge house which he purchased to bring a bride to, he would not remove from the village he had chosen for a home.

In the thirty-four months covered by this volume Emerson's intellectual and artistic growth is visible largely in a growing maturity and firmness of style, in a constant effort toward compression and aphorism. Except for the journals of travel his record is still more focused on his inner than upon his outer experiences. It is seldom indeed that we get the bald living fact of his entry for March 29, 1832: "I visited Ellen's tomb & opened the coffin." The diaristic personal note is usually lacking. For example, though by 1834 he was solidifying his acquaintance with Lydia Jackson, a relationship which would result in marriage, her name does not appear in the year's journal entries. And when in October, 1834, he received the news of his beloved brother Edward's death in Puerto Rico his response is brief, even muted: "So falls one pile more of hope for this life. I see I am bereaved of a part of myself."

The structure of his journals is obviously built on ideas rather than personalities. As he was to write later to Carlyle: "I dot evermore in my endless journal, a line on every knowable in nature; but the arrangement loiters long, and I get a brick-kiln instead of a house." The ideas "knowable in nature" are emphasized above the daily facts of human nature. Yet the journals are the advancing record of his mind; in them one can trace the growth of his major and repeated ideas: the examinations of compensation, friendship, history, heroism, the Christian minister, the American scholar, the genuine and self-reliant man, the relation of science to morality, the ancient problems of the individual in society and in solitude.

And always the journals contain the record of his reading. For in spite of all disclaimers of reading as secondary to action or to nature or as an activity for the "scholar's idle times," Emerson delighted in books. In Naples, mournful in his "black lodgings," he read Goethe for consolation; he apparently had Cicero in his pocket in Sicily; in the rich welter of paintings and opera at Florence he finished Manzoni's *I Promessi Sposi*; and he seems to have carried his Byron with him throughout Europe. If books were so important in travel they were more so when he found himself at home in comparative quiet. He records his reading of the past as he found it "luminous with manifold allusions." In these years his old favorites still appear. The writers whom he had always cited — Shakespeare, Milton, Dryden, Pope, Samuel Johnson and Ben Jonson, Scott — are accompanied more and more by Wordsworth (near to the major gods but often a disappointment); by Coleridge, whose influence grows through *The Friend, The Statesman's Manual, On the Constitution of Church and State*, and finally the *Biographia Literaria*; by Burns and Byron (the latter especially apposite during the travels because of *Childe Harold's Pilgrimage*); by Madame de Staël, more and more cited because of her comments on Germany, whose literature by the fall of 1832 had become an object of high interest to Emerson; by Goethe, whom Emerson had been trying to read for a couple of years and whom now under Carlyle's influence he was actually beginning to admire; and above all by Carlyle, that "Germanick" Scotsman whom Emerson had learned to know first only as an anonymous magazine author in such periodicals as *The Foreign Quarterly Review, The Foreign Review*, and *Frazer's Magazine*.

To indicate the width of Emerson's reading in these months as well as the breadth of his curiosity one need only turn the pages of these journals. He is still reading his old periodicals eagerly, *The North American Review, The Edinburgh Review, The Christian Examiner*; but he has widened his field not only to the British magazines in which he found Carlyle but more and more to volumes of science: the *Philosophical Transactions of the Royal Society*, the innumerable records of exploration and travel to be found in the outpourings of the new family and cabinet libraries, the flowering literature aimed at making science intelligible as it appeared in the publications of the various Societies for the Diffusion of Useful Knowledge. Besides these works which explained hydrostatics and astronomy, volcanic action and what every young naturalist should know, Emerson ranged from Cousin to Swedenborg, from Jeffrey to Montaigne, from such minor female poets as Felicia Hemans and Mrs. Letitia Barbauld to their equally obscure male counterparts, Ebenezer Elliott and John Wilson. Above all there was Plutarch, whose *Morals* in these months becomes an ever-increasing storehouse for wisdom; and always there was the Bible, whose accents continue to echo, often without any acknowledgement in the way of quotation marks, through Emerson's maturing style.

Volume IV consists of eight regular journals, six of which tend to fall into the category of diaries of travel, and three miscellaneous notebooks. Of the latter, "France and England" contains jottings on travel and on his study of the Italian language; some of the entries here are drafts for later and more developed entries in the regular journal Italy and France. "Pocket Diary 2," though used mainly as a memorandum book for addresses and appointments, contains illuminating book lists and a charming record of a chance meeting with Burns's son. "Composition" is really a partial compilation from these and earlier journals of materials pertinent to any study of writing. One other notebook exists containing entries which in part cover this period, but "Notebook 1833" is omitted here since only a very small section of its miscellaneous entries actually come from the years 1832–1834. It will appear in a later volume.

Editorial technique. The editorial process followed here is that begun in volume I and slightly modified in volumes II and III. Journal passages appearing within the sermons are indicated here as they have been discovered, but no careful parallel passage study has been undertaken and no claim for completeness is here offered. In the same way many journal passages later incorporated into the printed essays are noted by reference to title and page of the Centenary Edition. In correlating like passages the editor is indebted especially to Edward W. Emerson, who habitually indicated his father's use of journal material either by notations within the manuscript or by notes within the printed text. The findings of other scholars have also been utilized, especially the careful studies of the late Stephen E. Whicher, and the work of Wallace Williams and Kenneth W. Cameron. In many instances further locations have been made by the editor; no obligation, however, to provide a record for every journal passage which may appear in the essays has been felt, for in some instances the passages are not used until the compilations put together in the last stages of Emerson's career. Emerson's use marks are, however, always fully described as potential clues to later studies of his habits of composition.

CHRONOLOGY 1832–1834

1832: March–June 20, Emerson carries on his regular ministry but with increasing uneasiness; June 2, he sends his church a letter requesting a change in the communion ceremony; June 20, his request is refused but since repairs close the church for six weeks he is free to travel to the White Mountains, where he preaches at Fryeburg, Maine, on July 1 and 8 and decides on July 15 to resign his pastorate; July 20, he returns to Boston afflicted by a stubborn diarrhoea which incapacitates him for preaching during August; August 19, he is becoming better acquainted with Goethe and reading German literature in translation; September, he is well enough to preach on the first two Sundays, but his second sermon is his explanation of his unwillingness to celebrate the Eucharist and his apologia for his resignation; September 11, he sends in a formal letter of resignation; October 1, he praises the anonymous author of a review of *The Corn Law Rhymes* whose work he has already unknowingly quoted on May 11; within the month he discovers that his author's name is Carlyle and he reads most of his articles on German literature; October 21, he delivers his final sermon as pastor of the Second Church, having been too ill since September 16 to enter the pulpit; October 28, his resignation is voted upon and accepted; by December 10, still ill and suffering, he decides to sail to Europe in search of health; December 25, he clears for Malta aboard the *Jasper*.

1833: December 25, 1832–October 7, he travels abroad, visiting Malta, Sicily, Italy, France, England, and Scotland; January–February 2, en route to Malta he enjoys increasing good health even though the voyage is stormy; February 15, he disembarks at La Valetta after two weeks of miserable quarantine; February 21, after touring Malta he sails on *Il Santissimo Ecce Homo* for Sicily; February 27–March 9, he tours Sicily, visiting its principal cities, Syracuse, Catania, Messina, and Palermo; March 9 or 10, he boards the steamer *Re Ferdinando* on which he had traveled from Messina to Palermo and sails for Naples; March 12–25, he visits the major tourist sites in Naples, Vesuvius, Pompeii, Herculaneum and is horrified by the misery of the beggars; March 26–April 23, he is in Rome over the Easter season, experiencing the glories of both religion and art; his companions are mainly American artists; April 23–29, he is en route to Florence where he remains from April 29 to May 28, not only seeing the art treasures but visiting twice with Walter Savage Landor; May 28–June 14, he travels from Florence to Venice for a three-day visit and then across Italy to Milan for another three days and finally over the Alps to Geneva; June 14–20, he is in Geneva and en route to Paris; June 20–July 18, he is sightseeing in Paris where he attends a Fourth of July dinner for Lafayette, goes often to the Jardin des Plantes and to lectures on science at the Sorbonne, and attends the theater; July 18–20, he travels from Paris to London via Boulogne; July 20–August 9, he is in London, seeking out Coleridge at Highgate on August 5; August 9–16, he is en route to Edinburgh, visiting Kenilworth and Warwick on the way with his cousin Orville Dewey; August 16–20, he is in Edinburgh, where he preaches in the Unitarian Chapel and meets Alexander Ireland, who acts as a guide to the city; August 21–29, he is en route to Liverpool through the Scottish Lochs to Glasgow, and then to Craigenputtock to see Carlyle on August 25, and from Scotland to the English Lake District where on August 28 he visits Wordsworth at Rydal Mount, arriving in Liverpool after an exciting ride on the new fast trains; September 4, he sails aboard the *New York* for America after a four-day delay in which he meets and talks at length on science with Jacob Perkins, the inventor; October 7, he disembarks in New York; October 9, he arrives in Boston where he stays first with his friend George Sampson and then by October 20 moves to Newton to live with his mother and aunt; October 27, he preaches again at his former church; November 5, he delivers a lecture, "The Uses of Natural History," at the Masonic Temple; November 9–December 9, he is in New Bedford supplying his cousin Orville Dewey's church; December 11, he moves into rooms adjoining those of his brother Charles at the home of James Pelletier; December 15, he preaches again at the Second Church and works on lectures.

1834: January 6, Emerson lectures in Boston "On the Relation of Man to the Globe"; January 17, he lectures to the Mechanics Institution on "Water"; January 26, he returns to New Bedford to preach for Orville Dewey for a month; February 3–7, he visits Plymouth and probably meets Lydia Jackson; February 19–early March, he preaches in Boston; March 9–early April, he preaches again in New Bedford, where he probably also delivers two lectures on Italy, though he visits Plymouth as well on March 12–13; April, he moves to his Aunt Ladd's in Newton to join his mother and preaches in Cambridge, Boston, and Waltham; May 7, he lectures to the Boston Natural History Society on "The Naturalist"; May 14, he gives an unidentified lecture at Concord; June, he preaches each Sunday at one or another church near Newton; July 3–27, he takes a trip into Maine to Bangor, returning to preach the funeral sermon for his friend George Sampson, who had died en route to join him; August–September, he preaches at Newton, Waltham, and New Bedford; October 10, he moves with his mother to Concord to live at the Manse with his grandfather Ripley; October 17–early November, he is in New York serving as a supply minister and lecturing on November 3 in Brooklyn; October 18, he hears of his brother Edward's death on the first of the month in Puerto Rico; December, he is working diligently preparing lectures on biography.

SYMBOLS AND ABBREVIATIONS

⟨ ⟩	Cancellation
↑ ↓	Insertion
/ /	Variant
‖ . . . ‖	Unrecovered matter, normally unannotated. Three dots, one to five words; four dots, six to fifteen words; five dots, sixteen to thirty words. Matter lost by accidental mutilation but recovered conjecturally is inserted between the parallels.
⟨‖ . . . ‖⟩	Unrecovered cancelled matter
‖msm‖	Manuscript accidentally mutilated
[ ]	Editorial insertion
[. . .]	Editorial omission
[ ]	Emerson's square brackets
⌞ ⌝	Marginal matter inserted in text
[ ]	Page numbers of original manuscript
n	See Textual Notes
∧	Emerson's symbol for intended insertion
[R.W.E.]	Editorial substitution for Emerson's symbol of original authorship. See volume I, plate VII.
*	Emerson's note

epw   Erased pencil writing

☞
✒   Hands pointing
🖐

ABBREVIATIONS AND SHORT TITLES IN FOOTNOTES

E t E   Kenneth W. Cameron. *Emerson the Essayist.* Raleigh, N.C.: The Thistle Press, 1945. 2 vols.

J   *Journals of Ralph Waldo Emerson.* Edited by Edward Waldo Emerson and Waldo Emerson Forbes. Boston and New York: Houghton Mifflin Co., 1909–1914. 10 vols.

JMN   *The Journals and Miscellaneous Notebooks of Ralph Waldo Emerson.* Edited by William H. Gilman, Alfred R. Ferguson, Merrell R. Davis, Merton M. Sealts, Jr., and Harrison Hayford (Volume I edited by William H. Gilman, Alfred R. Ferguson, George P. Clark, and Merrell R. Davis). Cambridge: Harvard University Press, 1960–

L   *The Letters of Ralph Waldo Emerson.* Edited by Ralph L. Rusk. New York: Columbia University Press, 1939. 6 vols.

Lectures   *The Early Lectures of Ralph Waldo Emerson,* volume I, 1833–1836, edited by Stephen E. Whicher and Robert E. Spiller. Cambridge: Harvard University Press, 1959.

Life   Ralph L. Rusk. *The Life of Ralph Waldo Emerson.* New York: Charles Scribner's Sons, 1949.

W   *The Complete Works of Ralph Waldo Emerson.* With a Biographical Introduction and Notes, by Edward Waldo Emerson. Centenary Edition. Boston and New York: Houghton Mifflin Co., 1903–1904. 12 vols. I — *Nature Addresses and Lectures;* II — *Essays, First Series;* III — *Essays, Second Series;* IV — *Representative Men;* V — *English Traits;* VI — *Conduct of Life;* VII — *Society and Solitude;* VIII — *Letters and Social Aims;* IX — *Poems;* X — *Lectures and Biographical Sketches;* XI — *Miscellanies;* XII — *Natural History of Intellect.*

YES   *Young Emerson Speaks.* Edited by Arthur C. McGiffert, Jr. Boston: Houghton Mifflin Co., 1938.

"Emerson's Reading." Kenneth W. Cameron, *Ralph Waldo Emerson's Reading.* Raleigh, N. C.: The Thistle Press, 1941.

PART ONE

The Journals

Q

1832–1833

Journal Q is both a regular and a miscellaneous journal. Emerson began it on March 10, 1832, and made regular entries in the volume, largely of drafts for sermons or ideas which might be later used for sermon material, until early winter when illness and the imminent prospect of travel stopped all his journal keeping. No entries appear from December 1, 1832, until February 3, 1833, when at Malta Emerson began to use the book again for supplementary and miscellaneous entries on his European travels. Though most of Emerson's record of his travels is to be found in four small pocket journals, Journal Q served for some scattered entries during the tour and for a more complete account of the first months after Emerson's return to New England in the fall of 1833. The last dated entry in the volume is November 19, 1833.

The notebook is home-made: 36 sheets folded folio into a single gathering that is sewed from the outside into the center with cobbler's wax thread. A cream-colored outer wrapper serves as a covering for the volume; the back leaf of the wrapper is torn off and missing. The leaves measure 20 x 24.2 cm apiece. Besides the 144 pages of the notebook, there is one insert sheet, folded into 2 leaves and pinned to the lower left inside margin of page 121. The leaves of this sheet measure 18.6 x 22.7 cm; its pages are unnumbered and the editors have added subscript letters a, b, c, d, to 120, the number of the page which the insert sheet follows. The paper of the insert sheet is the same letter paper, watermarked "London Superfine Satin," as that used by Emerson for the journal Sea, 1833, with its overlapping record of the return to America. The pages of Journal Q are irregularly numbered, generally in ink. Numbers are given for all even-numbered pages except for pages 142 and 144. Odd-numbered pages are given numbers in ink consistently through page 17 and after that only to pages 25, 27, 35, 39, 45, 71, 73, 83, 113, and 125. Pages 123 and 131 carry page numbers in pencil.

3

[front cover]   March, 1832.

———
1832
———
Q
———

[front cover verso] Biographical heads. Socrates, Phocion, Alfred, Luther, Thomas More, George Fox.

EBE's texts [1]
Eccle[s.]

[1][2] March 10, 1832.   Chardon Street, Boston.

Temperance is an estate. I am richer, the Stoic migh‖t‖ say, by my self command than I am by my income. And literally, for his acquaintance spends at the confectioner's what ⟨will buy the⟩ pays the bookseller's bill of the Stoic & makes him rich indeed. Then the ⟨liquor dealer⟩ sum withholden from the liquor dealer enables the Stoic to be magnificent in expenses of charity & of taste. To say nothing of the doctor's & apothecary's accounts.

A good way to look at the matter is to see how it figures in the le⟨ger⟩dger. Bacon says — Best spend in the most permanent ways, such as buying Plato.[3] This year I have spent, say ⟨12.00 in cider & porter⟩ $20 in wine & liquors which are drunk up, & the drinkers are the worse. It would have bought a beautiful print that would have pleased for a century; or have paid a debt that makes me wince whenever I remember the person & may make me wince this hundred years. And so on[.]

But every indulgence weakened the moral faculty, hurt at least for the time ⟨your⟩ the intellect, lowered the man in the estimation

———

[1] An actual listing of these biblical texts associated with Edward Bliss Emerson is given on p. 36 below.

[2] The lower right corner of this page is torn and mended with modern transparent tape under which are visible the initials "C C E" (Charles Chauncy Emerson) in faint pencil. On the verso of the leaf, p. [2], the tear cuts through the first word in each of the last two lines.

[3] Possibly Emerson's variation of the comment in "Of Expense" that "extraordinary expense must be limited by the worth of the occasion."

of ⟨those⟩ the spectators though sharers, injured them, & diminish‖ed‖ the means of beneficence.

———

Εις οιωνος αριστος αμυνεσθαι περι πατρης [n] [4]

———

Vacat Temperantia [5]

[2] One would think that the hog, that walking sermon upon Gluttony, was enough to turn the stomachs of all men from intemperate eating. Then was ever the full feeder ready for religion?

> ——— "Swinish Gluttony
> Ne'er looks to Heaven amidst his gorgeous feast
> But with besotted base ingratitude
> Crams & blasphemes his Feeder."
> [Milton] Comus [ll. 775–778]

Then is there in the world so illustrious an ornament as Temperance? It does not need any explanation to make it admired by a savage tribe or by kings & nobles or by the mob or by wise men. If I ⟨carry⟩ choose a diamond breast pin for my ornament, I cannot deny, it is very beautiful, & will attract much attention; but my servant or a ruffian may pilfer it & then it is gone forever, tho' it cost me much. But this ⟨gem⟩ decoration no man can take from me, & ⟨‖ . . . ‖⟩no law can oblige me to conceal it. No rev‖o‖lution in society can make it of less current ‖val‖ue than it has now. It will be a per‖pet‖ual letter of recommendation and [3] really possesses the virtues falsely ascribed to amulets ⟨& charms⟩ that of making the bearer healthful & beloved. See Sermon 147[.] [6]

Yes[,] it is continually in use & note & all men are judges of it.

March 14, 1832.   Tu cura tibi. [7]

Any thing ⟨to⟩ not base is desireable to bring about so good an

[4] "One omen is best, to fight for one's country." Homer, *Iliad*, XII, 243.

[5] "Temperance is void" (Ed.). The tag is from Seneca according to Robert Leighton, *Select Works*, 2 vols. (London, 1823), I, 503n. These volumes, apparently Emerson's immediate source, are in his library.

[6] The whole foregoing entry for March 10 on "Temperance" is used almost verbatim in this sermon, first preached March 18, 1832.

[7] The full line, from Ovid, *The Heroides*, Epistle XIII, l. 166, is "si tibi cura

end as this of personal purity. Be master of yourself, and for the love of God keep every inch you gain. No man who has once by hatred of excess mastered his appetites would be bought back to his bondage by any possessions.

28 March my food per diem weighed 14 ¼ oz
29 —   —   — 13 oz
2 April   12 ½

What ails you gentlemen said Jupiter — What ails you my wobegone friend? ⟨s⟩Speak, what are you? — 'Bilious' — And you? '⟨a⟩A slave'. And you? 'Hypp'd' And you? ⟨po⟩ —— 'Poor.' And you? 'Lame.' And you? 'A Jew'

[4] Ann H. Bryant.   Frances G. Bryant. Deborah Townsend
Sarah S. Loring, sa mere [8]

[5] March 23. What did Pestalozzi every where seek to know? Himself. How did Niederer befriend him? By helping him to the knowledge of himself[.]

"With all the anxiety of one who carries an unborn universe within his bosom Pestalozzi never was able, often as he attempted it, to explain himself fully & clearly to others or even to himself" — — — — — "he saw at once that Niederer was the man who like a mirror would place his own ideas & feelings before his consciousness & enable him to pursue his course securely & successfully." Biber, p 52 [9]

---

mei, sit tibi cura tui!" — "if thou carest ought for me, then care thou for thyself!" The tag itself is proverbial and Emerson may have found it ascribed to Greene's *Groatsworth of Wit* in Thomas Fielding's *Select Proverbs of all Nations* (New York, 1825), p. 121.

[8] Sarah Stewart (Collins) Loring (1774–1846), the wife of Henry Loring and the mother of Anna Haldane Loring, married George W. Bryant in 1825. She was in 1832 a widow living at 22 Richmond Street. See C. H. Pope and K. P. Loring, *Loring Genealogy* (Cambridge, Mass., 1917), p. 174. Frances Bryant and Deborah Townsend are unidentified, though a widow named Deborah Townsend lived on Pond Street according to the Boston *Directory* for 1830. A line to the right of "Bryant." and "sa mere" below it obviously connects Anna Bryant and Sarah Loring and separates them from the rest of the entry.

[9] Edward Biber, *Henry Pestalozzi and his Plan of Education; being an account of his life and writings . . .* (London, 1831), pp. 51–52.

29 March. I visited Ellen's tomb & opened the coffin.

"There is little justice & little friendship in tyrannies but most of both in republics; because among equals there are most common rights & most common enjoyments." Aristotle [10]

[March] 30. I am your debtor, Sir James Mackintosh, for your Ethics & yet, masterly book as it is, highly as I esteem the first account of the Conscience that has ever been given (see p.   ) [11] yet is it at last only an Outline, nor can suffice to my full satisfaction. Thus I believe in the formation of the Secondary desires but you have not shown me the laws by which one secondary desire becomes paramount instead of another as for instance the love of skill in the Sculpto‖r‖ [6] rather than the love of gain or of beneficence or of superiority. And though I admit that you have defined for the first time the Conscience or Moral Sentiments yet have you not told how it was formed, which seems incumbent on one who affirms it of secondary formation.

Omnis Aristippum decuit color et status et res. [12]

Horace [*Epistles*, I, i, 23]

[7]   "Be not Almighty, let me say,
                Against — but for me."

Herbert. ["The Search," ll. 51–52]

An ingenious & pleasing account of human nature is Hartley's successive passions as expounded by Mackintosh. [13] Each becomes the

[10] Slightly misquoted from *Aristotle's Ethics and Politics*, trans. John Gillies, 2 vols. (London, 1797), I, 346, "Ethics," Bk. VIII.

[11] Emerson may have left this page reference incomplete because of the difficulty of assigning a single page to Mackintosh's extensive treatment of conscience, examined at some length in connection with Butler, Hutcheson, Hartley, Dugald Stewart, and Thomas Brown. Sir James Mackintosh, *A General View of the Progress of Ethical Philosophy* (Philadelphia, 1832), pp. 119–124, 126–127, 163–175, 222–228, and 253–269. On pp. 253–254 Mackintosh calls his own examination "something . . . more modestly tried towards an outline."

[12] "To Aristippus every form of life was fitting, every condition and circumstance."

[13] Mackintosh considers Hartley's *Observations on Man* in *A General View of . . . Ethical Philosophy*, 1832, pp. 157–176. The discussion of the successive passions is to be found on pp. 173 ff.

7

parent of a new & higher passion & itself dies. If the Scheme of Necessity must be admitted, then let that doctrine also be the anti-dote — the gradual glorification of man.

The analogies of the lower creation, the caterpillar & tadpole with temporary organs which perish when their object is answered, & the creature advanced, come in; & the temporary constitution of the foetus in the womb; the building of nests; & all ⟨prote⟩ systems of prospective protection. The parent bird turns her young out of doors when they can shift for themselves. Very costly scaffoldings are pulled down when the more costly building is finished. And God has his scaffoldings. The Jewish Law answered its temporary purpose & was then set aside. Christianity is completing its purpose as an aid to educate man. And Evil is a scaffolding on which universal good is reared. God shall be all in all.

[8] Secondary passions are formed out [of] primary ones yet wholly different — not mixture but combination. The bee makes honey out of thyme & marjoram, but it is then honey & neither thyme nor marjoram. The union of hydrogen & oxygen is like neither one but is water. On this theory ought not *emulation* to be employed in edu-cation?

Moore to Crabbe

    "True bard! ⟨yet⟩ ——, & simple, as the race
        Of true born poets ever are
  When, stooping from their starry place,
      They're children, near, though gods afar."
        ["Verses to the Poet Crabbe's Inkstand," st. 8]

of Campbell —

    "In whose sea odes — as in those shells
      Where Ocean's voice of majesty
  Seems sounding still, — immortal dwells
    Old Albion's spirit of the sea."

    "Yet next to Genius is the power
      Of feeling where true genius lies. ——"
       [*Ibid.*, st. 14 and st. 18, ll. 1–2]

8

[9] 'The world' is an academy to the scholar, a butt to the satirist, a church to the devotee, 'the scaffold of the divine vengeance'[14] to the Calvinist, good society to the fashionist, a market to the merchant, a conquest to Alexander.

2 April. Write a sermon upon Animals. They are to man in life what fables about them are in Ethics. Draw the moral then of the bee, ant, fox, hedgehog, ermine, swine, roe, woodpecker, pigeon, worm, moth, mite.
a frozen snake.[15]

"Deus anima brutorum."[16]

"No one can guess what kind of vision belongs to the fly. There are probably 25000 hexagonal lenses or menisci on its surface or the same number of distinct visual organs as some comparative Anatomists would lead us to believe." Abernethy, p. 265.

"*oestrum equi.* this fly never deposits its eggs but ⟨on⟩ ↑in↓ those parts of the horse to which that animal can apply its mouth so that they may be swallowed. By this means the larvae are provided with a warm lodging & plenty of food during the winter season & are not expelled till spring in order to undergo their metamorphosis into perfect flies" Abernethy [p. 320]

'Welcome is the best cheer.' Proverb.[17]

[14] Jacques Saurin (1677–1730) is the author of the phrase, probably made familiar to Emerson through his Aunt Mary. See *JMN*, II, 225 and 307.

[15] Emerson drew the moral fully and with expansive example in Sermon 152, first preached on April 22, 1832. There he cited at some length Réaumur's demonstration of design in the bee-cell and Abernethy's commentary on the eye of the fly. The separate phrase "a frozen snake" may be a memory of a speech by Queen Elizabeth to Leicester, in ch. 40 of *Kenilworth*, where Leicester begs: "Tread not upon a crushed worm" and the queen replies, "A worm, my lord . . . nay a snake is the nobler reptile . . . a frozen snake."

[16] "God is the soul of brutes" (Ed.). The tag is quoted in John Abernethy's *Physiological Lectures exhibiting a general view of Mr. Hunter's physiology and of his researches in Comparative Anatomy, delivered before the Royal College of Surgeons in the year 1817* (London, 1817), p. 272. The following two paragraphs of quotation come from the same source.

[17] Vicesimus Knox, *Elegant Extracts . . . in Prose*, 7th ed., 2 vols. (London, 1797), II, 1026. From April 2 through May 12 Emerson entered a great many proverbs in his journal. Though he knew such other collections as Fielding's *Select Proverbs . . .* , 1825, John Ray's *A Complete Collection of English Proverbs . . .* (London, 1817), George Herbert's *Jacula Prudentum, or Outlandish Proverbs* (1640,

9

"Hospitality with cloudless brow"

Burns ["The Brigs of Ayr," l. 224]

[10] In the sweat of thy face thou shalt eat bread[.] [18]

Sermon on idleness. Galileo's eye, ⟨Galen's hand⟩ He that does nothing is poorer than he that has nothing.[19] 'The devil tempts others, an idle man tempts the devil.' 'An idle brain is the devil's shop.' 'He hath no leisure who useth it not.' The busy man is entirely ignorant of what was doing this morning all over the city. Working in your calling is half praying. What keeps the world from being a horrid Poneropolis? What divides & conquers? Necessity of all; Labor; 'Poverty is a good which all hate.' Give us no leisure until we are fit for it.

blundering rhetorician seeking in the tones or gestures of Chatham or Adams or in the circumstances of the parties present or concerned the electricity that ⟨lurked⟩ lay ⟨in⟩ only in the breast of Chatham & Adams. Pectus est disertum et vis mentis.[20]

[11]   April 6, 1832.

"It was the comparing the mechanism of the hand & the foot that led Galen, who, they say, was a skeptic in his youth to the public declara-

---

1651), and Charles G. Colton's *Lacon, or Many Thoughts in Few Words* (New York, 1822), most of the proverbs cited during this period are obviously from Knox's treasure house. See Kenneth Cameron, "Emerson, Thoreau, *Elegant Extracts*, and Proverb Lore," *Emerson Society Quarterly*, I Quarter, 1957, pp. 28–39.

[18] Slightly misquoted from Gen. 3:19, the passage was included in Sermon 156 on May 20, 1832, and became the text for Sermon 161, first preached on September 2, 1832, which is the sermon on "idleness" referred to by Emerson. In this sermon remarks on Galileo, Galen, and some proverbs were included.

[19] In Encyclopedia, p. [137], Emerson lists this proverb as his own under the heading "My Proverbs." The remaining sentences within the paragraph mix Emerson's own comments with proverbs drawn from Knox, *Elegant Extracts . . . in Prose*, 1797, II, as follows: "'The devil . . . devil.'" 1025; "'An idle . . . shop.'" 1026; "'He hath . . . it not.'" 1024; "'Working . . . half praying.'" 1030; "'Poverty . . . all hate.'" 1031. Emerson's question about the world as a "horrid Poneropolis" was derived from his memory of Plutarch, "Of Curiosity." See the *Morals*, trans. from the Greek by Several Hands, corrected and revised by W. W. Goodwin, 5 vols. (Boston, 1870), II, 437: "the city Poneropolis (or Rogue-town), so called by King Philip after he had peopled it with a crew of rogues and vagabonds."

[20] The preceding paragraph is struck through with a diagonal use mark. The

tion of his opinion that intelligence must have operated in ordaining the laws by which living beings are constructed." Abernethy's Lectures p. 152

"In explaining these things," he says, "I esteem myself as composing a solemn hymn to the great architect of our bodily frame, in which I think there is more true piety than in sacrificing hecatombs of oxen or burning the most costly perfumes for I first endeavour from his works to know him myself & afterwards by the same means to show him to others, to inform them how great is his Wisdom, his goodness, his Power."

Galen. Apud Abernethy [*Lectures*, pp. 152–153] [21]

Hunter like Pestalozzi; each lived to an idea which was their guide & genius, but Abernethy is hardly a Niederer. So Jussieu wrote nothing yet had an idea.[22] ——

April 17. A strange poem is Zoroastrism. It is a system as separate & harmonious & sublime as Swedenborgianism. congruent. One would be glad to behold the truth which they all shadow forth. For it cannot but be truth that they typify & symbolize as the play of every faculty reveals an use, a cause, & a law to the intelligent. One sees in this & in them all the [12] element of poetry according to Jeffrey's true theory — the effect produced by making every thing outward only a sign of something inward.[23] Plato's *forms* or *ideas* which seem almost tantamount to the Ferouers of Zoroaster. "Of all the Ferouers of beings that should exist in the world the most precious in the eyes of Ormuzd were that of Law, that of Iran & that of Zoro-

---

Latin tag, from Quintilian, *Institutio Oratoria*, X, vii, 15, should read "Pectus est enim, quod disertos facit, et vis mentis" — "For it is feeling and force of imagination that make us eloquent."

[21] These two citations from Abernethy Emerson used in Sermon 151, first preached two days after this entry, on April 8, 1832.

[22] John Hunter (1728–1793) and Johann Heinrich Pestalozzi (1746–1827) were notable respectively in the fields of comparative anatomy and education; John Abernethy and Johannes Niederer were disciples and commentators on the works of their masters, although Abernethy, unlike Niederer, was famous in his own right. The Jussieu is probably Bernard (1699?–1777), one of a family of famous botanists. From his work with the Jardin des Plantes came the system of plant classification and arrangement which Emerson admired in 1833.

[23] Francis Jeffrey's actual phrase in a review of Felicia Hemans' verse in *The Edinburgh Review*, L (Oct. 1829), 35, was "that subtle and mysterious analogy which exists between the physical and the moral world — which makes outward things and qualities the natural types and emblems of inward gifts and emotions . . . ."

aster." Acad. des Inscrip. vol 37, p. 623.[24] But what I would have quoted just now to illustrate the poetry theory is this.

"Fire, the son of Ormuzd was also created. He represented tho' imperfectly the original Fire which animates all beings[,] forms the relations which exist between them & which in the beginning was a principle of union between Ormuzd & Time-sans-bornes." (which is the first name in their Theodicaea)

By the way I cannot help putting in here an exquisite ⟨morsel⟩ specimen of the vraisemblance in fiction. Among the evil persons & things produced by Ahriman it is said. "Ahriman produisit même une espèce de feu ténébreux, dont vient celui de la fièvre." [*Ibid.*,] p. 628.

[13] Do we not feel in reading these elemental theories that these ⟨ficti⟩ grotesque fictions are the gallipots of Socrates[,] that these primeval allegories are globes & diagrams on which the laws of living nature are explained? Do we not seem nearer to divine truth in these fictions than in less pretending prose?

Here is one of the sentences. Goschoronn rejoicing before Ormuzd at the prospect of the creation of Zoroaster, says, "I said to heaven in the beginning when there was no night, that there must be ↑qu'il falloit avoir↓ purity of thought, of word, & of action." [*Ibid.*,] p. 643

I am quoting from the Histoire de l'Academie des Inscriptions Vol. 37[.]   Prometheus archaic, 'Jupiter an upstart'

The foolish took no oil in their vessels with their lamps. Pestalozzi said, "that no man was either willing or able to help any other man." He that does nothing is poorer than he who has nothing. "Wit once bought is worth twice taught." [25]

[24] Emerson is apparently making his own translation from *Histoire de l'Académie des Inscriptions et Belles Lettres avec les mémoires de littérature*, 50 vols. (Paris, 1736–1808). He withdrew vol. 37 from the Boston Athenaeum from April 18 to May 8, 1832.

[25] The four sentences within the paragraph are drawn respectively from Matt. 25:3–4; Biber, *Henry Pestalozzi and his Plan of Education*, 1831, p. 203; Emerson's own proverbial sayings in Encyclopedia, p. [137] (see p. 10 above); and Knox, *Elegant Extracts . . . in Prose*, 1797, II, 1026.

[14] Chardon St. 29 April, 1832. You may chuse for yourself or let others chuse for you, in things indifferent. You may give the law or take it. Let a man set down his foot & say, "this or that thing I can't & won't do," — & stand it out, it shall be counted to him not only for innocency, but for righteousness, whilst a poor craven stands by omitting the same thing & apologizing for it, & receives the hearty contempt & round abuse of all observers.

You had better begin small, sail in an eggshell, make a straw your mast, a cobweb all your cloth.[26] Begin & proceed on a settled & not to be shaken conviction that but little is permitted to any man to do or to know, & if he complies with the first grand laws he shall do well. He had better stick by what he knows *sartain*[,] that humility & love are always to be practised, but there is no such pressing reason for his asserting his opinions, but he had better be humble & kind & useful today & tomorrow & as long as he lasts. Count ⟨M⟩ ⟨the⟩ from yourself in order the persons that have near relation to you up to ten or fifteen & see if you can consider your whole relation to each [15] without squirming. That will be something. Then, have you paid all [27] your debts? Then have you paid to the world as much kindness as you received from early benefactors? It were a sort of baseness to die in the world's debt. Then can you not, merely for the very elegancy, the *eruditus luxus* [28] of the thing, do an unmixed kindness or two?

May 3. Sir J. Mackintosh said well, that every picture, statue, and poem was an experiment upon the human mind.[29] I hunt in Charles's dish of shells each new form of beauty & new tint, & seem, as Fontenelle said, "to recognize the thing the first time I see it." [30]

---

[26] Emerson is quoting from Ben Jonson's *The Sad Shepherd*, III, v, 9–11: "But you must wait occasions, and obey them:/ Sail in an Egg-shell, make a Straw your Mast,/ A Cobweb all your Cloth, and pass unseen. . . ."

[27] From this point the paragraph is struck through with a wavy diagonal use mark in pencil.

[28] "Accomplished extravagance" (Ed.). Emerson may have remembered the classical tag from Bacon where it is quoted from Tacitus, *Annals*, Bk. XVI, xviii. See *The Advancement of Learning*, Bk. II, in *The Works of Francis Bacon*, 10 vols. (London, 1824), I, 118.

[29] *A General View of . . . Ethical Philosophy*, 1832, pp. 42–43, slightly paraphrased.

[30] See Pt. IV, ch. 2 of Madame de Staël-Holstein's *Germany*, 3 vols. (London,

Every knot of every cockle has *expression*, that is, is the material symbol of some cast of thought.

To ⟨understand the⟩ analyze a foolish sermon ⟨needs much⟩ may require much wisdom. Strange that so ⟨wise⟩ ↑learned↓ & gifted a man as my friend should please himself with drawing for an hour such gingerbread distinctions.

[16] May 7. Charles says that Porto Rico is a place where one is never pestered with cold feet & never needs a pocket-handkerchief, ⟨& there ⁿ is no glass window in the island.⟩ and never is unwilling to get out of bed in the morning.

Mutato nomine de te fabula narratur.[31] To be at perfect agreement with a man of most opposite conclusions you have only to translate your language into his. ⟨That⟩ The same thought which you call *God* in his nomenclature is called *Christ*. In the language of William Penn moral sentiment is called *Christ*.

May 11. There is no country so extensive as a thought.

"He who contemplates hath a day without night." [32]

I suppose an entire cabinet of s⟨e⟩hells would be an expression of the whole human mind; a Flora of the whole globe would be so likewise; or a history of beasts; or a ⟨collection⟩ painting of all the aspects of the clouds. Every thing is significant.

"Next to the satisfaction I receive in the prosperity of an honest man I am best pleased with the confusion of a rascal." [33]

1813), III, 284. Fontenelle is quoted there, however, as saying "a truth" rather than "the thing." Emerson had recorded Fontenelle's thought in Journal 1826–1828 (see *JMN*, III, 55).

    [31] "Change but the name, and the tale is told of you." Horace, *Satires*, I, i, 69–70.
    [32] Knox, *Elegant Extracts . . . in Prose*, 1797, II, 1024.
    [33] Though the author of this aphorism is unidentified, it was apparently widely used, for it appears as one of the "select sentences" in *The Speaker: or Miscellaneous Pieces . . .* , ed. William Enfield (Philadelphia, 1799), p. 30, as well as in Noah Webster's even more widely-known school collection. See *An American Selection of Lessons in Reading and Speaking calculated to improve the mind and refine the taste of youth*, 4th ed. (Boston, 1793), p. 24.

[17] That man has taken advantage, you say, of the doctrine of the high calling to play the fool. I say, no; he is a craven deserter. Whom has he deserted? Himself; ask him & he will own it. Appeal from Philip drunk to Philip sober.[34]

Reduce the body to the soul. Make the body ⟨but⟩ the instrument thro' which that thought is uttered. It is counted disgraceful in the ambassador not to represent in the dignity of his carriage the power of his country. If your manners are false to your theory, cut them off as Cranmer burnt the offending hand.[35] Don't shrink from your work. It will never be an example *further* than it should be: for no other man has the same freak.

Do not believe that possibly you can escape the reward of your action. You serve an ungrateful master, serve him the more. Be wholly his. Embrace any service, do what you will, & the Master of your master, the Law of laws will secure your compensation. ↑'Every man is valued as he makes himself valuable.' proverb↓ [36]

He that rides his hobby gently must always give way to him that rides his hobby hard.

[18] "Genius is always a secret to itself." "Of the wrong we are always conscious, of the right never." "Already my opinion my conviction has gained infinitely in sureness in force the moment another has adopted it." [37]

[34] The proverb is to be found in Valerius Maximus, VI, 2, Externa, I. The "doctrine of the high calling" is apparently an echo of the comparison of soul and body emphasized in Phil. 3:14.

[35] The story of Cranmer burning his own offending hand might have been found in many sources familiar to Emerson, such as David Hume, *The History of England*, 8 vols. (Oxford, 1826), IV, 379–380.

[36] " 'Every . . . proverb" is squeezed onto the page in a smaller handwriting, apparently as a later addition. Its source is Knox, *Elegant Extracts . . . in Prose*, 1797, II, 1028.

[37] The three quotations within the paragraph are Emerson's first citations from Carlyle, from "Characteristics," *The Edinburgh Review*, LIV (Dec. 1831), 354, 356, and 359. Carlyle in his turn was apparently translating the sentences from German sources, respectively Schiller's letter of August 23, 1794, to Goethe; Bk. VII, ch. 9, of Goethe's *Wilhelm Meister's Apprenticeship*; and Novalis, *Die Schriften*, 2 vols. (Berlin, 1826), II, 104.

"Pectus est disertum et vis mentis" [38]   Fabius

Is it not better to intimate our astonishment as we pass through this world if it be only for a moment ere we are swallowed up in the ye[a]st of the abyss? I will just lift my hands & say Κοσμος[.] [39]

[May] 12. Burns' remark about fine women too true in my experience.[40] Is not affluence or at least easy circumstances essential to the finish of the female character — not to its depth & resources perhaps but to the *beauty* of mind & manners? Is it not because woman is not yet treated properly but some taint of Indian barbarity marks yet our civilization? ⁿ She was made not to serve but to be served & only wealth admits among us of that condition. — Or is it that an eye to interest is a fatal blot to the female character & the poor scarce can help it?

[19] Write a sermon upon Blessed Poverty. Who have done all the good in the world? Poor men. 'Poverty is a good hated by all men.' [41]

⟨Spanish⟩ Proverbs.[42]

_____

God comes to see us without a bell
A wall between both, best preserves friendship

[38] "For it is feeling and force of imagination that makes us eloquent." Quintilian, *Institutio Oratoria*, X, vii, 15, slightly misquoted. See p. 10 above. In *J*, II, 472, Edward Emerson notes that Emerson by adding "Fabius" attributed the statement to Quintus Fabius Pictor, the "Father of Latin History."

[39] "Order" or "world" (Ed.).

[40] Possibly Emerson here refers to a remark of Burns quoted by Francis Jeffrey in a review of R. H. Cromek's *Reliques of Robert Burns* in *The Edinburgh Review*, XIII (Jan. 1809), 273: "One of Burns' remarks was . . . that between the men of rustic life and the polite world he observed little difference . . . but a refined and accomplished woman was a being almost new to him, and of which he had formed but a very inadequate idea."

[41] Knox, *Elegant Extracts . . . in Prose*, 1797, II, 1031. See p. 10 above. No sermon on poverty seems to have been written, but at this time Emerson certainly went through Knox's collection of folk sayings carefully, as his quotations indicate. Certainly he had also long conceived of poverty as blessed. See *JMN*, III, 357: "Poverty is distinguished[,] is blessed."

[42] This phrase is not only spaced as a title, it is also set off by ink lines drawn above and below it. "Spanish" is no doubt canceled because finally Emerson drew not only from the section in Knox called "Old Spanish Proverbs" but from that entitled "Old Italian Proverbs" also. The first nine proverbs in the list are called Spanish and come from vol. II, pp. 1035–1039; then apparently Emerson went back

There is no ill thing in Spain but that which can speak.
God doth the cure, & the Physician takes the money for it.
Whither goest thou, Grief? Where I am used to go.
Make the night night, & the day day⟨,⟩.
I wept when I was born, & every day shows why.
A cheerful look & forgiveness is the best revenge of a↑n↓ affront.[43]
The love of God prevails forever; all other things come to nothing
A man is valued as he makes himself valuable
Working in your calling is half praying
The wise hand doth not all which the foolish tongue saith
There's no fool like a learned fool
When you are all agreed upon the time, quoth the curate, I will make it rain.
If you would have a thing kept secret, never tell it to any one & if you would
not have a thing known of you, never do it.

Would you be revenged on your enemy, live as you ought & you have done
it to purpose.

Oil & truth will get uppermost at last

He counts very unskilfully who leaves God out of his reckoning.

---

[20] A good man is ever at home wherever he chance to be.

Spare diet & no trouble keep a man in health

Welcome is the best cheer. 'Hospitality with cloudless brow'

'He that's in, will grin. He that's out, will pout.'

---

to p. 1028 under "Old Italian Proverbs" and from "A man . . . valuable" to
"A good man . . . to be." quoted in order from pp. 1028, 1030, 1031, 1032, 1033,
and 1034. For "Spare diet . . . health" he returned again to p. 1028 and for
"Welcome . . . cheer." to p. 1026. No source has been found for " 'He that's in . . .
pout.' " "It is better . . . cheep." is to be found in several sources, though not in
Knox. It is in Fielding's *Select Proverbs* . . . , 1825, p. 85; in Sir Walter Scott's
Tales of a Grandfather (1831), ch. 9; and in a work of Isaac D'Israeli which
Emerson knew, *Curiosities of Literature*, 2nd. ser., 3 vols. (London, 1824), I, 432.
"When there . . . way." is found in slightly different wording in Ray, *A Complete Collection of English Proverbs*, 1817, pp. 18 and 26. For "working . . . pray-
ing," see p. 10 above, n. 19.
    [43] The cross on the "t" in "affront" is extended into a series of connected, curved
lines running beyond the middle of the page.

It is better to hear the lark sing than the mouse cheep.

———————

"When there is a will, there is a way."

———————

[21] 13 May.[44] *There remaineth a rest for the people of God.*[45] A rest, as the New Jerusalem hath it, not *in* evils ⟨f⟩but *from* evils. 'Vacat temporantia,' vacat veritas, vacat virtus, vacat ⟨amicitia⟩ caritas.' [46]

"Truth never is, always is a-being." [47] Does not that word signify that state in which ⟨ever⟩ a man ↑ever↓ finds himself, conscious of knowing nothing but being just now ready to begin to know? [n] He feels like one just born. He is ready to ask the first questions.

Strange how abysmal is our ignorance. Every man who writes a book or pursues a science seems to conceal ambitiously his universal ignorance under this fluency in a particular.

———————

The higher the subjects are, which occupy your thoughts, the more they tax yourself; and the same thoughts have least to do with your individuality, but have equal interest for all men. Things moreover are permanent in proportion to their inwardness in your nature.

———

[22] 16 May, 1832. Shakspear's creations indicate no sort of anxiety to be understood. There is the Cleopatra[,] an irregular, unfinished, glorious, sinful character, sink or swim — there she is —

———————

[44] The date is enclosed in a half box, probably to separate it from the *italic* sentence following.

[45] Heb. 4:9, slightly misquoted. Emerson's reference is to a commentary on Rev. 14:13 ("Blessed are the dead who die in the Lord. From henceforth now, saith the Spirit, that they may rest from their labours for their works follow them") in *New Jerusalem Magazine*, IV (Sept. 1830), 11.

[46] " 'Temperance is void,' as are truth and virtue and ⟨friendship⟩ affection" (Ed.). See p. 5 above for the phrase that made the pattern for this Latin tag. Apparently Emerson imitated the phrase attributed by Leighton to Seneca and added three parallel phrases of his own making.

[47] Thomas Carlyle, "Characteristics," *The Edinburgh Review*, LIV (Dec. 1831), 380. The sentence is there ascribed to Schiller: "Truth, in the words of Schiller, *immer wird, nie ist*; never *is*, always *is a-being*."

& not one in the thousand of his readers ⟨takes⟩ ↑apprehends↓ the noble dimensions of the heroine. Then Ariel, Hamlet, & all — all done in sport with the free daring pencil of a Master of the World. He leaves his children with God.

It is a good sign in human nature the unmixed delight with which we contemplate the genius of Shakspear & if it were ten times more should be glad.

17 May, — King James liked old friends best, as he said his old shoes were easiest to his feet.[48] We are benefitted by coming to an understanding, as it is called, with our fellow men, and with any fellow man. It empties all the ill blood; it ventilates, purifies the whole constitution. And we always feel easiest in the company of a person [23] to whom the whole nature has been so made known. No matter what, but how well known.

The moment you present a man with a new idea, ⟨it⟩ he immediately throws its light back upon the mass of his thoughts, to see what new relation it will ⟨call out⟩ ↑discover↓. And thus all our knowledge is a perpetually living capital, whose use cannot be exhausted, as it revives with every new fact. There is ⟨support⟩ proof for noblest truths in what we already know but we have not yet drawn the distinction which shall methodize our experience ⟨af⟩ in a particular combination[.]

[May] 18. Shall I not write upon Envy?[49] upon the wisdom of Christ which ranks envy with robbery, which is only envy in act; upon the folly of envy which seeks an impossible ⟨good⟩ thing, viz., to draw another man's good to itself. In the sweat of *thy* brow shalt thou eat bread.[50] Upon the nobleness which converts all the happiness of the world into my happiness ⟨shall[?]⟩ and makes Mr Davis' house agreeable to me. Pestalozzi's melancholy [24] paradox that

[48] See John Selden, "Friends," in *Table Talk*, ed. Edward Arber (London, 1868), p. 51.
[49] Most of the material within the entry for May 18 is used in Sermon 156, first delivered May 20, 1832.
[50] Gen. 3:19. See p. 10 above.

no man is able or willing to help any other man,[51] should set men right[.]

Who receive hospitality? the hospitable; who receive money? the rich. Who receive wisdom? the wise. ↑To↓ whom do opportunities fall? to the opportune. Unto him that hath shall be given.[52] Malthus coops up indomitable millions. Spiritual world not so. We rejoice unmixedly in Shakspear's genius. Ardor with which we desire a friend — a teacher of prima philosophia. Admiration warms & ⟨magnifies⟩ exalts. The lover is made happier by his love than the object of his affection[.]

"No revenge is more heroic than that which torments envy by doing good." [53]

Would you be revenged? Live well.

Who hath envy? I do not envy any one in the sense of wishing their goods mine. But I am capable I may easily see of ⟨wishing evil⟩ malevolence to those who have injured me or ⟨wh⟩ before whom I have played the fool. Charles saith, The Jackson Party hath envy, and doubtless the low idle hate the high rich. It is a very low passion if we have to look so hard to find it. It is as rare as robbery, its bad son.

[25] 19 May.

Because sentence is not executed speedily &c &c

How has the soldier acquired his ⟨admirable⟩ formidable courage[,] by a rare occasional action[,] effort? No; by eating his daily

---

[51] See p. 12, n. 25 above. Pestalozzi's principle, as explained by Biber referring to the novel *Leonard and Gertrude* (1781), is actually that men will by his educational methods learn to help themselves, since "there is no one . . . that is willing or able to help them." The quotation is used in "The American Scholar," *W*, I, 113.

[52] Luke 19:26, slightly misquoted.

[53] The original version for both this and the following line was probably Plutarch, *Morals*, "How to Profit by our Enemies," Several Hands edition, 5 vols. (London, 1718), I, 270–271, in which Diogenes answered "one that asked him, how he might be revenged of his Enemy: The only way, says he, to gall and fret him effectually, is, for your self to appear a good and an honest man." "No revenge . . . good." can be found as a "Select Sentence" in the school collections. See Noah Webster, *An American Selection of Lessons in Reading* . . . , 1793, p. 18. The second version may be Emerson's variation on Knox, *Elegant Extracts . . . in Prose*, 1797, II, 1024: "Living well is the best revenge we can take on our enemies."

bread in danger of his life[,] by having seen a thousand times what resolution & combination can accomplish[.]

Well is any other virtue to be gained in any other way? How is a firm cheerful conversation to be got? Not by one effort, but by spending days & *years* well, & so having a divine support for such a frail nature to lean upon,[n] a divine support of all the virtue of his life. ↑the bubble of the present is every moment hardening into the flint of the Past

The Watch-watch.↓ [54]

[55] What makes the majesty of Brougham, Webster, & Mackintosh? ↑No brass resembles gold.↓ The consciousness of an innocent life & the cumulative glory of so many witnesses behind. There they all stand, & shed an united light on the advancing actor. He is attended as by a visible escort of angels to every man's eye.

Therefore if you feel ashamed as you walk in the street it is because It nerves my arm it steels my sword[.] [56]

That is it that throws music into Channing's voice & dignity into Washington's port & America into Adams' eye. Blot out the memory of the spectators & the heroes would lose a great deal yet not all. Character not extempore but cumulative.

[26][57] If you would not be known to do any thing, never do it.[58] A man may play the fool in a pantry & say who can possibly

---

[54] See Emerson's comment in Blotting Book III (*JMN*, III, 281): "There is an engine at Waltham to watch the watchmen of the factory. Every hour they must put a ring on the wheel or if they fall asleep and do not, the machine will show their neglect & which hour they slept." Emerson referred again to the machine able to tell of the "doing & failing of every hour" in a letter to Charles, December 4 and 5, 1834. See *L*, I, 426.

[55] "What makes . . . man's eye." is struck through with three light use marks in pencil. "Therefore . . . sword" is struck through with a heavy use mark in ink: used in "Self-Reliance," *W*, II, 59–60. Though not marked with a use line in the text here, "That is . . . Adams' eye." was included in the version in "Self-Reliance."

[56] "It nerves . . . sword" is slightly misquoted from Scott, *Lady of the Lake*, V, 14.

[57] Each of the two paragraphs on this page is struck through with a wavy diagonal use mark in pencil. "If you would . . . Seneca?": used in "Spiritual Laws," *W*, II, 159.

[58] Obviously a variation on a proverb earlier quoted from Knox, *Elegant Extracts . . . in Prose*, 1797, II, 1032. See p. 17 above.

tell it, but he will betray his own secret ⟨himself⟩ unawares; pimples shall tell; a swinish look shall tell; incapacity of generous acts, ↑this↓ want of knowledge he ought to have acquired in that hour of self-indulgence[,] all these shall blab. Can a Cook[,] a Chiffinch be mistaken for ↑a↓ Seneca? Reputation is no extempore advocate[.]

The vanishing volatile froth of the present which any shadow will alter, any thought blow away, any event annihilate, is every moment converted into the Adamantine Record of the past — the fragility of man into the Eternity of God. The present is always becoming the Past. We walk on ⟨lava⟩ molten lava on which the claw of a fly or the fall of a hair makes its impression which being received, the mass hardens to flint & retains every impression forevermore.

[27] There is a great *parallax* in human nature ascertained by observing it from different states of mind. If I look at an action from the low ground of the effect upon the immediate actors & neighbors, it appears important. If I look at it from the high ground of the re⟨al⟩lation of the actors to the Universe & the Eternal generation of Beings it is too insignificant for thought. Yet each of those views is perfectly just.

[59] Who thinks kindly of the world? Always those who do well themselves. For who receive hospitality? the hospitable. For whom are the doors of the great flung wide open but for the diligent & the magnanimous? ⁿ Who ⟨are likely to⟩ see the sweetest smiles of beauty? the insignificant dangler whom ⟨al⟩every one would shake off or the brave & just man who cuts a straight path to whatever is most precious in the world? ⁿ And does the world bow to the cook, & the taster, & the Iachimo & the self despised or to the selfcommander?

[28] Letter to Eleazar Howard: ⟨Mrs Dix hymn book⟩: Mrs Wheelock's Select tracts: A book for Mrs Howe, sen[io]r ⟨Dict[ionary] for Miss More⟩. & Dea. Foster ⟨Mrs. Cook⟩

[59] The following paragraph is struck through with a wavy diagonal use mark in pencil. The material is drawn on for Sermon 156.

May 22. The philosophical grandmother of Frederic the Great declined the offer of religious counsel in her last hours, saying, Laissez moi mourir sans disputer. Seeing one of ⟨her⟩the ladies of honour weeping by her bedside she said — Ne me plaignez pas, car je vais a present satisfaire ma curiosite sur les principes des choses que Leibnitz n'a jamais pu ⟨a⟩ m'expliquer.

Ed. Rev. no 107. p. 246 [60]

' "Here sit the Pope of Germany & Cardinal Pomeranus" said Luther, laughingly, as he stepped into the carriage of Pomeranus.'

———

Jortin said in his Tracts that they who uphold the orthodox doctrine of the Trinity must be prepared to assert "that Jesus Christ is his own Father & his own Son. — The consequence will be so, whether they like it, or whether they like it not[.]"
He also said in a letter to Gilbert Wakefield[,] "There are propositions contained in our liturgy [29] & articles which no man of common sense among us believes."

"You send out to the Sandwich islands one missionary & twenty five refutations in the crew of the vessel" said Mr Sturgis[.] [61] ———

May 23. Fuseli painted Macbeth ↑going to↓ meet⟨ing⟩ the witches in the cave[:]
"I have endeavoured" ↑he said↓ "to show a colossal head rising out of the abyss, & that head Macbeth's likeness. What, I would ask, ⟨you⟩ would be a greater object of terror to you, if some ↑night↓ on going home, you were to find yourself sitting at your own table, either writing, reading, or otherwise employed? Would not this

---

[60] As he notes, Emerson's source for this anecdote was "The State of Protestantism in Germany," *The Edinburgh Review*, LIV (Sept. 1831), 246. The quotations from Luther and from Jortin come from the same article, pp. 241–242 and 240.
[61] Probably William Sturgis (1782–1864) of the firm of Bryant and Sturgis which carried more than half the trade of the U.S. with the Pacific Islands from 1810 to 1840. See Charles G. Loring, *Memoir of the Hon. William Sturgis* (Boston, 1864), p. 14. Seven missionaries with their families sailed for the Islands on October 23, 1819, as perhaps Emerson remembered. See Samuel Morison, "Boston Traders in the Hawaiian Islands, 1789–1823," *Mass. Hist. Soc. Proc.* LIV (1920–1921), 9.

make a powerful impression on your mind?" — He told Northcote 'he (N) was an angel at an ass but an ass at an angel.' [62]

"There is no armour against fate."
[Shirley, *The Contention of Ajax and Ulysses*, Sc. III, l. 3]

Indeed is truth stranger than fiction.[63] For what has imagination created to compare with the science of Astronomy? [64] What is there in Paradise Lost to elevate & astonish like Herschel or Somerville? [n] The contrast between the magnitude & duration of the things observed & the animalcule observer. ⟨The⟩ It seems a mere eye sailing about space in an eggshell & for him to undertake to weigh the formidable masses, [30] to measure the secular periods & ⟨give a⟩ settle the theory ⟨out⟩ of things so vast & long, & out of the little cock-boat of a planet to aim an impertinent telescope at every nebula & pry into the ⟨order⟩ plan and state of every white spec that shines in the inconceivable depths. Not a ⟨dot⟩ ↑white spot↓ but is a lump of Suns[,] the roe[,] the milt of light & life[.]
Who can be a Calvinist or who an Atheist[?] —
God has opened this knowledge to us to correct our theology & educate the mind.

"How many centuries of observations were necessary to render the motion of the earth suspected!"
Am. Encyc. ["Trap Rocks," XII, 323]

"There can be no true valor in a bad cause" ancient gleeman [65]

---

[62] Emerson no doubt read in *The Edinburgh Review*, LIV (Sept. 1831), 165, this quotation, which was copied into a review of John Knowles, *The Life and Writings of Henry Fuseli*, 3 vols. (London, 1831). But since the anecdote concerning Northcote is not in the magazine, he must have expanded his reading to the volume itself where the two quotations are to be found respectively in I, 189–190, and I, 364–365.

[63] From Byron, *Don Juan*, XIV, ci.

[64] Though this entry precedes the delivery of Sermon 157, on astronomy, by only four days, almost no echo from the journal is audible in the sermon; but Emerson returns to the subject of the heavenly spaces on May 26 and almost all the entry for that day is incorporated into his sermon. See pp. 25–27 below.

[65] Emerson's "ancient gleeman" has not been located but a version of the line may be found in Shakespeare: "In a false quarrel there is no true valour." *Much Ado About Nothing*, V, i, 120–121.

"A good naturalist cannot be a bad man"
                 Bewick [66]

"Bonus orator bonus vir" [67]
So Galen so Abernethy so Davy

Has not some astronomer said Young's sentiment of astronomy[?] [68] Newton

I hope the time will come when there will be a telescope in every street.

[31][69] Every form is a history of the thing. The comparative anatomist can tell at sight whether a skeleton belonged to a carnivorous or ⟨gramin⟩↑herb↓ivorous animal. A climber, a jumper, a runner, a digger, a builder. The Conchologist can tell at sight whether the shell covered an animal that fed on ⟨fish⟩ animals or on vegetables, whether it were a river or a sea shell, whether it dwelt in still or in turbid waters. Every thing is a monster till we know what it is for[;] a ship, a telescope, a surgical instrument are puzzles & painful to the eye until we have been shown successively the use of every part & then the thing tells its story at sight & is beautiful. A lobster is monstrous but when we have been shown the reason of the case & the color & the tentacula & the proportion of the claws & seen that he has not a scale nor a bristle nor any quality but fits to some habit & condition of the creature he then seems as perfect & suitable ⟨as a glove⟩ to his sea house as a glove to a hand. A man in the ⟨sea⟩ rocks under the sea would be a monster but a lobster is a most handy & happy fellow there.

[32] 26 May. Astronomy hath excellent uses. The first questions it

[66] Quoted from James L. Drummond, *Letters to a Young Naturalist*, 2nd ed. (London, 1832), which Emerson withdrew from the Athenaeum in May, 1832. The quotation is part of the motto on the title page as well as being the closing phrase in the book (p. 281).

[67] "The good orator is the good man" (Ed.).

[68] See Edward Young, *Night Thoughts*, "Night IX," l. 773: "An undevout astronomer is mad." Emerson may have recalled the phrase from Abernethy, *Physiological Lectures* . . . , 1817, p. 331.

[69] The entry on this page, struck through with a diagonal use mark, is used almost verbatim in "The Uses of Natural History," *Lectures*, I, 17.

suggests[,] how pregnant! Do you believe that there is boundless space? Just dwell on that gigantic thought. Does not idealism seem more probable than a space ⟨compared with⟩ ↑upon↓ whose area what is, the family of being[,] is a ⟨dot⟩ mere dot, & the thought of men or angels can never fathom more than its verge. All is lost in the bosom of its great night.

Next see how it corrects the vaunty speculations of men. It was ⟨said⟩ ↑an old sarcasm↓ If the triangles had a god, they would paint him with three sides.[70] And men take man of course for the type of the highest beings & suppose whatever is intelligent & great must be like him in nature. Astronomy gives the lie to all this, & shows that whatever beings inhabit Saturn, Jupiter, Herschel, Venus, even in this little neighborhood of social worlds that so nearly resemble ours must be of entirely different structure from man. The human race could not breathe in the moon nor exist in the cold of Saturn nor move in the gravity of [33] Jupiter[.]

Well then it irresistibly modifies all theology.

> Not to earth's contracted span
> Thy goodness let me bound
> Nor think thee Lord alone of man
> When thousand worlds are round[.]
>   [Pope, "The Universal Prayer," st. 6, ll. 21–25]

Calvinism suited Ptolemaism. The irresistible effect of Copernican Astronomy has been to make the great scheme for the salvation of man absolutely incredible. Hence great geniuses who studied the mechanism of the heavens became unbelievers in the popular faith: Newton became a Unitarian. Laplace in a Catholic country became an infidel, substituting Necessity for God but a self intelligent necessity is God.

⟨It⟩ Thus Astronomy proves theism but disproves dogmatic theology. The Sermon on the Mount ⟨would⟩ must be true throughout all the space which the eye sees & the brain imagines but St Paul's epistles[,] the Jewish Christianity[,] would be unintelligible. It operates steadily to establish the moral laws[,] to disconcert & evapo-

---

[70] Emerson's paraphrase of Montesquieu. See *Lettres Persanes*, ed. Henri Barckhausen, 2 vols. (Paris, 1932), Letter 59, I, 114, and *JMN*, I, 268–269.

rate temporary systems. At the touch of time errors scatter[;] in the eye of Eternity truth prevails.

[34] June 2, 1832. Cold cold. Thermometer Says Temperate. Yet a week of moral excitement.[71] ⟨But only⟩

———

It is years & nations that guide my pen[.]

———

I have sometimes thought that in order to be a good minister it was necessary to leave the ministry. The profession is antiquated. In an altered age, we worship in the dead forms of our forefathers. Were not a Socratic paganism better than an effete superannuated Christianity?

———

Does not every shade of thought have its own tone so that wooden voices denote wooden minds? [n]

———

Whatever there is of Authority in religion is that which the mind does not animate.

Conway, ↑N. H.↓ 6 July. Here among the mountains the pinions of thought should be strong and one should see the errors of men from a calmer height of love & wisdom. What is the message that is given me to communicate next Sunday? Religion in the mind is not credulity & in the practice is not form. It is a life. It is the order & soundness of a man. It is not something else *to be got*[,] to be *added*[,] but is a new life of those faculties you have. It is to do right. It is to love, it is to serve, it is to think, it is to be humble,[72]

[35][73] Ethan Allen Crawford's. White Mountains, 14 July 1832.

There is nothing to be said. Why take the pencil? I believe something will occur. A slight momentum would send the planet to

———

[71] Edward Emerson conjectures that during this week Emerson had first raised the problem of the communion service and its modification within his church, a matter referred to a committee for consideration (*J*, II, 491n.).

[72] Here Emerson left a blank space followed by a comma, perhaps with the idea of filling out his series and completing the thought later.

[73] "Ethan Allen . . . ⟨‖ . . . ‖⟩." is in pencil. The first line of the entry ("Ethan . . . 1832.") is underlined in blue crayon, probably by Edward Emerson.

roll forever. And the laws of thought are not unlike. A thought I said is a country wide enough for an active mind. It unrolls, it unfolds, it shows unlimited sense within itself. A few pains[,] a few pleasures[,] how easily we are amused[,] how easily scared. A too benevolent man is at the mercy of every fop he meets & every householder. His willingness to please withdraws him from himself. Sure he ought to please but not please at the expense of his own view by accomodation of ⟨|| . . . ||⟩.

"Imitation is a leaning on something foreign; incompleteness of individual development, defect of free utterance." Ed. Rev. No CX.[74]

Ah me, said the mourner to me, how natural he looked when they had put on his dickey! It was this that caught him, said the wife to me touching her pearl earring.

[36]   The golden days of youth are gone
          The hours of sun & hope, And round thee ——

How hard to command the soul or to solicit the soul. Many of our actions[,] many of mine are done to solicit the soul. Put away your flesh[,] put on your faculties ⟨never⟩. I would think — I would feel. I would be the vehicle of that divine principle that lurks within & of which life has afforded only glimpses enough to assure me of its being. We know little of its laws — but we have observed that a north wind clear cold with its scattered fleet of drifting clouds braced the body & seemed to reflect a similar abyss of spiritual heaven between clouds in our minds; or a brisk conversation moved this mighty deep or a word in a book was made an omen of by the mind & surcharged with meaning or an oration or a southwind or a college or a cloudy lonely walk — "striking the electric chain wherewith we are darkly bound." [75] And having this experience we strive to avail ourselves ↑of it↓ & propitiate the divine inmate to speak ⟨with⟩ to us again out of clouds & darkness. Truly whilst it speaketh not man is a pitiful being. He whistles, eats, sleeps, gets his gun,

----

[74] Carlyle's review of *The Corn Law Rhymes*, 3rd ed. (London, 1831), in *The Edinburgh Review*, LV (July 1832), 351.

[75] Byron, *Childe Harold's Pilgrimage*, IV, xxiii. Cf. *JMN*, II, 254.

makes his bargain, lounges, sins, and when all is done is yet wretched. Let the soul speak & all this drivelling & ↑these↓ toys are [37] thrown aside & man listens like a child[.]

The good of going into the mountains is that life is reconsidered; it is far from the slavery of your own modes of living and you have opportunity of viewing the town at such a distance as may afford you a just view ⟨nor can you have any⟩ nor can you have any such mistaken apprehension as might be expected from the place you occupy & the round of customs you run at home.⁷⁶

He who believes in inspiration will come here to seek it. He who believes in the woodloving muses must woo them here. ⟨Nor⟩ And he who believes in the reality of his soul will therein find inspiration & muses & God & will come out here to undress himself of pedantry & judge righteous judgment & worship the First Cause[.]

The reason why we like simplicity of character, the reason why grown men listen with untiring interest to a lively child is the same, viz it is something more than man[,] above man[,] & we hearken with a curiosity that has something of awe. We should so listen to every man if his soul spake, but it does not; his fears speak, his senses speak, & he himself seldom.

[38] July 15, 1832, White Mountains. A few low mountains, a great many clouds always covering the great peaks, a circle of woods to the horizon, a peacock on the fence ⟨&⟩or in the yard, & two ⟨or th⟩ travellers no better contented than myself ⟨mak⟩ in the plain parlor of this house make up the whole picture of this unsabbatized Sunday. But the hours pass on — creep or fly — & bear me and my fellows to the decision of questions of duty; to the crises of our fate; and to the solution of this mortal problem↑.↓ ⟨to be[?]⟩ Welcome & farewell to them, fair come, fair go. God is, & we in him. ⟨Est deus in nobis agitante calescimus ille⟩ ⁷⁷

---

⁷⁶ "nor can you . . . at home." is struck through with two ink marks, possibly signs here of cancellation rather than of use.

⁷⁷ "There is a god within us. It is when he stirs us that our bosom warms." Ovid, *Fasti*, VI, 5. See *JMN*, III, 12, 139.

The hour of decision. It seems not worth while for them who charge others with exalting forms above the moon to fear forms themselves with extravagant dislike. I am so placed that my aliquid ingenii [78] may be brought into useful action. Let me not bury my talent in the earth in my indignation at this windmill. But though the thing may be useless & even pernicious, do not destroy what is good & useful in a high degree rather than comply with what is hurtful in a small degree. The Communicant celebrates on a foundation either of authority or [n] of tradition an ordinance which has been [39] the occasion to thousands, — I hope to thousands of thousands — of contrition, of gratitude, of prayer, of faith, of love, & of holy living. Far be it from any of my friends, — God forbid it be in my heart — to interrupt any occasion thus blessed of God's influences upon the human mind. I will not, because we may not all think alike of the means, fight so strenuously against the means, as to miss of the end which we all value alike. I think Jesus did not mean to institute a perpetual celebration, but that a commemoration of him would be useful. Others think that Jesus did establish this one. We are agreed that one is useful, & we are agreed I hope in the way in which it must be made useful. viz; by each one's making it an original Commemoration[.] [79]

[80] I know very well that it is a bad sign in a man to be too conscientious, & stick at gnats. The most desperate scoundrels have been the over refiners. Without accomodation society is impracticable. But this ordinance is esteemed the most sacred of religious institutions & I cannot go habitually to an institution which they esteem holiest with indifference & dislike.

[40] Mrs Wheelock's Tracts
(Hannah Ladd's schoolbooks)
Mr Blanchard

---

[78] "Something of genius" (Ed.). Emerson may have drawn the tag from Cicero's "aliquid immensum infinitumque" via Bacon. See Vivian C. Hopkins, "Emerson and Bacon," *American Literature*, XXXIX (Jan. 1958), 413.

[79] "I think . . . Commemoration": used in Sermon 162, "The Lord's Supper," September 9, 1832, in *W*, XI, 7–8.

[80] "I know . . . impracticable." is struck through with a wavy diagonal use mark in pencil, although the sentences so marked are not to be found in Sermon 162.

Mrs Tucker
Mrs Homer
Book promised to Hannah Haskins
David Reed for Dr Ripley
Crombie [81]

[41] George Fox born 1624 son of a weaver was put out to a shoemaker & for him tended sheep. In   he began his wander· ings dressed always in leather clothing for strength's sake & suffering much from hunger, thirst, want of lodging, imprisonment, & abuse. He taught 'that the Ss [Sacred Scriptures] could not be understood but by the same spirit that gave them forth.' Rails had been built about the communion table in churches about   and the ⟨ch⟩ house in which the episcopalians worshipped of course was only called 'the Church'. These things moved George's indignation very much. He called them steeple houses, & on almost all occasions preferred to preach out of doors. When the church was manifestly the only con- venient place, he went in. He told the priests that he was no man- made priest[.]

"The visible," he said "covereth the invisible sight in you." [82]

[81] The eight items in the list can be partially identified as follows: (a) see p. 22 above for Emerson's earlier reminder to send "Select tracts" to Mrs. Wheelock; (b) probably Emerson's cousin in Newton, daughter of William and Mary Haskins Ladd; (c) Joshua P. Blanchard (1793–1841), past secretary of the Auxiliary of the American Unitarian Association and frequent officer in the Massachusetts Peace Society; (d) two Mrs. Tuckers, both widows, are listed in the Boston Directory for 1833: Eleanor on Summer Street and Mehitable on Poplar; (e) possibly the wife of Dr. Jonathan Homer, pastor of the First Church of Newton until 1839; (f) Emerson's double first cousin in Waterford, Me. (see *L*, I, 169); (g) the editor of *The Christian Register* and formerly general agent of the American Unitarian Asso- ciation; on October 12, 1832, Emerson noted in his Account Book, 1828–1835, a pay- ment "to David Reed for Dr. Ripley" (Emerson's stepgrandfather); (h) Alexander Crombie (1762–1845), author of *Natural Theology, or Essays on the Existence of Deity and Providence* . . . , 2 vols. (1829).

[82] The material on Fox is a mixture of summary, paraphrase, and direct quota- tion from William Sewel, *The History of the Rise, Increase, and Progress of the Christian People Called Quakers*, 3rd ed., 2 vols. (Philadelphia, 1823), which Charles Emerson owned. "George Fox . . . abuse." appears in I, 31, 40; " 'that the Ss . . . forth.' " is a close paraphrase of I, 115 (see *JMN*, III, 236 for an earlier use of the same phrase); "Rails . . . priest" is a summary, especially of I, 32; and " 'The visible . . . in you.' " is a quotation from I, 73.

"It pleased the Lord to show him that the natures of those things which were hurtful without were also within in the minds of wicked men,[n] & that the natures of dogs, swine, vipers, &c & those of Cain, Ishmael, Esau, Pharaoh, &c were in the hearts of many people. But since this did grieve him he cried to the Lord [42] saying — Why should I be thus, seeing I was never addicted to commit those evils? ⟨"⟩ And inwardly it was answered him   That it was needful he should have a sense of all conditions." — "About that time it happened that walking in the town of Mansfield by the steeple house side it was inwardly told him 'That which people trample ⟨on⟩upon must be thy food.' & at the saying of this it was opened to him that it was the life of Christ people did trample on & that they fed one another with words, without minding that thereby the blood of the Son of God was trampled under foot" [Sewell, vol 1, p 44]

Thoroughly consistent he was[,] how much more than other reformers. A consistent reformer. The natural growth by reaction of a formal church. Words[,] words[,] ye feed one another with words, — he said.[83] ⟨They put him in prison he applied the same pro⟩ He would have the substance of religion seen & obeyed. All his prophetic rhapsodies are directed at some moral offence. They put him in prison. He saw the evils of the jail, "& laid before the judges what a hurtful thing it was that prisoners should lie long in jail because they learned wickedness one of another in talking of their bad deeds; & that therefore speedy justice ought to be done." [Ibid., I] (p. 87)

He also wrote to them about the evil of putting to death for stealing. (see [ibid., I,] p. 86)

[43] In jail there was a conjurer who threatened to raise the devil & break the house down. But George went to him & said[,] "Come let us see what thou canst do, & do thy worst; the devil is raised high enough in thee already; but the power of God chains him down." At this undaunted speech, the fellow slunk away. [Ibid., I, 88] They gave him liberty to walk a mile from jail, hoping he would escape. [Ibid., I, 71] Socrates-like he would not. They offered him bounty if he would serve against Charles. He said his weapons were not carnal. ⟨They⟩ A band of volunteers chose him their captain. Still he refused[.] [Ibid., I, 84]

Col. —— threatened to kill the Quakers. — 'Here's my hair said G Fox here's my cheek, & here's my shoulder.' The Colonel & his com-

[83] Ibid., I, 44, a paraphrase.

panions stood amazed,[n] & said "if this be your principle as you say we never saw the like in our lives." To which G. Fox said — "What I am in words, I am the same in life." [*Ibid.*, I, 460]

Practical good sense he had when at the request of some one he lay down on a bed to refute the rumor that he never slept in a bed. [*Ibid.*, I, 103]

A reformer putting ever a thing for ⟨f⟩ a form. "My allegiance," he said "doth not consist in swearing but in truth & faithfulness." [*Ibid.*, II, 102, and 186–187]

[44] [blank]

[45] Swedenborg "considered the visible world & ↑the relation of↓ its parts as the dial plate of the invisible one." [83a] quoted in N[ew]. J[erusalem]. M[agazine]. for July 1832 p. 437[,] [Vol. V, "Emanuel Swedenborg"]

I have complained that the ⟨worship⟩ ⟨sense of God's⟩ acknowledgment of God's presence halts far behind the fact. What is it intended to be but the tribute to one without whose movings no tribute can be paid for no tributary can be? One without whom no man or beast or nature subsists; One who is the life of things & from whose creative will our life & the life of all creatures flows every moment, wave after wave, like the successive beams that every moment issue from the Sun. ⟨T⟩ Such is God, or he is nothing. What is God but the name of the Soul at the centre by which all things are what they are, & so our existence is proof of his. We cannot think of ourselves & how our being is intertwined with his without awe & amazement.

[46] August 11. — A stomach ache will make a man as contemptible as a palsy. Under the diarrhoea have I suffered now one fortnight & weak am as a reed. Still the truth is not injured[,] not touched though thousands of them that love it fall by the way. Serene, adorable, eternal it lives, though Goethe, Mackintosh, Cuvier, Bentham, Hegel die in their places which no living men can fill.

[83a] The quotation is used in *Nature*, *W*, I, 33.

Repairs [84]

The errors that the moon & earth make in the heavens in a long period of time an equal period repairs[;] the seventh pleiad was lost & is found[;] the sweet fern dies but revives[;] as much rain as the mountain sheds in foaming torrents is replenished by visiting clouds. But these are far off signs of compensation. Before tea I counted not myself worth a brass farthing & now I am filled with thoughts & pleasures and am as strong and infinite as an angel. So when one of these days I see this body going to ruin like an old cottage I will remember that after the ruin the resurrection is sure.

[47] "Who is he that can harm you if ye be followers of that which is good?" [85] 'An ancient gleeman has said that true valour cannot be shown in a bad cause.' [86] Devotion becomes idolatry. The better the worse. Saints & angels & God can well be invoked in aid of the right with a certainty that something is meant — that real assistance exists & may be hoped for, which these words may express accurately or may not; but the thing *is*. But let the cause be bad & the whole invocation would be superstitious, the words[,] the worship types of nothing. The principle of repairs is in us [87] [—]

[Patrick Henry's speech full of religion]

(Our upstart antiquities ⟨l⟩hide themselves like little children between the knees of such a fatherly place as London. The bishop of London sits in his cathedral by a regular succession of twelve hundred years. Read Palgrave's account of Saxon religion Vol 1. p 55 God = good, Man = wickedness. They believed in future state.)

[84] This paragraph is written first in faint pencil and then partially overwritten in heavy ink with a few minor variations. The reading in ink is here printed; the different readings in pencil are as follows: "in heaven a long"; "as much ⟨dew⟩ rain"; "from visiting clouds"; "strong as an angel & infinite like him."; "So when I see this body to be but an old tin pot going to rack"; and "ruin comes a sure resurrection."

[85] I Peter 3:13, slightly misquoted.

[86] For the variant of Shakespeare's *Much Ado About Nothing*, V, i, 120–121, see p. 24 above.

[87] The broken-off thought is picked up again in proper order in the manuscript after six lines. The interruption, except for the bracketed reference to an unlocated speech of Patrick Henry, consists of notes from Francis Palgrave's *History of England: Volume I, the Anglo-Saxon Period* (London, 1831), pp. 62 and 55.

the remedial principle. Every body perceives greatest contrasts in his own spirit & powers. Today he is not worth a brown cent — tomorrow he is better than a million. He kicks at riches & could be honoured & happy with nothing but arrowroot & balm tea. This we call being in good or bad spirits. It is only in the bad fit, that we doubt & deny & do ill, & we know well at that time that sorrow will come for the bad action, & sorrow is repairs and belief in the powers & perpetuity of man will return & we shall be magnified by trust in God. When therefore I doubt & sin I will look up at the moon & remembering [48] that its errors are all periodical, I will anticipate the return of my own spirits & faith[.]

[August] 12. ⟨A⟩The British Plutarch [88] ↑& the modern Plutarch↓ is yet to be written. They that have writ the lives of great men have not written them from love & from seeing the beauty that was to be desired in them. But what would operate such gracious motions upon the spirit as the ⟨life⟩ death of Lord Cobham & of Sir Thomas More & a censure of Bacon & a picture of ⟨Fox⟩ George Fox & Hampden, & the chivalrous integrity of Walter Scott & a true portrait of Sir Harry Vane, & Falkland, & Andrew Marvell? [n] I would draw characters[,] not write lives. I would evoke the spirit of each and their relics might rot. Luther, Milton, Newton, Shakspear. Alfred a light of the world. Adams. I would walk among the dry bones & wherever on the face of the earth I found a living man I would say here is life & life is communicable. Jesus Christ truly said my flesh is meat indeed[.] I am the bread.[89] For of his life or character have the nations of the earth been nourished. Socrates I should like well if I dared to take him. I should repeat Montaigne though. I wouldn't.

> "Eyes that the beam celestial view
> Which evermore makes all things new."
> [John Keble, "Morning," ll. 3–4]

These I claim sole qualification, ewe lamb. [49] I would make Milton shine. I would mourn for Bacon. I would fly in the face of every

---

[88] Emerson knew Francis Wrangham's *British Plutarch*, 6 vols. (London, 1816), of which vol. 3 is noted in "Catalogue of Books Read," *JMN*, I, 397.

[89] John 6:55 and 6:48, slightly misquoted.

cockered prejudice[,] feudal or vulgar[,] & speak as Christ of their good & evil[.]

"There are very few examples of life full & pure, & we wrong our instruction every day to propose to ourselves those that are weak & imperfect, scarce good for any one service, that pull⟨s⟩ us back, & that are rather Corrupters than Correctors of Manners." Montaigne Vol 3. p. 548 [90]

↓When we look at the ⟨past⟩ world of past men, we say, What a host of heroes but when we come to particularize, it is like counting the stars which we thought innumerable, but which prove few & rare. Bacon, Shakspear, Caesar, Scipio, Cicero, Burke, Chatham, Franklin, none of them will bear examination or furnish the ⟨m⟩ type of a *Man.*↑

E. B. E.'s texts.[91] Eccles. VI.12
VII.9
29
VIII.
Isaiah 41.21, 22
Prov. 14.14
Ps.   119.100
80.14, 15
Luke 16.16
Jer.   9.23, 24
1 Chron. 29 — Scripture

What we say ⟨must⟩ however trifling must have its roots in our-

---

[90] The passage is marked in the margin in Emerson's own copy of *The Essays of Michael Seigneur de Montaigne*, trans. Charles Cotton, 3 vols. (London, 1693 and 1700). Emerson owned vols. 1 and 3 in the edition of 1693 and vol. 2 in the edition of 1700.

[91] See front cover verso, p. 4 above, for a truncated beginning of this list. The initials "EBE" are written ornately into a crosshatched rectangle in the left margin beside the column of texts. The final text is circled faintly in ink. The names of the famous men in the preceding entry, perhaps a later insertion, are crowded into the right margin beside the texts, running as far down as "VIII." A penciled line separating the names from the texts is possibly an addition by Edward Emerson. The texts themselves apparently have in common only a concern for wisdom, understanding, and the intelligent conduct of the human being.

selves or it will not move others. No speech should be separate from our being like a plume or a nosegay, but like a leaf or a flower or a bud though the topmost & remotest, yet joined by a continuous line of life to the trunk & ⟨root⟩ the seed.

[50]   Aug. 17.
    Cholera times. It would be good to publish Girard's heroism in yellow fever at Philadelphia & Dr Rush's account of his own practice to stimulate the cowed benevolence of this dismal time. We are to act doubtless ⟨as if there⟩ in our care of our own health as if there were no other world. We are to be punctilious in our care. No caution is unseemly. This is the design of Providence. But we are to recognize in every instant of this creeping solicitude that happy is the lot of those to whom the unspeakable secrets of the other state are disclosed. When our own hour comes[,] when every medicine & means ha⟨ve⟩s been exhausted we are then to say to the Angel Hail! All hail! & pass to whatever God has yet to reveal to the conscious spirit. Why should we dread to die when all the good & the beautiful & the wise have died & earth holds nothing so good as that which it has lost[?]
    [51] But oh let not life be valued when that which makes the value of life is lost. It is only a clean conscience[,] the knowledge that we are beloved by our friends & deserve to be beloved that can persuade an honorable mind to pray that its being may be prolonged an hour, but to ⟨live⟩ out live your own respect[,] to live when your acquaintance shall shrug their shoulders & count it a disgrace ↑to you↓ the breath that is yet in your nostrils.[92] I shall be glad to be told what is the pleasure ⟨th⟩ what is the profit that is worth b⟨y⟩uying at such a price.

[52] 18 Aug.
    To be genuine. Goethe they say was wholly so. The difficulty increases with the gifts of the individual. A ploughboy can be, but a minister, an orator, an ingenious thinker, how hardly! George Fox was. "What I am in words," he said, "I am the same in life." Swedenborg was. "My writings will be found," he said, "another self."

[92] Cf. Isaiah 2:22.

37

George Washington was; 'the irreproachable Washington.' Whoever is genuine, his ambition is exactly proportioned to his powers. The height of the pinnacle determines the breadth of the base.[93]

Sept. 5 — Hypocrisy is the attendant of false-religion. When people imagine that others can be their priests, they may well fear hypocrisy. Whenever they understand that no religion can do them any more good than they actually taste, they have done fearing hypocrisy.

[53] Aug. 19   A Subject for a Sermon.[94]

Reverence man, & not Plato & Caesar. Wherever there is sense, reflexion, courage[,] admit it to the same honour — embrace it, — quote it from a truckman as quick as from Webster. If you cannot get the habit of seeing qualities except in the great, — if any thing new should spring up, it ⟨is⟩ ↑will be↓ lost to you. "Socrates", says Montaigne, "makes his soul move a natural & common motion. 'A country peasant said this; a woman said that;' he has never any thing in his mouth but Carters, Joiners, Cobblers & Masons. — — We should never have entertained the nobility & splendor of his admirable Conceptions under so vile a form." "Do but observe by what reasons he rowzes his Courage, &c. — You will find nothing in all this borrowed from Arts & Sciences. The simplest may there discover their own means & power; 'tis not possible more to retire or to creep more low. He has done human nature a great kindness in showing it how much it can do of itself. We are all of us richer than we think we are, but we are taught to borrow & to beg, & brought up more to make use of what is another's than our own." Vol 3 p 421 [pp. 418–421]

"He was content to stand by, & let reason argue for him." [95]

[93] The quotations on Fox and Swedenborg (the latter really a paraphrase) are respectively from Sewel, *The History of the . . . Quakers*, 1823, I, 460 (see p. 33 above), and Nathaniel Hobart, "Life of Swedenborg," *New Jerusalem Magazine*, II (1828–1829), 36. "Whoever is . . . base." is struck through with a wavy diagonal use mark in pencil.

[94] The subject of the geninue man, treated in the following entry as well as in the entry for August 18 above, becomes the theme of Sermon 164, first preached October 21, 1832. See *YES*, pp. 180–190. Apparently, however, only the quotations concerning Fox, Swedenborg, and Lowndes were actually transferred to the sermon itself.

[95] In a speech on the tariff Richard Henry Wilde assessed the qualities of some

[54] "Potentissimus est qui se habet in potestate."

Seneca [96]

The sublime [97] of morals seems ever to be of this kind ⟨implying⟩ ↑frail man intimating↓ this defiance of the universe & gathering himself into his shell. Every grand sentiment of religion far as it flies comes back to self. As when you say "the gods approve the depth but not the tumult of the soul" the sublime of it, is, that 'to the soul itself depth not tumult is desireable.' When you say "Jupiter prefers integrity to charity" your finest meaning is 'the soul prefers.' &c. When Jesus saith "he that giveth one of these little ones a cup of cold water ⟨he⟩ shall not lose his reward," is not the best meaning 'the love at which the giver has arrived'?⟨"⟩ "Every plant which my heavenly Father hath not planted shall be rooted up"[;] 'every thing is transitory but what ⟨is inmost in⟩ hath its life from the interior of the soul.' And so on through the N[ew]. T[estament]. there is not a just or grand thought but is made more round & infinite by applying it to the soul considered as the Universe living from God within. ⟨The⟩ Consider the sense of such propositions as "the pure in heart shall see God[.]" [98]

---

of the most distinguished members of the Fourteenth Congress. William Lowndes of South Carolina he called "no less remarkable for gentleness of manners and kindness of heart, than for that passionless, unclouded intellect which rendered him deserving of the praise, if ever man deserved it, of merely standing by and letting reason argue for him." See R. W. Griswold, *The Prose Writers of America* (Philadelphia, 1847), p. 261, for a partial reprint of the speech. Emerson quoted the phrase in Sermon 52, October 18, 1829 (see YES, p. 65) and was to use it again in Sermon 164 on October 21, 1832 (see YES, p. 186).

[96] The passage in *Ad Lucilium Epistulae Morales*, Epistle XC, 34, actually reads "potentissimum esse" — "that he is most powerful who has power over himself." Emerson may have found the sentence in Montaigne, who quotes it in "Of Physiognomy."

[97] The matter on the page is struck through from here with a wavy diagonal use mark in pencil.

[98] Emerson has apparently used double quotation marks in the passage to indicate quotation and single marks to indicate his own paraphrase or commentary. The first and third Biblical citations, however, are slightly misquoted even within the double marks. The sources are respectively (a) Wordsworth, "Laodamia," ll. 74–75; (b) unlocated, but ascribed by Emerson to Socrates. Cf. "Natural Religion" (1869), reprinted from a contemporary newspaper report in *Uncollected Lectures by Ralph Waldo Emerson*, ed. Clarence Gohdes (New York, 1932), p. 50: " 'Integrity,' said Socrates, 'is better than charity.' " (c) Matt. 10:42; (d) Matt. 15:13; and (e) Matt. 5:8.

Is not then all objective theology a discipline[,] an aid to the immature intellect until it is equal to the truth, & can poise itself? [n] Yet God forbid that I should one moment lose sight [55] of his real eternal Being[,] of my own dependence, my nothingness, whilst yet I dare hail the present deity at my heart.

The understanding speaks much; the passions much; the soul seldom. The only friend that can persuade the soul to speak is a good & a great cause. — Out it comes now & then like the lightning from its cloud & with an effect as prodigious.

Sept. 14. The true doctrine respecting forms is this is it not? that Christianity aims to form in a man a critical conscience, & that being formed he is constituted a judge[,] the only & absolute judge of every particular form that the established religion presents to him. The discretion he exercises is like the discretion of the bench which hath nothing arbitrary[.]

Every man feels the strain of duty in a different place; L. in domiciliaries, I in paraeneticks.

"Architecture reminds me of frozen music"

De Stael [99]

"People who know how to employ themselves can always find leisure moments; while those who do nothing, are forever in a hurry."

Mme Roland [100]

[56] "Think of living." [101] ⟨I do not believe in the justice of

[99] *Corinne, ou l'Italie*, Bk. IV, ch. 3: "La vue d'un tel monument est comme une musique continuelle et fixée." In 1834 Emerson traced the origins of this phrase much further. See p. 337, n. 250 below.

[100] Mrs. Lydia Maria Francis Child, *The Biographies of Madame de Staël and Madame Roland* (Boston, 1832), p. 212, slightly misquoted.

[101] The original phrase, "Gedenke zu Leben," appeared in Goethe's *Wilhelm Meister's Apprenticeship*, Bk. VIII, ch. 5, whose translation by Carlyle provided the English version. Emerson might also have found the phrase quoted by Carlyle in "Goethe's Portrait," *Fraser's Magazine*, V (March 1832), 206. The entry introduced by the quotation and continuing through the page is a rough draft of material used in Sermon 163, first preached September 16, 1832.

the⟩ Don't tell me to get ready to die. I know not what shall be. The only preparation I can make is by fulfilling my present duties. This is the everlasting life. To think of mortality makes us queasy — the flesh creeps at sympathy with its kind. What is the remedy? to ennoble it by animating it with love & uses. Give the Soul its ends to pursue & death becomes indifferent. It saith[,] What have I to do with death? ⁿ

The vice of Calvinism has been to represent the other world wholly different from this. So that a preparation to live ⟨here⟩ ↑in this↓ was all lost, for that. A true teaching shows that ↑true↓ fitness for this, is an education or development of the soul, & therefore so much accomplishment for all its theatres[.]

I do not think that people are rightly urged to a good life because their future well being depends on it, for, that which is not wholly desireable now, I may well doubt if it ever will be.

But a good life hath a perfect motive evidence now and we say it always will be because it is perfect now.

[57] I would very temperately speak of future delight's employments, not at all by foreign pictures[,] not at all by description[,] solely from the ⟨ex⟩ prophecy of the powers that are immortal. Not by description to captivate for the impenetrable veil not to be lifted has been shut down for that reason to confine us to the present where all duty & excellence ↑for us↓ lies.

"in seipso totus terres atque rotundus." ¹⁰²
[Horace, *Sermones*, 2.7.86]

⟨I⟩

Truth & virtue teach the same thing. It is in being good to wife & children & servants that the kingdom of heaven begins. It is in settling punctually with your tailor and not holding out false hopes to young men. It is in not overpraising your goods or underrating your debtor's goods. It is in forming your own judgment

---

¹⁰² "A man perfect in himself, polished and round as a globe." Emerson probably remembered the Horatian tag from his reading in a review of Palgrave's *Rise and Progress of the English Commonwealth* in *The Edinburgh Review*, LV (July 1832), 314.

upon questions of duty. It is in preferring a just act to a kind one, & a kind act to a ⟨timid⟩ ↑graceful↓ one.

It is in thus trying your powers & bringing out each one in order until the whole moral man lives & acts & governs the animal man[.]

It is no argument against the future state, the ignorance of man ⟨But the ignorance⟩ no more than the lifelessness of the egg is a proof ⟨against its⟩ that it shall not be a bird, or the ⟨igno⟩ ⟨un⟩ ↑want of↓ intelligence of the human embryo a proof [58] that it shall not be a reasoning speaking man. But this ignorance is argument as significant as a visible finger out of the sky that we should not fabricate a heaven in our heads & then square life to that fiction.

These powers & these powers alone contain the revelation of what you can do & can become. It is writ in no book. ⟨Th⟩ It can be never foretold or imagined. Theirs is your secret. They are your ⟨or⟩ heaven, ↑or↓ they^n are your hell. And their hell shall be whatever part of heaven you miss of. i.e. it is the perversion of a good power that makes your misfortunes.[103]

Sept. 17. I would gladly preach to the demigods of this age (& why not to the simple people?) concerning the reality of truth & the greatness of ⟨trusting it⟩ believing in it & seeking after it. It does not shock us when ⟨f⟩ ordinary persons discover no craving for truth & are content to exist for years exclusively occupied with the secondary objects of house & lands & food & company [59] & never cast up their eyes to inquire whence it comes & what it is for, wholly occupied with the play & never ask after the design. But we cannot forgive it in the Everetts & Cannings that they who have souls to comprehend the magnificent secret should utterly neglect it & seek only huzzas & champagne. My quarrel with the vulgar great men is that they do not generously give themselves to the measures which

---

[103] Between this and the following entry Emerson has written "H 436 481" in an angled column. The numbers are references to hymns in F. W. P. Greenwood's *A Collection of Psalms and Hymns for Christian Worship* (Boston, 1831). The hymns, one by Jeremy Taylor and one by James Montgomery, are concerned with man's attitude toward death. They are referred to by number at the top of Sermon 163, for which this journal entry is a draft. For Emerson's practice of listing the numbers of hymns accompanying each sermon, see *YES*, p. 246, n. 4.

they meddle with; they do not espouse the things they would do; live in the life of the cause they would forward & faint in its failure, but they are casting sheep's eyes ever upon their own by[-]ends[;] their pert individuality is ever & anon peeping out to see what way the wind blows & where this boat will land them[,] whether it is likely they will dine nicely & sleep warm. That for the *first* thing, that choosing action rather than contemplation, they only half act, they only give their hands or tongues & not themselves to their works.

My *second* charge ⟨upon⟩ ↑against↓ them is, that they lack faith in man's moral nature. They can have no enthusiasm, for, the deep & infinite part of man out of which only sublime thought & emotions can proceed, is hid from them.

[60] Socrates believed in man's moral nature & knew & declared the fact, that Virtue was the supream beauty.[104] He was capable therefore of enthusiasm. Jesus Christ existed for it. He is its Voice to the world. ⟨P⟩
Phocion felt it, recognized it, but was a man of action true in act to this conviction[.]

Luther, More, Fox, Milton, Burke, every great man, every one with whose character the idea of stability presents itself had this faith.

Shakspear

You[,] we[,] are not interested in the artificial fellows, however considerable they are grown; however good work their mechanism turns off, it would give you no uneasiness if you never should see them again. You have no Curiosity about their homes. But a true man is more fascinating the closer he is seen.

The⟨y a⟩ true men are ever following an invisible Leader & have left the responsibleness of their acts with God. But the artificial men have assumed their own bonds & can fall back on nothing greater than their finite fortunes. The first are formers of their characters on a divine plan; the second empirics with [61] expedients for a few years — reputation instead of character & fortune instead of wisdom.

[104] Cf. *The Republic*, III, 401 and *The Symposium*, 212.

⟨Reason st⟩ The true men stand by, & let reason argue for them. I talk with Sampson & see it is not him but a greater than him, "My Father is greater than I." [105] Truth speaks by him. (Can my friend wish a greater eulogy?)

Whatever I say that is good on the Sundays[,] I speak with fervor & authority, — surely not feeling that it rests on my word or has only the warrant of my faulty character but that I got it from a deeper & common source & it is as much addressed to me as to those I speak to.

Lucas on Holiness
Lucas on Happiness
Bp. Patrick's Parable of a Pilgrim [106]

"The Prometheus is the grandest poetical conception that ever entered into the heart of man. ⟨Homer⟩ x x x x Critics talk most about the visible in sublimity. . the Jupiter, the Neptune. Magnitude & power are sublime but in the second degree, managed as they may be. Where the heart is not shaken, the Gods thunder & stride in vain. True sublimity is the perfection of the pathetic, which has other sources than pity; generosity, for instance, & self-devotion." *Landor*. [*Imaginary Conversations*] Vol 3 p. 205

"There are few who form their opinions of greatness from the individual.[. . .] Ovid says 'The girl is the least part of herself:' of himself certainly the man is."

[*Ibid.*, vol. 3] p. 220

[62] "While I remember what I have been, I never can be less. External power can affect those only who have none intrinsically. I have seen the day, Eubulides, when the most august of cities had but one voice

[105] For the reference to R. H. Wilde's phrase concerning William Lowndes, who "let reason argue", see p. 38 above. The "Sampson" referred to is probably Sampson Reed. For Emerson's relationship to Reed and Swedenborgianism at this period, see *EtE*, I, 248–249. The following Biblical reference is to John 14:28.

[106] These three citations are crowded into a space above the quotation from Landor, by whom all were apparently suggested, since all appear on the same page in "Duke de Richelieu, Sir Fire Coats, and Lady Glengrin," *Imaginary Conversations*, 1st ser., 3 vols. (London, 1828), III, 193. The works recommended are in order: two by Richard Lucas, *Practical Christianity, or an Account of the Holiness which the Gospel enjoins* . . . (1685) and *An Enquiry after Happiness*, 2 vols. (1685); and a volume by Bishop Simon Patrick, *The Parable of the Pilgrim: Written to a Friend* (1664).

within her walls; & when the stranger, on entering them, stopped at the silence of the gateway, & said, 'Demosthenes is speaking in the assembly of the people.' "

[*Ibid.*] Vol 3. p. 545 —

October 1. I am cheered & instructed by this paper on Corn Law Rhymes in the Edinburgh by my Germanick new-light writer whoever he be.[107] He gives us confidence in our principles. He assures the truthlover everywhere of sympathy. Blessed art that makes books & so joins me to that stranger by this perfect railroad.

Has the doctrine ever been fairly preached of man's moral nature? The whole world holds on to formal Christianity, & nobody teaches the essential truth, the heart of Christianity for fear of shocking &c. Every teacher when once he finds himself insisting with all his might upon a great truth turns up the ends of it at last with a cautious showing *how* it is agreeable to the life & teaching of Jesus — as if that was any recommendation. As if the blessedness of Jesus' life & teaching were not because they were [63] agreeable to the truth. Well this cripples his teaching. It bereaves the truth he inculcates of more than half its force by representing it as something secondary that can't stand alone. ⟨Its tr⟩ The truth of truth consists in this, that it is selfevident[,] selfsubsistent. It is light. You don't get a candle to see the sun rise. ⟨You⟩ Instead of making Christianity a vehicle of truth you make truth only a horse for Christianity. It is a very ⟨cumbrous⟩ operose way of making people good. You must be humble because Christ says, 'Be humble'. 'But why must I obey Christ?' 'Because God sent him.' But how do I know God sent him? 'Because your own heart teaches the same thing he taught.' Why then shall I not go to my own heart at first?

[64]–[65] [blank]

[66] 2 Oct.
It well deserves attention what is said in N. J. M. concerning

[107] Though Emerson had quoted from Carlyle's review, "Corn Law Rhymes," *The Edinburgh Review*, LV (July 1832), 338–361, on July 14, 1832 (see p. 28 above), he had obviously not yet identified his "Germanick" writer.

External Restraint.[108] It is awful to look into the mind of man & see how free we are — to what frightful excesses our vices may run under the whited wall of a respectable reputation. Outside, among your fellows, among strangers, you must preserve appearances, — a hundred things you cannot do; but inside, — the terrible freedom!

True freedom is his only who has learned to live within as he would appear without[.]

There are men — are there not? — who are more afraid of their opinions than their will, who are more afraid to express their own opinions than to trust themselves to this inland sea. Good it is to grow familiar with your own thoughts & not shun to speak them.

9 October

'I teach by degrees,' says Landor's Epicurus.[109] It is not the will but the necessity of the wise. None are wise enow to teach otherwise. All this pedantry about the peoples not bearing the whole truth, — what ↑else↓ does it mean ⟨but⟩ than that the teacher has not yet arrived at the safe, that is, the *true* statement of the particular doctrine which he would oppose to the ruling error. He knows in general there is an error; he [n] has not yet found its boundary lines.

[67] How do we ⟨make⟩ attain just views? In conversation somebody says something about God or heaven which makes us feel uneasy. It is so specious we cannot contradict it. It is so false we cannot assent to it & we get off the best we may. Take that remark for your thesis, & work upon it till you detect the fallacy.

The true statement concerning retribution, is, that human nature is self retributive. Every moment is a judgment day, because, every act puts the agent in a new condition.

"The mighty tread

[108] "External Restraint," *New Jerusalem Magazine*, VI (Sept. 1832), 30–32. The article insists that natural man is saved from savagery by the external restraints of law and society, that men and societal laws are both essentially evil, and that only God is good. The laws of the spiritual world demand no restraints, but ultimately (p. 32) "things without represent the true quality of things within."

[109] "Epicurus, Leontion, and Ternissa," *Imaginary Conversations*, 2nd ser., 2 vols. (London, 1829), II, 187.

Brings from the dust the sound of liberty."

"Wisdom & goodness to the vile seem vile
Filths savour but themselves"

↑"The true↓⟨?"⟩ Philosophy is the only true prophet" [110] rose colour

All our art is ⟨to prepare⟩ ↑how↓ to use the good God provides us. There is water enough; we ⁿ are only so to shape aqu⟨a⟩educts as to bring it to our door. There is air enough; we must only so build as that it shall ventilate our house. So with man's education. There is truth enough; only open the mind's door, & straighten the passages. There are men enough; only so place yourself to them in true position (en rapport) i.e. by amity, as to suck the sweetness of society. There is power & happiness enough[.]

[68]   I will not live out of me
             I will not see with others' eyes
             My good is good, my evil ill
             I would be free — I cannot be
             While I take things as others please to rate them
             I dare ⟨aspire⟩ ↑attempt↓ to ⟨walk in⟩ ↑lay out↓ my own
                 road
             That which myself delights in shall be Good
             That which I do not want, — indifferent,
             That which I hate is Bad. That's flat
             Henceforth, please God, forever I forego
             The yoke of men's opinions. I will be
             Lighthearted as a bird & live with God.

[110] For the first of the three quotations cf. John Wilson (Christopher North), "On Reading Mr. Clarkson's History of the Abolition of the Slave Trade," ll. 47–49:
                    ". . . noble shapes,
             Kings of the desert, men whose stately tread
             Brings from the dust the sound of liberty!"
Emerson was to use part of the quotation years later in "Address to Kossuth, at Concord, May 11, 1862," W, XI, 398. The second quotation is from Shakespeare, *King Lear*, IV, ii, 38–39. The third quotation is from Landor, "Barrow and Newton," *Imaginary Conversations*, 2nd ser., 1829, II, 49. Landor's actual words, as the errata sheet indicates, were "The true philosopher is the only true prophet."

I find him in the bottom of my heart
I hear continually his Voice therein
And books, & priests, & worlds, I less esteem
Who says ⟨it is⟩ ↑the heart's↓ a ⟨false⟩ ↑blind↓ guide?
        It is not.
My heart did never counsel me to sin
I wonder where it got its wisdom
For in the darkest maze amid the sweetest baits
↑Or↓ Amid horrid dangers never once
Did that gentle Angel fail of his oracle
The little needle always knows the north
The little bird remembereth his note
And this wise Seer never errs
I never taught it what it teaches me
I only follow when I act aright.
Whence then did this Omniscient Spirit come?
From God it came. It is the Deity.[110a]

[69] 13 Oct. "If thou lovest true glory, thou must trust her truth."
                Landor ["William Penn and Lord Peterborough,"
                        Imaginary Conversations, 2nd ser., II, 258]

'She followeth him who doth not ⟨stop⟩ turn & gaze after her.' [*Ibid.*]

"Our national feelings are healthy & strong by the closeness of their intexture. What touches one class is felt by another: it sounds on the rim of the glass, the hall rings with it, & it is well if the drum & the trumpet do not catch it."

                Landor. [*Ibid.*, II, 269–270]

"The true philosophy is the only true prophet."[111] He that hath insight into principles alone hath commanding prospect of remotest results.

"No men are so facetious as those whose minds are somewhat perverted. ⟨"⟩Truth enjoys good air & clear light, but no playground."
                        [Landor, "Barrow and Newton,"
                        Imaginary Conversations, 2nd ser., II, 68]

↑"Since all transcendent,↓ all true & genuine greatness must be of a man's own raising & only on the foundations that the hand of God has

[110a] Cf. "Self-Reliance," *Poems, W*, X, 394.   [111] *Ibid.* See p. 47 above.

laid, do not let any touch it; keep them off civilly, but keep them off."

Landor [*Ibid.*, II, 91]

"Abstinence from low pleasures is the only means of ⟨inher⟩↑mer↓iting or ↑of↓ obtaining the higher.

Kindness in us is the honey that blunts the sting of unkindness in another."

Landor's Epicurus. [*Ibid.*, II, 204]

"I found that the principal" ↑(↓means ⟨"(⟩ of gratifying the universal desire of happiness) "lay in the avoidance of those very things which had hitherto been taken up as the instruments of enjoyment & content, such as military commands, political offices, clients, adventures in commerce, & extensive landed property."

L's Epicurus [*Ibid.*, II, 212, slightly misquoted]

[70] "The heart in itself is free from evil but very capable of receiving & too tenacious of holding it" [*Ibid.*, II, 224]

13 October. Exhortations & examples are better than psalms & sermons.

We have thoughts but we don't know what to do with them, materials, that we can't manage or dispose. We cannot get high enough above them to see their order in reason. We cannot get warm enough to have them exert their natural affinities & throw themselves into crystal. We see a new Sect devoted to certain ideas & we go to individuals ↑of it↓ to have them explained. Vain expectation! They ⟨follow⟩ ↑are possessed with↓ the ideas but do not ⟨embrace or command⟩ ↑possess↓ them.

Chardon St. Oct. 14, 1832. The great difficulty is that men do not think enough of themselves, do not consider what it is that they are sacrificing, when they follow in a herd, or when they cater for their establishment. They know not how divine is a Man. I know you say such a man thinks too much of himself. — Alas! he is wholly ignorant. He yet wanders in the outer darkness in the skirts & shadows of himself & has not seen his inner light[.]

[71] Would it not be the text of a useful discourse to Young men, ⟨"⟩*that, every man must learn in a different way?* ⁿ⟨"⟩⟩ How

much is lost by imitation. Our best friends may be our worst enemies. A man should learn to detect & foster that gleam of light which flashes across ⟨it⟩ his mind from within far more than the ⟨w⟩ lustre of ↑whole↓ firmament without. Yet he dismisses without notice his peculiar thought *because* it is peculiar. The time will come when he will postpone all acquired knowledge to this spontaneous wisdom & will watch for this illumination more than those who watch for the morning.[111a] For this is the principle by which the other is to be arranged. This thinking would go to show the significance of self-education; that in reality there is no other; for, all other is nought without this.

A man must teach himself because that which each can do best, none but his maker can teach him. No man yet, knows what it is, nor can, till that person has exhibited it. Where is the master that could have taught Shakspear? ⁿ Where is the master that could have instructed Franklin or Washington or Bacon or Newton? ⁿ

[72] Every great man is an unique. The Scipionism of Scipio is just that part he could not borrow. Corregiosity

Every man comes at the common results with most conviction in his own way. But he only uses a different vocabulary from yours[;] it comes to the same thing.

An imitation may be pretty, comical, popular, but it never can be great. Buonaparte mimicked Themistocles.

If any body will tell me who it is the great man imitates in the original crisis when he performs a great act — [112] ↑who Muley Molok imitated or Falkland, or Scipio, or Aristides or Phocion or Fox or More, or Alfred or Lafayette,ⁿ↓ I will tell him who else can teach him than himself.

Self Education treats on the importance of *humanity*. "How is he greater than I if he be not more just? [113] ↑detaching the man from

[111a] Cf. Ps. 130: 6.

[112] The insertion is crowded into the right side of the page under "tell . . . can" and to the right of "himself." A pointing finger is drawn into the space between "act" and "I will" as a direction for the order of insertion. The entry for October 14 is obviously concerned with self-reliance. From p. [71] "that which each can" through p. [72] "part he could not borrow." is used in "Self-Reliance," *W*, II, 83.

[113] The story of the response of Agesilaus to the word *great* applied to the

his exteriors. & whatever "*dat*" that lesson benefits the world.↓

    treats of the increase of all knowledges in the increase of the soul in one; as he that goes up a hill to see a fire in a distant village sees the whole country. & Landor knows many things[.]

    treats of the continual appeal that is made from the facts to the feelings[,] from the world to the high inward infallible ⟨self⟩ Judge ever suggesting a grander creation.

A man has got to learn that he must embrace the truth or shall never know it[,] that to be thankful for a little is the way to get more.

He is to work himself clear of how much nonsense & mischief[.]

He is to learn like the Persian to speak the truth.[114]

[73] Do ⟨w⟩you say that a mechanic must attend to language & composition? ⁿ ⟨Strong⟩ You are looking the wrong way & seeking the source in the river. Strong thinking makes strong language; correct thinking correct speech[.]

A man must teach himself because he can only read according to his state. All the chemists may blab their secrets to a carpenter & he shall be never the wiser.

S. gave a sad definition of his friend in saying he resembled a ⟨set⟩ ↑nest↓ of Indian boxes, ⟨puzzling to open,⟩ one ⁿ after the other, each a new puzzle, & when you come to the last there's nothing in it. So with each man, a splendid barricade of circumstances, the ⟨glitte⟩ renown of his name, the glitter of his coach, then his great professional character, then comes another fine shell of manners & speech but go behind all these & the Man [—]the self — is a poor, shrunken, distorted, imperceptible thing.

Persian king was a favorite with Plutarch. Emerson may have found it in the life of Agesilaus (xxiii, 5) or in the *Morals*, in any one of the following essays: "The Apophthegms of Kings and Great Commanders," "How a Man may be sensible of his Progress in Virtue," and "How a Man may Praise himself without being Envied." See Plutarch's *Morals*, 1870, I, 219; II, 455; II, 319.

[114] Herodotus in *The History*, I, 136, tells of the ancient Persian youths who were taught to ride, draw a bow, and speak the truth. Emerson may have found the idea either in Herodotus or in Byron's *Don Juan*, XVI, i.

[74] 17 Oct.

The surveyor goeth about taking positions to serve as the points of his angles, & thereby afterwards he finds the place of the mountain. The philosopher in like manner ⟨fixes tries to⟩ selects points whence he can look on his subject from ⟨a⟩ different sides & by means of many approximate results he at last ⟨deter⟩ obtains an accurate expression of the truth.

⟨I only learn that⟩ [115] That statement only is fit to be made public which you have got at in attempting to satisfy your own curiosity. For ⟨a man⟩ himself, a man only wants to know how the thing is; it is for other people that he wants to know what may be said about it.

All true greatness must come from internal growth.

If it be agreed that I am ↑⟨ever⟩ always↓ to express my thought, what forbids me to tell the company that a flea bites me or that my occasions call me behind the house? Plainly this, that my thoughts being rightly ordered these will appear to ⟨ourselves⟩ ↑myself↓ insignificant compared with those that engage my attention.

[75] 19 October. Landor said, "The true philosophy is the only true prophet." May I not ↑add↓ *the whole Future is in the bottom of the heart.*[116]

Jung Stilling said of Goethe, "the man's heart, which few know, is as true & noble as his genius, which all know." [117]

[118] If Carlyle knew what an interest I have in his persistent Goodness, would it not be worth one effort more, one prayer, one ⟨c⟩ ⟨hou⟩ meditation? ⁿ ↑But will he resist the Deluge of bad example in England?↓ One manifestation of goodness in a noble soul ⟨plunges⟩

[115] The rest of the paragraph is struck through with a wavy diagonal use mark in pencil.

[116] For the epigram from Landor, see pp. 47 and 48 above. The italicized additional apophthegm is Emerson's own, as he points out by including it in his Encyclopedia, p. [137], under the heading "My Proverbs."

[117] Quoted by Carlyle in "Schiller," *Fraser's Magazine*, III (March 1831), 138.

[118] The paragraph is struck through with a vertical use mark in pencil.

↑brings↓ him in debt to all the beholders that he shall not betray their love & trust which he has awakened.

'Praise,' said Landor, 'Keeps good men good.' [119]

Every thought is a world, — is a theory of the whole.

Fraser's Magazine. Vol 3 [pp. 127–152] March, 1831. Carl⟨is⟩yle's Notice of Schiller.

Mr. N. K. G. Oliver died on board U. S. ship Potowmac[,] Com[modore] Downes. He was Commodore's Secretary. The crew subscribed $2080.00 for the relief of his destitute family[.] [120]
The sum raised in Boston for the relief of the Cape de Verd islanders suffering from famine was about $6800.00[.]

My aunt [Mary Moody Emerson] had an eye that went through & through you like a needle. 'She was endowed,' she said, 'with the *fatal* gift of penetration.' She disgusted every body because she knew them too well.

[76] To live in a field of pumpkins yet eat no pie[.]
Oct. 27. "Luther's words were half battles." At Worms to the Diet he said "Till such time as either by proofs from Holy Scripture or by fair reason & argument I have been confuted & convicted I cannot & will not recant. It is neither safe nor prudent to do aught against conscience. Here stand I, I cannot otherwise. God assist me. Amen!"
V. Fraser's Mag. Vol 2 p 743 [121]

[119] *Imaginary Conversations*, 1st ser., 1828, III, xiii–xiv. The phrase in the dedication to vol. III is marked in Emerson's own copy.
[120] Nathaniel K. G. Oliver (1790–1832) served under Commodore John Downes (1784–1854) in the campaign against pirates in the Pacific who had violated the American ship *Friendship*; on May 2, 1832, he died of consumption. See *Niles' Weekly Register*, XLIII, 146–147, quoting *The Boston Daily Advertiser*, Nov. 3, 1832.
[121] Carlyle's version of Luther's famous statement in "Luther's Psalm," reviewing Luther's *Geistliche Lieder* (Berlin, 1817). The phrase " 'Luther's words . . . battles.' " Carlyle used also in "Goethe's Works," *Foreign Quarterly Review*, X

Oct. 28, 1832. The Vote on the question proposed to the Proprietors of the Second Church this ev.g, ⟨wa⟩stood thus — Ayes 25; Nays 34; blanks 2. On the acceptance of the pastor's letter — Ayes 30; Nays 20; blanks 4.[122]

"Look at the biography of Authors! Except the Newgate Calendar, it is the most sickening chapter in the history of man." [Carlyle] Life of [Friedrich] Schiller p. 66 [1825 ed.]

"He who would write heroic poems should make his whole life a heroic poem." Milton [123]

We want lives. We want characters of worthy men[,] not their books nor their relics. As the cultivation of an individual advances he thinks less of condition[,] less of offices & property & more keenly hunts for characters. Was it Henry who loved *a man?* [123a] ⟨I⟩So do men who would not have admitted him to their presence but for charity. There are very few finished men in the history of the world. To be sure the very expression is a solecism against faith. But there are none finished as far as they go[.] ——

[77][124] I propose to myself to read Schiller of whom I hear

---

(Aug. 1832), 31, and in "Jean Paul Friedrich Richter," *Foreign Review*, V (1830), 42, noting there its origin in Richter's *Vorschule der Aesthetik.*

[122] The question proposed and first voted on was whether the connection between the minister and the church should be dissolved. The second vote was on whether to accept Emerson's letter of September 11 in which he had requested a "dismission from the pastoral charge." A third motion was voted upon and carried: to continue the pastor's salary for the time being, that is actually until the end of the year. See Rusk, *L*, I, 356, n. 45.

[123] The quotation is struck through with a diagonal use mark in pencil. See *The Works of John Milton*, ed. F. A. Patterson, 23 vols. (New York, 1931–1940), III, Pt. I, 303–304 for the sentence in *An Apology for Smectymnuus* which is being paraphrased here: "he who would not be frustrate of his hope to write well hereafter in laudable things, ought himself to be a true Poem . . . not presuming to sing high praises of heroick men, or famous Cities, unlesse he have in himselfe the experience and practice of all that is praiseworthy." Emerson's version is, however, a quotation from Carlyle's paraphrase which Emerson had read both in *The Life of Friedrich Schiller*, 1825, p. 69, and in "The Life of Robert Burns," *The Edinburgh Review*, XLVIII (Dec. 1828), 310.

[123a] Cf. *I Henry IV*, III, iii, 107–108.

[124] The entry for the page is struck through with a wavy diagonal use mark in pencil.

much. What shall I read? His Robbers? oh no, for that was the crude ⟨production of a⟩ fruit of his ⟨unripe⟩ ↑immature↓ mind. He thought little of it himself. What then: his Aesthetics? oh no, that is only his struggle with ⟨|| ... ||⟩Kantean metaphysics[.]

His poetry? oh no, for he was a poet only by study. His histories[?] & so with all his productions[,] they were the fermentations by which his mind was working itself clear, they were the experiments by which he got his skill & the fruit[,] the bright pure gold of all was — Schiller himself.

[78] [blank]

[79] Carlyle says it was complained of Schiller's Robbers that ⟨it had⟩ the moral was bad or it had none & he saith — "but Schiller's vindication rests on higher grounds than these. His work has on the whole furnished nourishment to the more exalted powers of our nature; the sentiments & images which he has shaped & uttered, tend in spite of their alloy, to elevate the soul to a nobler pitch; & this is a sufficient defence. x x x x The writer of a work which in-terests & excites the spiritual feelings of men, has as little ↑need↓ to justify himself by showing how it exemplifies some wise saw or modern instance as the doer of a generous action has to demonstrate its merit by deducing it from the system of Shaftesbury, or Smith or Paley or whichever happens to be the favourite system of the age ⟨or⟩& place. The instructiveness of the one & the virtue of the other exist independently of all systems ⟨&⟩ or saws & in spite of all."

Life of Schiller p 35–6

This is tantamount — is it not? — to Aristotle's maxim 'We are purified by pity & terror.' [125] And thus is Shakspear moral not ⟨by formal intent⟩ of set purpose but by "elevating the soul to a nobler pitch." [126] So too are all great exciters of man moral; in war & plague & shipwreck greatest virtues [80] appear. Why but that the inmost soul ⟨is moved⟩ which lies tranquil ⟨in ordinary⟩ every day, ↑is moved↓

---

[125] A paraphrase of *The Poetics*, VI, 2.
[126] Thomas Carlyle, *The Life of Friedrich Schiller*, 1825, p. 36.

& speaks. But the inmost soul is God. —   The spark passes
where the chain is interrupted.

⟨O⟩Nov. 1. N. J. Magazine had a fine remark on Sleep. "Were
not the will alternately active & quiescent, it could never be brought
to a sense ⟨of its⟩ ↑&↓ acknowledgment of its dependence ⟨up⟩on the
divine Will." [127]

"Purified through suffering." [128]

> [129] ↑⟨Is it⟩↓ hard is it to persuade the public mind of its
>   plain ⟨interest⟩ ↑duty↓ & ⟨high⟩ ↑true↓ ⟨offices⟩ interest
> ⟨tis⟩And hard to find a straight road to renown
> And hard for young men to get ↑honest↓ gold ⟨enough⟩
> And hard to find a perfect wife
> And mid the armies of ⟨weak & evil⟩ ↑imperfect↓ men
> To find a friend hardest of all
> ↑All good is hard to come by↓
> Yet all these are easilier done
> Than to live well one day — to be a Man.
> Who speaks the truth outspeaks ⟨Demosthenes⟩ ↑our
>   ⟨‖ . . . ‖⟩ Everett↓
> Who acts his thought takes place of Washington
> ↑And↓ Who ⟨hears the⟩ ↑prefers↓ ⟨whisper⟩ ↑music↓ of
>   his ⟨Conscience⟩ ↑Reason↓
> Above the thunder of all men's example
> Embraces the beatitude of God.
> ⟨Ah me⟩ Alas! ⟨how ever in act⟩ ↑that evermore↓ the
>   worldly hands
> Hang back behind the charitable Will.

[81] Nov. 6. Pope is said to have preferred this couplet among
his writings

"Lo where Maeotis sleeps & hardly flows

[127] Sampson Reed, "Sleep," *New Jerusalem Magazine*, VI (Nov. 1832), 88.
[128] Aristotle, *Poetics*, VI, 2, paraphrased. See p. 55 above.
[129] The entire poem is canceled by a heavy crosshatch of X marks.

The freezing Tanais mid a waste of snows" [130]

A part of our anxiety for the welfare of the state — that the elections should go well — proceeds peradventure from our consciousness of personal defect[.]

If the soul globe itself up into a perfect integrity — have the absolute command of its desires — it is less dependent on other men, & less solicitous concerning what they do, albeit with no loss of philanthropy. At least, that is my thought from reading Milton's beautiful vindication of himself from the charge of incontinence & intemperance. (See Vol. 1, p. 239, &c) [131] Yet seemeth it to me that we shall all feel dirty if Jackson is reëlected.

11 November. What is the grief we feel when a man dies? Is it not an uneasiness that nothing can be said? He has done nothing; he has been merely passive to the common influences that act on all men. And now that the great endowments proper to every man have passed away from this flesh we feel that the nothingness of life & character is sad dispraise. And the affectionate expressions of friendship are apologetic. [82] Certainly the feeling would be very different if the departed man had been an earnest self cultivator scattering streams of useful influence on every side of him. Then every tear that flowed would be a tribute of eulogy. Friends would not ⟨send[?]⟩ need to say any thing — his acts would speak for him. They would keep a proud silence: a rich Consolation would shine in all eyes. But now let our tears flow for the vanity of man[,] for the poor issues of a God's charity.

—— Nov. 11
Mr Walker preached today on the government of the thoughts.[132]

[130] The couplet is from *The Dunciad*, III, 87–88. For the comment, see Samuel Johnson, *Life of Pope*, in *Lives of the English Poets*, ed. G. B. Hill, 3 vols. (Oxford, 1905), III, 250.
[131] The "vindication" is in *An Apology for Smectymnuus*; Emerson is citing from an edition which he owned: *A Selection from the English Prose Works of John Milton*, ed. Francis Jenks, 2 vols. (Boston, 1826), I, 239–241.
[132] The Reverend James Walker (1794–1874) was minister of the Unitarian church in Charlestown, 1818–1839, editor of *The Christian Examiner*, 1831–1839,

Thought I, what thunders mutter in these commonplaces. Suppose
he had rolled back the cloud of ceremony & decency & showed us
how bad the smooth plausible people we meet every day in society
would be if they durst, nay how *we* should behave if we acted our
thoughts, — not how devils would do, but how good people that
hope to be saved would do if they dared, — I think it would shake
us. There are the real terrors. I wrote the same thought above.
(Oct. 2.) [133]

[83] Nov. 13.

We think so little that we are always novices in speculation. We
think so little that every new thought presented to us[,] even every
old thought in a new dress of words takes us by surprize and we are
thus at the mercy of Goethe, Kant, Cousin, Mackintosh, & even of
Burton. If from their natural centre our thoughts had taken a natural
arrangement by frequent & free exercise, we should detect the falsehood at sight in whatever was proposed to us on all the primary
questions. As it is, we can hardly stand our ground against the ready
advocate of a proven lie.

Excellence is always brand new[.]

A kingdom has the rig of a man of war; a republic the rig of
a merchantman.

Men ↑in our day↓ consent to war because the antagonists are
strangers. I know my neighbor but the Frenchman, the Malay, the
Buenos Ayrean are no more to me than *dramatis personae.*

The chief mourner does not always attend the funeral.

A fine day is not a weather breeder, but a fine day.

The whole future is in the bottom of the heart.[134]

---

and, finally, Professor of Moral and Intellectual Philosophy at Harvard, 1839–1853,
and President, 1853–1860.

[133] See pp. 45–46 above.

[134] "Excellence . . . new" is one of Emerson's own proverbial sayings, noted

[84]   " 'What shall I teach you the foremost thing?'
        — Could'st teach me off my own shadow to spring?"
                              Goethe apud Carlyle.[135]

Nov. 14.[136]

What is *called* ⁿ practical is not always so but what is felt to be
practical is so. I have heard a man call himself a practical man &
yet ⟨s⟩he said nothing to the purpose; but a mere ⟨s⟩ recluse that
could not tie a beau knot threw out the very word; ⟨out⟩ ↑forth↓ it
came, alive & ran from mouth to mouth[,] from street to street &
the whole city obeyed it. His name was Luther or Taylor or Fox
or Phillips or a thousand names besides. But you say this was a
practical man who by chance became a scholar. Yea verily, but I
say unto you that all Truth is practical,ⁿ and that there is not a man
in this multitude, gentle or simple, worker or writer who is not
practical if he pleases, when he pleases, is always practical somewhere & always is unpractical, hollow, pedantic thro' his own fault.
↑(See J. 1833 p. 91)↓

[85] ——
        Unconsciously we are furnishing comic examples, ⟨of⟩ to all
spectators, of cobwebbed ethical rules. I go to the Atheneum & read
that "man is not a clothes-horse," [137] & come out & meet in Pearl
St. my young friend who, I understand, cuts his own clothes, &
who little imagines that he points a paragraph ⟨of⟩ for Thomas

---

in Encyclopedia, p. [137], under the heading "My Proverbs" as "Excellence is new
forever". "A Kingdom . . . merchantman." is marked in Encyclopedia, p. [227],
with Emerson's symbol of authorship. "The chief mourner . . . funeral.", "A fine
day . . . day.", and "The whole future . . . heart." are all listed under "My
Proverbs". For the final apophthegm, see p. 87 below and p. 52 above.

[135] Goethe's couplet in the *Zahme Xenien* (see *Die Werke*, Cotta edition, 55 vols.,
Stuttgart and Tübingen, 1828–1835, IV, 319) reads: " 'Was lehr' ich dich vor allen
Dingen?' / Möchte über meinen eignen Schatten springen!" Carlyle translated the
couplet in "Goethe's Works," *Foreign Quarterly Review*, X (Aug. 1832), 37.

[136] The rest of the page is struck through with a wavy diagonal use mark in
pencil. Within the paragraph "His name . . . besides." is struck through with a use
mark in ink. The cross reference at the end of the page is in a different ink and was
obviously added at a later date. The passage referred to is in Journal A; see p. 327
below.

[137] Carlyle, "Goethe's Works," *Foreign Quarterly Review*, X (Aug. 1832), 6.

Carlyle. Goethe says, 'Others will never spare you.' [138] So true is it that I ⟨do not spare⟩ ↑am not reminded of↓ my own unfaithfulness when I ⟨see⟩ ↑animadvert upon↓ it ⟨large⟩ in C[arlyle].

Saturday, 11 h[our]. A. M. 24 November, 1832. Died my sister Margaret Tucker. Farewell to thee for a little time my kind & sympathizing sister. Go rejoice with Ellen, so lately lost, in God's free & glorious universe. Tell her if she needs to be told how dearly she is remembered[,] how dearly valued. Rejoice together that you are free of your painful corporeal imprisonment. I may well mourn your loss, for in many sour days I had realized the delicacy & sweetness of a sister's feeling. I had rejoiced too, as always, in the gifts of a true lady in whom was never any thing little or mean seen or suspected[,] who was all gentleness, purity, & sense with a rare elevation of sentiments. ⟨I⟩ God comfort the bitter lonely hours which the sorrowing mother must spend here. Twice a mother has she been to ⟨them⟩ all but Paulina.[139]

[86] 27 November. Instead of lectures on Architecture I will make a lecture on God's architecture, one of his beautiful works, a Day. I will draw a sketch of a Winter's day. I will trace as I can a rude outline of the foundation & far assembled influences[,] the contribution of the Universe whereon this magical structure rises like an exhalation, the wonder & charm of the immeasurable Deep. ⟨Its as⟩ The ⟨gr⟩ bed of a day ↑is eternity↓, the groundplan is Space. The account of its growth is Astronomy. Its nearer phenomena are Chemistry, Optics, Agriculture, Hydrostatics, Animated Nature. It ends again in Astronomy when it has carried forward by its few rounded hours the immense Beneficence.

This magic lanthorn with fresh pictures, this microcosm, this Bridal of the earth & sky, this God's wonder — we cannot take to pieces like a machine but we may study its miracles apart, one at a time, & learn how to find the whole world & every one of its pebbles a tongue.

---

[138] Possibly a version of some unlocated translation from Goethe's *Reinecke Fuchs*, 8,173: "Aber sie (die geistliche Herren) schonen uns nicht, uns andere Laien."
[139] Paulina Tucker Nash, now the only one of the Tucker sisters for whom the mother, Margaret Tucker Kent, had not overseen both birth and death.

The *snow* is a selfweaving blanket with which the ⟨cold⟩ parts of the globe exposed to the cold cover themselves in pile proportioned to their exposure, what time the animated creation in the same parts whiten & thicken their fleeces. The snow crystal. hexagon ↑nix columnaris↓ densum vellus tacitarum aquarum[.] [140]

[87] provision for keeping the waters of the globe fluid, immense force of crystallizing water, riving of granite blocks[,] powers of the arctic winter.

beneficent effects upon the animal, vegetable, mineral creation. most, unknown. defence of trees. Vegetable heat. e.g. last winter.

Domestic effects. ↑*crunching of the snow under the wood sled*↓ *pump frozen.* thawed by salt. *Water pitcher cracked.* leave it empty. *Clock too fast* ⟨short⟩ lengthen the pendulum. *Gloves not thick enough.* exchange them for mittens. *frost on the windows*[,] *wood splits better, & stone, worse.* ↑*cat's back & flannel vest sparkles*↓ flowers, bees, ants, flies none. ↑but instead,↓ the social apple, the breakfast honey, the good proverb.ⁿ & the flies plainsuited we are willing to spare. & their cousins the musquitoes that make men draw up the foot.

ice trade, fur trade, & country trade by means of universal rail road ↑& conservative powers of frost↓. fuel wood brought out of the wood lots. game easier procured. lime ⟨slow⟩ kiln burned.

Games. skating, sledding snowbuilding ⟨snowshoes⟩ ↑Esquimaux↓ hunting with snowshoes.

Winter Evening. Reading, Astrono⟨|| ... ||⟩mical observations. electricity.

indiarubber shoes [141]

---

[140] For "rises . . . exhalation," in the first paragraph on the page, see Milton, *Paradise Lost*, I, 711; for "Bridal . . . sky," in the second paragraph, see Herbert, "Virtue," st. 1, l. 2; the phrase in the third paragraph, "hexagon ↓nix columnaris↑" (hexagonal snow column) is drawn from Edward T. W. Polehampton and John M. Good, *The Gallery of Nature and Art, or a Tour through Creation and Science*, 6 vols. (London, 1821), IV, 167–168n. The remaining Latin phrase, "thickly the still fleecy shower [flows down]", is from Martial, *Epigrams*, IV, iii, I. See *JMN*, II, 370, n. 57.

[141] The entry "indiarubber shoes . . . beautiful." is in pencil, probably a later addition. On the next page, [88], another penciled note "Consult . . . Black" appears as an addition after the interruption of the farewell to Margaret Tucker, under a penciled line running across the page.

Winter less interesting here than in the north or in the south, but beautiful.

[88] Farewell dear girl. I have a very narrow acquaintance & of it you have been a large part. We anchor upon a few. & you have had the character & dignity that promised every thing to the esteem & affection of years. Think kindly of me. I know you will, but perchance the disembodied can do much more — can elevate this sinking spirit & purify & urge it to generous purposes[,] teach me to make trifles, trifles, & work with consistency & in earnest to my true ends. The only sister I ever had — pass on, pure soul! to the opening heaven.

Consult for "The Winter's day" Audubon
                                 Polar Regions
                                 Polehampton
                                 Daniell
                                 Black [142]

[89]   The bee upsprings
            On trumpeting wings
            The worm crawls still in the grass

            O'er the cold November grave
            Which not one kindred eye beheld
            Which strangers saw & strangers gave
            ⟨To thy poor earth dear Margaret⟩
            ⟨Over that grave the sun's cold eye⟩

The cholera cost the city of New York 110,000 dollars. & a

[142] The works to be consulted for the projected essay on winter were probably the following: John J. Audubon, *Ornithological Biography* . . . , I (Edinburgh, 1831); John Leslie, Robert Jameson, and Hugh Murray, *Narrative of Discovery and Adventure in the Polar Seas and Regions*, 3d ed. rev. (Edinburgh, 1832), a work which in the Harper Family Library edition (New York, 1833), Emerson recommended highly in letters to Elizabeth Tucker, February 1, 1832, and to Abby Larkin Adams, December 2, 1833; Polehampton and Good, *The Gallery of Nature and Art* . . . , 1821; John F. Daniell, *Meteorological Essays and Observations* (London, 1823); and Joseph Black, *Lectures on the Elements of Chemistry*, 2 vols. (Edinburgh, 1803).

vast additional expense to individuals. ⟨Sp⟩ The Holy days are said to cost Spain £7,000,000 sterling a year.

Dec. 1. I never read Wordsworth without chagrin. — A man of such great powers & ambition, so near to the Dii majores to fail so meanly in every attempt. A genius that hath epilepsy, a deranged archangel. The Ode to Duty conceived & expressed in a certain high severe style does yet miss of greatness & of all effect by such falsities or falses as

"And the most Ancient heavens thro thee are fresh
                                                    & strong" [l. 48]

which is throwing dust in your eyes because they have no more to do with duty than a dung cart has. So that fine promising passage about "the mountain winds being free to blow upon thee" &c flats out into *me & my benedictions.* [143] If he had cut in his Dictionary for words he could hardly have got worse.

[90] ――――――――――
    Among things to be reformed is this miserable practice at college of leading ingenuous youth blindfold thro' trigonometry & the other mathematics. The first scholar tells me that 'he can understand a page at a time.' & young Appleton [144] himself suggests the great good of having a preliminary treatise often referred to in the main body apprizing the reader what it all drives at. Now he has no idea. There are two sorts of *Cui bono* however. If the boy sees the truth & beauty of the problem he may well remain ignorant & indifferent for a time as to its practical applications. But if he discern neither necessary truth nor utility, he has got stone for bread.[145]
Teach me, said the young Syracusan to Archimedes[,] the divine art by which you have saved your country. " 'Divine' do you call it,"

[143] Emerson is misquoting, perhaps from memory, "Lines composed a few miles above Tintern Abbey," ll. 136–137 and ll. 144–146: "And let the misty mountain winds be free/To blow against thee; and in after years . . . with what healing thoughts/ Of tender joy wilt thou remember me,/And these my exhortations!"
[144] Edward Emerson suggested that the reference was either to Thomas Gold Appleton (Harvard, 1831) or to William Channing Appleton (Harvard, 1832). See J, II, 535n.
[145] For the allusion, cf. Matt. 7:9 or Luke 11:11.

said A., "It is indeed divine, but so it was before it saved the city. He that woos the goddess must forget the woman." —— [146]

It is not certainly to gratify any impatience of domestic sorrow by a ⟨poor⟩ parade of departed merits that this ⟨little⟩ notice of a worthy woman is offered but it is offered merely because many wet eyes will look in the obituary & ask if there is no word to be spoken over a dear & honored benefactress[,] a most gentle & virtuous lady[.]

[91] ⟨It is not⟩

In the death of Miss Margaret Tucker one ⟨is passed [n] away⟩ who was /formed/fit/ to be an ornament of Society yet has passed away almost unknown to ⟨those to whom she wished & provided according to her ability every blessing⟩ ↑it↓. A ⟨member of⟩ beloved member of a gifted family to whom uncommon accomplishments & most attractive manners ⟨belonged⟩ were the ornament & riches of a most delicate frame she has ⟨been little known to⟩ spent her few years in retirement. ⟨& her name has yet been little known.⟩ But in that family & in the much larger circle of her acquaintance she was revered & loved in an uncommon degree and as she deserved. For she possessed the charm & respect that always attaches to a strong sense when united with ⟨right the purest & most⟩ elevated sentiments. ⟨She⟩ Never was anything little or mean either seen or suspected in her. She was the ⟨judicious⟩ ↑considerate↓ but most liberal friend of all who ⟨most⟩ needed assistance & ⟨those who knew her best⟩ ↑many↓ know how ingeniously ↑sometimes↓ her ⟨fr⟩ open hand sought the luxury of beneficence. ⟨No⟩ Her extreme delicacy & sweetness never suffered ⟨sha⟩ her to wound the feelings of another & though almost

[146] Edmund Berry, *Emerson's Plutarch* (Cambridge, Mass., 1961), p. 216, suggests that this anecdote is a combination by Emerson of at least two sources, vaguely remembered. But since F. H. Hedge, in a review, "The Progress of Society," *The Christian Examiner*, XVI (March 1834), 17, tells the story exactly, calling it a "tradition concerning Archimedes," and ending with "He who would woo the goddess, must forget the woman," the tale must have been current. Hedge drew it, no doubt, from a version by Schiller, "Archimedes und der Schüler," whose final lines are " 'Göttlich nennst du die Kunst? Sie ist's,' versetzte der Weise;/ Aber das war sie, mein Sohn, eh' sie die Stadt noch gedient."

all her life the victim of slow but disheartening disease [92] it is not easy to remember that she ever complained. ⟨Possessed of ⟨ample means of generosity⟩ ↑wealth↓ she understood the office of dispensing relief & never needed any interference of friends unless to restrain her bounty.⟩ Few have preserved such dignity & gentleness thro so long a term of sickness or gone out of the world to join the friends she had never forgotten, more affectionately remembered by those whom she has left in it. ⟨Malta 3 February, 1833⟩

> None spares another yet it pleases me
> That none to any is indifferent
> No heart in all this world is separate
> But all are cisterns of one central sea
> All are mouthpieces of the Eternal Word

The good Earth[,] the planet on which we are embarked & making our annual voyage in the unharboured Deep carries in her bosom every good thing her children need on the way for refreshment, fuel, science, or action. She has coal in the hold & all meats in the larder & [is] overhung with showiest ⟨tapestry⟩ ↑awning↓. The progress of art is to equalize all places; [n] reindeer, caoutchouc ↑glass windows↓, anthracite coal, Nott stoves, ⟨wine⟩ ↑coffee↓ [147] & books will ⟨make⟩ ↑give↓ Greenland the air & ease of London. Ice, fruits, baths, refrigerators, linen will fan the hot forehead of Cuba, to the 56 degree.

presented him with a basket of provision to keep the soul & the body together one day more.[148]

[93] *Dangers.* The snowstorm
　　　Capt. Parry's *frozen men*
degree of Cold tolerable[;]−58 temperature of the celestial spaces [149]

---

[147] The inserted word and the cancellation marks through "wine" are in pencil.
[148] The fragmentary entry seems to fit no context and differs in ink from the rest of the page.
[149] "Dangers . . . spaces" is apparently a further note for the essay on "The Winter's Day" developed on pp. 60–62 above.

⟨Γλωσσης προ των αυτων κρατει θεοις επομενος
Γλωσσης προ των αλλων κρατει θεοις επομενος Pythagoras⟩
Γλωσσης προ των αλλων κρατει θεις επομενος

Pythagoras [150]

Let us draw near with a true heart in full assurance of faith, having our hearts sprinkled from an evil conscience. He[brews]. X.22

18 Oct. It occurred last night with much force that we are all guarded often from our worst enemies by ⟨our greatest weaknesses as we all⟩ what we think our greatest weaknesses. ⟨The fable⟩ Aesop's stag who praised his horns & despised his feet aptly paints the truth. The stammering tongue & awkward formal manners which hinder your success in social circles keep you true to the mark which is your own — to that particular power which God has given you for your own & others' benefit.[151]

[94] 29 Nov. I wrote to G. A. Sampson.[152] Are they not two worlds, your solitude & your society? one, heaven; the other, earth; one, real, the other apparent. And that society is best & unobjectionable which does not violate your solitude but permits you to communicate the very same train of thought. And then will our true heaven be entered, when we have learned to be the same manner of person to others that we are alone, say the same things to ⟨others⟩ them, we think alone, & to pass out of solitude into society without ⟨any⟩ change or effort. When an awkward man is alone he is graceful, all his motions are natural. When a vain man is alone, his thoughts are wise. It is the presence of other people which embarrasses them by overexciting them & they do & say ungracious things. The reason is, himself is a peppercorn & his relations to other people are the whole world in his imagination. ⟨I⟩The only remedy must be from the growth of his true self, & its mastering predominance over him so

[150] "Before others he controls the tongue, following the gods" (Ed.). A saying about Pythagoras; see Iamblichus, *Protrepticus*, ed. H. Pistelli (Leipzig, 1888).

[151] This paragraph is used in "Compensation," *W*, II, 117. The fable, "The Stag Drinking," is no. 13 in Robert Dodsley, *Select Fables of Esop and other Fabulists* (London, 1809), pp. 19–20. See also p. 329 below for a later rewording.

[152] Though what follows may be, as Rusk suggests (*L*, I, 358), a partial paraphrase of a letter actually sent to George Sampson, no original of the letter has been found; and since what is here may be meditation on the subjects raised in such a letter it has been included in the journal.

that the men [95]¹⁵³ ↑Dew Fog. Am. Almanack 1831 — p.↓ & things which looked so great shall shrink to their true dimensions as already the house in which we lived & the hills on which we ran in childhood appear smaller than they were.

[96] [blank]

[97] Nobody can teach more than he knows.

[98] Harbor of Malta, Marsa ⟨Marsatto⟩ ↑Muscetto↓ 3 February, 1833. Here in the precincts of St John, the isle of old fame under the high battlements ⟨of the⟩ once of the Knights & now of England I spend my Sunday, which shines with but little Sabbath light. 'Tout commence', as Pere Bossuet says.¹⁵⁴ It is hardly truer of me at this point of time when I am setting foot on the old world & learning two languages than it is of every day of mine so rude & un↑tr↓eady am I sent into this world. Glad very glad to find the company of a person quite the reverse of myself in all these particulars in which I fail most, who has all his knowledge & it is much & various, at his sudden command. I seem on all trivial emergences, to be oppressed with an universal ignorance. If I rightly consider that for this point of time which we call a Life, tout commence, I shall rejoice in the omen of ⟨o⟩a boundless future & not be chagrined, oh heavens, no. It is however a substantial satisfaction to benefit your companions with your knowledge, a pleasure denied me. 'Time' said friend Carlyle, 'brings Roses.'¹⁵⁵ A capital mot putting a little rouge on the old skeleton's cheeks.

[February] 10. Perhaps it is a pernicious mistake yet rightly seen I believe it is sound philosophy, that wherever we go[,] whatever

¹⁵³ The citation, occupying the top center of the page and interrupting the regular entry, apparently refers to *The American Almanac and Repository of Useful Knowledge . . .* , for 1831, ed. J. E. Worcester (Boston), pp. 77ff., which contained an essay "The Natural History of the Weather," drawing heavily on Daniell's *Meteorological Essays* and reprinted from *The Companion to the British Almanac for 1830.* Dew and fog are treated on pp. 80, 91–92, 95–96.

¹⁵⁴ Emerson first used this tag in his journals in 1824. See *Discours sur l'histoire universelle* (Paris, 1892), p. 7, cited in *JMN*, II, 217, n.15.

¹⁵⁵ "German Literature in the 14th and 15th Century," *Foreign Quarterly Review,*

we do[,] self is the sole subject we study & learn. Montaigne said, himself was all he knew.[156] Myself is much more than I know, & yet I know nothing else. The chemist experiments upon his new salt by trying its affinity to all the various substances he can ⟨col-lect⟩command arbitrarily selected & thereby discloses the most won-derful properties in his subject [99] & I bring myself to sea, to Malta, to Italy, to find new affinities between me & my fellowmen[,] to observe narrowly the affections, weaknesses, surprises, hopes, doubts, which new sides of the panorama shall ⟨operate⟩ call forth in me. Mean sneakingly mean would be this philosophy[,] a rep-tile ⟨train[?]⟩ unworthy of the name, if *self* be used in the low sense, but as self means Devil so it means God. I speak of the Universal Man to whose colossal dimensions each particular bubble can by its birthright expand. Is it the hard condition upon which the love of highest truth is given, such extreme incapacity for action & common conversation as to provoke the contempt of the bystander, even of kindred & debtors? [n] Or is it that we will put off upon our ⟨gifts⟩ nature the bad ⟨effect⟩ consequence of our faults? Hang out your temperance, my friend, as your amulet, your benevolence as your shield, your industry as your advocate and perhaps you will not have so much reason as you think to complain of ⟨the⟩ your re-ception among men. I am a full believer in the doctrine that we always make our own welcome.

Naples, 13 March. When I was at home & felt vaunty I pestered the good folks with insisting on discarding every motive but the highest. I said you need never act for example's sake; never give pledges; &c. But I think now that we need all the advantages we can get, that our virtue wants all the crutches; that we must avail

---

VIII (Oct. 1831), 391. The phrase is of course a translation of a German proverb, "Zeit bringt Rosen," as W. G. Benham notes, *Book of Quotations* (Philadelphia, 1907).

[156] The comment is a paraphrase of a commonplace in Montaigne's thought. Cf. the "preface of author to reader": "It is myself I paint . . . . Myself am the matter of my book." In the *Essays* proper he noted: " 'Tis now many years since that my thoughts have had no other aim and object than myself, that I have only pried into and studied myself." *Essays of Michael Seigneur de Montaigne*, trans. Cotton, 1700, II, 75.

ourselves of our strength & weakness & want of appetite & press
of affairs & of calculation & of fear as well as of the just & sublime
considerations ⁿ [100] of the love of God & of self respect. Not that
any others will bear comparison with these but because the tempta-
tions are so manifold & so subtle & assail archangels as well as coarser
clay that it will not do to ⟨part⟩ spare any strength.

The remembrance of the ↑affectionate↓ anxious expectation ⟨others
have⟩ with which others are intent upon your contest with temptation is a wonderful provocative to virtue. So is it when in a vast city
of corrupt men you ask who are the elegant & great men, to reflect
that in all & by all you may be making yourself the elegant, the
great, the good man, day by day. —

We are what we are made & every following Day
Is the Creator of our human mould
Not less than was the first; the all wise God
Gilds a few points in every several life
And as each flower upon the fresh hillside
And every coloured petal of each flower
Is sketched & dyed each with a new design
Its spot of purple & its streak of brown
So each man's life shall have its own ⟨beauty⟩
And a few joys, a few peculiar charms,
Round in the hours
And reconcile him to the common days.

Not many men see beauty in the fogs
Of close low pinewoods in a river town
Yet unto me not morn's magnificence,
Nor the red rainbow of a summer eve,
Nor Rome, nor joyful Paris, nor the halls
Of rich men blazing hospitable light
Nor wit↑,↓ ⟨of man⟩ ↑nor eloquence,↓ no nor even the song
Of any woman that is now alive
Hath such a soul, such divine influence
Such resurrection of the happy past
As is to me when I behold the morn

[101]

Ope in such low moist roadside, & beneath
Peep the blue violets out of the black loam
Pathetic silent poets that sing to me
Thy elegy, sweet singer, sainted wife! [157]

[102] What is it to sail
Upon the calm blue sea
To ride as a cloud
Over the purple floor
With golden mists for company?

And Day & Night are drest
Ever in their jocund vest,
And the water is warm to the hands,
And far below you see motes of light
By day, & streams of fire by night.

What is it to sail
Upon the stormy sea,
To drive with naked spars
Before the roaring gale,
Hemmed round with ragged clouds,
Foaming & hissing & thumping waves
The reeling cabin is cold & wet,
The masts are strained, & the sail is torn,
The gale blows fiercer as the night sets in
Scarce can the seaman aloft master his struggling reef,
Even the stout captain in his coat of storms
Sighs as he glances astern at the white, white combs
And the passenger sits unsocial
And puts his book aside
And leans upon his hand.
        Yet is the difference less
Between this gray sea & that golden one
Than twixt the moods of the man that sails upon it
        Today & yesterday.

[157] Cf. "Written at Naples," in *Poems*, W, IX, 395–396.

[103] March 22. Judge of your natural character by what you do in your dreams. If you yield to temptation there, I am afraid you will, awake. If you are a coward then, I jalouse of your courage by day.

> Alone in Rome! why Rome is lonely too,
> Besides you need not be alone, the Soul
> Shall have society of its own rank,
> Be great, be true, and all the Scipios
> The Catos the ⟨glorious men⟩ wise patriots of Rome
> Shall flock to you & tarry by your side
> And comfort you with their high company.
> Virtue ⟨& truth⟩ is company enough
> It keeps the key to all heroic hearts
> And opens you a welcome in them all
> You must be like them if you desire them
> Scorn trifles & embrace a better aim
> Than wine or sleep or other men's applause
> Hunt knowledge as the lover woos a maid
> And ever in the strife of your own thoughts
> Obey the nobler impulse. That is Rome
> That shall /command/call/ a Senate to your side
> For there is no force in the Universe
> That can contend with love   It reigns forever.
> Wait then sad friend wait in majestic peace
> The hour of heaven ⟨its hour will come⟩
> ⟨Its man appear⟩ Generously trust
> The web of thy fortune to the beneficent ⟨hand⟩ ↑one↓
> That until now has [n] not forgotten thee
> He watches for thee still his restless tender love
> Broods over thee and as God liveth in heaven
> However long ⟨thy⟩ thou walkest solitary

[104]   The hour of heaven will come, the man appear.[158]

Rome

21 April. I went this morn to the Church of Trinita di Monte to

---

[158] Cf. "Written at Rome," in *Poems, W*, IX, 396–397.

see some nuns take the veil. Can any ceremony be more pathetic than to see youth, beauty, rank thus self devoted to mistaken duty? [n]

[104]–[106] [Letter omitted] [159]

———

[106]   "How small of all that human hearts endure
       The part that laws or kings can cause or cure
       Still to ourselves in every place consigned
       Our own felicity we make or find."
             [Samuel Johnson, "Lines added to Goldsmith's
                'The Traveller,' " ll. 429–432]

[107] Florence
7 May. To-day I heard by Charles's letter of the death of Ellen's mother. Fast fast the bonds dissolve that I was so glad to wear. She has been a most kind & exemplary mother, & how painfully disappointed. Happy now. And oh what events & thoughts in which I ⟨have⟩ should have deepest sympathy does this thin partition of flesh entirely hide. Does the heart in that world forget the heart that did beat with it in this? Do jealousies, do fears, does the ⟨know⟩ observation of faults intervene? [n] Dearest friends, I would be loved by all of you: dearest friend! we shall meet again.

[May] 11. How little is *expressed* [n] or can be! In the least action what an infinity is *understood*! [n] I heard La Straniera performed last night. Moreover cannot a lesson of wisdom & glory be got even from the hapless   prima donna of an Italian opera? [n] At least one is informed of the extent of female powers & warned not to be too easily satisfied with the accomplishments of vulgar pretty women.

[108] I have heard that the old king George was so impatient of his state that he delighted to dress himself plainly & escape in a morning from Windsor to the market or the lanes & mix in a crowd. Well I have seen a man[,] the lord of quite another sort of prin-

---

[159] The omitted letter to Mary Moody Emerson dated Rome, April 22, is a partial copy of a letter of April 18 and May? c. 17? printed in full in *L*, I, 375–376. The partial copy, which is printed in *J*, III, 100–103, with variations only in punctuation, differs from the original in minor wording and in the omission of the beginning, of the end, and of some phrases within the letter.

cipality[,] forced to pay the same price for all his knowledge & to unking himself & take knocks from such "parmaceti" gentlemen in order to have a peep at men.

May 18.[160] I told Landor I thought it an argument of weak understanding in Lord Chesterfield, his slippery morality. It is inexcusable in any man who pretends to greatness to confound moral distinctions. ⟨Truly wise men,⟩ True genius, whatever faults of action it may have, never does. Shakespear never does, though a loose liver. But such fry as Beaumont & Fletcher & Massinger do continually. And Chesterfield did. Well for him if he had often thought & spoken as when he said — "I judge by every man's truth of his degree of understanding." [161]

[109] I think it was of Socrates that Landor dared to say, so far can a humoursome man indulge a whim, "he was a vulgar sophist & he [Landor] could not forgive vulgarity in any body; if he saw it in a wise man he regretted it the more."

"un ⟨uomo⟩ ↑tale↓ le cui mani giugnevano spesso dove non arrivava la vista degli altri." I Promessi Sposi Vol. 2. p. 121.[162]

I like the sayers of No better than the sayers of Yes.

On bravely thro' the sunshine or the showers
Time hath his work to do & we have ours.[163]

"Il tempo il suo mestiere, ed io il mio" I promessi sposi

[160] "108" with the 8 overlying the o is written above "May 18." The number may be a cancellation and miswriting of the date or possibly a repetition of the page number.
[161] A slight misquotation of a remark by Chesterfield in letter 41, September 21, O.S., 1747. See *The Letters of Philip Dormer Stanhope, Lord Chesterfield*, ed. J. Bradshaw, 3 vols. (London, 1892), I, 59.
[162] Still in Emerson's library is a 3-volume edition of Alessandro Manzoni's *I Promessi Sposi* (Torino, 1827). But neither in this Italian edition nor in the 1828 edition (Piacenza) does the citation fall on the page given. Either Emerson made an error in numbering or used some other edition than that in his library, where the quotation is in ch. 18, II, 139.
[163] By Emerson? The couplet is printed as the motto for "The Man of Letters," in *Lectures and Biographical Sketches*, W, X, 239.

"Dorremmo pensare piu a far bene che a star bene."

Uomo di studio, egli non amava nè di comandare ne di obbedire.[164]

[110] 25 May. Is not Santa Croce a grand church! Nobody knows
how grand who only sees it once. Its tombs! Its tombs! And then the
mighty windows of stained glass which a man sees at noon & thinks
he knows what they are worth & comes back after sunset & finds to
his delight (I did) a wholly novel & far more beautiful effect. They
should be seen just ⟨after⟩ about the hour of candlelight. —— We
come out to Europe to learn what man can,[n] —— what is the utter-
most which social man has yet done. And perhaps the most satisfactory
& most valuable impressions are those which come to each individual
casually & in moments when he is not on the hunt for wonders. To
make ⟨a⟩ ↑any↓ sincere good use, ↑I mean what I say,↓ of what he sees,
he needs to put a double & treble guard upon the independency of
his judgments. The veriest Luther might well suspect his own
opinion upon the Venus or the Apollo.

[111] Venice. 2 June, 1833. The ancient metropolis of the merchants. In coming into it, it seemed a great oddity but not at all
attractive. Under the full moon, later in the evening St Mark's piazza
showed like a world's wonder, but still I pity the people, who are
not beavers, & yet are compelled to live here. But what matter where
& how, as long as all of us are estranged from truth & love, from
Him who is truth & love[?] Sometimes I would hide myself in the
dens of the hills, in the thickets of an obscure country town[,] I am so
vexed & chagrined with myself, — with my weakness, with my guilt.
Then I have no skill to live with men, that is, with such men as the
world is made of, & such as I delight in, I seldom find. It seems to
me, no boy makes so many blunders or says such awkward, contrary,
disagreeable speeches as I do. In the attempt to oblige a person I
wound & disgust him. I pity the hapless folks that have to do with
me. But would it not be cowardly to flee out of society & live in the
woods? I comfort myself with a reference to the great & eternal

[164] The three Italian quotations are from Manzoni's *I Promessi Sposi*, chs. 37, 38,
and 27 respectively, or III, 292, III, 327, and III, 60 in the 1827 edition in Emerson's library.

revolution which, under God, bears the good of us all, — thine & mine — & that of each by the instrumentality of the other, on the wings of these dull hours & months & years.

[112] I collect ↑nothing that can be touched or tasted or smelled,↓ neither cameo, painting, nor medallion; nothing in my trunk but old clothes, but I value much the growing picture which the ages have painted & which I ⟨s⟩ reverently survey. It is wonderful how much we see in five months, ⟨how⟩ in how short a time we learn what it has taken ⟨ages⟩ so many ages to teach.

↑Milan, 10 June.↓

Architecture, — shall I speak what I think, — seems to me ever an imitation. Accustomed to look at our American churches as imitative I cannot get it out of my head that these which I now see are only more splendid & successful imitations also. I am perplexed with my inveterate littleness. I must & will see the things in detail & analyze all, every noble sentiment to the contrary notwithstanding. It seems to me nothing is truly great, nothing impresse⟨d⟩s us, nothing overawes, nothing crowds upon us, & kills calculation[.] We always call in the effect of imagination, coax the imagination to hide this & enlarge that & even St Peter's, nor this frostwork cathedral at Milan with its 5000 marble people all over its towers ⟨nor⟩ can charm down the little Imp.

[113] It is in the soul that architecture exists & Santa Croce & this Duomo are poor far-behind imitations. I would rather know the metaphysics of architecture as of shells & flowers than anything else in the matter — But one act of benevolence is better than a cathedral, so do you duty, yours. Architecture[,] said the lady[,] is frozen music.[165] And Iarno says in Wilhelm that he ⟨‖ ... ‖⟩ who does the best ⟨does⟩ in each one thing he does, does all. For he sees the connexion between all good things.[166]

[165] Mme. de Staël, *Corinne*, Bk. IV, ch. 3. See p. 40 above.

[166] A paraphrase from Carlyle's translation of Goethe's *Wilhelm Meister's Travels*, ch. 6. See *The Works of Thomas Carlyle*, Centenary ed. (London, 1896–1901), XXIV, 228: "For the highest [mind], in doing one thing, does all; or, to speak less paradoxically, in the one thing which he does rightly, he sees the likeness of all that is done rightly."

Paris. It shall be writ in my Memoirs (as Aunt Mary would say) as it was writ of St Pachomius "Pes ejus ad saltandum non est commotus omni vita sua." [167] The worse for me in the gay city. Pray what brought you here, grave sir? the Moving Boulevard seems to say.

Paris, July 4, 1833. The two gifts of the Old World to the New — Columbus & Lafayette.[168]

"Aimer pleurer mourir" c'est la vie de la femme. Title of a novel just published.[169]

It is not the confidence in our own opinion but our conviction of our neighbor's error.

July 9. How does everybody live on the outside of the world? All young persons thirst for a *real* existence[,] for an object, — for something great & good which they shall do with all their heart. Meantime they all pack gloves, or [114] keep books, or travel, or draw indentures, or cajole old women.

[July] 11 Does any man render written account to himself of himself? I think not. Those who have anything worth repeating, ah! the sad confession! Those who are innocent have been employed in tape & pins. When will good work be found for great spirits? When shall we be able without a blush & without harm to utter to the world our inmost thought?

Thus shall I write memoirs? A man who was no courtier but loved men went to Rome & there lived with boys. He came to France & in Paris lives alone & in Paris seldom speaks. If he do not see

---

[167] "He had never shaken his foot in dancing in his whole life" (Ed.). St. Pachomius was a 3rd-century Egyptian saint who first wrote down the monastic rule.

[168] Emerson enters this sentiment as a toast in Encyclopedia, p. [39], but does not mark it with his sign of authorship.

[169] The *Bibliographie de la France* lists the following under Saturday, April 27, 1833: "*Aimer, pleurer, mourir*, par Mme. la baronne de M. Deux volumes, Paris, 1833."

Carlyle in Edinburgh he may go to America with out saying anything in earnest except to Cranch & to Landor.

The errors of traditional Christianity as it now exists, the popular
faith of many millions, need to be removed to let men see the divine
beauty of moral truth. I feel myself pledged if health & opportunity
be granted me to ⟨maintain⟩ demonstrate that all necessary truth is
its own evidence; that no doctrine of God need appeal to a book;
that Christianity is wrongly received by all such as take it for a
system of doctrines, — its stress being upon moral truth; it is a rule
of life not a rule of faith.

And how men can toil & scratch so hard for things so dry,
lifeless, unsightly as these famous dogmas [115] when the divine
beauty of the truths to which they are related lies behind them, how
they can make such a fuss about the case & never open it to see the
jewel — is strange, is pitiful.

——— ↑Paris, 12 July.↓ [170]
Is it not true that in every season of excited thought when a
man has a strong conception of God, it is wholly new to him, he
perceives that he has never penetrated so far before into the Holy
of holies? And yet every time.

St Charles Borromeo — what a man was he! what a priest!

———
You cannot answer at the hour the argument of little men which
insists on the unavoidableness of sensual pleasure to such constitu-
tions as ours but St Charles Borromeo is answer enough[,] any great
& noble man is answer enough[,] any one who will not be little,
who will bestir himself, who will use his faculties & do his duty.

Be cheerful. What an insane habit is this of groping ⟨& scraping⟩
always into the past months & scraping together every little pitiful
⟨f⟩instance of awkwardness & misfortune & keeping my nervous [116]

[170] The dated heading differs in color of ink from the rest of the entry. The
paragraph following it is struck through with a wavy diagonal use mark in pencil.

system ever on the rack. It is the disease of ⟨an⟩a ⟨ill⟩ man who is at the same time idle & too respectful to the opinions of others.

Il tient son affaire

London, July 24. Here in the great capital it needs to say some thing of the creature immortal that swarms on this spot. Coming to Boulogne, I thought of the singular position of the American traveller in Italy. It is like that of a being of another planet who invisibly visits the earth. He is a protected ⟨seer⟩ witness. He sees what is that boasted liberty of manners — free of all puritan starch — & sees what it is worth — how surely it pays its tax. He comes a freeman among slaves. He learns that old saws are true which is a great thing. He is not now to be answered any longer in his earnest assertions of moral truth by the condescending explanation that these are his prejudices of country & education. He has seen how they hold true through all the most violent contrasts of condition & character.

[117] 28 July. Attended divine service at Westminster Abbey. The bishop of Gloucester preached. It is better than any church I have seen except St Peter's.

Happy the man who never puts on a face but ⟨always⟩ ⟨‖ . . . ‖⟩ receives every visiter with that countenance he has on.

Liverpool, 1 September, 1833. I thank the great God who has led me through this European scene[,] this last schoolroom in which he has pleased to instruct me from Malta's isle, thro' Sicily, thro' Italy, thro' Switzerland, thro' France, thro' England, thro' Scotland, in safety & pleasure & has now brought me to the shore & the ship that steers westward. He has shown me the men I wished to see [—] Landor, Coleridge, Carlyle, Wordsworth [—] he has thereby comforted & confirmed me in my convictions. Many things I owe to the sight of these men. I shall judge more justly, less timidly, of wise men forevermore. To be sure not one of these is a mind of the very first class, but ⟨the⟩ what the intercourse with each of these suggests is true of intercourse with better men, that they never *fill the ear* — fill the mind — no, it is an *idealized* portrait which always we

78

draw of them. ⟨To⟩ Upon an intelligent man, wholly a stranger to their names, they would make [118] in conversation no deep impression — none of a world-filling fame — they would be remembered as sensible well read earnest men — not more. Especially are they all deficient all these four — in different degrees but all deficient — in insight into religious truth. They have no idea of that species of moral truth which I call the first philosophy. [Peter Hunt [171] is as wise a talker as either of these men. Don't laugh.]

The comfort of meeting men of genius such as these is that they talk sincerely. They feel themselves to be so rich ⟨in thought⟩ that they are above the meanness of pretending to knowledge which they have not ↑& they frankly tell you what puzzles them↓. But Carlyle. Carlyle is so amiable that I love him. But I am very glad my travelling is done. A man not old feels himself too old to be a vagabond. The people at their work, the people whose avocations I interrupt by my letters of introduction accuse me by their looks for leaving my business to hinder theirs.

These men make you feel that fame is a conventional thing & that man is a sadly 'limitary' spirit. You speak to them as to children or persons of inferior capacity whom it is necessary to humor; adapting our ⟨rem⟩tone & remarks to their known prejudices & not to our knowledge of the truth.

[119] I believe in my heart it is better to admire too rashly, as I do, than to be admired too rashly as the great men of this day are. They miss by their premature canonization a great deal of necessary knowledge, & one of these days must begin the world again (as to their surprize they will find needful) poor. I speak now in general & not of these individuals. God save a great man from a little circle of flatterers. I know it is sweet, very sweet, rats bane.

Today I heard Mr Hinckes, Mr Martineau, & Mr Yates, preach.

---

[171] Benjamin Peter Hunt had been one of Emerson's 18 students in his school at Chelmsford in 1825. Of him Emerson had remarked, "He was a philosopher whose conversation made all the social comfort I had." See *J*, II, 355, n. 1. After a hiatus in their relationship from 1830–1835, Emerson reinvoked the friendship through correspondence. See *L*, I, 431–432.

Yates who wrote against Wardlaw.[172] He preached the best sermon I have heard in England — a great deal the best. Here at my Hotel, the Star & Garter, Paradise Street, I have found Jacob Perkins[,] the inventor of so many improvements in steam engines. He has been illuminating me upon the science of heat[.]

Could not Wordsworth have kept to himself his intimations that his new edition was at the bookseller's & contained some improvements? [n] John Milton was a poet not a bookmaker, although The Muse made Shakspear, Milton made his Muse.[173]

[120] True elevation which nothing can bring down is that of moral sentiment. All C[arlyle]'s intellect did not hinder an unpleasant emotion at hearing about ⟨the⟩ his occupation. But Johnson's school or Peter Hunt's are above contempt and an act of heroism[,] 'a Roman recovery'[,] would have enshrined C. a saint for me. I love his love of truth. The spot is the preference of such a scrub as Mirabeau to Socrates.

At sea. Sunday, 8 September, 1833. I wrote above my conviction that the great men of England are singularly ignorant of religion. They should read Norton's Preface to his new book who has stated that fact well.[174] Carlyle almost ⟨covets⟩ ↑grudges↓ the poor peasant his Calvinism. Must I not admit in the same moment that I have practical difficulties myself? [n] I see or believe in the wholesomeness of Calvinism for thousands & thousands. I would encourage or rather

[172] To hear these three well-known Unitarian preachers, Emerson probably attended the Paradise Street Chapel, to which James Martineau (1805–1900) had come as pastor in 1832. William Hincks (1794–1871) had been minister at Renshaw Street, Liverpool, 1822–1827, and was in 1833 Professor of Natural History at Manchester College, York. James Yates (1789–1871) had become pastor of the Carter Lane Chapel in London in 1833, having become famous within his sect for *Vindicating Unitarianism* (1815), his reply to Ralph Wardlaw's attack, *Discourses on the Principal Parts of the Socinian Controversy* (1814). Yates's text was I Pet. 5:5, "Be clothed with humility." See pp. 236–237 below.

[173] Possibly an unlocated quotation or Emerson's own phrase, since he makes a similar though less aphoristic remark on Milton and Shakespeare in "Milton," *W*, XII, 276.

[174] Andrews Norton, *A Statement of Reasons for not believing the Doctrines of Trinitarians concerning the Nature of God and the Person of Christ* (Boston, 1833).

I would not discourage their scrupulous religious observances. I dare not speak lightly of usages which I omit. And so with this hollow obeisance to things I do not myself value I go on not pestering others with what I do believe & so ↑I am↓ open to the name of a very loose speculator, ⟨the⟩ ↑a↓ faint heartless supporter of a frigid & empty theism, a man of no rigor of manners[,] of no vigor of benevolence. Ah me! what hope of reform[,] what hope of communicating religious light to benighted Europe if they who have what they call the Light are so selfish & timid & cold & their faith so unpractical &

[120ₐ]¹⁷⁵   Liverpool, 2 September, 1833.
No sailing today, so you may know what I have seen & heard in the four days I have been here. Really nothing external, so I must spin my thread from my bowels. It must be said this is the least agreeable city to the traveller in all England — a good packet office — no more. Glad I bid adieu to England, the old, the rich, the strong nation, full of arts & men & memories[;] nor can I feel any regret in the presence of the best of its sons that I was not born here. I am thankful that I am an American as I am thankful that I am a man. ⟨It can only⟩ It is its best merit to my eye that it is the most resembling country to America which the world contains. ———— The famous burden of English taxation is bearable. Men live & multiply under it, though I have heard a father in the higher rank of life speak with regret of the increase of his family.

⟨B⟩That is all I can say. I am at a dead stand. I can neither write nor read more[.] If the vessel do sail they say we shall be drowned on the lee shore[;] if she do not sail I perish waiting. What's the odds? I have plainly said my last word[;] it is the prodigality of ink[,] the wanton destruction of paper to add another syllable & withal a singular exhibition of what fatuity a man is capable who reckons himself sometimes an educated & thinking man. Yet must I write still. Why — these lines are the expectants of the dinner[;]

---

¹⁷⁵ The broken-off entry is continued on p. [121]. The interruption resulted from the insertion of a sheet folded folio into four pages, the last of which is blank, pinned to the left bottom margin of p.[121]. See the headnote, p. 3 above. The pinned-in sheet has been folded vertically at some time, apparently for easier carriage within a pocket or wallet. Page numbers for the insert (120ₐ, 120ᵦ, 120ᵧ, and 120ᵨ) have been added by the editor. The insert may have been the draft of a letter.

it is cold & I cannot go out — Why should I? I have bid goodbye
to all the people. Shall I make them repeat their tears & benedictions?
There are no books in the [120$_b$] house. I have digested the newspaper. I have no companion. Even Mr P[erkins]. when at home has
finished his communications, & we have got to theology at last. If it
won't rain after the soles & cutlets I will brave one family whom I
have parted from. Ah me Mr Thomas Carlyle I would give a gold
pound for your wise company this gloomy eve. Ah we would speed
the hour. Ah I would rise above myself[.] What self complacent
glances casts the soul about in the moment of fine conversation esteem-
ing itself the author of the fine things it utters & the master of the
riches the memory produces & how scornfully looks it back upon the
plain person it was yesterday without a thought. It occurs forcibly[,]
yea some what pathetically[,] that he who visits a man of genius
out of admiration for his parts should treat him tenderly. ⟨The o⟩
'Tis odds but he will be disappointed. That is not the man of genius's
fault. He was honest & human but the fault of his own ignorance
of the limits of human excellence. Let him feel then that his visit
was unwelcome & that he is indebted to the tolerance & good nature
of his idol & so spare him the abuse of his own reacting feelings[,]
the backstroke.

3 Sept. No sailing still, but sitting still. I went to the railroad & saw
Rocket & Goliath [120$_c$] & Pluto & Firefly & the rest of that vulcanian
generation. Mr Perkins says they should not go faster than 15 miles
the hour, it racks the engines so to go faster. There are 30 locomotives
upon the road. Three only have the Circulators. There is no such
thing as latent heat. The thermometer indicates all the heat that is
present. Only when the particles of the water expand in vapor, the
particles of the heat expand also. High pressure steam engines are
safer than low.

He says that he confidently expects the time will come when
the Ocean will be navigated by merchantmen *by steam* as the most
economical means but there is a great deal to be done first[;] that
now very little advantage is taken of the *expansion* of steam[,] its
most important property. Mr P. recited with glee his victory over
one of the directors of the Manchester road. Mr P. showed that his

engine had beat the ⟨s⟩Sun (Stephenson's) all last week doing more work with less coke. Director said that was because Sun had been out of order. Mr P. reminded him of the quantity of coke which the Director had alleged was needful always to the ton & the hour for said engine, to which Director assented. Well[,] said Mr P.[,] I have here certificates of your servants to show that the Sun[n] performed the same work all last week with a fraction less coke. The Director acknowledged it could not be much out of order.

[120$_a$] [blank]

[121] in their judgment so unsuitable for the middling classes. I know not, I have no call to expound, but this is my charge plain & clear to act faithfully upon my own faith, to live by it myself, & see what a hearty obedience to it will do.

[Carlyle deprecated the state of a man living in rebellion as he termed it with no worship, no reverence for any body. Himself he said would worship any one who showed him more truth. And Unitarians he thought were a tame limitary people who were satisfied with their sciolistic system & never made great attainments — incapable of depth of sentiment.]

Back again to myself. I believe that the error of religionists lies in this[,] that they do not know the extent or the harmony or the depth of their moral nature, that they are clinging to little, positive, verbal, formal versions of the moral law & very imperfect versions too, while the infinite laws, the laws of the Law, the great circling truths whose only adequate symbol is the material laws, the astronomy, &c, are all unobserved, & sneered at when spoken of, as frigid & insufficient. I call Calvinism such an imperfect version of the moral law. Unitarianism is another, & every form of Christian and of Pagan faith in the hands of incapable teachers is such a version. On the contrary in the hands of a true Teacher, the falsehoods, the pitifulnesses, the sectarianisms of each are dropped & the sublimity & the depth of the Original is penetrated & exhibited to men. I say also that all that recommends each of these established ⟨creeds⟩ systems of opinion to men is so much of this Moral Truth as [122] is in them, & by the instinctive selection of the preacher is made to shine forth when the system is assailed.

And because of this One bottom ⟨it is⟩ that the eminent men of each church, Socrates, A Kempis, Fenelon, Butler, Penn, Swedenborg, Channing think & say the same thing[.]

But the men of Europe will say, Expound; let us hear. What is it that is to convince the faithful & at the same time the philosopher? Let us hear this new thing. It is very old. It is the ⟨af⟩old revelation that perfect beauty is perfect goodness[;] it is the development of the wonderful congruities of the moral law of human nature. Let me enumerate a few of the remarkable properties of that nature. A man contains all that is needful to his government within himself. He is made a law unto himself. All real good or evil that can befal him must be from himself. He only can do himself any good or any harm. Nothing can be given to him or taken from him but always there is a compensation. There is a correspondence between the human soul & everything that exists in the world, — more properly, everything that is known to man. Instead of studying things without the principles of them[,] all may be penetrated unto within him. Every act puts the agent in a new condition. The purpose of life seems to be to acquaint a man with himself. He is not to live to the future as described to him but to live to the real future by living to the real present. The highest revelation is that God is in every man. I [176]

[123] 1833, February.

Malta. I am now pleased abundantly with St John's Church in Valetta. Welcome these new joys. Let my American eye be a child's again to these glorious picture books. The chaunting friars, the carved ceilings, the Madonnas & Saints, they are lively oracles, quotidiana et perpetua.[177]

Silver gates

[176] After the incompleted entry a quarter of the page is left blank, perhaps as space for a later addition to or completion of the thought.

[177] "daily and continually" (Ed.). The entry is obviously a note from about February 16 or 17, 1833, when he first visited St. John's Church in Valetta and read of indulgences. See pp. 116–121 below for his other comments on sightseeing in Malta.

Louis Debeaujolais [178]

You have one inner rule. You leave that & measure your actions by a laxer rule of others. In vain. They won't judge you by theirs but will hold you to your own. Spite of themselves they will find out & use that secret inner rule of yours cobwebbed up in thickest darkness of nature as you thought.
Everything intercepts us from ourselves[.] [179]

[124] Liverpool, 10 September. I have heard the proverb that there is no evil but can speak.[180] Especially in these days when every sentiment & ↑every↓ class of opinions & interests has its organ & voice is there no evil but speaks. Also consider that every week Europe sends this voice of all its opinions & interests by its periodical press or occasional works into America[;] it ⟨wo⟩ follows that one can better know what transpires there by reading here (with more accuracy & in a shorter time) than by the slow & partial method of personal observation in travelling. It seems to argue great simplicity then for a traveller to undertake to inform us upon Europe because he has seen it. So it would. You have ⟨seen more⟩ learned more by contenting yourself with this abbreviated tabulated method. I will then say what I have to say merely in confirmation of your results & by no means pretending to state new views or theories.[181]
                                                            ☞

The whole creation groaneth until now waiting for that which shall be revealed.[182]

[178] Both fragmentary notes refer to St. John's Cathedral in Malta whose Chapel of the Virgin possessed "large silver gates which form a pierced screen," according to William Talleck, *Malta under the Phenecians, Knights, and English* (London, 1900), p. 68. The so-called French Chapel contained a sarcophagus in memory of Louis-Charles-d'Orleans, Comte de Beaujolais, a younger brother of Louis Philippe, who died in Malta in 1808 and whose full-length recumbent statue, as well as the silver gates, was no doubt pointed out as a memorable sight.

[179] Possibly an echo of a phrase Emerson may have read in Montaigne, "Of Vanity," *Essays*, 1693, II, 359: "Look into your self, discover your self, keep close to your self . . . . Men steal you from your self."

[180] "There is no ill thing in Spain but that which can speak." Knox, *Elegant Extracts . . . in Prose*, 1797, II, 1035; see p. 17 above.

[181] Below and to the right of "theories." is a pointing hand directed toward the lower half of the facing page, which is, however, blank.

[182] A paraphrase of Rom. 8:22–23.

[125] Loud winds last night but the ship swam like a waterfowl betwixt the mountains of sea. The wise man in the storm prays God not for safety from danger but for deliverance from fear. It is the storm within which endangers him[,] not the storm without. But it is a queer place to make one's bed in, the hollows of this immense Atlantic; Mazeppalike we are tied to the side of these wild horses of the Northwest. But this rough breath of Heaven will blow me home at last, as once it blew me to Gibraltar. The powerful trumpet of the blast finds a response to all its stops in the ⟨men⟩ bottom of the heart of the men in the cabin[.]

[126] At sea. 17 September. Yesterday I was asked what I mean by Morals. I reply that I cannot define & care not to define. It is man's business to observe & the definition of Moral Nature must be the slow result of years, of lives, of states perhaps of being. Yet in the morning watch on my berth I thought that Morals is the science of the laws of human action as respects right & wrong. Then I shall be asked — And what is Right? Right is a conformity to the laws of nature as far as they are known to the human mind. — These for the occasion but I propound definitions with more than the reserve of the feeling abovenamed — with more because my own conceptions are so dim & vague. But nevertheless nothing darkens, nothing shakes, nothing diminishes my constant conviction of the eternal concord of those laws which are perfect music & of which every high sentiment & every great action is only a new statement & therefore & insomuch speaks aloud to the whole race of man. I conceive of them by no types but the apparent hollow sphere of the whole firmament wherein this ball of the earth swims. Not easy are they to be enumerated but he has some idea of them who considers such propositions as St. Bernard's, Nobody can harm me but myself,[183] or who developes the doctrine in his own experience that nothing can be given or taken without an equivalent[.]

---

[183] A misquotation of an epigram that Emerson was fond of: "For after all, nothing can work me mischief except myself." The sentiment was found in a book which he owned, George Stanhope's translation, *Pious Breathings, Being the meditations of St. Augustine . . . to which are added Select Contemplations from St. Anselm and St. Bernard* (London, 1818), p. 401. See *JMN*, III, 339.

[127] Milton describes himself in his letter to Diodati as enamoured of moral perfection.[184] He did not love it more than I. That which I cannot yet declare has been my angel from childhood until now. It has separated me from men. It has watered my pillow[;] it has driven sleep from my bed. It has tortured me for my guilt. It has inspired me with hope. It cannot be defeated by my defeats. It cannot be questioned though all the martyrs ⟨turn⟩ apostat⟨e⟩ize. It is always the glory that shall be revealed; it is the 'open secret' of the universe; [185] & it is only the feebleness & dust of the observer that makes it future, the whole *is* now potentially in the bottom of his heart.[186] It is the soul of religion. Keeping my eye on this I understand all heroism, the history of loyalty & of martyrdom & of bigotry, the heat of the methodist, the nonconformity of the dissenter, the patience of the Quaker. But what shall the hour say for distinctions such as these — this hour of southwest gales & rain dripping cabin? ⁿ ⟨It can only be pretended that the⟩ As the law of light is fits of easy transmission & reflexion [186a] such is also the soul's law. She is only superior at intervals to pain, to fear, to temptation[,] only in raptures unites herself to God and Wordsworth truly said

> Tis the most difficult of tasks to keep
> Heights which the soul is competent to gain.
> [*The Excursion*, IV, 138–139]

What is this they say about wanting mathematical certainty for

[184] Letter VII, to Charles Diodati, September 23, 1637, in *Works*, 1931–1940, XII, 25–26.

[185] Though the phrase is proverbial and may be traced back through Schiller, Gozzi, and Calderon to the *Miles Gloriosus* of Plautus (1. 1014), it undoubtedly came to Emerson from Goethe via Carlyle. Goethe spoke of "ein offenbares Geheimnis" (see *Maximen und Reflexionen*, ed. H. Hech, Goethe Gesellschaft, Weimar, 1907, XXI, no. 201); Carlyle found the tag so useful that he employed it in five different essays between 1827 and 1832, all of which Emerson probably knew: "The State of German Literature" (1827); "Goethe" (1828); "Jean Paul Friedrich Richter Again" (1830); "Biography" (1832); and "The Death of Goethe" (1832). See *The Works of Thomas Carlyle*, Centenary ed., XXVI, 41; XXVI, 225; XXVII, 131; XXVIII, 58; and XXVII, 377. The version in "The State of German Literature" is identical with Emerson's.

[186] Emerson is paraphrasing his own proverb. See pp. 52 and 58 above.

[186a] The phrase is Newton's. See David Brewster, *The Life of Sir Isaac Newton* (New York, 1831), pp. 78, 272.

moral truths? ⁿ I have always affirmed they had it. Yet they ask me whether I know the soul immortal. No. But do I not know the now to be eternal?

[128] Is it not a sufficient reply to the red & angry worldling colouring as he affirms his unbelief — ⟨is⟩ to say Think on living? [187] I have ⟨no⟩ to do ↑no↓ more than you with that question of another life. I believe in this life. I believe it continues. As long as I am here I plainly read my duties as writ with pencil of fire[;] they speak not of death. They are woven of immortal thread.

Men seem to be constitutionally believers & unbelievers. There is no bridge that can cross from a mind in one state to a mind in the other. All my opinions, affections, whimsies, are tinged with belief, — incline to that side. All that is generous, elegant, rich, wise, looks that way. But I cannot give reasons to a person of a different persuasion that are at all adequate to the force of my conviction. Yet when I fail to find the reason, ⟨is not⟩ my faith ↑is not↓ less.

Unpalatable must be always the argument based upon the text, "If ye do my Father's will ye shall know of the doctrines[,]" [188] & almost incapable of being used in conversation.ⁿ It is felt as a gross personality. Yet it is a good topic for the preacher & a better topic for the closet. I believe that virtue purges the eye[,] that the abstinent, ⟨humble⟩ meek, benevolent, industrious man is in a better state for the fine influences of the great universe to act upon him than the cold, idle, eating disputant. The ⟨barr⟩ rocky, dry, fallow ⟨field⟩ ↑ground↓ says "I can produce nothing — nothing will grow — yet I see the sun & feel the rain as much as you." Aye replies the cornfield but they have plucked away my stones & turned up my surface & let in the watercourses & now [129] the sun & the air[,] the heat & the snow all serve me.

Is it not singular & not at all unpleasing the fact that almost all great men have been so yoked together by the accidents of their lives & few or none stand alone but all in genial constellation? ⁿ John Evelyn gave a pension to Jeremy Taylor. Jeremy Taylor & John Milton both did homage to the same lady ↑Countess of Carbery↓

---

[187] Goethe's phrase from *Wilhelm Meister's Apprenticeship*. See p. 40 above.
[188] John 7:17, slightly misquoted.

one in his Dedication[,] the other in his Comus.[189] Milton & Galileo.
⟨Hume⟩ Clarke, Butler, & Hume. Cervantes & Shakespear. Sir Henry
Wotton was a hoop of gold to what a company! ⟨Dante, Boccacio, &
Petrarch⟩ Dante died at Ravenna[,] 1321. Fifty one years after[,]
Boccacio was made professor at Florence to lecture upon the Divine
Comedy & in 1351 Boccacio was sent by the Florentines to Padua
to intreat Petrarch to return & end his days ⟨there⟩ in his native city.
These are God's mnemonics. ↑Newton was born the year Galileo died.
Cuvier, Scott, & Mackintosh were born & died in the same years[.]↓[190]

———

It were a good topic for a sermon to preach upon serenity of
mind; manners; countenance; according to the sentiment of ⟨a⟩ some
pretty verses on "Consider the lilies of the field how they grow" —
verses contained in The Pious Minstrel (& which also have the fine
line, "Christ's blessing at your heart is warm;") and according to
the sentiment of Herbert's Verses upon Rest.[191] "Study to be quiet"
[I] Thess. [52:7]

[130]   I will not hesitate to speak the word
             Committed to me. It is not of men
             It is not of myself — no vain discourse
             Empty oration, tinkling soulless talk

[189] Actually Emerson is in error, confusing the second with the third Countess
of Carbery. Richard Vaughan, second Earl of Carbery, married three times. To his
second wife, Frances, Jeremy Taylor dedicated the first edition of *The Great Exemplar*
(1649) and announced in the Epistle Dedicatory of *Holy Dying* that the volume was
meant for the Lady Frances, who had forestalled the dedication by her death. The
third wife of the Earl was Lady Alice Egerton, daughter of the Earl of Bridgewater,
who represented the Lady in *Comus* in the first performance of the masque. Vaughan
married her in 1652, two years after the death of the Lady Frances.

[190] "Newton . . . . years" is added in pencil to the end of the paragraph, apparently as a later and further illustration of "God's mnemonics."

[191] "Consider the lilies of the field how they grow" is the title given to a poem
in *The Pious Minstrel: Sacred Poetry* (Boston, 1832), p. 37, an American reprint of
an 1831 London edition. The line Emerson praises is the next to the last of the 4th
stanza. Though the poem is printed in *The Pious Minstrel* as anonymous, it is actually
by John Keble and is the poem appointed for the first Sunday after Trinity in his
volume *The Christian Year* (Oxford, 1828), p. 233. The original version contains
two further stanzas omitted from the American reprint. The Biblical source for the
verses is, of course, Matt. 6:28. The "sentiment of Herbert's Verses upon Rest" probably refers to the lines from "The Pulley" which Emerson quoted years later in
Parnassus (Boston, 1874), p. 144.

My heart lies open to the Universe
I read only what there is writ I speak
The sincere word that's whispered in my ear
I am an organ in the mouth of God
My prophecy the music of his lips.
Tho' harsh in evil ears 'tis harmony
To patient wise & faithful hearts whose love
Cooperates with ⟨the⟩ his
Concord of heaven & earth. Author divine
Of what I am & what I say, vouchsafe
To cleanse me that my folly may not hide
Thy truth nor my infirmity disguise
The Omnipotence that animates my clay.
Thou Lord dost clothe thy attributes with flesh
And named it man a morning spectacle
Unto the universe exhibiting
A manifold & mystic lesson

[131] The pure in heart shall see God. [cf. Matt. 5:8]

In Rome it is not the diameter nor the circumference of the columns[,] it is not the dimensions nor the material of the temples which constitute their chief charm. It is the name of Cicero[;] it is the remembrance of a wise & good man[;] it is ↑the remembrance↓ [of] Scipio & Cato & Regulus — the ↑influence of↓ human character, the heroes who struggled, the patriots who fell, the wise men who thought —— the men who contended worthily in their lifetime in the same trials which God in this city & this year is placing before each of us. Why are you dazzled with the name of Caesar? A ^{n} part as important, a soul as great, a name as dear to God as his or any other's is your own.

It will take you long to learn another tongue so as to make yourself fully understood by those who speak it but your actions are easy of translation. ↑They understand what you do↓. Temperance is good English & good French & good Italian. Your courage, your kindness, your honesty are as plain to a Turk as his own alphabet.

In Boston they have an eye for improvement, a thing which does not exist in Asia nor in Africa[.]

Newtown, 20 October. A Sabbath in the country but not so odoriferous as I have imagined. Mr. Bates [192] a plain, serious Calvinist not winning but not repelling: one of the useful police which God makes out of the ignorance & superstition of the youth of the world. I dare not & wish not speak disrespectfully of these good, abstemious, laborious men. [132] Yet I could not help asking myself how long is the society to be taught in this dramatic or allegorical style? When ⟨are⟩ is religious truth to be distinctly uttered — what it is, not what it resembles? Thus every Sunday ever since they were born this congregation have heard tell of *Salvation*, and of going to the door of heaven & knocking, & being answered from Within, "Depart, I Never Knew You" [193] & of being sent away to ⟨ruin⟩ eternal ruin. ⟨Who⟩ What hinders that instead of this parable the naked fact be stated to them? Namely that as long [as] they offend against their conscience they will seek to be happy but they shall not be able, they shall not come to any true knowledge of God, they shall be avoided by good & by wise men, they shall become worse & worse.

God defend me from ever looking at a man as an animal. God defend me from the vice of my constitution, an excesstive↓ ⟨of⟩ desire of sympathy. Let me be content with the consciousness of innocency & the desire of ⟨improve⟩ worth without stretching myself upon the rack whenever any man, woman, or child passes by until he, she, or it is ⟨assured⟩ possessed of my intention.
The nine solids.

[133] An impulse as irresistible as is in the acorn to germinate is in the soul ⟨to⟩ of the prophet to speak.

[192] The Reverend James Bates (1799–1865) was colleague pastor to Dr. Jonathan Homer at the First Parish Church of Newton from 1827 to 1839. See *The History of Newton*, ed. Henry K. Rowe (Newton, Mass., 1930), pp. 69, 98, 107, and 110.
[193] Cf. Matt. 7:23.

Mr Blanchard said that labor had kept him well 11 years at the desk[.] [194]

[October] 21. I am sure of this that by going ↑much↓ alone a man will get ↑more of↓ a noble courage in thought & word than from all the wisdom that is in books. ⟨He acquires⟩ He will come to hear God speak as audibly through his own lips as ever ⟨h⟩He did by the mouth of Moses or Isaiah or Milton. "For nature never did betray the heart that loved her." [195] Such revelations as were made to George Fox or Emanuel Swedenborg are only made in the woods or in the closet. They were no common madmen. They wanted but little or if you please they exceeded but little of being true prophets.

———

EBE quotes from St Pierre the saying that "when the chain is put upon a slave the other end is rivetted around the neck of the master" & sanctions warmly the observation.[196]

———

When a man goes into the woods he feels like a boy without loss of wisdom.[196a] To be sure a dandy may go there, & Nature will speak to a dandy.

[134] It seems to me that ⟨Time helps us as to⟩ the perspective of time as it sets every thing in the right point of view does the same by Christianity. We learn to look at it now as a part of the history of the world,[n] to see how it rests in the broad basis of man's moral nature & is not itself that basis. I cannot but think that Jesus Christ will be better loved by being less adored. He has had an unnatural[,] an artificial place for ages in human opinions[,] a

[194] Joshua P. Blanchard; see pp. 30–31 above.
[195] Wordsworth, "Lines Composed a Few Miles Above Tintern Abby," ll. 122–123.
[196] Though Emerson had in his library four volumes of James-Henry Bernardin de Saint-Pierre's *Studies of Nature*, trans. Henry Hunter, 5 vols. (London, 1796), and though both in this work (which included as volume V the celebrated *Paul and Virginia*) and in *A Voyage to the Isle of France . . .* (London, 1800), Bernardin de Saint-Pierre condemned slavery violently, the particular passage Edward Bliss Emerson cited has not been located. Cf. "Compensation," *W*, II, 109.
[196a] "When a man . . . wisdom.": used in *Nature*, *W*, I, 9, and also in "The Uses of Natural History," *Lectures*, I, 21.

place too high for love. ⟨W⟩There is a recoil of the affections from all authority & force. To the barbarous state of society it was thought to add to the dignity of Xt[Christ], to make him king, to make him God. Now that ⟨a⟩ the SS[Sacred Scriptures] are read with purged eyes, it is seen he is only to be loved for so much goodness & wisdom as was in him, which are the only things for which a sound human mind can love any person. ⟨Now he⟩ As the world [135] waxes wiser he will be more truly venerated for the splendor of the contrast of his character to the opinions & practices of his age[;] he will attract the unfeigned love of all to whom moral nature is dear because he planted himself in the face of the world upon that sole ground, show-ing that noble confidence in the reality & superiority of spiritual truths, that simplicity & at the same time enthusiasm in declaring them which is itself one of the highest merits & gives confidence to all thinkers that come after.

But will not this come to be thought the chief value of his teaching, that is, of Christianity, to wit, that it was a great stand made for man's spiritual nature against the sensualism, the forms, & the crimes of the age in which he appeared & those that preceded it. Like every wise & efficient man he spoke to /the/his/ times in all their singular peculiarities. His instruction is almost [136] as local as personal as would be the teaching in one of our Sunday Schools. He speaks as he thinks, but the is↓ thinking for them. Yet such is the extraordinary truth of his mind that his sentences have a fulness of meaning, a fitness to human nature, & an universality of application that has commended them to the whole world.

They must be looked upon as one /affirmation/proclamation/ glorious of moral truth but not as ⟨a⟩ the last affirmation. There shall be a thousand more. Very inconsistent would it be with a soul so pos-sessed of this love as his to set bounds to that illimitable ocean. None knew better than he that every soul occupies a new position & that if the stars cannot be counted nor the sands of the sea neither can those moral truths be numbered & ended of which the material creation is only the shadow[.]

[137] 24 Oct., Newton. The teacher of the coming age must occupy himself in the study & explanation of the moral constitution

of man more than in the elucidation of ⟨obs⟩ difficult texts. He must work in the conviction that the Scripture can only be interpreted by the same spirit that uttered them. And that as long as the heart & the mind are illumined by a spiritual life there is no dead letter but a perpetual Scripture.

I expect everything good & auspicious from the studies & the actings of good men in the course this thought shall guide them. It will be inspiration to prophet & to heroes. It will bring the heavens near & show a calm sky always overhead.

[138]¹⁹⁷ 31 Nov. [October] Sir J. Mackintosh has well said that every picture, statue, poem ⟨are⟩ ↑is an↓ experiment ⁿ on the human mind.¹⁹⁸ And if such slight & transient things often produce in us deepest results[,] if a paragraph of a newspaper or ⟨a word⟩ ⁿ an eloquent word touch us so to the quick as we know they often do, what may we not expect from a familiar & full comprehension of the amazing discoveries that the Naturalists of this day have made: ⁿ from the wonderful application of polarized light to the discovery of periodical colors in refrangible substances & so to the uncovering of nature's primary forms in the secret architecture of bodies. Or the great long expected discovery of the identity of electricity & magnetism lately completed by ⟨the obt⟩ ⁿ Dr Faraday obtaining the spark from the magnet & the opening

> The heart must have the heart. When the sun shines
> One passing guest is welcome as another

almost a ⟨th⟩ door to the secret mechanism of life & sensation in the relation of the pile of Volta to the electrical fish[.]

---

¹⁹⁷ The entry, written in an unusually large, sprawling hand, is markedly careless. The dating is in error. Other evidences of inattention are the inadequate cancellations on the page. Across the center of the page from "have made" above to "⟨the obt⟩" below are double parallel vertical lines; a single horizontal cross line intersects the vertical lines below "colors"; "42" appears under "application" and above "uncovering"; "the heart . . . as another" is written upside down in pencil between lines of ink entry, apparently prior to their inscription.

¹⁹⁸ The actual phrase in *A General View of . . . Ethical Philosophy,* 1832, pp. 42–43, is "Every poem . . . every picture, every statue is an experiment on human feeling. . . ." See p. 13 above.

[139] 2 November. Bacon said man is the minister & interpreter of nature:[199] he is so in more respects than one. He is not only to explain the sense of each passage but the scope & argument of the whole book. He is to explain the attractiveness of all[.]

There is more beauty in the morning cloud than the prism can render account of. There is something in it that resembles the aspects of mortal life[,] its epochs & its fate. There is not a passion in the human soul[,] perhaps not a shade of thought but has its emblem in nature. And this does not become fainter this undersong, this concurrent text, with more intimate knowledge of nature's laws[,] but the analogy is felt to be deeper & more universal for every law that is revealed. It ↑almost↓ seems as if an unknown ⟨wisdom⟩ ↑intelligence↓ in us ⟨was satisfied with⟩ ↑expressed its recognition of↓ each new disclosure.

Let a man under the influence of strong passion go into the fields & see how readily every thought clothes itself with a material garment. [Is it not illustration to us of the manner in which every spirit clothes itself with body[?]] Now I say is it not time something was done to explain this attractiveness which the face of nature has for us renewed this 2d [140] day of November of the 6000th year of the world ↑as it has been every day of the 6000 years,↓ to the reality of which every age has testified? [n]

Nature is a language & every new fact that we learn is a new word; but rightly seen, taken all together it is not ⟨only⟩ ↑merely↓ a language ⟨but a scripture which contains the whole truth.⟩ but the language put together into a most significant & universal book. I wish to learn the language not that I may know a new set of nouns & verbs but that I may read the great book which is written in that tongue.[200]

[199] The statement appears twice in Bacon's *Magna Instauratio*, in the "Arguement of the Several Parts" and in Aphorism I. See *The Works of Francis Bacon*, ed. James Spedding, Robert Ellis, and Douglas Heath, 15 vols. (Boston, 1860–1864), VIII, 53 and 67.

[200] The whole preceding entry for November 2 looks forward to *Nature*, W, I, 25–32, but since no use marks appear on the passage Emerson may not have drawn upon it. Three passages within the entry are, however, unmarked and yet used in "The Uses of Natural History," *Lectures*: "There is more beauty . . . fate.": used I, 24; "And this does not become fainter . . . revealed.": used I, 25; and "Nature is a language . . . tongue.": used I, 26.

The ⟨thin⟩ grey leaves fall around me[.]

The glutton wrote for his epitaph[:]

> What I have eat is mine; in words my will
> I've had & of my lust have ta'en my fill[.]

Crates the philosopher altered it for himself[:]

> What I have learned is mine, I've had my thought,
> And me the Muses noble Truths have taught.[201]

To an instructed eye the universe is transparent. The light of higher laws than its own shines through it.[202]

[141] New Bedford, 19 Nov. Stubler [203] said the difference between brother Witherlee's preaching & his, was this[:] Brother W. said 'If you do not become good you shall all be whipt' and himself said, 'If you will become good, you shall not be whipt.'

Wrote to Charles yesterday of the amount of meaning in life: *dum tacet clamat*.[204] He would feel it if he should suppose Shakspear should go with him to Mr Peabody's or Aunt Cook's. If a susceptible man should lay bare his heart, it would show theories of life, thoughts of unutterable tenderness, & visions of beauty that were suggested from the most ⟨a⟩seemingly inadequate & mean occasions, from hearing an unwashed boy spell or cipher ⟨at a district school⟩ ↑in his class↓ or seeing the blush upon the cheek of a school girl or watching the transmission of the candle light through his closed fingers, or listening long to the sound made by tinkling a glass tumbler or

---

[201] Plutarch, "How a Man may praise Himself without being Envied." See the *Morals*, 1870, II, 370.

[202] "the universe . . . . shines through it.": used in *Nature*, *W*, I, 34.

[203] Apparently Edward Stabler (1769–1831), druggist and Quaker preacher in Alexandria, Va., whom Emerson had met years earlier on the boat in Delaware Bay. See *JMN*, III, 185, n. 56.

[204] "While he is silent he speaks" (Ed.). Apparently this is Emerson's version of Cicero's phrase from *In Catilinam*, I, viii (21): "Cum tacent clamant" — "By their silence they cry aloud."

touching the key of a piano. Is it not true that no persons meet[,] of what inequality soever, but a quick apprehension can straightway bridge over the distance between them & see ⟨the⟩ how they may stand in most strict & amicable relations[?]

"Thomas, I know what thee is thinking of." If you do, Micah, you don't feel flattered.

"Mary, it has been revealed to me that I should marry thee." — — Abner, when it is revealed to me I will tell thee.

["]William, I am sent to tell thee thou hast a divided heart.["] [205]

[142] Hymn for the Ordination of Chandler Robbins.[206]
                We love the venerable house
                Our fathers built to God
        In heaven are heard their grateful vows
                Their bones are in the sod.

        Here ⟨beamed⟩ holy thoughts a light have shed
                From many a radiant face,
        And prayers of humble virtue made
                The perfume of the place.

        And anxious hearts have pondered here
                The mystery of life,
        And prayed the eternal Spirit to clear
                Their doubts, & aid their strife.

[205] The versions of Quaker dialogue apparently represent Emerson's experiences at New Bedford, a strongly Quaker community where he boarded with Mrs. Deborah Brayton, a Quaker landlady, while he preached at Orville Dewey's church. See L, I, 400.

[206] The hymn was written for Chandler Robbins, Emerson's successor at the Second Church, whose ordination was on December 4, 1833. This version of the hymn is identical with that sent by Emerson on November 18 to Horace Scudder (see L, I, 399). A version differing in the first and last stanzas appears in Poems, W, IX, 223–224; what were apparently the first attempts at composing the hymn appear in Blotting Book IV (see JMN, III, 370–375).

From humble tenements around
  Came up the pensive train,
And in the church a blessing found
  Which filled their homes again;

For, faith & peace & mighty love
  That from the Godhead flow,
Showed them the life of heaven above
  Springs from the life below.

They live with God; their homes are dust;
  But here the children pray
And, in our fleeting lifetime, trust
  To find the narrow way.

On him who by th⟨is⟩e altar stands,
  On him thy spirit send;
Speak through his lips thy pure commands,
  Our Father & our Friend!

[143] *Dampier*

"This retarded our business, for I did not find Price Morrice very intent on work; for 'tis like he thought he had logwood enough. And I have particularly observed there, & in other places, that such as had been well bred were generally most careful to improve their time, & would be very industrious & frugal when there was any probability of considerable gain. But on the contrary, such as had been inured to hard labor & got their living by the sweat of their brows, when they came to have plenty, would extravagantly squander away their time & money in drinking & making a bluster[.]" Ap[ud] Early Eng[lish] Navigators[,] Ed. Cab-[inet] Lib[rary] [207]

To the same purpose the fact that the Esquimaux will sell his bed in the morning; ⟨And the remarkable fact that at sea we always estimate the length of the voyage by the weather of the present

[207] Emerson is quoting from the "Life of Dampier" in *Lives and Voyages of Drake, Cavendish, and Dampier; including an introductory view of the Earlier Discoveries in the South Sea, and the History of the Bucaniers* (Edinburgh, 1831), p. 306.

moment.) [208] The Buccaneer shows his wealth instantly & as long as it lasts in his dress, in his food, & his profuseness. The merchant hangs out no sign to show you whether he has made a good bargain today or lost a ship.

[144]

Legenda [209]

Article Croker's Boswell's Johnson, in Ed Rev
Essays on Pursuit of Truth
Hazlitt's Essays on Principles of human action
Hobbes' Treatise on Human Nature
Hume's Dissertation on the passions; & Enquiry
Shaftesbury's Enquiry
Sir Charles Bell's Animal mechanics
Sir Samuel Romilly's Article on Codification   Ed. Rev. Hartley
Tucker's Chapter on Pleasure & Paley's on Happiness
Cousin's Tenneman[n]
Turner's Elements of Chemistry   Affinity

---

[208] "And . . . moment." is struck through with five diagonal lines, apparently indicating a cancellation rather than use.

[209] It is probable that this list of materials to be read was largely suggested by Mackintosh, *A General View of . . . Ethical Philosophy*, 1832, a volume which Emerson owned and from which he began to make citations as early as March, 1832. Ten of the items on the list are discussed or mentioned in Mackintosh and for one of them, Romilly's article in *The Edinburgh Review*, the name of the writer is revealed, apparently for the first time. The list is identified as follows; after relevant items a bracketed reference to Mackintosh's mention or treatment is appended: (a) Thomas Babington Macaulay's review of the 5-volume, 1831, edition of Boswell's *Life of Johnson* by John Wilson Croker in *The Edinburgh Review*, LIV (Sept. 1831), 1–38. (b) [Samuel Bailey], *Essays on the Pursuit of Truth, on the Progress of Knowledge, and on the Fundamental Principles of all Evidences and Expectation* (London, 1829, or Philadelphia, 1831). (c) *Essays on the Principles of Human Action . . . . To which are added, Some Remarks on the Systems of Hartley and Helvetius* (London, 1805) [praised in a note, p. 119]. (d) Possibly the first discourse in *Tripos in Three Discourses*, which was called "Human Nature" (see *The English Works of Thomas Hobbes*, ed. W. Molesworth, 11 vols., London, 1839–1845, vol. IV), or *Humane Nature or the Fundamental Elements of Policy* (1650) [Hobbes' "tract" on Human Nature is discussed at length, pp. 55–70, and 160]. (e) Probably "A Dissertation on the Passions" and "An Enquiry concerning the Principles of Morals" in *Essays and Treatises on Several Subjects* (Edinburgh, 1817 or 1825), vol. II, but possibly

On Peace.

"It hath pleased Almighty God (saith Cavendish to Lord Hunsdon) to suffer me to circumpass the whole globe of the world entering in at the strait of Magellan & returning by the Cape of Buena Esparança; in which voyage I have either discovered or brought certain intelligence of all the rich places ⟨in⟩ of the world which were ever discovered by any Christian. I navigated along the Coast of Chili, Peru, & New Spain *where I made great spoils. I burnt & sunk ⟨2⟩19 sails of ships small & great. All the villages & towns that ever I landed at I burned & spoiled.* And had I not been discovered upon the coast I had taken great quantity of treasure. The matter of most profit unto me was a great ship of the King's which I took at California &c &c[."] [210]

He arrived in Plymouth[,] 9 Sept., 1588, 2 years 50 days from the time of depa‖rt‖ing from same place.[211]

---

a further essay in the same volume, "An Inquiry concerning Human Understanding [the first two essays are considered on pp. 153 and 140–146, respectively, while Hume's *Treatise on Human Nature*, Bk. II of which is called "Of the Passions," is considered on pp. 136ff.]. (f) Anthony Ashley Cooper, Earl of Shaftesbury, "An Inquiry concerning Virtue and Merit," Treatise IV in *Characteristics* (multiple editions after 1711) [discussed at length, pp. 88–95]. (g) *Animal Mechanics, or Proofs of Design in the Animal Frame*, contributed to the Library of Useful Knowledge (London, 1828) [p. 182]. (h) "Bentham on Codification," *The Edinburgh Review*, XXIX (Nov. 1817), 217–237 [a note to pp. 192–193 calls the article "beautiful" and comments: "It need no longer be concealed that it was contributed by Sir Samuel Romilly."]. (i) *Observations on Man* (1749 or 1791 or 1801) or possibly Hartley's *Theory of the Human Mind* . . . (1775) [the former volume is discussed at length on pp. 157–176]. (j) Abraham Tucker [Edward Search], *The Light of Nature Pursued*, 4 vols. (Cambridge, Mass., 1831), I, 256–268 contains ch. 22, "Pleasure." [p. 178 points out this chapter as probable stimulus to Paley's "good" chapter on Happiness; the two works are linked again on p. 180]. (k) William Paley, *The Principles of Moral and Political Philosophy* (1785) in *Works*, 5 vols. (Boston, 1811), III, 37–51, contains as Bk. I, ch. 6, a chapter on Happiness [p. 178 and p. 180]. (l) Victor Cousin translated William Gottlieb Tennemann's *Geschichte der Philosophie* (1811) under the title *Manuel de l'histoire de la philosophie*, 2 vols. (Paris, 1829) [p. 216]. (m) Edward Turner, *Elements of Chemistry*, 3rd American ed. (Philadelphia, 1830), in Pt. II, sect. I, pp. 102–114, contains a chapter "Affinity." Emerson had in his library the 4th Am. ed., Philadelphia, 1832.

[210] "The Life of Cavendish," ch. 6, in *Lives and Voyages of Drake, Cavendish, and Dampier* . . . , 1831, pp. 204–205. The quotation is an extract of a letter from Cavendish to Lord Hunsdon.

[211] *Ibid.*, p. 203, a paraphrase.

"No peace beyond the ⟨l⟩Line." "No prey no pay." [212]

[inside back cover] [213]   Nomenclatur

mutato nomine [214]

[Index material omitted]

[212] Both the phrases appear in *The Lives and Voyages* . . . , 1831, as maxims of the Buccaneers, the first on p. 228 and the second on p. 238 and again on p. 451.

[213] The back cover is missing from the manuscript; the transcript is made from a typescript which in turn was made from the journal in the 1920's by the Ralph Waldo Emerson Memorial Association.

[214] A truncation of "mutato nomine de te fabula narratur," Horace *Satires*, Bk. I, i, 69–70 — "change but the name and the tale is told of you." See p. 14 above.

Sicily

1833

Emerson prepared for his European trip by purchasing two small leather-covered pocket notebooks from Simpkins and Company in Boston. The first of these, Sicily, he began after five days at sea on January 2, 1833. By early March when he had experienced his ocean voyage and had passed through the first flood of impressions of Europe at Malta and Sicily, his notebook was full. The little journal was small enough to be slipped into a pocket; many of the entries were obviously made in pencil and then revised with great care and in his most legible hand later in ink, perhaps even on his return voyage from England to Boston when he speaks of "posting" his Italian journals.

The small pocket notebook is covered with limp reddish-brown leather. A square of paper bearing "1" in ink is pasted to the upper right corner to indicate that the volume is the first of four travel journals progressively numbered. A reddish-brown label on the inside front cover reads "Sold by N.S. Simpkins and Co. *Boston.*" Strips of modern transparent tape now hold the cover to the single gathering of 16 sheets. There are 65 numbered pages since the back inside cover is included in the faint pencil pagination. The leaves measure 10 x 15.8 cm. Partially erased or blurred pencil writing underlies the ink entry on many pages; no traces of this earlier pencil writing appear on pages 1, 2, 27–31, 33–41, or 43–56.

[front cover] 1833 Sicily

[front cover verso] [blank]

[1] At Sea. Jan. 2, 1833. Sailed from Boston for Malta Dec. 25, 1832 in Brig Jasper, Capt Ellis, 236 tons laden with logwood, mahogany, tobacco, sugar, coffee, beeswax, cheese, &c[.]

A long storm from the second morn of our departure consigned all the five passengers to the irremediable chagrins of the stateroom, ↑to wit,↓ nausea, darkness, unrest, uncleanness, harpy appetite & harpy feeding, the ugly sound of water in mine ears, anticipations of going to the bottom, & the treasures of the memory. I remembered up nearly the whole of Lycidas, clause by clause, here a verse & there a word, as Isis in the fable the broken body of Osiris.[1] —

Out occasionally crawled we from our several holes, but hope & fair weather would not, so there was nothing for it but to wriggle again into the crooks of the transom. Then it seemed strange that the first man who came to sea did not turn round & go straight back again. Strange that because one of my neighbors had some trumpery logs & notions which would sell for a few cents more here than there he should thrust forth this [2] company of his poor countrymen to the tender mercies of the northwest wind.

We study the sailor, the man of his hands, man of all work; all eye, all finger, muscle, skill, & endurance[;] a tailor, a carpenter, cooper, stevedore, & clerk & astronomer besides. He is a great saver, and a great quiddle by the necessity of his situation[.]

The Captain believes in the superiority of the American to every other countryman. "You will see[,] he says[,] when you get out here how they manage in Europe; they do everything by main strength & ignorance. Four truckmen & four stevedores at Long Wharf will load my brig quicker than 100 men at any port in the Mediterranean." It seems the Sicilians have tried once or twice to bring their fruit to America in their own bottoms, & made the passage, he says, in 120 days.

P.M. A crop of meditations in the berth. Thought again of the sailor & how superficial the differences — How shallow to make much of mere coat & hat distinctions. You can't get away from the radical, uniform, interior experiences which peep out of the new faces identical with those of the old. New tongues repeat the old proverbs, primeval truths. The thought occurred, full of consolation,[n] [3][2] that if he would deal towards himself with severest truth, man must acknowledge the Deity. So far from being a conventional idea, built

---

[1] Cf. Plutarch, "Of Isis and Osiris," *Morals*, 1870, IV, 80.

[2] Faint traces of earlier pencil writing underlie the ink entry on the page. Beneath "with severest truth" is "Jan 2 1833" and in the empty line between "snowflake." and "3. Jan." is "Lycidas I nearly", apparently a version of the comment on Lycidas now on p. [1]. These traces of pencil entry continue without a break until p. [27] and will be indicated again only when there is recovered material.

on reason of State, it is in strict soliloquy, in absolute solitude when the soul makes itself a hermit in the creation, that this thought naturally arises. This unavoidable acknowledgment of God, this valid prayer puts the soul in equilibrium. In this state the question whether your boat shall float in safety or go to the bottom is no more important than the flight of a snowflake.

3 Jan. I rose at sunrise & under the lee of the spencer sheet had a solitary thoughtful hour. All right thought is devout. 'The clouds were touched & in their silent faces might be read unutterable love.' [3] They shone with light that shines on Europe, Afric, & the Nile, & I opened my spirit's ear to their most ancient hymn. What, they said to me, goest thou so far to seek —— painted canvass, carved marble, renowned towns? But fresh from us, new evermore, is the creative efflux from whence these works spring. You now feel in gazing at our fleecy arch of light the motions that express [n] [4] themselves in Arts. You get no nearer to the principle in Europe. It animates man. It is the America of America. It spans the ocean like a handbreadth. It smiles at Time & Space. Yet welcome young man! the Universe is hospitable. The great God who is Love hath made you aware of the forms & breeding of his wide house. We greet you well to the place of History as you please to style it; to the mighty Lilliput or ant hill of your genealogy, if, instructed as you have been, you must still be the dupe of shows, & count it much, the three or four bubbles of foam that preceded your own on the Sea of Time. This strong-winged sea gull & striped sheer-water that you have watched as they skimmed the waves under our vault [—] they are works of art better worth your enthusiasm[,] masterpieces of Eternal power strictly eternal because now active & ye need not go so far to seek what ye would not seek at all if it were not within you. Yet welcome & hail! So sang in my ear the silver grey [5] mists & the winds & the sea said Amen.

Thursday 3 Jan. N. lat 37.53. Dr Johnson rightly defends conversation upon the weather. [4] With more reason we at sea beat

[3] Wordsworth, *The Excursion*, I, 225–227, slightly misquoted.
[4] *The Idler*, No. 11.

that topic thin. We are pensioners of the wind. The weather cock is the wisest man. All our prosperity, enterprize, temper come & go with the fickle air. If the wind should forget to blow we must eat our masts. Sea farmers must make hay when the sun shines. The gale collects plenty of work for the calm. Now are we all awaiting a smoother sea to stand at our toilette. A headwind makes grinning Esaus of us. Happy that there is a time for all things under the moon, so that no man need give a dinner party in a brig's cabin, nor shave himself by the gulf lightning.

Sat. Eve. 5 Jan. I like the latitude of 37° better than my bitter native 42°. We have sauntered all this calm day at one or two knots the hour & nobody on board well pleased but I. And why should I be pleased? I have [6] nothing to record. I have read little. I have done nothing. What then? Need we be such barren scoundrels that the whole beauty of heaven, the main, & man cannot entertain ⟨me⟩us unless ⟨I⟩we too must needs hold a candle & daub God's world with a smutch of our own insignificance? ⁿ Not I, for one. I will be pleased though I do not deserve it. I will act in all up to my conceit of last week when I exulted in the power & art with which we rode tilting over this January ocean, ⟨while⟩ ↑albeit↓ to speak truth, our individual valours lay very sick the while, lodged each in the waistcoat pocket of the brave brig's transom. So that each passenger's particular share in the glory was much the same as the sutler's or grocer's who turns his penny in the army of Leonidas or Washington. The southing latitude does not yet make early mornings. The steward's lanthorn & trumpery matutinal preparations are to me for the rosy ray, the silver cloud, or chaunt of earliest bird. But days will come.

[7] Poor book this Scelta di Goldoni.⁵ He is puffed in the Preface and also by Sismondi as the Restorer ⟨of⟩ or Reformer of

⁵ From the title Emerson appears to have been reading an Italian version of Goldoni, perhaps one of the editions prepared especially for the beginner in the language, such as *Scelta di alcune commedie per uso di dilettanti della lingua Italiana* (Perugia, 1813, and many editions thereafter). For Sismondi's praise, see J.C.L. Simonde de Sismondi, *Historical Views of the Literature of the South of Europe*, trans. Thomas Roscoe, 4 vols. (London, 1823), II, 368–369.

the Italian stage. &c &c not a just sentiment or a well contrived scene in the book. His highest merit [is] that of a good phrase book. Perrin [6] might as well knit his conversations into a dialogue & call it a Drama[.]

Sunday 6 Jan. lat 37 23. long. 39 59 w. Last ev'g fair wind & full moon suddenly lost in squall & rain. There are no attractions in the sailor's life. Its best things are only alleviations. "A prison with the chance of being drowned." [7] It is even so and yet they do not run blind into unmeasured danger as seems to the landsman; those chances are all ⟨weighed⟩ counted & weighed & ⟨a⟩ experience has begotten this confidence in the proportioned strength of spars & rigging to the ordinary forces of wind & water which by being habitual constitutes the essence of a sailor's fearlessness. Suppose a student confined to a ship, I see not why he might not trim his lamp to as good purpose as in college attic. Why should he be less efficient in his vocation than the poor steward who ingloriously deals ever in pork & beans[,] [8] let the quadrant or the chart or the monsoon say what they will? [n] The caboose is his Rome.[8]

It occurred forcibly this morning whether suggested by Goldoni or Bigelow [9] or some falsetto of my own that the thing set down in words is not affirmed. It must affirm itself or no forms of grammar & no verisimilitude can give it evidence. This is a maxim which holds to the core of the world.

Storm, storm; ah we! the sea to us is but a lasting storm. We have had no fine weather to last an hour. Yet I must thank the

[6] John Perrin, *The Elements of French and English Conversation* (Philadelphia, 1807).

[7] See *Boswell's Life of Johnson*, ed. George B. Hill, revised and enlarged edition by L. F. Powell, 6 vols. (Oxford, 1934–1950), I, 348; II, 438; V, 137 and 249.

[8] In the space to the right of this word is faintly visible in overwritten pencil: "of a good phrase book I do not find." The comment is apparently part of an earlier version of the entry on Goldoni on p. [7].

[9] Andrew Bigelow, *Travels in Malta and Sicily with Sketches of Gibraltar in 1827* (Boston, 1831), a volume from which Emerson cites in his Italian journal. See p. 136 below.

sea & rough weather for a truckman's health & stomach, — how connected with celestial gifts!

The wind is the sole performer in these parts of nature & the royal Aeolus understands his work well, &, to give him his due, shifts the scene & varies the accompaniment as featly & as often as the audience can desire. Certainly he rings his few chimes with wondrous skill of permutation. Sometimes we his pets are cross & say 'tis nought but salt & squalls & [9] sometimes we are ourselves & admit that it is divine Architecture.

⟨Mon⟩ 7 Jan. w long. 36.11. n. lat. 37.4. Sailors are the best dressed of mankind. Convenience is studied from head to heel, & they have a change for every emergency. It seems to me they get more work out of the sailor than out of any other craftsman. His obedience is prompt as a soldier's & willing as a child's, & reconciles me to some dim remembrances of authority I wondered at. Thin skins do not believe in thick. Jack never looks an inch beyond his orders. "Brace the yards," quoth the master; "Ay Ay, sir," answers Jack, and never looks over the side at the squall or the sea that cometh as if it were no more to him than to the capstan.

But though I do not find much attraction in the seaman yet I can discern that the naval hero is a hero. It takes all the thousand thousand European voyages that have been made to stablish our faith in the practicability of this our hodiurnal voyage. But to be Columbus, to steer WEST steadily day after day, week after week, for the first time, and wholly alone in his opinion, shows a mind as solitary & [10] self-subsistent as any that ever lived.

I am learning the use of the quadrant. Another voyage would make an astronomer of me. How delicately come out these stars at sea. The constellations show smaller & a ship though with the disadvantage of motion is a fine observatory. But I am ashamed of myself for a dull scholar. Every day I display a more astounding ignorance. The whole world is a mill stone to me. The experiment of the philosopher is but a separation to bring within his optics the comprehension of a fact which is done masterly & in harmony in God's laboratory of the world.[10]

[10] In the space at the end of the paragraph after "world." in blurred pencil is

Wednesday 9 Jan. w. long 28 58. Still we sail well & feed full & hope tomorrow to make St Mary's[,] the southernmost of the Azores. When the Abbey grew rich the fat monk cut up all his quills for toothpicks. So do we.

Thursday Eve at 9 o'clock passed St Mary's[,] a dim black hummock of land. Our dead reckoning agreed with its longitude in the bearings to a mile.

[11] 13 Jan. We have but 14 degrees of longitude to make to reach the rock of Gibraltar but the fickle wind may make these fourteen longer measure than all we have meted. A gale day before yesterday; yesterday a heavy sea & a cold head wind today. Yet still we hope & drift along. In the Ocean the vessel gains a large commission on every mile sailed even with a wind dead ahead. In a narrow sea much less. A sea voyage at the best is yet such a bundle of perils & inconveniences that no person as much a lover of the present moment as I am would be swift to pay that price for any commodity which any thing else would buy. Yet if our horses are somewhat wild & the road uneven & lonely & without inns yet experience shows us that the coward eye magnifies the dangers[.] [11]

[12] Sunday W. long. 17° 4'. Let us insist on having our say. We but half express ourselves[,] but ever draw diagonals between our own thought & the supposed thought of our companion & so fail to satisfy either. Now God made the model & meant we should live out our idea. It may be safely trusted as proportionate & of good issues so that it be faithfully expressed but God will not have his work made manifest by cowards. And so it takes a divine man

"that then ‖ . . . ‖ see that the naval officer[?] is a hero." Apparently the erased entry is an earlier version of the comment on the naval hero now on p. [9]. In the space at the bottom of the page under "longitude . . . mile." is the semi-erased entry: "a shame that the Muses should ‖ . . . ‖ ". In Emerson's text, the word "longitude" is broken between the last two lines of p. [10], and the semi-erased entry actually is under "gitude . . . mile.", the last line of the page.

[11] Below the ink paragraph in very faint pencil is "the southernmost of the Azores Thursday night at 9 o'clock passes St Mary's a dim black hummock of land ‖ . . . ‖ reckoning agreed with its longitude in ‖ . . . ‖ ". At the bottom of the page is "Saturday long. 19.55". The erased entry is apparently an earlier version of that for Wednesday, January 9, on p. [10].

to exhibit any thing divine [—] Socrates, Alfred, Columbus, Wordsworth or any other brave preferrer of the still voice within to the
roar of the populace (a thing very easy to speak of & very hard to
do for 24 hours.) The rest are men potentially not actually[,] now
only pupas or tadpoles[,] say rather quarries of souls, heroes that
shall be, seeds of gods,[12]

[13] [...] [13]

[14][14] 14 Jan. W. long. 14° 14′
Well blithe traveller what cheer[?]
What have the sea & the stars & the moaning winds & your discontented thoughts sung in your attentive ears? Peeps up old Europe
yet out of his eastern main? hospitably ho! Nay the slumberous
old giant cannot bestir himself in these his chair days to loom up
for the pastime of his upstart grandchildren as now they come shoal
after shoal to salute their old Progenitor[,] the old Adam of all.
Sleep on, old Sire, there is muscle & nerve & enterprise enow in us
your poor spawn who have sucked the air & ripened in the sunshine
of the cold West to steer our ships to your very ports & thrust our
inquisitive American eyes into your towns & towers & keeping-rooms.
Here we come & mean to be welcome. So be good now, clever old
gentleman.

[15] I comfort the mate by assuring him that the sea life is

[12] "We but half . . . cowards.": used in "Self-Reliance," *W*, II, 46–47. To
the right and below "gods," is the following in very faint pencil: "what time
& place to give a dinner party. Yet if ‖ . . .‖ But is ‖ . . .‖ new ‖ . . .‖".
The entry, perhaps similar to the one now found on p. [5] for Thursday, January 3,
continues on the top of p. [13].

[13] The page contains an almost totally blurred pencil entry, the first part of which
is apparently a continuation of the blurred pencil from p. [12] as follows: "scope,
new phases of that for one life like the spinner ‖ . . .‖ stuff his web, makes all the
difference with the whereabouts of sunshine or shade, squall or calm." Then in a
new paragraph the pencil entry continues in language identical to the ink entry on p.
[12]. The only legible variations between the blurred pencil and the ink entry are
"God drew the model", "work be shown by cowards", and a reversal of names to
"Columbus Alfred Socrates" in the pencil version.

[14] The entry, not recopied, remains in its original pencil writing.

excellent preparation for life ashore. No man well knows how many fingers he has got nor what are the faculties of a knife & a needle or the capabilities of a pine board until he has seen the expedients, & the ambidexterous invincibility of Jack Tar. Then he may buy an orchard or retreat to his paternal acres with a stock of thrifty science that will make him independent of all the village carpenters, masons, & wheelwrights & add withal an enchanting beauty to the waving of his yellow corn & sweetness to his shagbarks in his chimney corner. No squally ⟨ca⟩ Twelve o'clock Call the Watch shall break his dreams.

Tuesday.[15] 15 Jan. W. Long 13°. 27. Calm, clear, warm, idle day; holiday to the senses, rest to the sailor, vexation to the captain, dubiously borne by the passenger. Yesterday or day before saw three sail, one Englishman.   Today one French brig & saluted them both by exchanging the sight of our colours.   John Bull, they say is very sulky at sea as assuredly[?] [16] sometimes very rude. But how comes my speculative pencil down to so near a level with the horizon of life, which commonly proses above?

[16] I learn in the sunshine to get an altitude & the latitude but am a dull scholar as ever in real figures. Seldom I suppose was a more inapt learner of arithmetic, astronomy, geography, political economy than I am as I daily find to my cost. It were to brag much if I should there end the catalogue of my defects. My memory of history — put me to the pinch of a precise question [—] is as bad; my comprehension of a question in technical metaphysics very slow, & in all arts practick, in driving a bargain, or hiding emotion, or carrying myself in company as a man for an hour, I have no skill. What under the sun canst thou do then, pale face! Truly not much, but I can hope. "In a good hope," said Bias, "the wise differ from

---

[15] The entry is in legible pencil writing, not recopied. The prior paragraph ("I comfort . . . dreams.") is an ink recopying done above the lines of the pencil version, which is still partially visible.

[16] The original pencil word is almost totally rubbed out; Edward Emerson has inserted above the blurred word, in pencil, "assuredly?" Actually only "ass . . . ly" is visible.

the unwise." [17] I am content to belong to the great *all*, & look on & see what better men can do, & by my admiration realize a property in their worth. I did not put me here, yet God forbid I should therefore decline the responsibility into which I am born. Space & Time & venerable Nature & beautiful Stars & all ye various fellow beings, I greet ye well, & will not [17] despond but even out of my acre God shall yet rear himself some tardy fruit. If not still is it not sublime unprofitably to pray & praise? [18]

Wednesday, 16 Jan. W. long. 11.30 North latitude 30 || . . . ||

16 Jan. I rose betimes & saw every fold of the banner of the morning unrolled from starlight to full day. We are as poor as we are rich. We brag of our memory but in the lonely night watch it will not always befriend us but leaves the scholar's brain [18] as barren as the steward's. But that I sat in the confessional last night I should parade my rags again. The good Captain rejoices much in my ignorance. He confounded me the other day about the book in the Bible where God was not mentioned & last night upon St Paul's shipwreck.[19] Yet I comforted myself at midnight with Lycidas. What marble beauty in that classic Pastoral. I should like well to see an analysis [n] of the pleasure it gives. ↑That were criticism for the gods.↓

The inconvenience of living in a cabin is that people become all eye. 'Tis a great part of wellbeing to ignorize a good deal of your fellowman's history & not count his warts nor expect the hour when he shall wash his teeth.

[17] Diogenes Laertius, "Chilon," *Lives of Eminent Philosophers*, I, 69: "Being asked wherein lay the difference between the educated and the uneducated, Chilon answered, 'In good hope.' " But Emerson also remembered vaguely, perhaps, a second anecdote from Diogenes Laertius, "Bias," I, 87: "Being asked, 'What is sweet to men,' he answered, 'Hope.' " The final anecdote then telescopes the two.

[18] Between "praise?" and "Wednesday" sixteen lines of the page are lacking an ink entry. But an original pencil entry underlies on the whole page and is partially legible in the open space. Of the pencil entry only the last line, "Wednesday . . . latitude" is fully recoverable. The following scattered phrases or words at the beginning and end of lines are still legible: "you"; "we are great"; "trite as any other"; "have an orange[?]"; "who being"; "said to him he would"; "and the rich"; "When he thought"; "replied when he"; "The wise || . . . || the unwise".

[19] Esther and Acts 27.

17 Jan. n. lat 36 29 w long 9.48 Another day as beautiful as ever shines on the monotonous sea but a wind so soft will not fill our sails & we lie like a log so near our haven too. Ατρυγετη θαλασση [20] [—] the sea is a blank & all the minstrelsy of nature rings but a few changes on the instrument. The more it should send [19] us to the inner Music; but that is a capricious shell which sometimes vibrates wildly with multitudinous impulses & sometimes is mute as wood. The inner shell is like its marine archetype which murmurs only where there is already noise.

Friday 18 Jan. lat 36 36 long 8 20 w.

Well thou navigating Muse of mine 'tis now the hour of Chinese inspiration, the post-tea-cup-time, the epical creative moment to all thinking heads of the modern world & what print have the ⟨bright⟩ ↑ethereal↓ footsteps of Night & Morn left upon your tablets? [n] Another day, another profusion of the divine munificence yet taken & spent by us as by the oysters. The boar feeds under the tree & never looks up to see who shakes down the mast & I glide in leisure & safety & health & fulness over this liquid Sahara & the Invisible Leader so venerable is seldom worshipped & much a stranger in the bosom of his child. We feel sometimes as if the sweet & awful melodies we have once heard would never return. As if we [were deaf?] [21] and fear we shall not again aspire to the glory of a moral [20] life, of a will as punctual as the little needle [22] in the binnacle over my head. The sea tosses on the horns of its waves the framework of habits so slight & epicurean as mine & I make the voyage one long holiday which like all holidays is dull.

Sat. 19 Jan. Mem. No trust to be put in a seaman's eye. He can see land wherever he wishes to see it & always has a cloud & "the stuff" ready to cover up a mistake. No wor[d] suits the sea but I hope. Every sign fails.

[20] Possibly Emerson's memory of the *Iliad*, XIV, 204, ἀτρυγέτοιο θαλάσσης, — "unresting sea."

[21] The bracketed emendation to correct the sense of the text is added above the line in pencil, probably by Edward Emerson.

[22] The page is apparently recopied in ink. Under "life . . . needle" are the same words faintly visible in pencil.

20 Jan. Straits of Gibraltar. Last evening they saw land from the mast-head & this morn[in]g broke over the bold & picturesque mountains of Africa behind Cape Spartel & Tangiers. On the left was Cape Trafalgar & Spain. The passengers greeted each other & mused each in his own way on this animating vision. But now as Tarifa light opened upon us we have encountered an adverse current[,] a thing unknown in the books or to the sailors in these waters where they say the current always sets from the Ocean into the Mediterranean. Meantime [21] all the other craft great & small are flying by us & we seem anchored in the middle of the stream. What is this to me beyond my fellowfeeling for the master? Shall not I be content to look at the near coast of Andalusia & Morocco? I have seen this morn the smokes of Moorish fishers or mountaineers on one side & of Spanish on the other. We could not quite open Tangier Bay enow to see that Mauritanian town, but the watch towers & the cultivated enclosures & the farm houses of the Spaniard are very discernible. Not many weeks ago I should scarce have been convinced that I should so soon look on these objects, yet what is their poetry or what is it not? Is not a hut in America a point that concentrates as much life & sentiment as a hut in Europe or on the ragged side of Mount Atlas? [n] Ah! it is all in the Anointed eye. Yet will not I refine overmuch on the love of the remote & the renowned, nor affirm them both to be only a mixture of colors upon [22] the retina of the eye, nor say of a man he is mammiferous & of beauty it is but gelatine & oxygen.

21 Jan. A squall with copious rain helped us out of our Straits & last eve[nin]g I saw the lights of the barracks at Gibraltar on one side & at Ceuta on the other. ⟨This day we s⟩ The summit of the hill at Gibraltar is 1500 feet high.

This day we sail bravely 5, 6, & 7 knots. Sunrise was charming; the pillars of Hercules astern[;] the Barbary Coast on the lee quarter; & the mountains of Grenada covered with snow, having white villages half way up their sides on the left hand. A grand show they make. The Sierra Nevada is the name of the range, & the easternmost summit which we saw is the highest in Spain & except the Alps in Europe to wit 11,690 ft. We glided by Malaga the country of the finest grape but were too far seaward to spy the town. Twenty one sail were in sight at sunrise.

[23][23] These cold Alpine hilltops remind us of New England though far higher than any of our snow banks. Noble Sierra Nevada! All the afternoon we have watched the sublime peak of Cumbre de Mulahacin & fast as we go we scarce change our bearings from it.

[January] 22d. Off the snowy mountains blew not so cold breath yesterday as this day from the Northeast. "Fire," well said the ancient, "is the sauce of life." [24] If you diminish the temperature, it infuses ague into my inner as well as outer Self. Yet since the first ten days of the voyage I have scarce worn my great coat except at evening or to sit still in the shade.

[24] 25 Jan. N. Lat. 37° 31 E. long. 1° 20′ [25] Head winds are sore vexations & the more passengers the sorer. Yesterday the Captain killed a porpoise & I witnessed the cutting up of my mammiferous fellow creature.

When men & women sit mum by the hour & week, shall I doubt the doctrine that every natural character is interesting? By no means[;] there is always sweet music in the pipe but it needs a skilful player to draw it out, else month by month we may be packed in the same closet, & shall be all only so much ash & ebony.

If the sea teaches any lesson it thunders this through the throat of all its winds "That there is no knowledge that is not valuable." [26] How I envied /the/my/ fellow passenger who yesterday had knowl-

[23] That the entry has been recopied and revised in ink is evident from the few recovered pencil words underlying the present writing: "were out of sight"; "cold hill"; "New England"; and "temperature".

[24] Plutarch, "The Symposiacs"; see the *Morals*, 1870, III, 362, slightly misquoted.

[25] "25 Jan . . . 20′" is underwritten by the same words in pencil. Yet the pencil entry originally on the page must have been somewhat different from the present entry since still faintly visible in pencil are the following fragments: "And for want of"; "shall all be"; "Cheerful is it to"; "swell from"; "lessons of our ignorance"; "at the Ocean of truth"; and "of our faculties thereby".

[26] See *The Works of the Right Honorable Edmund Burke*, rev. ed., 12 vols. (Boston, 1865–1867), II, 38. The aphorism comes from the "Speech on American Taxation," 1774; see *JMN*, I, 192.

edge & nerve enough to prescribe for the sailor's sore throat & this morning to bleed him. In this little balloon of ours, so far from the human family and their sages & colleges & manufactories every accomplishment, every natural or acquired talent, every piece of information is some time in request. And a short voyage will show the difference [n] [25][27] between the man & the apprentice as surely as it will show the superior value of beef & bread to lemons & sugar-plums. Honour evermore aboard ship to the man of action, — to the brain in the hand. Here is our stout master worth a thousand philosophers — a man who can strike a porpoise, & make oil out of his blubber, & steak out of his meat; who can thump a mutineer into obedience in two minutes; who can bleed his sick sailor, & mend the box of his pump; ⟨&⟩ who can ride out the roughest storm on the American coast, &, more than all, with the sun & a three cornered bit of wood, & a chart, can find his way from Boston across 3000 miles of stormy water into a little gut of inland sea 9 miles wide with as much precision as if led by a clue.

2 Feb. Made St Elmo's light at 1 o'clock this morng; lay to in a gale till daylight & then sailed into St Paul's bay. The pilot boat was quickly followed by a procession of boats who after a short loud wrangling with the unflinching captain [26][28] came into his terms & took the rope & brought us in. So here we are in Malta, in the renowned harbor of Marsa Muscette the Quarantine roads for a fortnight, imprisoned for poor dear Europe's health lest it should suffer prejudice from the unclean sands & mountains of America. The

[27] A few pencil words, apparently part of an entry that was not recopied, are visible faintly beneath the ink of the upper part of the page: "passenger ∥ . . . ∥ casts his eye"; "bubbles to see ∥ . . . ∥ fast"; and "but it is welcome to sight". In the middle of the page with a new paragraph is a pencil entry that is apparently an early version of the ink entry beginning "2 Feb." below: "2 February Made La Valletta light this morng at 4 o'clock lay to in a gale till daylight & then sailed into St Paul's bay".

[28] Emerson is still apparently rewriting and revising the original pencil entry, for faintly visible beneath the ink are the following fragments: "Then came the Merchant Paul Eynaud. Here we learn that ∥ . . . ∥ imprisonment for ∥ . . . ∥ says ∥ . . . ∥ I went to the ∥ . . . ∥ a real life scene was ∥ . . . ∥ Greeks English, Maltese, friars ∥ . . . ∥ & poor ∥ . . . ∥ like a picture ∥ . . . ∥ 15 Feb. God has put every man's credentials in his ∥ . . . ∥ has no ∥ . . . ∥ to originate any thing ∥ . . . ∥". The dated pencil entry for February 15 seems not to have been worked into the final ink version.

truth is it is all pro forma on the part of the English government[,] this quarantine being enforced in accordance with the rules of Naples & Trieste merely that vessels quarantined here may be admitted to full pratique in those ports.

We were presently visited by the Harbor-master, then by the boats of the grocer & ship chandler presenting their cards at the end of a pole to us leprous men, then the clamorous *Spenditori* to offer their services, then by the merchant signor Paul Eynaud.

This P.M. I visited the Parlatorio where those in quarantine converse with those out across barriers. It looked to me like the wildest masquerade. There jabbered Turks, Moors, Sicilians, Germans, Greeks, English, Maltese, with friars & guards & maimed & beggars.ⁿ [27]²⁹ And such grotesque faces! It resembled more some brave antique picture than a congregation of flesh & blood. The human family can seldom see their own differences of color & form so sharply contrasted as in this house. I noticed however that all the curiosity manifested was on our part. Our cousins of Asia & Europe did not pay us the compliment of a second glance.

In Quarantine, our acquaintance has been confined chiefly to the Maltese boatmen, a great multitude of poor, swarthy, goodnatured people, who speak their own tongue, not much differing from the Arabic, & most of them know very few words of Italian & less of English.

[28] 16 February, La Valetta. Yesterday we took pratique & found lodgings once more on dry ground with great joy. All day with my fellow travellers I perambulated this little town of stone. It is from end to end a box of curiosities. & though it is very green & juvenile to express wonder, I could not hinder my eyes from rolling continually in their sockets nor my tongue from uttering my pleasure & surprize. It is an advantage to enter Europe at the little end so we shall admire by just degrees from the Maltese architecture up to St Peter's. I went to St John's Church & a noble house it is to worship God in; full of marble & mosaic & pictures & gilding; the walls are eloquent with texts & the floor covered with epitaphs. The Verger led me down into a dim vault full of solemn sculpture

---

²⁹ No pencil writing exists beneath the ink entries on pp. [27]–[31].

& showed me the tomb of L'Isle Adam, the Grand Master of the Knights of St John, to whom Charles V gave the island of Malta when ⟨they⟩ he & his knights had been driven by the Turks from Rhodes. Next to him, rests the body of La Valetta [29] who so bravely defended the island against the Sultan   in [30]

But I shall ⟨le⟩have more to say about this fine temple when I have paid another visit. Every where as I went, the wretched beggars would steal up beside me, with, "Grazia, Signore, sono miserabile, uno grano per carita." Look hard at a Maltese, said my friend, Mr H[olbrook]. & he instinctively holds out his hand. I went to the churches of St Popilius & St Thomas. The first is no other than 'Publius, the chief man of the island' in Acts XXVIII & much honor hath he in Malta at least on the walls of his church.

↑In↓ all [n] these churches there were many worshippers continually coming in, saying their prayers, & going their way. I yielded me joyfully to the religious impression of holy texts & fine paintings & this soothfast faith though of women & children. How beautiful to have the church always open, so that every tired wayfaring man may come in & be soothed by all that art can suggest of a better world when he is weary with this.

[30] I hope they will carve & paint & inscribe the walls of our churches in New England before this century, which will probably see many grand granite piles erected there, is closed. To be sure there is plenty of superstition. Every where indulgence is offered, and on one convent on our way home I read this inscription over the gate, "Indulgentia plenaria, quotidiana, perpetua, pro vivis et defunctis." [31] This is almost too frank, may it please your holiness.

[February] 17. Visited St John's again & attended mass. The bishop [32]
          a venerable old man was present but did not officiate.

---

[30] La Valetta, the 6th Grand Master of the Knights of St. John, 1557–1568, defended against the Turkish siege of 1565. Space is left to fill in the information later.

[31] "Indulgence, full, daily, perpetually, for the living and the dead" (Ed.).

[32] A line space is left after these two words, evidently so that the name could be filled in later. A penciled comma and line linking "bishop" to "venerable" in the line below are probably insertions by Edward Emerson.

This noble temple was built by the grand Master La Cassiera & chiefly adorned with painting by Preti who lies buried here (V[ide]. Abela).[33] Mrs Davy told me it was built about 1560. The lordly heads of the Grand Masters still command the eye in marble or on canvas around the walls & their notched cross surmounts or underlies every ornament.[34] The music of the organ & chaunting friars very impressive, especially when we left the kneeling congregation in the nave, & heard it at [31] distance, as we examined the pictures in a side oratory. I went into several churches which were all well attended. How could any body who had been in a catholic church, devise such a deformity as a pew?

Went at 11 o'clock to Mr Temple's plain chapel on the third story of his dwelling house & heard with greedy ears the English bible read, & Watts' psalms sung, & a good sermon. A small congregation of English; one Armenian, who is translating the bible into his tongue. Mr Temple & Mr Halleck conduct the Missionary press here & print in modern Greek, in Italian, in Armenian, & Turkish. The Maltese is Arabic with a mixture of Italian. They have translated Adams' Arithmetic & Peter Parley's Geography (πετρου Ωμιλητου) & the best tracts into Greek. The names look odd enough. "Η δυναμις της αλεθειας" and "Η θυγατηρ του γαλακτοπωλου" are droll masks for Scott's Force of Truth & the Dairyman's Daughter.[35] I brought away Scougal's "Life of God in the Soul of Man" in Italian.[36]

The Missionary press for the Mediterra [37]

---

[33] John de la Cassière, 8th Grand Master from 1572–1581, opened the Cathedral church in 1578. Some of Emerson's information apparently came from reading Giovanni Francesco Abela, *Malta Illustrata*, 2 vols. (Malta, 1772), a history of Malta in Italian and Latin which he read in on February 20. See p. 120 below.

[34] A rough Maltese cross is sketched into the line here.

[35] The works whose titles were translated into odd Greek were as follows: Daniel Adams, *The Scholars' Arithmetic* (Keene, N. H., 1802, 1807, 1816, 1824) or its revised edition, *The New Arithmetic* (Keene, N.H., 1827); probably Samuel G. Goodrich, *A System of School Geography* . . . (Hartford, Conn., 1830); Thomas Scott, *The Force of Truth, An Authentick Narrative*, 5th ed. (London, 1798); [Legh Richmond], *The Dairyman's Daughter; an authentic and interesting narrative* (London and Dublin, 1810, and multiple editions thereafter).

[36] Henry P. Scougal, *The Life of God in the Soul of Man* (1774) was, as Emerson remarked in a letter to Elizabeth Tucker, February 1, 1832 (*J*, II, 459), a book which he valued highly. He owned the Boston, 1823, edition.

[37] This entry, interrupted by what is evidently an original pencil entry on p.

[32] 13 January, Sunday. In the wonderful store of the memory carry we power & peace. It is the monument of how high antiquity. The sides of the pyramids cannot contain the story of half so much time nor be inscribed with any thing like the magic of its method. Its method is myriad fold. Its order comprehends a thousand lines right, left, oblique, curved & waving. Every point lives & is centre or extreme in turn. As the lightning shineth out of one part of heaven even unto the other part, so one thought in this firmament flashes its light over all the sphere.

A man looks upon himself as a mere circumstance & not as the solid, adamant, mundane groundplan of a universal man. He thinks his internals are evanescent opal shades & won't bear criticism & description. Let him turn the telescope on them. Let him compare them with durable things. He will find they outshine the sun & will grind to powder the iron & the stone of outward permanence.

[33] nean is established here for the sake of the protection of this government. There is only protection, no countenance. It was a stipulation of the Maltese in their capitulation to the English in [38] that the scriptures should not be printed in the Maltese.   (?)

[February] ↑20.↓ I went to the terrace on the top of Mr Temple's house. All the ⟨houses⟩ ↑roofs↓ are flat & afford this valuable accomodation. I saw many persons walking on the tops. Last Friday, Mr T. said he saw Mt Etna very distinctly from hence & it is very frequently seen↑.↓ ⟨from⟩ It is 150 miles distant. He is sure the atmosphere is much more transparent than with us; that Venus & Jupiter give more light.

Mr T. rents his lofty house for $140 containing his chapel & Press. It rented once for 1000 scudes, = $400. Noble houses every where, thanks to the beautiful material for building which constitutes the soil of the island. The Maltese stone is very soft & easily wrought & when well selected ⟨will⟩ the house will last a thousand years.

---

[32] for January 13, continues with the completion of the broken word on the top of p. [33]. No more pencil entries, either untouched or overwritten, occur until p. [42].

[38] Emerson left space for a later insertion of the missing date.

The architecture is in fine taste[,] the apartments 20 or 30 [34] feet high — floors, walls, stairs, all of this cold, clean, sightly stone, the balconies supported with sculptured work & the openings adorned with vases. Instead of paper the walls & ceilings are covered with ordinary frescoes wherein Æsop & the Old Testament furnish the subjects.

Visited the Armoury in the Palace & saw the arms of the old knights of every form & size, much the same show I suppose as is in the Tower of London. The hall might be 200 ft. long[.]

The library of the Knights contains 40000 volumes, and a venerable ptolemaic bookstall it is. I sat down & read in Abela's old folios — 'Melita Illustrata.'

Through the politeness of Mr Eynaud the American Consul, I received a card of invitation from Sir Frederick Ponsonby the Governor to attend a fancy dress ball at the Palace — A very gay & novel scene but hardly equal to the place & expectation. As the consul did not appear very early my friends & I presented each other to Sir Frederick who [35] conversed a few moments very pleasantly. We thought he resembled George IV.

A few beautiful faces in the dancing crowd, & a beautiful face is always worth going far to see. That which is finest in beauty is *moral*. The most piquant attraction of a long descended maiden is the imputation of an immaculate innocence, a sort of wild virtue (⟨I⟩if I may so term it) wild & fragrant as the violets. And the imagination is surprised & gratified with the strong contrast — meeting the Divinity amidst flowers & trifles.

Called upon Mrs Davy, a very agreeable woman. Dr Davy, (brother to Sir Humphry) is given to chemical pursuits.[39] Much younger than I expected, and of simple manners. I was sorry I could not accept of their invitation ⁿ to dine, as they were well named, well educated, well mannered, & well acquainted with Malta.

Visited the workshop of Sigismundo Dimeck a sculptor in Mal-

[39] John Davy (1790–1868), a surgeon who saw much foreign service, married Margaret Fletcher in 1830 and wrote his observations of Malta in *Notes and Observations on the Ionian Islands* . . . (London, 1842).

tese stone. Beautiful work. If I had a great house in America, I would send to the Signor for a pair of vases which I saw [—] 4 ft high, 2 ft diam., richly carved with [36] ornaments a la Raffaello, price $8.00 apiece. Another pair of the same size & as good to my eye though with less costly ornament[,] price $5.00. Venetian oil is put in them to make them hold water. A *Bocale* 1 ft high & beautiful $⟨1.00⟩ .75. Vaso Etrusco $1.00

———

Convicts in chains sweep the streets in Malta.

———

The Maltese milkman drives his goats through the street & milks you a pint at your door. Asses & mules *passim*.

———

Sigismondo Dimeck, Sculptor, Strada Teatro, No 69

[37] 21 Feb. At 8 o'clock P.M. we embarked for Syracuse in a Sicilian brigantine "⟨The⟩Il Santissimo Ecce Homo," and a most ridiculous scene our ship's company offered, they to us & we to them. The little brig was manned with 14 men who were all on a perfect level with each other. The steersman sat down at the helm & when they brought him his supper the captain affectionately took his post whilst he ate. The boy was employed in sitting down by the steersman & watching the hour glass so that he might turn it when it ran out. But the whole interest of master & men was concentrated on us his five passengers. We had hired for $30 ⟨d⟩ the whole cabin, so they put all their heads into the scuttle & companionway to behold all that we did, the which seemed to amuse them mightily. When any thing was to be done to sails or spars they did it who had a mind to it & the captain got such obedience as he could. In the morning the mate brought up his gazetteer to find Boston ⟨which⟩ the account of which he read aloud, and all the crew gathered round him whilst he read. They laughed ⟨as⟩ heartily at the captain & passed jokes upon him & when the little boy did something amiss every [38] body gave him a knock. A cask of blood red wine was on tap, ⟨wh⟩ from which every body drank when it pleased him in a quart measure. Their food was a boiled fish called *purpo* (which looks like an eel & tastes like lobster) with

bread & green onions eaten raw. Their little vessel sailed fast & in 16 hours we saw the ancient city of Syracuse. Abundance of fuss & vexation did the Sanita & the Dogana give us before we were suffered to land our baggage but our Captain & mate helped us all they could, & our money opened all the gates at last.

[39]   Syracuse 23 Feb.

Shall I count it like the Berber at Rome the greatest wonder of all to find myself here? [n] I have this day drank the waters of the fountain Arethusa & washed my hands in it. I ate the very fragrant Hyblaean honey with my breakfast. ⟨Af⟩ I have been into the old temple of Minerva praised for its beauty by ⟨T⟩Cicero [40] & now preserved & concealed by having its pillars half buried in the walls of the Cathedral. A modern facade conceals the front but the severe beauty of a Parthenon peeps from the sides in projecting flutes & triglyphs. It was 7 in the morning, & I found the priests ⟨cele⟩ saying mass in the oratories of the church. The American Consul called upon our party in the forenoon & we rode with him into the country. We stopped at a crumbled arch reputed as the spot where Cicero [41] found the globe & cylinder, the tomb of Archimedes. Did I hold my breath for awe? Then went we to the Catacombs ⟨old enough⟩ — old enough — nothing else — mere excavations in the ⟨stra⟩ living rock for cemeteries, but the air was soft & the [40] trees in bloom & the fields covered with beautiful wild flowers to me unknown and amidst ruins of ruins Nature still was fair. Close by we found the Aqueduct, which once supplied the magnificent city of Hiero[,] now turning a small grist mill. Then we went to Dionysius' Ear; a [n] huge excavation into the hard rock which I am not going to describe. Poor people were making twine in it & my ear was caught on approaching it by the loud noise made by their petty wheels in the vault. A little beyond the entrance the floor was covered with a pool of water. We found a twine maker who ⟨was⟩ very readily took us, one after another on his shoulders into the recess 250 ft, & planted us on dry land at the bottom of the cave. We shouted & shouted & the cave bellowed & bellowed; the twine maker tore a

[40] *Against Verres*, II, iv, 53 and 55–56.
[41] See *Tusculan Disputations*, V, xxii, 63.

bit of paper in the middle of the cave, & very loud it sounded; then
they fired a pistol at the entrance & we had our fill of thunder.

[41] I ⟨eagerly⟩ inquired for the tyrant's chamber in the wall,
the focus of sound where he was wont to hear the whispers of his
prisoners, — but in this unvisited country it is inaccessible. High up
the rock, ⟨they⟩ seventy or eighty feet, they pointed to a little inlet [42]
to which once there was a stair, but not now. If we had time & spirit
would we not go up thither in baskets, as sundry English have done?
I affirm not. ⟨Then⟩ A little way off, along the same quarry of rock
we found another great excavation in which they were making salt-
petre. It was the place from which the great pillars of the Temple
of Minerva, it is said, were taken. Then we visited the ⟨t⟩Theatre
or rather the rows of stone benches which are all of it that remains.
From this spot we looked down upon the city & its noble harbour
and a beautiful sad sight it was. The town stands now wholly within
the little peninsula, the ancient Ortygia ⟨& the three great sub⟩ (not
a third of the size of the peninsula of Boston, I judge) [43]

[42][44] What is a passenger? He is a much enduring man who
bends under the load of his leisure. He fawns upon the Captain,
reveres the mate, but his eye follows the Steward; scans accurately
as symptomatic, all the motions of that respectable officer.

The species is contemplative, given to imitation, viciously inquisitive, immensely capable of sleep, large eaters, swift digesters,
their thoughts ever running on men & things ashore & their eye
usually squinting over the bulwark, to estimate the speed of the
bubbles.

[42] A sketch of the opening in the form of a truncated triangle follows within
the line.

[43] The entry, broken off by the interruption of an original pencil entry overwritten and revised in ink on p. [42], continues on p. [43].

[44] Underlying pencil writing on this page is partially visible at the top and
bottom of the ink entry. The pencil words at the top are apparently not a part of
the revised entry. But from "Captain" through "bubbles." the pencil entry seems
to have been identical. At the top of the page in pencil is "‖ . . . ‖ the merchant Signor
Paul Eynaud ‖ . . . ‖ our imprisonment forthwith"; beneath "reveres the mate," is
"What is a passenger?"; beneath "large eaters" is "The species is"; after "bubbles."
and below it is "their eye generally squinting over the bulwark to estimate the
speed of the bubbles."

[43] and the three great suburbs or parts[,] Neapoli, Tycha, & Acradina [,] have almost no house or church where they stood. And Syracuse is very old & shabby, with narrow streets & few people & many, many beggars. Once 800000 people dwelt together in this town. Its walls were according to historical measurements twenty two English miles in circuit. ⟨Its⟩ Of its two ports, the northern was called the Marmoreus because surrounded with marble edifices. The southern is 5 miles round, & is the best harbor in the Mediterranean Sea.

In the old time every Sicilian carried honey & wheat & flowers out of the port & threw them into the sea as soon as he lost sight of the statue of Minerva aloft on her temple. Once Dion, once Timoleon, once Archimedes dwelt here & Cicero dutifully visited their graves.

[44] I lodge in the Strada Amalfitan[i]a. In a Caffé in our street, they have had the good taste to paint the walls ⟨with⟩ ↑in↓ very tolerable frescoes with Archimedes drawing the famous galley by means of a windlass. ⟨& a few ⁿ doors off from the Locanda⟩ A sign over ⟨a⟩our Locanda contains this sentence of Cicero's 4th Oration in Verrem "Urbem Syracusas elegerat[."] [45]

[45] Was it grand or mournful that I should hear mass in this Temple of Minerva this morn? Though in different forms, is it not venerable that the same walls should be devoted to divine worship for more than 2500 years? ⁿ Is it not good witness to the ineradicableness of the religious principle? With the strange practice ⁿ that in these regions every where confounds pagan & Christian Antiquity & half preserves both, they call this cathedral the Church of 'our Lady of the pillar.'

Abundance of examples here of great things turned to vile uses. The fountain Arethuse, to be sure, gives name to the street Via Aretusa in which it is found: but an obscure dark nook it is & we walked up & down & looked in this & that court yard in vain for some time. Then we asked a soldier on guard Where it was? He only knew that "Questa e la batteria," — nothing more. At last

---

[45] "He selected the city of Syracuse . . ." is actually from *Against Verres*, II, 5 (not 4), 26. This paragraph is centered on the page.

an old woman guided us to the spot and I grieve — I abhor to tell — the fountain was bubbling up in its world renowned [46] waters within four black walls serving as one great washing tub to fifty or sixty women who were polluting it with all the filthy clothes of the city.

It is remarkable ⟨at⟩ now as of old for its quantity of water springing up out of the earth at once as large as a river. Its waters are sweet & pure & of the colour of Lake George.

All day from the balcony, Mount Etna is in sight, covered with snow. From the parlor window I look down on the broad marshes where the Carthaginian army that came ⟨perished⟩ to rescue Syracuse from the Romans, perished.

They say in this country you have but to scratch the soil & you shall find medals, cameos, statues, temples.

[47] [February] 24. Visited the Latomié of the Gardens of the Capuchins — a strange place — . It is a large & beautiful garden full of oranges & lemons & pomegranates in a deep pit[,] say 120 feet below the surrounding grounds. All this is a vast excavation in the solid rock, & we first came upon it from above & peeped down the precipice into this fragrant cellar far below us. "Opus est ingens magnificum regum ac tyrannorum. Totum [est] ex saxo in mirandam altitudinem depresso, &c" Cicero. [Against Verres, II, v, 27] [46] All this excavation is manifestly the work of art — Cyclopean all. After circumambulating the brink above we went to the Convent & got admission to the garden below. A handsome & courteous monk conducted us, & showed us one huge arch wherein he said the Athenian prisoners recited the verses of Euripides for their ransom. Wild &

[46] "An immense and splendid piece of work, carried out by the kings and tyrants. The whole thing is a profound excavation in the rock . . ." "Opus . . . Cicero." is actually written below and to the right of "perished." on p. [46]. The quotation is set in to the center of the page, enclosed with a large ink bracket on the left margin, and has a carefully sketched, red-crayoned hand with a pointing finger directed toward "us." on p. [47]. There, to show precisely the point of insertion, is another hand with a pointing finger, sketched roughly but colored red again. Apparently Emerson found and inserted the comment from Cicero at a later date.

grand effect. All Syracuse must have been built out of this enormous quarry. Traces of works on a vast scale in oldest time.

Went into the Convent & the Fathers set before us bread, olives, & wine. Our conductor then showed us the ⟨sleeping rooms⟩ dormitories [48] (over each of which was a latin inscription from the bible or the Fathers,) the Chapel, &c. of the House. There is no better spot in the neighborhood of Syracuse than the one they have chosen. The air, the view, the long gallery of the chambers, the peace of the place quite took me & I told the Padre that I would stay there always if he would give me a chamber. He said, 'I should have his,' which he opened — a little neat room, with a few books, "Theologia Thomae ex Charmes," & some others. My friend's whip-cords hung by the bed side.

There are only 22 or 23 persons in this fine old house. We saw but 4 or 5. I am half resolved to spend a week or fortnight there. They will ↑give me↓ board, ⟨me,⟩ I am informed, on easy terms. How good & pleasant to stop & recollect myself in this worn out nook of the human race, to turn over its history & my own. But, ah me!

Hence we went to the Campo Santo where several Americans have been buried; & thence to other [49] Latomie, the gardens of the Marquis di Casal. Similar to those we had left but the rich soil is now filled with flowers in wildest profusion of scent & color. The bergamot ⟨oran⟩ lemon, the orange, the citron, we plucked & ate; & lavender & rosemary & roses & hyacinths & jasmine & thyme, which were running wild all over the grounds we filled our hands & hats with.

Here we found the Marchesino or son of the Marchese, who was very polite to us, & Mr Baker, the English consul, & his family, whom we greeted warmly for the love of the father-land & language. Well pleased we came back to the Locanda where we received the American Consul Signor Nicosia & his friend Signor Giuseppe Ricciardi to dine. ⟨I⟩

[February] 25. Still, melancholy, old metropolis! under the moon, last eve, how wan & grey it looked. Took a boat this morning & crossed the Porto Maggiore & sailed up the mouth of the river Anapus; full of canes & bulrushes & [50] snails & a very little, narrow, mean puddle to be famed in song. We did not go up so far as the fountain Cyane, but disembarked about 3 miles lower, where the stream was an oar's length wide. It was a pretty fable of Pluto's metamorphosis of Cyane [47] & if we had more time should have stamped on the very ground where "gloomy Dis" stamped, & the rather that our 'plan' afterwards showed us this was the spot of the Athenian Encampment. No wonder Proserpine gathered flowers; they grow everywhere of prettiest forms & liveliest colors now in February, & I stopped ever & anon to pick them.

On the banks of the Anapus grows the Papyrus — the immortal plant. — ⟨The⟩ It is a sightly, clean, green, triangular stem 20 feet high surmounted by a bunch of threads which the people call par↑r↓oc⟨c⟩a (perriwig). We cut down a good many, & then crossed the fields to the columns of the Temple of Olympian Jove.

Here stand two broken shafts [51] the sole remains of the temple which Gelo enriched with the spoils of the Carthaginians 2500 years ago.[48] The site is a commanding one, facing the centre of the ⟨G⟩ mouth of the Great Harbor. Seven of these fluted columns were standing in the last century, but Earthquakes are added to Time here in the work of destruction.

We crossed the bridge of the Anapus & went home by way of the Catacombs. We sat down on the benches of the Theatre which was entire in the days of Nero. We asked a goatherd who smoked his pipe on the same bench what they were for? "per il mulino", mulino. We could not easily get him by our questions beyond the Mill; at last he said, "antichita!" On the lowest circuit of benches we read the inscriptions ΒΑΣΙΛΙΣΣΑΣ ΦΙΛΙΣΤΙΔΟΣ and ΒΑΣΙΛΙΣΣΑΣ ΝΕΡΗΙΔΟΣ. There are medals with the first inscription [n], supposed to denote the daughter of Philistus, wife of the elder Dionysius.[49]

In the afternoon, I went to the Museum & saw the Venus Kallipyg⟨ie⟩e, dug up here [52] in 1810, a headless beauty.

---

[47] See Ovid, *The Metamorphoses*, V, 420–429.

[48] Gelo, son of Deinomenes, tyrant of Syracuse, enriched his city by the spoils won in the battle of Himera (see Herodotus, *History*, vii).

[49] "Basilissas Philistidos" and "Basilissas Nereidos" are transcriptions of title and name, meaning the Lady Philistidos and the Lady Nereidos. Mariana Starke, *Travels in Europe between the Years 1824 and 1828* (London, 1828), p. 386, prints the four inscriptions as they appeared on the benches from the second to the fifth circuit. Emerson apparently mixed the order somewhat and wrote an English L instead of a Greek Λ.

[February] 27. At dinner, a Frate dei Padri Capuccini was announced who brought olives & lemons in his hand, & would accompany us to the Latomié of the Church of St John. Thither we went, ⟨with⟩ and descended into subterranean caverns cut regularly in the living rock. Two Fathers & two boys attended with torches. On each side of the main passages were catacombs[,] some larger, some less. Occasionally the ceiling was vaulted up to admit light & air. I asked how far these long passages extended; the friar said, he knew not how far, but the air was bad, & no one went further than we. Cicero visited them before us.

Then went to the Church — very old, small, & poor; but by stone stairs descended into one far older, ⟨of⟩ ⟨with⟩ which they say is St John's Church, & coeval with the planting of Christianity in Sicily. The bold ⟨gr⟩ carving of the granite all around made me think it o⟨n⟩f Greek age & afterwards converted to this use.

[53] Signor Ricciardi, a friend of the Consul Nicolini's,[50] ⟨and⟩ was very civil to us & spoke good English. At parting he gave each of us a handful of sugar plums.

[54] Catania, ⟨28⟩ 1 March. Fine strange ride & walk yesterday coming by mules from Syracuse hither, 42 miles,[n] thirteen hours. Our party (3 gentlemen 2 ladies) [51] were accomodated with seven beasts[,] 2 for the Lettiga containing the ladies, 2 for the baggage, one for each saddle. The morning road led us by catacombs without number. What are they but evidences of an immense ancient population that every rock should be cut into sepulchres. The road, a mere mule-path through very stony soil[,] was yet not so rough but that I preferred walking to riding, & for an hour or two kept up easily with the caravan. Fine air, clear sun, Mount Aetna right before us, green fields — laborers ploughing in them, many flowers,[n] all the houses of stone. Passed the trophy of Marcellus,[52] a pile of broken masonry and yet it answers its purpose as well as Marcellus

---

[50] Consul Nicolini mentioned here is Emerson's second thought. On February 24 he had called the American consul Signor Nicosia (see p. 126 above).

[51] The party was still the five passengers from the *Jasper*: Mr. and Mrs. Silas Holbrook, their daughter, Mr. Samuel Kettell, and Emerson.

[52] The so-called "trophy of Marcellus" was connected with the conqueror of Syracuse only by legend.

could have hoped. Did he think that Mr Emerson would be reminded
of his existence & victory this fine spring day 2047 years to come?
[55] Saw the town of Mellili. Dined from our own knapsack at the
strangest tavern; hills of olive trees all around, an oil mill or press
adjoining, & a dozen big Morgiana jars thereby; ⟨and⟩ what seemed
the remains of some most ancient church or temple with the stumps
of pillars still standing, in the rear and the hostelry itself a most
filthy house of stone[,] more stable than house, the common dwelling of men, women, beasts, & vermin. "Siamo pronti, Signore," then
said the muleteer, which he of our party to whom it was said, mis-
apprehending to be a call for *brandy,* we waited yet a little. The
afternoon ride was pleasanter much — flowers abounding, the road
smooth and Aetna glorious to behold with his cap of smoke, & the
Mountainettes like warts all over his huge sides. Then wound the
road down by the seaside and for many miles we traversed a beach
like that of Lynn ⟨floored⟩ paved with pretty shells. We crossed the
Simaethus in a ferry & going a little inland [56] we tramped through
miles of prickly pears gigantic[,] but though Catanea had been in
sight much of the time since twelve o'clock nothing could be ruder
than this mule path from Syracuse to a city of 70000 souls. Had I
opened my eyes from sleep here almost under the shadows of the
town I might have thought myself near Timbuctoo. Yet has Nature
done all it could for this drowsy nation. I suppose the bay of Naples
cannot be so beautiful as the spacious bay, round the shore of which
we straggled & stumbled with tinkling mules, & sighing & shouting
drivers. Tzar, Tzar, gia, hm, and many an odd, nondescript, despair-
ing sound they ⟨make[?]⟩ utter to that deliberate animal. As the day
went down the mules began to tire, & one slipt into the mud, & was
with difficulty ⟨rescued⟩ got out. Another fell down with the lettiga.
The sun set, the moon rose, & still we did not reach the town so
near at noon till eight o clock.

------

[57]   men [53]   as   math   instrum[ents].   one   quadr[ant]   one

[53] The first entry ("men . . . degree") is in unblurred pencil writing, apparently a later insertion than the rest of the entry, which is in very faint, blurred pencil.
The poem is an early version later copied and revised into Journal Q, pp. [100]–
[101] (see pp. 69–70 above) and printed with variations in *Poems, W,* IX, 395.

sext[ant]. This wants the prolonged scale & ranges at one sweep
from the highest to the lowest degree[.]

> We are what we are made & every following day
> Is the Creator of our human mould
> Not less than was the first. God
> Gilds a few points in every several life
> And as ⟨in⟩ each flower ⟨a new design⟩
> And every varied leaf is sketched each with a new design
> A spot of purple & a streak of brown
> So each man's life its own beauty shall have
> And a few peculiar delights ⟨within[?]⟩
> ⟨|| . . . ||⟩& reconcile him to the common days
> Not many men I suppose see any pleasure in
> The fogs of close low ⟨woods⟩ pine woods in a river
> town Yet unto me not star's magnificence
> nor the red rainbow of a summer's day nor Rome
> nor Paris nor splendid festal parlours nor
> the wit of man nor angels' music hath such a
> soul a resurrection of the happy past
> As comes to me when I see the morning in
> such low moist roadside where blue violets peep[?]
> as[?] magic remembrances out of the black loam

[58]⁵⁴ Catan[ia]

Today & Yesterday

[59] Town of lava of earthquakes. The mountain is at once a
monument & a warning. Houses are built, streets paved with lava;
it is polished in the altars of the churches. Huge black rocks of it

---

[54] Under the incompleted ink entry "Catan" and covering the rest of the page
is a very faint blurred pencil draft of a poem. The fragments that can be read
indicate that the poem is a draft, apparently almost unchanged later, of "What is it
to sail," which is copied in ink into Journal Q, p. [102], after Emerson's return to
the United States. See p. 70 above. "Today & Yesterday" at the bottom of the page
is an ink repetition of the penciled words, the final phrase in the poem, which underlie "Town of lava" on the top of p. [59].

line the shore, & the white surf breaks over them. A great town full of fine old buildings, long regular streets thronged with people, a striking contrast to the sad solitude of Syracuse. Cathedral church of St Agatha. What exhilaration does the mere height of these prodigious Churches produce! We feel so little & so elated upon the floor. All the interior & exterior of this edifice is costly & the cost of ages. The ancient ⟨Greek⟩ ↑Roman↓ Amphitheatre was robbed for the columns & bas reliefs of its porch & much of its walls. Its niches & altars shine with many colored marbles & round the whole ample square ⟨on⟩whereon the church stands runs a large marble fence[.]

[60] But what is even this church to that of the Benedictines? [n] Indeed, my holy Fathers, your vows of poverty & humility have cost you little. Signor Ricciardi of Syracuse gave me a letter to Padre Anselmo Adorno, the Celleraio of this monastery & this morn I waited upon his reverence in his cell, & the kings of France & England, I think, do not live in a better house. The Padre with great courtesy showed us the church & its paintings, & its organ, here reputed the finest in Europe. It imitates sackbut, harp, psaltery, & all kinds of music. The Monk Donatus who built it, begged that he might be ⟨be⟩ buried under it, & there he lies. To my ignorance, however, the organ neither appeared very large nor very richly toned. But the Church shall be St Peter's to me till I behold a fairer shrine. Have the men of America never entered these European churches that they build such mean edifices [61] at home? Contini was the Architect but Father Anselm only knew that it was more than a hundred years old. But O the marbles! & oh the pictures & oh the noble proportions of the pile! A less interesting exhibition was the Treasury of the Convent, some silver richly wrought, seats & stools embroidered & gilt, & a wardrobe, — drawers full of copes & things of cloth-of-gold & silver. Then the long lofty cloisters, galleries of chambers, then gardens, too artificially laid out. About 50 monks are laid up in clover & magnificence here. They give bread twice in a week, one roll to every comer. I saw hundreds of women & children in the yard each receiving her loaf & passing on into a court, that none should come twice to the basket.

Visited the Museum of the Prince of Biscari, one of the best collections of the remains of ancient art. Bronzes, marbles, mosaics, coins, utensils dug up all over Sicily [62] of Greek & Roman manufacture are disposed with taste & science.

A head of Scipio took my fancy. & some more heads. The Prince of Biscari is a venerable name here. He was the Roscoe, the Petrarch of the town. Everywhere his beneficent hand is shown in restoring the old & saving the new.

I have been under the Cathedral into the ancient baths: and into the subterranean ruins of the ancient theatre, & now I will leave this primeval city, said to have been built by the Siculi 85 years before the destruction of Troy! & engage with the Vetturo for a visit to Messina.

I have been to the Opera, & thought three taris, the price of a ticket, rather too much for the whistle.[55] It is doubtless a vice to turn one's eyes inward too much, but I am my own comedy & tragedy. Did ye ever hear of a magnet who thought he had lost his virtue because he had fallen into a heap of shavings? Our manners are sometimes so mean, [63] our blunders & improprieties so many and mulish that it becomes a comfort to think that people are too much occupied with themselves to remember even their neighbor's defects very long.

Messina. March [5]. From Catania my ride to this city was charming. The distance is but ⟨50⟩60 miles but that is two days' journey here. Mount Etna was ⟨The first day⟩ the grand spectacle of the first day & a fine sight it is. This monarch of mountains they say supports a population of 115000 souls, & is 180 miles in circuit. And its ample sides are belted with villages & towers up almost to the snow. As the wind blew fresh I *smelt* the snowbanks. Village of Giarre; old country; catholic all over; scare a house or a fence but hath a shrine or cross or inscription. "Basta a chi non ha. Basta a chi morra." Another, "Viva la Divina Providenza," & a thousand more. It is a poor philosophy that dislikes these sermons in stones.[56] ⟨"⟩ But what green fields, & trees in bloom, & thick villages the turns in the

---

[55] Emerson apparently is remembering Franklin's famous story, "The Whistle." See *The Complete Works, in Philosophy, Politics, and Morals, of the Late Dr. Benjamin Franklin* . . . , 3 vols. (London, 1806), III, 480–483.

[56] Cf. Shakespeare, *As You Like It*, II, i, 17.

road showed; & my ⟨Italian⟩ ↑Sicilian↓ companions would break out
"O che bella veduta!"

These companions were four, ⟨the⟩a priest of the [64] Church
of St Iago in Messina, named Itellario, his two nephews Lorenzo &
Gaetano, & Francesco Nicolosi, a tailor. I name them all because
they were very kind to me. They speedily found I was a stranger &
took great pleasure in hearing my bad Italian & in giving me the
names of things & places. They brought their viveri with them & at
Giardini, where we spent the night, they made me dine with them
& paid all reckonings in the morng. It was amusing enough first, to
see how a Sicilian dines. Then their intercourse with me was all a
comedy. [their pronunciation & dialect are very different from Tus-
can] When I could not understand they would raise their voices,
& then all say the same thing, & then the worthy priest after a con-
sultation among them inquired if I could understand Latin, & I
declaring that I could, he essayed to communicate in that tongue,
but his Sicilian accent made his Latin equally unintelligible to me.
All the household collected gradually around us. At last I hit upon
the sense of what they would say, & much acclamation & mutual
congratulation there was. Coachey came in too, [65][57] & he told
them I was a *Sacerdote*[,] a *preté*[,] in my own country, a fact he had
picked up in Catania. This was wonders more. Then at every sentence which I forged & uttered was profound silence followed by
acclamations "che bravo Signore!" so modulated as only Italians can.

The little dark Locanda was on the beach of cape   & the
roar of the sea lulled me to sleep. Next morning I awoke right early
& found myself in the most picturesque of places. High overhead
was Taormina, so high & steep that it seemed inaccessible, & if men
could get there, not safe to live on the edge of a rock. Presently we
set forth & every step of the road showed new beauty & strangeness.
The ruins of the ↑amphi↓theatre at Taormina in very good preservation, I saw. & much I doubt if the world contains more picturesque
country in the same extent than in the thirty miles betwixt Giardini
& Messina[.]

[57] Some pencil figures, evidently records of latitude, underlie the ink entry on
the page, which is glued to the inside back cover. Below "by acclamations" is "La
Valette 35.5"; below "Italians can." is "observed at 32° 35′ ".

Italy

1833

The journal fills the second of the two companion volumes purchased in Boston in preparation for Emerson's European tour. Its dated entries begin at Palermo on March 7, 1833, a day or so after the final entry in the first notebook, and run through April 17, toward the end of Emerson's stay in Rome. He apparently still continued his practice of making entries first in pencil and then later recopying or revising in ink.

In make-up and dimensions this notebook is the same as the first in the series of the travel journals. Its limp leather cover is, however, dark blue instead of reddish brown. Two labels are on the front cover. Centered toward the top is a pasted-on white label with "1833" written within an inked-in rectangle. In the upper right corner a similar but smaller label is marked "2". Once more there are 16 folded sheets, making 64 pages plus a back inside cover. Modern transparent tape holds the cover to the final page. Unlike Sicily this notebook is without page numbers, which have been supplied in sequence by the editor. The sale tag from N. S. Simpkins and Company is pasted to the upper left-hand corner of the front cover verso as it is in Sicily. Page sizes are identical to those in the earlier notebook: 10 x 15.8 cm.

[front cover verso]   R. W. Emerson.

franc of France	= $0.18 ¾
ounce of Sicily	2.46 = 30 tarins = 600 grains
pezza of Leghorn	.90 76/100 = 20 soldi
livre — —	.15 ¾
new livre of Genoa	.18 ¾
ducat of Naples	.80 = 10 carlins = 100 gr.
scudo of Malta	.40 = 12 taris = 240 gr.

rix dollar of Bremen   .75
   of Prussia   .68 29/100
florin of Trieste   .48
pound sterling of
  Great Britain   4.80

Italy.

---

1 rotolo = 1 ¾ lb.[1]

[1][2] "Italy is naturally divided by variety of surface & climate into
4 distinct zones or regions which are thus distinguished. *1.* comprising
Lombardy & a part of Romagna to the slopes of the Appenines on the side
of Florence is about 260 mls. in length[,] 150 in greatest breadth from
Alps to the gulfs of Genoa & Venice & the Appenines; lying between the
parallels 46° 30′ & 43° 30′. The winter here often severe, thermom falling
several deg. below freezing. Neither olive nor orange tree flourishes except on the sheltered shores of Genoa, & some favored spots.

 2d extends over Tuscany & the Papal dominions from Florence to
Terracina & the course of the Sangro; descending 2 deg. of latitude
nearer the Equator. Here the winters are mild enough to allow the olive
& wild orange tree to flourish; but the sweet orange & other delicate fruits
not brought to perfection in the open air. Summer heat at Florence & Rome
often rises to 90° Fahr but at Florence winter is prolonged by the vicinity
of the Appenines. *3d* climate lying between the parallels of 41 30 & 39 30
comprehends the N part of the kingdom of Naples. In this region the
Seville orange & the lemon thrive almost without culture & without shelter.
Yet in winter frosts occur in places raised but little above the level of the
sea. & at Naples the thermom [2] occasionally descends a few degrees below
the freezg point while in summer it often rises to 96°. *4th* region, that of
Further Calabria & Sicily, thermom rarely sinks to the freezg pt. snow
seldom seen except on Etna. Palm, aloe, Indian[3] fig grow in open air &
sugar cane in low grounds. Vegetation resembles that of finest parts of
Africa. S. wind extremely disagreeable in this burning climate but sirocco,
(S.E. wind) in highest degree oppressive." Malte Brun[4]

---

 [1] "1 rotolo = 1 ¾ lb." is in pencil.
 [2] The pages are unnumbered in the manuscript; sequential pagination is supplied by the editor.
 [3] Beneath "Etna . . . Indian" are three illegible pencil words.
 [4] Though ascribed to Conrad Malte-Brun, whose *Universal Geography, or a
Description of all the Parts of the World on a new Plan*, 8 vols. in 17 (Boston,
1824–1831) Emerson owned, the source of this passage is Josiah Conder, *Italy*,

[3] Malta, Gozzo & Comino form a superficies of 22 sq. leagues. Malta is a calcareous rock 5 leagues in length[,] 3 in breadth. 60 mls. from Sicily. Population of the group 94,000 ↑200 [mls.] from Africa↓ ↑in 1798 [pop.] acc. Bigelow 110,000↓ [5]

A. D. 1523 [1530] ceded by Charles V to the Knights of Rhodes
                under the Grand Master L'Isle Adam
    1565   repelled the Turks
    1798   submitted to France
    1800   capitulated to England

        1 scudo = 12 taris = $0.40
        1 tari = 2 carlins = .0333
        1 carlin = 10 grains ⟨.033⟩ .0166
        1 grain   .00⟨3⟩16
        1/2 Sicily Dollar   15 taris
        1 shilling   7 taris 4 gr.
           6 pence   3 taris 12 gr
           1 penny

[4]–[5] [blank]

[6] *Sicily*, length from S.E. to N.W. 155 miles; breadth, 62;
    Continental provinces. sq. mls. 3910   pop. in 1826; 5,690000
    Sicily & the islands   sq. mls. 1610; pop. in 1826; 1,780000
                                5,520   7,420000

    Population of Palermo ⟨400⟩   168,000
                  Messina   60,000 [6]
    Messina, lat. 38°.11′N. long. 15°34′E. rebuilt since the earth-
quake, 1783.

---

3 vols. (London, 1831), I, 4–6. Emerson drew much of his factual material from Conder though he often listed the original rather than the actual debt. Conder is summarizing and paraphrasing Bk. 131 of Malte-Brun (VII, 246), as he acknowledges.

    [5] This line and the rest of the entry on the page are in pencil. The geographic and demographic details are a compilation from at least three sources, only two of which have been identified. "Malta . . . breadth." is based on Malte-Brun, *Universal Geography*, 1829, VII, 602; "in 1798 . . . 110,000" comes from Bigelow, *Travels in Malta and Sicily* . . . , 1831, p. 145.

    [6] Malte-Brun, *Universal Geography*, 1829, VII, 598, 770, and 772.

Palermo lat 38°.6′ long. 13° 21′E.
500 foreign ships yearly enter

[7] [blank]

[8] Naples. Vedi Napoli et poi muori
The lazzaroni obtain as much macaroni as they can eat for 3 half-
pence & quench their thirst with iced water for a farthing.[7]
Population, 354,000 In 1824; 349,190. Goodrich [8]

"The Francavilla palace contains a few pictures [9] of the 1st order —
'2 wonderful Dead Christs by Schidone; a Madonna in Raffael's largest
manner; a St John Baptist by Da Vinci' — *Forsyth.* 'Prince Leopold
has also an unrivalled collection of Salvator Rosas. The Dead Christ by
Spagnolet at S. Martino's[,] a sumptuous Church[,] is a firstrate pro-
duction & the 3 statues of which the Neapolitans boast much are at least
curiosities in art.' *Sass.* The best building is the new Church of S. Francesca
by Bianchi.   Alfonso's arch in Castel Nuovo[,] a mixed composition
of XV Cent." [Forsyth]
'At the Studii; Madonna &c with the Rabbits by Corregio & the Charity
of Schidone deserve all their fame.' Statues = The famous Hercules; the
lovely Flora; Juno, Bacchus; noble statue of Aristides. "The collection
of Greek & Etruscan vases & of bronzes from Herc[ulaneu]m is the most
valuable in Europe[.]" [*Conder*] [10]

[9] Rome, population in 1825, 138,370 [11]

[7] "Vedi . . . muori", though used in Goethe's *Italienische Reise* (Letter of
March 2, 1787, *Werke*, 1829, XXIX, 25), which Emerson was apparently reading
during his journey, caught his eye in Malte-Brun, *Universal Geography*, 1829, VII,
706, perhaps when he was taking down the information on the lazzeroni, a direct
quotation from *ibid.*, VII, 707.
      [8] "In . . . Goodrich" is in pencil. Samuel Goodrich, *A System of Universal
Geography* (Boston, 1832), p. 625, gives the 1824 figure, as does Malte-Brun, *Universal Geography*, 1829, VII, 773. The more recent figure Emerson evidently obtained from other sources.
      [9] Beneath the ink entry " 'The . . . pictures" are almost illegible pencil words,
apparently in Greek.
      [10] The source for the whole passage is Josiah Conder, *Italy*, 1831, III, 419–
421. Conder in turn cites his sources, which were Joseph Forsyth, *Remarks on Antiquities, Arts, and Letters during an Excursion in Italy, in the years 1802 and 1803*
(Boston, 1818) and Henry Sass, *A Journey to Rome and Naples performed in 1817
. . .* (New York, 1818).
      [11] Malte-Brun, *Universal Geography*, 1829, VII, 769.

[10] Grand Dutchy of Tuscany including 36 towns, 135 burghs, 6017 villages

sq. geog. leagues 1098; Pop. in 1826; 1,275000
population ↑of Florence↓ 80,000 [12]

[11]–[12] [blank]

[13] ⟨Messina, 7 March, 1833. Yesterday at noon I left⟩ Palermo, 7 March, 1833. Yesterday at noon I left Messina in the Steamboat and passed betwixt Scylla & Charybdis which have long lost their terrors probably fabulous at first. Then saw I Stromboli, & the Lipari islands, & ⟨stea⟩ smoke ascending from the Crater of the first &, as night grew darker, a faint light of fire. Three very pleasant Englishmen recently from Naples & ⟨bou⟩ about to travel in Greece were on board. All the English I have yet seen, I have found courteous, contrary to report. Palermo is a fine sight from the sea. Bold mountainous coast like all the North & East of Sicily. 1⟨5⟩60,000, inhabitants. Arrived on shore at 9 o'clock, & passed the usual gauntlet of petty extortions. My lessons cost me much. Visited the Consul —

I have visited the Cathedral built in 1158. ⟨&⟩ A rich & stately church with some fine bas reliefs. Saw the tombs of four sovereigns. The first was Roger the first King of Sicily 1154; Emperor Henry 6, 1197; Constantia 1198; Frederic II 1250.[n]

[14] At the Viceroy's Palace, I saw nothing but a small chapel which they vaunted much. ⟨A⟩ I went to the Capuchin Convent. That pleased me better. I like these Capuchins, who are the most esteemed of the Catholic clergy. Their profession is beggary but they distribute large alms to the poor. You approach their houses thro' a regiment of beggars. The Fathers were at dinner so I took a turn in their sober garden. Then came a monk & led me down into their Cemetery. A strange spectacle enough. Long aisles ⟨thr⟩ ↑the↓ walls of which on either side are filled with niches & in every niche the standing skeleton of a dead Capuchin; the skull & the hands appearing, the rest of the anatomy wrapped in cearments. Hundreds & hundreds of

---

[12] *Ibid.*, VII, 765. See also Goodrich, *A System of Universal Geography*, 1832, pp. 618, 617.

these grinning mortalities were ranged along the walls, here an abbot, there a General of the Convent. Every one had his label with his name, when in [15] the body, hanging at his breast. One was near 300 years old. On some the beard remained, on some the hair. I asked the monk how many there were? He said, since 300 years half a million; and he himself would stand there with his brothers in his turn.

My cicerone conducted me next to the Spedale dei Pazzi. I did not ↑know↓ where I was going or should not have visited it. I could not help them & have seen enough of their sad malady [13] without coming to Sicily.ⁿ Then to the pleasant gardens of the Prince di Buttera. At the tavola rotonda of the Giacheri perhaps 8 persons dined. I believe no one but I, spoke English. So I sat mute. ⟨Others spoke alternately in⟩ The same gentlemen spoke alternately French, Spanish, & Italian. A traveller should speak all the four & his pocket should be a wellspring of taris & bajochhi.

Noble ⟨public⟩ Flora or public garden; parterres & fountains & statues; and the Marina fine, far better than the good one of Messina.

Mr Gardner tells me there are 400 churches [16] & convents in Palermo. I have visited several beautiful ones. Art was born in Europe & will not cross the ocean, I fear. In the University, a good collection of casts & pictures; one Rubens, one Vandyke, one Domenichino; & many things from Pompeii, & Sicilian excavations.

Mr Gardner the American Consul lives in a fine house. Mrs G. has a rich collection of shells & fossils. She tells me, all her society is English; none native. If you ask a Sicilian to your house, he will bring twenty more. They will always accept your invitations, but never ask you in return to visit them but at their box at the opera. Their pride is in an equipage to ride on the Marina. Even shoemakers & hairdressers will go hungry to keep a carriage.

No learned or intelligent men or next to none. Abate Ferrara is. The daughters are sent to a convent for their education, & learn to make preserves & needlework. The English here, & now some Sicilians, send their ⟨chi⟩ sons to Switzerland, to excellent schools.

[13] The "sad malady" was tuberculosis of which the Emerson family had had more than its share.

[17] The steamboat must stay another day & I must use philosophy. So I have been to the Monte Reale on foot & I suppose the world has not many more beautiful landscapes than the plain & the port of Palermo as seen therefrom. Olive & orange & lemon groves wide around. After visiting St Simon's Church & the Benedictine Convent, I followed my vivacious little guide Raimondo to his house & he set before me wine & olives & oranges & bread.

At the tavola rotonda with eight persons we had five languages. At the opera in the evening I had a thought or two that must wait a more convenient page. I do not know whether I can recommend my domestique de place Michele Beleo to the patronage of my friends, but I promised to remember his name. And now for Naples.

At sea[14] in the steamboat Re Ferdinando 11 March. I tried last night in my berth to recal what had occurred at the opera. Ποιημα.[15] What is really good is ever a new creation. I could not help pitying the performers in their fillets & shields & togas, & saw their strained & unsuccessful[n] [18] exertions & thought on their long toilette & personal mortification at making such a figure. There they are — the same poor Johns & Antonios they were this morning, for all their gilt & pasteboard. But the moment the Prima donna utters one tone or makes a gesture of natural passion, it puts life into the dead scene. I pity them no more. It is not a ghost of departed things, not an old Greece & Rome but a Greece & Rome of this moment. It is living merit which takes ground with all other merit of whatever kind, — with beauty, nobility, genius, & power. O trust to Nature, whosoever thou art, even though a strutting tragedy-prince. Trust your simple self & you shall stand before genuine princes. The play was tedious, & so ⟨it may be⟩ are the criticisms[.]

Two pleasant young Englishmen, who had just ascended Etna, on board the boat. One named Barclay, ↑the other, Hussey↓ fond of

---

[14] Faint traces of erased pencil writing underlie the ink entry from "At sea" to "& shields" below. The underlying pencil writing continues on p. [18] as far as "tragedy-prince."

[15] "Poem." Apparently a comment on the opera as a poem of action. For the phrase in full, ποιημα πραξεως ("a poem of action") see p. 158 below.

geology. Kind domestic manners are more elegant than too civil ones. "This is the most capital place of all —" was better than twenty Sirs & scrupulosities.

[19] Naples, 12 March. And what if it is Naples, it is only the same world of cake & ale — of man & truth & folly. I won't be imposed upon by a name. It is so easy, almost so inevitable to be overawed by names that on entering this bay it is hard to keep one's judgment upright, & be pleased only after your own way. Baiae & Misenum & Vesuvius, Procida & Pausilippo & Villa Reale sound so big that we are ready to surrender at discretion & not ⟨bandy⟩ stickle for our private opinion against what seems the human race. Who cares? Here's for the plain old Adam, the simple genuine Self against the whole world. Need is, that you assert yourself or you will find yourself overborne by the most paltry things. A young man is dazzled by the stately arrangements of the hotel & jostled out of his course of thought & study of men by such trumpery considerations. The immense regard paid to clean shoes & a smooth hat impedes him, & the staring of a few dozens of idlers in the street [20] hinder[s] him from looking about him with his own eyes; & the attention which he came so far to give to foreign wonders, is concentrated instead, on these contemptible particulars↑.↓ ⟨immediately around him.⟩[16] Therefore it behooves the traveller to insist first of all upon his simple human rights of seeing & of judging here in Italy as he would in his own farm or sitting room at home.

[March] 13. Howbeit Naples is a fine city, though it rains very fast today, — a beautiful city beyond dispute. But merely from its wonderful situation & its chiaia & not from the magnificence of Streets or public buildings. I have not yet found St Martin's, but have straggled into several ⟨ordinary⟩ churches nowise remarkable.

[March] 14. I climbed up this morn to St Martin's sumptuous church & saw the fine bold paintings of Spagnoletto, excepting the dead Christ, for that chapel was shut & the keeper gone to the city.

[16] The period after "particulars" is inserted and "immediately . . . him." is canceled in pencil.

But what pomp of marble & sculpture & painting. A nativity by Guido. I staid long alone.

[21] There is a fam⟨o⟩ed view of the city from the adjoining monastery & what a noise came up from its 400000!

[March] 15. A nation of little men[,] I fear. No original art remains. I have been to the Academia & seen the works of Raffaelle, Titian, Guido, Correggio. ⟨All⟩ A good many artists were making indifferent copies of the best. I hear nothing of living painters, but perhaps there are. A rich collection of marble & bronze & frescoes, &c from Herculaneum, Pompeii, & the Baths of Caracalla. — ⟨S⟩ Many fine statues, Cicero, Aristides, Seneca, and Dianas, Apollos, &c without end. Nothing is more striking than the contrast of the purity[,] the severity expressed in these fine old heads, with the frivolity & sensuality of the mob that exhibits & the mob that gazes at them. These are the countenances of the first born,[n] the face of man in the morning of the world & they surprize you with a moral admonition as they speak of nothing around you but remind you of the fragrant thoughts & the purest resolutions of your Youth.

[22] 16 March. Last night stayed at home at my black lodgings in the Croce di Malta & read Goethe. This morn[,] sallied out alone & traversed I believe ↑for↓ the seventh time that superb mile of the Villa Reale; then to the tomb of Virgil. But here ↑the effect of↓ every Antiquity is spoiled by ↑the contrast of↓ ridiculous or pitiful circumstances. The boy who guided me was assailed by men, women, & children with all manner of opprobrium. A gang of boys & girls followed me, crying, "Signore, C'e un mariolo." Yea the venerable silence of the poet's sepulchre must be disturbed with the altercation of these Lilliputians. The tomb is well enough for so great a name, but its rich ashes are long ago scattered. It has an aperture which looks down into the entrance of the Grotto of Posilippo. Then descending, I passed through this Cyclopean excavation to the bright & beautiful country of vineyards & olive groves beyond with the fine ridges of Camaldoli[.]

Presently I met a company of muleteers who set up a shout [23] of "ladre" & "mariolo" when they saw my cicerone; so I hasted

to get rid of my suspicious companion, & engaged another to conduct me to the Grotto del Cane. Through lanes of plenty he led me
to the beautiful Lake of Agnana & the Grotto where they expose a
dog to the sulphurous vapor & the animal in a short time loses all
signs of life, but is restored by being brought out. They offered the
poor dog for the experiment if I would pay six carlines; & I told
them I would not; so the dog was saved his fainting. A pleasant
place is this little lake.

Thence I followed my guide for two or three miles to the Sol-
fatura of Pozzuoli & saw these volcanic springs of ever boiling sulphur. The soil was hot under my feet & the mountain smoked above
at different openings. ⟨I⟩We always look at volcanoes with great
respect. Thence to Pozzuoli & the well preserved remains of the
Coliseum [24] or Amphitheatre. Here underground I could have a
lively recollection of that great nation for whose amusement these
fabrics were reared, but above ground in Pozzuoli, it is impossible
to connect the little dirty suburb full of beggars, & beggar-boatmen,
& beggar-coacheys with the most ancient city which the Cumaeans
founded, the old Dicearchia, & long after the Puteoli of Cicero, his
'little Rome', as he affectionately called this garden of palaces.

Alas! no! here by the temple of Serapis one stout fellow tried to
pick my pocket of my torn handkerchief & here too my guide worried me with demanding three or four times ⟨his dues⟩ as much as
his due and a swarm of boys settled on me with 'antiquities' to sell,
old coins & fragments of brass & copper. & beggars as usual a regiment. Ah sirs of Naples! you pay a high price for your delicious
country & famed neighborhood in this swarming, faithless, robber
population [25] that surrounds & fills your city today. I was very
glad to see no more antiquities, ⟨today⟩ but to get home as fast as
I could. I dined with Mr Rogers [17] and found some pleasant gentlemen at his hospitable house.

One must be thoroughly reinforced with the spirit of antiquity
to preserve his enthusiasm through all the annoyances that await the
visitor of these ruins. Long ago when I dreamed at home of these
things, I thought I should come suddenly in the midst of an open
country upon broken columns & fallen friezes, & their solitude would

[17] Rogers was Emerson's banker in Naples. See *L*, I, 369.

be solemn & eloquent. Instead of this, they are carefully fenced round like orchards ⟨& these vermin of ciceroni & padroni are let loose upon the unhappy traveller the moment he approaches any of them⟩ and the moment the unhappy traveller approaches one of them, this vermin of ciceroni & padroni fasten upon him, a class of people whose looks & manners are more like those of Mac Guffog [26] & the duke of Alsatia [18] than the vain & flippant character I had imagined as the exhibitor *con amore*. What with these truculent fellows, & the boys & the beggars & the coachmen all sentiment is killed in the bud, & most men clap both hands on their pockets & run.

[March] 17. This morning under the kind guidance of Mr Durante I have visited six or seven churches the finest in the city. They are truly splendid & compare with the best I have seen. The Cathedral is a suite of churches & there the blood of St Januarius is annually liquefied. Its wealth must be immense. They showed me thirty busts of saints, large as life, composed of solid silver, & lamps, & angels, & candelabra, many more. Huge gates of brass richly carved admitted us to this chapel. It was thronged with worshippers, so was the nave of the cathedral.

Then the private chapel of the family of the Severini, ⟨co⟩ in the Strada St Severino, contains [27] the famous veiled statues, which are wonders in their way.

Then ⟨An⟩ Santa Clara, Santo Geronimo, St Laurentio, Gesu Nuovo, St Gaetano[.]

All which, I trust, I shall find again, for they were superb structures & of their ornaments was there no end. Such churches can only be finished in ages. They were all well attended this Sabbath morn. Who can imagine the effect of a true & worthy form of worship in these godly piles? [n] It would ravish us. I do not mean the common protestant service, but what it should be if all were actual worshippers. It would have something of this Catholic ceremony too & yet ⟨be⟩ not show a priest ⟨trotting⟩ hither & thither, & buzzing now on this side then on that.

[18] McGuffog is the "thief-taker," constable, and jailor in Scott's *Guy Mannering* (see especially chs. 33, 44, and 57); the duke of Alsatia is Duke Jacob Hildebrod, the lord of Whitefriars (Alsatia), the refuge of thieves, in *The Fortunes of Nigel*, especially ch. 17.

[28] These mighty dwelling houses rise to 5 & 6 tall stories
& every floor is occupied by a different family. Opposite my window
at the Crocelle, on the 4th story, a family lived with poultry cackling
around them all day, 40 feet from the ground; & today I observe
a turkey in the chamber across the street stepping about the 2d story.
A goat comes up stairs every day to be milked. But the woes of this
great city are many & conspicuous. Goethe says 'he shall never again
be wholly unhappy, for he has seen Naples.' [19] If he had said '*happy*,'
there would have been equal reason. You cannot go five yards in any
direction without seeing saddest objects & hearing the most piteous
wailings. Instead of the gayest of cities, you seem to walk in the
wards of a hospital. Even Charity herself is glad to take a walk in
the Villa Reale, & extricate herself from beggars for half an hour.
Whilst you eat your dinner at a Trattoria, a beggar stands at the
window, watching every mouthful[.]

[29] [March] 18. Left my watch this morning with Signor Tavassi,
Largo di Gesa Nuovo, to be repaired.[20]

[March] 19. It rains almost every day in showers, to the great dis-
comfiture of all the inhabitants of a town where people live out of
doors. The streets are full of tables & stands of all sorts of small
tradesmen. When the shower comes, the merchant takes out his
pocket handkerchiefs & covers up his table-full of goods. Then rises
the cry of "La Carozza! la Carozza" from the thousands of hackney
coachmen that infest every street & square.
    It takes one 'Grand tour' to learn how to travel.

[March] 20. And today to the Lake Avernus, to the Lucrine Lake,
to Baiae, the Arco Felice or gate of Cuma; and at Baiae to the Temple
of Venus, the Temple of Mercury, & many many nameless ruins.
A day of ruins. The soil of Baiae is crumbled marble & brick. Dig
anywhere, & they come to chambers & arches & ruins. What a sub-

---

[19] *Die Werke*, 1829, XXVIII, 18: "so konnte man umgekehrt von ihm sagen,
dass er nie ganz unglücklich werden konnte, weil er sich immer wieder nach Neapel
dachte."
    [20] The entry for March 18 is in very faint pencil.

terranean taste those Roman builders had. On each side I saw [30] structures peeping out of the ground that must have been originally built into the side of the hill. Here & there could be traced for some distance in the hill-side the remains of a ⟨mosaic⟩ floor composed of small pieces of white marble. I broke some out. It is a most impressive spot. ⟨& b⟩ Before you is this ever beautiful bay, & Capri (always more like a picture than a real island) & Vesuvius with his smoke; and about you are the great remains of this pleasure-ground of the Roman Senators, their magnificent Nahant not only broken by time but by earthquakes & covered even with new soil by the volcanic action which has raised Monte Nuovo, a large hill within a fourth of mile from this spot. Then to what base uses turned. The temple of Venus which is almost all standing, & even some delicate bas-reliefs remain upon the ceiling, is now a cooper's shop, & asses bray in it. They turn the chambers of the Roman ladies into [31] little stables for the goats & all Baiae & Pozzuoli swarm with the gang of ciceroni & beggars. I saw the lake of Avernus, a beautiful little sheet of water — but what gave it its evil classic name, it is not easy to see. Nor did the Acherontian Marsh at all suggest the images of the sheeted dead & the Judges of Hell. As to the Lucrine lake, it is not above three times the size of Frog Pond, nor quite three times as pretty.

21

[March] 21. Well I have been to Herculaneum & Pompeii. Herculaneum is nothing but a specimen of the mode of destruction, a monument of the terrors of the volcano. Nothing is excavated but ⟨the⟩ a path or tunnel through the stone around the Theatre[,] for besides the immense cost & labor of excavation through hard stone, all Portici & Resina are built overhead & the [32] habitations of the existing generation must not be endangered to explore those of the past. But at Pompeii one ⟨three[?]⟩ quarter⟨s⟩ ↑part↓ of a town ⟨3⟩three miles in circumference, is [n] opened to the sun, 1700 years after it had been hid under a mountain of ashes. Here is the resurrection of a Roman town. I walked in the shops, the bake-houses, ↑the mills,↓ the baths, the dining halls, the bed chambers, the theatre,

the court of justice, the prison, the temples of this ancient people, &
read the inscriptions, & scribblings on the walls, & examined the frescoes, as if in houses not twenty years vacant. In the temple of Venus
I climbed a ruin which commanded a view of almost the whole excavation. The whole world has no such other view; for half a mile
around me on every side were rows of columns, & streets of roofless
houses. The houses are all built much in the same way, & only of
one story. The frescoes are very pretty & in almost ⟨all the⟩ ↑every↓
house⟨s⟩. Yellow & [33] red are the prevailing colours. The marble
baths in some private houses were very rich & the mosaic painting,
⟨in⟩ ↑on the floor of↓ one chamber, of Alexander & Darius, of the
highest beauty. The statues & utensils have all been carried away to
the Museums of Naples & Sicily. Pity they could not be left here,
— 'twould make so impressive a spectacle.

The theatre is very [21] perfect & the view from its top made me
wish to sit down & spend the day. Far around is this green & fertile
land sprinkled plentifully with white villages & palaces[,] washed
by the sea adorned with islands[,] & close at hand on the other side
the solemn mountain, author of all this ruin, & now black with recent
streams of lava, without a green shrub, or so much as a blade of
grass upon its side and a little smoke stealing out of the summit as
if to say — The fire that once & again has ravaged this garden, is not
⟨out⟩ quenched.

About a quarter of a mile from this building by a road leading
through well cultivated fields where corn & wine grow [34] above
the buried city, we came to the Amphitheatre in almost perfect
preservation. All the intermediate space remains to be explored, as
the Amphitheatre is on the edge of the town. Here we were reminded
of a new distinction in property. This land is Signor Aquila's to plant
cauliflowers & brocoli, but as fast as it is excavated, & the work goes
on every day, it is the king's. Signor Aquila may have the surface,
but all underneath, the king owns, to the centre.
We drank wine that grew here and gave our guide a piastre & returned home.

[21] "His mighty ‖ . . . ‖ Whenever the Lazzaroni ‖ . . . ‖ his eyes" in faint pencil
underlies the ink entry from "they could not" above through "is very" below.

[35] [March] 23. Tired am I with a visit to Vesuvius. But it is well paid fatigue. I left the coach at Resina & was accommodated with a braying ass who but for his noise was a good beast & thus ascended about a mile above the Hermitage. Thence we climbed with good staves straight up thro' the loose soil wholly composed of lava & cinders. The guide showed us the limits of the different eruptions down to that of December 1832. Presently we came to the top of the old crater. Out of this has risen a new mass which is fast filling up & will soon probably obliterate the old crater. The soil was warm & smoking all around & above us. The ascent from this point to the summit looked dangerous & was not easy. The wind blows the smoke & fumes in your face almost to suffocation & the smoke hides all your party much of the time from your sight. We got to the top & looked down into the red & yellow pits, the navel of this volcano. I had supposed [n] [36] there was a chasm opening downward to unknown depths, but it was all closed up; only this hollow of salt & sulphur smoking furiously beneath us. We ⟨se⟩put paper between the stones & it kindled & blazed immediately. We found many parties going up & down the mountain & ladies are carried in chairs to the top.

Sunday. [March 24] Attended service in the English Chapel. Rev Mr Bennett read the prayers very well & the liturgy sounded well & kindly in my ear. But nothing could be more insipid[,] inane than the Sermon. It ⟨answer⟩ was a counterpart of the "Noodle's Oration" or the "Song by a person of Quality." [22] I thought how always we are beginning to live, & how perfectly practicable at all times is the sublime part of life, the high hours, for which all the rest are given.

---

[22] "Noodle's Oration" is a term used to describe a speech full of all possible absurdities and fallacies. Emerson probably found the phrase in Sydney Smith's article, "The Book of Fallacies: From Unfinished Papers of Jeremy Bentham," *The Edinburgh Review*, XLII (Aug. 1825), 386: "The whole of these [already described] fallacies may be gathered together in a little oration, which we will denominate the *Noodle's Oration* . . ." "Song of a Person of Quality" is an amphigouri or nonsense poem sometimes attributed to Swift but more accurately to Pope. See *The Works of Alexander Pope*, ed. Whitwell Elwin and William Courthope, 10 vols. (London, 1871–1889), IV, 489.

[37] 25 [26] March.[23] I left Naples in Angresani's coach with my townsmen Messrs Grant & Warren,[24] & two English people. We dined at Molo di Gaeta; & think I have seen nothing since I stood on the Monte Reale at Palerm⟨a⟩o, which was richer than this view from the pleasant Locanda. Strange costumes upon the road ↑at Fondi↓. But we rode all night & passed in safety the Pontine marshes molested neither by malaria nor by robbers. As we drew nigh to the imperial city, the stately ruins of the aqueducts began to appear, then the tomb of Cecilia Metella, and we entered the city by the Gate of St John.

[38] Rome. 27 March. It is even so; my poor feet are sore with walking all this day amongst the ruins of Rome.

[March] 28. We came hither Tuesday a little after noon. But that day I saw nothing but a passing view of the Coliseum as we entered the city & afterwards the yellow Tiber. Yesterday morn at 9 I set forth with a young Englishman Mr Kingston[25] & crossed the Tiber & visited St Peter's. Another time I will say what I think about this temple. From St Peter's to the Chambers of Raffaelle & saw the pictures of the great master. It was a poor way of using so great a genius to set him to paint the walls of rooms that have no beauty &, as far as I see, no purpose. Then we threaded our way through narrow streets to the Temple of Vesta & the house of Rienzi, 'last of Romans'[,] [26] then to the FORUM & the Coliseum. Here we spent some hours in identifying ruins & fixing in mind the great points of the old topography.

[23] The entry obviously could not have been made until Tuesday, March 26, since it includes the arrival in the afternoon at Rome after an all-night ride. The dating of entries then proceeds accurately with a brief entry on March 27, after a day of sightseeing and a long summary on March 28. Apparently within this entry, however, Emerson added a "29", perhaps after leaving his journal-keeping for a while. He errs again in the entry for March 29, calling it 30.

[24] Probably Patrick Grant, Harvard graduate of 1828, Charles C. Emerson's class, and James Sullivan Warren, Harvard, 1832, friend of Oliver Wendell Holmes.

[25] Possibly one of the "two English people" mentioned in the entry for March 25[26] as coach companions from Naples to Rome.

[26] Byron, *Childe Harold's Pilgrimage*, IV, cxiv: "Rienzi! last of Romans!"

29. [March 28] I went to the Capitoline hill then to its Museum &
saw the Dying Gladiator, The Antinous, the Venus. —— to the Gallery. then to the Tarpeian Rock. then to the vast & splendid museum
of the Vatican. A wilderness of marble. After traversing many a
shining chamber & gallery I came to the Apollo & soon after to the
Laocoon. 'Tis false to say that the casts give no idea of the originals.
I found I knew these fine statues already by heart & had admired
the casts long since[,] much more than I ever can the originals.

Here too was the Torso Hercules, as familiar to the eyes as
some old revolutionary cripple. On we went from chamber to chamber through galleries of statues & vases & sarcophagi & bas reliefs
& busts & candelabra — through all forms of beauty & richest materials — till the eye was dazzled & glutted with this triumph of the
arts. Go & see it, whoever you are. [40] It is the wealth of the civi-
lized world. It is a contribution from all ages & nations of what is
most rich & rare. He who has not seen it does not know what beautiful
stones there are in the planet, & much less what exquisite art has
accomplished on their hard sides for Greek & Roman luxury.

In one apartment there were three statues of Canova, the Perseus, & two fighting gladiators. Then lions & horses & fauns & cupids
& cars. Then the sitting philosophers & such Scipios & Caesars. It is
vain to refuse to admire. ⟨or⟩ You must in spite of yourself. It is
magnificent.

Even all this unrivalled show could not satisfy us. We knew
there was more. Much will have more. We knew that the first picture in the world was in the same house & we left all this pomp to
go & see the Transfiguration by Raphael.

A calm benignant beauty shines over all this picture and goes
[41] directly to the heart. It seems almost to call you by name.
How the father of the poor mad boy looks at the apostles! And the
sister. And the sweet & sublime face of Jesus above, is beyond praise,
& ranks the artist with the noble poets & heroes of his species — the
first born of the Earth. I had thought in my young days that this
picture & one or two more were to surprize me with a blaze of
beauty[,] that I was to be delighted by I know not what bright
combination of colours & forms, but this familiar simple home-
speaking countenance I did not expect.[26a]

   [26a] "A calm benignant . . . expect." : used in "Art," W, II, 362.

After the pictures St Peter's again.

30. [March 29] I have seen St John Lateran,^{n}⟨'s⟩ & the Pantheon & the Baptistery of Constantine & the sad remnants of the Palace of the Caesars. & many many ruins more. Glad I was amidst all these old stumps of the past ages to see Lewis Stackpole[27] as [42] fresh & beautiful as a young palm tree in the desert. Rome is very pleasant to me, as Naples was not, if only from one circumstance, that here I have pleasant companions to eat my bread with & there I had none.

31 [March 30] This morng went with young Warren & Grant to Thorwaldsen's Studio & saw his fine statue of Byron. 'Tis good as a history. I saw three or four rooms of stone things but nothing else to look at. Then to the Barberini Palace & saw the Beatrice Cenci of Guido[28] & the Fornarin⟨i⟩a of Raffaelle[.]

Thence to the Borghese Palace & saw Raffaelle's portrait of ⟨|| ... ||⟩ Caesar Borgia & many fine things but nothing that pleased me more than a Madonna by Andrea del Sarto. Whoso loves a beautiful face, look at this.

Then to the Colonna palace[,] a proud old mansion of this ancient ^{n} [43] family — the finest suite of apartments I have ever seen & hung around with master pictures & many of them portraits of the heroes & the beauties of their own line. Two fine portraits of Luther & Calvin by Titian & the Martyrdom of St Sebastian by Guido. But I liked the whole show — the hall itself, better than any part of it. William Pratt[29] very kindly acted the part of cicerone & introduced me to his relatives.

Then I found under the Capitoline hill the famous Mamertine Prison[,] the scene of the death of Cethegus & Lentulus & of the captivity of St Peter & St Paul, & the reputed dungeon of the 'Roman daughter.'[30]

[27] Joseph Lewis Stackpole, a Bostonian and Harvard graduate, 1824, in Edward B. Emerson's class.

[28] "Guido" and the "a" of "Fornarina" are added in darker ink; the name of the painter is obviously inserted into a space left vacant for later completion.

[29] Another of Edward Emerson's college classmates (Harvard, 1824), who, according to *Life*, p. 189, gave Waldo letters of introduction to England.

[30] The two accomplices of Catiline in his conspiracy, strangled on orders of

This P.M. I went to the ⟨house⟩palace of Cardinal Wield [Weld], where Bishop England [31] delivered a discourse in explanation of the ceremonies of the Catholic church tomorrow [n] [44] (Palm Sunday) to the English & American residents. I was led in the evening, so easy is it to be led, to a violin concert. I was glad however to learn the power of a fiddle. It wailed like a bugle & reminded me of much better things & much happier hours.

Sunday, [March] 31. I have been to the Sistine Chapel to see the Pope bless the palms & hear his choir ⟨s⟩chaunt the Passion. The Cardinals came in one after another, each wearing a purple robe, an ermine cape, & a small red cap to cover the tonsure. A priest attended each one to adjust the robes of their Eminences. As each Cardinal entered the chapel, the rest rose. One or two were fine persons. Then came the Pope in scarlet robes & a bishop's mitre. After he was seated the cardinals went in turn to the throne & kneeled & kissed his hand. After this ceremony the attendants divested the cardinals of their robes & [45] put on them a gorgeous cope of cloth of gold. When this was arranged a sort of ornamental baton made of the dried palm leaf was brought to his holiness & blessed and each of the cardinals went again to the throne & received one of these from the hands of the pope. They were supplied from a large pile at the side of the papal chair. After the Cardinals, came other dignitaries, bishops, deans, canons, I know them not — but there was much etiquette, some kissing the hand only, & some the foot also of the pope. Some received Olive branches. Lastly several officers performed the same ceremony. When this long procession of respect was over and all the robed multitude had received their festal palms & olives his

Cicero; the reputed captivity of the Christian saints is probably only a legend like that of the " 'Roman daughter' ", celebrated example of filial tenderness who kept her mother alive in prison by feeding her at the breast. Pliny tells the story in *Natural History*, VII, 36. Emerson probably recalled the tale from Byron, *Childe Harold's Pilgrimage*, IV, cxlviii–cli, who, following Festus (*De Verborum Significatu*, xx), changed the mother to a father.

[31] The English Cardinal Thomas Weld (1773–1837) made the Odescalchi Palace a center of the best Roman and foreign society after 1830 when he became Cardinal Priest of San Marcellus. Bishop John England (1786–1842) of Charleston, S.C., was in Rome in the spring of 1833 to report on his recent mission as Papal Legate to Haiti.

Holiness was attended to a chair of state & being seated was lifted up by bearers & preceded by the long official array & by his chaunting choir he rode out of the chapel[.]

[46] It was hard to recognize in this ceremony the gentle Son of Man who sat upon an ass amidst the rejoicings of his fickle countrymen. Whether from age or from custom, I know not, but the pope's eyes were shut or nearly shut as he rode. After a few minutes he reentered the chapel in like state. And soon after retired & left the Sacred College of Cardinals to hear the Passion chaunted by themselves. The ch⟨urch⟩apel is that whose walls Michel Angelo adorned with his 'Last Judgment.' But today I have not seen the picture well.

All this pomp is conventional. It is imposing to those who know the customs of courts & of what wealth & of what rank these particular forms are the symbols. But to the eye of an Indian I am afraid it would be ridiculous. There is no true majesty in all this millinery & imbecility. Why not devise ceremonies that [47] shall be in as good & manly taste as their churches & pictures & music?

I counted twenty one cardinals present. ⟨Evg⟩ Music at St Peter's in the afternoon & better still at ⟨Ge⟩ Chiesa Nuova in the evg. Those mutilated wretches sing so well it is painful to hear them.

Monday. [April 1] Today at the Grotto of Egeria whence came the laws of Rome[,] then to tomb of Cecilia Metella 'the wealthiest Roman's wife'.[32] A mighty tomb; the wall is 30 feet thick. Then to the tomb of Scipio, then to the Spada Palace, & saw the statue of Pompey, at whose base great Caesar fell. Then to the Palace Farnesina, to see Raffaelle's frescoes. Here Raffaelle painted whilst Michel Angelo ⟨was⟩ locked himself up in the Sistine Chapel. Then to the Vatican. And at night to an American Soirée.

[48] Tuesday, 2 Apr. What is more pathetic than the Studio of a young Artist? Not rags & disease in the street move you to sadness like the lonely chamber littered round with sketches & canvass &

[32] Byron, *Childe Harold's Pilgrimage*, IV, ciii. The tomb was actually built to honor the daughter of Metellus Creticus (not Cecilia Metella), the daughter-in-law, rather than the wife of Crassus, of the first Triumvirate, famous for his riches.

colourbags. There is something so gay in the art itself that these rough & poor commencements contrast more painfully with it. Here another enthusiast feeds himself with hope[n] & rejoices in dreams & smarts with mortifications. The melancholy artist told me that if the end of painting was[33] to please the eye, he would throw away his pallet. And yet how many of them not only fail to reach the soul with their conceptions, but fail to please the eye.

These beggarly Italians! If you accept any hospitality at an Italian house a servant calls upon you the next day & receives a fee, & in this manner, the expense of your entertainment is defrayed. In like [49] manner, if you are presented to the Pope, it costs you five dollars.

Plain good manners & sensible people — how refreshing they are. A bashful man is cramped among the fine people who have ⟨good⟩ ⟨m⟩polished manners but ⟨heavy⟩ ↑dull↓ brains; but he is relieved & recreated by a better influence & regains his natural shape & air & powers.

Today I have seen the fine church of Sta Maria Maggiore, the third best in Rome. Then the Doria Palace. There was Nicholas Machiavel by Titian & landscapes of Claude Lorraine[.]

3 Apr. Wednesday. The famous Miserere was sung this afternoon in the Sistine Chapel. The saying at Rome, is, that it cannot be imitated not only by any other choir but in any other chapel in the world. The Emperor of Austria sent Mozart to Rome on purpose to have it sung at Vienna with like effect, but it failed.

[50] Surely it is sweet music & sounds more like the Eolian harp than any thing else. The pathetic lessons of the day relate the treachery of Judas & apply ⟨fine⟩ select passages from the prophets & psalms to the circumstances of Jesus. Then whilst the choir chaunt the words "Traditor autem dedit eis signum, dicens, Quem osculatus

---

[33] An erased pencil draft of a poem underlies the ink entry from "with sketches" above to "painting was" below. Of the nine lines only the following has been conjecturally recovered: "The day the diamonded sight The echo ‖ . . . ‖ of sound The ‖ . . . ‖ night The livid lightnings ‖ . . . ‖ The seven ‖ . . . ‖ glittering ring ‖ . . . ‖ less changed".

fuero, ipse est, tenete eum," ⁿ ³⁴ ⟨they⟩ all the candles in the chapel
are extinguished but one. ⟨which is put behind the altar whilst⟩ During the repetition of this verse, the last candle is taken down & hidden under the altar. Then out of the silence & the darkness rises
this most plaintive & melodious strain, (the whole congregation
kneeling) "Miserere mei, Deus, &c.³⁵ The sight & the sound are very
touching[.]

Every thing here is in good taste. The choir are concealed by
the high fence which rises above their heads. We were in a Michel
Angelo's chapel which is full of noblest scriptural ⟨an⟩ forms & faces.

[51] Thursday. [April 4] These forms strike me more than I expected, & yet how do they fall short of what they should be. Today
I saw the Pope wash the feet of thirteen pilgrims, one from each
nation of Christendom. One was from Kentucky. After the ceremony
he served them at dinner; this I did not see. But Gregory XVI is
a learned & able man; he was a monk & is reputed of pure life. Why
should he not leave one moment this formal service of ⟨a⟩ fifty
generations & speak out of his own heart[,] the Father of the Church
to his Children[,] though it were but a single sentence or a single
word? ⁿ One earnest word or act to this sympathetic audience would
overcome them. It would take all hearts by storm.

To night I heard the Miserere sung in St Peter's & with less
effect than yesterday. But what a temple! When night was settling
down upon it & ⟨the⟩a long religious procession moved through a
part of the Church[,] I got an idea of its immensity [52] such as I
had not before. You walk about ⟨in⟩on its ample marble pavement as
you would on a common[,] so free are you of your neighbors; &
throngs of people are lost upon it. And what beautiful lights & shades
on its mighty gilded arches & vaults & far windows & brave columns,
& its rich clad priests, that look as if they were the pictures come down
from the walls & walking. ⟨O⟩Thence we came out (I was walking
with two painters Cranch & Alexander) ³⁶ under the moon & saw the

---

³⁴ Matthew 26:48: "Now he that betrayed him gave them a sign, saying, Whom-
soever I shall kiss, that same is he; hold him fast." Cf. also Mark 14:44.
³⁵ "Lord, pity me" (Ed.).
³⁶ John Cranch, elder brother of Christopher P. Cranch, was studying art in

planet shine upon the finest fountain in the world. & upon all the
↑stone↓ saints on the piazza & the great church itself. This was a
spectacle which only Rome can boast — how faery beautiful! An
Arabian night's tale —

Good Friday. [April 5] The Mystery of the Tre Ore [37] is said
& shewn in all the churches, in some with scenic representations; [n]
I have seen nothing affecting tho' it is [53] sometimes, I am told,
very much so. Many religious processions in the streets muffled in
black with staves surmounted by death's-heads.
This night I saw with Cranch the great Coliseum by moonlight. It
is full of dread.

Saturday. [April 6] I did not go to the baptism of the Jew
today. Usually it is a weary farce. ↑'Tis said↓ they [n] buy the Jews at
150 scudes the head, to be sprinkled. This man was respectable.
This P.M. I heard the Greek Mass. The chaunts are in Armenian[.]

Sunday. [April 7] This morng the Pope said Mass at St Peter's. Rich
dresses, great throngs, lines of troops, but not much to be said for
the service. It is Easter & the curtains are withdrawn from the pictures
& statues to my great joy & the Pope wears his triple crown instead
of a mitre.

At twelve o clock the benediction was given. A canopy was hung
[54] over the great window that is above the principal door of St
Peter's & there sat the Pope. The troops were all under arms & in
uniform in the piazza below, & all Rome & much of England &
Germany & France & America was gathered there also. The great
bell of the Church tolled, drums beat, & trumpets sounded over the
vast congregation.

Presently, at a signal, there was silence and a book was brought
to the Pope, out of which he read a moment & then rose & spread

---

Italy in 1833; Francis Alexander (1800–1881), portrait painter and lithographer,
had been in Italy two years. He was later to accompany Emerson from Paris to
London.
    [37] The "three hours," a special service formerly widely celebrated on Good
Friday.

out his hands & blessed the people. All knelt as one man. He repeated
his action (for no words could be heard,) stretching his arms gracefully to the north & south & east & west — pronouncing a benediction
on the whole world. It was a sublime spectacle. Then sounded drums
& trumpets, then rose the people, & every one went his way.

[55] This evening I have seen the illumination of the Church.
When it was ⟨dark I set out⟩ dark, I took the wellknown way and on
reaching the Bridge of St Angelo ⟨I⟩ found the church already hung
with lights from turret to foundation. But this was only partial. At
the moment when the bell in the tower tolled 8 o'clock out flashed
innumerable torches in the air & the whole edifice blazed with fires
which cast the first lamps into shade & lit up every face in the multitude on the piazza as with daylight. But it is very melancholy to
see an illumination in this declining church & impoverished country[.]

⟨Alas the young men that come here & walk in Rome without
one Roman ⟨thought⟩ thought! they unlearn their English & their
morals, & violate the sad solitude of the mother of the nations.

They think the Coliseum is a very *nice* place.⟩

[56] I love St Peter's Church. It grieves me that after a few days
I shall see it no more. It has a peculiar [37a] smell from the quantity
of incense burned in it. The music that is heard in it is always good
& the eye is always charmed. It is an ornament of the earth. It is
not grand, it is so rich & pleasing; it should rather be called the
sublime of the beautiful.

Tuesday. [April 9] Today I went with Cranch & Wall [38] to the
Palazzo Chigi — a good gallery; ↑there is ⟨Titian's⟩ ↑the↓ Laura of
Paul Veronese↓ to the Farnese, a fine palace where are Annibal
Caracci's frescoes but saw no pictures besides. Then ⟨to the⟩ we
crossed the Tiber in a boat to the Corsini Palace whose noble gardens
ascend the side of Mons Janiculum. Pleasant walk & far prospect of

---

[37a] "I love . . . a peculiar" is written above an earlier pencil entry, now
illegible.
[38] William Wall. See *J*, III, 97, n.2: "a young artist of New Bedford, Mass., . . .
[whose] copy of the Three Fates in the Pitti Palace, then attributed to Michael Angelo, always hung over the fireplace in Mr. Emerson's study."

the Apennines & of Mount Soracte. Then to the Sciarra Palace whose gallery is one of the best in Rome. Quick eye had Cranch to detect a Titian every where. He admires him as an [57] *original* painter. Here was Guido's Magdalen; Leonardo da Vinci's Modesty & Vanity; Titian's Mistress; Rafaelle's portrait of himself; & fine pictures by Garofalo.

All the Americans are gone & I who lately knew them not, now feel quite alone — my countrymen & country-women have been so civil & social. Miss Bridgen [39] is a most intelligent & excellent lady & young Grant has made me much a debtor by his courtesy.

10 Apr. Walked alone in the spacious grounds & fine groves of the Villa Borghese, whilst the birds sang to me. I thought it would be good to spend an hour there by myself every day. ποιημα πραξεως.[40]

[April] 11. How have all nations & ages contributed to the magnificence of the Vatican. If we could only know the history of each marble there, ⟨for whom ⟩ when, & ⟨for⟩by whom, & for whom it was carved; of what luxurious villa it formed an ornament, it would open to us the story of the whole world. [58] Each has figured in splendid scenes & served the pleasure of the lords of mankind[.]

Then again most gladly would I know the place of all these works in the history of art, how this vase & that statue were designed, what the sculptor & what his patron thought of them & the marks of the eras of progress & decline. But now they amaze me & beget a vague curiosity which they cannot satisfy, nor can any living man.

I went up to the top of St Peter's & climbed into the copper ball. It is necessary to go up into the dome in order to estimate the prodigious dimensions of the edifice. It takes one's breath away, to look down into the church from the Giro within the cupola, & at first the temptation is terrible to throw yourself down, though the walk is wide, & the railing is high. With some pauses & some conversation I succeeded in getting round the dizzy promenade; but like many

---

[39] Anna Bridgen and her sister were from Albany. See *Life*, 179.
[40] "a poem of action" (Ed.). See p. 140 above.

things in Rome, it is a quite unimaginable spot. [59] The view from
the exterior of the cupola, of the ⟨c⟩Campagna di Roma is delicious,
from the Ap⟨enn⟩penines on one side to the Sea on the other, &
Tiber flowing through his marble wilderness below.

[April] 13. Rome fashions my dreams. All night I wander
amidst statues & fountains, and last night was introduced to Lord
Byron! It is a graceful termination to so much glory that Rome
now in her fallen state should be the metropolis of the arts. Art is
here a greater interest than any where else. The Caffés are filled with
English, French, & German artists, both sculptors & painters. The
number of Mosaicist↑as↓ ⟨shops⟩ & print shops is surprizing. Rinaldi
has just finished a Mosaic picture of Paestum which is valued at a
thousand louis d'ors.

I am indebted to my new found countryman [41] for some most
pleasant hours — a grateful relief to sights of ruins. I do not yet
fall in [60] with that class of English I had hoped to see, these best
educated gentlemen, namely, who are not bred with a view to any
profession nor even to politics, but only to maintain the old honours
of their houses. In such a class one would hope to find chivalry &
learning & sense; but I am not so fortunate as to meet them, but of
dandies an abundance. A gentleman, I suppose is as rare as a genius.
Those who usurp the name are often masses of selfishness & littleness.

Sunday, 14 Apr. Attended divine service at the English Chapel.
To preach well you must speak the truth. It is vain to say what has
been said every Sunday for a hundred years, if it is not true.

[April] 15. Few pictures please me more than the Vision of St
Romoaldo by Andrea Sacchi in the Vatican. What a majestic form
is the last Carmelite in the train who ascends the steps. One is greater
for knowing that such forms can be. What a cant of the head has this
same figure! Look at him.

I shall I think remember few sculptures better when I get
[61] back into my Chimney Corner than the beautiful head of the

---

[41] Probably John Cranch (see p. 155 above), whom Emerson called a "valuable"
and a "most agreeable and sensible companion & a great comfort to me." See L, I,
374 and 380.

Justice who sits with Prudence on the monument of Paulus III on the left of the Tribuna in St Peter's. It was designed by Michel Angelo, executed by William de la Porta, but where in the Universe is the Archetype from which the Artist drew this sweetness & grace? [n] There is a heaven.

I have been to see the library of the Vatican. I think they told me the hall was a quarter of a mile long. Afterwards, the Elgin marble⟨s⟩-casts. What heads & forms!

In Rome all is ruinous. In the garden before my window the flowerpots stand upon blocks made of the capitals of old columns, turned upside down.[42] Everywhere you may see in the walls & the foundations of houses fragments of carved & fluted stone ⟨used with other || ... || ornaments formerly⟩ ↑now cemented in with rough stones, but↓ once the ornament of the Luculli or Scauri or even of Vesta or Jove.

[April] 17. I have been to the Church of St [62] [43] Onofrio to see the tomb of Tasso. Then in the convent the courteous fathers showed us his bust in wax. He died in the convent & this head was taken ⟨in⟩at the time from the corpse. A noble head it is, full of independence & genius. It resembles strongly the prints I have seen of his head, but is better, I should think than any. I shall always like him the better for having seen this face. I have never yet learned to feel any strong interest in a poet so imitative, but since God marked him I will attend to him.

In the convent was also a beautiful Madonna by Leonardo da Vinci.

I neglected ↑on the 15th↓ to record my visit to the Church Araceli, once the Temple of Jupiter Capitolinus; a [n] dim lighted spacious & lofty temple worthy of its name & fame & location. Here if I rightly remember, Gibbon says, he conceived the design of writing

---

[42] After this sentence Emerson has sketched in the left margin a flower pot resting on an inverted capital.

[43] Erased pencil writing underlies the ink entry on pp. [62] and [63]. Only a few scattered words at the top of p. [63] are legible: "From ↑to↓ Florence Rome to || ... || by Parmigiano[?] with vetturino || ... || at Florence || ... || a || ... || hotel || ... || a day". The entry at the bottom of p. [63] listing addresses ("Piazza . . . trinita") is also in pencil and is perhaps a continuation of the earlier overwritten pencil entry.

his History.[44] Its Scala might be called the Giant's Staircase, and on some [63] of the steps were half effaced inscriptions. What a memorandum is each step to the historical eye that can see the priest of Jove, ages back, climbing the same hill burning incense on the same spot.

What pleasant fountains all over Rome in every villa, garden, & piazza. An eye for beauty is nature's gift to this people; they delight in bright colours & in all ornaments. As we sat in the Caffé, we agreed that it was decorated & furnished with a beauty & good taste which could not be rivalled in America.

No man should travel until he has learned the language of the country he visits. Otherwise he voluntarily makes himself a great baby — so helpless & so ridiculous.

Piazza Santa Maria Novella 6002 6004[?]
      Restaurants. Marchi   Porta Rossa
                  Vigne   d[itt]o
      Caffe delle colonne in piazza della Trinita

[64]   Largo de Gesu Nuovo
                  Palazzo Monteleone
                        Sig[nore]. Tavassi
                        Orologiajo

              Sig[nore] Cicognani
                  Via di Pr⟨o⟩efetti, No 23.[45]

In Rome at the best Trattoria you may get a good dinner for 15 bajocchi. Thus today & yesterday I have dined at the Lepri on this

[44] See *Autobiography*, ed. J. B. Bury (London, 1907), p. 160. Actually Gibbon says he was "musing amidst the ruins of the Capitol, while the bare-footed friars were singing vespers in the Temple of Jupiter." But Conder (*Italy*, 1831, III, 343) cites the Aracoeli Church as the place where the History was conceived.

[45] "Largo . . . No 23." is in pencil, probably a further continuation of the penciled material begun on p. [62] and carried through p. [63] beneath the ink entry.

fashion; 'Maccaroni a la Napolitana' 3; 'Mongana con spinnagio' 5; 'Crema in piatta', 5; & two rolls of bread to eat with it, 2; = 15 cents for a good dinner in the best house. ↑Add one or two for waiter.↓ My breakfast at the most expensive Caffé in Rome costs 16 cents. Coffee in the evg 5 & my chambers at the Gran Bretagna 50 cents.

[inside back cover] [46]

————

Beethoven's Waltz called *Le Desir* with any thing; if possible with *Le Soupir*. for F. Cunningham[.] [47]

————

Small edition of Dante for Mrs R.[48]

————

Population of the United States in 1830

	12,856,165
Increase per cent in 10 years	33.4
Population of Massachusetts	610,014
of S. Carolina	581,458
Slaves in S. C.	315,665
population of Charleston	30,289
Population of Georgia	516,567
Slaves in Ga.	217 470
Population of ⟨M⟩Boston	61,392
City of New York	203,007
Pop. of State of N. Y	1,913 508

[46] At the top center of the page "keep the straight road" is written in a circle completed by x marks. Over the writing and x marks is then drawn a heavy ink line, possibly as a cancellation. "Beethoven's . . . Mrs. Ripley" is immediately below the ink circle, written in pencil.

[47] Francis Cunningham, later minister of the Third Church in Dorchester (1834–1842), filled the pulpit of the Second Church for Emerson once in November and on four Sundays during December, 1832. Emerson, though his resignation had been accepted, was still in charge of supplying a pastor. Emerson had apparently been commissioned to buy a music box which would play two Beethoven selections. See p. 195 below.

[48] Probably Mrs. Sarah Alden Bradford Ripley, notable reader and scholar who early inspired in Emerson a delight in poetry (see *L*, I, 4).

Italy and France

1833

Emerson apparently bought this small volume in Rome in late April, 1833, as a companion to the two pocket notebooks he had already filled. Its entries begin on April 20, three days after the last record in the journal Italy, and cover the rest of Emerson's continental tour, ending with his arrival in London on Sunday, July 20. Some of the material in the journal Italy and France overlaps the rough jotted records of the notebook France and England, which apparently was sometimes used as a source for the more careful entries of this volume.

The journal is a pocket-sized notebook with a hard brown-marbled cover and a darker brown leather spine decorated by 4 gold stripes. The cover measures 10 x 17.7 cm. Counting the flyleaf there are 120 pages, all lined except for the flyleaf and measuring 9.5 x 16 cm. The pages are unnumbered; pagination is supplied by the editor.

[front cover verso]

R. W. Emerson.
Rome, 1833
April
Piazza di Spagna
Hotel di Gran Bretagna

May, Florence
Piazza d. Maria Novella
No 4599. —

Qui a de soi parfaite connaissance,
N'ignore rien de ce qu'il faut savoir;

163

Mais le moyen assuré de l'avoir
Est se mirer dedans la patience.[1]

[i][2] Florence
      Casa Fiacchi
         Borgo SS. Apostoli
next house to the Baths called Terme Antiche & opposite to the
Palace Turchi — first floor.

Piazza Santa Maria Novella
6002   6004
Restaurants
         Marchi, Porta Rossa
         Vigne   d[itt]o

Caffe delle Colonne in piazza della Trinita

4599 — Santa Maria Novella
      Casa Testina —

[ii] La pianta uomo nasce piu robusta in Italia che in qualunque altra
terra, — e quegli stessi atroci delitti che vi si commettono, ne sono una
prova.

                                      Alfieri.[3]

[1][4] Rome, April 20, 1833.
Yesterday I went with Cranch & Smith & Wall to Tivoli. I cannot describe the beauty of the Cascade nor the terror of the Grotto
nor the charm of the iris that arched the torrent. The Temple of
Vesta is one of the most beautiful of ruins & in a chosen place. The

---

[1] The quotation appears on a clipping from a newspaper or magazine, 6 x 1.8
cm, pinned vertically to the top left margin of the front cover verso.
  [2] The flyleaf is a continuation of a sheet which is pasted in as a front cover
verso. The entries here are in pencil.
  [3] Quoted in Italian in Byron's letter to Hobhouse prefixed to *Childe Harold's
Pilgrimage*, IV, with "che gli" for Emerson's "quegli."
  [4] The ink for this entry and for those through p. [5] "in Vinculo," is black,
as is that used for the name and date on the front cover verso. On April 21 Emerson
apparently changed inks. He then used a light brown. This light brown also appears in the addresses on the front cover verso, added, therefore, after this date.

whole circuit of about four miles which we make with the Cicerone, showed everywhere a glorious landscape. All was bright with a warm sun. The ground was sprinkled with gay flowers, & among others that pink thing with a spicy smell we used to call 'Rabbit's ears.' Then there was the great aloes with its formidable fleshy spine growing about, & (which is a rare sight,) one of these plants [2] was in bloom. We found the remains of the villa of Catullus, then the reputed site of the house of Horace, & hard by, the arched ruins of the Villa of Q[uintilius]. Varus. Here too, they say, M[a]ecenas lived; & no wonder that poet & patron should have come to this fair specular mount escaping from the dust of the Capitol. The Campagna lies far & wide below like a sea. Then we went to the Villa d'Este whose beauty in my eyes outshone the beauty of the cascade. Such trees, such walks, such fountains, such grottoes, such adornments, the long long house — all its empty halls painted in fresco; the piazza [3] with its vast prospect, the silver river, the sun that shone, & the air that blew — I would fain keep them in my memory the fairest image of Italy. The Villa belongs to the Duke of Modena who never saw it & it is occupied only by a custode.

I have paid a last visit to the Capitoline Museum & Gallery. One visit is not enough, no, nor two to learn the lesson. The dying Gladiator is a most expressive statue but it will always be indebted to the muse of Byron for fixing upon it forever his pathetic thought.[5] Indeed Italy is Byron's debtor, and I think no one knows how fine a poet he ⟨was⟩is who has not seen the subjects of his verse, & so learned to appreciate the justness of his thoughts & at the same time the↑ir↓ great superiority to other men's. I know well the great defects of Childe Harold.

[4] In the Gallery I coveted nothing so much as Michel Angelo's Portrait by himself.

[5] [April] 21. I went this afternoon to see Michel Angelo's statue of Moses at the Church of San Pietro in Vinc⟨o⟩ulo, and ⟨very⟩ it is grand. It seems he sought to embody the Law in a man. Directly under the statue, at the side where the whole face is seen, the ex-

---

[5] Byron described the "Dying Gladiator," "butchered to make a Roman holiday," in *Childe Harold's Pilgrimage*, IV, cxl–cxli.

pression is terrible. I could wish away those emblematic horns. "Alzati, parla!" said the enthusiastic sculptor.[6]

[6] Foligno   E B E 26 [7]

[7] And so I left on the twenty third of April the city built on seven hills[:] [8] the Palatine, the Capitoline, Coelian, Aventine, Quirinal, Viminal, & Esquiline.

"Won't you go to America with me little fellow?" "Non, Signore." — "In America all the little boys are taught to read & write." — "In Terni, auzi," he replied.

[8] 28 April. I arrived in Florence. —

1 May. Of my journey from Rome to this city I cannot give a good account. I came in a vetturo with Messrs Wall, Walsh, ⟨Cranch⟩ & Mayer, Mr O Flanagan [9] an Irish priest, and Signor Dracopoli, a Greek, returning to New Smyrna after an absence of ten years for his education in Rome. The journey occupied five days & a half. The first night was spent at Civita Castellana. The second day we arrived a little after noon at Terni and visited the great Cascade of Velino.

---

[6] Emerson tells more fully this legend of Michelangelo striking the statue Moses with his hammer and saying "Alzate, parla," in a letter to William, April 21, 1833 (*L*, I, 379); no printed source for the story has been discovered.

[7] The cryptic memorandum is in pencil. Emerson left Rome for Florence on April 23, 1833, and spent the night of April 25 at Foligno. Hence the "26" may be merely a month date. But with the "EBE" (Edward Bliss Emerson) it might be Waldo's memory that his brother passed from Rome to Florence through Foligno in 1826. No letter to Edward Emerson is listed for the date, according to Rusk.

[8] Written in pencil below "I left on the" is "fountains"; below "city . . . hills" "Pincian hill" is penciled in.

[9] Traces of erased penciled numbers appear under the ink entry from "cannot" above to "O Flanagan" below, apparently a jotting of dates or expenses. The identifiable companions were William Wall (see p. 157 above), Robert M. Walsh, son of a well-known Philadelphia editor, and Brantz Mayer of Baltimore (see *L*, I, 374 n). For the agreement signed with the Italian carriage driver, see L. H. Naylor, "Emerson and an Italian Carriage Driver, 1833," *Emerson Society Quarterly*, IV Q (1955), pp. 3–4.

Nature never disappoints us. Her grand & beautiful things always
satisfy the eye, and this does. Still I think the Grotto under the cascade at Tivoli better deserves the name of "the hell of waters" — [10]
has more of the terrible in it than any thing I saw here.

[9] Great abundance of the spicy red flowers which they call
capuccini. Terni was the birthplace of Tacitus. The next morning we
came to Spoleto where Hannibal received a repulse after his victory
at Thrasimene and we were shown the Porta di Fuga, named from
that event. Here too was a prodigious aqueduct 300 feet high. From
Spoleto to Foligno where we passed the night. All the streets of this
town have been shaken by earthquakes; the houses lean, and are kept
from falling by timbers which cross the street from house to house.
↑Between↓ ⟨Next morn from⟩ Foligno ⟨to⟩& Vene we saw the 'temple
of small & delicate proportion' [11] dedicated to Clitumnus. Strange
dreams at F[oligno].

Next morn from Foligno to Assisi through fertile fields, & up
the mountain to Perugia. Perugia has outgrown its walls which [10]
are far within the town. It commands a wide prospect of cultivated
territory. The difference of cultivation is very great between the fat
Umbria & the lean Sabina. On we came to the little hamlet of Passignano on [the] margin of the lake of Thrasimene and passed a
peaceful night close by the dreadful field of Hannibal & Flaminius.
In the morning we crossed the Sanguinetto, & left the pontifical state.
We passed by ⟨c⟩Cortona the venerable Etruscan town, then by
Arezzo, the birthplace of Petrarch, & stopped at night at Levane.

Next morn through the beautiful Val d'Arno we came to Figline,
to Incisa, & ⟨at⟩in the afternoon to fair Florence.

And how do you like Florence? Why, well. It is pleasant to see
how affectionately all [11] the artists who have resided here a little [12]
while speak of getting home to Florence. And I found at once that
we live here with much more comfort than in Rome or Naples. Good
streets, industrious population, spacious well furnished lodgings,

---

[10] Byron, *Childe Harold's Pilgrimage,* IV, lxix.

[11] *Ibid.,* IV, lxvii.

[12] From "little" through "comfort" below, penciled jottings underlie the ink
entry: "Terni Ap 25 By vetturino 8.00[?] Passignano [April] 27 pd d[itt]o
[vetturino] 1.00 Foligno 26 Apr EBE in ‖ ... ‖"

⟨C⟩elegant & cheap Caffés, the cathedral & the Campanile, ↑the splendid galleries↓ and no beggars — make this city the favorite of strangers.

How like an archangel's tent is this great Cathedral of many-coloured marble set down in the midst of the city and by its side ⟨this⟩ its wondrous campanile! I took a hasty glance at the gates of the Baptistery which Angelo said ought to be the gates of Paradise "degne chiudere il Paradiso" [13] and then of his own David & hasted to the Tribune & to the Pitti Palace. I saw the statue that enchants the world.[14] And [12] truly the Venus deserves to be visited from far. It is not ⟨f⟩ adequately represented by the plaster casts as the Apollo & the Laocoon are. I must go again & see this statue. Then I went round this cabinet & gallery & galleries till I was well nigh "dazzled & drunk with beauty." [15] I think no man has an idea of the powers of painting until he has come hither. Why should painters study at Rome? Here, here.

I have been this day to Santa Croce which is to Florence what Westminster Abbey is to ⟨L⟩England. I passed with consideration the tomb of Nicholas Machiavelli but stopped long before that of Galileus Galileo, for I love & honor that man, except in the recantation, with my whole heart.[16] But when I came to Michel Angelo [13] Buonaroti my flesh crept as I read the inscription. I had strange emotions, I suppose because Italy is so full of his fame. I have lately continually heard of his name & works & opinions; I see his face in every shop window, & now I stood over his dust.

[13] The Duomo, also known as the Santa Maria del Fiore. The comment of Michelangelo on the Baptistery gates is quoted in most guide books, though usually in English. See Starke, *Travels in Europe* . . . , 1828, p. 73. The praise in slightly different wording, as Rusk notes, appears also in Giorgio Vasari's life of Ghiberti in *Vite de' Più Eccellenti Pittori, Scultori, e Architetti*, 16 vols. (Milan, 1808), IV, 139 (see *L*, I, 382).
[14] Thomson, *The Seasons*, "Summer," l. 1346, of the Venus de'Medici: "So stands the statue that enchants the world. . . ."
[15] Byron, *Childe Harold's Pilgrimage*, IV, 1.
[16] Cf. Jonson's comment on Shakespeare in *Timber or Discoveries made upon Men and Matter* (*Ben Jonson*, ed. C. H. Herford and Percy Simpson, 10 vols., Oxford, 1925–1950, VIII, 583–584): "for I loved the man and doe honour his memory (on this side Idolatry) as much as any."

Then I came to the empty tomb of Dante who lies buried at
Ravenna. Then to that of Alfieri.

2 May. I revisited the Tribune this morning to see the Venus & the
Fornarina and the rest of that attractive company. I reserve my admiration as much as I can; I make a continual effort not to be pleased
except ⟨with⟩ ↑by↓ that which ought to please *me*. And I walked
coolly round & round the marble lady but when I planted myself at
the iron gate which leads into the [14] chamber of Dutch paintings & looked at the statue, I saw & felt that mankind have had
good reason for their preference of this excellent work, & I gladly
gave one testimony more to the surpassing genius of the artist.

    Today I had a singular pleasure. Mr Ritchie's kindness procured
me the privilege of seeing the apartments occupied by Lord Byron
when he was in Florence. They are part of the palace of the Duke of
San Clementi who is Mr R's neighbor. The rooms were ⟨w⟩very
richly furnished & hung with tapestry. There were five in a range
& the last opening into a large dining hall. Below was a large hall
which Byron fitted up as a theatre. The palace is in the Via S. Sebas-
tiano[.]

[15] How bare & poor are these Florentine churches after the
sumptuous temples of Naples & Rome. Ah! ah! for St Peter's, which
I can never more behold. Close by my door is the Church of Santa
Maria Novella which Michel Angelo called his *bride*; ⟨I have⟩ ↑my
eye has↓ not yet learned why; it still looks naked & unfinished to me.
The Church of St John's in Malta, he might well have distinguished
by such a name.

    ↑Evg.↓ Beautiful days, beautiful nights. It is today one of the
hundred festas of this holiday people; so was yesterday; so is tomorrow. The charming Cascina, & the banks of the Arno are thronged,
but moonshine or sunshine are indispensable to a festa; as they say
in France, "there will be no revolution today, for it rains."

[16] Tuesday, 7 May.
        "Ah! l aurora della vita
        E l'aurora del dolor."

[May] 9. I rode out this ev.g with Mr Miles [17] in the beautiful Cascina. Its walks & groves extend from the Prato gate of the city out for miles along the right bank of the Arno. It is full of sweetsinging birds — the robin & the nightingale, and of quails, partridges, & rabbits kept for game by the Gran↑d↓duke.

I saw Jerome Buonaparte on horseback. He resembles the pictures of his brother Napoleon though utterly devoid of ⟨the⟩ ↑this↓ energy of expression. His brother Louis also lives in Florence. The emperor of Austria is responsible for the good behaviour of the family.

[17] I went last night to a theatre & heard a whole opera very respectably performed, with all scenic pomp & music & numbers & paid one paul ↑10 cents↓ for my seat. A seat in the pit costs 2 crazies.
                                    — E perchè questo cristallo?
         "Perchè cosi vuole il Principe."
I have visited the palace & gallery of ⟨P⟩ the Principe ⟨de⟩ Corsini, where are Carlo Dolcis & Salvator Rosas in plenty; the original sketch by Michel Angelo of his Last Judgment; a fine portrait by Rembrandt of himself, & some other good pictures in many fine rooms. The Prince himself is gone to Naples as proxy for the Grand-duke to marry the sister of the King.

All night the street echoes with the songs of this musical people, they have fine voices & repeat the airs of the operas. But the *boys*.

[18] [May] 10. Visited Professor Amici [18] & saw his optical instruments. He is reputed the maker of the best microscopes in Europe. He has also made a telescope for Herschel in London. He has a microscope wh⟨ich⟩ose magnifying power is 6000 diameters, or 36,000,000 superficies. To instruments of this enormous power he applies the camera lucida & then draws the outline of the object with pencil. His experiments upon polarised light are beautiful.
The price of his best instruments is 800 francs. He has just made one for Dr Jarvis [19] for 45 dollars.

---

[17] Henry Miles, an American merchant of Florence, to whom Emerson had a letter of introduction. See *Life*, p. 180.
[18] Giovanni Battista Amici (1784–1863), Italian optician, astronomer, and instrument maker, created the famous Amici achromatic microscope in 1827.
[19] Dr. Edward Jarvis (1803–1884) took his A.B. at Harvard in 1826 and his

Speak out, my boy, speak plain, non capisco. "Ed io anche non intendo lei," said the beggar.

[May] 11. Last night I went to the Pergola, and to my eyes, unused to theatres, it was [19] a glorious show. The prima donna, Signora Delsere, is a noble Greek beauty, full of dignity, & energy of action & when she sang the despair of Agnes,[20] she was all voice. ⟨The⟩ She had moreover so striking a resemblance to a valued friend in America, that I longed to know who & what Signora Delsere was, much more than the issue of the play. But nobody knew. The whole scenery & the dresses of the performers were in admirable taste, everything good but the strutting of the actors. Is it penal for an actor to *walk*? Before the play was done, my eyes were so dazzled with the splendor of light & colors that I was obliged to rest them & look at my shoes for half an hour, that I might keep them for the [20] last act.

For my seat in the pit, where ladies sit also, I paid three pauls, 30 cts.

I ought not to forget the ballet between the acts. Goethe laughs at those who force every work of art into the narrow circle of their own ⟨judgme⟩ prejudices & cannot admire a picture as a picture & a tune as a tune.[20a] So I was willing to look at this as a ballet, & to see that it was admirable, but I could not help feeling the while that it were better for mankind if there were no such dancers. I have since learned God's decision on the same, in the fact that all the *ballerine* are nearly ideotic.

---

medical degree in 1830. See Emerson's letter of recommendation for him in *L*, II, 49–50.

[20] The opera was Bellini's *La Straniera*.

[20a] Cf. "How difficult, though it seems so easy, is it to contemplate . . . a fine picture simply in and for itself; to watch the music for the music's sake; to admire the actor in the actor. . . . Most men are wont to treat a work of art, though fixed and done, as if it were a piece of soft clay. The hard and polished marble is again to mould itself . . . according as their inclinations, sentiments, and whims may dictate." *William Meister's Apprenticeship*, Bk. VII, ch. 7, Carlyle trans. See the *Works of Thomas Carlyle*, Centenary ed., XXIV, 152. See also Vivian C. Hopkins, "The Influence of Goethe on Emerson's Aesthetic Theory," *Philological Quarterly*, XXVII (Oct. 1948), 337.

[May] 12. I dined today with Mr Askew at his villa seven miles out of Florence and all the road was through a garden.ⁿ [21] We rode on our return through a *shower* of flies, all the way.

I gladly hear much good of the order of Misericordia. I see these philanthropists now with quite new feeling, when they carry by the dead with their hasty chaunt. This order is composed of men of all professions & ages & ranks who for a penance or for love enter into it for a longer or shorter period. They devote themselves to all works of mercy especially to the care of the sick. They watch & ↑at↓tend them but never speak, & their faces are never seen being always covered with a silken hood. ↑They are not known to each other.↓ Cardinals & princes sometimes take the dress of this order for a time. ↑The last Grand duke was once a member.↓ Miss Anna Bridgen tells me that she saw in Rome a coachman driving a splendid coach with chasseurs attendant, who attempted to pass directly through a funeral procession, when one of [22] the Misericordes ran forward & laid a powerful arm upon the rein of the horse & lifted his veil to the coachman who instantly drew up his horses & waited with the utmost respect for the train to pass.

They have taken down the old marble bench on which Dante used to sit & look at the beautiful Campanella, & set it into the pavement with the inscription "Sasso di Dante." Well he might sit and admire that charming tower which is a sort of poem in architecture. One might dream of such a thing, but it seems strange that it should have been executed in lasting stone. Giotto built it[,] that old Gothic Painter. ⟨His tomb is in the Cathedral.⟩ [21]

[May] 13. At the Arena di Goldoni this afternoon I saw a Hercules of a man lie on his back & raise [23] his feet upon which two men stood, upon the men two boys climbed; two women then stood, one upon each of his hands, & he held them all up in the air. Afterwards he lifted a weight of 1500 lbs.

[May] 15. Today I dined with Mr Landor at his villa at San

---

[21] The sentence is canceled in pencil.

Domenica di Fiesole.[22] He lives in a beautiful spot in a fine house full of pictures & with a family most engaging. He has a wife & four children. He said good & pleasant things & preferred Washington to all modern great men. He is very decided, as I might have expected, in all his opinions, & very much a connoisseur in paintings. He was not very well today & I go to breakfast with him next Friday. He thinks that no great man ever had a great son, if Philip & Alexander be not [24] an exception, & Philip he calls the greater man. Montaigne he likes very much, & praised Charron. He thought Degerando indebted to Lucas on Happiness! & Lucas on Holiness! Sir James Mackintosh [23] he would not praise, nor my Carlyle. He pestered me with Southey; what is Southey? And the Greek histories he thought the only good, & after them Voltaire's. In art he loves the Greeks & in sculpture them only. He prefers the Venus to every thing else, & after that the head of Ale⟨ss⟩xander in the gallery here. He prefers John of Bologna to Michel Angelo. In painting, Raffaelle & Perugino & Giotto. Mr Hare was present, the author of 'Guesses at Truth'; [24] & Mr Worsley.

[May] 1⟨7⟩6. ⟨Visited Mr L[andor] again yesterday⟩ This day is the festival of the Ascension which is a great annual holiday of the Florentines & pours them [25] all out under the trees & along the lawns of the beautiful Cascina. There they keep a sort of rural Saturnalia. The Grand duke came up towards evening & took a turn round the Square in his coach & bowed gracefully to the bowing multitude. His little children were with ⟨the⟩him in the coach.

[22] Horatio Greenough procured the invitation for Emerson. Most of the details of the entries for May 15 and May 18 are used in *English Traits, W*, V, 7–9.

[23] Pierre Charron (1514–1603) was a French philosopher and theologian; Emerson himself had read and extensively extracted Marie Joseph de Gérando, *Histoire comparée des systèmes de philosophie*, 4 vols. (Paris, 1822–1823) as his entry in his Blotting Book for October 27, 1830, shows (see *JMN*, III, 360–370); he perhaps remembered that under the influence of Landor he had jotted down references to Richard Lucas' *Enquiry After Happiness*, and the *Practical Christianity* . . . (see p. 44 above, for September 17, 1832); Mackintosh's *A General View of . . . Ethical Philosophy*, 1832, Emerson owned and had cited with high praise on March 30, 1832 (see p. 7 above).

[24] Julius Charles Hare (1796–1855), coauthor with his brother Augustus William Hare. Emerson had first cited *Guesses at Truth* in June, 1831. See *JMN*, III, 264.

In the evening the grounds were light as day with countless lamps hung in the trees & in the centre of all an obelisk of flambeaux. Then played the band, & all the people danced. I believe this rude ball was continued all night. I left them in full activity about 10 o'clock.

[May] 18. Visited Mr Landor again yesterday. He talked with spirit & learning & quoted some half a dozen hexameters of Caesar,[n] from Donatus.[25] He glorified Lord [26] Chesterfield more than was necessary. And Burke he undervalues. But far worse, he undervalues Socrates. He spoke of ⟨the⟩ three of the greatest men as Washington, Phocion, & Timoleon, & remarked the similar termination of their names.* [26] "A great man should make great sacrifices," he said, "he should kill his hundred oxen without knowing whether they would be eaten, or whether the flies would eat them." He spoke contemptuously of entomology, yet said that 'the sublime was in a grain of dust.' & the second thought should have condemned the first. He spoke of Wordsworth, Byron, Massinger, Beaumont & Fletcher, ↑&↓ Davy. Herschel he knew nothing about, not even his name.[27]

Cyclamen —. of Pope, Sterne[?] ↑Tooke↓
↑He lives in the Villa Ghirardesca.↓

[27] Mr L. has a fine cabinet of pictures & as Greenough remarked, he, in common with all collectors, imagines that ⟨he ha⟩his

* He might have added Bacon, Newton, &   .

[25] The six hexameters are printed and their source is given by Edward Emerson in his notes to *English Traits*. See *W*, V, 326.

[26] The footnote is added by Emerson under a long rule at the bottom of the page, with space left for a third example.

[27] Emerson had read Sir John F. W. Herschel's *A Preliminary Discourse on the Study of Natural Philosophy* (London, 1831), as he notes in a letter to William, December 25, 1831 (*L*, I, 342–343) in which he praises the book as a "noble work." He may at the time have read only the part of the *Discourse* printed in the American Library of Useful Knowledge, Boston, 1831, as "The General Nature and Advantages of the Study of the Physical Sciences." Either then or soon after, however, he probably acquired the 1831 edition which is in his library. In his library is also Herschel's *A Treatise on Astronomy* (London, 1833), no. 43 in the Cabinet Encyclopedia; this volume he acquired in London and apparently read on the ship during the return to America.

are the only masterpieces. "Ne sutor" — and I remembered the story of Voltaire & Congreve.[28] Mr Hare told me that Mr L. has not more than twelve books in his library.

Noon. I went to the Museum of Natural History & ⟨saw⟩to the representation in wax of the *Plague* of *Florence,* & saw how man is made & how he is destroyed. This museum contains an accurate copy in wax from nature of every organ & process in the human frame, & is beautiful & terrible. For in life nature never intends that these things should be uncovered.

[28] I have looked into Santa Croce this afternoon & if I spoke ill of it before I will unsay it all. It is a grand building, and its windows of stained glass charm me. It is lined & floored with tombs, & there are two or three richly furnished Chapels. In one is a fine painting of the Last Supper by Vasari. While we were walking up & down the church the organ was played & I have never heard a more pleasing one. I saw the bust of ⟨A⟩Michel Angelo & his eight wrinkles.

When I walk up the piazza of Santa Croce I feel as if it were not a Florentine no nor an European church but a church built by & for the human race. I feel equally at home within its walls as the Grand duke, so *hospitably* sound to me the names of its mighty dead. Buonaroti & Galileo lived for us all. As Don Ferrante says of Aristotle, "non è nè antico nè moderno; è il filosofo, senza piu." [29]

[29] I met the fair Erminia today. These meetings always cost me a crazie & it is fit that she should not be slighted in the journal.

---

[28] Pliny, *Natural History*, XXXV, xxxvi, 85, tells the story of Apelles, speaking to the cobbler who criticized his drawing of a leg: "Ne supra crepidam sutor judicaret" — "a shoemaker in his criticism must not go beyond the sandal." The phrase became a common Latin proverb as "ne sutor ultra crepidam" — "the cobbler should stick to his last." The story of Voltaire and Congreve is the account of a famous visit by Voltaire to Congreve, who refused to take his writing seriously and asked to be thought of as a "mere gentleman." Voltaire's response was one of disgust; such a figure as a mere gentleman he would not have visited.

[29] Manzoni, *I Promessi Sposi,* 1827, ch. 27, III, 61. This Italian edition in Emerson's library is probably the text he finished reading on May 21, 1833 (see p. 177 below).

Erminia is a flower-girl who comes to the Caffé every morning & if you will not buy her flowers she gives them to you & with such a superb air. She has a fine expression of face & never lets her customers pass her in the street without a greeting. Every coach too in Florence that ventures to stop near the Piazza di Trinita is a tributary of Erminia's. I defy them to escape from her nosegays. She has a rich pearl necklace worth I know not how much, which she wears on festas. Mr Wall wishes to paint her portrait but she says she is not handsome enough. "E brutto il mio ritratto."

[30] Went again to the Opera to see a piece called Ivanhoe.[29a] What a miserable †ab↓use to put a woman of dignity & talent into men's clothes to play the part of Wilfrid. The Signora Delsere who delighted me so much the other night was strutting about ineffectually with sword & helmet. They had spoiled a fine woman to make a bad knight. I came home disgusted.

The Italians use the Superlative too much. Mr Landor calls them the nation of the *issimi*. A man to tell me that this was the same thing I had before, said "E l'istessissima cosa;" and at the trattoria, when I asked if the cream was good, the waiter answered, "Stupendo." They use three negatives; it is good [31] Italian to say, 'Non dite nulla a nessuno'[.] [29b]

[May] 19. Hot weather steadily for three weeks past & Florence is a degree of latitude farther north than Boston. Six or seven blazing hours every day, when, as the Florentines say, 'there's nobody but dogs & Englishmen in the streets.' Then the pleasant evening walk from 6 to 7 or 8 o'clock upon the Cascina, or the banks of the little sylvan Mugnone, or in the Boboli gardens. And wherever I go, I am surrounded by ⟨these⟩ beautiful objects; the fine old towers of the city; the elegant curve of the Ponte ⟨Sa⟩Trinità; the rich purple line of the Appenines; broken by the bolder summits of the marble

---

[29a] Two operas by this name might fit the circumstances: "Ivanhoe" by Rossini (1826) and Giovanni Pacini's "Ivanhoe" (1832). The latter is the more probable.

[29b] As his sample of the negative in Italian, Emerson is slightly misquoting Manzoni, *I Promessi Sposi*, 1827, I, 273: "Lo prega, e vero, di non dir nulla a nessuno."

mountains of Carrara. And all all is Italian; not a house, not a shed, not a field that the eye can for a moment imagine to be American.

[32] Miss Anna Bridgen said very wittily, "that so inveterate were her Dutch instincts, that she sees almost no work of art in Italy, but she wants to give it a good scrubbing; the Duomo, the Campanella, & the statues."

[May] 21. Rose early this morng. & went to the Bello Sguardo out of the Roman gate. It was a fine picture this Tuscan morning and all the towers of Florence rose richly out of the smoky light on the broad green plain. I passed the Michelozzi Villa, where Guicciardini wrote his history.[30] Returning I saw the famous fresco painting on the wall within the city, directly opposite the Roman gate, the work of Giovanni da S. Giovanni; executed, they say, to show the skill of Tuscan art. A story is told that some Roman painter having been sent [33] for to execute a public work in Florence, the Florentine Artists painted this wall that he might see it on his entrance into the city. When he came & saw this painting he inquired whose work it was; & being informed it was done by Florentines, he returned immediately to Rome, saying that they had no occasion for foreign artists.

———

"Birbo, sì ma profondo," * says Manzoni of Machiavelli. I have finished ⟨with⟩ the "Promessi Sposi", and I rejoice that a man exists in Italy who can write such a book. I hear from day to day such hideous anecdotes of the depravity of manners, that it is an unexpected delight to meet this elevated & eloquent moralist.

Renzo, & Lucia, Fra Cristoforo, & Federigo Borromeo [31] — all are excellent &, which is the highest praise, all excite the reader to virtue.

* "diceva don Ferrante" [*I Promessi Sposi* (1827), ch. 27, III, 64]

[30] Francesco Guicciardini (1483–1540), *The History of Italy from the year 1490 to 1532* (1564).
[31] The hero, heroine, and two of the important secondary characters in *I Promessi Sposi.*

[34] May 25. It is the Festa of San Zenobio once bishop of Florence.[n] And at the churches, the priests bless the roses & other flowers which the people bring them, & they are then esteemed good for the cure of head ache & are laid by for that purpose. Last night in the Duomo I saw a priest ⟨w⟩carrying a silver bust of San Zenobio which he put upon the head of each person in turn who came up the barrier. This ceremony also protects him from the head ache for a year. But, asked I of my landlady, do you believe that the bust or the roses ⟨are⟩ do really cure the head ache of any person? "Secondo alla fede di ciascuno," she replied.
It is my Festa also.

[35] I wrote to G. A. S.[32] yesterday what I have found true[,] that it is necessary ↑for the traveller↓ in order to see what is worth seeing & especially *who* is worth seeing in each city, to go into society a little. Now no man can have society upon his own terms. If he seek it, he must serve it too. He immediately & inevitably contracts debts to it which he must pay at a great expense often of inclination & of time. ↑& of duty.↓ [33]

[36] "Comanda niente Signore?" — Niente. — "Felice notte, Signore." — Felice notte. Such is the dialogue which passes every evening betwixt Giga   & me when the worthy woman lights my lamp, & leaves me to Goethe & Sismondi,[34] to pleasant ⟨hours⟩study hours, & to sound sleep.

I have been to the Academia delle belle Arti, & there saw an unfinished work of Michel Angelo's. His opinion was asked concerning

[32] George A. Sampson, Boston merchant, one-time parishioner of Emerson's at the Second Church, had been a close friend ever since he opened his house to his new pastor during the first months of 1829.

[33] The phrase is crowded into the end of the line in pencil, obviously as a later addition to the thought.

[34] Emerson was apparently reading Goethe both to practice German and for information, turning to parts relevant to his travels in the *Italienische Reise* and perhaps the *Tag-und-Jahres Hefte*. Since the early 1820's he had been familiar with Simonde de Sismondi's work (see *JMN*, I, 134–135, and *passim*, for translations from *De la littérature du midi de l'Europe*, 4 vols., Paris, 1829, and from *L'Histoire des républiques Italiennes au moyen age*, 16 vols., Paris, 1818).

a block of marble, whether it were large enough to make a statue of?
"Yes," he said, "a Colossus." And the inquirers doubting, he went
to work, & cutting a little here & a little there, rudely sketched a
figure of gigantic dimensions & left it so, a sort of sculptor's puzzle.[35]

[37] 26 April, 1833.[36] Passignano. Here sit I this cold eve, ↑by
the fire↓ ⟨o⟩in the Locanda of this little town on the margin of the
lake of Thrasimene & remember Hannibal & Rome. Pleases me well
the clear pleasant air which savors more of New England than of
Italy. Today we came from Spoleto to Perugia on the top of how
high a hill with mighty walls & towers far within the gates of the
town. Old cathedral & all around architectural ornaments of the
middle ages. But were I a proprietor in Perugia I would sell all &
go & live upon the plain. ⟨Wh⟩ How preposterous too it is to live in
Trevi where the streets must make with the horizon an angle of 45
degrees. Yet here in Umbria every height shows a ⟨grand⟩ wide prospect of well cultivated country!

[38] At Terni, Tacitus. At Arezzo, Petrarch. Civita Castellani =
Veii

For Galileo's house go out the Roman Gate beyond the Poggio
Imperiale & inquire for the Casa Caparina near to the Torre Gallo.
I did not [37] climb Fiesole beyond Mr Landor's residence which is at
San Domenica di Fiesole. I was consoled for my omission by the
following dialogue which passed betwixt my companions who did.

Mr W. Have you been to Fiesole Mr H.? [38]

Mr H. Yes.

[35] Two lines of unrecovered erased pencil writing follow the ink entry.

[36] The entry, out of chronological order, is in pencil, apparently part of the
record written at the time of the journey from Rome to Florence and later revised
in ink. See the entry for May 1, on pp. 166–167 above. Perhaps because of its precise
detail this section of the first notes for the travel record was not erased and recopied.
The penciled entry continues through "Veii" on p. [38], where Emerson is noting
the birthplaces of Tacitus and Petrarch and the somewhat doubtful identification of
Civita Castellani with the ancient city of Veii.

[37] "I did not . . . Mr H. Yes." is written in ink over a cramped penciled version of the same anecdote, in which the names "Holbrook" and "Wall" are written
in full.

[38] Probably William Allen Wall and S. P. Holbrook, with whom and Thomas
Stewardson of Philadelphia Emerson was about to set out via diligence from Florence across the Alps.

Mr W. Steep

Mr H. Quite.

and here the conversation dropped.

[39]³⁹ Tuesday Morn, 28 May. Sad I leave Florence, the pleasant city. I have not even seen it all & between negligence & mishap have failed to see the library. The system of mezzeria or metayer is universal in the agriculture of Tuscany. The introduction of the potato into general use & the culture of Saracenic grain has done much to alleviate the distress of the peasantry. Labor is dog cheap. The hat manufacture is almost peculiar. Mr Miles tells me that it takes one woman one week to make a hat & he usually orders a thousand hats in a week. The taxation seems very irregular & sometimes enormous, every ox that enters the gates of Florence pays eleven francesconi at the gate.

[40]⁴⁰ Left Florence 28th May. Stopped at the Pratolino five miles out of the city to see the colossal statue of Father Appenine [Apennine] by John of Bologna. It is grand if only from its size. They call it 60 ft high, meaning probably that in a standing posture it would be so high. I got up into his neck & head & looked out of his ear. Fine mountain scenery to the frontier of the Roman state. At last on reaching a new height we saw the Adriatic sea. We slept at Lacca the first village on the Roman territory 36 miles from Florence.

[May] 29. At 4 a.m. we set forward & passing thro' a picturesque country arrived at Bologna (25 miles) at 10 ½ o clock. Here we

---

³⁹ "The system . . . at the gate." is apparently a later, more detailed version of a canceled entry in the notebook France and England, pp. 404–405 below. The system of mezzeria or métayer was an arrangement by which tenants worked the land on shares. The ill effects of this variety of share-cropping were described at length in Simonde de Sismondi, *Nouveaux Principes d'économie politique.* . . . , 2 vols. (Paris, 1819), I, 186–201. See also Edward Everett, "An Address delivered at Brighton before the Massachusetts Agricultural Society, 16th October, 1833" in *Orations and Speeches on Various Occasions* (Boston, 1836), pp. 420–421.

⁴⁰ The ink entries from here through p. [51] are copied from earlier, half-erased penciled entries. Emerson apparently merely recopied and slightly revised the original notes to make a permanent record.

visited the celebrated statue of Neptune by John of Bologna — (good enough — but why so famous?)[,] the Gallery of the Academy & of the Palazzo Lambacari both rich in Guidos, Caraccis, Guercinos; the Museum & Library founded by Marsilius,[n] [41] 100000 volumes, the Cathedral, the Church of San Domenico where is Guido's fresco Paradise, [41] & where lie the bones of Guido, of the two Caraccis, & also of St Dominick[.]

Here too are two leaning towers[,] one deviating 9 ft. from the perpendicular[,] & a good story is told of their building.[42] All the streets are lined with porticos so that the inhabitants walk always under cover which in the rain & under this dangerous sun is a great public convenience. From the gate of the city a portico three miles in length formed of 650 arcades leads to the Church of the Madonna della Guardia. In the piazza ⟨stand⟩ were planted some pieces of artillery which have stood there since the soi disant *Revolution,* two years ago. There are here 7500[0] [43] souls.

[May] 30. From Bologna to Ferrara 32 mls. Nearly all the way the road was paved & lined with trees.[44]

Arrived at Ferrara at 4, P M. Visited Tasso's [42] prison[,] a real dungeon.[45] There I saw Byron's name cut with his penknife in the wall. The guide said his father accompanied him & that Byron staid ⟨half⟩ an hour & a half in the prison & there wrote. We visited the Cathedral — fine old Gothic exterior built in 1100[,] then the library where is Ariosto's tomb, his inkstand, medals, & chair. I sat in his chair. They were shown by an old man who entered into the spirit of his profession as the showman. Thence to the Campo Santo passing through the Jews' quarter of whom there are 2800 who are shut up every

[41] Luigi Ferdinando Marsigli (1658–1730), an Italian naturalist and mathematician, one of the founders of the Society of Sciences and Arts at Bologna, 1712.

[42] The two towers are called the Asinelli and the Torre degli Garisendi, but the "good story" of their building remains unlocated.

[43] In copying the population figure Emerson evidently omitted one zero by error. The underlying penciled version reads: "In Bologna are said to be 75 000 souls." Only the ink version includes the sentence: "In the piazza . . . years ago."

[44] Under "Nearly all . . . trees." are the same words in pencil with the addition of "on both sides. It was haying time & fragrant all".

[45] In the Hospital of S. Anna.

night as in Rome like dogs. At the Campo Santo, two monuments by Canova. What a desolate town! The streets appeared like State street on Sunday, & the grass grew. There are 24000 inhabitants. Under the dukes there were 70000[.]   It is the native place of Garofalo, Guercino, Canova. A prolegate of the Pope administers the government.

[43] [May] 31. From Ferrara to Rovigo across the Po in a Ferry. The stream was wide & strong, about as wide as the Connecticutt at Hartford. The road all day was lined with poplars on each side. Fine bold taste displayed in all their architecture. Every church is a new & pleasing plan. Every chimney is built on an ornamental design. At night we reached Monselice after crossing the Adige. — Saw our honest countryman the Indian corn growing well.

Monselice is the most picturesque town I have seen in Italy. It has an old ruin of a castle upon the hill & thence commands a beautiful & extraordinary view. It lies in the wide plain — a dead level — whereon Ferrara, Bologna, Rovigo, [44] Este, Padua stand & even Venice we could dimly see in the horizon rising with her tiara of proud towers. What a walk & what a wide delightful picture. To Venice 38 miles.

1 June. This morn we stopped half a mile this side of the village of Battaglia on the road to Padua, sent the vettura on to the market place, & walked over to Arqua to see the tomb of Petrarch, & the house where he spent his latter days. Both are striking & venerable objects. The house is vacant & clean[,] its windows look out upon mountains. His portrait & his interviews with Laura are painted in fresco on the walls. They show his chair & the chamber where he died. Good good place. It does honor to his head & heart[;] there grow the pomegranate & fig & olive.

At noon at Padua. Three rich churches as usual in Italy unlike all others:[n] the Duomo, & San Antonio, & San Justin. Visited the grand Hall[,] the ancient Sala di Giustizia[,] 300 ft long, 100 wide, 100 high [45] without other support than the walls. Stewardson, Wall, & I then went for our breakfast to the most beautiful Caffe in Europe. Nothing can exceed the taste & splendor of this room.

182

Visited the University. 1600 students 62 professors. Heard the professor Caldania [Caldani] lecture upon anatomy with a subject. The form of the Lecture room was an inverted cone. Saw the Museum. The quadrangle of the University is a venerable place covered with armorial bearings.

From Padua to Venice 20 miles. Crossed the Brenta & passed a profusion of fine villas — all the grounds full of statues not quite as thick as they could stand. Far the most splendid of all was the Villa Imperiale built by Palladio.   Arrived at Mestre the place of embarcation for Venice 5 miles off. Here we took a boat & sailed for the famous city. It looked for some time like nothing but New York. We entered the Grand Canal & passed under the Rialto & ⟨were⟩ presently stepped out of the boat into the front entry of the Grande Bretagna.[46] The front entry of the Grande Bretagna opens also upon a little bridge which connects by a narrow alley with the Piazza [46] of St Mark so out we went under the full moon to see the same. It was all glorious to behold. In moonlight this arabesque square is all enchantment — so rich & strange & visionary.   June 2. Again I have been to St Mark's & seen his horses & his winged lion, the bridge of sighs, the doge's palace, the piazza, the canals. We took a gondola — three of us — (that is, one too many for the perfect enjoyment of that cunning vehicle) & proceeded to the Churches & the Academy. There is Titian's picture of the Assumption of the Madonna — so glorified by the painters. The young men whom I converse with prefer it to Raphael. There also is another of Titian's[,] the Presentation of the Virgin yet a child to the High priest[,] a very large picture, and I thought I might call it the *handsomest* picture I have seen but certainly not the best. It lacks the expression of Raffaelle. It will not do to compare any thing, in my opinion, with his Transfiguration. A great man will find a great subject or which is the same thing make any subject great & what tenderness & holiness beams from the face of the Christ in that Work. [47] What emotion[!] I have never yet seen the face copied in all the soi disant copies of that picture.

[46] According to Mariana Starke La Gran-Bretagna was the best hotel in Venice, even though cold and gloomy in the winter and early spring (*Travels in Europe*, 1828, p. 418).

In the Academy is a cast of the Hercules of Canova. The original is in the Torlonia Palace at Rome. It is a tremendous action. Here too are casts of his best works. The chair in which he has seated Mme Buonaparte is the same beautiful form I admired in the Caffe at Padua. Grand pictures here of Paul Veronese, Tintoretto, & Titian[.]

These churches of Venice surpass all the churches in Florence in splendor. The Chiesa dei Carmeliti has eight chapels built at the expense of eight families & they are superb. The Chiesa dei Gesuiti is a most costly imitation in marble of tapestry hangings throughout the interior. Hiram & Solomon could not beat it.

In the Chiesa della Salute is a monument of Canova built from Canova's design of a tomb for Titian. Canova's design, however, if that little model I saw in the Academy be it, is more impressive than this gorgeous marble [48] *execution*[n] of the same in the Salute. These churches are all rich with monuments on many of which is figured the horned bonnet worn by the Doges of Venice. From these we came to the Ducal Palace up the ⟨g⟩Giant Stair⟨s⟩Case.

At the side of the door we were shown the 'Lion's Mouth,' a hole in the wall into which anciently were thrown the anonymous accusations of any citizen for the eye of the Council of State. Thence we were conducted to the Library, then to the Hall — a grand chamber whose whole walls & ceiling are adorned by the best pictures of great size by Paul Veronese & his son and Tintoretto & Palma Vecchio & Palma Giovane & Bonifacio. All the paintings are historical. This hall & the adjoining chambers contain in this splendid way a chronicle of the republic. The portraits of 116 doges hang around on high[,] among which is the black [49] board where should be the head of Marino Faliero.[47] On the ceiling, most of the pieces are allegorical — (which is as bad in painting as it is in poetry). And at one extremity of the Hall a Paradise by Tintoretto a picture of amazing size. From this hall to the Audience Chamber where the Doge & his Council received foreign ambassadors — then to the Council Chamber of the 300,[n] with its rostrum & other realities. After seeing these noble apartments we were conducted to the prisons below and all the hideous economy & arrangement of them explained.

[47] Byron tells the story in *Marino Faliero, Doge of Venice*; the so-called "black board" over Faliero's portrait he speaks of as a "painted black veil."

I saw the little blackened chamber from those walls Lord Byron had those sad inscriptions copied [48] and passed the dreaded door opening on the bridge of Sighs down to the third noisome story of the subterranean dungeon. It is a sickening place, & 'tis enough to make one dance & sing that this horrid tyranny is broken in pieces. [50] To be sure the Austrians are here but their rule is merciful to ⟨the Venetian⟩ that whose story is written here in stone & iron & ⟨clay⟩ ↑mire↓.[49] The policy of the Venetian government kept even the existence of their state prison a secret & on the approach of the French in 1796, they hastily built up the secret passages. The French acted with good sense in opening these damnable holes to the day & exposing them to the public in order to make their own invasion popular.

After leaving the Ducal palace we climbed the stairs of the Campanile to the lookout,[n] an essential part of the traveller's duty at Venice for as in the city you are always in a gutter it needs to get up into this tower to have any sight of its shape & extent. The day was not very clear but the view was noble[.]

[51] The Campanile itself is [a] beautiful tower but it cannot compare with Giotto's wonder at Florence — the poem in stone. I should attempt to describe St Mark's Piazza[,] the glory of Venice & without which the city would not be worth visiting[,] but that the common prints of it are so good. There stand the painted masts whereon the republic hung her banners. As its is the only piece of ground in the city where a thousand men could find elbow room, its ↑daily↓ importance can easily be conceived.

We took a long sail across the harbor to the immense arsenal, a place of all manner of naval works three miles in circuit. The Bucentaur [50] is gone but there they show a model of it & upon it all the places of state & the garrulous showman tells all the story of the annual marriage of the Adriatic.[51]

[48] Byron spoke of and printed the "sad inscriptions" taken from the Venetian dungeon in his notes to *Childe Harold's Pilgrimage*, IV, i.

[49] "mire" is inserted above "clay" in a different color of ink, apparently as a change made at a later reading.

[50] The underlying penciled entry which through the earlier part of the journal has been partially erased and then rewritten in ink ends here. Evidently Emerson now abandoned his practice of writing first in pencil and then revising in ink, perhaps because he had caught up his journal.

[51] Cf. Byron, *Childe Harold's Pilgrimage*, IV, xi.

[52] Here too is an armory where they show without a blush the golden keys of Venice that were made in 17↑97↓ [52] to be presented to Napoleon. Worse things are various inventions for torture & a nameless thing for an incredible indecent cruelty ascribed to Francesco da Carrara.

I am speedily satisfied with Venice. It is a great oddity — a city for beavers — but to my thought a most disagreeable residence. You feel always in prison, & solitary. Two persons may live months in adjoining streets & never meet, for you go about in gondolas and all the gondolas are precisely alike & the persons within commonly concealed; then there are no Newsrooms; ⟨no⟩except St Mark's piazza, no place of public resort. — It is as if you were always at sea. And though, for a short time, it is very luxurious to lie on the eider down cushions of your gondola [n] [53] & read or talk or smoke, drawing to now the cloth lined shutter, now the venetian blind, now the glass window, as you please, yet there is always a slight smell of bilgewater about the thing, & houses in the water remind me of a freshet & of desolation — any thing but comfort. I soon had enough of it.

The board-nail men, as Mr Wall called them, was a new form of beggary. At every frequented landing place[,] as a church or palace[,] stood on the shore a beggar with a nail in the end of a stick by which he held the boat to the shore whilst the passenger stepped out, & then held out his hat for a copper.

As you sail up the streets ⟨at every new⟩ on approaching every opening the gondolier calls aloud to warn any gondola that is round the corner. I ought not to forget that I went to the Manfrini Palace & saw its famous gallery of paintings & Giorgione's picture. [54] And so we left the ocean-Rome.

[55] Tuesday, 4 June. With our trusty Vetturino who brought us from Florence, we left Mestre this morn for Padua, & then for Vicenza, where we pass the night. This is the city of Palladio and embellished with his architecture. The Campo Marzo is a beautiful

---

[52] The "97" in the date is inserted in a different color of ink into the space which Emerson originally left to be filled in.

public walk. Went thence to the Duomo & the Basilica. Many fine palaces in this town.

5 June. To Verona 30 miles. The chief object of interest is the Amphitheatre built in Trajan's time — a smaller Coliseum — but in excellent preservation & still used as a theatre. A play was getting up in the arena when we came away. Then to what is called Juliet's tomb — a very apocryphal sepulchre; then to the Duomo to see an Assumption of the Madonna by Titian[,] to San Giorgio to see pictures of Paul Veronese. This is his own town & of Maffei also. Saw the Roman [56] bridge built by Vitruvius over the Adige.

There are 12000 soldiers now in this town. A large part of them are employed in rebuilding the ancient walls. The population — from 50 to 60,000. This place suffered much in the French invasion in 17   [53] and I saw many walls honey combed with musket shot.

We do not make many miles in a day but our journey has many alleviations & we are very companionable travellers and some of our Tuscan conversations with the Vetturino ludicrous enough. "Vetturino!" shouted my friend S[tewardson] from within the coach, "Vetturino! Perché non arrangiate questo window?" Then we find a hospitable Caffé every evening where we find an ice and the oriental narcotic & W[all] & S[tewardson] their cigar[.]

[57] 6 June. Today from Verona to Brescia, 40 miles. From Verona in the morning to Lago di Guarda & crossed the smooth sliding Mincio & spent our three hours of nooning at Desenzano. 'Tis Corpus Christi day & for a week past wherever we have been we have seen preparations for celebrating this festa with what pomp each city could. A splendid procession is every where made under awnings & in many places I believe over carpets laid along the streets. Even in this little village every house has hung out its quilts & damask & brocade, & the walls are lined. ⟨al⟩At the altar in the church officiate little girls dressed out in white & gold with wings for angels. We passed today many beautiful villas and what was new & pleasant we saw no beggars. The women in this country universally wear in their [58] hair silver pins with heads as large as eggs: they remind

[53] Lacking the precise date Emerson left the space open and the date incomplete.

one of an electrical machine. All the way they were stripping the mulberry trees of leaves for the food of the silkworms which are in every house. I went into a house & begged to see the animals; the padrona led me up stairs & showed the creatures in every age & state. She had given up the whole of the primo piano or what we call the second story to them.

Then to Brescia. All the Italian towns are different & all picturesque, the well paved Brescia. The Church of the Madonna dei Miracoli [—] how daintily it is carved without to the very nerves of the strawberry & vine leaf! Italy is the country of beauty but I think specially in the northern part. Every thing is ornamented. A peasant wears a scarlet cloak. If he has no other ornament he ties [59] on a red garter or knee band. They wear flowers in the hat or the buttonhole. A very shabby boy will have the eye of a peacock's feather in his hat. In general the great coats ⟨of⟩ & jackets of the common people are embroidered. And the other day I saw a cripple leaning on a crutch very finely carved. Every fountain, every pump, every post is sculptured, and not the commonest tavern room but its ceiling is painted. ↑Red is a favorite color and on a rainy morning at Messina the streets blazed with red umbrellas.↓ [54]

In Brescia they have lately made some excavations of their antiquities & laid open the floor & shafts of the pillars of a Roman temple of Hercules. They have found a fine bronze Victory there. At a fountain in the piazza was a statue of Canova's. I thought a clever mason might make as good a one.

In Brescia 4000 soldiers. Porticoes in all these towns in North of Italy.

[60] [55] Paris. I arrived in Paris at noon on Thursday 20 June. The eye is satisfied on entering the city with the unquestionable tokens on every side of a vast, rich, old capital. I crossed the Seine by the Pont Neuf ⟨V⟩ and was very glad to see my old acquaintance Henry

---

[54] The insertion, in a different color of ink and probably of a later date, is crowded between the lines after "painted."

[55] The entry on this page is struck through with a heavy diagonal use mark, probably because the material interrupts the account of the Italian trip and is repeated with slight revision and expansion in a more suitable chronological order. For the second version see p. 196 below.

IV very respectably mounted in bronze upon his own bridge — but a little mortified to see that the saucy faction of the hour has thrust a tricolor into the monarch's hand as into a doll's & in spite of time & decency & the grave the old monarch must be Vicar of Bray [56] in the whirligig politics of his city. From the bridge saw the Louvre & the Thuilleries.

[61] [57] ⟨O⟩The roads seem the best & costliest I have ever seen. But there are no bad roads in Italy. Buonaparte with whatever intent was a great benefactor to this whole peninsula from Naples northward.

I notice that the new buildings erected or erecting are in as bold and as beautiful a style as old ones. Every church every villa is original. And what gates they can make to a villa or a palace!

7 June. Today crossed the Mela. In all this Lombard region they write on a sign post the name of each town thus; "Commune di Ospedaletto
            Capo luogo del secondo distretto
               Provincia di Brescia."
and ⟨the⟩ ↑a↓ similar threefold inscription in every village. We begin to see goitres on both men & women. The Vettura stopped at noon at Calcio. [62] Wall & I have walked on towards Triviglio & now whilst he sketches I sit upon an arch that crosses a brook & listen to a bird's song; 'tis surely the nightingale. —

8 June. This morn at 10 o'clock entered Milan by a broad & splendid street. Saw the top of the Cathedral from far upon the road. & got a nearer view of its glories ⟨u⟩before arriving at the hotel.

[56] The Reverend Symon Aleyn, Vicar of Bray, c. 1575, is reported to have said (see Thomas Fuller, "Berkshire," *The History of the Worthies of England*, 3 vols., London, 1662, I, 113), "The Vicar of Bray will be Vicar of Bray still." Samuel Butler in *The Tale of the Cobbler and the Vicar of Bray* (c. 1660) immortalized the character with the lines "I shall still be Vicar of Bray,/ whichever side prevails."

[57] A penciled entry originally occupied the upper part of the page, running down to "7 June." It was apparently an entry dealing with Venice, perhaps a truncated early version of that now found pp. 183–186 above, since the following scattered words are visible: "Venice to Mestre[?]"; "Paolo Veronese"; "Arsenal ‖ . . . ‖ of Bucentaur"; "And they are of Francesco Carrera[?]".

[June] 9. This Cathedral is the only church in Italy that can pretend to compare with St Peter's. It is a most impressive & glorious place, without & within. And its exterior altogether as remarkable & deserving minute attention as its interior. It was begun by Andrea Commodia in 1386 & is not yet finished though always being built. When completed [n] [63] it will have 7000 statues great & small upon the outside. There are now 5000. It is all built, to the minutest part, of white marble, and, as the showman asserted, would have cost a mountain of gold, but that the founder had left to it a quarry of marble. Forty two artists are perpetually employed upon it. The walk upon the top of the church is delightful from the novelty & richness of the scene. Neighbored by this army of marble saints & martyrs, with scores of exquisitely sculptured pinnacles rising & flowering all around you, the noble city of Milan beneath, and all the Alps in the horizon, — it is one of the grandest views on earth.

Then inside the church the grand Gothic perspective of the aisles, the colour of the light which all enters through stained glass, the richness & magnitude of all the objects [—] truly it is good to be there.

An immense surface in this cathedral is glass window. Thus behind the great altar [64] are three huge windows only separated by sashes ⟨of wh⟩ each of which is wide by 12 panes (each pane 1 foot) & high by 12 panes (each pane 2 feet) & over all a great arch in which the glass is of irregular shape. These huge windows contain the whole history of Mankind from Adam & Eve down, each pane being a separate picture.

Underneath the church is the sum↑p↓tuous ⟨church⟩ ↑tomb↓ of St Charles Borromeo whose history is the glory of Milan and has furnished Manzoni with a hero in "I promessi Sposi." [58]

The kindness of the Conte del Verme has shown me & my friends all the curiosities of Milan. In his coach we have made the circuit of the City and as travellers say 'killed it thoroughly.' We visited not less than eight churches beside the Cathedral. Some of them very rich. At one they showed me tapestry between [65] two & three cen-

[58] Emerson finished the novel and praised the character of Federigo Borromeo on May 21 (see p. 177 above).

turies old which was as delicately pictured as if done by a camel's hair pencil. We went to the Ospitale Grande which is the most considerable institution of the sort in Europe — a magnificent charity. There are 2500 beds and almost all are full. Its aid is gratuitous. Every body is received who applies. & we walked through corridor after corridor of beds where↑on↓ lay the sick of all manner of diseases ⟨w⟩ — great and good and sad. This hospital is a little city in itself.

A very different spectacle was the Palazzo di Brera which has a rich gallery of paintings, a great public Library, and an astronomical observatory which were all shown us. Then we visited the Triumphal Arch l'Arco del Sempione designed & begun by Napoleon as the termination of the road of the Simplon from Paris to Milan. It[s] [66] finishing by the Austrian Government[,] of course with some variation in the bas reliefs.   Then to the Ambrosian Library & Museum where I saw Petrarch's copy of Virgil all written by himself; and to the Ospitale dei Frati Fatebenefratelli and to the Castle, & to the Arena, & to a Collegio, & to a Registry office, &c, &c.ⁿ

My friend the Count speaks with no good will of the Austrian government — so jealous, so rapacious, which holds Italy down by the pointed cannon. There are 96 or 97000 Austrian troops in Lombardy. When he solicited a passport to go to the United States of America it was 16 months before it was granted him.

I visited the Church of San Domenico [59] to see the famous fresco painting of the Last Supper by Leonardo da Vinci. It is sadly spoiled by time & damp. The face of Christ [67] is still very remarkable.

Milan is a wellbuilt town with broad streets and a little railroad of stone for the wheels to run upon in the middle of the street. It looks too modern to be so conspicuous in European history as it has been[,] for Lombardy was the theatre of every war.

There is an advantage which these old cities have over our new ones that forcibly strikes an American. Namely that the poorest inhabitants live in good houses. In process of time a city is filled with palaces, the rich ever deserting old ones for new, until beggars come to live in what were costly & well accommodated dwellings. Thus all the trattorias, even of little pretension, have their carved work &

[59] "San Domenico" is apparently filled in later in a different color of ink within a space left open.

fresco painting, as this of the Marino where I dine with my companions.

[68] [blank]

[69] Left Milan Tuesday, June 11, in the diligence, with Wall & Stewardson & the Misses Bridgen. Before sunset, we arrived on the beautiful banks of the Lago Maggiore, & crossed the Adda ⟨or⟩ which is there an arm of the lake, at Sesto Calendo, & stopped at Arona to dine. Though we passed directly below the famous colossal statue of San Carlo Borromeo, after leaving Arona, it was so dark that I could not see it, which I regretted much. We rode all night and reached Domo d'Ossola next morn to breakfast[,] the town at the foot of the Alps. The maitre d'hotel here spoke English, & we were much cheated, two facts which are said to be concomitant. The whole of the day, 12 June, was spent in crossing the mountain by the celebrated road, of the Simplon, cut & built by Buonaparte. Let it be a glory to his name,[n] him, the great Hand of our age. Truly [70] it is a stupendous work passing thro' every variation of ragged mountain scenery, now thro' the earth or solid rock in the form of a tunnel, now in successive easy ↑inclined↓ planes called galleries climbing the sides of a precipice, now crossing some rift in the mountain on a firm bridge, & so working its way up from the hot plain of Lombardy to cold waterfalls & huge snowbanks & up & upward to the bleak hamlet of Sempione which almost crowns the top. Here we see our own breath, & are very glad to get into the house & avoid the cold air. Over a wild mountain cascade & within a gallery cut thro' the rock Buonaparte has had the honesty to write "Italo Aere, Nap. Imp. MDCCCV." [60] Céard was his principle engineer.

And these, I thought, are the mountains[n] [71] of freedom. This queer ridge of matter is of such proved moral efficiency. Let their Spartan hymn ascend. I saw a good many of the Swiss peasantry on the hill sides: how different from the Italians on on[e] side, or the French on the other, but exactly resembling the faces & dresses of their countrymen who emigrate to the United States. It is marvellous to see their houses on such narrow lodgments, half way up a

[60] "In the Italian Era, Nap[oleon] Emp[eror] 1805" (Ed.).

192

mural precipice, as was said of Cortona, "like a picture hanging on a wall." [61] What can they do with their children[?]

We dined at Sempione & soon began the descent of the mountain[.] The wheel of the diligence is chained & shod with a heavy log of green wood; yet the descent at some points looks perilous enough. The mountain views are very fine. No extensive prospect is commanded in the ascent or from the [72] top but we see many noble summits of the chain as we come down toward Briga. We arrived safely at Briga at the foot of the mountain after sunset. We have left the Italian speech behind us & though in Switzerland, all is French. After supper we set forward again, and unluckily having taken my place outside by day I was compelled to ride the whole cold night *sub Jove frigido*,[62] & was very thankful to one of my fair friends within, who loaned me a *shawl* for the occasion. At dawn we reached Sion & in the forenoon Martigny. We had taken our places for Martigny intending to visit Mont Blanc from thence. But the sky was overcast & it rained a little & we were afraid ⟨to stop⟩ of a storm, so we relinquished our purpose or at least postponed it for consideration at Geneva. 13 June. On we came [73] passing the fine Cascade of Pissevache & stopped an hour at St Maurice. Thence in more convenient vehicles thro' a country of grandest scenery passing thro' Clarens & along the banks of Lake Leman, by the Castle of Chillon then through Vevay & we reached Lausanne before nightfall.

The repose & refreshment of a good hotel were very welcome to us after riding two nights; but the next morning (14th) was fine, and Mr W[all]. & I walked out to the public promenade[,] a high & ornamented grove which overlooks the Lake & commands the view of a great amphitheatre of mountains.

We are getting towards France. In the café where we breakfasted we found a printed circular inviting those whom it concerned to a rifle-match, to the intent, as the paper stated, "of increasing their

---

[61] The phrase may be from some unidentified poem, but it more probably reflects the common guide-book response to the mountainous situation of Cortona. Joseph Forsyth (*Remarks on Antiquities . . . in Italy*, 1818, p. 101) speaks of the town "like a picture hung upon a wall," and Conder (*Italy*, 1831, III, 93) refers to Cortona as "a picture hung against a wall."

[62] "under the cold, open sky" (Ed.). See Scott, *The Bride of Lammermoor* (1818), ch. I.

skill in that valuable accomplishment, & of drawing more closely the bonds of [74] that regard with which we are, &c." After breakfast I inquired my way to Gibbon's house & was easily admitted to the garden. The summerhouse is removed but the floor ⟨is⟩ of it is still there, where the History was written & finished. I stood upon it & looked forth upon the noble landscape of which he speaks so proudly. I plucked a leaf of the limetree he planted, & of the acacia — successors ⟨no doubt⟩ of those under which he walked. I have seen however many landscapes as pleasant & more striking.

At 10 o'clock we took the steamboat for Geneva & sailed up lake Leman. The passage was very long — seven hours — for the wind was ahead, & the engine not very powerful. We touched at Coppet. The lake is most beautiful near Geneva. It was [75] not clear enough to see Mont Blanc or else it was not visible. Mount Varens & Monte Rosa were seen.

Geneva, 16 June. Here am I in the stern old town[,] the resort of such various minds [—] of Calvin, of Rousseau, of Gibbon, of Voltaire, of De Stael, of Byron [—] on the blue Rhone by the placid Lake Leman. Mont Blanc towers above the Alps on the east sublimely with his three summits; Jura on the west is marking the line of France, & the lake lies in beauty before me. Every body is polite.

Yesterday to oblige my companions & protesting all the way upon the unworthiness of his memory I went to Ferney to the chateau, the saloon, the bed chamber, the gardens of Voltaire, the king of the scorners. His rooms were modest & pleasing & hung with portraits of his friends. Franklin & Washington were there. [76] The view of the lake & mountains commanded by the lawn behind the chateau is superior to that of Gibbon's garden at Lausanne. The old porter showed us some pictures belonging to his old master & told a story that did full justice to his bad name. Yet it would be a sin against faith & philosophy to exclude Voltaire from toleration. He did his work as the bustard & tarantula do theirs.

We had a fine ride home, so royally towers up Mont Blanc with his white triple top. On the way we passed the stone which

marks the boundary of France which made Dr S[tewardson] crow
like chanticleer, — and the grass he thought greener.

Visited the music box manufactory & the watch-maker's. The
music man offered to make a box with two airs of Beethoven for
50 francs, to be received by me in Paris.

Prices of the best watches that [77] they can make are 500 francs.
Of the second class without a compensation but esteemed as good
for all ordinary purposes, 300 francs. S. bought one for 275 the
difference of value being in the weight of the case. They speak of
smuggling with perfect simplicity & offer to send you the watch to
Paris (via smuggler, that is) for a few francs.

Through the Misses Bridgens' acquaintance in Mr Wolf's family I was carried away to hear M. Gissot a very worthy Calvinist
who has been ejected from the National Church. His exercise was a
catechism & exhortation of a large class of children. Then I was introduced to Mr Cordis & others of their brethren[,] very worthy
men they seemed. I spent the day at the house of Mr Wolf. The
daughter told me that "if I was, as I said, a seeker, she thought I
ought to make it a point of duty to stop longer at Geneva," & offered
in very pretty broken English "to intrude me to the minister [78]
who bégun the exercise." She had learned English because her house
was destined to receive boarders, &c, &c.

I owed them all much kindness but if I had known any thing
I should have made acquaintance with M. Cheneviere first. After
all this kindness it would have been great violence to have gone away
to him.

The Established Church of Geneva is now Unitarian & the three
Calvinistic clergymen of the city are ejected.[63]

[79] Left Geneva in the Diligence for Paris Monday morning at 4
o'clock & presently crossed the line of France & began the ascent of

[63] The quarrel between Calvinists and Unitarians at Geneva had been reported
at length in the religious magazines; see especially "Historical Notices of Geneva,"
The Christian Examiner, IV (Jan.–Feb. 1827), 37–61; "Recent Events in Geneva,"
ibid., XI (Nov. 1831), 225–240; "Theological Essays of M. Chenevière," *ibid.*, XII
(March 1832), 39–47; and "M. Chenevière on the Use of Reason," *ibid.*, XV
(Nov. 1833), 137–153. Chenevière was the spokesman for the Unitarians. The central Calvinists were M. Malan, M. Gaussen, M. Cellérier the elder, and M. Gissot.

Mount Jura. As we rose toward the top what noble pictures appeared on the Swiss side. The Alps, the Alps, & Mont Blanc in all his breadth towering up so cold & white & dim towards heaven all uninhabitable & almost inaccessible. Yet more than Saussure [64] have reached the top.

France France. It is not only a change of name [—] the cities, the language, the faces, the manners have undergone a wonderful change in three or four days. The running fight we have kept up so long with the fierté of postillions & ⟨v⟩padroni in Italy is over & all men are complaisant. The face of the country is remarkable[,] not quite a plain but a vast undulating [80] champaign without a hill, and all planted like the Connecticutt intervales. No fences,[n] the fields full of working women. We rode in the Coupée of a Diligence by night & by day, through [65]   for three days & a half & arrived in Paris at noon Thursday[.]

Paris, 20 June. My companions who have been in the belle ville before, & wished it to strike me as it ought, are scarce content with my qualified admiration. Certainly [66] the eye is satisfied on entering the city with the unquestionable tokens of a vast, rich, old capital.

We crossed the Seine by the Pont Neuf & I was glad to see my old acquaintance Henry IV very respectably mounted in bronze on his own bridge but the saucy faction [n] [81] of the day has thrust a tricolor flag into his bronze hand as into a doll's & in spite of decency the stout old monarch is thus obliged to take his part in the whirligig politics of his city. Fie! Louis Philippe.

We were presently lodged in the Hotel Montmorenci on the Boulevard Mont Martre. I have wandered round the city but I am not well pleased. I have seen so much in five months that the magnificence of Paris will not take my eye today. The gardens of the

[64] Horace Bénédict de Saussure (1740–1799), eminent Swiss naturalist, professor of philosophy at Geneva, author of *Voyages dans les Alpes*, 4 vols. (1796), climbed Mont Blanc in 1788.

[65] Emerson left a long space here to be filled in later with his itinerary.

[66] "Certainly . . . Louis Philippe." is a repetition with slight variations of the use-marked entry on p. 188 above. The inclusion of the revised version here supplies continuity of time to the journal record.

Louvre looked pinched & the wind blew dust in my eyes and ⟨after a short time⟩ ↑before I got into the Champs Elysees↓ I turned about & flatly refused to go farther. I was sorry to find that in leaving Italy I had left forever that air of antiquity & history which her towns possess & in coming hither had come to a loud modern New York of a place.

[82] I am very glad to find here my cousin Ralph Emerson [67] who received me most cordially & has aided me much in making my temporary establishment. It were very ungrateful in a stranger to be discontented with Paris, for it is the most hospitable of cities. The foreigner has only to present his passport at any public institution & the doors are thrown wide to him. I have been to the Sorbonne where the first scientific men in France lecture at stated hours every day & the doors are open to all. I have heard Jouffroy, Thenard, Gay Lussac[.] [68]

Then the College Royale de France is a similar institution on the same liberal foundation. So with the College du Droit & the Amphitheatre of the Garden of Plants[.]

I have been to the Louvre where are certainly some firstrate pictures. [83] Leonardo da Vinci has more pictures here than in any other gallery & I like them well despite of the identity of the features which peep out of men & women. I have seen the same face in his pictures I think six or seven times. Murillo I see almost for the first time with great pleasure.

[84] July. It is a pleasant thing to walk along the Boulevards & see how men live in Paris. One man has live snakes crawling about him & sells soap & essences. Another sells books which lie upon the ground. Another under my window all day offers a gold chain. Half a dozen walk up & down with some dozen walking sticks under the

---

[67] Ralph Emerson, brother of George Barrell Emerson, lived in Puerto Rico, then in France after 1831, and then in California. He was a second cousin.

[68] "Gay Lussac" is inserted in faint pencil into a part of the space left open for later completion. Théodore Jouffroy was lecturing in the second semester, 1833, at the Sorbonne on the Greek language and philosophy; Louis Jacques Thénard and Joseph-Louis Gay-Lussac were giving their lectures on chemistry at the Jardin des Plantes.

arm. A little further, one sells cane tassels at 5 sous. Here sits Boots brandishing his brush at every dirty shoe. Then you pass several tubs of gold fish. Then a man sitting at his table cleaning gold & silver spoons with emery & haranguing the passengers on its virtues. Then a person who cuts profiles with scissors "Shall be happy to take yours, Sir." Then a table of card puppets which are made to crawl. Then a hand organ. Then a wooden figure called [69]
which can put an apple in its mouth whenever [n] [85] a child buys a plum. Then a flower merchant. Then a bird-shop with 20 parrots, 4 swans, hawks, & nightingales. Then the show of the boy with four legs &c &c without end. All these are the mere boutiques on the sidewalk, moved about from place to place as the sun or rain or the crowd may lead them.[70]

4 July. Dined today at Lointier's with Gen Lafayette & nearly one hundred Americans. I sought an opportunity of paying my respects to the hero, & inquiring after his health. His speech was as happy as usual. A certain Lieut. Levi   did what he could to mar the day.[71]

13 July.[72] I carried my ticket from Mr Warden [73] to the Cabinet of Natural History in the Garden of Plants. How much finer things are in composition than alone. 'Tis wise in man to make Cabinets. When I was [86] come into the Ornithological Chambers, I wished I had come only there. The fancy-coloured vests of these elegant

[69] Emerson left a space here to be filled in with the French word if it occurred to him.

[70] "It is a pleasant . . . lead them." is an expanded and revised version of an entry written originally in the notebook France and England. The latter notebook, though much of it covers the period immediately following that included in the journal Italy and France, has some notes on the French visit which were later revised and transferred. Though the two versions are similar, both are printed in order to show the slight but significant variations in style. See pp. 406–407 below.

[71] See John T. Morse, *Life and Letters of Oliver Wendell Holmes*, 2 vols. (Boston, c. 1896), I, 105, for the episode.

[72] The entry for this date is a revised and expanded version of a similar entry in the notebook France and England. See pp. 405–406 below. Much of the entry was later used in a lecture, "The Uses of Natural History." (See especially *Lectures*, I, 7–10).

[73] David Bailie Warden (1778–1845), an Irishman who became an American citizen, was for forty years American consul in Paris, constantly promoting knowledge of America among the French and of France among American travellers.

beings make me as pensive as the hues & forms of a cabinet of shells, formerly. It is a beautiful collection & makes the visiter as calm & genial as a bridegroom. The limits of the possible are enlarged, & the real is stranger than the imaginary. Some of the birds have a fabulous beauty. One parrot of a fellow, called *Psittacus erythropterus* from New Holland, deserves as special mention as a picture of Raphael in a Gallery. He is the beau of all birds. Then the hummingbirds little & gay. Least of all is the Trochilus Niger. I have seen beetles larger. The *Trochilus pella* hath such a neck of gold & silver & fire! Trochilus Delalandi from Brazil is a glorious little tot — la mouche magnifique.

[87] Among the birds of Paradise I remarked the Manucode or P. regia from New Guinea, the Paradisaea Apoda,[n] & P. rubra. Forget not the Veuve à epaulettes or Emberiza longicauda, black with fine shoulder knots; nor the Ampelis cotinga nor the Phasianus Argus a peacock looking pheasant; nor the Trogon pavoninus called also Couroncou pavonin.

I saw black swans & white peacocks, the ibis the sacred & the rosy; the flamingo, with a neck like a snake, the Toucan rightly called *rhinoceros*; & a vulture whom to meet in the wilderness would make your flesh quiver[,] so like an executioner he looked.

In the other rooms I saw amber ⟨with⟩ containing perfect musquitoes, grand blocks of quartz, native gold in all its forms of crystallization, threads, plates, crystals, dust; & silver [88] black as from fire. Ah said I this is philanthropy, wisdom, taste[74] — to form a Cabinet of natural history. Many students were there with grammar & note book & a class of boys with their tutor from some school. Here we are impressed with the inexhaustible riches of nature. The Universe is a more amazing puzzle than ever as you glance along this bewildering series of animated forms, — the hazy butterflies, the carved shells, the birds, beasts, fishes, insects, snakes, — & the upheaving principle of life everywhere incipient in the very rock aping organized forms. Not a form so grotesque, so savage, nor so beautiful

---

[74] Beneath the ink entry "this is philanthropy, wisdom, taste —" are the words in faint pencil: "Le moment où je parle est deja loin de moi". See the *Œuvres complètes de Boileau*, 4 vols. (Paris, 1872), II, 163, Épitre III, à M. Arnauld, Docteur de Sorbonne. The phrase Boileau ascribes to Persius, *Satires*, V, 153: "hoc quod loquor inde est" — "that of which I speak is already hence" (Ed.).

but is an expression of some property inherent in man the observer, — an occult relation between the very scorpions [89] and man. I feel the centipede in me — cayman, carp, eagle, & fox. I am moved by strange sympathies, I say continually "I will be a naturalist."

There's a good collection of skulls in the Comparative anatomy chambers. The best skull seemed to be English. The skeleton of the Balena looks like the frame of a schooner turned upside down.

The Garden itself is admirably arranged. They have attempted to classify all the plants *in the ground*,[n] to put together, that is, as nearly as may be the conspicuous plants of each class on Jussieu's system.[75]

Walk down the alleys of this flower garden & you come to the enclosures of the animals where almost all that Adam ⟨No⟩ named or Noah preserved are represented. Here are several lions, two great elephants walking out in open day, [90] a camelopard 17 feet high, the bison, the rhinoceros, & so forth [—] all manner of four footed things in air & sunshine, in the shades of a pleasant garden, where all people French & English may come & see without money. By the way, there is a caricature in the printshops representing the arrival of the giraffe in Paris, exclaiming to the mob "Messieurs, il n'y a qu'⟨n⟩un bete de plus." It is very pleasant to walk in this garden.

As I went out, I noticed a placard posted on the gates giving notice that M. Jussieu would next Sunday give a public herborisation, that is, make a⟨n⟩ botanical excursion into the country & inviting all & sundry to accompany him.

[91] 15 July.[76] I have just returned from Pere le Chaise. It well deserves a visit & does honour to the French. But they are a vain nation. The tombstones have a beseeching importunate vanity and

---

[75] Antoine Laurent de Jussieu (1748–1836), Professor of Rural Botany at the Museum of Natural History, developed the natural system of plant classification. His son Adrien L. H. de Jussieu (1797–1853) succeeded him in 1826 and, as Emerson noted, conducted public botanical excursions in the summer of 1833.

[76] The following two paragraphs through "*Francais*" on p. [92] are a revision with slight changes of earlier notes on the same date entered in the notebook France and England. The earlier version added further small notes on epitaphs not included here. See pp. 408–409 below.

remind you of advertisements. But many are affecting. One which
was of dark slate stone had only this inscription, 'Mon Pere.' I prefer
the "Ci git" to the "Ici repose" as the beginning of the inscriptions
but take the cemetery through I thought the classics rather carried
the day. One ⟨inscription⟩ epitaph was so singular, or so singular
to be read by *me*, that I wrote it off.

"Ici repose Auguste Charles Collignon mort plein de confiance
dans la bonte de Dieu à l'age de 68 ans et 4 mois le 15 Avril 1830.
Il aima et chercha à faire du bien et mena une vie douce et heureuse,
en suivant autant qu'il put, la morale et [92] les lecons des essais de
Montaigne et des Fables de la Fontaine." — I notice that, universally, the French write as in the above, "*Here lies Augustus, &c.*"
& we write, "*Here lies the body of, &c*" [n] a more important distinction than *roi de France* & *roi des Francais*.

I live at *pension* with Professor Heari at the corner of Rue
Neuve Vivienne directly over the entrance of the Passage aux Panorames. If I had companions in the City it would be something better
to live in the Café & Restaurant. These public rooms are splendidly
prepared for travellers & full of company & of newspapers.

This Passage aux Panorames was the first Arcade built in Paris
& was built by an American Mr Thayer. There are now probably
fifty of these passages in the city. And few things give more the
character of magnificence [n] [93] to the city than the suite of these
passages about the Palais Royal.

Notre Dame is a fine church outside but the interior quite naked
& beggarly. In general, the churches are very mean inside.

I went into the Morgue where they expose for 24 hours the
bodies of persons who have been drowned or died in the streets,
that they may be claimed by their friends. There were three corpses
thus exposed, & every day there are some.

Young men are very fond of Paris, partly, no doubt, because
of the perfect freedom — freedom from observation as well as interference, — in which each one walks after the sight of his own
eyes; & partly because the extent & variety of objects offers an unceasing entertainment. So long as a man has francs in his pocket he
needs consult neither time nor place nor other men's convenience;
wherever in the vast city he is, he is within a stone's throw of a

patissier, a cafe, a restaurant, [94] a public garden, a theatre & may enter when he will. If he wish to go [to] the Thuilleries, perhaps two miles off, let him stop a few minutes at the window of a printshop or a bookstall, of which there are hundreds & thousands, and an Omnibus is sure to pass in the direction in which he would go, & for six sous he rides two or three miles. Then the streets swarm with Cabinets de Lecture where you find all the journals & all the new books. I spend many hours at Galignani's [77] & lately at the English Reading Room in the Rue Neuve Augustine where they advertise that they receive 400 journals in all languages & have moreover a very large library.

Lastly the evening need never hang heavy on the stranger's hands, such ample provision is made here for what the newspapers call "nos besoins recreatifs." ↑More than↓ twenty [n] theatres are blazing with light & echoing with fine music every night [95] from the Academie Royale de la Musique, which is the French Opera, down to the Children's Drama; not to mention concerts, gardens, & shows innumerable.

The Theatre is the passion of the French & the taste & splendour of their dramatic exhibitions can hardly be exceeded. The Journal in speaking of the opera last night, declares that "Mme D. was received by the dilettanti of Paris with not less joy than the lost soul by the angels in heaven." I saw the Opera Gustave [78] performed the other night & have seen nothing anywhere that could compare with the brilliancy of their scenic decoration. The moonlight scene resembled nothing but Nature's; ⟨A⟩and as for the masked ball, I think there never was a real fancy-ball that equalled the effect of this.

At the Theatre Francais where Talma played & Madame Mars plays I heard Delavigne's new piece Enfans d'Edouard excellently performed; for [96] although Madame Mars speaks French beautifully & has the manners of a princess yet she scarcely excels the acting of the less famous performers who support her. Each was perfect in his part.

---

[77] A well-known reading room operated by the publishers John and William Galignani.

[78] Rusk suggests that the opera was *Gustave III, ou le bal masqué*, a work by Auber performed in this year.

Paris is an expensive place. Rents are very high. All Frenchmen in all quarters of their dispersion never lose the hope of coming hither to spend their earnings, and all the men of pleasure in all the nations come hither, which fact explains the existence of ⟨these⟩ ↑so many↓ dazzling shops full of most costly ⟨t⟩articles of luxury. Indeed it is very hard for a stranger to walk with eyes forward ten yards in any part of the city.

I have been to the Faubourg St. Martin to hear the Abbe Chatel[,] the founder of the Eglise Catholique Francaise.[79] It is a singular institution which he calls his church with newly invented dresses for the priests & martial music performed by a large ⟨choir⟩ orchestra, relieved ⁿ [97] by interludes of a piano with vocal music. His discourse was far better than I could expect from these preliminaries.

Sometimes he is eloquent. He is a Unitarian but more radical than any body in America who takes that name.

I was interested in his enterprize for there is always something pathetic in a new church struggling for sympathy & support. He takes upon himself the whole pecuniary responsibilities of the undertaking, & for his Chapel in the Rue St Honoré pays an annual rent of 40,000 francs. He gave notice of a grand funeral fête which is to be solemnized on the anniversary of the Three Days at that Chapel.

In the printshops they have a figure of the Abbe Chatel on the same picture with Pere Enfant, & Le Templier.[80]

I went this evening into Frascati's[,] long the most noted of the gambling houses or hells of Paris, & which a gentleman had promised to show me. This establishment is in a very [98] handsome house on the Rue Richelieu.

Several servants in ⟨L⟩livery were waiting in the hall who took our hats on entering, & we passed at once into ⟨the⟩a suite of rooms in all of which play was going on. The most perfect decorum & civility prevailed[;] the table was covered with little piles of Napoleons which seemed to change masters very rapidly but scarce a word

[79] Ferdinand Toussaint François Chatel (1795–1857), French religious reformer and author of *Profession de foi de l'église catholique française* (1831).

[80] Emerson may have felt it odd to connect a socialist with a protestant reformer if his "Enfant" is a version of Le Père Enfantin (1796–1864), socialist leader of the Saint Simonists. "Le Templier" is unidentified.

was spoken. Servants carry about lemonade, &c but no heating liquor. The house, I was told, is always one party in the game. Several women were present, but many of the company seemed to be mere spectators like ourselves. After walking round the tables, we returned to the hall, gave the servant a franc for our hats, & departed. Frascati has grown very rich.

Go to the Champs Elysées after sunset & see the manifold show. An orchestra, a roundabout, a tumbler, sugar-plum-gambling-tables, harpers, dancers, [99] and an army of loungers.

I went to the Mazarine Library, & Mr Warden kindly introduced me to the seance of the Class of Science in the Institute, & pointed out to me the conspicuous men. I saw Biot, Arago, Gay Lussac, Jouffroy, & others.[81] Several Memoirs were read & some debate ensued thereon.

Visited St Cloud[.]

[100]–[101] [blank]

[102] 18 July. Left Paris in the Diligence for Boulogne. Rode all night through St Denis, Moiselles, Beauvais, breakfasted at Abbeville, passed thro' Montreuil[,] Samur & reached Boulogne about sunset. At Abbeville we picked up Signore Alessandro [82]   an Italian emigrant[.]

At Boulogne on Saturday Morn 19th[20] took the steam-boat for London. After a rough passage of 20 hours we ⟨reached⟩ arrived at London & landed at the Tower Stairs.

We know London so well in books & pictures & maps & traditions that I saw nothing surprizing in this passage up the Thames. A noble navigable stream lined on each side by a highly cultivated country, full of all manner of good buildings. Then Greenwich &

[81] Jean Baptiste Biot (1774–1862), celebrated astronomer and natural philosopher, was professor of physical astronomy. Domenique-François Arago (1786–1853) had carried on well-known geodesical measurements of the meridian in 1806 with Biot and had founded the periodical *Annales de Chemie et de Physique* (1816). For the other scientists see p. 197 above.
[82] Space is left after the name, no doubt so that the last name of the Italian emigrant could be added if remembered.

Deptford, hospital, docks, [103] arsenals, fleets of shipping, & then the mighty metropolis itself, old, vast, & still. Scarce any body was in the streets. It was about 7 o'clock Sunday Morning & we met few persons until we reached St Paul's. A porter carried our baggage, & we walked through Cheapside, Newgate St., High Holborn, and found lodgings (according to the direction of my friend in Paris) at Mrs ⟨C⟩Fowler's No 63 Russell Square. It was an extreme pleasure to hear English spoken in the streets; to understand all the words of Children at play, & to find that we must not any longer express aloud our opinion of every person we met, as in France & Italy we had been wont to do.

[104]–[105] [blank]

[106][83]

[107]–[112] [blank]

[113][84] Milan. 96 or 97000 Austrian troops in Lombardy || ... || in Bologna & Milan. 16 months to get a passport. — Cathedral built by Andrea Commodia in 1386. 7000 statues great & small when finished. 2000 lacking, all marble[;] it would take a mountain of gold but that the founder left a quarry of marble. 42 artists employed. glory of the interior[?] each window divided in 12 each 1 ft wide[?] || ... || 12 panes high each 2 ft & arching over all|| ... || Great advantage of an old city in giving good houses to the humblest inhabitants. Trattoria del Marino.

[114][85] ⟨Pd. boatmen 5 ½ swanz.⟩
Pd for Wall to padrone at Venice 12 ½ franks
At Milan 1 ½ swanziger
At Domo d'Ossole ⟨recd.⟩ pd. 1.4 f

---

[83] The page is occupied by a detailed pencil sketch of a medieval castle with two towers, wall, and moat through which leads what may be an entrance like the Traitor's Gate in the Tower of London.

[84] The entry is in almost indistinguishable pencil writing, apparently partial notes on the Milan cathedral, reworked later for the ink entry on p. 190 above.

[85] All the entries through p. [118] are in pencil.

At ⟨Domo d Ossole⟩ ↑Simplon↓ recd 7.10 f.s.
Briga pd for Misses B[ridgen] 2.10
      recd   3.
      pd to postillion   ⟨4.4⟩ 5.
At Lago Maggiore   3.5

[June] 13. Recd. of Miss B. .50 f.
↑Sion 1 f.↓
St Maurice for the ladies at the hotel 3. f
Postillion   1 f 2
Porter for three   2 f 10
Postillion
At Simplon   5.
      Chambermaid   .10

       3
     18   15

      6.5

[115][86]

Milan some deficit 4 f.
Milan   1 ½ swanziger
surpoids —   — 11.10
on the road recd & pd. 1 swanz
Lago Maggiore recd 4 swanz. &
pd for supper all but 7 sold. — waiter
At Domo d'Ossola pd. 1 f. 5s.
— do — surpoids
[At Simplon recd f.10
At Simplon pd 5.
    chambermaid ⟨10⟩0.10
At Briga pd   2.10
[— — recd   3.
 — — pd postillion   5.00

[86] A penciled sketch of a chair with a curved back is centered at the top of the page, above and overlapping the first line of the continued accounts.

206

Sion	1.
St Maurice	3 f
↑Postillion↓	
Postillion	1.2
⟨At Simplon⟩	

[116]

At Lausanne		
postillion		
porter	0.33	
custode Gibbon	.⟨05⟩	10
Hotel	8.	
↑Cameriere↓ ⟨Valet⟩	.26	
Valet de place	1.	
Coach & porter	3.8	
Coach to Preleveque	5.	

[117] [blank]

[118]   For London

———

Mrs Fowler's, 63 Russell Square, recommended by Mr Webb
of Albany.

———

Mrs Wright   12 Adam St
                        Adelphi [87]

———

[inside back cover]
          Son caduto qui per terra,
          Sol del vin la causa fu,
                    La sua virtù
                    E la mia rovina,
                    Cara Bettina
                    Ajutami tu.

———

[87] After the short rule below "Adelphi" are traces of erased pencil jottings, possibly further accounts or addresses.

John Webb[,] James & Co
    Leghorn
    for
       H. Miles
             Florence
George [88] Wiles & Co
Plough Court Lombard St.
William Allen

10 Howland St. Fitzroy Square

[88] "George Wiles . . . Fitzroy Square" is in pencil. At the left of "Plough . . . Allen" is a heavy pencil bracket.

Scotland and England

1833

Emerson numbered this volume as the fourth of his travel journals, though it is like the other three only in being pocket-size. It is home-made rather than purchased and was used briefly in 1832 (January through March) for miscellaneous notes and accounts before the European voyage. During the voyage (February and March) it was used for accounts. Though Emerson inscribed it "Journal in Europe 1833" it covers only a part of his visit to Scotland and England, from August 23 through August 30, 1833.

The manuscript is made up of a single gathering of 17 sheets folded folio and sewed from the outside spine into the center fold. Leaves 26 and 27 are raggedly torn out, leaving only 64 pages in this gathering. The leaves may have been blank since no writing is visible on the irregular stubs. Pages measure 10 x 15.6 cm and are unnumbered. The paper in the regular gathering is faintly ruled. Pagination is supplied by the editors.

Besides the 64 pages of the regular gathering the notebook contains 2 loose inserts, only one of which is in Emerson's hand. Between pages 16 and 17 is a gathering of 8 pages made from 2 sheets of unruled paper irregularly folded folio, and one slipped into the other. The pages measure approximately 9.8 x 15.3 cm apiece and are numbered in ink by Emerson from 1 to 8, though physically, because he apparently skipped a leaf in writing, then came back to fill in the 2 empty pages, and was thus forced to revise his numbering to fit the facts, the numbers run 1, 2, 3, 5, 6, 4, 7, and 8. The inserted pages are indicated in the present text by subscript letters (a, b, c, d, e, f, g, h) added to page 17, the number given to the page which they should follow in chronological order.

A second insert, not in Emerson's hand and therefore not printed here, is tucked sideways between pages 42 and 43. This scrap of paper is a financial memorandum from Emerson's Paris bankers, Welles and Company, recording his drafts and payments in English and French currency on July 24, 26, and 30, 1833. It measures 12.1 x 7 cm with somewhat irregular edges.

The journal is only partially filled. Pages now numbered 6, 13, 14, 16, 31, 33, 36, 37, 45, 49, 50, 53, 54, 55, and 58 are blank. A thin brown-paper wrapper, once sewed to the gathering but now attached by modern transparent tape, serves as a cover; it may have been added at a later date since the front and back pages of the volume seem discolored by use.

[front cover]   No. 4

Journal in Europe 1833

[1] Jan., 1832.

"Nothing can work me mischief except myself." St. Bernard.[1]

'You cannot eat your cake & have it.'[2] You cannot have the pleasures of ⟨temper⟩gluttony and the pleasures of abstinence.

> [3] Left N.Y. at 4 P.M. 10 Nov.
> Left Providence at 11 h. 20 m. A.M.
> Left Canton at 3 h. 10 m. P M
> Arrived at Boston 3 h. 42 m P M
> Arrived at 276 Washn St at 4 P.M.

[2]   No chronic tortures racked his aged limb
            For luxury & sloth had nourished none for him [4]

Cruelty & Sensuality are brothers.[5]

⟨Catania 97[?]⟩
Cornaro satisfied himself with 12 oz. solid food & 14 oz. wine per day.

---

[1] *Pious Breathings* . . . , trans. Stanhope, 1818, p. 401. See also p. 86 above and *JMN*, III, 339, n. 3.

[2] The proverb is given in approximately this wording in Anthony Ashley Cooper, Third Earl of Shaftesbury, *Characteristicks of Men, Manners, Opinions, Times*, 3 vols. (London, 1711), I, 130. George Herbert gives it as a question ("Couldst thou both eat thy cake and have it?") in "The Size."

[3] The rest of this page and p. [2] through "none for him" is in pencil. The brief itinerary was for 1834.

[4] William Cullen Bryant: "The Old Man's Funeral," st. 6, ll. 5–6. Emerson probably remembered these lines from the volume he had recommended to Ellen: Emily Taylor's *Sabbath Recreations; or, Select poetry of a religious kind, chiefly taken from the works of modern poets* (Boston, 1829), p. 102. This edition is still in Emerson's library with notes in Ellen Tucker's hand.

[5] The aphorism was, perhaps, created by analogy with Montaigne's chapter title, "Cowardice the Mother of Cruelty" (ch. 27) and his further remark (*Essays*, 1700, II, 630) that "Abstinency is the sister of Constancy."

He passed his 100th year. H. Daggett, his editor, finds ⟨12⟩ less than 12 oz. vegetable food, sufficient.[6]

28 March, 1832. I consume 15 oz solid food & ⟨3⟨0⟩2⟩ ↑32↓ oz. liquid./ 29th 13 oz.

1 sized blue plate	13 ½ oz
cut glass tumbler	9 ½ oz
containing water	6 ½ oz
1 Jamieson	½ oz
1 roll	5 ½ oz
baker's biscuit	

[3] St John's Ch[urch]. created by the Gr. Master La Cassiera[,] consecrated by Lodovico Torres.[7]

[8 Oct. 1833.]

My God who dost animate & uphold us always on the sea & on land, in the fields, in cities & in lonely places, in our homes & among strangers[,] I thank thee that thou hast enlightened & comforted & protected me to this hour. Continue to me thy guard & blessing. May I ⟨to⟩ resist the evil that is without by the good that is within. May I rejoice evermore in the consciousness that it is by Thee I live. May I rejoice in the Divine Power & be humble. O that I might show forth thy gift to me by purity, by love, by unshrinking industry & unsinking hope & by unconquerable courage. May I be more thine, & so more truly myself every day I live. —

8 Oct. 1833.

[4] "Quant a ce qui me concerne, je me contente de la conviction que je serai eternellement sous la garde du Supreme Remunerateur, qu'une sainte et juste Providence veillera sur moi dans l'autre monde, comme elle l'a fait dans celui ci, et que ma véritable félicité consiste dans la beauté et la perfection de mon ame." Socrates.

Mendelsohn's Phedon.[8]

[6] Luigi Cornaro (c. 1463–1566?), a Venetian noted for his diet and longevity. Emerson owned *An Abridgment of the Writings of Lewis Cornaro, a nobleman of Venice, on Health and Long Life*, ed. Herman Daggett (Andover, Mass., 1824).

[7] "St John's . . . Torres." is in pencil.

[8] Moses Mendelssohn, *Phédon, ou entretiens sur la spiritualité et l'immortalité de l'ame*, trans. M. Junker (Paris, 1772), pp. 290–291, slightly misquoted.

'suavissima vita indies sentire se fieri meliorem'.[9]

[5] He that promiseth runs in debt.[10]
⟨But know thyself to be⟩
"But know thyself a man, & be a god."
                              an inscription ⟨Athens⟩within a gate of Athens [11]
'Working in thy calling is half praying.'
"Would you be revenged on your enemy? live as you ought, & you have done it to purpose."

A cheerful look & forgiveness is the best revenge of an affront.[12]

Never assume. Be genuine. Sept. 1832.[13]

Stand by & let reason argue for you.[14]

---

[6] [blank]

[7] My children, said my Grandfather, you will never see any thing worse than yourselves.[15]

[9] Francis Bacon, *The Advancement of Learning*, in *The Works*, 1824, I, 62. The phrase may be translated as "the sweetest life, to feel himself each day a better man than he was the day before." (*The Works of Francis Bacon*, ed. Spedding et al., 1860–1864, VI, 165.) The passage is based on Xenophon, *Memorabilia*, I, VI, 9.

[10] Knox, *Elegant Extracts . . . in Prose*, 1797, II, 1035. See also Fielding, *Select Proverbs . . .* , 1825, p. 100 and Ray, *English Proverbs . . .* , 1818, p. 19.

[11] Plutarch, "Life of Pompey," *Lives*, trans. John and William Langhorne, 8 vols. (Philadelphia, 1822), V, 113. Emerson had seven volumes of this eight-volume set in his library.

[12] Apparently Emerson went back to Journal Q to recopy these proverbs which he had first put down on May 12, 1832 (see p. 17 above). All three proverbs come from Knox, *Elegant Extracts . . . in Prose*, 1797: II, 1030; II, 1033; and II, 1036.

[13] Looking back at his journal for late August and September, 1832, Emerson apparently reread in Q not only proverbs but his extensive comments on the true or genuine man, on the vice of hypocrisy, and on the folly of the artificial (see pp. 37–38 and 42–45 above).

[14] R. H. Wilde's phrase concerning William Lowndes of South Carolina, slightly modified. Lowndes served Emerson as a notable exhibit of the genuine man. See Sermon 164 (*YES*, p. 186) and p. 38 above.

[15] Edward Emerson, in *J*, III, 234n, noted that the "Grandfather" might refer to William Emerson of Concord, his father Joseph Emerson of Malden, or possibly John Haskins of Boston. It is possible that Dr. Ezra Ripley of Concord as a step-grandfather might also suit. The sentence is used in "Spiritual Laws," *W*, II, 148.

[8] 21 Feb. [1833] recd of S. P. Holbrook   116 00

> ounce of Sicily   2.46 = 30 ↑tarins↓ 600 ↑gr[ains]↓
> ducat of Naples   .80 = 10 carlins = 240 gr [16]

> Pd S. P. H.   38   38
>   Muleteers   9.75   975
> Supposed to have pd.
> S[amuel]. Kettell at Syra-
>   cuse   15
>   ───────
>   62 75
> Pd S. P. H. at Catania   38.
>   ───────
>   100.75
>   116.
>   ───────
>   1⟨6⟩5.⟨7⟩25

[9] 1833
Malta

15 Feb.	Pd Capt Ellis for board 15 days [17]	
	at 2 scudes	10.40
”	Washerwoman for 30 pieces	.37 ½
	Mr Eynaud for 5 passports	10.00
”	black cap	1.50
	Armoury 12, St John's 12, Coach 62	.87
	boat 5 times	.10
	hairdresser 12, pocket inkstand .50	62
	Vases & Candlesticks. Malta stone	2 15
	Cesarii.	7 00
	chambermaid 25 do. 25	50
	Waiter 50 figs 3	53

---

[16] "ounce . . . 240 gr" is in pencil.
[17] The board payment to Captain Cornelius Ellis of the brig *Jasper* was for the days spent in quarantine at Malta.

[February] 22 Custom house Syracuse   *75*
               Carita 6d
               [Due me at this date from S Kettell
               2.25; from ↑me to↓ S. P. Holbrook
               ⟨14.23⟩11.90   ⟨14.23⟩11 90
               Due ↑from↓ Mr H ⟨from⟩ to me   6.30
               _____

               R. W. E. indebted to S. P. H.   ⟨7.73⟩5.60]

               Joint expenses of the party at
               Vickary's in Malta 1 week $48.16
               My share   ⟨|| ... ||⟩9 63
               postage 12, boat 12 Dr
               Consul 33

[10] 1833. Malta
Feb. 21.   For pair candlesticks of Malta stone
                   3 s[cudi].
               1 pr. vases 4 s[cudi]. & packing   2.12
               Passage from Malta to Syracuse   6.00
               At St John's Church; boat 16   ⟨ 7⟩53
↑Syracuse↓
[February] 26 Pd S. P. Holbrook   38.00
               At M. di Casal's 2 sc[udi] 37
                   Capuchins 25 Dionys[ius] 30
                   Museum 24 [18]

Catania
[February] 29 Pd Muleteers ↑Recd of↓ S. Kettell .50 [19]   9⟨|| ... ||⟩75
               At Cathedral 12 ½
               for 3 passports 3 taris   25
               for guide to Sicily   1 25

_____

[18] "At . . . Museum 24" is in pencil. The note covers sightseeing fees paid February 24 on a visit to the beautiful gardens of the Marquis di Casal, the Capuchins, and other points of interest in Syracuse. See pp. 125–128 above.

[19] "Recd of" is written above the line and linked to "S. Kettell .50" by an irregular semicircle.

March 2	Pd. S. P. Holbrook	38 00
	Locanda	4 30
	buckle .9 waiter 24	33
	beggars 24 waiters 16	40
Messina		
	carozza 2. & comp 38 & boy 6	2 43
	beggars .12 Police knaves 1.00	1 12
	vest 2.50 barber & soap 20	2 70

By settlement with S P Holbrook this
date it appears that I owe him $34.79 & I
owe S. Kettell [20]

[11] ↑Messina	Brought from home cash 48.00↓	
March 5	recd of S. P. H.	34.79
	in purse	82.79
⟨All thine are mine.⟩		16.80
↑to this date↓ expended.		65 99

6 March. I owe S. P H
Pd S. P. H. $34 64
    remaining due .15
Pd S Kettell   1 92
    He owes me .48
Pd passage in steam boat   23.

Recd., of Mr Payson [21] 100 Sicily dollars.

Expenses in Palermo   say   8 00

Naples.

---

[20] A single bracket encloses "By settlement . . . Kettell" at the left margin, and
a half line beyond "Kettell" is left open for later entry of an accurate reckoning.
    [21] John L. Payson was the American consul at Messina.

March 13.	Pd. Crocelle [22]	2 16
	pr shoes	88
[March] 18.	Pd circ. lib 1.00 &	
	⟨depos[ited] 2.00⟩	⟨3⟩1.00
[March] 21.	Pd guide at Pompeii	1 00
	Pd for a dinner 8 grains!	
	for mending watch	.80
[March] 23.	Pd Hermit for the party	32
	↑S. P. H. pd 16↓	
	basketer on mountain	16

↑S. K[ettell]. pd. 16↓

	Pd Salvatore	2 00
	Pd Mr Hammatt [23] for passport	4 00
[March] 25.	Pd Angrisani for passage to Rome	14 00
	Pd Mr Trapp at Croix di Malte	
	for 12 days at	
	4 carlins pr day	3.84
	9 breakfasts at 3 carlins	2.16

[12]	Naples/for service 12 days at 1 carlin	1.00
	To circulating library	

Rome

[13]–[14] [blank]

[15] Why can we find a spiritual meaning in every natural fact? [24]

[16] [blank]

[17] Sunday School

---

[22] Starke, *Travels in Europe* . . . , 1828, p. 501, mentions this hotel as having only back rooms, "damp and unwholesome."

[23] Alexander Hammett (the spelling given by *L*, I, 369) was consul at Naples.

[24] "Why can we . . . fact?": used in *Nature*, *W*, I, 20.

The young bee up to the time he leaves the hive has never seen light. Yet he launches at once into the air, flies far from home, wanders to many flowers, yet comes back with unerring certainty to the hive. Who pilots him?

Loch Lomond 24 miles

[17ₐ]²⁵   Glasgow, 23 Aug. 1833.

May I send you an account of my romancing from Edinburgh to the Highlands? ⁿ I was told it was so easy at an expense of two days to see that famous country of Ben Lomond, Loch Katrine, & the rest. So up the Forth sailed I, in the steamboat, for Stirling. Cold rainy wind in our teeth, all the way; ⁿ ⟨so, tho'⟩ we past Alloa & Falkirk, yes close by Bannockburn I quietly reading my book in the cabin. ⟨all the way.⟩ At Sterling, I saw the ruin of the Abbey of Cambus Kenneth & ⟨then visited⟩ ↓the view from↑ Sterling Castle↓.↑ ⟨which commands a noble prospect on every side.⟩

At night, in a car, being too late for the coach, I rode through ⟨such⟩ ↓the↑ rain⟨s⟩ ten miles to Doune & Callender. ⟨↓Of↑ The⟩ Of the [17ᵦ] scenery ⟨both man & books assured me was fine but⟩ I saw little more than my horse's head. At Callendar I slept hard from 10 till 5, & was then waked to hasten to the Trosachs Inn. This passage was made in a⟨n⟩ ↓uncovered↑ car again & the rain ⟨fell in torrents &⟩ wet me thro' my own coat & my landlord's over that, & tho' ⟨the scenery was exquisite ⟨↓famed↑⟩ as the first lock ⟨↓being↑⟩ we passed was⟩ ↓we passed ⟨was⟩↑ Loch Vennachar, & ⟨the second was⟩ ↓then↑ Loch Achray, yet the scenery of a shower bath must be always ↓much↑ the same & perpendicular rather than horizontal. ↓Once↑ when ⁿ the flood intermitted, I peeped out from under the umbrella, & it was a pretty place. ⟨Arrived &⟩ ↓Wet↑ dried ↓& breakfasted↑ at the Trosachs. I walked with a party a mile & a half to the head of

---

²⁵ For a description of the letter occupying pp. [17ₐ]–[17ᵦ], see the bibliographical note, p. 209 above. The material is printed in *J*, III, 176–180, with no cancellations or revisions. The number of revisions would seem to indicate that this account is a first draft of a letter whose fair copy is lost, rather than a copy of a letter as both Rusk (*L*, I, 393) and Edward Emerson (*J*, III, 176) have suggested. The complexity of the revisions makes the description a good example of Emerson's stylistic experiments.

Loch Katerine. [17c] It had cleared up ⟨7⟩ tho' the wind blew ⟨strongly. It is a beautiful walk.⟩ ↓stoutly and I had the satisfaction of the Trosachs.↑ The ⟨great⟩ ornament of ⟨the⟩ Scottish scenery is the heather, which colours the ⟨whole⟩ country to the hue of a rose. ⟨Well we embarked⟩ In ⁿ two ⟨row⟩ boats with four oars each ⟨&⟩↓we↑ pushed into ⟨the bosom of⟩ the lake ⁿ ↑and↓ ⟨We⟩ got as far as Helen's Island, the Isle of the Lady of the Lake. ⟨We⟩ Ben Venue & Ben An rise on either side. ⟨But⟩ The ⁿ lake was ⟨so⟩ rough, ⟨&⟩ the wind ⟨so⟩ ↑twas↓ strong, ⟨that⟩ ↑⟨and⟩↓ our party were ⟨more⟩ spattered, ⟨than gratified⟩ & the rowers made such little way that it seemed impracticable ⟨&⟩ⁿ & [17d]²⁶ ⟨dangerous withal⟩ to attempt to go thro' the lake which is nine miles ²⁷ long. They put into the first ⟨little harbor⟩ ↑cove↓ the shore afforded, ⟨& here a⟩ part of the company ⟨determined to⟩ return↑ed↓ to the Trosachs, & a part who were bent on ⟨getting before⟩ ↑reaching that↓ night ⟨to⟩ Glasgow, had nothing for it but to walk to the end of the lake, which following the windings of the shore, is fourteen miles. ⟨This was no easy task for⟩ There ⁿ was no ↑better↓ road ⟨more⟩ than a sheep track thro' every variety of soil, now sand, now morass, now fern, & br⟨ush⟩ake, now stones. But the day was fine & on we fared[,] one of the boat men acting as guide[.] [17e] We embarked in the boat at 9 o'clock. ⟨We⟩ ↑Five out of fifteen↓ reached the little hut at the end of the lake at 12 ½. Here we dried our shoes, & drank (I drank) whiskey, & eat oat cake. It was ⟨now⟩ five miles to Inversnaid, where we must take the steam boat on Loch Lomond. ⟨This was to be walked also & was walked.⟩ ↑There was no conveyance but our legs, which served us again.↓ A country as bare almost as a paved street ⟨but I don't re⟩ [—] mountains mountains but I don't remember that I saw a sheep. At Inversnaid a hut full of Highlandmen & women talking Gaelic. ⟨There was⟩ No ⁿ chimney & the ↑peat↓ smoke escaped [17f] as it could. ⟨Back of⟩ ↑Behind↓ the house was a roaring cataract.ⁿ ⟨the Falls of Inversnaid.⟩ The steamboat came (& through much fear & tribulation on the rough waves) we were transported in a little boat & embarked therein. And

---

²⁶ Emerson inadvertently skipped two pages in composing his description (the verso of leaf 2 and recto of leaf 3) and then apparently corrected his numbering system to fit the order of his composition (see the bibliographical note, p. 209 above).

²⁷ "23" is written under the last two letters of "miles" in faint ink.

so on we fared thro' this ⟨fine⟩ lake about 15 miles to Balloch. ⟨But⟩ The ⁿ wind blew my cap off ⟨& the dear affectionate thing⟩ which had travelled with me from Malta where it was ma⟨id⟩de ⟨to those ⟨rainy⟩ ↑stormy↓ highlands was found a watery grave. Better ↑it↓ so than its master.⟩ & it fell into Loch Lomond. ⟨But⟩ ↑My hat was with↓ the baggage ⟨was⟩ all at Glasgow, & the loss not to be repaired so I shivered & sweltered ⁿ [17g] when need was in the rain & wind with a handkerchif on my head. We landed at Balloch & took coach 5 miles farther to Dumbarton. At Dumbarton we were carried to the steam boat on the Clyde & ↑went↓ up ⟨the stream we sailed⟩ to Glasgow where we arrived about 10 o'clock at night. My own appearance was ⟨more⟩ ↑no doubt↓ resolute ⟨than elegant.⟩ arriving at an inn (where my ⟨baggage⟩trunk ⟨to my consternation⟩ had not ⟨arrived⟩) in /the/an/ old ⟨& failing⟩ surtout without a hat & without a rag of baggage.

[17h] They put me in a little room ⟨abov⟩ aloft. I was in no condition to dictate & crept to bed. This morn came ⟨the clean shirt in⟩ the trunk & ⟨so⟩ armed with razors & clean shirt I recovered courage ⟨& ⁿ had my way⟩ ⟨took mine ease in mine inn⟩.²⁸ I visited the Cathedral ⟨the fine old church⟩ of 1123 spared by Knox, & now a Presbyterian church. In the vaulted cellar of the same is ↑laid↓ the scene of part of Rob Roy. Then ⟨I went⟩ to the Saltmarket & to the Hunterian Museum & to the walks behind the College ⟨where Rashleigh met Frank⟩. A little girl named Jeanie was my guide to the tower of the Church. Broad Scotch she spake but she said her name was not Deans.²⁹

[18]³⁰ Carlisle in Cumberland. Aug. 26.

I am just arrived in merry Carlisle from Dumfries. A white day in my years. I found the youth I sought in Scotland & good & wise & pleasant he seems to me. Thomas Carlyle lives in the parish of Dunscore 16 miles from Dumfries amid wild & desolate heathery hills & without a single companion in this region out of his own

²⁸ Cf. Shakespeare, *I Henry IV*, III, iii, 91–92.
²⁹ The two preceding sentences are struck through with a vertical use mark.
³⁰ The entry on the visit to Carlyle is used in much detail in *English Traits*, W, V, 15–19 and n., p. 333.

house. There he has his wife a most accomplished & agreeable woman. Truth & peace & faith dwell with them & beautify them. I never saw more amiableness than is in his countenance. He speaks broad Scotch with evident relish. "in London yonder," "I liked well," "aboot it," ↑Ay Ay↓, &c &c. Nothing can be better than his stories [—] the philosophic phrase — the duchess of Queensb⟨err⟩ury was appointed to possess this estate — by God Almighty added the lady — Wordsworth. The Earl of Lonsdale, the town of Whitehaven, the Liverpool duellist — [.]

[19] Coleridge, Allan Cunningham; Hazlitt, Gigman,[31] Walter Scott, Sheriff of Selkirk. *One idea.* "W. Wordsworth wishes to see W. Scott." Mud magazine. Sand magazine[.] grave of the last sixpence.[32] Coronation of K. William. Jane Baillie Welsh. John Welsh son in law of Knox. K Jamie said "Canna I mak him a bishop?" "I had rather toss his head here" she said, holding up her apron.[33] Irongray   Criffell.[34] T.C. was born in Annandale. His reading multifarious [—] Tristram Shandy, Robinson Crusoe,   Robertson's America. Rousseau's Confessions discovered to him that he was not such an ass as he had imagined. 10 years ago he learned German.

London. Heart of the world. Wonderful only from the mass of human beings. Muffins. Every event affects all the future[,] e.g. Christ died on the tree, that built Dunscore Church yonder & always

[31] Carlyle invented the pejorative term "Gigman" for the narrow-minded wealthy snob. Cf. "Instead of a man we have but a gigman," in "Goethe's Works," *Foreign Quarterly Review*, X (Aug. 1832), 16.

[32] Cf. Emerson's expansion of these cryptic notes of Carlyle's conversation in *English Traits*, W, V, 15–16. "Mud magazine" was Carlyle's term for *Fraser's Magazine*; "Sand magazine" for *Blackwood's Magazine*. The "grave of the last sixpence" was a phrase to describe a failed enterprise nearby.

[33] King William IV was crowned June 26, 1830, succeeding George IV. Carlyle refers to him and to his queen as William and Adelaide Guelph (see p. 221 below). Jane Baillie Welsh is, of course, Jane Welsh Carlyle, and the anecdote is about her ancestress, daughter of John Knox. Carlyle used the anecdote in "Aprons," Bk. I, ch. 6 of *Sartor Resartus*. See also J. A. Froude, *Thomas Carlyle: A History of the First Forty Years of his Life, 1795–1835*, 2 vols. (New York, 1910), I, 87. These items are omitted from the treatment of the visit in *English Traits*.

[34] A granite mountain in Kirkcudbrightshire visible from near Carlyle's house. Emerson remarks in *English Traits*, W, V, 18 that Criffel was "without his cap." Since the mountain is granitic and was not snowcovered at the time, the "Irongray" might be a description of its top. The location of the word, however, links it to "apron" and so the head of Knox.

affects us two. The merely relative existence of Time & hence his faith in his immortality.

Books, puffing Coulburn & Bentley. £ 10000 per ann[um] pd. for puffing. ⟨They⟩ Hence it came to be that [20] no newspaper is trusted & now no books are bought & the booksellers are on the eve of bankruptcy. Pauperism crowded country[;] government should direct poor men what to do. Poor Irishmen come wandering over these moors[;] my dame makes it a rule to give to every son of Adam bread to eat & supply his wants to the next house but here are thousands of acres which might give them all meat & nobody to bid these poor Irish go to the moor & till it. They burned the stacks & so found a way to force the ↑rich↓ people to attend to them. Liverpool man that fought a duel[.]
Splendid bridge from the new world to the old built by Gibbon.
Domestic animals. Man the most plastic little fellow on the planet[.]
Nero's death 'qualis artifex perio'[.] [35]

T.C. had made up his mind to pay his taxes to William & Adelaide Guelph with great cheerfulness as long as William is able to compel the payment [21] & he shall cease to do so the moment he ceases to compel them.

Landor's principle is mere rebellion & he fears that is the American principle also. Himself worships the man that will manifest any truth to him.

Mrs C. told of the disappointment when they had ⟨p⟩determined to go to Weimar & the letter arrived from the bookseller to say the book did not sell & they could not go.

The first thing Goethe sent was the chain she wore round her neck, & how she capered when it came! but since that time he had sent many things.

Mrs. C. said when I mentioned the Burns piece [35a] that it always had happened to him upon those papers to hear of each two or three years after.

T.C. prefers London to any other place to live in. John S. Mill the best mind he knows, more purity, more force — has worked himself clear of Benthamism[.]

---

[35] "What an artist the world is losing!" Suetonius, *De Vita Caesarum*, VI, 49.
[35a] "Burns," *The Edinburgh Review*, XLVIII (Dec. 1828), 267–312.

The best thing T.C. thought in Stuart's book was the story of the bootblack [—] that a man can have meat for his labor.[36]

[22][37] Ambleside, 28 August, 1833.
This morng. I went to Rydal Mt & called upon Mr Wordsworth. His daughters called in their father[,] a plain looking elderly man in goggles & he sat down & talked with great simplicity. A great deal to say about America[,] the more so that it gave occasion for talk upon his favorite topic, which is this[,] that Society is being enlightened by a superficial tuition out of all proportion to its being restrained by moral Culture. Schools do no good. Tuition is not education. He thinks far more of the education of circumstances than of tuition. It is not whether there are offences of which the law takes cognisance but whether there are offences of which the law does not take cognisance[.] [23] Sin, sin, is what he fears. ⟨He thinks there may be in Ameri⟩ & how society is to ⟨get on⟩ ↑escape↓ without greatest mischiefs from this source he cannot see.

He has even said what seemed a paradox [38][,] that they needed a civil war in America to teach them [the] necessity of knitting the social ties stronger.

There may be in America some vulgarity of manner but that's nothing important; it comes out of the pioneer state of things; but, 1. I fear they are too much given to making of money & secondly to politics;[n] that they make political distinction the end & not the means. And I fear they lack a class of men of leisure — in short of gentlemen to give a tone of honor to the community. I am told that things are boasted of in the second class of society there that in Eng-

---

[36] See James Stuart, *Three Years in North America*, 2 vols. (Edinburgh, 1833), II, 27: "I went into a shoe-black's apartment . . . and there I found him and his wife, both persons of colour . . . at dinner, consisting of one of the fattest roast geese I had ever seen, with potatoes, and apple-pie."

[37] A capital "W" appears in the upper left corner of the page, perhaps a false start for Wordsworth, the subject of the entry. The report of the visit to Wordsworth is used in detail in *English Traits, W*, V, 19–24.

[38] "paradox . . . America some" is underlaid with erased pencil writing, of which only slight fragments are legible, one of them apparently some cipher variation on initial letters: "Send to chamber 35 ‖ . . . ‖ &c ‖ . . . ‖ t s[?] o f o t d gt. l f h g t i[?] o d d m". Cf. *JMN*, III, 140.

land (God knows are done in England every day) but never would be spoken of here.

[24] Carlyle he thinks insane sometimes. [I stoutly defended Carlyle[.]]

Goethe's Wilhelm Meister he abused with might & main [—] all manner of fornication. It was like flies crossing each other in the air. He had never got further than the first book, so disgusted was he. I spoke *for* the better parts of the book & he promised to look at it again.

Carlyle he said wrote the most obscurely. Allowed he was clever & deep but that he defied the sympathies of everybody. ↑Even↓ Mr Coleridge wrote more clearly though he always wished Coleridge would write more to be understood.

He carried me out into his garden & showed me the walk in which thousands of his lines were writ. His eyes are inflamed [—] no loss except for reading because he never writes prose & [39] poetry [25] he always carries even hundreds of lines in his memory before writing it. He told me he had just been to Staffa & within a few days had made three sonnets upon Fingal's Cave & was making a fourth when he was called in to see me. He repeated the three to me with great spirit. I thought the second & third more *beautiful* than any of his printed poems. The third is addressed to the flowers which, he said, especially the ox-eye daisy, are very abundant above it. The second alludes to the name of the Cave which is Cave of Music; the first to the circumstances of its being visited by the promiscuous company of the steamboat.

> "calm as the Universe"

> as the supreme Geometer ordained [40]

[39] In the manuscript a comma in different and very faint ink is inserted after "prose"; an ink caret and "of" are inserted after the ampersand. The addition was probably made by Emerson when he revised his comment for *English Traits* (see *W*, V, 22).

[40] As Emerson notes, there were four Staffa sonnets among the Itinerary Poems of 1833. Emerson heard XXVII and XXX certainly. These two poems are the first and third of which he speaks. Whether the second, alluding to music, is Sonnet XXVIII or XXIX is undetermined since neither makes the exact allusion he describes and both are concerned with music. Wordsworth described the abundance of ox-eyed daisies in his notes to Sonnet XXX, subheaded "Flowers on the top of the Pillars at the En-

[26]   ⟨*Cathedra*

G[reenwood]
83   O God we praise thee & confess
145   Greatest of Beings Source of life
323   To keep the lamp alive⟩ [41]

I hoped he would publish his promised poems. He said he never was in haste to publish[,] partly because he altered his poetry much & every alteration is ungraciously received but what he wrote would be printed whether he lived or died. I said Tintern Abbey was the favorite poem but that the more contemplative sort preferred the Excursion & the sonnets. He said yes they were better to him. He preferred himself those of his poems which touched the affections to any others[,] for what was more didactic[,] what ⟨referred⟩ ↑was↓ to theories of society & so on might perish fast but the others were a κτημαεσαε [42] [—] what [27] was good today was good forever. He preferred the Sonnet on the feelings of a high minded Spaniard to any other (I so understood him) & the "two Voices" & quoted with great pleasure some verses addressed to the skylark.[43]

He spoke of the Newtonian theory as if it might be superseded & forgotten & of Dalton's atomic theory.

The object of his talking upon political aspects of society was to impress it upon ⟨al⟩ me & all good Americans to cultivate the moral[,] the conservative &c &c & never to call into action the physical strength of the people as lately in the Reform — — &c[,] a thing prophesied by De Lolme.[44]   making a fortune.

---

trance of the Cave." This sonnet is not only highly praised; Emerson quotes it in the two fragments. "Calm as the Universe" is part of l. 9, and l. 14 actually reads, "As the supreme Artificer ordained." The misquotation was perhaps a later addition since its ink color differs from that of the rest of the entry.

[41] The canceled matter written in faded brown ink is a list of hymns from Greenwood's *Collection of Psalms and Hymns for Christian Worship* which Emerson reviewed in the *Christian Examiner*, X (March 1831), 30–34 and which was adopted by the Second Church under his urging on October 16, 1831. Emerson normally appended such a list to the top of his sermons, though this specific list has not been located there.

[42] "a gain forever" (Ed.).

[43] "Indignation of a High-Minded Spaniard"; "Thoughts of a Briton on the Subjugation of Switzerland"; and "To a Skylark."

[44] John Louis De Lolme (1740?–1807), Swiss lawyer, emigrated to England as

He had broken a tooth lately walking with two lawyers & said he was glad it did not happen 40 years ago whereupon they praised his philosophy. [28] Lucretius's poem far better than any other poem in Latin[,] far more a poet than Virgil [—] his system nothing, but his illustrations[.] —

Faith he said was necessary & ⟨faith in the vulgar genius[?]⟩ to explain anything[,] to reconcile the foreknowledge of God with human evil[.] —

Cousin he knew nothing about but the name[.]

In America he wished to know not how many churches or schools but ⟨how many⟩ ↑what↓ *newspapers?* He had been told by a friend of his [Colonel Hamilton] at the bottom of the hill who was a year in America that the newspapers were atrocious, & openly accused members of the Legislature of stealing silver spoons, &c. He was against taking off the tax upon newspapers in England which the Reformers represented as a tax upon knowledge[n] [29] for this reason; they would be inundated with base prints.

Then to show me what a common person in England could do, he carried me into the inclosure of his clerk[,] a young man whom he had given this slip of ground which was laid out[,] or its natural capabilities shown[,] with great taste.

He then walked near a mile with me talking and ever & anon stopping short to impress the word or the verse & finally parted from me with great kindness & returned ⟨by the⟩ across the fields.

His hair is white, but there is nothing very striking about his appearance.

[30] The poet is always young and this old man took the same attitudes that he probably had at 17 — whilst he recollected the sonnet he would recite.

His egotism was not at all displeasing — obtrusive — as I had heard. To be sure it met no rock. I spoke as I felt with great respect of his genius.

He spoke very kindly of Dr Channing, who, he said, sat a long time in this very chair, laying his hand upon an armchair.[45]

---

a political refugee and wrote *The Constitution of England or an Account of the English Government* . . . (1775).

[45] For William Ellery Channing's visit to Grasmere and Wordsworth in the

He mentioned Burns's sons.[46]

[31] [blank]

[32] 30 August. Liverpool [47]

I talked commonplaces today with a man at this hotel who told me
he had lived in Boston, until I found ⟨t⟩out it was Jacob Perkins.[48]
He says it is not true that he had failed for want of material strong
enough to hold his force. He says he has succeeded in every thing
↑he has undertaken↓ but in making money.

[33] [blank]

[34] 29 Aug. From Kendal this morng to Lancaster; ⟨from⟩
thence to Manchester & there was deposited with my luggage in the
coach on the railway to Liverpool. We parted at 11 minutes after
six, & came to the 21st milestone at 11 minutes after seven. Strange
it was to ⟨see⟩ meet the ⟨other⟩ return cars; to see a load of timber[,]
six or seven masts[,] dart by you like a trout. Every body shrinks
back when the engine hisses by him like a squib. The fire that was
dropped on the road under us all along by our engine looked as we
rushed over it as ⟨f⟩a coal swung by the hand in circles not distinct
but a continuous glare. Strange proof how men become accustomed
to oddest things[:] the ⟨passengers⟩ laborers did not lift their umbrellas to[n] look as we flew by them [35] on their return at the side
of the track. It took about 1 ½ hour[s] to make the journey[,]
32 miles. It has been performed in less than the hour.

---

spring of 1822 see Madeleine H. Rice, *Federal Street Pastor: The Life of William
Ellery Channing* (New York, 1961), pp. 112–113.

[46] Four days earlier at Dumfries Emerson himself had seen and commented on
one of Burns's sons. See pp. 425–426 below.

[47] The entry is out of order chronologically, probably because Emerson wished
to leave a blank page for a possible further entry on Wordsworth and then inadvertently skipped two leaves rather than one in continuing. Then he posted the August 30
entry after the blank page rather than in its proper order.

[48] An American inventor (1766–1849) who established a plate-making factory
in England, developed the steam-engine boiler on English trains, and published the
results of many experiments in steam and heat.

The Council of Lateran decrees that every believer shall receive the Com[munion]. at least at Easter. Gratian & the master of the sentences prescribed as a rule for the laity to communicate 3 times a year[:] Easter, Whitsuntide, & Christmas. In the 13 century it was the practice never to approach the Euch[arist] but at Easter. The Council of Trent renewed the injunctions & recommended frequent Communion.[49]

[36]–[37] [blank]

[38][50]   Always day & night
Day before me
Night behind me

This I penned
Sitting on two stakes
Under the apple tree
Down in the swamp
To guard a friend

[39] First questions always to be asked. Even Goethe, Newton, Gibbon seem to me nothing more than expert spinners of a[n] extended superficies to hide the Universe of our ignorance. Poems, Histories with some are expedients to get bread & with others to conceal their bottomless & boundless ignorance. So that scarce can I blame the man who frankly ⟨says it who⟩ affects to philosophize on the matter as some sensualists do, & says my ⟨part⟩ ↑fun↓ is profound calculation.

Deep sense of Socrates' famous saying. It is the recantation of Man.[51]

---

[49] The paragraph is written upside down in pencil. The badly blurred notes probably represent Emerson's inquiry into the historical problem of the Eucharist in the spring and early summer of 1832.

[50] The entries from here through p. [43] are all in pencil, from the summer of 1832.

[51] Emerson may be making a connection between the famous admonition of Socrates, "Know thyself," and a phrase he has already quoted from "The Life of Pompey" (Plutarch's *Lives*, 1822, III, 104), "But know thyself a man, and be a

[40] 1832.

July 16.[52] Left Crawford's house at   8th.↓,10′
Arrived at top of Mt Washington   ⟨12th↓ 8′⟩
at 25 minutes after noon   12 25 = 4th↓.15
remained there 43 minutes   1,8
arrived at Crawford's   5 o'clock

[41] 1832.

June 21.	Fare to Portsmouth	6 00
	Dinner at Newburyp[or]t	75
	expenses at Portsmouth	2 00
	hairdresser 12 book 40	58
22.	fare to Portland	6 00
23.	expenses at Portland	1 75
	fare to Waterford	2 00
	dinner at Raymond	50
	straw hat 30 straps 12 ½	
	⟨wash'g &c 75⟩	42
	washing &c	75
30.	fare to Fryeburg	1 67
	fare of M[ary].M[oody].E[merson].	83
	Cash to Reuben 25 to oats 12	37
July 3.	Cash to C[harles].C[hauncy].	
	E[merson].	10 00
7.	postage	25
10.	cash to Reuben	25
12.	board — 15 days	6 00
	cash to Eunice	25
	postage	42
13.	fare to E. Crawford's	4 00
	recd of M.M.E. .50	
	pd .6 + 10 M M E	16

---

god." Emerson recurs to this linking of Socrates and the "recantation" of man in
June, 1834 (see p. 298 below).

[52] Emerson was at Ethan Allen Crawford's in the White Mountains during July,
1832, deciding on whether to resign from the Second Church. See Journal Q, pp. 29–
30 above, for the entry of July 15 which preceded Emerson's report of his climb up
Mt. Washington.

14.	cash to M.M.E.	10 00
	expenses at Crawford's	4 50
		——————
		59 45

[42]

July 17.	⟨expense for M M E⟩	⟨50 00⟩59 45
	wagon to T. Crawford	25
	dinner &c	42
	Harvey	25
	stage to Conway	2 00
	expenses at Conway	50
18.	Breakfast at Ossipee	25
	dinner at Meredith Bridge	25
	fare to Concord	3 00
19.	expenses at Concord	87
	fare to Boston	3 00
	dinner at Lowell	37
	expense for M.M.E.	1 00
		——————
		71 61

	deduct	10
		——————
		61

[43][53] Linnaea
      Diervilla
      Angelica
      Spergula Corn Spurrey

[53] Between pp. [42]–[43] is the loose insert described in bibliographical note p. 209 above. The penciled list of plants probably reflects Emerson's trip into the White Mountains during late June and early July, 1832, since all the plants mentioned flower in June or July and several are described by Bigelow as native to the White Mountains. All the items are to be found in Jacob Bigelow, *Florula Bostoniensis: A Collection of Plants of Boston and its Vicinity* (Boston, 1824) with which Emerson was familiar, having withdrawn it from the Harvard Library August 1, 1828, and again for a month, June 15–July 15, 1830, from the Boston Athenaeum.

Oxalis
Ledum.   Labrador tea
Dracaena Borealis
Arethusa

[44] 1832.
Sept. 26.   Fare to Hopkinton Springs
      Mrs R.E. & Self   3 50
      dinner at H. Village   75 [54]
      expenses 3 days at Springs   6 50
      chaise to Westborough   75
      conveyance to stage at Hopk'n 1 00
      Fare to Boston   2 75

                                   15.25

[45] [blank]

[46] [55] Florence should have its history in Boston. Bardi[,] Medici. Early local democratic glory. Tribuna its Fanueil Hall. Country of beauty. Hence painters Raffaelle, Titian[.] System of Mezzeria[.]
Opera
Last Granduke, present, Modena
"Lombard's borrowed legs" [56]
Amerigo Vespucci's house
Santa Croce, Galileo, Michael Ang[elo], Dante, Boccacio, Alfieri, Machiavelli

Amici

---

[54] "1832 . . . H. Village 75" was first written in pencil and then copied over in ink.

[55] Pages [46]–[48] are in pencil, apparently raw notes from the European journey and jottings from reading, intended perhaps for lectures.

[56] The phrase, quoted from an address of praise to Queen Elizabeth for freeing England from foreign traders, is in the "Life of Cavendish," *Lives and Voyages of Drake, Cavendish, and Dampier* . . . , 1831, p. 171.

[47] Hist. of Commerce
Hist. of Arts
Landor — Leopold
Hallam [57]

[48] The Sea.
Drops make it. Expansion by cold[,] specific gravity. phosphores-
cence[,] gulf weed — birds — petrel.

[49]–[50] [blank]

[51][58]–[53] [blank]

[54]		Taris
Messina　T⟨ea⟩he [59]		3
March 3 [1833]. Alloggio		4
4.	Colazione	3
	Pranzo	6
	Alloggio	4
5.	Colazione	3
	Pranzo	6
	Alloggio	4
6.	Colaz[ione]	3
		————
		3.00

[55] Giacheri's Palermo

		gr[ains].
March 9.	Pranzo	70
10.	Colazione	30
	Alloggio	60
	Colazione	30
	Pranzo	70

---

[57] Possibly Henry Hallam, author of *View of the State of Europe during the Middle Ages,* a volume Emerson had long known. See *JMN,* II, 8, n. 10[a].

[58] Between pp. [50] and [51] two leaves have been irregularly torn out, leaving large stubs with no indication of any writing.

[59] The cancellation suggests that Emerson shifted from English to Italian in his account of dining expenses in order to practice the language of the country.

Alloggio	60
Pranzo	70
Allogio	60
Colazione	30

ducats

4 80

Trattoria Venez[ia].

Brodo Bianca	4
Pollo fricass	12
Amandole	4
vino	4
pane	3

27

[56] [blank]

[57]   Atheneum [60]
    Prison Regulations
    Shipwreck Regulations
    Army d[itt]o.

    Gibbon's Memoirs [61]
    Sir Everard Home on the Egg. *Philosoph*. Transactions for year
1816 [62]
    Hatchett [63]

[60] Except for this word the entry on the page is in pencil, as is the entry on p.
[58], where the apparent heading "*College Library*." is half circled from below.

[61] Perhaps *The Miscellaneous Works of Edward Gibbon, with Memoirs of his
life and writings, composed by himself*, ed. J. B. Holroyd, Lord Sheffield, 5 vols.
(London, 1814), which Emerson had taken out from the Boston Public Library in
1822.

[62] "On the formation of fat in the intestine of the tadpole, and on the use
of the yolk in the formation of the embryo in the egg," *Philosophical Transactions*
(1816), II, 301–311.

[63] Charles Hatchett was a frequent contributor to the *Transactions of the Royal
Society*, especially in physiology. Sir Everard Home wrote in his essay on the egg of
"the assistance of my friend and fellow labourer in animal chemistry, Mr. Hatchett,"

Abernethy's Physiological Lectures [64]
Memoires de l'Academie de la Litterature. Tome 46. 47. 50.
51. 56. 57. cited in Upham's Letters.[65]

[58]   *College Library.*

North's Examen.
Butler's Life of Erasmus [66]
[59] Turner's Chemistry. Chapter on Affinity [67]
Baber's Commentaries [68]

[60] [...] [69]

[61] Tax on pew no. 1 pr. ann. 26.00

A horse power is equal to 33,000 lb raised 1 foot in one minute.

[62] [March, 1832] Bunker Hill

---

and Coleridge praised him as Emerson probably read in *The Friend*. See *The Complete Works of Samuel Taylor Coleridge*, ed. W. G. Shedd, 7 vols. (New York, 1853), II, 431.

[64] Abernethy, *Physiological Lectures*, 1817. Emerson cited this work on April 2, 1832. See p. 9 above.

[65] Charles W. Upham, *Letters on the Logos* (Boston, 1828), p. 78. In "Memoires . . . 57." Emerson reproduced a footnote in Upham's work.

[66] Roger North (1653–1734), *Examen: or, an Enquiry into the Credit and Veracity of a Pretended Complete History . . . . All Tending to vindicate the Honour of the late King Charles II* . . . (London, 1740), and Charles Butler, *Life of Erasmus with historical remarks* (London, 1825).

[67] Edward Turner, *Elements of Chemistry*, 4th Amer. ed. (Philadelphia, 1832); the chapter on Affinity is in Pt. II, "Inorganic Chemistry," sect. I, pp. 109–121.

[68] Emerson evidently found a note in Mackintosh's *A General View of . . . Ethical Philosophy*, 1832, p. 232, which discussed William Erskine as a translator of Baber's *Commentaries* and praised highly a review by M. Silvestre de Sacy in the *Journal des Savans*, May–June 1829, pp. 296–308 and 330–345, of these same *Commentaries*. This name is not used elsewhere to describe the volume referred to, which Francis Jeffrey had reviewed at some length in *The Edinburgh Review* of June 1827: *The Memoirs of Zehir-ed-Din Muhammed Baber, Emperor of Hindustan* (London, 1826). Mackintosh not only referred to the work by the odd title *Commentaries* rather than *Memoirs*; he also praised it as "perhaps the best . . . work of modern Eastern prose."

[69] "Baber's Commentaries" is repeated here from p. [59], a single entry in large penciled writing.

Wash'n Statue $8000 sub[scribe]d. increased to 16000 [70]
Pictures of Washn & Lady W. by Stuart $1250.

1830.[71] Population of England 13,039,338

[63] 1832.

Feb. 19.   Rode in a sulky to Cambridge with the horse Driver
⟨1832⟩   From ↑1st↓ toll house to Stimpson's   15.'
            ↑thro' the Port↓ [72]
            From Stimpson's to Barnard's   20'
March 11.   same horse & sulky from Chardon St to Mr
            Francis' house Watertown — —   40'
            In the evg. from Mr R[ipley].'s Waltham, to
            Barnard's   60'
Apr. 15.   From Chardon St to W. Cambridge m[eeting].
            h[ouse]. in horse & chaise   41'
Apr. 13.   Walked from Lincoln m.h. to Concord m.h. in 1 h. 3'

Clematis to Canton sailed 9281 ↑stat. miles↓ in 41 days. 200 pr. d.

        [64] T[homas].C[arlyle]. 5 Great Cheyne Row, Chelsea, London

Copernopi, Keplupa, Miltsyk, Cer-sas-Shake, Lutzasid, Galsit, Newtsod [73]

---

[70] On March 5, 1832, Emerson wrote his brother Charles about a reported mortgage on the Bunker Hill monument, the purchase by the Washington Statue Society of Stuart portraits of Washington and his wife, and the success of the Society in raising funds for a statue, $8000 subscribed by the public and another $8000 given by P. C. Brooks. See Rusk, L, I, 347.

[71] The date represents the time of the census rather than of entry.

[72] "thro' the Port" is inclosed in markings resembling reversed angle brackets.

[73] "Copernopi . . . Newtsod" is an example of a cipher to aid the memory which Emerson originally found in Dr. R. Grey's *Memoria Technica or Method of Artificial Memory* . . . , *to which are subjoined Lowe's Mnemonics Delineated in Various Branches of Literature & Science*, 8th ed. (London, 1806), p. 5. Emerson wrote the cipher down on the flyleaf of his copy of Sir James Mackintosh's *History of England*, vol. I (Philadelphia, 1830), in Lardner's *Cabinet History of England, Scotland, and Ireland*:

a	e	i	o	u	au	oi	ei	ou	y	th
1	2	3	4	5	6	7	8	9	0	00
b	d	t	f	l	s	p	k	n	z	

[74] Copernicus born 1543 Copernopi
  Kepler   born 1571 Keplupa
  Newton   born 1642 Newtsod
    Lutz*asid*
    Swed*seik*
    Kant*oido*

  Shakspear & Cervantes died 1616
  Milton b. 1608   Milt*syk*
  Washington 1732
  Bonaparte
  Biot b. 1774
  Webster 1782
Sir J Mackintosh 1765. Oct. 24. in Dover, Inverness
Sir W. Scott

[inside back cover] [blank]

The letters added to the truncated version of the name served to recall important dates to Emerson as follows: (a) the birth date of Copernicus, 1473; (b) Kepler's birth date, 1571; (c) Milton's birth date, 1608; (d) the death date for both Cervantes and Shakespeare, 1616; (e) the Battle of Lutzen, 1632; (f) the date of Galileo's recantation, 1633; (g) Newton's birth date, 1642. See *JMN*, III, 265, for an earlier use of this mnemonic device.

[74] "Copernicus" to the end of the page is in pencil. "Copernicus" underlies "Galsit, Newtsod" and was an earlier version of the memory cipher. Emerson gave in error the death date rather than the birth date for Copernicus (1473–1543). Then he worked out, again in order, the Battle of Lutzen, 1632; the birth date of Swedenborg, 1688; and Kant's birth date, 1724.

Sea 1833

1 8 3 3

The small notebook, home-made from letter paper, is a record of Emerson's return voyage from England to America covering one month (September 4–October 4) though the trip itself lasted until October 7. The record overlaps that given in Journal Q of the same voyage.

For the bibliographical description, see p. 396 below in the headnote to the notebook France and England, within which the journal Sea 1833 is laid loose.

[1] Wednesday
September 4, 1833 at 2 o'clock left Liverpool in the New York of N.Y. 14 cabin passengers, 16 steerage. Ship 516 tons.

[September] 5. Thursday. Calm fine day. I remember that Mrs H[olbrook]. my fellowpassenger to Malta told me that she sailed from Boston to Charleston S.C. & never saw the water. One other fact occurred in my seasick ruminations to be recorded, that namely, which Carlyle mentioned, that Colburn & Bentley the London publishers expended in one year £ 10 000 in puffing.[1] This morn I saw the last lump of England receding without the least regret. I saw too for the first time a piece of Ireland. It was the Wicklow Mountains. ⟨I⟩As I came down to the waterside in Liverpool I noticed the announcement of the wind at Holyhead — "At Holyhead N.E. wind blowing fresh" [—] this communication was telegraphed from Holyhead 60 miles from Liverpool. Noble docks. Heard Mr Yates preach on Sunday the best Sermon I heard in England. "Be clothed

---

[1] See p. 221 above.

with humility." [2] ⟨When I came out⟩ ↑After service↓ I stood [2] waiting for him to come out when he spoke to me at my side. "Oh" said I surprised "how do you do Mr *Wardlaw* — I mean — Mr Yates."

Is it not strange that every book begins with "no science deserves more attention than" whether astronomy, geology, civil history, geometry, algebra, commerce, or what not? [n] Even wise Herschel after a saving flourish begins with a "no science —" [3]

We were towed out of Liverpool harbor by steamboat. Admirable contrivance for ⟨citi⟩ ports in deep bays like this or Philad. or Baltimore for they might lie weeks waiting to get out with the wind ⟨as⟩ fair for the voyage all the time. At one moment the boat & the ship had nearly struck. [4] Every ship every man has all but struck[,] been within an inch of destruction a thousand times. It is such a narrow line that divides an awkward act from the finish of gracefulness. Every [3] man eats well alone. Let a stranger come in & he misses his mouth & spills his butterboat & fails of finding the joint in carving & that by so little.

See page X ☞

Friday [September] ⟨5⟩6. Fair fine wind, still in the Channel — off the coast of Ireland but not in sight of land. This morning 37 sail in sight.

I like my book about nature & wish I knew where & how I ought to live. God will show me. I am glad to be on my way home yet not

---

[2] 1 Pet. 5:5. Emerson had entered this high praise for Yates and his sermon of September 1 in his overlapping record of the period, Journal Q (see p. 80 above). The anecdote of Emerson's error in greeting Yates is based upon his fame as defender of Unitarianism against Robert Wardlaw.

[3] Herschel, *A Treatise on Astronomy*, 1833, p. 1, begins with the phrase. Emerson evidently bought the book in England and read it on his voyage, as he refers to it again on September 8. The edition is in his library.

[4] The passage from "Every ship" on p. [2] through "See page X" on p. [3] is struck through with use marks. According to Emerson's directions the passage then continues on p. [17] below after the "X" in the left margin of the page. The "X" is lined on top and bottom as though to indicate a Roman numeral, but it may be a sign rather than a number since it is on neither page nor leaf 10. The continuation of the passage on p. [17] is also struck through with a use mark from "I wrote" through "was seized by"; perhaps through inadvertence the use mark does not continue through the completion of the passage on p. [18].

so glad as others & my way to the bottom I could find perchance with less regret for I think it would not hurt me[,] that is the ducking or drowning.

Saturday [September] 6 [7]. Gentle ⟨f⟩airs. Wind still & what is perhaps good — no events. At 12 o'clock south of Cape Clear.

Sunday [September] 7 [8]. ⟨I⟩The solitary keeper of the lighthouse of the Smalls in the Eng. Channel which stands on three pillars of Cast iron[,] the waves washing through them. There were two — one sickened & died[;] the other kept his body lest they should say he murdered him, until somebody came to the spot & the body was quite rotten.[4a] Bread must be well mixed to keep sweet[;] man well tempered to keep his spirit clear.

"A rum place" says an Englishman[.]

[4] ⟨Captai⟩ It is pleasant to know that our ship is renowned for fast sailing. Captain Hoxie tells me that in three successive days he sailed in this ship 275, 273 & 276 miles, = 824.

Astronomy[,] I thank Herschel[,] promises every thing. It refers me to a higher state than I now occupy. I please myself rather with contemplating the penumbra of the thing than the thing itself. But no moralities now[,] the good the holy day[.]

Sept. 9.[5] Monday. The road from Liverpool to New York as they who have travelled it well know is very long, crooked, rough, & eminently disagreeable. Good company even[,] Heaven's best gift[,] will scarce make it tolerable. Four meals a day is the usual expedient (& the wretchedness of the expedient will show the extremity of the case) & much wine & porter [—] these are the amusements of wise men in this sad place. The purest wit may have a scur⟨y⟩vy stomach[.]

[5] The letterbag is our captain's best passenger. ⟨He⟩It neither eats

---

[4a] Cf. *The Imperial Magazine and Monthly Record*, 2nd ser. II (May 1832), 217: "Once, on relieving this forlorn guard, one of the men was found dead, his companion choosing rather to shut himself up with a putrefying carcase than, by throwing it in to the sea, to incur the suspicion of murder."

[5] The first two entries under this date, here and on p. [5], are struck through with use marks.

nor drinks & yet pays at least in Liverpool a passenger's fare. Capt. H. tells me that he usually carries between 4 & 5,000 letters each way. At the N.Y Post Office they count his letters & pay him two cents for every one. At Liverpool two pence. The last time he received in Liverpool £ 39. for them.

Fraser's Magazine states that Lord Clarendon wrote a sketch of ⟨Ch⟩the life of Charles Cotton[,] father of Charles Cotton[,] doubtless the translater of Montaigne.[6] I have never seen it.

Sept. 11. Wednesday. I have been nihilizing as usual & just now posting my Italian journal. Admirable story of Grizel Cochrane in Chambers' Mag.[7] Never was a regular dinner with all scientific accompaniments so philosophic ⟨as⟩ a thing as at sea. I tipple with all my heart here. May I not?

Sept. 13. Friday. The sea to us is but a lasting storm. How it blows, how it rocks. My [6] sides are sore with rolling in my berth[;] the ⟨bl⟩coverlet is not wide enough that a man should wrap himself in it. It is only strange that with such a sea & wind & rain[,] such wild distressful noisy nights, no harm should befal us. We have torn a sail & lost a hencoop & its inmates but the bulwarks are firm, & I often hear of the sea breaking the bulwarks of ships. Capt Fox who went in 14 days from Liverpool to Boston [7a] slept in the ⟨pier chain⟩ ↑cable tier↓ to keep the mate from taking in sail. ⟨Th⟩Running in for Boston harbor it was very misty & the passengers besought him to lay to, in vain. Presently the man before cried — a sail! "Pooh," said Capt F. " 'tis the lighthouse — Starboard helm." It was the light & he ran round it & came to anchor within the bay.

---

[6] "Ancient Country Gentlemen of England," *Fraser's Magazine*, VII (June 1833), 651.

[7] *Chambers's Edinburgh Journal*, no. 84, September 7, 1832, pp. 250–252. Grizel, whose father was under penalty of death, robbed the mail coach of the final execution papers, hoping to gain delay and a pardon. Her ruse worked, and her father was finally spared.

[7a] See the *Columbian Centinel*, Boston, March 18, 1824, for the news that the *Emerald*, Captain Philip Fox, Master, had made the trip from Liverpool to Boston in 15 days and 14 hours. See *Emerson Society Quarterly*, III Q, 1960, p. 35.

What a machine is a ship changing so fast from the state of a butterfly all wing to the shape of a log — all spar.

Poor Ireland! they told a story of ↑an↓ Irish boy at school asking a holiday to go to the market town. "What to go for?" "To see Uncle hanged."

Monday, [September] 16th. Gale & calm — pitch & rock — merrily swim we, the sun shines bright. The mate says they took up ↑about where we are now↓ a year ago the crew of Leonidas, a Portland vessel loaded with salt which sprang a leak. The Capt would not [7] leave the ship after putting quadrant & compass & his own things in the boat, & saw the boat leave the ship.

One of this line of packets struck an island of ice, ⟨bu⟩& the whole company with 35 passengers escaped in the boat.

Dull stormday yesterday. I kept Sunday with Milton & a Presbyterian magazine. Milton says, "if ever any was ravished with moral beauty, he is the man." [8]

It occurred with sad force how much we are bound to be true to ourselves — (the old string) — because we are always judged by others as *ourselves* & not as those whose example we would plead. ⟨You⟩A read↑s↓ in a book the praise of a wise man who could unbend & make merry & so he tosses off his glass whilst round him ⟨you⟩ are malicious eyes watching his guzzling & fat eating, & ⟨‖ . . . ‖⟩ The truth is, you can't find any example that will suit you, nor could, if the whole family of Adam should pass in procession before you, for you are a new work of God.

[8]   Time & the hour wear through the roughest day [9]

America, my country, can the mind
Embrace in its affections realms so vast
(Unpeopled yet the land of men to be)
As the great oceans that wash thee enclose

[8] See Letter VII, to Charles Diodati, September 23, 1637, in *The Works*, 1931–1940, XII, 25–26. The phrase is used in "Milton," *W*, XII, 263, and in "English Reformers," *Uncollected Writings* (New York, 1912), p. 93.

[9] See Carlyle, *The Life of Friedrich Schiller*, 1825, p. 323, slightly misquoted, or possibly Shakespeare, *Macbeth*, III, iii, 147, with *wear* for *runs*.

⟨It⟩ 'Tis a↑n↓ ⟨most⟩ ambitious charity ↑that makes
⟨That seeks↑⟨meets⟩↓ to entertain⟩ its arms ⟨about⟩ meet
    round↓ a continent
⟨In an embrace as strict, as man his friend.⟩
And yet, the sages say, ⟨the love of home⟩
⟨The tenderness⟩ the preference
Of our own cabin to a stranger's wealth
The insidious love & hate that curls the lip
Of ⟨f⟩the frank Yankee in the tenements
Of ducal & of royal rank abroad
His supercilious ignorance
Of heraldry & ceremony
And his tenacious recollection
Amid the coloured treasuries of Art
That enrich the Louvre or the Pitti house
Tuscany's unrivalled boast
Of the brave steamboats of New York
The Boston Common & the ⟨Meadow⟩ ↑Hadley↓ farms
Washed by Connecticutt.
Yea if the ↑ruddy↓ Englishman speak true ⟨upon the
    floor⟩
Of the vast Roman Church, and underneath
The ⟨Firmament⟩ ↑frescoed sky↓ of its majestic dome
⟨My countryman⟩ ↑The American↓ will ⟨calculate⟩ ↑count↓
    the cost
And build the shrine with dollars ⟨o'er again⟩ ↑in his head↓
And all he asks ↑arrived↓ in Italy ⟨is whether⟩
↑Has↓ the ⁿ starbearing squadron ⟨yet has⟩ left Leghorn

[9]   Land without history land lying all
In the plain daylight of the temperate zone
⟨Without⟩   thy plain acts
Without exaggeration, done in day
Thy interests contested by their manifest good sense
⟨Not⟩ ↑In their own clothes↓ without ⁿ the ornament
Of bannered Army harnessed in uniform
Land where ⟨man asks the questions⟩ ↑and 'tis in Europe
    counted a reproach↓

↑Where↓ man ⁿ asks ⟨the⟩ question ↑—↓ for which man
    was made.
A land without nobility or wigs or debt
No castles no Cathedrals and no kings
Land of the forest[.]

I walk upon the deck
My thought recurs upon the uncertain sea
To what is faster than the solid land.[10]

[10]–[11] [blank]

[12] In this world, if a man sits down to think, he is immediately asked if he has the headache.⟨?⟩

Sunday, 22 September. Gales & headwinds ⟨in⟩ ↑producing↓ all
the variety of discomfort & ennui in the Cabin. We try in vain to
⟨lo⟩keep bright faces & pleasant occupation below, heedless of the
roar of the tempest above. We are too nearly interested in every
rope that snaps & every spar that cracks overhead to hear the ruin
with philosophy. We may keep our eyes on the Cicero or Addison in
our hands but that noise touches our life. I would I were in the bushes
at Canterbury, for my part. Yesterday was too fine a day to lose at
sea. Calm shining after the wild storm of two preceding days. This
time I have not drawn the golden lot of company. And yet far
better than the last voyage. But that little one to Charleston from
St. Augustine with Murat was worth all the rest.[11] Yet thanks to the
good God who leads & protects me for the measure of comfort &
intellectual occupation that is possible in the valleys of the sea by
means of this wonderful chef d'oeuvre of human Art [13] the ship.
Sad for the steerage passengers[,] old women & children ⟨lyin⟩ sitting
up all night or lying in wet berths. The poor cow refuses to get up
& be milked, & four dogs on board shiver & totter about all day, &
bark when we ship a sea.

[10] "I walk . . . solid land." is in a different color of ink from that of the preceding poetry and was apparently entered at a later time.
[11] See *JMN*, III, 77–78, for the account of this voyage on the sloop *William* and
Emerson's relation to Achille Murat, in April, 1827.

[September] 25. It was a good jest which a passenger quoted from a sea song in ⁿ which two sailors ⟨sing⟩ in a storm at sea ↑express their↓ pity [for] the poor landsmen.

> "My eyes what tiles & chimney pots
>   About their heads are flying
> Whilst you & I upon the deck
>   Are comfortably lying."

It is like the "being thankful for the board blanket." [12] What a gale that was on the night of the 19th. The second mate says that if an 18 pounder had been fired on deck it could not have been heard aloft & the only way he got the Captain's orders was by putting his ear to his mouth.

[14]   Dear brother [13] would you know
         Sitting ⟨beneath⟩ under a gold September sun
         How we plough the Atlantic wave
         Under the stars & under the clouds
         With swimming deck & singing shrouds
         Climbing the steep slope of the cabin floor
         Or peeping timid into the rain
         Out of the round house door
         Shall I not tell you to kill the time
         How we spend the day
         Dull the bard & sad the lay
         Uneasy rolls the ship ⟨irregular⟩ ↑uneven↓ runs the rhyme
             ⟨When the day dawns⟩
         ↑Dimly↓ the ⁿ morning breaks
         Upon the skylight of my berth
         ↑Where↓ I had dreamed myself at peace
         My feet upon my Maker's Earth
         But the Muse doth refuse
         To recollect these trumpery cares

[12] Edward Emerson notes (*J*, III, 214n.) that this reference is to one of Emerson's favorite stories. A poor widow added a board door to the thin blanket she had to cover her children. One child responded, "What do those poor little children do who haven't got a door to cover them?"

[13] Edward Emerson suggests (*J*, III, 215n.) that this poem is a verse letter to Edward B. Emerson in Puerto Rico. The entry was apparently written on September 25.

The waking bell that tragic knell
That calls us back to recognition
Of our deplorable condition
Out we come unshaven faces
And with what look forlorn
Pass the greetings of the morn
Each to the other in the wellknown places
We climb the gangway walk the deck
Survey the wide horizon round
There's not a sail there's not a wreck
There's not a wreck there's not a sail
Nor land nor waterspout nor whale

[15]   The only living thing
Sometimes a gull with snowy wing
A shoal of porpoises come wheeling
Across the bows thro' the grey waves
Or Mother Carey's chickens stealing
On wings that never rest, their forlorn food
Poor little wanderers outcasts of nature
Where have you been in the drowning storm
Here is no bush to hide you from whirlwinds
Here is no perch to rest your little footies

Going Alway
By night and by day,
Under starlight, under clouds,
With swimming deck & singing shrouds

I have read what Shakspeare wrote
Of bloated Fal⟨l⟩staff royal Lear [14]

[16]   There is a dulness proper to great wit.
⟨Wit⟩And Jonson hath his ample share of it

[14] The preceding 6 lines are in a different color of ink than that of the rest of the verses and may well be two separate entries rather than part of the verse letter to Edward. "Going Alway . . . shrouds" is also written into Pocket Diary 2 (see p. 424 below) under the date October 2 and may therefore have been composed a week after the preceding verse.

It needs much skill to write so dull a piece [n]
⟨And⟩ Draw [n] ⟨its⟩ ↑learned↓ faults from Italy &
Greece

Beautiful songs B[en]. J[onson]. can write, & his vocabulary is so
rich & when he pleases so smooth that he seems to be prosing with
a design to relieve & display better the bright parts of the piece. Then
he shows himself master of the higher[,] the moral taste & enriches
himself occasionally with those unquestionable gems which none but
the sons of God possess. Strange that among his actors, & not the
first is Will Shakspeare. He never was dull to relieve his brilliant
parts. He is all light — sometimes terrestrial, sometimes celestial —
but all light.

[17] "Take away that empty marine," said the D[uke] of York.
"What do you mean sir?" said an officer of marines. "I mean that
fellow who has done his duty, & is ready to do it again," replied
the Duke.
      It can [15]

"O c'est grande! magnifique! dat is, vat you call *pretty well*," [n] said
Monsieur arrived in London.

X [16] ☞
      I wrote above something concerning the golden mean wherein
grace & safety lies. In peaceful pursuits in cities we do not consider
how great is the distance between danger & death. A man in his parlor
thinks that to meet a lion in the desart or to stumble over an alli-
gator in wading thro' a watered savannah is certain destruction. They
who are familiar with these rencontres think no such thing & in that
discrimination their safety lies. See the story of the ⟨girl⟩ Indian girl
who put out the Cayman's eyes [17] & in the accurate Dampier the
acc[oun]t of the Irishman whose knee was seized by [18] [an] alli-

---

[15] The entry is left incomplete and the following anecdote is in a different ink.
[16] As directed by his sign Emerson here picks up the entry from p. [3] above.
[17] William Mac Gillivray, *Travels and Researches of von Humboldt*, Harper's
Family Library, no. 54 (New York, 1833), p. 181. Emerson apparently used this
edition for most of his material connected with Humboldt.

gator — he quietly waited till the animal loosened his teeth to take a new & surer hold, & when it did so, snatched away his knee interposing the butt end of his gun in its stead which the animal seized so firmly, that it was jerked out of the man's hand & carried off.[18] — See also the marvellous expedient of righting the ship ⟨by⟩ when lying in the trough⟨s⟩ of the sea by going up the fore shrouds & spreading out their coats.

(Early. Eng. Navig. Ed. Cab. Lib. p 344)

When the French fleet under Count d'Estrées was wrecked, those of the ordinary seamen who got ashore died of fatigue & famine, while those who had been Buccaneers ⟨lived⟩ ↑&↓ were wrecked here, ⟨lived merrily⟩ being used to such accidents, lived merrily, — for they kept a gang by themselves & watched when the ships broke up to get the goods, that came out of them & tho' much was staved against the rocks, yet abundance of wine & brandy floated over the reef where they waited to take it up. "There were about 40 Frenchmen on board one of the ships, in which was good store of liquor till the after part of her broke & was floated over the reef & was carried away to sea with all the men [19] drinking & singing[,] who being in drink did not mind the danger but were never heard of afterwards —" [*ibid.*,] p 338[.]

In the ↑selecting↓ unknown ⟨places⟩ ↑wildfruits↓ they were guided by birds[,] freely eating whatever kind had been pecked. [*Ibid.*, p. 335]

[20]–[22] [blank]

[23]   At sea.
Thursday, 26 Sept. Longit. 49 Lat 44
On the banks; found bottom at 49 fathoms & fished in vain with 70 fathoms of line. ⟨The⟩ Saw a fishing schooner. They fish from June to October. It may take 2 months to get full & they bring home

---

[18] "The Life of Dampier," *Lives and Voyages of Drake, Cavendish, and Dampier,* 1831, p. 301. "he quietly . . . carried off." is a quotation, almost verbatim. Emerson usually referred to this volume as "Early English Navigators," as he did below in the next anecdote.

20 or 25 000 fish. The ⟨w⟩colour of the water has changed, the birds fly about, & we have fogs. Yesterday a little petrel caught in the end of a rope & was drowned — webfooted[,] a pretty bird with a white belt upon the tail.

Sept. 29. Storm storm storm[,] but only this can show the virtues of the ship which behaves well & carries these tender bodies tucked up in boxes along its side without injuring a hair through these wild cold savage waters. Strange that any body who has hands to work should be willing to spend two months in that ⟨bleak⟩ Bank exposed to such storms as yesterday's. "That fellow has got a bleak place," said the Captain. Much indebted to Mr H's conversation.[19] Story of the Duc de Bourdeaux[,] infant son of Duc de Berri[,] being carried to Louis XVIII[:] Le roi pue; l'enfant a raison otez l'enfant. Qui pius est summe philosophatur.[20] I notice that we always judge of the length of the passage by the weather of the present moment.[21]

[24] Friday, 4 October. Long. 67, je crois.

Our month expires today, & therefore 'tis time to look for land. The poor Malay saith to the wind in his petulance "Blow, me do tell you blow" but not of that mind are we, but contrariwise, very glad of this fine weather. Capt's merry account of his capture by pirates in S. America in 1822 when they cut up his sails for trowzers & ripped off the copper sheathing of the vessel for French horns & appointed him fifer. He played in that capacity the dead march of two priests, whom the worthy lieut. gen. shot for smuggling.

"Chap from Wiggin, Manchester man, & a gentleman from Liverpool" said Coachey. — Sea of all colours. Today indigo, yesterday grass green, & day before grey.

A terrible child bed hast thou had my dear

[19] The source for the French anecdote was apparently either J. H. Henley of Dublin or John Hudson of New York, both of whom were passengers aboard the *New York* during Emerson's voyage. See *The New York Commercial Advertiser*, October 8, 1833, p. 2, col. 6.

[20] "He who is pious plays the philosopher best" (Ed.).

[21] The lower right corner of the page is torn away from "to spend" through "moment." On p. [24] the tear runs from "Chap" through "And aye"; the entries are unmutilated and must have been made after the page was torn.

No light no fire. The unfriendly elements
Gave thee no help. And now, for hallowed rites
And aye remaining lamps, I must cast thee [22]

[22] The speech from Shakespeare, *Pericles, Prince of Tyre*, III, i, 57–63, is badly misquoted and telescoped after the first two lines and is then left unfinished.

A

1833–1834

Journal A introduces a new pattern of order into Emerson's journal-keeping. Recognizing that his journals were his "Savings Bank," he began to letter them in alphabetical order, to buy rather than to make them, to choose books of relatively uniform size for his records, and to increase his somewhat sporadic indexing into a major activity. Dated entries in Journal A begin on December 11, 1833, about three weeks after the final entry in Q, which had been used for journal-keeping after the return to America in October. The last dated entry in A comes on December 29, 1834.

The cover of the volume, brown marbled boards with a diced Russia leather spine in darker brown, is marked with a large "A" on both front and back and measures 21.4 x 24.8 cm. Originally the volume contained 184 pages faintly lined after page 6 and measuring 21 x 24 cm apiece. The 9 leaves that precede the final leaf in the volume have been cut away, probably at two different periods, leaving 166 pages plus the inside back cover, which is numbered as page 167.

The journal is paginated in ink with some omissions. The following pages are unnumbered: 1, 2, 4, 8, 16, 70, and 165. Pages 2, 23, 61, 69, 149, and 160 are blank. A misnumbering occurs on leaves 13–14. After numbering the recto of leaf 13 "25" Emerson skipped the verso and then repeated the number 25 on the recto of leaf 14. The sequence of numbering is continued properly with the verso of leaf 14 as page 26. An attempt to correct the misnumbering is supplied in pencil, possibly by Emerson himself. On the unnumbered verso of leaf 13 "24a" is added in pencil; the repeated page number "25" on the recto of leaf 14 has an "a" added to it in pencil. The editor has supplied subscript numbers to indicate the repeated and confused pagination as follows: "24"–24_1; "25"–25_1; "24a"(in pencil)–24_2; "25"("a" in pencil)–25_2.

A loose leaf measuring 12.6 x 20.2 cm presently lies between pages 40 and 41. The leaf is numbered "40a" in pencil, probably by Edward Emerson, and is not printed since the material on the recto (40a) is apparently a set of notes belonging to Emerson's lectures on the philosophy of history in 1839 and the content of the unnumbered verso consists of penciled index references to Journal B of 1835–36.

A loose clipping found between pages 102 and 103 and a loose leaf, 16.3 x 20.4 cm, found between pages 130 and 131 and numbered in pencil "130a" and "130b" may belong to this period and are printed.

An index occupies pages 161–162. Following page 162 are the stubs of 9 cutout leaves. The first stub, larger than the others, bears traces on its verso of writing in the same order as that of the rest of the journal. This cutout leaf probably carried page numbers 163–164 since these two numbers are missing from the numbering. The 8 following stubs could not have been numbered within the existing pagination and carry traces of upside-down writing. Perhaps Emerson used these pages of A in reverse and then cut them out when he began his journal at the other end.

[inside front cover]

Ch' apporta mane, e lascia sera.[1] [Dante, *Paradiso*, xxvii, 138.]

[1][2]   R. Waldo Emerson

———

Journal. A
1833–4.   Amber?
                                                            Ambergris

———

Not of men neither by man.[3]

May ^{n} I "consult the auguries of time
And through the human heart explore my way
And look & listen" [4]

[index omitted]

[2] [blank]

[3] This Book is my Savings Bank. I grow richer because I have somewhere to deposit my earnings; and fractions are worth more to

---

[1] The quotation is in pencil. Emerson cites the line again slightly misquoted and expanded. See p. 362 below.

[2] "Amber?", and "Ambergris" are in pencil. Four index headings are penciled into the lower portion of the page.

[3] Gal. 1:1.

[4] Wordsworth, "Not 'mid the World's vain objects," (on the Convention of Cintra, 1808), in *Sonnets dedicated to Liberty*, Pt. II, Sonnet V, ll. 11–13. The passage is marked in Emerson's copy of *The Poetical Works of William Wordsworth*, 4 vols. (London, 1824), II, 340.

me because corresponding fractions are waiting here that shall be made
integers by their addition.

Memoranda [5]

Mariners Society — Taylor

Dr Reynolds.

School books

Library of Ch. in Concord, N.H.

Nov. 3. promised Mr Center to give notice of A.U. Assocn. at Ch.
& solicit subss.

Dr Channing's Works to Miss Lincoln

Magnetism — to Miss Hayden

Offering of Sympathy to Mrs Davis

[4] 'In being silent & hoping consisteth our strength,' so Luther
quotes Isaiah.[6]

> 'For every gift of noble origin
> Is breathed upon by hope's perpetual breath'   Wordsworth.[7]

J. M. Saunders [8]
Joan Putnam

[5] "*Memoranda* . . . Mrs Davis" is written upside down in the lower right
corner of the page and is struck through with two diagonal lines, perhaps as an indication that the reminders had been taken care of. The identifiable memoranda relate
to (a) "Father" Edward T. Taylor, the seaman's minister who preached at the
Mariner's Church (Sailor's Bethel) and whom Emerson later (see p. 381 below)
called "that living Methodist, the Poet of the Church"; (b) Dr. Edward Reynolds,
Boston physician; (c) the church in Concord, New Hampshire, where Emerson had
preached often when he was courting Ellen Tucker; (d) Mr. Center, apparently an
official in the American Unitarian Association; (e) probably William Ellery Channing's *Discourses* (Boston, 1832) or *Discourses, reviews, and miscellanies* (Boston,
1830), since the first American edition of Channing's *Works* was 1841; (f) perhaps
John Farrar's *Elements of Electricity, Magnetism, and Electro-Magnetism . . . ,
Being the Second Part of a Course of Natural Philosophy . . .* (Cambridge, Mass.,
1826–1827), which Emerson listed in 1829 as among books to be purchased,
according to *JMN*, III, 346; (g) [The Rev. Francis Parkman] *An Offering of
Sympathy to Parents Bereaved of their Children and to others under affliction* (Boston,
1830).

[6] *Colloquia Mensalia or Dr. Martin Luther's Divine Discourses at his Table,*
trans. Henry Bell (London, 1652), p. 235. The phrase is a variation of Isa. 30:15.

[7] Wordsworth, "These times strike monied worldlings with dismay," ll. 10–11,
slightly misquoted, in *Poems Dedicated to National Independence and Liberty,* Pt. I,
Sonnet 20, 1803.

[8] "J. M. Saunders . . . 121 & 76" is written in pencil with the first name in

⟨Abby Adams⟩
John T. Saville
Mr & Mrs Chamberlain $100
R.E. Hamlin

New Bedford Jan. 26 [1834], 154 & 95
              Feb. 2, 122 & 126
              Feb. 9, 104 & 163
              Feb. 16, 124 & 117
              March 9 [127 & 79]
Plymouth   March 13 [160]
New Bedford March 16 1[65 & 33]
              March 23, 121 & 76

[5]   Boston, 11 December, 1833.
The call of our calling is the loudest call. There are so many worthless lives, apparently, that to advance a good cause by telling one anecdote or doing one great act seems a worthy reason for living. —— When a poor man thanked Richard Reynolds for his goodness, he said, "Do you thank the clouds for rain?" The elder Scipio said, "he had given his enemies as much cause to speak well of him as his friends." Fontenelle said "I am a Frenchman. I am sixty years old, & I never have treated the smallest virtue with the smallest ridicule." [9]

---

the column falling between the two lines of the Wordsworth quotation. The penciled entry is, however, later than the ink. The identity of all the persons named is not established although in Account Book (1828–1835) Emerson records paying a Saville a debt for Charles Emerson (August 4, 1830) and a cash payment to Mrs. Saunders (September 6, 1830). Joan Putnam was perhaps a daughter of Israel Putnam of Chelmsford who was taking charge of Bulkeley Emerson. Abby Larkin Adams of New Bedford was the adopted child of Emerson's friend Abel Adams; Emerson's cousin Phebe Ripley Haskins married John Chamberlain in 1824. The record of dates is Emerson's memorandum of his preaching engagements with the number of the sermons which he gave on each occasion. The bracketed numbers added to fill out the account are supplied from his own list in his School and Preaching Record.

  [9] The anecdote concerning Reynolds Emerson may have found in either *A Sketch of the Life of the late Richard Reynolds of Bristol, The Great Philanthropist* . . . (Bristol, 1816), p. 24, or in *Fragments to the Memory of the late Richard Reynolds, Esq., the Philanthropist* . . . (London, 1817), p. 8 and pp. 24–25; the phrase of Scipio, slightly misquoted, he no doubt found in Montaigne, "Of Vanity,"

—— Took possession of my chamber at Mr Pelletier's,[10] Tuesday 10 Dec.

Alexander gave away the conquered provinces, — "And what have you left for yourself?" "Hope"; replied the hero.[11] — ⟨The reason not for this low & vulgar application of the sentiment but for the sentiment itself⟩ "How do the wise differ from the unwise?" ⟨were⟩was the question put to Bias. He replied, "In a good hope." [12] It is the true heroism & the true wisdom. Hope. The wise are always cheerful. The reason is, (& it is a blessed reason,) [13] that the ⟨enlightened⟩ eye sees that the ultimate issues of all things are good. There is always a presumption in favor of a cheerful view.

14 Dec. I please myself with contemplating the felicity of my present situation. May it last. It seems to me singularly free & it invites me to every virtue & to great improvement.

The plough displaces the spade, ⟨&⟩ the bridge the watermen, ⟨and⟩ the press the scrivener.

[6] The Siphon. Reaumur's angles of bee-cells[.] [14] Smeaton [15] built Eddystone lighthouse on the model of an oaktree as being the

---

Essays, 1693, III, 306; and the Fontenelle remark came from Madame de Staël's *Germany*. See *Germany*, ed. O. W. Wight, 2 vols. (New York, 1859), II, 365.

[10] James Pelletier, a French teacher, at 276 Washington St., Boston, where Charles Emerson was already living.

[11] Plutarch, "Of the Fortune or Virtue of Alexander the Great"; see the *Morals*, 1870, I, 511. The story with slight variation is told also in Bacon's *The Advancement of Learning* (see *The Works*, 1824, I, 56).

[12] Diogenes Laertius, "Chilon," *Lives of Eminent Philosophers*, I, 69. See pp. 110–111 above for the possibility that Emerson is mixing two anecdotes, one on Chilon, one about Bias. The apophthegm appears also in William Penn, *The Christian Quaker, Select Works* (London, 1782), I, 217.

[13] The parenthesis and its internal punctuation are a later addition, differing markedly in color of ink from the rest of the entry.

[14] René A. F. de Réamur (1683–1757) had discovered that bee cells were always made with the same angles and six equal sides. Emerson had read this comment often, particularly in any argument of the period for design, such as Henry, Lord Brougham, "Preliminary Treatise: Objects, Advantages, and Pleasures of Science," in *Natural Philosophy*, 4 vols. (London, 1829), I, 31.

[15] "Smeaton . . . shin bone.": used in "Art," *W*, VII, 41.

form in nature designed to resist best a constant assailing force. Dollond (?) formed his ⟨te⟩ achromatic telescope on the model of the human eye. The Caraibs in Guiana use the sheaths of their palm tree to evaporate seawater for its salt, drawing the hint from Nature. Du Hamel built a bridge by letting in a piece of stronger timber for the middle of the under surface[,] getting a hint from the shin bone. See Bell on the Hand.[16]

[December] 19. The moral of your piece should be cuneiform & not polygonal. Judge of the success of the piece by the exclusive prominence it gives to the subject in the minds of all the audience.

2 January, 1834. The year, the year, but I have no thoughts for time. It occurs that a selection of natural laws might be easily made from botany, hydraulics, natural philosophy, &c. which should at once express also an ethical sense. Thus, 'Water confined in pipes will always rise as high as its source'. 'A hair line of water is a balance for the ocean if its fount be as high'. "Durable trees make roots first," C[harles]. reads.[17] A cripple in the right road beats a racer in the wrong ↑road↓.[18] "Fractures well cured make us more strong." Action

[16] John Smeaton published his own account of his work in *A Narrative of the building, and a description of the construction of the Eddystone Lighthouse, . . .* (London, 1791), but Emerson knew the story probably from such a secondary source as John Kidd, *On the Adaptation of External Nature to the Physical Condition of Man* (Philadelphia, 1833), pp. 127–129. John Dolland's achromatic telescope was well known. See Sir David Brewster, "Optics," in *Natural Philosophy,* 1829, I, 27. Of these notes on natural law, only the final entry on Jean-Pierre-François Guillot du Hamel and his bridge building comes from Sir Charles Bell, *The Hand, its Mechanism and vital endowments as evincing design* (Philadelphia, 1833), pp. 178–179. This volume, like Kidd's work cited above, is one of the famous Bridgewater Treatises intended to demonstrate the "Power, Wisdom, and Goodness of God, as manifested in the Creation" (see Kidd, p. viii).

[17] The natural laws could of course be found in most handbooks of science. " 'Water . . . its source.' " is a commonplace of hydrostatics that Emerson may well have read in Lord Brougham, "Hydrostatics," in *Natural Philosophy,* 1829, I, 3 and 6. The volume is the first of a 4-volume edition put out in the Library of Useful Knowledge and is made up of ten separate essays, by different authorities and separately paged. Emerson drew on the volume excessively for his lecture on "Water." " 'A hair line . . . as high.' " is a version of material in *ibid.,* p. 6. " 'Durable trees . . . first.' " is a statement from Charles Emerson's reading: used in *Nature, W,* I, 33.

[18] Emerson's paraphrase of Bacon, *The Advancement of Learning,* Bk. II (see *The Works,* 1860–1864, VI, 172 and *JMN,* III, 124). The aphorism is used in *Nature, W,* I, 33.

& reaction are equal.[19] Concentrated nourishment is unhealthy; there must be mixture of excrement.

[January] 3. To Goethe [20] there was no trifle. Glauber picked up what every body else threw away. Cuvier made much of humblest facts. The lower tone you take the more flexible your voice is. The whole ⟨prospect⟩ landscape is beautiful though the particulars are not. "You never are tired whilst you can see far." [21]

[7] [22] There is no weakness no exposure for which we cannot find consolation in the thought — Well 'tis a part of my constitution, part of my relation & office to my fellow creature. I like to see the immense resources of the creature. — 5 January. "Newton", says Fourrier, "knew not yet the perfections of the Universe." "What La Place called great, was really great." [23] I read in Herbert a beautiful verse, a high example of what the rhetorician calls the moral sublime.

> "Ah, my dear ⟨Lord⟩ God! though I am clean forgot,
> Let me not love thee, if I love thee not." [24]

[19] See William Enfield, *Institutes of Natural Philosophy, Theoretical and Practical*, 3rd Am. ed. (Boston, 1820), p. 12. "To every action . . . there is an equal and contrary re-action."

[20] "To Goethe . . . facts." is struck through with a use mark. "He [Goethe] knew no such thing as a trifle . . ." is in Sarah Austin, *Characteristics of Goethe*, 3 vols. (London, 1833), III, 323.

[21] Johann Rudolf Glauber (1604–1688), a German physician and alchemist who discovered muriatic acid and Glauber's salts. "Cuvier . . . facts.", like much of the material on science in the entries for December 14, January 2, and January 3, was later to be used and expanded in "The Uses of Natural History." See the *Lectures*, I, 18. Emerson had in his own library Georges Cuvier, *Discourse on the Revolutions of the Surface of the Globe, and the Changes thereby produced in the Animal Kingdom* (Philadelphia, 1831). "You . . . see far." is separated by a slash mark from the preceding entry and is in ink of a different color. It may be a later addition. According to Emerson the epigrammatic phrase was coined by his brother Charles. In Encyclopedia, p. [138], "You never are tired whilst you can see far enough" is ascribed to C[harles]. C[hauncy]. E[merson]: used in *Nature*, W, I, 16.

[22] "There is no weakness . . . fellow creature.": used in "Heroism," W, II, 261.

[23] Jean Baptiste Joseph Fourier, "Éloge historique de M. le Marquis de la Place," *Mémoires de l'institut* (1831), X, lc[xc] and lcxviii[xcviii]: used in "The Naturalist," *Lectures*, I, 73.

[24] "Affliction," ll. 65–66: used in "Ben Jonson, Herrick, Herbert, Wotton," *Lectures*, I, 352.

12 January. I was well pleased with Dr Bradford's [25] view of ⟨exper⟩ judgment the other day. Particular men are designated as persons of good judgment. It is merely that they are persons of experience in such affairs as interest most men. Their opinion on any question where they have not experience is worthless. ⟨Some men reserve thei⟩ Men of good sense act in certain conjunctures in a most imbecile manner. It is because it is their first trial. Others act with decision & success. It is because they have made many trials before & of course got through their failures. Then some men reserve their opinion & so never speak foolishly. Others publish every opinion they hold, & so though the first thoughts of all w⟨ill⟩ere equally ineffectual & foolish yet the abstemious have the credit of forming sound opinions the first time & the prompt speakers[,] if of active & advancing minds[,] are always uttering absurdities.

[January] 19. What is it that interests us in biography? [n] Is there not always a silent comparison between the intellectual & moral endowments portrayed & those of which we are conscious? [n] [8] The reason why the Luther, the Newton, the Bonaparte concerning whom we read, was made the subject of panegyric, is, that in the writer's opinion, in some one respect this particular man represented the idea of Man. And as far as we accord with his judgment, we take the picture for a standard Man, and so let every line accuse or approve our own ways of thinking & living by comparison. — At least I thought thus in reading Jeffery's fine sketch of Playfair the other evening.[26]

[January] 21. Is not the use of society to educate the Will which never would acquire force in solitude? [n] We mean Will, when we say that a person has a good deal of character. Women generally

---

[25] Gamaliel Bradford (Harvard A.B., 1814; A.M., 1819) took a medical degree and later became Superintendent of the Massachusetts General Hospital.

[26] From January 10 to January 18 Emerson had withdrawn from the Boston Athenaeum volume I of *The Works of John Playfair . . . with a memoir of the author*, 4 vols. (Edinburgh, 1822). The conclusion of the biographical memoir was a "Notice and Character of Professor Playfair," first published in an unidentified Edinburgh newspaper, by Francis Jeffrey. See Jeffrey's *Contributions to the Edinburgh Review*, 4 vols. (London, 1844), IV, 542–550, for a reprinting of this sketch.

have weak wills, sharply expressed perhaps, but capricious unstable. When the will is strong we inevitably respect it,[n] in man or woman. I have thought that the perfection of female character ⟨is⟩ seldom existed in poverty, at least where poverty was reckoned low. ⟨because⟩ Is not this because the rich are accustomed to be obeyed promptly & so the will acquires strength & yet is calm & graceful? [n] I think that involuntary respect which the rich inspire in very independent & virtuous minds, arises from the same circumstance[,] the irresistible empire of a strong will. There is not nor ever can be any competition between a will of words & a real will. Webster, ↑Adams,↓ Clay, Calhoun, Chatham, and every statesman who was ever formidable are wilful men. But Everett & Stanley & the Ciceros are not; want this ↑backbone.↓ Meantime a great many men in society speak strong but have no oak, are all willow. And only a virtuous will is omnipotent[.]

[January] 31[21]. I add that in a former ⟨of⟩age the men of might were men of will[,] now the men of wealth.

[9] [January] 22. Luther & Napoleon are better treatises on the Will than Edwards's. Will does not know if it be cold or hot or dangerous[;] he only goes on to his mark & leaves to mathematicians to calculate whether a body can come to its place without passing through all the intermediates. "Men have more heart than mind."
    Buy land by the acre & sell it by the foot.

Different faces things wear to different persons. Whole process of human generation how bifronted! To one it is bawdy, to another wholly pure. In the mother's heart every sensation from the nuptial embrace through the uncertain symptoms of the quickening to the birth of her child is watched with an interest ⟨as⟩ ↑more↓ chaste & wistful than the contemplations of the nun in her cloister.[n] Yet the low minded visiter of a woman in such circumstances has the ignorant impertinence to look down & feel a sort of shame.

———

    "⟨In⟩The Emperor Nicholas lately delivered a speech to the Council of Administration of Warsaw assembled at Modlin in which the following remarkable words occurred; "Gentlemen, you must persevere in your

course; and as to myself, as long as I live, I will oppose a will of iron
to the progress of liberal opinions. The present generation is lost, but we
must labor with zeal & earnestness to improve the spirit of that to come.
It may perhaps require a hundred years. I am not unreasonable. I give
you a whole age; but you must work without relaxation." "Boston Mer-
c[antile]. Jour[nal]." Jan. 21.

—————

Akin to the pathetic sublime of the two lines of Herbert on the
last leaf, are the lines in the last Canto of Il Paradiso, thus translated;
"O virgin mother, daughter of thy Son!
Created beings all in lowliness
Surpassing, as in height above them all." [27]

[10] 23 Jan. I cannot read of the jubilee of Goethe,[28] & of such a
velvet life without a sense of incongruity. Genius is out of place
when it reposes fifty years on chairs of state & ⟨breathes⟩ ↑inhales↓ a
continual incense of adulation. Its proper ornaments & relief are
poverty & reproach & danger. & if the grand-duke had cut ⟨his⟩
Goethe's head off, it would have been much better for his fame than
his retiring to his rooms after dismissing the obsequious crowds to
arrange tastefully & contemplate their gifts & honorary inscriptions.

New Bedford. 29 Jan. Michel Angelo's life in the Lib. Usef.
Knowl.[29] & his poetry by Signor Radici in the Retrospective Review
Vol 13. These elevate my respect for the artist. His life, they say
too, was a poem. Beautiful is his Platonic passion, before that word
had been perverted by affectation & hypocrisy. Heroic is his treaty
with the pope on assuming the charge of the building of St Peter's.
No fee & no interference.[30] Like my admirable Persian who would

[27] XXIII, 1–3. Emerson probably took the quotation from [Radici], "Review
of the *Rime*," *Retrospective Review* (London), XIII (1826), 260, since he cites the
article a week later. Emerson compares Dante to Herbert's poem, "Affliction," quoted
one "leaf" or two pages earlier.

[28] The entry is struck through with a vertical use mark in pencil. For an account
of the Jubilee, see Austin, *Characteristics of Goethe*, 1833, III, 50–51 and 100–116.

[29] [Thomas Roscoe], "The Life of Michael Angelo Buonaroti," in *Lives of
Eminent Persons* (London, 1833), 72 pp. The entry that follows is used in "Michel
Angelo Buonaroti," *Lectures*, I, 111, 115–117.

[30] "The Life of Michael Angelo Buonaroti," *Lives of Eminent Persons*, 1833,
pp. 44 and 48.

neither serve nor command; or like (is it not) Don ⟨Abbondio⟩ ↑Ferrante↓ 'Uomo di studio, non amava ni comandare ni ubbedire.' [31] Towards his end seems to have grown in him an invincible appetite of dying, for he knew that his spirit could only enjoy contentment after death. "Bel fin fa, Che vien amando more," said Petrarch. So vehement was this desire that 'his soul could no longer be appeased by the wonted seductions of painting & sculpture.' He blames his nephew for celebrating the birth of a son with pomp, saying "That a man ought not to smile when all those around him weep, & that we ought not to show that joy when a child is born which ought to be reserved for the death of one who has lived well." [32] He nothing vulgar did or mean.[33] He had a deep contempt of the vulgar, not of [11] "the simple inhabitants of lowly streets or humble cottages, but of that abject & sordid crowd of all classes & all places, who *obscure*, as much as in them lies, *every beam of beauty in the Universe.*" He had intense love of solitude & the country & rejoices in the remembrance of his residence with the hermits in the mountains of Spoleti so much that, he says, he is only half in Rome; 'since, truly, peace is only to be found in the woods.' [34] Berni said of him, "*Ei dice cose*, e voi dite parole." [35] He sought to penetrate by just degrees to the centre of that eternal radiance in which is hidden "l'amor che move il sole e l'altre stelle." [36]

Are not his struggles & mortifications a more ⟨splendid⟩ ↑beautiful↓ wreath than the milliners made for Goethe?

In reference to this appetite for death, shall I say it is sometimes

[31] The admirable Persian is Otanes, who pronounced himself "equally averse to govern or obey," in Emerson's personal copy of William Beloe's translation of Herodotus, *History*, 3 vols. (London, 1830), II, 75–76: used in "The Conservative," *W*, I, 307. Don Ferrante is a character in Manzoni's *I Promessi Sposi* whose actual remark in ch. 27 (1827, III, 60) was: "Uomo di studio, egli non amava nè di comandare nè di obedire."

[32] A pastiche of quotation and paraphrase from [Radici], "Rime," *Retrospective Review*, XIII (1826), 261–264 and "Michael Angelo Buonaroti," *Lives of Eminent Persons*, 1833, p. 61.

[33] Cf. Andrew Marvell, "An Horatian Ode upon Cromwell's Return from Ireland," l. 57: "He nothing common did or mean."

[34] "Michael Angelo Buonaroti," *Lives of Eminent Persons*, 1833, pp. 59 and 62 and [Radici], "Rime," *Retrospective Review*, XIII (1826), 256–257.

[35] "Rime," *Retrospective Review* (1826), XIII, 255.

[36] Dante, *Paradiso*, XXXII, 145.

permissible? that the object of life is answered when the uses of time are discovered; when the soul has so far discovered its relation to external truth, that time can never more be a burden, & nothing but the evils inseparable from human condition prevent⟨s⟩ it from being a heaven? —

1 Feb. In viewing the greatness of men of the first ages, Homer & Alfred equal to Goethe & Washington, does it not seem a little additional force of Will in the individual is equivalent to ages-ful of the improvements we call civilization? [n] But these Anakim do yet yield to the sad observer of his race real & great consolation (I am thinking now of Michel Angelo & his Platonism) for they seem to him himself without his faults & in favorable circumstances he recognizes ⟨these⟩ their lofty aspirations as the thoughts of his own childhood[;] he looks at these heroes as nothing peculiar & monstrous but as only more truly men, & he perceives that a heaven of truth & virtue is still possible. Some thoughts always [12] find us young,[n] and keep us so.[37] Such a thought is the love of the universal & eternal beauty. Every man leaves that contemplation with the feeling that it rather belongs to ages than to mortal life.

2 Feb. How often our nature is conscious of & labors with its own limits. In the very act of pretension it is oppressed with secret humiliation.

[February] 3. I have read Corinne [38] with as much emotion as a book can excite in me. A true representation of the tragedy of woman which yet (thanks to the mysterious compensation which nature has provided) they rarely feel. The tragedy of genius also. The story labors with the fault of an extravagant I may say ridiculous filial passion in Oswald which no man of such intelligence can carry so far & then with the second impossibility of his rapid marriage. No

---

[37] "Some thoughts . . . us so.": used in "Ode to Beauty," *Poems, W,* IX, 89.

[38] Emerson had withdrawn Madame de Staël's *Corinne ou l'Italie,* 3 vols. (Paris, 1812), from the Boston Library Society four times during 1820–1822. He may now have been reading the novel in English as *Corinna: or Italy,* 2 vols. (Boston, 1808), the edition he withdrew from the Boston Society Library in May, 1841.

matter; though the circumstances are untrue the position & the feelings of Corinne are possible, &, as Plato would say, more true than
history.[39]

New Bedford. 7 Feb. I have been to Plymouth & stood on the
Rock & felt that it was grown more important by the growth of
this nation in the minutes that I stood there. But Barnabas Hedge
ought not — no man ought — to own the rock of Plymouth.

[13][40] Mr Bond said he had learned that men can never learn by
experience. In the last depression of trade he had resolved never
to be caught again; and now amid his perplexities resolves again. At
sea we always ⟨determine⟩ ↑judge↓ by the present weather the probable length of the voyage.

10 Feb. The Newspapers say they might as well publish a
thunderstorm as a report of Webster's speech in answer to Wright.[41]

---

[39] *JMN*, III, 314, noted that in 1831 Emerson copied two quotations from a
review, one from Plato, one from Aristotle. "Action comes less near to vital truth
than description" was ascribed to Plato's *Republic*, V, [473]. This passage, Cornford,
a modern translator, renders as "Is it not the nature of things that action should come
less near to truth than thought?" (*The Republic of Plato*, New York, 1945, p. 178).
The second passage, "Poetry is something more philosophical and excellent than
history" was properly assigned to Aristotle, *The Poetics* [IX, 3]. Having copied the
two statements together Emerson in time began to blend them and ascribe the com-
posite to Plato, even though it is perhaps closer in idea to Aristotle. This tendency
he exhibits here and more fully in *Nature*, *W*, I, 69, where he ascribes to Plato
this mixed version: "Poetry comes nearer to vital truth than history."

[40] Mr. Bond . . . voyage." is struck through with a vertical use mark. Another
use mark runs from "last night" downward through "scaffold." In the left margin
from "10 Feb." to "were like" below are parallel ink lines, one straight, one wavy.
The first paragraph for February 10 is struck through with a wavy diagonal use mark
in pencil, and a second pencil use mark runs upward within the paragraph from
"tumult," to "last night"; within the second paragraph "It is . . . been poor." is
marked by a heavy line in the left margin. "Mr Bond" is probably George Bond,
early director of the Boston and Worcester Railroad and later a founder of the New
England Mutual Life Company, who in 1825 was involved in establishing the
American Unitarian Association. For Emerson's earlier use of "At sea . . . voyage."
see p. 247 above.

[41] Webster's speech "On the Removal of the Deposits," given in support of the
United States Bank on January 31, 1834, in response to Silas Wright of New York,
who had presented a resolution against the bank, contained the famous wordplay on the
phrase "the natural hatred of the poor to the rich."

His tones were like those of a commander in a battle. Times of eloquence are times of terror. I wrote to C[harles?]. last night that the obstinate retention of simple & high sentiments in obscurest duties is hardening the character to that temper that will work with honor, if need be, in the tumult, or on the scaffold. Yet perhaps the courage of heroes in revolutions is extemporary and what seems superhuman fortitude is the effect of an ecstasy of sorrow. Evil times have the effect of making men think. I suppose in the last few weeks men have thrown more searching glances at the structure & interdependence of society than in years of prosperous times. They begin to trace the path of an ear of ↑corn from ⟨the⟩its stalk to their table.↓

G.A.S[ampson]. confirms the views (21 Jan.) of the education of the Will,[42] by saying, that in his experience a very great change is produced in men by the possession of property, a great addition of ⟨energy⟩ force, which would remain to them if their property were taken away. It is not the possession of ⟨wealth⟩ luxuries but the exercise of power which belongs to wealth that has wrought this effect. The possession of Office has the same effect. What a pepper corn man is B.S. if he had been poor. By this education of things & persons he is now a person of decision & influence.

How imbecile is often a young person of superior intellectual powers for want of acquaintance with his powers[;] [14] bashful, timid, he shrinks, retreats, before every confident person & is disconcerted by arguments & pretensions he would be ashamed to put forward himself. Let him work as many merchants do with the forces of millions of property for months & years upon the wills of hundreds of persons & you shall see him transformed into an adroit fluent masterful gentleman, fit to take & keep his place in any society of men. This is the account to be given of the fine manners of the young Southerners brought up amidst slaves, & of the concession that young Northerners make to them, yes, & old Northerners to old Southerners. The story of Caesar among the Corsairs who took him prisoner [43] — rehearsing his speeches to them, abusing them if they did not admire, & threatening to crucify them one day, *which he did,* —

---

[42] See pp. 256–257 above.

[43] Plutarch, "Apothegms of Kings and Great Commanders"; see the *Morals,* 1870, I, 246.

is a good illustration of the natural empire of a strong Will. They had caught a Tartar.

This part of education is conducted in the nursery & the playground, in fights, in frolics, in business, in politics. My manners & history would have been very different, if my parents had been rich, when I was a boy at school. Herein is good ground for our expectation of the high bearing of the English nobleman.

B[enjamin].R[odman]. called his friend the naval architect, a perfect ship. Mr Hillman

[15] New Bedford, 12 February, 1834. The days & months & years flit by, each with his own black riband, his own sad reminiscence. ⟨&⟩ Yet I looked at the Almanack affectionately as a book of Promise. These last three years of my life are not a chasm — I could almost wish they were — so brilliantly sometimes the vision of Ellen's beauty & love & life come out of the darkness. Pleasantly mingled with my sad thoughts the sublime religion of Miss Rotch [44] yesterday. She was much disciplined, she said, in the years of Quaker dissension and driven inward, driven home, to find an anchor, until she learned to have *no choice,* to acquiesce without understanding the reason when she found an obstruction to any particular course of acting. She objected to having this spiritual direction called an impression, or an intimation, or an oracle. It was none of them. It was so simple it could hardly be spoken of. It was long, long, before she could attain to anything satisfactory. She was in a state of great dreariness, but she had a friend, a woman, now deceased, who used to advise her to dwell patiently with this dreariness & absence, in the confidence that it was necessary to the sweeping away of all her dependence upon traditions, and that she would finally attain to something better. And when she attained a better state of mind, its beginnings were very, very small. And now it is not any thing to speak of. She designed to go to England with Mr & Mrs Farrar,[45]

[44] Miss Mary Rotch, liberal Quaker of New Bedford, involved in the disputes of 1823–1824. According to Zephaniah W. W. Pease, ed. *Life in New Bedford a Hundred Years Ago* . . . (New Bedford, Mass., 1922), p. 26, Emerson is reported to have boarded with her, though his own account names Mrs. Deborah Brayton as his hostess.

[45] John Farrar, professor at Harvard, after the death of his first wife, Lucy Buckminster, married Eliza Rotch, sister of "Aunt" Mary Rotch of New Bedford.

& the plan was very pleasant and she was making her preparations & the time was fixed, when she conceived a reluctance to go for which she could not see any reason, but which continued; and she therefore suspended her purpose, and suffered them to depart without her. She said she had seen reason to think it was best for her to have [16] staid at home. But in obeying it, she never felt it of any importance that she should know now or at any time what the reasons were. But she should feel that it was presumption to press through this reluctance & choose for herself. I said it was not so much any particular power, as, a *healthful state of the mind,* to which she assented cordially. I said, it must produce a sublime tranquillity in view of the future — this assurance of higher direction; and she assented.

Can you believe, Waldo Emerson, that you may relieve yourself of this perpetual perplexity of choosing? & ⟨l⟩by putting your ear close to the soul, learn always the true way. I cannot but remark how perfectly this agrees with the Daimon of Socrates, even in that story which I once thought anomalous, of the direction as to the choice of two roads.[46] And with the grand Unalterableness of Fichte's morality. Hold up this lamp & look back at the best passages of your life. Once there was *choice*ⁿ in the mode, but *obedience* in the thing. In general there has been pretty quiet obedience *in the main,* but much recusancy *in the particular.*

> "Hamlet. But thou woulds not think how ill all's here
> about my heart:
> but it is no matter.
> Hor. If your mind dislike any thing, obey it."
> [Shakespeare, *Hamlet*, V, ii, 222–224 and 228]

"The barber learns his art on the orphan's face." Arabian Proverb.[47]

The walls of houses are transparent to the architect[.]

[48]Providence[:] men apply themselves to events & according to

---

[46] Plutarch, "A Discourse concerning Socrates' Daemon"; see the *Morals*, 1870, II, 388–389. Socrates, warned by his Daemon to change his road, walked another way saying that the change was the "will and admonition" of his Daemon. His friends went laughingly on but were overturned by a herd of swine. So it was shown that Socrates' Daemon never forsook him.

[47] The proverb occurs in D'Israeli, "The Philosophy of Proverbs," *Curiosities of Literature*, 1824, I, 449, and in a slightly varied form in Fielding, *Select Proverbs,* 1825, p. 54.

[48] The following paragraph is in pencil.

their affinities that is sweet or bitter. Good man is obedient to the
laws of the world & so successful. The angel rather. Conversation
with W.W. Swain.[49] The fish that swims round the world, then into
a little brook, & that is polluted by a dead horse may with reason
call that event as much a part of his life as the barnacle on a rock
in the same brook must call it a⟨n⟩ part of his circumstances[.]

[18] Boston, Feb. 19. A seaman in the coach told the story of
an old sperm whale which he called a white whale which was known
for many years by the whalemen as Old Tom & who rushed upon
the boats which attacked him & crushed the boats to small chips in
his jaws, the men generally escaping by jumping overboard & being
picked up. A vessel was fitted out at New Bedford, he said, to take
him. And he was finally taken somewhere off Payta head by the
Winslow or the Essex. He gave a fine account of a storm which I
heard imperfectly. Only 'the whole ocean was all feather white.' A
whale sometimes runs off ⟨3⟩three rolls of cord, three hundred fathom
in length each one. A sperm whale

[February] 20.

> "Self contradiction is the only wrong
> For by the laws of spirit in the right
> Is every individual character
> That acts in strict consistence with ⟨him⟩itself."
> Coleridge's Wallenstein [IV, vii].[50]

[19] [February] 21. The true reasons for actions are not given.
G[eorge].P.B[radford] says that he is so well understood at Plymouth that he can act naturally without being reckoned absurd. That
is a valid reason for going there. But how many would not understand it & how many understanding it would hoot at it? They
think a cheaper board is a good reason for going to one house or
the prospect of making acquaintance that give parties, or the like;
but such a reason as this which affects happiness & character seems

[49] William W. Swain, ship owner of New Bedford, was called "Governor"
Swain because he "ruled" jointly with John M. Forbes over the island of Naushon.
[50] Emerson is probably quoting these lines from Austin, *Characteristics of Goethe*,
1833, II, 181. He borrowed all three volumes of the work from the Athenaeum on
February 20, 1834, keeping the first two volumes out until April 17.

unworthy attention. As George says, it is agreed in society to consider realities as fictions & fictions realities.

[February] 22. It were well to live purely, to make your word worth something. Deny yourself cake & ale [51] to make your ⟨witness⟩ testimony irresistible. Be a pure reason to your contemporaries for God & truth. What is good in itself ⟨no circumstances can make bad⟩ can be bad to nobody. As I went to Church I thought how seldom the present hour is seized upon as a new moment. To a soul alive to God every moment is a new world. A new audience[,] a new Sabbath affords an opportunity of communicating thought & moral excitement that shall surpass all previous experience, that shall constitute an epoch a revolution in the minds on whom you act & in your own. The awakened soul[,] the man of genius makes every day such a day, ⟨but the professional mob⟩ by looking forward only but the professional mob look back only to custom & their past selves.

[20] [February] 25th. "The day is immeasureably long to him who knows how to value & to use it." said Goethe.[52]

2 March.[53] It is very seldom that a man is truly alone. He needs to

[51] Cf. Shakespeare, *Twelfth Night*, II, iii, 124.

[52] Austin, *Characteristics of Goethe*, 1833, II, 297. The "lustre" is a good example of Emerson's later remark in "Self-Reliance," that "a stranger will say with masterly good sense precisely what we have thought and felt all the time." About June 7, 1830, Emerson had entered in his journal, "The year is long enough for all that is done in it." (*JMN*, III, 188) On December 20, 1831 (*JMN*, III, 313) he had returned to his idea, deciding that if one could die or kill in an instant, "What can't then be done in a year? Life is long enough for any good purpose; a year long enough." After finding his idea well stated in Goethe, he reverts to it twice more later in Journal B, pp. [259] and [275] as "I am glad of a day when I know what I am to do in it."

[53] The entries for March 2 and March 15 are struck through with several vertical use marks, indicating, perhaps, a record of several stages of use: (a) through both entries but broken to omit the sentence "one illustration . . . the other."; (b) through both entries but very light and tentative over the sentence omitted in (a); (c) penciled through the March 2 entry, broken to omit "I have been . . . pines.", and then continued in pencil through the rest of the page; (d) through the March 15 entry, "I have been . . . once; '—'" and "Another illustration . . . world." No use marks appear on the final sentence of the March 15 entry on p. [21]. "He needs . . . great they are!": used in *Nature*, W, I, 7.

retire as much from his solitude as he does from society into very loneliness. While I am reading & writing in my chamber I am not alone though there is nobody there. There is one means of procuring solitude which to me & I apprehend to all men is effectual, & that is to go to the window & look at the stars. If they do not startle you & call you off from vulgar matters I know not what will. I sometimes think that the atmosphere was made transparent with this design to give man in the heavenly bodies a perpetual admonition of God & superior destiny. Seen in the streets of cities, how great they are! When I spoke of this to G.A.S[ampson]. he said, that he had sought in his chamber a place for prayer & could not find one till he cast his eye upon the stars. —

New Bedford, 15 March. I have been again to Plymouth and the families & the faces are almost as tranquil as their pines. The blue ocean reminded me of Goethe's fine observation that "Nature has told every thing once;" [54] — one illustration of it is Playfair's bough of a tree which was perfect wood at one end, and passed through imperceptible gradations to perfect mineral coal at the other.[55] Another illustration of it was to me this noble line of sea by which Nature is pleased to reveal to the asking eye the dimensions of the globe by showing the true outline of the world. Fine objects [21] in Plymouth from men & women down to vegetables, & saw & relished all even to the epigaea & the byssus or pulvis simplicissimus, ground pine, sabbatia, & empetrum.

"I will cast about for the causes of my disposition to take this view."
Mary Rotch

"I found though the sympathy of friends was most pleasant, yet the little faith I had, tho' but a grain of mustard seed, nothing could shake, and I found that nothing could confirm it." [56]

[54] Emerson's paraphrase of Goethe's remark in Austin, *Characteristics of Goethe*, 1833, I, 64, "that Nature accidentally and as it were against her will became the telltale of her own secrets; that everything was told — at least once; only not in the time and place at which we looked for or suspected it . . .": used in "The Relation of Man to the Globe," *Lectures*, I, 29.

[55] Playfair, *Illustrations of the Huttonian Theory of the Earth*, in *Works*, 1822, I, 161.

[56] "Mary Rotch" is written to the left of the quotations, possibly as a later ad-

"Nature tells every thing once." Yes our microscopes are not necessary[.] [57] They are a mechanical advantage for chamber philosophers[;] she has magnified every thing somewhere. Each process, each function, each organ is disproportionately developed in some one individual. Go study it there, instead of wearing your eyes out in your 6 million magnifier.

I count no man much because he cows or silences me. Any fool can do that. But if his conversation enriches or rejoices me, I must reckon him wise. Being & Seeming.[58]

[22] New Bedford, 21 March. I have been much interested lately in the Mss Record of the debates in the Quakers' Monthly Meetings here in 1823, when Elizabeth Rodman & Mary Rotch were proposed to be removed from the place of Elders for uniting in the prayers of Mary Newhall.[59] I must quote a ⟨wo⟩sentence or two from two of these speakers. Feb. 1823, "M[ary].N[ewhall]. rose in the meeting & began with As the stream does not rise higher than the fountain, &c spoke of the Mosaic dispensation in which the performance of certain rituals constituted the required religion, the more spiritual dispensation of our Saviour, of the advent of Christ & the yet more inward & spiritual dispensation of the present day. These dispensations she compared to the progressive stages of the human heart in the work of religion, from loving our neighbor as ourselves to loving our enemies & lastly arriving at that state of humility when self would be totally abandoned & we could only say Lord be merciful to me a sinner."

---

dition. The whole entry dealing with Mary Rotch is written and encircled in pencil. Emerson returns to this remarkable Quaker woman of New Bedford in the entry for March 21. She was, according to Orville Dewey, Emerson's cousin at New Bedford, called "Aunt Mary" Rotch and may well have resembled Mary Moody Emerson. See *Autobiography and Letters of Orville Dewey, D.D.*, ed. Mary E. Dewey (Boston, 1883), p. 67 and *Life in New Bedford*, ed. Pease, 1922, *passim*. For other remarks on her, see p. 263 above.

[57] "'Nature . . . necessary": used in "Country Life," *W*, XII, 160.

[58] "I count . . . wise." is enclosed in slash marks and struck through with a wavy diagonal use mark in pencil. "Being & Seeming." is one of Emerson's index headings on p. [161] below; it appears here in a different color of ink and may be a later addition.

[59] A noted Quaker from Lynn, she upset the Quaker meeting at New Bedford by her preaching. See *Life in New Bedford*, ed. Pease, 1922, pp. 14, 15 and *passim*.

[23] [blank]

[24₁] [60] New Bedford. My Swedenborgian friend Dr Stebbins [61] tells me that "he esteems himself measureably excused for not preaching whilst I remain here, as I am giving as much New Jerusalem doctrine as the people will bear." —

[25₁] Fine thought in the ⟨fine⟩ old verse by Barbour describing Bruce's soldiers crowding around him as with new unsated curiosity after a battle.

> "Sic wordis spak they of their king;
> And for his hie undertaking
> Ferleyit & yernit him for to see,
> That with him ay was wont to be." [62]

22 March. The subject that needs most to be /presented/ developed/ is the principle of Self reliance, what it is, what is not it, what it requires, how it teaches us to regard our friends. It is true that there is a faith wholly a man's own, the solitary inmate of his own breast, which the faith↑s↓ of all mankind cannot shake, & which they cannot confirm. But at the same time how useful, how indispensable has been the ministry of our friends to us, our teachers, — the living & the dead.

I ask advice. It is not that I wish my companion to dictate to me the course I should take. Before God, No. It were to unman, to un-god myself. It is that I wish him to give me information about the facts, not a law as to the duty. It is that he may stimulate me by his thoughts to unfold my own, so that I may become *master of the facts* still. My own bosom will supply, as surely as God liveth, the direction of my course.

This truth constitutes the objection to *pledges*. They are advo-

---

[60] An error in pagination begins here and runs to p. [26]. Repeated page numbers are indicated by a subscript number. For a description of the misnumbering, see the bibliographical note above.

[61] Dr. Artemas Stebbins (1787–1871) was both a doctor of medicine and a sporadic preacher in the Independent Tabernacle at New Bedford. In 1824 he became a follower of Swedenborg and organized a New Church Society in Bridgewater, Mass.

[62] See *The Bruce and the Wallace*, 2 vols. (Edinburgh, 1820), I, Bk. IV, 118, ll. 977–980.

cated on the principle that men are not to be trusted. They are to be trusted. They can never attain to any good, until they are trusted with the whole direction ⁿ [24₂] [63] themselves & therefore it is pernicious[,] it is postponing their virtue & happiness whenever you substitute a false principle for the true ⁿ in a mind capable of acting from a right motive.

[March] 23. It occurs that the distinction should be drawn in treating of Friendship between the *aid of commodity*, which our friends yield us, as in hospitality, gifts, sacrifices, &c. & which, as in the old story about the poor man's will in Montaigne,[64] are evidently esteemed ⟨the highest⟩ by the natural mind (to use such a cant word) the highest manifestations of love; and, secondly, the spiritual aid — far more precious & leaving the other at infinite distance, — which our friends afford us, of confession, of appeal, of social stimulus, mirroring ourselves. [March] 26.[65] As the ⟨bud⟩ ↑flower↓ prece⟨e⟩des the ⟨flower⟩ ↑fruit↓, & the ⟨flower⟩ ↑bud↓ the ⟨fruit⟩ ↑flower↓ ⟨26⟩ so ⟨L⟩long before the knowledge, comes the opinion, long before the opinion, comes the instinct, that a particular act is unfriendly, unsuitable, wrong. We are wonderfully protected. Much wisdom is in the fable of the stag who scorned his feet & praised his horns.[66]

[March] 27. We ⟨are taught⟩ ↑learn↓ to esteem our own censure above any other from the consideration that we shall always dwell with ourselves, & may abide with one another only a short time. ⟨Then we⟩ ⟨|| . . . ||⟩ There are two purposes with which we may seek each other's society — for finite good as when we desire protection, aid in poverty, furtherance in our plans, even political ⁿ societ⟨y⟩ies & philanthropical. All have relation to present well being. But there is a de-

---

[63] The page number, originally omitted, was supplied in pencil: "24a".

[64] "Of Friendship," *Essays*, 1693, I, 298. Eudamides, a poor Corinthian, had two close friends. He left a will in which he bequeathed to one friend the maintenance of his mother and to his other friend he left the care of his daughter and the obligation to provide her with an adequate dowry.

[65] The entry for this date is struck through with a diagonal use mark in pencil. The first sentence in the entry for March 27 is also struck through with a use mark, wavy, diagonal, and in pencil.

[66] "The Stag Drinking," in R. Dodsley, *Select Fables of Esop*, 1809, pp. 19–20. See p. 66 above.

270

sire of friends for the sake of no finite mercenary good ⟨gre⟩ small or great. There is a seeking of friends that thoughts may be exchanged, sympathies ⟨established⟩ ↑indulged↓, & a purity of intercourse established that would be as [25₂]⁶⁷ fit for heaven as it is for earth. The object of this intercourse is, that a man may be made known to himself ⟨by⟩ to an extent that in solitude is not practicable. ⟨The⟩Our faculties ⟨we possess⟩ are not called out except by means of the affections.

But we do not seek ⟨or⟩friends for conversation. We act for, with, upon ⟨th⟩each other. Our duty our necessity is continually forcing us into active relations with others. Very well. This serves the same purpose to make you master of your own powers. The service you render to others may be accomplished in another manner, but only by it can your own faculties & virtues be trained[.]

[March] 28. Wherever the truth is injured, defend it. You are there on that spot within hearing of that word, within sight of that action as a Witness, to the end that you should speak for it.

[March] 29. In the Am. Quarterly Review in an article on Parisian society occurs the remark, "The French have unquestionably carried society to as high a degree of perfection as it can well be brought."!!! ⁶⁸

> "My Heritage how ⟨far⟩long & wide
> Time is my heritage my field is Time." ⁶⁹

---

⁶⁷ The page number was repeated by error; later a penciled "a" was added. The repeated number is indicated by 25₂.

⁶⁸ *The American Quarterly Review*, XV (March 1834), 131–167: a review of Emma Willard's *Journal and Letters from France and Great Britain* (Troy, N. Y., 1833). Mrs. Willard considered French society immoral; on p. 155 the reviewer decidedly disagreed!

⁶⁹ Goethe's *West-Östlicher Divan* (*Werke*, 1828, V, 119) contains the original couplet: "Mein Erbteil wie herrlich, weit und breit! / Die Zeit ist mein Besitz, mein Acker ist die Zeit!" Carlyle, fascinated by the phrase, employed it in a variety of versions: (a) as the motto of his translation of Wilhelm Meister (1824): "My inheritance how wide and fair, / Time is my estate, to Time I'm heir." (b) This same version he used in "Jean Paul Friedrich Richter," *Foreign Review*, V (1830), 30. (c) In "Characteristics," *The Edinburgh Review*, LIV (Dec. 1831), 383, he changes his version to "My inheritance how wide and fair,/ Time is my fair seedfield, of Time I'm heir." (d) In *Sartor Resartus* he uses the tag as the title page

Boston, 10 April. Is it possible that in the solitude I seek I shall have the resolution the force to work as I ought to work — as I project in highest most farsighted hours? Well, & what do you project? Nothing less than to look at every object in its relation to Myself.

[26] E[dward].B.E[merson]. wrote on the back of Alexander's portrait of mother taken in 1825 at the age of 57 — ⟨C[harles].C. E[merson]. alters a few words⟩ Faeminae uxoris viduae matris optimae laudatae benedictae vita pulchra similitudo tam similis pretiosa. Ipsa mulier ⟨in⟩ad coelum ibit. Umbra picta inter amicos, Deo volente, nunquam inter inimicos, quia tales non sunt, vivis ⟨imaginem⟩ ↑descriptionem↓ ⟨purae⟩ ↑sine↓ error⟨is⟩e mortalis quondam, tunc angeli dabit.[70]

C.C.E. proposes an improved ⟨version⟩ reading of the second sentence. Ipsa mulier in coelum ibit: umbra picta inter amicos, Deo volente, non unquam cum tales nulli sint, inter inimicos, errore purae mortalis quondam tunc animae beatae imaginem servabit.[71]

"Placuit omnibus cui satis uni placuisse" epitaph on Olivia Buckminster Emerson[.] [72]

[27] 11 April. Went yesterday to Cambridge & spent most of the day at Mount Auburn,[73] got my luncheon at Fresh Pond, & went back again to the woods. After much wandering & seeing many things, four snakes gliding up & down a hollow for no purpose that I could

---

motto: "Mein Vermächtniss, wie herrlich weit und breit!/ Die Zeit ist mein Vermächtniss, mein Acker ist die Zeit." Since Emerson misquotes any version, his variation is no doubt done from memory.

[70] "The life of this woman, wife, widow, and mother, one of highest praise and blessed, is a beautiful likeness, so like a precious one. This woman will go into heaven. Her shade depicted among friends, God willing, never among enemies, because such do not exist, to the living she will give the appearance once of a pure mortal without error, now of an angel" (Ed.).

[71] "This woman will go into heaven: her shade depicted among friends, God willing, never among enemies, since such do not exist, she will preserve the image once of a pure mortal without error, now of a blessed soul" (Ed.).

[72] "She was pleasing in all things to one for whom it would have been enough to have pleased in one alone" (Ed.). Olivia B. Emerson, the wife of George Barrell Emerson, died in 1832.

[73] Cf. "May Day," Poems, W, IX, 169: "And dream the dream of Auburn dell."

see — not to eat, not for love, but only gliding; then a whole bed
of Hepatica triloba, cousins of the Anemone all blue & beautiful
but constrained by niggard Nature to wear their last year's faded
jacket of leaves; then a black capped titmouse who came upon a tree
& when I would know his name, sang *chick a dee dee*[;] then a far
off tree full of clamorous birds, I know not what, but you might
hear them half a mile. I forsook the tombs & found a sunny hollow
where the east wind could not blow & lay down against the side of
a tree to most happy beholdings. At least I opened my eyes & let
what would pass through them into the soul. I saw no more my relation how near & petty to Cambridge or Boston, I heeded no more
what minute or hour our Massachusetts clocks might indicate — I
saw only the noble earth on which I was born, with the great Star
which warms & enlightens it. I saw the clouds that hang their significant drapery over us. — It was Day, that was all Heaven said.
The pines glittered with their innumerable green needles in the light
& seemed to challenge me to read their riddle. The drab-oak leaves
of the last year turned their little somersets & lay still again. And
the wind bustled high overhead in the forest top. This gay & grand
architecture from the vault to the moss & lichen on which I lay [28]
who shall explain to me the laws of its proportions & adornments?
↑See the perpetual generation of good sense:↓ [74]

Nothing wholly false, fantastic, can take possession of men who
to live & move must plough the ground, sail the sea, have orchards,
hear the robin sing, & see the swallow fly.

Today I found in Roxbury the Saxifraga Vernalis[.]

12 April. Glad to read in my old gossip Montaigne some robust
rules of rhetoric: I will have a chapter thereon in my book. I would
Thomas Carlyle should read them. "In good prose (said Schlegel(?))
every word should be underscored." [75] Its place in the sentence should
make its emphasis. Write solid sentences & you can even spare punctuation. The passages in Montaigne are in Vol. 3. pp. 144–6. [76]

[74] "See . . . good sense:" is preceded by a long slash mark, is in ink different
from that of the rest of the page, and is inserted into space left between the two
paragraphs.
[75] Hare, *Guesses at Truth*, 2 vols. (London, 1827), I, 256; see *JMN*, III, 271.
[76] In Emerson's own copy of Montaigne, *Essays*, 1693, III, 144–147, the fol-

We are always on the brink of an ocean of thought into which we ⟨venture not⟩ do not yet swim. We are poor lords — have immense powers ↑which↓ we are hindered from using. I [77] am kept out of my heritage. I talk of these powers of perceiving & communicating truth, as my powers. I look for respect as the possessor of them. & yet, ⟨mo⟩ after exercising them for short & irregular periods, I move about without them — quite under their sphere — quite unclothed. " 'Tis the most difficult of tasks to keep Heights — which the soul is competent to gain." [78] A prophet waiting for the word of the Lord. Is it the prophet's fault that he waits in vain? [n] Yet how mysterious & painful these laws. Always in the precincts — never [29] admitted; always preparing, — vast machinery — plans of life — travelling — studies — the country — solitude — and suddenly in any place, in the street, in the chamber will the heaven open & the regions of boundless knowledge be revealed; as if to show you how thin the veil, how null the circumstances. The hours of true thought in a lifetime how few! And writing they say makes the feet cold & the head hot. And yet are we not ever postponing great actions & ineffable wisdom? [n] We are ever coming up with a group of angels still in sight before us,[n] which we refer to when we say 'the Truth' & the Wise Man, & the corrections these shall make in human society.

All the mistakes I make arise from forsaking my own station & trying to see the object from another person's point of view. I read so resolute a self-thinker as Carlyle & am convinced of the riches of wisdom that ever belong to the man who utters his own thought with a divine confidence that it must be true if he heard it there.

We live[,] animals in the basement story[,] & when Shakspeare or Milton or even my fantastical Scotchman who fools his humour

---

lowing passages are marked in the margin: "no more words of air but of flesh and bone, they signify more than they express." (p. 144); "The handling and utterance of fine Wits . . . motions." (p. 144); "And the forms of speaking . . . transplanted" (p. 145); "but that takes . . . understanding man" (pp. 145–146); "I would as much *naturalise* art, as they *artifie* Nature." (p. 146); "I can hardly be without a Plutarch . . . either a Leg or a Wing." (pp. 146–147).

[77] "I am kept" through "head hot" on p. [29] is struck through with wavy diagonal use marks in pencil.

[78] Wordsworth, *The Excursion*, IV, ll. 139–140, slightly misquoted. See p. 87 above. The passage is marked in Emerson's copy of *The Poetical Works of William Wordsworth*, 1824, IV, 134 and indexed under its page on the back flyleaf.

to the top of his bent [78a] — call[s] us up into the high region, we feel & say 'this is my region, they only show me my own property — I am in my element[,] I thank them for it.' Presently we go about our business into the basement again, cumbered with serving & assured of our right to the halls above, we never go thither.

[30] I had observed long since that to give the thought a just & full expression, I must not prematurely utter it. Better not talk of the matter you are writing out. It was as if you had let the spring snap too soon. I was glad to find Goethe say to the same point, 'that he who seeks a hidden treasure must not speak.' [79]

[April] 13. ↑Sabbath.↓ There are some duties above courtesy. And were it not lawful for the discontented unfed spirit sometimes to cry out 'Husks, Husks, Ye feed the people with words,' [80] even in their solemn assembly? [n] They distress me by their prayers, and all the discourse was an impertinence. There sat too, the gifted man, and if he unlawfully withheld his word, this wearisome pros⟨ing⟩e was his just punishment.

Elsewhere, certainly not there, but from M.M.E., from Carlyle, or from this delicious day, or whatever celestial fingers touched the divine harp, — I woke to a strain of highest melody. I saw that it was not for me to complain of obscurity, of being misunderstood; it was not for me even in the filthy rags of my unrighteousness to despond of what I might do & learn. Can you not do better than clear your action to the highest of these puppets or these potentates around you, by clearing it to your Creator? by being justified to yourself?

Absolve yourself to the universe, &, as God liveth, you shall ray out light & heat, — absolute good. [81]

[31] Were it not noble gratitude since we are the fruit of ⟨t⟩Time & owe all to the immeasureable past — its nations & ages guide our pen — to live for the world; to inspect the present &, in

---

[78a] Cf. Shakespeare, *Hamlet*, III, ii, 401.

[79] Quoting from Goethe's *Tag und Jahres Hefte*, 1803, Austin, *Characteristics of Goethe*, 1833, II, 322, actually wrote: "A man in search of hidden treasure must work in utter silence, must not speak a word."

[80] A paraphrase of Sewel, *The History of the . . . Quakers*, 1823, I, 44. See p. 32 above.

[81] "Absolve . . . good.": used in "Self-Reliance," *W*, II, 50.

the present, report of the future for the benefit of the existing race; & having once seen that Virtue was beautiful, count that, portion enough without higgling for our particular commodity to boot? [n] Down with that fop of a Brutus. Peace to the angel of Innocency for evermore.

It occurs how much friction is in the machinery of society.[82] The materiel is so much that the spirituel is overlaid & lost. ⟨In preaching⟩ A man meditates in solitude upon a truth which ⟨he proposes⟩ seems to him so weighty that he proposes to impart it to his fellowmen. Immediately a society must be collected & books consulted & ⟨paper⟩ much paper blotted in preparation of his discourse. Alien considerations come in, personal considerations — & finally when he delivers his discourse, 'tis quite possible it does not contain the original message ↑so that it was no superfluous rule he gave who said, When you write do not omit the thing you meant to say.↓ [83] The material integuments have quite overlaid & killed the spiritual child. ⟨A⟩ Not otherwise it falls out in Education. A young man is to be educated & schools are built & masters brought together & gymnasium erected & scientific toys & Monitorial Systems & a College endowed with many professorships & the apparatus is so enormous & unmanageable that the e-ducation or *calling out of his faculties* [32] is never accomplished, he graduates a dunce. See how the French Mathematics at Cambridge have quite destroyed the slender chance a boy had before of learning Trigonometry.

Is it otherwise in our philanthropic enterprizes? They wish to heal the sick, or emancipate the African, or convert the Hindoo, and immediately agents are appointed, & an office established, & Annual Reports printed, and the least streamlet of the Vast contributions of the public trickles down to the healing of the original evil. The Charity becomes a job.[84]

Well now is it otherwise with life itself? We are always getting ready to live, but never living. We have many years of technical edu-

[82] "Seeming disproportionate" is written above "much friction is in the"; broken lines arching over the two words apparently link them to the sentence underneath. They may be meant to be modifiers to "friction" or to be inserted in another fashion within the sentence.

[83] Hare, *Guesses at Truth*, 1827, I, 248; see *JMN*, III, 271.

[84] "Is it . . . job." is struck through with a vertical use mark in pencil.

cation; then, many years of earning a livelihood, & we get sick, & take journeys for our health, & compass land & sea for improvement by travelling, but the work of self-improvement — always under their nose, — nearer than the nearest, is seldom seldom engaged in. A few few hours in the longest life.

Set out to study a particular truth. Read upon it. Walk to think upon it. Talk of it. Write about it. The thing itself will not much manifest itself, at least not much in accommodation to your studying arrangements. The gleams you do get, out they will flash, as likely at dinner, or in the roar of Faneuil Hall, as in your painfullest abstraction.

Very little life in a lifetime.

[33] M.M.E. writes, that "the world is full of children, & what in our hearts we take no merit in — blush that it is no more generous — we expose to the weak as justification[.]"

[April] 15.[85] The least change in our point of vision gives the whole world a pictorial air, ⟨or⟩ shall I say, dramatizes it. Thus get into a stage coach & ride through Boston and what a ludicrous pathetic tragical picture will the streets present. The men, the women, those that talk earnestly, the hammering mechanic, the lounger, the beggar, the boys, the dogs are unrealized at once, or at least wholly detached from ↑all↓ relation to the observer & seen as phenomenal not actual beings. ↑V. p. 87↓ [86] Get into the railroad car & the Ideal Philosophy takes place at once. —

20 April. A good Inaugural Sermon from Mr Stearns at Old South this morning; & from Mr Frothingham this P.M. a good unfolding of the Parting of Elijah & Elisha. Elijah said "Ask What thou wilt." ⟨& Elisha⟩ Who could have stood this test? To whom would it not have been a snare? But Elisha said, "Let a double portion of thy spirit be on me".[87] The preacher should have added, I

[85] The entry for this date is struck through with three diagonal use marks. "The least change . . . actual beings.": used in *Nature, W*, I, 50–51, as is the continuation of the idea on September 17, p. 323 below, "Make . . . barnyard."

[86] The cross reference, inserted in a different ink, refers to the continuation of the idea on p. 323 below, where a further reference leads back to this passage.

[87] Samuel H. Stearns (1801–1837) was pastor at the Old South Church from

think, that the blessing descended in the asking, the prayer answered itself, as all real prayers do.

Awake, arm of the Lord! Awake thou God-like that sleepest! dear God, that sleepest in Man I have served my apprenticeship of bows & blushes, of fears & references, of ⟨unworthy⟩ ↑excessive↓ admiration. The young man is guided as much by opinion of society as if he came to you & me, & said, what shall I read? what shall I wear? what shall I say? [88]

[34] The whole secret of the teacher's force lies in the conviction that men are convertible. And they are. They want awakening. Get the soul out ↑of bed,↓ out of her deep habitual sleep, out into God's universe, to a perception of its beauty & hearing of its Call and your vulgar man, your pros⟨ing⟩y ↑selfish↓ sensual↑ist↓ ⟨selfish Capitalist⟩ awakes a God & is conscious of force to shake the world. It seemed to me tonight as if it were no bad topic for the preacher to urge the talent of hearing good sermons upon their congregations. I can hear a good sermon where Surd shall hear none, & Absurd shall hear worse than none. Spend the Sunday morning well & the hours shall shine with immortal light, shall epitomize history, shall sing heavenly psalms. Your way to church shall be short as ⟨a walk⟩ the way to the playground is to a child, and something holy & wise shall sit upon all the countenances there & shall inspire the preacher's words with a wisdom not their own. Spend the Sunday morning ill, & you will hardly hear a good sermon anywhere. See The good Ear, J. 1831, 4 Jan.[89]

Could it be made apparent what is really true that the whole future is in the bottom of the heart,[90] that, in proportion as your life

---

1834 to 1837, following Benjamin Wisner. Nathaniel Frothingham of the First Church, Boston, took the story of the young prophet succeeding the old from II Kings 2. The specific text was II Kings 2:9.

[88] The preceding sentence is included at the end of the paragraph in ink of a different color and set off by slash marks at its beginning and end.

[89] The cross reference, inserted at the end of the paragraph in ink of a different color and set off by slash marks, refers to an entry of January 4, 1832. The passage is indexed on the inside back cover of Blotting Book III as "*The good ear.* — 4 Jan" and the relevant lines read: "More is understood than is expressed in the most diffuse discourse. It is the unsaid part of every lecture that does the most good." See *JMN*, III, 315.

[90] Emerson's own proverb. See above pp. 52, 58, and 87.

is spent within, — in that measure are you invulnerable. In proportion as you penetrate facts for the law, & events for the cause, in that measure is your knowledge real, your condition gradually conformed to a stable idea, & the future [35] foreseen. I have laid my egg, but 'tis either old or empty. It was nobly said by Goethe that he endeavored to show his gratitude to all his great contemporaries, Humboldt, Cuvier, Byron, Scott, or whosoever by meeting them half way in their various efforts by the activity & performances of his own mind.[91] It is like the worthy man whom I once took up in my chaise as I rode, & who, on parting, told me he should thank me by rendering the same service to some future traveller.

[April] 22. The most original sermon is adopted by each hearer's selflove as his old orthodox or unitarian or quaker preaching. —

There are people who read Shakspear for his obscenity as the glaucous gull (or burgomaster) is said to follow the walrus for his excrement. I would be as great a geographer as an eagle — & every winter like a bird or member of congress go south.[92]

23d April. ⟨T⟩ In desert lands the bird alights on the barrel of the hunter's gun, and many other facts are there, but that which I would say is that every teacher acquires ⟨a continually ⟨st⟩ increasing *stationary* force; an active⟩ ↑a ⟨growing⟩ cumulative↓ inertia; the more forcible the more eloquent have been his innovating doctrines, the more eagerly his school have crowded around him, ↑so much↓ the more difficult is it for him to ⟨stat⟩ forfeit their love, to compromise his influence by advancing farther in the same track. Therefore the wise man must be wary of ⟨feeli⟩ attaching followers. He must feel & teach that the best of wisdom cannot be communicated; must be acquired by every soul for itself. And the prudent [36] world cannot wish that the gifted Channing should advance one step, lest it be left without the confidence in its Conductor.

[91] "It was nobly . . . mind." is struck through with a vertical use mark in pencil. The passage is a paraphrase of Austin, *Characteristics of Goethe*, 1833, II, 323, quoting from the *Tag und Jahres Hefte*, 1813.
[92] The sentence is in pencil with "go south." overwritten in ink different from that used on the rest of the page.

April 26, Newton. The muses love the woods & I have come hither to court the awful Powers in this sober solitude. Whatsoever is highest, wisest, best, favor me! I will listen & then speak.[93]

To [94] be without God in the world — who devised that pregnant expression? [—] to wander all the day in the sunlight among the tribes of animals unrelated to anything better; to see the horse & cow & bird, & to foresee an equal & rapidly approaching limit to himself & them. No, the bird as it ⟨flew⟩ ⟨fluttered⟩ ↑hurried↓ by with bold & perfect flight would disclaim his sympathy & declare ⟨you⟩ ↑him↓ an outcast. To see men pursuing in faith their varied action, warm hearted, providing for their children, consulting the feelings of their friends, remembering the beggar, what are they to this chill, houseless, fatherless, aimless baboon with the image without the soul of man? — they are dupes & he is wise. To him Heaven & Earth have lost their beauty. Nothing to him is great. The words Great, Venerable, have lost their meaning and not only these but every word[,] every thought of his mind has lost all depth has become mere surface. ⟨He has⟩ There is no longer distinction between the value of thoughts. To be sweet as sugar is sweet, strong as iron is strong, wise as a miser, happy as a drunkard is the whole compass of his speculation. And he ⟨himsel[f] has become lonely⟩ ↑is left↓ in how terrible a solitude. The hopes that cheered him, [37] the glorious affections that made a sky over all he knew, the unseen powers ⟨that armed his action⟩ that watched with tenderness his education, that knit his yet imperfect endeavors to the great Cause of goodness & to the Universe that labors for it, the fellowship of all great men working earnestly in the world, the smiles & auspices of departed heroes, yea, & the right & power to rejoice in any thing that is won or done — all all depart from him, he is alone in a barren & mean solitude. He ⟨feels that⟩ bitterly feels that he must yield the palm

---

[93] The word "hawk" is written into the empty line between this paragraph and the next, below "favor me!" and above "who devised"; the word may be a particularization of the bird "with bold & perfect flight" in the following paragraph linking it to the extensive description of the hawk on p. 281 below.

[94] "To be without . . . mere surface." is struck through with two vertical use marks in pencil. Similar parallel and vertical use marks in pencil appear on "How gloomy . . . gone forever." on p. [37]. The two passages are used in "The Preacher," *W*, X, 221–222.

of real dignity to the meanest worm or fly for they are not tormented with a consciousness of total worthlessness as he is.

How gloomy is the day & ↑upon↓ yonder shining pond what melancholy light if you bereave me of the Deity. I cannot keep the sun in heaven if you take away the Spirit that animates him. The ball indeed is there but his power to cheer, his power to illuminate the heart, as well as the atmosphere, is gone forever. Do you not see that wherever the wise the good man goes, light springs up in his path[?] — he carries meaning to every dead symbol; the creator is in his heart, & illustrates & affects his world, through the hands of his servant. But the evil man, that is, the Atheist, goes up & down & all is dark & pernicious.

Rain rain. The good rain like a bad preacher does not know when to leave off.

[38] ⟨I am sorry to⟩ Good is promoted by the worst. Don't despise even the Kneelands [95] & Andrew Jacksons. In the great cycle they find their place & like the insect that fertilizes the soil with worm casts or the scavenger bustard that removes carrion they ⟨integrate⟩ perform a beneficence they know not of, & cannot hinder if they would.

⟨See that falcon how giddily high he soars see those⟩

I saw a hawk today wheeling up to heaven in a spiral flight & every circle becoming less to the eye till he vanished into the atmosphere. What could be more in unison with all pure & brilliant images? [n] Yet ⟨was⟩ is the creature an unclean greedy ⟨bird⟩ eater & all his geography from that grand observatory was a watching of ⟨farm⟩ barn yards, or an inspection of moles & field mice. So with the pelican crane & the tribes of sea-fowl — disgusting gluttons all. Yet observe how finely in nature all these disagreeable individuals integrate themselves into a ⟨ple⟩ cleanly & pleasing whole.

[95] The Rev. Abner Kneeland (1774–1844) was a notable atheist, according to the report of the Universalists whose parish in Charlestown he served from 1811 to 1814; he edited *The Christian Messenger* from 1819 to 1821 and finally became the leader of a group called the First Society of Free Enquirers. He was indicted for blasphemy in December 1833 and finally convicted in 1838. Emerson signed a petition for his pardon.

[April]↑26.↓

Here is a Mytilus Margaritiferus as large as a moon & of the same color, & a Tellina radiata which reminds the beholder of the rising sun. I think they should call one of these shells, Moon; & the other, Morn. Today I found also the ⟨little⟩ Andromeda Calyculata, Houstonia, Potentilla sarmentosa. This empetrum & smilax & kalmia [96] & privet I have wondered oft to what end they grew. How ridiculous! Ask wrens & crows & bluebirds. As soon as you have done wondering & have left the plant[,] the bird & the insect return to it as [39] to their daily table. And so it renews its race, for a thousand thousand summers.

[97] Nat. Hist gives *body* [n] to our knowledge.

No man can spare a fact he knows. The knowledge of nature is *most permanent*, clouds & grass are older antiquities than pyramids or Athens, then they are *most perfect*. Goethe's plant a genuine creation. Then they bear strange but well established affinities to us. Nobody can look on a cistus or a brentus without sighing at his ignorance. It is an unknown America. Linnaeus is already read as the Plato who described Atlantis. A classification is nothing but a Cabinet. The whole remains to be done thereafter.

The boy & the W.

A religion of forms is not for me. I honor the Methodists who find like St John all Christianity in one word, Love.[98] To the parishes in my neighborhood Milton would seem a free thinker when he says "they ↑(the Jews)↓ thought it too much license to follow the charming pipe of him who sounded & proclaimed liberty & relief to all distresses." [99]

[96] Jacob Bigelow, *Florula Bostoniensis*, 1824, identifies the plants as follows: (a) dwarf andromeda; (b) coerulea; (c) running cinquefoil; (d) Triandria, an evergreen shrub; (e) green briar; (f) laurel.

[97] "Nat. Hist . . . The boy & the W." is in pencil. Emerson apparently is referring within the paragraph to Goethe's Archplant or "Urpflanz," to the evergreen European rock-rose, and to the Brentus Anchorago, a tropical beetle with an elongated snout. He uses the latter examples of natural history in "The Naturalist," *Lectures*, I, 79–80. For "The boy . . . W." see the anecdote on p. 285 below.

[98] Cf. especially I John 3:10,14,16,18 and I John 4:18: "he that loveth not knoweth not God; for God is love."

[99] See "The Doctrine and Discipline of Divorce," Preface to Bk. I, *The Works*, 1931–1940, III, Pt. 2, 387.

Roger Rain
Come Again!

[40] 2⟨7⟩8 April. Vaccinium Tenellum, Pyrus Ovalis, Anemone nemorosa, Fragaria Virginiana.[100] The day [101] is as good for these as for oaks & corn. The air vibrates with equal facility to the thunder & to the squeak of a mouse[,] invites man with provoking indifference to total indolence & to immortal actions. You may even shun the occasions of excitement by withdrawing from a profession & from society & then the Vast Eternity of capacity of freedom, opens before you but without a single impulse. A day ⟨seems⟩ ↑is↓ a⟨n⟩ ↑rich↓ abyss ⟨so rich⟩ ⟨in⟩of means yet mute & void. It demands something godlike in him who has cast off the common yokes & motives of humanity & has ventured to trust himself for a taskmaster. High be his heart, faithful his will, vast his contemplations,[n] that he may truly be a world, society, law to himself,[n] that a simple purpose may be to him as strong as iron necessity is to others. It is a faithful saying worthy of all acceptation [102] that a reasoning Man conscious of his powers & duties annihilates all distinction of circumstances. What is Rome, what is royalty, what is wealth? His place is the true place & superior therefore in dignity to all other places. Linnaeus at Copenhagen, Oberlin on the high Alps, White at Selborne, Roger Bacon at Oxford, Rammohun Roy in India & Heber at Bombay, Washington in the Jerseys. — These are the Romes, the Empires, the Wealth of these men. The place which I have not sought but in which my duty places me is a sort of royal palace. ⟨of Almighty splendor.⟩ If I am faithful in it I move in it with a pleasing awe at the immensity of the chain of which I hold the last link in my hand & am led by it. I perceive my commission to ↑be↓ coeval

[40ₐ] [. . .] [103]

---

[100] Bigelow, *Florula Bostoniensis*, 1824, identifies the plants as (a) low blueberry; (b) swamp pyrus, related to the choke berry; (c) wood anemone; (d) wild strawberry. All are listed as flowering in late April or early May.

[101] "The day . . . circumstances." is struck through with a wavy diagonal use mark in pencil. "It demands . . . is to others." within the use-marked passage is used in "Self-Reliance," *W*, II, 74–75.

[102] Cf. I Tim. 1:15 or 4:9: "This is a faithful saying and worthy of all acceptation. . . ."

[103] Between pp. [40]–[41] is a loose leaf, 12.6 x 20.2 cm, numbered "40a" in

[41] with the antiquity of the eldest causes[.]

[104] The vulgar man seems to himself unmoored, the moment he has changed his scene & associates. He misses his chair & his hat peg. The wise man carries his spring & his regulator within, & is at home in untrodden wilds.

↑Order of Wonder (see p 1.) Cause & Effect. Means & Ends↓ [105]

[April] 29. Fontenelle said, if men should see the principles of Nature laid bare they would cry 'What! is this all?' [106] How simple are they. How is the Wonder perpetually lessened by showing the disproportionate effect upon the eye of simple combination. The shell is a marvel until we see that it was not one effort but each knot & spine has been in turn the lip of the structure. Shakspeare how inconceivable until we have heard what Italian Novels & Plutarch's Lives & old English Dramas he had, also what contemporary fund of poetic diction. A Webster's Speech is a marvel until we have learned that a part of it he has carried in his head for years, & a part of it was collected for him by young lawyers & that Mr Appleton furnished the facts, & ⟨the Alf⟩ a letter from Mr Swain turned the paragraph. St Peter's did not leap fullgrown out of the head of the Architect. The part that was builded instructed the eye of the next

---

pencil. The material on the recto "40a" is printed exactly, except for minor cancellations, in *J*, III, 286. These brief notes, however, belong to the 1836–1837 lecture series given at the Masonic Temple in Boston from December 8, 1836, to March 2, 1837, on "The Philosophy of History." The material is part of Lecture IV, "Literature." Cf. James Elliot Cabot, *A Memoir of Ralph Waldo Emerson*, 2 vols. (Boston, 1887), II, 725–726. The verso of the leaf, unnumbered and unprinted in *J*, contains a series of index references in pencil to pages in Journal B (1835–1836) which deal with art, literature, and genius, and two columns of addition. Because of the obvious reference of these index materials to a later date, they are not printed here.

[104] "The vulgar . . . untrodden wilds." is struck through with a vertical use line. Cf. Knox, *Elegant Extracts . . . in Prose*, 1797, II, 1034, "A good man is at home wherever he chance to be"; or the Latin proverb, "Fortunato omne solum patria est," — "The fortunate man is at home in every land" (Ed.).

[105] The insertion "Order . . . Ends" is in pencil, a cross reference to a short index in pencil, omitted on p. 250 above which lists these three headings for p. [41].

[106] Emerson is paraphrasing an anecdote which he probably found in Thomas Brown, *Lectures on the Philosophy of The Human Mind*, 3 vols. (Philadelphia, 1824), I, 92. See *JMN*, II, 347. Emerson had this single volume of the set in his library.

generation how to build the rest. Mirabeau has his Dumont. The tree did not come from the acorn but is an annual deposit of ⟨g⟩ vegetation in a form determined by the existing disposition of the parts. Every leaf contains the eyes which are sufficient to originate a forest.[107] The magnet is a marvel when we simply see it spontaneously wheel to the north & cling to iron like one alive. The wonder diminishes when it is shown to be only one instance of a general law that affects all bodies & all phenomena[:] light, heat, electricity, animal life. A ship, a locomotive, ↑a cotton factory↓ is a wonder until we see how [42] these Romes were not built in a day but part suggested part & complexity became simplicity. The poem, the oration, the book are superhuman, but the wonder is out when you see the manuscript. Homer how wonderful until the German erudition discovered a cyclus of homeric poems. It is all one; a trick of cards, a juggler's sleight, an astronomical result, an algebraic formula, amazing when we see only the result, cheap when we are shown the means. This it is to conceive of acts & works[,] to throw myself into the object so that its history shall naturally evolve itself before me. Well so does the Universe, Time, History, evolve itself, so simply, so unmiraculously from the All Perceiving Mind.

G. P. B[radford]. tells a ridiculous story about the boy learning his alphabet. That letter is A; says the teacher. A — drawls the boy. "That is B," says the teacher. "B," drawls the boy, & so on, "That letter is W," says the teacher. "The Devil! Is that W?" enquires the pupil. — Now I say that this story hath an alarming sound. It is the essence of Radicalism. It is Jack Cade himself. Or is it not ⟨the⟩ exquisite ridicule upon our learned Linnaean Classifications? What shell is this? "It is a strombus." "The devil! is that a strombus?" would be the appropriate reply.

———

⟨The fly & the musquito are as untameable as the hyena & jaguar⟩ The fly strikes against the window pane until at last he learns that tho' invisible there is an obstacle there. The soul of man by a thou-

[107] Cf. the sentence in "Goethe; or, the Writer," *Representative Men, W*, IV, 275: "Thus Goethe suggested the leading idea of modern botany, that a leaf or the eye of a leaf is the unit of botany . . . ."

sand offences learns at last that there is an invisible Law which [108]

[43] [April] 30. There are more purposes in Education than to keep the man at Work. Self-questioning is one; a very important end. The disturbance the self-discord which young men feel is a most important crisis indispensable to a free improvable / race / creature. / Give me the eye to see a navy in an acorn.

If I could write like the wonderful bard whose sonnets I read this afternoon I would leave all & sing songs to the human race. Poetry with him is no verbal affair[;] the thought is poetical & Nature is put under contribution to give analogies & semblances that she has never yielded before↑.↓ ⟨to man.⟩ ⟨It is a *fair* question⟩ ⟨w⟩Whether the same or an equal tone of natural Verse is now possible? Whether we are not two ages too late? [n] But how remarkable every way are Shakspear's sonnets! Those addressed to a beautiful young man seem to show some singular friendship amounting almost to a passion which probably excited his youthful imagination. They are invaluable for the hints they contain respecting his Unknown Self. He knew his powers; he loved Spen⟨c⟩ser; he deplored his ↑own↓ way of living &c &c. What said C[harles].C.E[merson]. the other day touching a common impression left by Jesus of Nazareth & this poet? [n] [109] . . .

The war of the telescope & the Microscope[,] the mass & the particular. Science ever ⟨individualizes⟩ ↑subdivides↓. It separates one star into two, a nebula into a constellation, a class into genera, a genus into species & ever the most interesting facts arise from ascertaining habits of an individual. We should find the individual traits of a robin or a bee probably far more interesting than their generic habits when once we arrive to know them, as much as the traits of

[108] "The fly . . . which" is struck through with a diagonal use mark. The passage is broken off abruptly but with ample space left for later completion. "⟨The fly . . . hyena": used in "Considerations by the Way," *W*, VI, 269.

[109] In his notebook devoted to Charles Emerson, Waldo recorded a lengthy comment from 1836 in which Charles opposed Christ and Shakespeare. The poet was "pagan," the "inspired tongue of Humanity," and concerned with the kingdoms of this world whereas Christ was heavenly and celestial. Perhaps Charles had voiced this contrast earlier in his conversation.

one dog [44] affect us more than, though interesting, the canine character. Newton & Webster charm us more than accounts of the character of the Saxon Race.

It occurred also in the forest that there is no need to fear that
the immense accumulation of scientific facts should ever incumber
us since as fast as they multiply they resolve themselves into a formula
which carries the world in a phial. Every common place we utter
is a formula in which is packed up an uncounted list of particular
observations. And every man's mind at this moment is a ⟨sort of⟩
formula ↑condensing↓ the result of ⟨ye⟩all his conclusions.[110]

1 May: In this still Newton we have seven Sabbaths in a week.
The day is as calm as Eternity — quite a Chaldean time.

[111]The philosophy of the Wave. The wave moves onward but
the Water of which it is composed does not. The same particle does
not rise from the valley to the ridge. Its unity is only phenomenal.
So is it with men. There is a revolution in this country now, is there?
Well I am glad of it. But it don't convert nor punish the Jackson
men nor reward the others. The Jackson men have made their fortunes; grow old; die. It is the new comers who form this Undulation.
The party we wish to /convince/condemn/ loses its identity. ⟨Get Mr⟩
↑Elect↓ Webster ⟨in for⟩ President, —— & find the Jackson party
if you can. All gone[,] dead, scattered, Webstermen, Southerners,
Masons, any & every thing. Judicial or even moral sentence seems
no longer capable of being inflicted. France we say suffered & learned;
but the red Revolutionists did not. France today is a new-born race
that had no more [45] to do with that ↑regicide France↓ than the
Sandwich islanders.

3 May. The Idea according to which the Universe is made is
wholly wanting to us; is it not? Yet it may or will be found to be
constructed on as harmonious & perfect a thought, self explaining,

[110] Vertical pencil lines beside the passage in the right and left margins mark
"Every common place . . . conclusions."

[111] The paragraph is struck through to the bottom of the page with a vertical use
mark in pencil. Probably the part of the final sentence continued on p. [45] should
have been included in the marking, since "The philosophy . . . islanders." is used
in "Self-Reliance," *W*, II, 87.

as a problem in geometry. The Classification of all ⟨scien⟩ Nat. Science is arbitrary I believe, no Method philosophical in any one. And yet in all the permutations & combinations supposable, might not a Cabinet of shells or a Flora be thrown into one which should flash on us the very thought? [n] We take them out of composition & so lose their greatest beauty. The moon is an unsatisfactory sight if the eye be exclusively directed to it & ⟨no⟩ ↑a↓ shell ⟨is⟩ retains but a small part of its beauty when examined separately. All our classifications are introductory & very convenient but must be looked on as temporary & the eye always watching for the glimmering of that pure plastic Idea. If Swammerdam [112] forgets that he is a man, &, when you make any speculative suggestion as to the habits or origin or relation of insects, rebukes you with civil submission that you may think what you please he is only concerned for the facts, ⟨then I say⟩ he loses all that for which his science is of any worth. He is a mere insect hunter, & no whit more respectable than the nut-hatch or titmouse who are peeping & darting about after the same prey.

This was what Goethe sought in his Metamorphosis of plants. The Pythagorean doctrine of transmigration is an Idea; the Swedenborgian of Affections Clothed, is one also.[113] Let the Mind of the ⟨observer⟩ student be in a natural, healthful, & progressive state[;] let him in the midst of his most [46] minute dissection, not lose sight of the place & relations of the subject. Shun giving it a disproportionate importance but speedily adjust himself & study to see the thing though with added acquaintance of its ⟨proximate⟩ intimate structure under the sun & in the landscape as he did before. Let it be a point as before. Integrate the particulars.

We have no Theory of animated Nature. When we have, it

---

[112] Jan Swammerdam (1637–1690), Dutch naturalist who described the red-blood cells in 1658 and the valves of the lymph vessels in 1664, and made microscopic examinations of the anatomy of insects.

[113] "This was . . . one also." is marked in the left margin by a heavy vertical pencil line. See pp. 342–343 below, the entry of November 23, 1834, for a fuller description of this Swedenborgian doctrine that the "affections" clothe themselves with appropriate garments, dwellings, or circumstances. So the natural world becomes a symbol for the spiritual and even animals are merely "incarnations of certain affections" as Emerson explained to Carlyle on November 20. (See *The Correspondence of Thomas Carlyle and Ralph Waldo Emerson, 1834–1872*, ed. Charles E. Norton, 2 vols., rev. ed., Boston, 1884, I, 32.)

will be itself the true Classification. Perhaps a study of the cattle on the mountainside as they graze, is more suggestive of truth than the inspection of their parts in the dissection-room.[114]

The way they classify is by counting stamens or filaments or teeth & hoofs & shells. A true argument, what we call the unfolding an idea, as is continually done in Plato's Dialogues, in Carlyle's Characteristics, or in a thousand acknowledged applications of familiar †ethical↓ truths,[115]   these are natural classifications containing their own reason in themselves, & making known facts continually. They are themselves the formula, the largest generalization of the facts, & if thousands on thousands more should be discovered this idea hath predicted already their place & fate. When shall such a classification be obtained in botany? This is evidently what Goethe aimed to do, in seeking the Arch plant, which, being known, would give not only all actual but all possible vegetable forms.[116] Thus to study would be to hold the bottle under water instead of filling it drop by drop. I wrote once before that the true philosophy of man should give a theory of Beasts & Dreams. A German dispatched them both by saying that Beasts are dreams, or "the nocturnal side of Nature." [117]

[47] 5 May. Monday — The parliamentary people say, we must not blink the question. There is an intellectual duty as impera-

---

[114] Double pencil lines run in the left margin from "be itself" above to "of truth" below. Probably they are meant to mark off the whole of the first paragraph on classification.

[115] Almost a line is left blank after this word, probably in order to have space for further illustrations of the point.

[116] See Austin, *Characteristics of Goethe*, 1833, I, 172, quoting a letter from Goethe to Herder: "The Archetypal Plant will be the strangest creature in the world . . . . With this model . . . one may then invent plants *ad infinitum*." See also p. 282 above.

[117] Madame de Staël, *Germany* (New York, 1814), II, 201, in talking about errors, superstitions, and the occult powers pleaded for a philosophy comprehensive enough to "embrace the universe" and wise enough not to despise "*the nocturnal side of nature*." In *Germany*, II, 322, discussing Daniel Schubert, she remarked: "How can we consider animals without being plunged into the astonishment which their mysterious existence causes? *A poet has called them the dreams of Nature, and man her waking.*" Emerson apparently linked the two statements in his memory, even though they are only distantly related.

tive & as burdensome as that moral one. I come ↑e.g.↓ to the present subject of Classification. At the centre it is a black spot — no line, no handle, no character; I am tempted to stray to the accessible lanes on the left hand & right, which lead round it — all outside of it. Intellectual courage, intellectual duty says we must not blink the question, we much march up to it & sit down ⟨at⟩before ↑it↓ ⟨the town⟩ & watch there incessantly getting as close as we can to the black wall, and watch & watch, until slowly lines & handles & characters shall appear on its surface & we shall learn to open the gate & enter the fortress, un⟨cover⟩↑roof↓ it & lay bare its ↑ground-↓plan ⟨& constitution⟩ to the day.

Mr Coleridge has written well on this matter of Theory in his Friend.[118] A lecture may be given upon insects or plants, that, when it is closed irresistibly suggests the question, 'Well what of that?' An enumeration of facts without method. A true method has no more need of firstly, secondly, &c. than a perfect sentence has of punctuation. It tells its own story, makes its own feet, creates its own form. It is its own apology. The best argument of the lawyer is a skilful telling of the story. The true Classification will not present itself to us in a catalogue of a hundred classes, but as an idea of which the flying ⟨insect⟩ ↑wasp↓ & the grazing ⟨cattle⟩ ↑ox↓ are developments.[119] Natural History is to be studied not with any pretention that its theory is attained, that its classification is permanent, but merely as full of tendency.[n]

[48] 6 May. Well, my friend, are you not yet convinced that you should study plants & animals? [n] To be sure the reasons are not very mighty; but words. To it again. ⟨T⟩Say then that I will study Natural history to provide me a resource when business, friends, & my country fail me, that I may never lose my temper nor be without soothing uplifting occupation. It will yet cheer me in solitude or I think in madness, that the mellow voice of the robin is not a stranger

---

[118] *The Friend, A Series of Essays* . . . , 3 vols. (London, 1818), III, 153–203. Essays V, VI, and VII are devoted largely to the questions of classification in the sciences, to theory, and to the problem of method.

[119] "The best . . . developments." is marked in right and left margin with vertical pencil lines.

to me, that the flowers are reflections to me of earlier, happier, & yet thoughtful hours[.]

Or again say that I am ever haunted by the conviction that I have an interest in all that goes on around me[,] that I would over-hear the powers what they say. — No knowledge can be spared, ⟨n⟩or ↑any↓ advantage we can give ourselves. And this is the knowledge of the laws by which I live. But finally ⟨all the reasons⟩ say frankly, that all the reasons seem to me ⟨f⟩to fall far short of my faith upon the subject, therefore — boldly press the cause as its own evidence; say that you love nature, & would know her mysteries, & that you believe in your power by patient contemplation & docile experiment to learn them.

8 May. The men of this world say ever of the Thinker, "How knoweth th⟨ese⟩is man these things, having never learned?" ⟨Nor can he⟩ Ho! every one that thirsteth! Come ye to the waters, & he that hath no money come buy wine & milk without money.[120]

"The recluse hermit ofttimes more doth see," &c. A few wise instincts [121]

[49][122] [May] 16. I remember when I was a boy going upon the beach & being charmed with the colors & forms of the shells. I picked up many & put them in my pocket. When I got home I could find nothing that I gathered — nothing but some ⟨old⟩ dry ugly mussel & snail shells. Thence I learned that Composition was more impor-tant than the beauty of individual forms to effect. On the shore they lay wet & social by the sea & under the sky.

[120] John 7:15, slightly misquoted, and Isa. 55:1.

[121] Donne's "Eclogue of Dec. 26, 1613," l. 1; the poem is quoted in Coleridge's *The Friend*, 1818, I, 192, with some alterations. Emerson apparently took his line from this version but is misquoting both Donne and Coleridge's variant. For the in-complete phrase, cf. Wordsworth, "Alas! What Boots the Long Laborious Quest," l. 11: "A few strong instincts and a few plain rules" (quoted also later in Journal B, p. [317]).

[122] "I remember . . . the sky." is struck through with a vertical use mark in pencil: used in "Each and All," *W*, IX, 5. "The sun . . . the child." is struck through with a diagonal use mark. "Ah that . . . the word!" is struck through with a diagonal use mark in pencil. "⟨C.C. . . . . benevolence.⟩" is heavily canceled with circular lines which begin with "RW" written over the underlying "C.C."

The sun illuminates the eye of the man but the eye & the heart of the child. His heart is in the right place[.]

Many eyes go through the meadow, but few see the flowers in it.

21 May. I will thank God of myself & for that I have. I will not manufacture remorse of the pattern of others, nor feign their joys. I am born tranquil[,] not a stern economist of Time but never a keen sufferer. I will not affect to suffer. Be my life then a long gratitude. I will trust my instincts. For always a reason halts after an instinct, & when I have deviated from the instinct, comes somebody with a profound theory teaching that I ought to have followed it. Some Goethe, Swedenborg, or Carlyle. I stick at scolding the boy, yet conformably to rule, I scold him. By & by the reprimand is a proven error. "Our first & third thought coincide." [123] I was the true philosopher in college, & Mr Farrar & Mr Hedge & Dr Ware [124] the false. Yet what seemed then to me less probable?

"There are three things," said my worthy friend W[illiam]. W[all?]. to me, "that make the gentleman, — the hat, the collar, & the boots."

Ah that Professor Teufelsdrock had heard the word! ⟨C.C.[E.] says that he never spends any thing on himself without deserving the praise of disinterested benevolence.⟩

[50] [May] 29.[125] Dr Darwin's work has lost all its consequence in the literary world. Why? not from Currie nor from Brown.[126] No. A dim venerable public decides upon every work. When it ⟨appears⟩ ↑offers itself↓, a sort of perplexity, ⟨a⟩ ↑an uneasy↓ waiting for judgment appears in the living literary judges, but ⟨it⟩ ↑the work↓ presently

[123] Dugald Stewart, *The Philosophy of the Human Mind*, probably quoted from Hare, *Guesses at Truth*, 1827, I, 143; see *JMN*, III, 265.

[124] John Farrar, Hollis Professor of mathematics and natural philosophy; Levi Hedge, author of *Elements of Logick*, who taught Lockean philosophy; and Dr. Henry Ware, Sr., professor of theology.

[125] The first paragraph of this entry is struck through with a vertical use mark.

[126] Dr. Erasmus Darwin's *Zoonomia, or the laws of organic life* (London, 1794–1796); probably Dr. James Currie (1756–1805), Scottish physician who wrote on fever and whose own case of pleurisy was discussed in Darwin's work; and Dr. John Brown (1735–1788), whose work on the elements of medicine reportedly provided material for Darwin.

takes its true place by no effort friendly or hostile, but by the real importance of its principles to the Constant Mind of Man. And this in a way that no individual ⟨seems⟩ can much affect, by blame or praise. It is the specific gravity of the atom.

⟨A young man who aspires⟩ An aspiring young man readily distinguishes in the first circles those who are there by sufferance & those who constitute them first circles, & attaches himself to the fountains of honor not to the conduits. The true aspirant goes one step further & ⟨mak⟩ discerns in himself the Fountain of these fountainlets & so becomes the giver of all fine & high influences. In him is the source of all the romance, the lustre, the dignity, that ⟨yet⟩ fascinates him in some saloons with an inexpressible charm; for, truth, honor, learning, perseverance are the Jove & Apollo who bewitched him[.] ↑see p. 84↓ [127]

30 May. Languages as discipline, much reading as an additional atmosphere or two, to gird the loins & make the muscles more tense. It seems time lost for a grown man to be turning the leaves of a dictionary like a boy to learn German, but I believe he will gain tension & creative power by so doing. Good books ⟨are⟩ have always a prolific atmosphere about them & brood upon the spirit. — [May] 31. ⟨One has foresight of dim mechanical advantages & ↑also↓ confirmation of the ideal philosophy that matter is phenomenal, [51] [128] when riding on the rail road, & seeing trees & men whiz by you as fast as the leaves of a dictionary as you hiss by them in your tea kettle.⟩ [129]

2 June. The life of women is unfortunately so much for exhibition that/every/the minutest/trait pleases which is wholly natural, even to a girl's crying because it thundered, et ce que disent les femmes

[127] Vertical lines in ink and pencil in the left margin apparently mark off "an inexpressible . . . see p. 84"; see p. 321 below.
[128] "What more . . . visit him." is struck through with a vertical use mark which actually descends, perhaps by error, to "yesterday" in the following paragraph. "When there is . . . should say." is struck through with a wavy diagonal use mark in pencil. At the foot of the page "See . . . Aug. 17" is in pencil, probably an inserted cross reference in further comment on the problems of genuineness, pp. 312–314 below.
[129] "⟨One has . . . tea kettle.⟩": used in *Nature*, *W*, I, 50–51. Canceled here, the passage is included in the entry for June 10, p. 296 below.

l'une de l'autre.   What more sensible than what they say of Mr Cushing that he sells his splendid Chinese house & goes to live at Watertown because he cannot make a bow & pleasantly entertain the crowd of company that visit him. ↑C[harles] C E[merson] says he should build a large room.↓

Preached at Waltham yesterday. Expect every day when some trenchant Iarno will come across me & read me such a lesson.[130] Is the preacher one to make a fool of himself for the entertainment of other people? would he say. When there is any difference of level felt in the foot board of the pulpit & the floor of the parlor, you have not said that which you should say. The best sermon would be a quiet conversational analysis of these felt difficulties, discords: to show the chain under the leather; to show the true within the supposed advantage of Christian institutions. There are several worthy people making themselves less because they would act the police officer, & keep the factory people at church. I say Be genuine. They answer, If we should, our society which has no real virtue, would go to pot. And so the yoke ⟨has⟩ it is confessed[,] is only borne out of fear. Suppose they should let the societies go down, and form new & genuine ones? Let such as ⟨saw &⟩ felt the advantage of a sermon & social worship meet voluntarily & compel nobody.

See further ⟨June⟩ Aug. 17

[52] 3 June.[131] The lower tone you take the more flexible your voice is.

5 June. What perpetual working & counterworking in us so that many good actions spring from bad motives & many bad actions from good motives. Verily. Then how slovenly & despite ourselves we are continually jostled into knowledge of truth. D.P. commends peace to the boys, the boys debate the matter & give such cogent reasons to the contrary, that D.P. in anger & fear to be put down, wades out

---

[130] On June 1, 1834, Emerson preached at Waltham using sermons 164 and 104 (see *YES*, 180–190 and 127–137). His discussion of the "genuine man" no doubt led him to his remark about Goethe's character, Iarno, in *Wilhelm Meister*, who warned Wilhelm to be himself without fear of appearance.

[131] The entry is a verbatim repetition of a sentence in the entry for January 3. See p. 255 above.

beyond his depth in the other direction, & gets unawares a knowledge of the infinite reason of love. Highest praise & happiness is it to go forward one step of our own ⟨accord⟩ ↑seeing↓ & find ourselves in a position whose advantages we foresaw.

Fatal tendency to hang on to the letter & let the spirit go.[n] We will debate the precept about 'turning the cheek to the smiter,' the 'coat & cloke,' the 'not taking thought what ye shall speak,'[132] &c & question whether it is now practicable, & is now obligatory. Yet every one of us has had his hours of illumination by the same spirit when he fully understood those commands & saw that he did not need them. He had the Commander; giving fresh precepts fit for the Moment & the Act. Yet it is[n] well that Christ's are recorded[;] they show how high the waters flowed when the Spirit brooded upon them & are a measure of our deficiency. The wonder that is felt at these precepts is a measure of our Unreason.

There are persons both of superior character & intellect whose superiority quite disappears when they are put together. They neutralize, anticipate, puzzle, & belittle each other.

⟨Antagonisms.[133]

[53] 8 June. The solitary bird that sung in the pine tree reminded me of one talker who has nothing to say alone, but when friends come in, & the conversation grows loud[,] is ⟨m⟩forthwith set into intense activity mechanically echoing & strengthening every thing that is said, without any regard to the subject or to truth. The soul has its diurnal, annual, & secular periodic motions like the needle. You may doubt ⟨o⟩for a day but you will believe before the week's end; you may abandon your friendships & your designs as you think on good advice for these months, but by & by it will come back ↑as↓ with thunder from all heaven, that God crowns him who persists in his purposes — no fair weather friend[n] [—] that the very armory of heroes & sages is in obscurity, conflict, high heart which

[132] Cf. II Cor. 3: 6, Luke 6: 29 or Matt. 5: 39–40, and Matt. 10:19, slightly misquoted.

[133] "Antagonisms" is centered beneath "put together. They" and is at the bottom of the page with a heavy ink bracket at the left which is apparently linked to a half bracket in the left margin around and above "There are persons"; the ink of the word and brackets differs from that of the rest of the entry.

sustained itself Alone. You are there in that place to testify. There was a man in Sais who was very good to all people but he could not be trusted alone. ⟨The moment⟩ When he was left alone all the devils associated themselves to him, & he robbed, murdered, committed adultery, blasphemed, lied, cringed.

10 June. One has dim foresight of ⟨what⟩ hitherto uncomputed mechanical advantages who rides on the rail-road and moreover a practical confirmation of the ideal philosophy that Matter is phenomenal whilst men & trees & barns whiz by you as fast as the leaves of a dictionary. As our teakettle hissed along through a field of may-flowers, we could judge of the sensations of a swallow who skims by trees & bushes with about the same speed. The very permanence of matter seems compromised & ⟨trees⟩ ↑oaks↓, fields, hills, hitherto esteemed symbols of stability do absolutely dance by you.[134] The countryman called it 'Hell in harness.'

[54] What habits of observation has my friend[,] what keen senses. It would seem as if nothing though under your nose was permitted to be visible to you until he had seen it. Thereafter, all the world may see it, & it never leaves your eyes.

Washington wanted a fit public. Aristides, Phocion, Regulus, Hampden had worthy observers. But there is yet a dearth of American genius[.]

I went to the Menagerie Tuesday & saw 14 pelicans, a sacred ibis, a gazelle, zebras, a capibra, ichneumon, hyena, &c. It seems to me like 'visiting the spirits in prison.' Yet not to '*preach.*'[135] There was the mystery. No *Word*[n] could pass from me to them. ⟨They⟩ ↑Animals↓ have been called by some German 'the dreams of Nature.'[136] I think we go to our own dreams for a conception of their consciousness. In a dream I have the same instinctive obedience, the same torpidity of the highest power, the same un-surprized assent to

---

[134] See p. 293, n.129 above.
[135] I Pet. 3:19, slightly misquoted.
[136] Madame de Staël, *Germany*, 1814, II, 322; see p. 289 above.

the Monstrous as these ⟨pythagorean⟩ ↑metamorphosed↓ Men exhibit. The pelicans remind one of Nick Bottom. One has a kind of compassionate fear lest they should ⟨fo⟩ have a glimpse of their ⟨own⟩ forlorn condition. What ⟨a⟩ horrible calamity would be to them one moment's endowment of reason[.]

Yet sometimes the negro excites the same feeling & sometimes the sharpwitted prosperous white man. You think if he could overlook his own condition he could not be kept from suicide. But to the contemplations of the Reason is there never penitence.

"Ma nel mondo non è se non volgo." Machiavelli [137]

[55] The scholar seeks the ingenuous boy to apprize him of the treasures within his reach, to show him poetry, religion, philosophy, & congratulate him on being born into the Universe. The boy's parents immediately call to thank him for his interest in their Son & ask him to procure him a Schoolmaster's situation. 18 June. Every thing teaches, even dilettantism. The dilettante does not, to be sure, learn anything of botany by playing with his microscope & with the terminology of plants but he learns what dilettantism is; he distinguishes between what he knows & what he affects to know & through some pain & self accusation he is attaining to things themselves[.]

Webster's speeches seem to be the utmost that the unpoetic West has accomplished or can. We all lean on England[,] scarce a verse, a page, a newspaper but is writ in imitation of English forms, our very manners & conversation are traditional & sometimes the life seems dying out of all literature & this enormous paper currency of Words is accepted instead. I suppose the evil may be cured by this rank rabble party, the Jacksonism of the country, heedless of English & of all literature — a stone cut out of the ground without hands — [137a] they may root out the hollow dilettantism of our cultivation in the coarsest way & the new-born may begin again to frame their own world with greater advantage. Meantime Webster is no imitator but a true genius for his work if ⟨not⟩that is not the highest. But every true man stands on the top of the world. He has a majestic under-

---

[137] See Coleridge's *On the Constitution of Church and State* . . . , ed. H. N. Coleridge (London, 1839), p. 99.
[137a] Cf. Dan. 2:34 and 45.

standing, which is in its right place the servant of the reason, & employed ever to bridge over the gulf between [56] the revelations of his Reason, his Vision, & the facts within in the microscopic optics of the calculators that surround him. Long may he live.

It is singular that every natural object how wearisome soever in daily observation is always agreeable in description & ⟨more so⟩ doubly so in illustration.[138]

20 June. What a charm does 'Wilhelm Meister' spread over society which we were just getting to think odious. And yet as I read the book today & thought of Goethe as the Tag und Jahres Hefte describes him, he seemed to me — all-sided, gifted,[n] indefatigable student as he is, — to be only another poor monad after the fashion of his little race bestirring himself immensely to hide his nothingness[,] spinning his surface directly before the eye to ⟨hide⟩ conceal the Universe of his ignorance. ↑See Journal 1832 13 May↓ The finest poems of the world have been expedients to get bread or else expedients to keep the writer from the madhouse & amuse him & his fellowmen with the illusion that he knew[;] but the ⟨Wisest⟩ greatest passages they have writ[,] the infinite conclusions to which they owe their fame are only confessions. Throughout Goethe prevails the undersong of confession & amazement; the apophthegm[n] of Socrates; the recantation of Man. The first questions are always to be asked, & we fend them off by much speaking & many books. So that scarcely can I blame the man who affects ↑to↓ philosophize as some sensualists do, & says ⟨t⟩his fun is profound calculation. And yet it is best in the poorest view to keep the powers healthy & supple by appropriate action. All things[,] complained the philosopher[,] hasten back to Unity.[139]

[57] The bells in America toll because Lafayette has died in France. The bells in all the earth, in church, monastery, castle, &

---

[138] "It is singular . . . illustration." is struck through with a wavy diagonal use mark in pencil. In the following paragraph for June 20, "indefatigable . . . the man who" is struck through with a similar use mark. Above "Universe of his ignorance." is an asterisk and the interlined note "See . . . May". The reference is to Journal Q, p. 18 above.

[139] Xenophanes, probably from Gérando, *Histoire comparée des systèmes de philosophie*, 1822–1823, I, 460; see *JMN*, III, 369.

38 July 15, 1832, White Mountains. A few low mountains, a
great many clouds always covering the great peaks,
a circle of woods to the horizon, a peacock on
the fence or in the yard, & two Travellers
no better contented than myself in the
plain parlor of this house make up the whole
picture of this unsabbatized Sunday. But the
hours pass on — creep or fly — & bear me and my fellows
to the decision of questions of duty; to the crises of
of our fate; and to the solution of this mortal
problem. Welcome & farewell to
them, fair come, fair go. God is, we in him.
Est deus in nobis ‸ Calecimus illo
The hour of decision. It seems not worth while for them
who charge others with exalting forms above
the moon to fear forms themselves with extravagant
dislike. I am so placed that my aliquid ingenii
may be brot into useful action. Let me not bury
my talent in the earth in my indignation at this
windmill. But though the thing may be useless &
even pernicious, do not destroy what is good & useful
in a high degree rather than comply with what
is hurtful in a small degree. The Communicant
celebrates on a foundation either of authority of
of tradition an ordinance which has been

Plate I   Journal Q, page 38   Text, pages 29–30

*In the silent mountains Emerson faces a crisis and
decides to resign his ministry rather than
to violate his inner integrity*

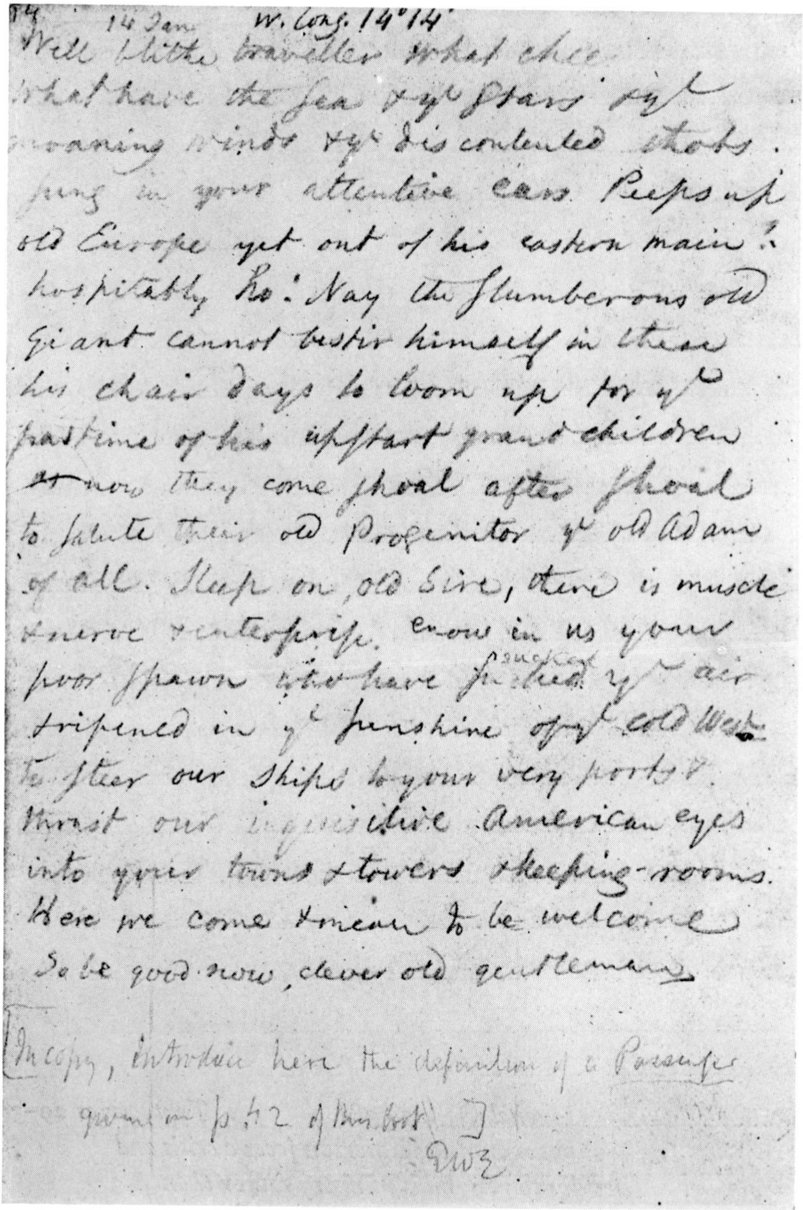

14 Jan W. Long. 14°14'
Well blithe traveller what cheer
What have the sea & ye stars sayd
moaning winds & ye discontented shots
sung in your attentive ears Peeps up
old Europe yet out of his eastern main?
hospitably ho! Nay the slumberous old
Giant cannot bestir himself in these
his chair days to loom up for ye
pastime of his upstart grandchildren
as now they come shoal after shoal
to salute their old Progenitor ye old Adam
of all. Sleep on, old Sire, there is muscle
& nerve & enterprise enow in us your
poor spawn who have sucked ye air
& ripened in ye sunshine of ye cold West
to steer our ships to your very ports &
thrust our inquisitive American eyes
into your towns & towers & keeping-rooms.
Here we come & mean to be welcome
So be good now, clever old gentleman.

[In copy, introduce here the definition of a Passenger given on p. 42 of this book]
RWE

Plate II *Sicily, page 14* *Text, page 109*

Emerson, voice of the youthful world of America, greets and challenges the old world of Europe

man eats well alone. Let a stranger come in & he misses his mouth & spills his butterboat & fails of finding the joint in carving, & that by so little.

See page X. 5

Friday 5. Fair fine wind, still in the Channel. off the coast of Ireland but not in sight of land. This morning 37 sail in sight.

I like my book about nature & wish I knew where & how I ought to live. God will show me. I am glad to be on my way home yet not so glad as others. & my way to the bottom I could find perchance with less regret for I think. it would not hurt me that is the ducking or drowning.

Saturday 6 Gentle fair. wind still & what is perhaps good — no events. at 12 o'clock South of Cape Clear.

Sunday 7. The solitary keeper of the light house of the Smalls in the Eng. Channel which stands on three pillars of Cast iron the waves washing through them. There were two — one sickened & died the other kept his body lest they should say he murdered him, until somebody came to the spot & the body was quite rotten. Bread must be well mixed to keep sweet. Man well tempered to keep his spirit clear. "a rum place" says an Englishman

Plate III   Sea 1833, page 3   Text, pages 237–238
Returning to his homeland Emerson meditates on mortality and on his future course

Concord 15 November 1834. Hail to the quiet fields of
my fathers! Not wholly unattended by supernatural friendship & favor let me come hither. Bless my purposes
as they are simple & virtuous. Coleridge's fine letter (in
London Lit. Gazette Sept. 13, 1834.) comes in aid of the very thoughts
I was revolving. And be it so. Henceforth I design not
to utter any speech poem or book that is not entirely &
peculiarly my work. I will say at public lectures &
the like, those things which I have meditated for their
own sake & not for the first time with a view. to
that occasion. If otherwise you select a new subject for
I labor to make a good appearance on the appointed
day, it is so much lost time to you & lost time to your
hearer. (You are your own dupe.) (It is a parenthesis
in your genuine life.) & for the sake of conciliating
your audience you have failed to edify them & winning their ear you have really lost their loved gratitude.

Respect a man! assuredly, but in general only as the potential God & therefore richly deserving of your pity
your tears. Now he is only a scrap an ort an end &
in his actual being no more worthy of your veneration than the poor lunatic. But the simplest person who in his integrity worships God becomes God: at
least no optics of human mind can detect the line
where man the effect ceases, & God the Cause begins.
Unhappy divorce of Religion & Philosophy

Plate IV Journal A, page 100 Text, page 335
Emerson announces the integrity of the self-reliant
man, potential god, who must speak his own
thoughts or be a worthless scrap

pagoda might well toll for the departure of so pure, faithful, heroic, secular a Spirit out of the earth to which it has been salt & spikenard. Go in, great heart! to the Invisible[,] to the Kingdom of love & faith. He has

> "Lingered among the last of those bright clouds
> Which on the steady breeze⟨s⟩ of Honor sail
> In long procession calm & beautiful." [140]

It occurred that the ⟨movements⟩ ↑gestures↓ of the Reason are grace-ful & majestic[,] those of the Understanding quick & mean. The ⟨ey⟩ uplifted eye of Memory, the solemn pace, perfect repose & simple attitudes of Meditation inspire respect, but the moment the senses call us back, & the Understanding directs us, we run, ↑start,↓ look askance, or turn & look behind us, we skulk, ⟨we⟩ fumble, exceed in manner & voice, & suffer. Live by Reason, & you will not make the foul mouths, nor utter the foul breath, nor drag ⟨heavy⟩ ⟨sleepyday⟩ disgracefully sleepy days that convince Alexander that he is mortal. When Minerva, they say, saw her distorted face in a brook she threw away her hautboy.[141] See p. 85[.]

[June] 26. If friendship were perfect there would be no false prayers. But what could Wilhelm [142] have done at the Crab's house? [n]

[143] The rare women that charm us are those happily constituted persons who take possession of society wherever they go & give it its form[,] its tone.[n] If they sit as we sit to wait for what shall be said we shall have no Olympus. To their genius elegance is essential. It is enough that we men stammer & mince words & play the clown & pedant alternately. They must [58] speak as cleanly & simply as a song. ⟨Then⟩ I say all this is a happiness not a merit, & few there be that find it. Society cannot give it, nor the want of society with-

[140] Wordsworth, *The Excursion*, VII, 1014–1016, slightly misquoted: used in "Boston," *W*, XII, 211.

[141] Both stories are from Plutarch, *Morals*: the first from "How to know a Flatterer from a Friend" (1870, II, 138), and the tale of Minerva from "Concerning the Cure of Anger" (1870, I, 41).

[142] Apparently the reference is to Goethe's *Wilhelm Meister*, but the significance is unclear.

[143] "The rare women . . . alternately." is struck through with a vertical use mark in ink and a wavy diagonal use mark in pencil.

hold it. Aunt Mary & S[arah].A.R[ipley]. ⟨a⟩never wait for the condescending influences of society, but seek it out, scrutinize it, amuse themselves with the little, sympathize with & venerate the great. And Ellen in a life of solitude was incapable of an inelegance.

Yesterday the attentions of the poor girl with flowers made me think how elegant is kindness. Kindness is never vulgar. Genius & strong Will may be only phenomena in the chain of causes & most men & women may grow up to be what they are as the cows & horses grow in the pastures but Kindness from a perfect stranger — a sudden will to benefit me & every body is a salient spring, it is ⟨the⟩ a hint of the presence of the living God. The condition of young women even the most favored excites sometimes a profound pity. 'When a daughter is born,' said the Sheking 'she sleeps on the ground, she is clothed with a wrapper, she plays with a tile, she is incapable either of evil or of good.' [144] But kindness[,] native courtesy redeems them at once out of your pity[;] they are happy & the objects of your joy & your respect.

> "Happy, happier far than thou,
> With the laurel on thy brow,
> She who makes the humblest hearth
> Lovely but to one on earth" [145]

Next door to us lives a young man who is learning to drum. He studies hard ⟨on⟩at his science every night. I should like to reward his music with a wreath of smilax peduncularis.[146]

[59] Goethe & Carlyle & perhaps Novalis have an undisguised

[144] The *Shi King* (*Shih Ching*), a compilation of poems ascribed to Confucius, Pt. II, Bk. IV, Ode 5, st. 9. According to James Legge, *The Chinese Classics*, 7 vols. (London, 1871), IV, Pt. II, 307, Emerson's version is apparently drawn from a mistranslation by Robert Morrison, perhaps in his *Dictionary of the Chinese Language*, 5 vols. (Macao, 1815–1823), three volumes of which (pts. 2 and 3) were in the Boston Athenaeum. The final line of the ode should read "it will be theirs neither to do wrong nor to do good." The reference is used in "Chaucer," *Lectures*, I, 280.

[145] The quatrain, squeezed into the space between two paragraphs and written in two divided lines, is the final stanza from Felicia Hemans, "To Corinna at the Capitol," included by Emerson in his anthology, *Parnassus* (Boston, 1874), p. 51.

[146] Bigelow, *Florula Bostoniensis*, 1824, describes the plant as long-stalked smilax with a highly offensive odor.

dislike or contempt for common virtue standing on common principles. Meantime they are dear lovers[,] steadfast maintainers of the
pure ideal ⟨of⟩ Morality. But they worship it as the highest beauty;
their love is artistic. Praise Socrates to them, or Fenelon, much more
any inferior contemporary good man & they freeze at once into
silence. It is to them sheer prose.

The *Tag und Jahres Hefte* is a book unparallelled in America,
an account of all events, persons, studies, taken from one point of
view. The problem to be solved, is, How shall this soul called *Goethe*
be educated? And whatever he does or ⟨meets⟩ whatever befals him
is viewed solely in relation to its effect upon the development of his
mind. ↑Even in the arms of his mistress at Rome he says he studied
sculpture & poetry.↓ [147]

To husband our admiration is an intellectual temperance indispensable to health. But Goethe was a person who hated words that
did not stand for things, & had a sympathy with every thing that
existed, & therefore never writes without saying something. He will
be Artist, & look at God & Man, & the Future, & the infinite, as a self-
possessed spectator, who believed that what he saw he could delineate.
Herder wisely questioned whether a man had a right thus to affect
the god instead of working with all his heart in his place.[148] Self-culti-
vation is yet the moral of all that G. has writ, & in indolence, intoler-
ance, & perversion, I think we can spare an olive & a laurel for him.

No man has drawn his materials ⟨of⟩ ↑of↓ fiction from so wide a
circuit. Very properly he introduces into the machinery of [60] his
romance whatever feeling or impulse the most rapt enthusiast has
trusted in. Coincidences, dreams, omens, ⟨&⟩ spiritual impressions, &
a habitual religious faith — all these are the materials which as a
wise Artist he avails himself of.

Nevertheless there is a difference between thought & thought,
& it is as ⟨much⟩ ↑real↓ a defect in a man not to perceive the right of
his moral sentiments to his allegiance, as it is not to be conscious of
moral sentiments. Yet Goethe with all his fine things about *Ent-
sagen* [148a] can write & print too like Rochester & Beranger.

[147] "Die Romische Elegien," V, 7–17, in *Die Werke*, 1828, I, 265–266.
[148] A paraphrase of Austin, *Characteristics of Goethe*, 1833, II, 31–33.
[148a] Cf. *Wilhelm Meister's Travels*, ch. 14 (Carlyle's trans.): ". . . the high

As to Carlyle, he is an exemplification of Novalis's maxim concerning the union of Poetry & Philosophy.[149] He has married them, & both are the gainers. Who has done so before as truly & as well? Sartor Resartus is a philosophical Poem.

↑Nov. 30.↓

Goethe is praised as μυριονους [150] or all-sided. And if I understand it this is the apology that is made for his epicurean life compared with his religious perceptions. To praise a man for such quality is like praising an observatory for being very low & massive & a very good fort. It is not more the office of man to receive all impressions, than it is to distinguish sharply between them. He that has once pronounced intelligently the word "Self-renouncement," "Invisible Leader," "Powers of Sorrow", & the like, is forever bound to the service of the Superhuman.

[61] [blank]

[62] We are wonderfully protected. We have scarce a misfortune, a hindrance, an infirmity, an enemy, but it is ↑somehow↓ productive of singular advantage to us. After groaning thro' years of poverty & hard labor the mind perceives that really it has come the shortest road to a valuable position, that though the rough climate was not good for leaves & flowers, it was good for timber. It has been saved from what associations. It has been introduced to what thoughts

---

meaning of Renunciation [Entsagen] by which alone the first real entrance into life is conceivable."

[149] Carlyle, "Novalis," *Foreign Review*, IV (1829), 129: "The division of Philosopher and Poet is only apparent, and to the disadvantage of both. It is a sign of disease, and of a sickly constitution."

[150] "ten thousand minded" (Ed.). The term is apparently to characterize Goethe as the myriad-minded or "clear and universal Man." See Austin, *Characteristics of Goethe*, 1833, I, 11, and Carlyle, "Goethe's Works," *Foreign Quarterly Review*, X (Aug. 1832), 42. The notes on Goethe appear between entries for June and for July but the date of November 30 seems correct, for the comments on Goethe echo remarks made in Emerson's letter to Carlyle dated November 20, 1834, which was finally sent off on December 14. "He that has once . . . Superhuman." is almost identical with a passage from this letter. See *The Correspondence of Thomas Carlyle and Ralph Waldo Emerson, 1834–1872*, ed. Norton, 1884, I, 31.

& feelings. 'He knows you not ye ⟨heavenly⟩ ↑mighty↓ Powers! who knows not sorrow.'[151] God brings us by ways we know not & like not into Paradise.

12 July. *On War*. ↑*Chap I.*↓ Assacombuit a sagamore of the Anasagunticook tribe was remarkable for his turpitude & ferocity. ⟨it⟩He was above all other known Indians inhuman & cruel. In 1705 Vaudreuil sent him to France, & he was introduced to the king. When he appeared at court, he lifted up his hand, & said, "This hand has slain 150 of your Majesty's enemies within the territories of New England." This so pleased the king that he forthwith knighted him, & ordered a pension of eight livres a day to be paid him during life. On his return home, he undertook to exercise a despotic sway over his brethren in which he murdered one & stabbed another, & thus exasperated their relations to such a degree, that they sought to take his life, & would have killed him, had he not fled his country. See Williamson, Hist. of Maine, Vol 2. p. 69.[–70][152]

On War Chap. II. At the close of the ten years' war in 1713 (after the treaty of Utrecht,) there was now in Maine "scarcely remaining a vestige of the fur trade, the lumber-business, or the fisheries. What we call enterprize excited no emulation. The virtues of ⟨men⟩ the people in these times were of another & higher order; — courage, fortitude, & brotherly kindness. These appeared in nameless exploits & in thousands of occurrences every year." See Williamson, p. 68. Vol 2.

[63][153] "Lincoln bell flings o'er the fen

[151] Goethe, *Wilhelm Meister's Lehrjahre*, Bk. II, ch. 13, the Harper's song. See also Carlyle, "Goethe," *Foreign Review*, II (1828), 105.

[152] William D. Williamson, *The History of the State of Maine from its earliest discovery, A.D. 1602, to the Separation, A.D. 1820, inclusive*, 2 vols. (Hallowell, Me., 1832). The inserted "*Chap I.*" at the beginning of the citation meant merely that material concerning war could be found there. The whole passage is a tissue of paraphrase and unindicated direct quotation.

[153] Traces of erased pencil writing are visible under the entry from "other men's senses" through "had given us rum." on p. [65]. The present entry is apparently a recopying and expansion of the original pencil, for still legible in pencil is the passage " 'Lincoln bell . . . Lincoln Cathedral" and beneath "When the wrong . . . beauty remind" on p. [64] is "They said of Sir Wm Pepperell that whatever he willed came to pass", recopied in pencil on p. [65].

His far renowned alarum." [154]

I read this & straight regret that I did not visit Lincoln Cathedral & hear the far renowned alarum; such ⟨power hath the⟩ superstitious preference do we give to other men's [n] senses. Undoubtedly something in my own sphere or spherule takes the place to me of that particular gratification. I have some 'Lincoln bell' — heard with joy in my ordinary movements. Yet I long to hear this other, simply out of deference to my fellows in England who have exalted it by their love. Better believe in the perfection of thine own ⟨nature⟩ lot. Retreat upon your own spontaneous emotions. Mark the occasions of them, & cheerfully believe that what has excited true & deep pleasure in one man is fitted to excite the same emotions in all men. So will I find my Lincolnshire in the next pasture & the 'bell' in the first thrush that sings. Napoleon sat back on his horse in the midst of the march to catch the fine tone of a bell.[155] With myself I shall always dwell, but Lincoln & Niagara & Cairo are less accessible. And yet and yet can aught approach the effect of the Sabbath Morn in quietest retreats? And yet is its sacredness derivative & alien. Some thoughts are ⟨der⟩superficial, — others have their root in your being. Always discriminate when you would write, between them & never chuse the first for a topic. Diogenes moved his tub in winter into the sun, & in summer into the shade, & compared himself to the Persian King who spent the one season at Susa & the other at Ecbatana.[156]

[64] "As many languages as a man knows, said Charles V., so many times is he a man." [157] Our eagerness to possess this gift of

[154] Wordsworth, "Peter Bell: A Tale," ll. 213–215: "And he had been where Lincoln bell/ Flings o'er the fen that ponderous knell —/ A far-renowned alarum."

[155] " 'Lincoln bell' . . . of a bell." is struck through with a diagonal use mark in pencil and is used in "Each and All," W, IX, 4. Possibly Emerson drew his anecdote of Napoleon and the bell from a slightly erroneous memory of a passage in Kidd, On the Adaptation of External Nature to . . . Man, 1833, pp. 140–143, in which Napoleon is described as being arrested in a march by the sound of the church clock at Brienne.

[156] Plutarch, "Of Proceedings in Virtue"; see the Morals, 1870, II, 455. See also JMN, III, 319. The passage is used in "History," W, II, 21.

[157] A proverbial statement frequently found in its Latin form as "Quot linguas calles, tot homines vales." See p. 417 below for Emerson's version of the apophthegm in Italian.

foreign speech rather hinders than helps us to it. I stand in a company where circulates how much wit & information, yet not one thought can pass from them to me, — I do not understand their speech. My countryman ⟨come⟩ enters who understands it & the communication between them & him, is perfect. ↑Stung with desire↓ I devote myself to the task of learning the language but this perpetual ⟨fairy⟩ ↑poetic↓ vision before me which is quite foreign from their experience, & which I shall lose ⟨th⟩ as soon as I master the speech, affords me so much entertainment as to embarrass every particular effort at dialogue & dispirits me & ⟨I lose that⟩ ↑unfits me for↓ simple ⟨feeling of desire⟩ ↑effort↓ to know the thing said to me, & to convey my ⟨ans⟩ thought in return, which is the best instructer. Ralph Emerson said ↑to me↓ in Paris, that the Americans think there is some magic in speaking & writing French. ⟨The master⟩ He who has mastered the tongue sees nothing behind him but simple addition of particulars, & this new knowledge blends harmoniously with all his ⟨knowledge⟩ experience; and, moreover, it has lost all its anticipated value.

When the wrong handle is grasped of comparative anatomy the tresses of beauty remind us of ↑a↓ mane⟨s⟩. How much is an assembly of men restrained! It seems often like a collection of angels, & a collection of demons in disguise.

> Come dal fuoco il caldo, esser diviso
> Non puo'l bel dall' eterno. *M. Angelo B*
> > [Sonnet 6, ll. 10–11]

[65] The great Spirit has given every tribe of Indians a goodly river with fine salmon. The Indian has rights & loves good as well as the Englishman. We have a sense too of what is kind & great. When you first came from the morning waters, we took you into our open arms. We thought you children of the sun. We fed you with our best meat. Never went white man cold & starving from an Indian wigwam. We are now told that the country spreading far from the sea is passed away to you forever — perhaps for nothing, — because of the names & seals of our sagamores. Such deeds be far from them! They never turned their children from their homes to suffer: their souls were too great. The English law-makers took our lands when they had given us rum.[158]

[158] Williamson, *The History of the State of Maine*, 1832, II, 112–113. The

It was an Indian maxim 'That the first blow is the best part of the battle.' They said of Sir William Pepperell "that whatever he willed came to pass." [159] Williamston↓ Hist. of Maine. [II, 341]

[66] Bangor. 15 July. The thoughtful man laments perhaps the unpliancy of his organization which draws down the corners of his mouth to ludicrous longitude, whilst all the company chat & titter around him. What matters it? He actually sympathizes with each of the company more truly than the liveliest chatterbox. For they are all going back from this smiling time to discipline, to silence, labor & anxiety, & then they recal the melancholy man with a fraternal remembrance.

A man does not consider that any dinge on his character, any feeling of smut ⟨is dear bought at⟩ cannot be paid for. He escapes by a suppression or an allowable phrase a tax of ⟨$50⟩fifty dollars. But he had better pay fifty & feel himself an honorable gentleman. They say this is not orthodoxy at Eastport.

In our plans of life an apparent confusion. We seem not to know what we want. Why, it is plain we can do best something which in the present form of society will be misconstrued & taken for another thing. I wish to be a true & free man, & therefore would not be a woman,[n] or a king, or a clergyman, each of which classes in the present order of things is a slave. ⟨The simple⟩ Mr Canning judged right in preferring the title of *Mister*, in the company of Alexander & Napoleon, to *My Lord*. The simple untitled unofficed citizen possessing manners, power, cultivation, is more formidable & more pleasing than ⟨all⟩ any dignitary whose condition & etiquette only makes him more vulnerable & more helpless.

[67] Noble strain of the revolutionary papers. See Williamson Vol 2 pp 408, 9, 10, 11. And when the port of Boston had been closed (in June 1774) 16 days they tolled the bells in the town of

---

quotation contains a number of unindicated omissions as well as a few minor variations in wording.

[159] "It was . . . pass." is in pencil. A vertical pencil line separates the two quotations, perhaps to indicate that only the second is to be found in Williamson's *History of Maine*.

Falmouth all day, & addressed an affectionate letter to the inhabitants of Boston. "We look upon you," they say, "as sufferers for the
common cause of American liberty. We highly appreciate your courage to endure privation & distress — sensibly aware that the season
puts to severest trial, the virtues of magnanimity, patience, & fortitude, which your example will honorably exemplify. We beg leave
to tender you all the encouragements which the considerations of
friendship & respect can inspire, & all the assurances of succor which
full hearts & feeble abilities can render."

[Williamson, *History of Maine*, II, 412]

[July] 18. The abomination of desolation [159a] is not a burned town nor
a ⟨wasted⟩ country wasted by war but the discovery that ⟨you have
been⟩ the man who has moved you, is an enthusiast upon calculation.

"Indeed all that class of the severe & restrictive virtues are at a
market almost too high for humanity." [160] May be so. That gives them
their worth. It is that we ourselves the observers have been imposed
upon & led to condemn ⟨them⟩ ↑the actor↓ before, & the farsighted
heroism of the sufferer has felt the ⟨su⟩ condemnation & yet persisted
in his own judgment & kept up his courage — it is that conviction that
adds eagerness to our commendation now.

What is there of the divine in a load of bricks? What is there
of the divine in a barber's shop or a privy? Much. All. Yesterday at
the installation they seemed like woodsawyers dressed up. It would
not out of my imagination. By & by a true priest spoke[.] [161]

[68] George A. Sampson died Wednesday evening 23 July,
1834[.]

[159a] Cf. Mark 13:14.
[160] Burke, "Speech on . . . A Plan . . . for the Economical Reformation of the
Civil and other Establishments." See *Works*, 1865–1867, II, 268, and *JMN*, II, 211.
[161] "What is there . . . spoke" is in pencil. The remains of a small red seal
to the left of the entry indicate that something has been pasted in over the writing at some time. The latter part of the entry is repeated with some expansion on p.
[70] below. The installation referred to was probably that of the Reverend John
Maltby of Sutton, Mass., at the Hammond Street Congregational Church in Bangor
on July 23, 1834.

[69] [blank]

[70] Newton 9 August. Carlyle says,[n] Society is extinct.[162] Be it
so. Society existed in a clan; existed in Alaric & Attila's time, in the
Crusades, in the Puritan Conventicles. Very well. I had rather be
solitary as now, than social as then. Society exists now where there
is love & faithful fellow working. Only the persons composing it are
fewer — societies of two or three, instead of nations. Societies[,]
parties are only incipient stages[,] tadpole states of man as caterpillars
are social but the butterfly not. The true & finished man is ever alone.
Men cannot satisfy him; he needs God, & his intercourse with his
brother is ever condescending, & in a degree hypocritical.

↑He charged them that they should tell no man.↓ [163] "Hold thy
tongue for one day; tomorrow thy purpose will be clearer." [164] Why
yea, & it would be good if the minister put off his black ⟨gow⟩ clothes
& so affirmed the reality of spiritual distinctions. When I was at the
ordination at Bangor the other day the men in the pulpit seemed
woodsawyers dressed up, as they stood up & spoke in succession. It
would not out of my head. By & by a true priest spoke. x x x Renounce.
Work hard. ⟨i⟩In the great heats why should you leave your labor
for a little sweat, since the haymaker does not? [n] ⟨leave his.⟩ He
cannot; therefore, if you are noble, you will not. Renounce. When
I was in the pasture & stopped to eat, the familiar cried, Eat not.
Tut, replied I, does Nemesis care for a whortleberry? I looked at
the world, & it replied, Yea. But the clock struck two & the table was
covered with fishes & fowls & confections. They are very good & my
appetite is ⟨excellent⟩ keen, & I could not see any good in refusing
the pleasure of a hearty meal that was as ⟨good⟩ ↑great↓ as the pleasure. [71] Look back, cried the familiar, at years of good meat in
Boston. Do you miss any thing that you forbore to eat? Nothing, replied I.

First thoughts are from God; but not the numerically first;

---

[162] *Sartor Resartus*, Bk. III, ch. 5. See *The Works*, 1896–1901, I, 184.

[163] "He charged . . . man." is a phrase found frequently in the New Testament;
see Matt. 9:30 and 16:20; Mark 8:30; Luke, 5:14.

[164] Carlyle, *Sartor Resartus*, Bk. III, ch. 3; see *The Works*, 1896–1901, I, 174,
slightly misquoted.

allow what space you may, for the mind to grasp the facts, then the thoughts that are first in place are divine & the second earthly.

Sunday, 10 Aug. At Mr Grafton's church [165] this P.M. and heard the eloquent old man preach his Jewish sermon dryeyed. Indeed I felt as a much worse spirit might feel among worshippers — as if the last link was severed that bound him to their traditions & he ought to go out hence. Strange ⟨w⟩that such ⟨hollow⟩ fatuity as Calvinism is now, should be able to stand yet — mere shell as it is — in the face of day. At every close of a paragraph it almost seemed as if this devout old man looked intelligence & questioned the whole thing. What a revival if St Paul should come & replace these threadbare rags with the inexhaustible resources of sound Ethics. Yet they are so befooled as to call this ↑sucked↓ eggshell ⟨of theirs⟩ hightoned orthodoxy, & to talk of anything true as *mere morality*. Is it not time to present this matter of Christianity exactly as it is, to take away all false reverence from Jesus, & not mistake the stream for the source? [n] 'It is no more according to Plato than according to me.' [166] God is in every man. God is in Jesus but let us not magnify any of the vehicles as we magnify the Infinite Law itself. We have defrauded him of his claim of love on all noble hearts by our supersti↑ti↓ous mouth honor. We love Socrates but give Jesus the Unitarian Association —.

[72] See two sincere men ⟨speculating⟩ conversing together. They deport themselves ⟨in⟩ as if self-existent. Are they not for the time two Gods? [n] For every true man is as if he should say, I speak for the Universe; I am here to maintain the truth against all comers[;] I am in this place to testify.[167]

[August] 11. Is not man in our day described by the very attributes which once he gave his God? [n] Is not the sea his minister; the clouds his chariot; the flame his wheels; & the winds his wings?

[August] 13. Blessed is the child; the Unconscious is ever the act of

---

[165] The Reverend Joseph Grafton was pastor of the First Baptist Church of Newton from 1788 to 1836.

[166] Montaigne, "Of the Education of Children," *Essays*, 1693, I, 225.

[167] "I am in . . . testify.": used in "Day by day returns," *W*, IX, 392.

God himself. Nobody can reflect upon his *unconscious* period or any particular word or act in it, with regret or contempt. Bard or Hero cannot look down upon the word or gesture of a child; it is as great as they. Little Albert Sampson asks when his father will come home, & insists that *his father can't die.*[168]

[August] 14. We look up sometimes with ⟨a sort of⟩ surprize to see that the tree, the hill, the schoolhouse are still there, & have not vanished in our mood of pyrrhonism. If there were many philosophers, the world would go to pieces presently[,] all sand, no lime. ⟨All⟩ Quam parva sapientia.[169] All society & government seems to be *making believe* when we see such hollow boys with a grave countenance taking their places as legislators, Presidents, & so forth. It could not be but that at intervals throughout society there are real men intermixed whose natural basis is broad enough to sustain these paper men in common times,[n] as the carpenter puts one iron bar in his banister to five or six wooden ones.

Yet when at other times I consider the capacities of [73] man & see how near alike they all are & that always [they] seem to be on the edge of all that is great & yet invisibly retained in inactivity & unacquaintance with our powers[,] it seems as if men were like the neuters of the hive every one of which is capable of transformation into the Queenbee, which is done with some one as soon as the sovereign is removed. The fourth chapter of my Meditation is the observation that the soul or the day is a turning wheel which brings every one of its manifold faces for a brief season to the top. Now this dunghill quality of animal courage[,] indomitable pluck[,] seems to be the supreme virtue; anon, patience; then elegance; then learning[;] then wit; then eloquence; then wealth; then piety; then beauty; each seems in turn the one desireable quality & thus every dog has his day.

It occurred furthermore that the fine verse of "Honorable

---

[168] Albert Sampson's father, Emerson's intimate friend George A. Sampson, had died on Wednesday, July 23, 1834, on his way to join Waldo in Bangor, Maine. See p. 307 above.

[169] "How little wisdom." Emerson is citing an abbreviated version of a Latin tag which he may originally have drawn from a letter of 1732 from Arbuthnot to Swift: "Quam parva sapientia regitur mundus!" — "With how little wisdom is the world ruled!" See *JMN*, II, 273.

age" &c in Wisd[om]. of Solomon [170] is quite Greek in its genius, not Jewish.

⇡For the Lecture on Nat. Hist.⇣

[August] 15.[171] Natural history by itself has no value; it is like a single sex. But marry it to human history, & it is poetry. ⟨at once.⟩ Whole Floras, all Linnaeus' & Buffon's volumes contain not one line of poetry, but the meanest natural fact, the habit of a plant, the ⟨noise⟩ ⇡organs,⇣ or work, ⇡or noise⇣ of an insect applied to ⇡the interpretation [of] or even associated⇣ [with] a fact in human nature is beauty, is poetry, is truth at once.

[August] 16, Saturday Eve. King Lear & Ant. & Cleopatra still fill me with wonder. Every scene is as spirited as if ⟨f⟩writ by a fresh hand of the first class and there is never straining; sentiments of the highest elevation are as simply expressed as the stage directions. They praise Scott for ⟨making⟩ taking kings & nobles off their stilts & giving them simple dignity but Scott's ⟨magnificoes⟩ ⇡grandees⇣ are all turgid compared [74] with Shakspear's. There is more true elevation of character in Prince Hal's sentence about the pleached doublet than in any king in the romances.[172] Another mastership of Shakspear is the immortality of the style; [n] the speeches of passion are writ ⟨in⟩ for the most part in a style as fresh now as it was when the play was published. The remarkable sentences of Lear, Hamlet, Othello, Macbeth, might as naturally have been composed in 1834 as in 1600.

[170] Wisd. of Sol., 4:8: "For honourable old age is not that which standeth in the length of time,/Nor is its measure given by number of years."

[171] All the insertions and cancellations in the entry for August 15 are in pencil except for "⟨at once.⟩" They may have been made when Emerson was preparing his lecture, *The Study of Natural History*, which he first gave at the Lyceum in Concord, Mass., on January 1, 1835. See William Charvat, *Emerson's American Lecture Engagements: A Chronological List* (New York, 1961), p. 15. The passage is used in *Nature, W*, I, 28.

[172] No reference to a "pleached doublet" exists in the Henry plays; Emerson is perhaps recalling somewhat mistakenly Prince Hal's speech concerning "peach-coloured" hose (*II Henry IV*, II, ii, 15–20), a passage cited approvingly later in "Heroism," *W*, II, 252–253: "Indeed these humble considerations make me out of love with greatness. What a disgrace it is to me to take note how many pairs of silk stockings thou hast, namely these and those that were the peach-coloured ones."

"I tax not you ye elements with unkindness
I never gave you kingdoms, called you daugh[ters]
You owe me no subscription &c" [*King Lear*, III, ii, 15–18]

[August] 17. Freedom. A very small part of a man's voluntary acts
are such as agree perfectly with his conviction & it is only at rare intervals that he is apprized of this incongruity — "so difficult is it to
read our own consciousness without mistakes." Whose act is this
churchgoing? Whose this praying? The man might as well be gone
so he leave a Maelzel machine [173] in his place[.]
                    ↑On the wisdom of ignorance.↓
Evg. Milton was too learned, though I hate to say it. It wrecked his
originality. He was more indebted to the Hebrew than even to the
Greek. Wordsworth is a more original poet than he. That seems the
poet's garland. He speaks by that right that he has somewhat yet
unsaid to say. Scott & Coleridge & such like are not poets[,] only professors of the art. Homer's is the only Epic. He is original yet he
⟨recedes⟩ ↑separates↓ before the German telescopes into two, ten, or
twenty stars. Shakspeare by singular similarity of fortune undeniably
an original & unapproached bard — first of men, — is yet infolded in
the same darkness as an individual Writer. His best works are ↑of↓
doubted authenticity [75] and what was his, & what his novelist's,
& what the players', seems yet disputed. A sharp illustration of that
relentless disregard of the individual in regard for the race which
runs through history. It is not an individual but the general mind of
man that speaks from time to time quite careless & quite forgetful
of what mouth or mouths it makes use ⟨of⟩. Go to the ⟨ma⟩ bard or
orator that has spoken & ask him if what he said were his own? No.
He got it he knows not where, but it is none of his. For example;
Edward Emerson whence had you those thunderous sentences in
your 'Master's ⁿ Oration'? [174] ↑There is nothing in Wordsworth so
vicious in sentiment as Milton's account of God's chariots, &c. stand-

---

[173] Johann Nepomuc Mälzel (1772–1838), German mechanician who made an
automaton called the Panharmonicon, able to play many instruments at once. Mälzel, who lived in the United States during the later part of his career, visited Boston
in 1826.
    [174] The reference is apparently to Webster's influence on Edward Bliss Emerson's
Master's oration, "The Importance of Efforts and Institutions for the Diffusion of
Knowlege," delivered on August 29, 1827. See *J*, III, 329, and *L*, I, 209.

ing harnassed for great days.[175] We republicans cannot relish Watts'
or Milton's royal imagery.↓[176]

Is it not true that contemplation belongs to us & therefore outward ⟨f⟩worship *because* our reason is at discord with our understanding? And that whenever we live rightly thought will express itself in
ordinary action so fully as to make ⟨extraordinary⟩ ↑a special↓ action,
⟨namely⟩ ↑that is↓, a religious form impertinent? ⁿ Is not ⟨the⟩ Solomon's temple built because Solomon is not a temple, but a brothel
& a change house? Is not the meeting-house dedicated because men are
not? ⁿ Is not the Church opened & filled on Sunday because the com-
mandments are not kept by the worshippers on Monday? ⁿ But when
he who worships there, speaks the truth, follows the truth, is the
truth's; when he awakes by actual Communion to the faith that
God is in him, will he need any temple[,] any prayer? The very fact
of worship declares that God is not at one with himself,ⁿ that there
are two gods. Now does this sound like high treason & go to lay
flat all religion? It does threaten our forms [177] [76] but does not that
very word 'form' already sound hollow? It threatens our forms
but it does not touch injuriously Religion. Would there be danger
if there were real religion? ⁿ If the doctrine that God is in man were
faithfully taught & received, if I lived to speak the truth & enact it,
if I pursued every generous sentiment as one enamoured, if the
majesty of goodness were reverenced: would not such a principle
serve me by way of police ↑at least↓ [178] as well as a Connecticutt
Sunday?

But the people, the people. You hold up your pasteboard religion for the people who are unfit for a true. So you say. But presently
there will arise a race of preachers who will take such hold of the
omnipotence of truth that they will blow the old falsehood to shreds
with the breath of their mouth. There is no material show so splendid,
no poem so musical as the great law of Compensation in our moral

---

[175] *Paradise Lost*, VI, 769–770.

[176] "There is nothing . . . imagery." is squeezed into a space between "Oration'?"
and the next paragraph as a later insertion.

[177] "Aug. 17" is centered beneath "religion?" in pencil at the bottom of the page.

[178] This insertion, probably of later date, is in pencil as is the wavy diagonal use
mark that crosses the passage from "timent" (a continuation within the line of
"sentiment") to "real anxious" at the end of the next paragraph.

nature. When an ardent mind once gets a glimpse of that perfect beauty & sees how it envelopes him & determines all his being, will he easily slide back to a periodic shouting about 'atoning blood'? [n] I apprehend that the religious history of society is to show a pretty rapid abandonment of forms of worship & the renovation & exaltation of preaching into real anxious instruction[.]

------

18 Aug. The Mussulman is right by virtue of the law of Compensations in supposing the scraps of paper he saves will be a carpet under his feet over the bridge of Purgatory. He has learned the lesson of reverence to the name of Allah.

[77] 19 Aug. Never assume. Be genuine. So wrote I for my own guidance months & years ago [179] but how vainly! Show me in the world the sincere man. Even the wit the sentiment that seasons the dinner is a sort of hypocrisy to hide the coarseness of appetite. ⟨God made⟩ The child is sincere, and the man when he is alone, if he be not a writer, but ⟨t⟩on the entrance of the second person hypocrisy begins.[180]

What mischief is in this art of Writing. An unlettered man considers a fact to ⟨see⟩ ↑learn↓ what it means; the lettered man does not sooner see it than it occurs to him how it can be told. And this fact of looking at it as an artist blinds him to the better half of the fact. ↑Unhappily he is conscious of the misfortune which rather makes it worse.↓ As cultivated flowers turn their ⟨stamens⟩stamina to petals so does he turn the practick part to idle show. He has a morbid growth of eyes; he sees with his feet. ⟨If such a⟩ What an unlucky creature is Dr Channing. Let him into a room; would not all the company feel that simple as he looked, the cat was not more vigilant, that he had the delirium tremens & its insomnolency, that he heard what dropped from any as if he read it in print? [n]

We sit down with intent to write truly & end with making a book

------

[179] See p. 212 above, the entry for c. October 8, 1833, which in turn refers backward to a treatment of the subject of the genuine man in Journal Q (pp. 37–44 above) in the entries from August 18 through September 17, 1832. The material was originally a preparation for Sermon 164 (*YES*, pp. 180–190).

[180] "The child . . . begins." is struck through with a wavy diagonal use mark in pencil; "and the man . . . hypocrisy begins." is used in "Friendship," *W*, II, 202.

that contains no thought of ours but merely the tune of the time. Here am I writing a ΦΒΚ poem free to say what I choose & it looks to me now as if it would scarce express thought of mine but be a sort of fata Morgana ⟨composed of ima⟩ reflecting the images of Byron, Shakspear, & the newspapers.

We do what we can, & then make a theory to prove our performance the best.

[78] 21 Aug.[181] How much alike are all sorts of excellence[:] Mr Webster's arguments like Shakspear's plays. One wakes up occasionally with a desire to unfold the simplest facts; to announce for example to the world the delight that is to be found in reading; & to commend to their especial attention Shakspear's Antony & Cleopatra.

[August] 22. The greatest men have been most thoughtful for the humblest. Socrates, of whom see the fine story told in Plutarch on Tranquillity,[182]   Alfred, Franklin, Jesus Christ, & all the Pauls & Fenelons he has made. It requires no ordinary elevation to go by the social distinctions & feel that interest in humanity itself which is implied in attentions to the obscure. Wordsworth is a philanthropist; Fox; Wilberforce; Howard; Montaigne. And, so keep me heaven, I will love the race in general if I cannot in any particular. ↑Washington introduced the ass into America.↓

30 August. Were it not a heroic adventure in me to insist on being a popular speaker & run full tilt against the Fortune who with such beautiful consistency shows evermore her back? Charles's naïf censure last night provoked me to ⟨remind⟩ ↑show↓ him ⟨of⟩ a fact apparently wholly new to him that ⟨together with⟩ my entire success, such as it is, is composed wholly of particular failures, — every

---

[181] The entry for this date is struck through with a wavy diagonal use mark in pencil which continues into "men" in the August 22 entry, probably by inadvertence.
[182] "Of the Tranquillity of the Mind"; see the *Morals*, 1870, I, 150. Socrates, hearing a friend complain of the high cost of living in Athens, of the prices demanded for wine, purple fish, and honey, took his companion to a shop where flour was sold for a penny and pointed out that the city was inexpensive for those who knew what to buy.

public work of mine of the least importance, having been (probably without exception) noted at the time as a failure. The only success (agreeably to common ideas) has been in the country & there founded on the false notion that here was a Boston preacher. I will take Miss Barbauld's line for my motto "And the more falls I get, move faster on." [183]

———

I never was ⟨i⟩on a coach which went fast enough for me.[184]

[79][185] It is extremely disagreeable, nay, a little fiendish to laugh amid dreams. ↑In bed↓ I would keep my countenance, ⟨in bed⟩ if you please.

A poem is made up of thoughts each of which filled the whole sky of the poet in its turn. ⟨with its lustre.⟩

Newton, ⟨August⟩ ↑Sept.↓ 13. There are some things which we should do if we considered only our own capacity & safety, which we stick at doing when we think of the estimates & prejudices of other people. For the freest man society still holds some bribe. He wants of it a living, or a friend, or a wife, or a fit employment, or a reputation correspondent to his self esteem. Is it not possible to draw in his importunate beggar hands & ask nothing but what he can himself satisfy? [n] In some respects certainly. In this matter of reputation — is it not possible to settle it in one's mind immoveably that ⟨the⟩ merit of the first class cannot in the nature of things be readily appreciated; that immortal deeds over which centuries are to pass as days, are not brought to light & wholly comprehended & decided upon in a few hours? [n] The wise man is to settle it immoveably in his mind, that he only is fit to decide on his best action; he only is fit to praise it; his verdict is praise enough, and as to ⟨the⟩society, 'their hiss is thine applause.' [186] It is an ordinary enhancement of our admiration

[183] Anna Letitia Barbauld, "[The Brook]," an untitled riddle; see *JMN*, III, 295.
[184] This sentence is struck through with a wavy diagonal use mark in pencil.
[185] "It is extremely . . . lustre.)" and within the entry for September 13 "the first class . . . ⟨the⟩society," are struck through with a wavy diagonal use mark in pencil.
[186] Thomas Randolph, "An answer to Master Ben. Jonson's Ode to persuade him not to leave the stage," st. 1, 1. 6.

of noble thinking & acting that it was done in wilful defiance of present censure out of a clear foresight of the eternal praise of the just.
Let others be born to castles & manners & influence. Be thou a noble
man. Be a man to whom meanness & duplicity are impossible. Overlook from thy judgment seat IN ETERNITY the titled & the untitled rabble, & in thy heart call them all rabble whilst they judge
externally, though their names be Scott & Canning & Brougham [80]
& Webster & England & America. Next, as to thoughts of the first
class. Do not cease to utter them & make them as pure of all dross
as if thou wert to speak to sages & demigods and be no whit ashamed
if not one, yea, not one in the assembly should give sign of intelligence. Make it not worthy of the beggar to receive but of the emperor to give. Is it not pleasant to you, unexpected wisdom? depth of
sentiment in middle life? Iarnos & Abbés [187] that in the thick of the
crowd are true kings & gentlemen without the harness & the envy
of the throne? Is it not conceivable that a man or a woman in coarse
clothes may have unspeakable comfort in being the only human
being privy to a virtuous action which he or she is in the act of con-
summating?

But the young gentlemen & ladies of the present day care not
for the worth of the action, so it *shines,* nor for the nobleness of
reputation, so the name be well-aired.

Perhaps you cannot carry too far the doctrine of self respect.
The story that strikes me; the joke that makes me laugh often; the
face that bewitches me; the flower, the picture, the building, that,
left to myself, I prefer [—] these I ought to remember, love, &
praise. For there is nothing casual or capricious in the impression they
make (Provided always that I act naturally,) but they make this
strong impression because I am fit for them & they are fit for me.
But if I forsake my peculiar tastes overawed by the popular voice
or deferring to Mr Everett's or Mr Wordsworth's [81] or Baron
Swedenborg's tastes I am straightway dwarfed of my natural dimensions for want of fit nourishment & fit exercise. It is as if you should
⟨feed⟩fill the stomach of a horse with the food of a fish. Lean ⟨I say⟩
without fear on your own tastes. Is there danger in the doctrine as if
it permitted self indulgence ⟨& listening to one's own passions⟩? Fool!

[187] Characters in Goethe's *Wilhelm Meister.*

Every man hath his own Conscience as well as his own Genius & if he is faithful to himself he will yield that Law implicit obedience. All these doctrines contained in the proposition Thou art sufficient unto thyself (Ne[c] te quaesiveris extra) [188] are perfectly harmless on the supposition that they are heard as well as spoken in faith. There is no danger in them to him who is really in earnest to know the truth but like every thing else may be a mere hypocrite's cloak to such as seek offence. Or to such as talk for talk's sake.

Lean without fear on your own tastes. But the young gentlemen of the day choose their profession by ⟨the⟩ what they call public opinion; & marry for the eyes of others; & ⟨reside⟩ ↑dwell↓ in town though they prefer the country & postpone what they love to what is popular.

↑Sunday, Sept. 14↓

What is the doctrine of *infallible guidance* if *one will abdicate choice*, but striving to act unconsciously, to resume the simplicity of childhood? [n] It is to act on the last impression derived from a knowledge of all the facts & not wilfully [82] ⟨open⟩ to secure a particular advantage. The single minded actor insists on the tranquillity of his own mind[.]

Aura. Translation. Lectures on moral philosophy. Cousin's theory. Sacred music in Straniera. Discipline[.] Blagden. On travelling [189]

Ne[c] te quaesiveris extra.[190] I would insist so far on my own tastes as to read those books I fancy & postpone reading those which offer me no attraction. If Dr Lindberg would have me study Swedenborg because I have respect for his doctrines, I shall hold it

---

[188] "Look to no one outside yourself." Persius, Satire I, 7.

[189] "Aura . . . travelling" is in pencil; the final phrase ("On travelling") is repeated again in pencil under "Ne te quaesiveris" within the following paragraph. The fragmentary notes are obviously explained in part by the following entry. "Aura . . . theory." apparently refers to Henning Gotfried Linberg's translation of Victor Cousin's *Introduction to the History of Philosophy* (Boston, 1832), a volume which Emerson owned. Linberg was a follower of Swedenborg. The remaining notes seem to refer to Bellini's opera *La Straniera*, which Emerson had seen in Florence on May 11, 1833 (see pp. 72, 171 above), and to George Washington Blagden, minister of the Salem Street Church, Boston, 1830–1836, whose sermon Emerson discusses below.

[190] See n. 188 above.

sufficient answer that the aura of those books is not agreeable to my intellectual state. ↑See p. 124↓ I will not so far do violence to myself as to read them against my inclination,ⁿ believing that those books which ⟨my best judgment⟩ at any time ↑I↓ crave⟨s⟩ are the books fittest at that time for me. This is Carlyle's justification for giving such humorous prominence to such incidents as George Fox's leather ⟨pantaloons⟩ suit of clothes.[191] ↑If I obey my passion instead of my reason that is another affair. The appeal is always open from Philip drunk to Philip sober.↓ [192]

Sept. 15. Heard Mr Blagden preach yesterday with much interest. What an orator would some extraordinary discipline of events make of him. Could some Socrates win him to the love of the True & the Beautiful; or extreme sorrows arouse the mighty interior reactions; or revolutionary violence call into life the best ambition; ⟨&⟩ ↑could any event↓ acquaint him⟨se⟩ with himself, ↑he would↓ with his rare oratorical talents ⟨he would⟩ absolutely ⟨thunder & lighten⟩ [193] command us. His manner is the best I know of, and seems to me unexceptionable. As to his preaching that was good too in the main. The skeleton of his sermon, or, as Charles called it, the frame of his kite, was fallacious[,] illogical after the most ordinary fashion of the Wisners & Beechers [194] [83] but his strong genius led him continually to penetrate this husk & leaning simply on himself speak the truth out of this ⟨deformed⟩ ↑unnecessary↓ mask. The conflict of the tradition & of his own genius is visible throughout. He gets his hands & eyes up in describing Jehovah exalted as in Calvinistic state, & then saves the whole by ending with — "in the heart's affections." I listen

---

[191] *Sartor Resartus,* Bk. III, ch. 1. See *The Works,* 1896–1901, I, 166: " 'Perhaps the most remarkable incident in Modern History' says Teufelsdröckh, 'is . . . George Fox's making to himself a suit of leather. . . .' "

[192] Valerius Maximus, VI, 2, 1; see p. 15 above.

[193] The phrase is both canceled and circled.

[194] Benjamin B. Wisner (1794–1835) was minister at Old South Church, 1821–1832, and then one of the three corresponding secretaries of the American Board of Commissioners for Foreign Missions, 1832–1835; two Beechers had recently moved from ministerial posts in Boston to the presidencies of Western educational institutions: Lyman Beecher (1775–1863), minister of the Hanover Street Church, 1826–1832; and Edward Beecher (1804–1895), pastor of the Park Street Church, 1826–1831.

without impatience because though the whole is literally false, it is really true; only he speaks Parables which I translate as he goes.[n] Thus, he says, 'the carnal mind ⟨in⟩hates God continually': & I say, 'It is the instinct of the understanding to contradict the reason.' [195] One phrase translates the other.

The charm of Italy is the charm of its names. I have seen as fine days ⟨bu⟩from my own window. Then what Boswellism it is to travel! Illustrate[,] eternize your own woodhouse. It is much cheaper & quite possible to any resolute thinker. What matters it I said to myself ⟨in the stage coach⟩ ↑on my journey↓ as the persons in the coach disputed as to the name of the town, whether this bunch of barberry bushes & birches ↑visible from the coach window↓ be called Bridgewater or Taunton. So, what matter whether this hill & yon green field be called Garofalo, Terni   or Ipswich & Cape Cod. Let the soul once be fully awake & its thought is so much that the place becomes nothing. ⟨The⟩ Remember the Sunday morning in Naples when I said 'This moment is the truest vision[,] the best spectacle I have seen amid all the wonders & this moment[,] this vision[,] I might have had in my own closet in Boston.' [196] Hence learn that it is an [84] unworthy superstition for seers to go to Italy or France & come home & describe houses & things[.] Let them see men & magnify the passages of common life. Let them be so Man-wise that they can see through the coat, the rank, the language & sympathize promptly with that other self that under these thin disguises wholly corresponds to their own. See what I wrote, p. 63, on Lincoln bell.[197]

You do not know any Socrates. Very likely. The philosopher whom you have admired in discourse makes a different impression

---

[195] Carlyle, "Novalis," *Foreign Review*, IV (1829), 117: "The elder Jacobi . . . says once, we remember — 'It is the instinct of the Understanding to *contradict* Reason.'" C. F. Harrold, *Carlyle and German Thought:1819–1834* (New Haven, 1934), p. 254, notes that though the statement ascribed to Jacobi is nowhere literally present in his work, it comes in essence from the Vorrede of his *Werke* (Leipzig, 1812–1825), II, 101 ff.

[196] Possibly Emerson is recalling his awareness of the spiritual church as opposed to physical churches, as he described it in his entry for Sunday, March 17, 1833 (see p. 144 above).

[197] See the entry for July 12, 1834, pp. 303–304 above.

in private life. Very likely. Most men do: their aims are not distinct enough. As his aim becomes more distinct it will ⟨more⟩ insensibly pervade & characterize his private action, his manners, his ↑table-↓talk ⟨at the tea-table⟩.

———

A brilliant young man easily becomes a satellite to some rich or powerful or eloquent man or set of men but as soon as he reflects, he is transformed from a Satellite into a central orb, & rich & great & kings & idols revolve around him. (See p. 50)

———

¹⁹⁸A man in the New Bedford coach told me a story of a lady who took an egg in her hand & the warmth of her body hatching it ⟨a parcel of⟩the little serpents came out & ran all over her hand.

¹⁹⁹The whole matter of Riches & Poverty is reversed by the act of reflexion, whenever it begins. The intellect at once takes possession of another's wealth & habits & performances as if it were its own. Who is rich in the room where Socrates sits but he? Whilst Webster speaks to the Senate who is formidable but he? The Intellect fairly excited [85] overleaps all bounds with equal ease & is as easily master of millions as master of one. With each divine impulse it rends the thin rinds of the ⟨local⟩ ↑visible↓ & finite & comes out into Eternity, inspires & expires its air. It converses with truths that have always been spoken in the world & becomes conscious of a closer sympathy with Phocion & Epictetus than with the persons in the house.

———

P.M.

No art can exceed the mellow beauty of one square rood of ground in the woods this afternoon. The noise of the locust, the bee, & the pine, the light, the insect forms, butterflies, cankerworms hanging, balloon spiders swinging, devil's-needles cruising, chirping grasshoppers; the tints & forms of the leaves & trees ⟨the⟩. Not a flower but its form seems a type, not a capsule but is an elegant seed box. Then the myriad asters, polygalas, and golden rods & through the bush the far pines, & overhead the eternal sky. All the pleasing forms

¹⁹⁸ "A man . . . her hand." is struck through with two diagonal use marks.
¹⁹⁹ The paragraph here, and its continuation on p. [85], is struck through with double use marks, vertical in ink and wavy, diagonal in pencil.

of art are imitations of these, & yet before the beauty of a right action all this beauty is cold & unaffecting.

——

Noble scene in "I promessi Sposi" the humiliation of Fra Cristoforo.[200] That is what we aim to teach in all our Christian rhetoric about the transforming power of godliness.

Ho! for the doctrine of Compensations.

Moreover saith the world 'Nothing venture, Nothing have.' [201]

The moulds & occasions of our virtues how contemptible often. Talked with Mr D. about the effect of a fine house & fine furniture in educating a ↑new↓ generation to fine manners.

[86] Young men struck with particular observations begin to make collections of related truths & please themselves as Burton did with thinking the wheel, an arc of whose curve they discern, will, by their careful addition of arc to arc as they descry them, by & by come full circle, & be contained in the field of their vision. By & by they learn that the addition of particular facts brings them no nearer to the completion of an infinite orbit.

Shall I say that the use of Natural Science seems merely ancillary to Moral? I would learn the law of the diffraction of a ray because when I understand it, it will illustrate, perhaps suggest, a new truth in ethics.

He knew what was in man. [John 2:25]

↑1⟨7⟩6 Sept.↓

How despicable are the starts, sidelong glances, & lookings back of suspicious men. Go forward & look straight ahead though you die for it. Abernethy says in his Hunter book, that the eye-sockets are so formed in the ⟨bes⟩ gods & heroes of Greek Sculpture that it would be impossible for such eyes to squint & take furtive glances on this side & that.[202] You have looked behind you at the passenger & caught

---

[200] Chs. 34 and 35.

[201] See Ray, *A Compleat Collection of English Proverbs* (London, 1768), p. 166.

[202] "How despicable . . . & that." is struck through with triple diagonal use

his eye looking behind also. What dastards you both are for that moment! The unconscious forever which turns the whole head or nothing!

[8⟨8⟩7] 17 Sept.[203] ⟨T⟩Make a very slight change in the point of view, & the most familiar objects are the most interesting. We read our own advertisement in the newspaper. In a camera obscura the butcher's cart & the figure of one's own barber or washerwoman delight us. Turn the head upside down by looking at the landscape through your own legs & how charming is the picture though of your own woodhouse & barnyard. See p. 33[.]

How truly has poetry represented the difficulty of reflexion in the story of Proteus or Silenus is it? & in that of Odin's Prophetess.[204] Any evasion, any digression, any thing but sitting down before the gates with immoveable determination that they must open. One of the forms the Proteus takes is that of civil self depreciation. 'You quite mistake, sir; I am not that you took me for. A poor evanescent topic really not worth your consideration; it was my resemblance to a relation that deceived you. Had you not better seek that?'

[September] 21. The poet writes for readers he little thinks of. Persons whom he could not bear, & who could not bear him, yet find passages in his works which are to them as their own thoughts. So Aunt Mary quotes the verses [205]

"That which Sir William Pepperel willed, came to pass." [206]

marks; "that the eye-sockets . . . that.": used in "History," *W*, II, 24. The passage is a slight paraphrase of Abernethy's *Physiological Lectures*, 1817, pp. 86–87.

[203] The following paragraph, struck through with several use marks, two wavy and diagonal in ink, one wavy and diagonal in pencil, is used in *Nature*, *W*, I, 51.

[204] Silenus was, as Virgil pointed out in Eclogue VI, prophetic. Proteus and Odin's Prophetess were apparently linked in Emerson's thought by their unwillingness to foresee the future unless forced to do so by grimly determined seekers. See the *Odyssey*, IV, 372–465 and Gray's "Descent of Odin," Ode IX, in which Odin sits immovably "right against the eastern gate" until the prophecy is forthcoming.

[205] A two-line space is left here, perhaps to include Aunt Mary's illustrative verses at a later date.

[206] Williamson, *The History of the State of Maine*, 1832, II, 341. See p. 306 above.

There is in some men as it were a preexistent harmony ⟨be⟩stablished between them & the course of events so that they *will* at the precise moment that which God *does*. They are pitched to the tune of the time. Or shall I say they are like the fly in the coach.

[88] 22 Sept. One is daunted by every one of a multitude of rules which we read in books of criticism but when we speak or write *unconsciously* we are carried through them all safely without offending ⟨one.⟩ or perceiving one[.]

[October] 6.²⁰⁷ In September the roads & woods were full of crickets & as fast as one falls by the way the rest eat him up. Wind & seed[.] Every thing may be painted [,] every thing sung. But to be poetized

The high prize of eloquence may be mine[,] the joy of uttering what no other can utter & what all must receive.

I thought how much not how little accomplishment in manners, speech, practick address an open eye discovers in each passenger. If an equal vitality is dealt out to each man how strange if diverging by all that force from your line your neighbor had not attained a degree of mastery in one sort admirable to you. Insist on yourself. Never imitate. For your own talent you can present every moment with all the force of a lifetime's cultivation but ⟨ta⟩ ↑of↓ the adopted stolen talent of anybody else you have only a frigid brief ⟨st⟩extempore half possession.²⁰⁸ Adhere to your own & produce it with the meek courage that intimates This possession is my all; is my inheritance from Almighty God & must have value.

To be poetized any object must be lifted from off its feet.

²⁰⁷ The "6" is in pencil. Beneath "September . . . up." is a half-erased pencil entry, apparently "German Lover Bob & J ‖ . . . ‖ Cricket Cannibals. Elements play with each other & themselves"; "Wind . . . poetized" is also in pencil and is apparently part of the earlier entry neither erased nor covered with an ink entry. Traces of unrecovered pencil writing underlie the present entry on the rest of the page.
²⁰⁸ "Insist . . . half possession.": used in "Self-Reliance," *W*, II, 83.

Disgusting to have genius treated as a medical fact[,] an inflammation of the brain[,] & thought & poetry as evacuations.

[89] "One first question I ask of every man; Has he an aim which with undivided soul he follows & advances towards? Whether his aim is a right one or a wrong one forms but my second question." [209]

14 Oct. Every involuntary repulsion that arises in your mind give heed unto. It is the surface of a central truth. Madame de Stael's Works & Plutarch & Bacon & Coleridge were a library to retire with[.]

18 Oct. New York. Received the tidings of the death of my dear brother Edward on the first day of this month at St John's, Porto Rico. So falls one pile more of hope for this life. I see I am bereaved of a part of myself.

> "Whatever fortunes wait my future life
> The beautiful is vanished & returns not." [210]

In Boston, at Second Church, George Sampson told me after I preached my sermon on Habit, that Mr Washburn said to him, that "he wished he was in the habit of hearing such sermons as that;" which speech I found to be good praise & good blame.[211]

[90] 27 October.[212] "Let them rave!" said Tennyson's Dirge. Thou art quiet in thy grave. ⟨I⟩Even so, how oft saith the spirit, that happier is the lot of the dead than of the living that are yet alive. Who that sees the Spirit of the Beast uppermost in the politics & the

[209] The paragraph is struck through with a diagonal use mark.

[210] Coleridge's translation of Schiller's *Death of Wallenstein*, V, i. See the *Works*, 1853, VII, 682.

[211] "In Boston . . . blame." is written in a different ink and in what appears to be the handwriting of Emerson's later years, as though it were a later recollection. Emerson delivered the sermon on Habit (Sermon 54) at the Second Church twice: November 8, 1829, and July 10, 1831. The "Mr. Washburn" is perhaps Abdiel Washburn Jr., one of Ellen Tucker's relatives.

[212] " 'Let them . . . Natural World." is struck through with a diagonal use line. " 'Let them . . . subjugated in him.": used in "Heroism," *W*, II, 263. "Let them . . . thy grave" is the refrain of Tennyson's "The Dirge," ll. 4 and 7 of each stanza, slightly misquoted. "how oft . . . yet alive." is a paraphrase of Eccles. 4:2: "Wherefore I praised the dead which are already dead more than the living which are yet alive."

movements of the time, but inly congratulates Washington that he is long already wrapped in his shroud & forever safe,[n] that he was laid sweet in his grave ⟨not yet⟩ the Hope of humanity not yet sub- jugated in him. And Edward's fervid heart is also forever still, no more to suffer from the tumults of the Natural World. And they who survive & love men have reason to apprehend that short as their own time may be they may yet outlive the honor, the religion, yea the liberty of the country. Yet yet is

"Hope the paramount duty which Heaven lays

For its own honor, on man's suffering heart." [213]

Otherwise one would be oppressed with melancholy & pray to die whenever he heard of the orgies of the Julien Hall or of the outrages of a mob.[214]

The best sign which I can discover in the dark times is the in- creasing earnestness of the cry which swells from every quarter that a systematic Moral Education is needed. Channing, Coleridge, Words- worth, Owen, Degerando, Spurzheim, Bentham. Even Saul is among the Prophets.[215] The gentleman will by & by be found to mean the man of Conscience.[216] Carlyle also. Pestalozzi[.]

"Where every man may take liberties there is little Liberty for any man." [217]

[91] All around us in vulgar daylight are hid (yes hid in day- light) sublimest laws. De Stael saw them.[218] Ours have not yet been seen. Do not multiply your facts but seek the meaning of those you have.

[213] Wordsworth, "Poems dedicated to National Independence and Liberty," Pt. II, no. 33, ll. 5–6.

[214] Emerson generally linked Julien Hall with political activity, particularly of the Jacksonians, or with the Society of the Free Enquirers, an atheistical group founded and led by Abner Kneeland. Julien Hall, erected in 1825 on the corner of Congress and Milk Streets, contained two halls, one of which was regularly used by the Free Enquirers.

[215] Cf. I Sam. 10: 11–12.

[216] "The gentlemen . . . Conscience." is struck through with a wavy diagonal use mark in pencil.

[217] See Coleridge, *On the Constitution of Church and State*, 1839, p. 102.

[218] Possibly a reference to "Almost all the axioms of physics correspond with the maxims of morals," *Germany*, 1859, II, 217–218. Cf. *Nature, W*, I, 33, and *JMN*, III, 255.

[219]This eternal superiority belongs to the contemplative man over his more forcible & more honored neighbor styled the practical man, that the former moves in a real world the latter in a phenomenal[,] that though the seasons of the former's activity may be ⟨sel⟩ rare & with intermissions of deepest gloom yet when he works it is life properly so called whilst the latter's endless activity & boundless pretension ⟨seems⟩ reminds him ↑too↓ often of the laborer at the poor-house who worked all winter shovelling ↑a ton of↓ coal from the yard to the cellar & then from the cellar to the yard. Euler's truth against all experience. ↑See Practical Man J. 1832, 14 Nov.↓ [220]

It is losing time to inquire anxiously respecting the opinions of another speculator. The way his opinions have attained any value is by his forbearing to inquire & merely observing.

Man is great not in his goals but in his transition from state to state. Great in act but instantly dwarfed by self-indulgence.

Not Universal Education but the Penny Magazine has failed. Brougham may have failed but Pestalozzi has not. Leibnitz said; "I have faith that man may be reformed, when I see how much Education may be reformed." Why not a moral Education as well as a discovery of America? [n]

[92] ⟨28 Oct. Do not seek to multiply your facts but seek the meaning of those you have⟩

The education of the mind consists in a continual substitution of facts for words, as in petrifaction a particle of stone replaces a particle of wood. But observe that what are called facts are commonly words as regards the fact-man.

It is rather humiliating to attend a public meeting such as this New York Caucus last evening & see what words are best received & what a low animal hope & fear patriotism is. There is however great unity in the Audience. What pleases the Audience *very much*, pleases every individual in it. What tires me, tires all.

---

[219] The paragraph is struck through with two diagonal use marks in pencil, one wavy, one straight.

[220] The cross reference is to Journal Q (see p. 59 above). Euler's comment Emerson had found repeated twice in Coleridge's *Aids to Reflection*, ed. James Marsh (Burlington, Vt., 1829), p. 274 and p. 285, in slightly differing versions.

Greatest care is taken instinctively on both sides to represent their own cause as the winning one. The word "Why then do we despond?" was manifestly a mistake in Mr Hone's speech.[221] This party-lie ⟨is m⟩ aims to secure the votes of that numerous class (whose veto *weighed* would kick the beam) of indifferent, effeminate, stupid persons who in the absence of all internal strength obey ↑whatever seems↓ the voice of their street, their ward, their town, or whatever domineering strength will be at the trouble of civilly dictating to them. But their votes count ⟨as⟩ like real votes.

Transcribe from Quarterly Review the sentences on the progressive influence of the man of genius[.] [222]
— If you kill them I will write a hymn to their memory that shall sing itself.[223] might Luther say[.]

[93] 29 October. — Michel Angelo Buonaroti: John Milton: Martin Luther: George Fox: Lafayette: Falkland: Hampden. Are not these names seeds? "Men akin unto the universe." The sentiment which like Milton's comes down to new generations is that which was no sham or half-sentiment to Milton himself but the utterance of his inmost self.

"———— plainest taught & easiest learnt
What makes a nation happy & keeps it so." [224]
                    [*Paradise Regained*, IV, 361–362]

[221] During a few weeks when he was preaching as a supply minister in the Second Unitarian Church in New York, Emerson apparently attended a Whig meeting, called by Philip Hone, who was one of the speakers, "the Merchants' Meeting at the Exchange." See *The Diary of Philip Hone*, ed. Allan Nevins, 2 vols. (New York, 1936), I, 139–140.

[222] "The Poetical Works of S. T. Coleridge," *The Quarterly Review*, LII (Aug. 1834), 36: "By and by, after years of abuse or neglect, the aggregate of the single minds who think for themselves, and have seen the truth and force of his genius, becomes important; the coterie becomes a sect; the sect dilates into a party; and lo! after a season, no one knows how, the poet's fame is universal."

[223] The paragraph is set off by vertical lines; the phrase "might Luther say" is in lighter ink and may be a later addition, perhaps of the time of the lecture on Luther when Emerson was recalling the martyrdom of Protestants at Brussels for which Luther composed a great hymn. See *Lectures*, I, 126.

[224] See "John Milton," *Lectures*, I, 162. Emerson may have been reminded of the quotation by Coleridge's citations of it in *On the Constitution of Church and*

Thanks for my sins, my defects as the stag should have thanked for his feet. As no man thoroughly understands a truth until he has first contended against it so no man has a thorough acquaintance with the hindrances or the talents of men until he has suffered from the one & seen the triumph of the other over his own want of the same.[225] I should not be a bard of common life, wants, individualities, in the pulpit, were I not the foolish parlor & table companion that I am.

Dr Gerard ascended on Himmaleh 20000 feet[;] Humboldt on Andes 19374. Gay Lussac in a balloon 23000 ft. "Galen is not medicine nor Herodotus history but Euclid is geometry."

⟨A ragged coat looks revolutionary⟩ We always idealize. Hard to find in Paul, Luther, Adams, Lafayette anything so fine as to bear out our praises. For said not Aristotle Action is less near to vital truth than description? ⁿ We tinge them with the glories of that Idea in whose light they are seen.[226]

[94] We should hold to the usage until we are clear it is wrong.[227]

How different is one man in two hours! Whilst he sits alone in his studies & opens not his mouth he is God manifest in flesh. Put him in a parlor with unfit company and he shall talk like a fool.[228]

[October] 31. It is not to be doubted that the subjectivity (to use the Germanic phrase) of man clothes itself with a different objec-

---

State (see 1839 ed., p. 41) and in *The Statesman's Manual* (see the *Works*, 1853, I, 424).

[225] "Thanks for . . . want of the same.": used in "Compensation," *W*, II, 117. See also the entry for October 18, 1832, p. 66 above, for an earlier version of the thought.

[226] "Hard to . . . seen." is written over an earlier erased pencil entry. The earlier entry may have been merely copied over, since pencil punctuation still remains and the few visible letters match the ink overwriting. But the pencil punctuation may be an addition by Edward Emerson and is not printed. The statement attributed to Aristotle is actually from Plato, *The Republic*, Bk. V. See p. 261 above.

[227] Beneath this sentence is an earlier penciled version, partially erased: "We should hold to those usages of whose wrong we are not yet clear."

[228] The paragraph is struck through with a wavy diagonal use mark in pencil.

tivity in every age. Satan who plays so prominent a part in the theology of the last age is a hollow word now but the evil principles which the word designated are no whit abated in virulence. I am bound by all my tastes to a reverence for Luther yet can I by no means find any but a subjective that is essential correspondence in me to his mind. I cannot reanimate & appropriate his difficulties & speculations. Socrates. Bacon. How then Jesus & the apostles? [n] Sometimes it seems nations[,] ages were the body of shades of thought. Wrote Mother of Edward what is true of all, that No words but his *name* can describe the peculiarities of any remarkable person.

But what shall be the action of society? How superficial are our fears & hopes! We meet with a single individual or read a single newspaper ⟨wh⟩expressing malignant sentiments & we despond for the republic. By one declaimer of an opposite character our confidence is renewed that all will go well. In these times a ragged coat looks sinister & revolutionary.

———

[95] "Who injures one threatens all." [229]

Luther says "Pull not by force any one person from the *mass*. Reflect on my conduct in the affair of the indulgences. I had the whole body of the papists to oppose. I preached, I wrote, I pressed on men's consciences with the greatest earnestness the positive declarations of the Word of God, but I used not a particle of force or constraint. What has been the consequence? This same Word of God has while I was asleep in my bed, given such a blow to papal despotism as not one of the German princes not even the Emperor himself could have done. It is not I, it is the divine Word that has done all." [230]

Sublimely is it said in Nat. Hist Fanaticism, of angry persons "Night does not part the combatants." [231]

At least let the good side of these truths be applied to the true Word which the Poet has uttered whilst he is asleep in his bed[,] &

———

[229] Cf. "Multis miniatur qui uni facit injuriam" — "He that injures one threatens many." Publius Syrus, 351. "He threatens many that hath injured one" is the version given by Jonson in *Sejanus*, II, iv, 53.

[230] John Scott, *Luther and the Lutheran Reformation*, 2 vols. (New York, 1833), I, 167, slightly misquoted: used in "Martin Luther," *Lectures*, I, 128–129.

[231] Emerson is actually combining the titles of two separate works by Isaac Taylor, both of which he knew: *The Natural History of Enthusiasm* (London, 1829; New York, 1831), and *Fanaticism* (London, 1833; Boston, 1834). The quotation is taken from p. 30 of the latter volume, 1834 ed.

when he is asleep in the grave it never halts or faints but prospers in the work whereto it is sent.

I believe in the ↑existence of the↓ material world as the expression of the spiritual or real, & so look with a quite comic & condescending interest upon the show of Broadway with the air of an old gentleman when he says ↑"Sir↓ I knew your father." Is it not forever the ⟨en⟩aim & endeavor of the real to embody itself in the phenomenal? ⁿ Broadway is Trade & Vanity made flesh. Therein should the philosophers walk as the impersonations of states as if Massachusetts, Carolina, Ohio, should go out to take ⟨a walk⟩ ⁿ an airing.

[96] [232] 1 November.

The Union of extreme sensitiveness & a defiance of ⟨the⟩ opinion is not very uncommon. Every man ⟨has⟩ is bipolar; never ⁿ a circle: somewhere therefore in each one of never so many million you shall find the contrariety[,] inconsistency of his nature. And as language translates language, verb verb, & noun noun so could their surfaces be adjusted to each other[,] might we find one age corresponding to another age in every minute peculiarity and every one man to every other man. This makes the interest of biography. ↑I have heard men say they were afraid to read the accounts of suicides in ⟨a⟩ the newspapers last year so remarkable for that crime↓[.]

Humboldt's scientific imagination will make the mnemonics of science. I read yesterday his designations of the sudden & violent disturbance of the magnetic equilibrium as "magnetic storms." So before of "Volcanic paps[.]" [233]

The speculations of one age do not fit another. The great man of one age is a showing how the great man of this time would have

---

[232] The first two paragraphs on the page are struck through with a diagonal penciled use mark. Under the ink entry for these paragraphs is an earlier erased entry in pencil with the following recovered words: under "circle: somewhere" is "upon the earth & sky"; under "each other" is "high way"; under "man" is "ball"; under "so before" is "& slow"; in the space below "magnetic storms" is "every where"; and beneath "the great men of" within the next paragraph is "those who sing". Penciled punctuation, either a remnant from the original entry or an insertion by Edward Emerson, is not printed. "I have heard . . . crime" is squeezed within the two paragraphs in a different ink.

[233] See Alexander von Humboldt, *Personal Narrative of Travels to the Equinoctial Regions of the New Continent*, 7 vols. (London, 1814–1819), IV, 43–44.

acted in that. Now & then comes a crisis when the contemporaries of one opinion become contemporaries of another & then the great man becomes the man of two ages as was Burke. Fault of our mortality we cannot act in a past age: we compensate ourselves by choosing out of that generation its most human individual & say 'Lo how man acted.'

[97][234] Some men stand on the solid globe[;] others have no basis but some one stands by & puts a shovel under their feet at any moment.

Euler having demonstrated certain properties of Arches, adds, "All Experience is in contradiction to this; but this is no reason for doubting its truth."[235]

Nov. 5. The elections. Whilst it is notorious that the Jackson party is the *Bad* party in the cities & in general in the country except in secluded districts where a single Newspaper has deceived a well disposed community, still, on all the banners equally of tory & whig good professions are inscribed. The Jackson flags say "Down with corruption!" "We ask for nothing but our Right." "The Constitution, the Laws," "the Laboring Classes," "Free trade," &c &c. So that they have not yet come to the depravity that says, "Evil be thou my good."[236] ⟨When⟩ ↑Should↓ the Whig party fail⟨s⟩, which God avert! the patriot will still have some confidence in the redeeming force of the latent i.e. deceived virtue that is contained within the tory party; and yet more in the ⟨reproductive⟩ remedial regenerative Nature of Man which ⟨reve⟩ ↑ever↓ reproduces ⟨the⟩a healthful moral sense even out of stupidity & corruption. Thus the children of the Convicts at Botany Bay are found to have sound moral sentiments.[237]

---

[234] Beginning at the top of the page under the present ink entry "stand on the solid globe" and continuing within the entry for November 5 as far as "Nature of Man which" is a penciled entry, almost completely erased, which appears by spacing and end words to have been a poem. Only the end words in the lines have been recovered as follows: " ‖ . . . ‖ on the good ‖ . . . ‖ choicest brotherhood ‖ . . . ‖ there may come to us ‖ . . . ‖ Duty gives us wings ‖ . . . ‖ exposed for sale ‖ . . . ‖ old ‖ . . . ‖ gone."

[235] "Euler . . . truth.' " is struck through with two wavy diagonal use marks: used in *Nature, W*, I, 56; for the source of the quotation see Coleridge's *Aids to Reflection*, 1829, p. 285. See also p. 327 above.

[236] Milton, *Paradise Lost*, IV, 110.

[237] Botany Bay in Cumberland County, New South Wales, was a penal colony

Mr H. says the Tories deserve to succeed, for they turn every stone with an Irishman under & pick him up.

Surprizing tendency of man *in action* to believe in his continuance. If these stormy partisans doubted their immortality in these hours as in others it would calm their Zeal.

[98] "The moral & intelligent instrumentality from which the Sovereign Grace refuses to sever itself, is nothing else than the Vital force which animates each single believer." [Isaac Taylor], *Fanaticism* p. 8

Noisy Election; flags, boy processions, placards, badges, medals, bannered coaches [—] everything to get the hurrah on our side. ⟨t⟩That is the main end. Great anxiety, pale faces are become florid. They count that 1600 minutes are all the time allowed in all three days. Indisposition to business & great promptness to spend.

The philosophy of the erect position[:] God made man upright.

The sublime of the Ship is that in ⟨a⟩the pathless ↑sea↓ it carries its own ⟨road⟩ ↑direction↓ in the chart & compass. See Herrick's verses[.] [238]

'Tis as hard to blow a flageolet [—] it takes so little breath [—] as to blow a flute which costs so much, so in writing poetry to speak simply enough in the abundance of thoughts & images is not easier than to be profound enough in their superficiality.

There is a way of making the biography of Luther as practical & pertinent today as ⟨an article upon the news price of cotton⟩ ↑the last paragraph↓ from Liverpool upon the price of cotton.

The children of this world are wiser than the children of light.[239] The good cause is always on the defensive, the evil assailant. Because the unscrupulous can not only avail themselves of innocent means to their ends but all evil ones likewise. The Whigs can put in their own votes. But the Tories can do this & put them in again in another ward or bring a ⟨dozen⟩ ↑gang of↓ forsworn gallows birds to boot,[n] to elect the officers that are to ↑hunt, try,↓ imprison, & execute them.

---

until 1840 when the transportation of criminals from England ceased. "Thus the children . . . sentiments.": used in "Politics," *W*, III, 211.

[238] Probably "The Way," the first two lines of which Emerson quoted in overwritten pencil writing on p. 343 below.

[239] Luke 16:8, slightly misquoted.

Let the worst come to the worst & the Whig cause be crushed for a season & the Constitution be grossly violated[,] then you should see the weak Whig become [99] irresistible. They would then acquire the gloom & the might of fanaticism & redeem America as they once redeemed England & ↑once aforetime↓ planted & emancipated America[.]

> Fight with the wild beasts
> Be so great as to be humble.[240]

> How many big events to ⟨shall⟩ shake the earth
> Lie packed in silence waiting for their birth.[241]

Mem. Write to Sidney Mason & offer services to Dr Armstrong[.]

Heard Mr Maxwell at the Masonic Hall[,] a thoroughly public soul[,] the mere voice of the occasion & the hour.[242] There are these persons into whom the general feeling enters & through whom it passes & finds never a hitch or hindrance; they express what is boiling in the bosoms of the whole multitude around them.

Plain is it too that there are people who justly make the impression of ability upon us & yet can neither speak nor write nor act well. There is a callus or paralysis somewhere[,] a slight excess or defect that neutralizes a fine genius.

It is a great step from the thought to the expression of the thought in action. Without horror I contemplate the envy, hatred, & lust that occupy the hearts of smiling well dressed men & women

---

[240] "Fight . . . humble." is written in pencil between the lines of the present entry above and below "fanaticism & redeem"; "Mem . . . Armstrong" is also in pencil following the couplet ("How many . . . birth.") and may have been inserted in late October following the receipt of the news of Edward's death on October 1, 1834, in Puerto Rico, since Sidney Mason, commercial agent and consul, was Edward's employer there and Dr. Francis Armstrong, Edward's companion in St. John's, was the author of an account of his friend's last days, sent to William Emerson. See Rusk, L, I, 422.

[241] This couplet, which appears a second time on p. [109] written in pencil between the lines of the ink entry (see p. 345 below) with slight variations, may be Emerson's version of a line in Othello (I, iii, 377): "There are many events in the womb of time, which will be delivered."

[242] Possibly Hugh Maxwell (1787–1873), long a leader in local politics among New York Whigs.

but the simplest most natural expressions of the same thoughts in action astonish & dishearten me. If the wishes of the lowest class that suffer in these long streets should execute themselves, who can doubt that the city would topple in ruins. Do not [n] trust man, great God!, with more power until he has learned to use his little power better. Does not ↑our↓ power increase exactly in the measure ⟨of⟩that ⟨our⟩we ↑learn how to use it? ↓

[100] Concord, 15 November, 1834. Hail to the quiet fields of my fathers! Not wholly unattended by supernatural [243] friendship & favor let me come hither. Bless my purposes as they are simple & virtuous. Coleridge's fine letter (in London Lit. Gazette Sept. 13, 1834.) [244] comes in aid of the very thoughts I was revolving. And be it so. Henceforth I design not to utter any speech, poem, or book that is not entirely & peculiarly my work. I will say at Public Lectures & the like, those things which I have meditated for their own sake & not for the first time with a view to that occasion. If otherwise you select a ↑new↓ subject ⟨for⟩ & labor to make a good appearance on the appointed day, it is so much lost time to you & lost time to your hearer. It is a parenthesis in your genuine life. You are your own dupe.[n] & for the sake of conciliating your audience you have failed to edify them & winning their ear you have really lost their love & gratitude.

Respect a man! assuredly, but in general only as the potential God & therefore richly deserving of your pity[,] your tears. Now he is only a scrap, an ort, an end & in his actual being no more worthy of your veneration than the poor lunatic. But the simplest person who in his integrity worships God becomes God: at least no optics of human mind can detect the line where man the effect ceases, & God the Cause begins.

Unhappy divorce of Religion & Philosophy

[101] Nov. 16. Our instincts, Sampson Reed thinks, would command

---

[243] Beneath "Not wholly unattended by supernatural" is "Lost time to make & fill up lecture" in faint blurred pencil; below "letter(in" "tho't's" is expanded in pencil between the lines into "thoughts", probably by Edward Emerson.

[244] *The London Literary Gazette and Journal of the Belles Lettres* (Sept. 13, 1834), pp. 628–629, reprinted in *EtE*, I, 155–156.

& Reason would gladly serve, "as the preceptor of a prince," if we were restored to primitive health.[245]

As soon as I read a wise sentence anywhere [246] I feel at once the desire of appropriation. How shall I use it? If I possessed the power of excluding all other readers from that sentence I should be conscious of some temptation to do it. At the same time I know the lower & the higher objections to this meanness. 1. That striking as the thought is to you at this moment yet to judge from your past experience it is more likely that you will forget it than that another will anticipate you in using it. 2 That though you should write the passage in light upon the firmament, yet would no other man or very few other men be able to read in it what you ⟨find there⟩ ↑read↓. 3. That however profound this thought may appear, it is really but a superficial statement of a truth whose depths are only to be sounded by unceasing & manifold consideration. 4 Every thought[,] every subject is capable of being presented with the same exclusive prominence that this now possesses and all that is known is nothing in comparison with what you are assured may be known.

I suppose the materials may now exist for a Portraiture of Man which should be at once history & prophecy. Does it not seem as if a perfect parallelism existed between every great & fully developed man & every other? [n] Take a man of strong nature upon whom events have powerfully acted [—] Luther or Socrates or Sam Johnson [—] & I suppose you shall find no trait in him, no fear, no love, no talent, no dream [247]

[245] "Review of Kirby and Spence," *New Jerusalem Magazine*, III (1829–1830), 140, concerning the value of instinct: "But what now appears to be the lowest, will, as it is purified and regenerated, become the most exalted part of our nature; and reason, like the preceptor of a prince, will delight to obey, where it had been accustomed to teach."

[246] Beneath "As soon as I read a wise sentence anywhere" are traces of erased pencil writing.

[247] "⟨See 6th. line next page)" is written under "love . . . dream" at the bottom of the page, perhaps by Edward Emerson. The canceled passage on p. [102] ("⟨I knew a . . . life.)") interrupts the sentence, "Take a . . . other." The interruptive passage is canceled by four ink lines but is not overmarked heavily, as are most of the passages which Emerson wished to eliminate. The passage appears to have been written on the page before the enclosing entry was written.

[102]²⁴⁸ ⟨I knew a man in the body in time past who was sub-limely generous within & frugal to meanness without; with a royal benevolence he was shabby to servants; ⟨with⟩ overflowing excessive sympathy ⟨with⟩for his fellowmen, he was frigid & disagreeable to them, an overscrupulous purist, he was justly regarded with jealousy for his self indulgent life.⟩

in one that did not translate a similar love, fear, talent, dream, in the other. Luther's Pope, & Turk, & Devil, & Grace, & Justification, & Catherine de Bore, shall reappear under far other names in George Fox, in John Milton, in George Washington, in Goethe, or, long before, in Zeno & Socrates. Their circles, to use the language of geom-etry, would coincide. Here & there, to be sure, are anomalous un-paired creatures, who are but partially developed, wizzeled ²⁴⁹ ⟨up⟩ apples, as if you should seek to match monsters, one of whom has a leg, another an arm, another two heads.

If one should seek to trace the genealogy of thoughts he would find Goethe's "Open Secret" ⟨to⟩ fathered in ⟨Alexander's⟩ Aristotle's answer to Alexander "that these books were published & not pub-lished." And Mme. De Stael's ⟨or Goethe's⟩ "Architecture is frozen music," borrowed from Goethe's "Arch[itectur]e. is dumb music," borrowed from Vitruvius, who said, 'the Architect must not only understand drawing but also Music'.* And Wordsworth's "plan that pleased his childish thought" got from Schiller's "Reverence the dreams of his youth[,]" got from Bacon's Primae cogitationes et consilia juventutis plus Divinitatis habent.²⁵⁰

[*] "——if those great Doctors truly said That th⟨e⟩' Ark to Man's proportion was made."

Donne. ["An Anatomy of the World; The First Anniversary," ll. 317–318]

²⁴⁸ Almost all the careful internal punctuation on this page as well as the passage "And Mme. De Stael . . . habent." is in ink different from the rest of the entry and may represent a later addition.
²⁴⁹ The word, not in Worcester's Dictionary, appears to be spelled as printed, though the first "e" is equal in size to the "l" that follows.
²⁵⁰ The "genealogy of thoughts" in the paragraph may be traced as follows: (a) for the phrase from Goethe, see p. 87 above; (b) for the remark of Aristotle, see Plutarch's Lives, 1822, V, 195, Alexander, slightly misquoted; (c) for the phrase

[103] 19 Nov. The aged grandsire [251] came out of his chamber last evening into our parlor for the first time since his sickness in cloak & velvet cap and attended prayers. In things within his experience he has the most robust erect common sense, is as youthful vigorous in his understanding as a man of thirty. In things without his circle often puerile. He behaved & spoke last evening as Jefferson or Franklin might. His prayer as usual with the happiest pertinence. "We have been variously disciplined; bereaved, but not destitute; sick, but thou hast healed, in degree, our diseases; and when there was but a step between us & death, thou hast said, Live." He ever reminds one both in his wisdom & in the faults of his intellect of an Indian Sagamore[,] a sage within the limits of his own observation, a child beyond. His discourse & manners so far fittest, noblest, simplest. ↑The↓ grace & dignity of a child. What could be better than his speech to me ⟨when⟩ ↑after↓ Grandmother's death? [n] "Well, the bond that united us, is broken, but I hope you & your brothers will not cease to come to this house. You will not like to be excluded, and I shall not like [to] be neglected." And his conversation with the Miles family after the death of their father I admired. The ⟨elder⟩ son was supposed to be intemperate in his habits. The family & friends were all collected for the funeral when we went in. "Madam, I condole with you; Sir, I condole with you; & with you all. I remember, Sir, when I came to this town Your Grandfather was ⟨a⟩ living on this farm and a most respectable citizen. ⟨Your⟩ His father lived here before him. Your father has stood in their place & lived a useful & respected life. Now, Sir, the name & respectability of your

---

from Madame de Staël, see pp. 40 and 75 above; (d) *Of Architecture*, Bk. I, ch. 1, secs. 3 and 8 (Emerson probably read the remark, however, in "Architecture," *The American Encyclopedia*, 1829–1833, I, 334); (e) "Character of the Happy Warrior," l. 5 (the phrase is not misquoted but is verbatim from an early version of the poem; see Emerson's own four-volume edition of 1824, III, 94); (f) *Don Carlos*, IV, xxi, probably at second hand from Madame de Staël (see *Germany*, 1859, I, 227); (g) *De Augmentis*, Bk. VI, ch. 3, Antithesis III, "For Youth." See the *Works*, 1864, IX, 157; Emerson translated the lines in Lecture V, on Human Culture, as "First thoughts and the contemplations of youth are from God." Within this paragraph "Architecture . . . Music'." is used in *Nature*, *W*, I, 43, and the anecdote of Aristotle's answer to Alexander in "Spiritual Laws," *W*, II, 146.

[251] Dr. Ezra Ripley; see *J*, II, 364, n. The entry is later used in "Ezra Ripley, D.D.," *W*, X, 387–388.

family rests on you. Sir if you fail — Ichabod — the glory is departed.[252] And I hope you will not." ——

[104] History teaches what man can do & not less what man can suffer & what he can believe. The slowness with which the stirps generosa seu historica [253] in Europe opened their eyes to the monstrous lie of Popery might startle us as to the possible depth of our own degradation through the sleep of Reason, & prompt a hope of what height we may yet attain.

There are ever & anon in history expressions uttered that seem to be fourfold-visaged ⟨to⟩& look with significant smile to all the quarters of time. Thus when ⟨C⟩Luther & Carolstadt had disputed publicly upon the new doctrines at Leipsic, the Duke George put an end to the controversy by declaring "Be his right divine, or be it human, he is still Pope of Rome." [254] Yet doubt not the same universality of application might be detected by a discerning eye in every homeliest utterance. This Duke George seems the Tory of the World.

Is it not an instructive fact in literary history that of Luther's /sending/writing/ from Wittemberg to Spalatin for the Elector's collection of gems to assist him in translating the 21 Chap. Revelations? [n] They were sent & after a careful examination returned. (V[ide]. Seckendorf p. 204) [255]

And here is another eulogy[,] a true eulogy of that great man. King Christian of Denmark passing through Saxony sent for Luther. He afterwards declared "Never have I heard the gospel so well explained as by Luther. So long as I continue to live I shall hold his discourse in remembrance, and shall submit with greater patience

---

[252] Cf. I Sam. 4:21.

[253] "A race noble or historical" (Ed.). Emerson perhaps was reminded of the Latin tag by its use in Coleridge's *On the Constitution of Church and State* (see the *Works*, 1853, VI, 46).

[254] The anecdote and quotation Emerson found probably in Alexander Bower, *The Life of Luther embracing an Account of the early progress of the Reformation* (Philadelphia, 1824), p. 133; used in "Martin Luther," *Lectures*, I, 123.

[255] Though Emerson's reference to Veit Ludwig von Seckendorf, *Commentarius Historicus et Apologeticus de Lutheranismo* . . . (Frankfurt and Leipzig, 1692) is a proper citation to a Latin work in which the letter to Spalatin is printed in full, his real source was no doubt Bower, *The Life of Luther*, 1824, p. 197, where the anecdote is found accompanied by a careful footnote to Seckendorf.

to whatever I am destined to endure." [256] Longinus could not improve the sentence, and the last clause should be writ in the diary of every preacher.

[105] The Marseilles Hymn and the Ballads of the Reformation and Watts' Hymnbook & the Ranz des Vaches.[257]

Be it remembered in the annals of Man under the Chapter of Incapacity to see ourselves as we see others that Henry VIII of England charged Luther with incest for marrying Catherine de Bore. 🖋 Even the divine Milton recurs with bitterness to tippet & surplice &c[.] [258]

⟨It occurred in church on Sunday with some force that⟩ The best cause has been seldom defended on its merits. Men are possessed by the Idea of liberty or right in the matter but the fewest are able to state in propositions that which makes the strength & soul of their party. The ⟨surfa⟩ idea is deep & pervades the whole mass of men & institutions involved but that which makes the surface is the names of certain men & other accidents. 🖋 These are what in words the antagonist party oppose & revile & therefore on these (as in European war, *on the Milanese*) the battle is fought.

Luther has never stated his thought so well as Mackintosh has done for him. ↑& dwelleth far more on the bald pates & gray cloaks of his opponents.↓

Luther was a great man & as Coleridge says, acted poems.[259] And his words, if they will, they may characterize as half-battles.[260] But the sublime of them, critically considered, is the material sublime not the moral. "If the heavens should pour down Duke Georges for nine days" &c. "If I don't burn them 'tis because I can't find fire" —

[256] *Ibid.*, p. 218.

[257] The ancient musical air of the Swiss mountain cowherds. Bernadin de Saint-Pierre, four volumes of whose *Studies of Nature* were in Emerson's library, noted (IV, 10) that the tune was prohibited in Holland and France because it made homesick Swiss mercenaries desert for love of their country. The story of the effect of the song is also in Alison's *Essays on the Nature and Principles of Taste* (see *JMN*, II, 226).

[258] See the *Works*, III, Pt. I, 61, for "Of Reformation," and VI, 98, for "Considerations touching the likeliest means to remove hirelings out of the church."

[259] *The Friend*, 1818, I, 237: "Luther did not *write*, he acted Poems."

[260] The phrase is Carlyle's; see "Jean Paul Friedrich Richter Again," *Foreign Review*, V (1830), 42, and "Luther's Psalm," *Fraser's Magazine*, II (Jan. 1831), 743.

"I'll go if all the devils are in the way" &c.[261] It is like Mahomet's description of the Angel whom he saw in heaven, 'It was nine days' journey from one of his eyes to the other.' [262] Mere sublimity of magnitude & number, but Landor says well, "where the heart is not moved, the gods stride & thunder in vain. The pathetic is the true sublime." [263] I speak of course of the homely monk's sayings as sentences.

[106] The purposes & character which they manifest is quite another consideration. There *is* something akin to sublimity. But there is no such force in all his sayings as in "Forgive his virtues too." [264]

Let a man have no presence[,] no manners. It takes some men so long to get through their preliminaries that every body avoids them for fear of the trouble. But be a mere Word[,] a mere action & when parade days come then do these long courtesies when there is time & expectation but spare working days & working people.

> O what is Heaven but the fellowship
> Of minds that each can stand against the world
> By its own meek but incorruptible will.[265]

The moral reformation of society certainly is remote but I hope is not out of sight[.]

November 21, 1834. Ah how shone the moon & her little spark-

---

[261] The three remarks are slightly misquoted from Scott, *Luther and the Lutheran Reformation*, 1833, I, 162; I, 95; and I, 126–127. "If I don't . . . find fire" Emerson may have found also in a slightly different version in Joseph and Isaac Milner, *The History of the Church of Christ*, 4 vols. (Boston, 1809–1811), IV, 466. Much of the material concerning Luther was taken over into the lecture. See *Lectures*, I, 137.

[262] The story of Mahomet and the angel is to be found in several sources known to Emerson, such as "The Life of Mahomet" in *Lives of Eminent Persons*, 1833, p. 19, and George Bush's *The Life of Mohammed* (New York, 1831), pp. 93–94. In these sources, however, the tale is Oriental and extravagant, with the distance between the angel's eyes given as 70,000 days' journey. Emerson may have misused the figure of nine days as an unconscious echo from his story of Luther and Duke George in the immediately preceding illustration.

[263] "Duke de Richelieu, Sir Fire Coats, and Lady Glengrin," *Imaginary Conversations*, 1st ser., 1828, III, 205, slightly misquoted.

[264] Young, *Night Thoughts*, IX, 2316; see *JMN*, III, 274.

[265] These lines Emerson usually wrote into an album if he were asked to supply a sample of his own verse. See *J*, III, 368.

lers last eve. There was the light in the selfsame vessels which contained it a million years ago[.]

⟨It occurred to me with a certain feel⟩ I perceived in myself this day with a certain degree of terror the prompting to retire. What! is this lone parsonage in this thin village so populous as to crowd you & overtask your benevolence? ⁿ The↑y↓ ⟨sensitiveness⟩ who urge you to retire hence would be too many for you in the centre of the desert or on the top of a pillar. How ²⁶⁶ dear how soothing to man arises the Idea of God peopling the lonely place[,] effacing the scars of our mistakes & disappointments. When we have lost our God of tradition & ceased from [107] our God of rhetoric then may God fire the heart with his presence.

2⟨4⟩3 Nov. The root & seed of democracy is the doctrine Judge for yourself. Reverence thyself. It is the inevitable effect of that doctrine ⟨if⟩ ↑where it has↓ any effect ⟨it have⟩ (which is ⟨only⟩ rare) to insulate the partizan, to make each man a state. At the same time it ⟨supplies⟩ ↑replaces↓ the dead with a living check in a true delicate reverence for superior congenial minds. ↑"How is the king greater than I, if he is not more just?"↓ ²⁶⁷

How does every institution, every man, every thought embody[,] clothe itself externally with dress, houses, newspapers, societies. As I sat in the Orthodox Church this day I thought how brick & laths & lime flew obedient to the master idea that reigns in the minds of many persons be that idea what it may, Jackson, Antimasonry, Diffusion of Knowledge, Farm School, or Calvinism. ⟨Well⟩ Why ⁿ then should the Swedenborgian doctrine be obnoxious that in the Spiritual world the affections clothe ²⁶⁸ themselves with appropriate garments, dwellings, & other circumstances? ⁿ Very philosophical was their tale that in the other world certain spirits tried to pronounce a word

---

²⁶⁶ "How dear" through "lost" at the bottom of the page is struck through with a wavy diagonal use mark in pencil. The use mark should have been continued through the first sentence on p. [107], since "How dear . . . his presence." is used in "The Over-Soul," *W*, II, 292.

²⁶⁷ For the question from Plutarch, a favorite saying of Emerson's, see p. 50 above.

²⁶⁸ Cf. the entry for May 3, 1834, p. 288 above. The Swedenborgian doctrine of "Affections clothed" is treated at length in *EtE*, I, 230, 236, 239, and 250.

representing somewhat which they did not believe. They twisted their lips into all manner of folds even to indignation but could not utter the word.[269]

What concerns me more than Orthodoxy, Antimasonry,[270] Temperance, Workingmen's party, & the other Ideas of the time?

Is the question of Temperance pledges a question whether we will in a pestilence go into quarantine?

[108] C. knew all law from the Constitution of his country to the usage of the next cider-mill[.]

Wonderful charm in the English elegiac verse for the expression of amatory sorrow & the shades of feeling of a mystic; but it is only in Newspapers & by second rate or third rate [271] poets that I have seen it used. A fine verse of this sort I chanced upon addressed to Music, in which ⟨s⟩after saying that Music links us to higher realities than we see around us, the unknown poet saith

"Therefore a current of sadness deep
Through the streams of thy triumph is heard to
sweep[.]" [272]

26 Nov. Goethe says of Lavater, that, "it was fearful to live near a man to whom every boundary within which Nature has seen fit to circumscribe us was clear." [273]

[269] Swedenborg, *The Apocalypse Revealed*, 3 vols. (London, 1832), I, 255. Emerson had in his library the Boston, 1836, edition, an exact reprint from the earlier London edition. "Very philosophical . . . the word.": used in "Spiritual Laws," *W*, II, 157.

[270] Underneath "Orthodoxy, Antimasonry," is an erased penciled notation, apparently: "If I were ‖ . . . ‖ "

[271] Beneath "third rate . . . links us" in faint pencil is
    " 'When I behold a ship sail on the Seas,
    Cuffed by those watery savages' Herrick" ["The Way," ll. 1–2, slightly
        misquoted].

[272] Felicia Hemans, "The Voice of Music," st. 6, ll. 21–22, slightly misquoted.

[273] Emerson probably found the remark, which he slightly misquotes, in "Goethe's Posthumous Works," *Foreign Quarterly Review*, XIV (Aug. 1834), 149, where the statement is assigned to the *Nachgelassene Werke* (Stuttgart, 1833), VIII.

"The world in which I exist is another world indeed but not to come." Coleridge [274]

O what a wailing tragedy is this world considered in reference to money-matters. Read EBE's letter of 6 July, 1833 & the other to his mother.

⟨r⟩Rather [275] melancholy after asking the opinion of all living to find no more receivers of your doctrine than your own three or four & sit down to wait until it shall please God to create some more men before your school can expect increase[.]

Show a head of Cuvier, Goethe, or Milton to vulgar people & they see nothing but resemblances to Deacon Gulliver or Mr Gibbons.

A year ago on 13 Nov. little Ezra Ripley started up in bed & told his father all the stars were falling down.[276] His father bid him sharply go to sleep but the boy was the ↑better philosopher.↓ [277]

---

[274] See the dialogue between Demosius and Mystes in *On the Constitution of Church and State*, 1839, p. 186.

[275] This paragraph and the next are struck through with wavy diagonal use marks in pencil.

[276] November 13, 1833, was the night of a remarkable meteoric shower. Ezra Ripley, son of Samuel Ripley and grandson of Dr. Ezra Ripley, died in 1863 on active duty in the Civil War.

[277] Slipped between pp. [108]–[109] is a clipping, measuring 8.7 x 7.1 cm and containing a poem entitled "Indian Seranade." The advertisements on the reverse indicate that the clipping is from an edition of the *New York Daily Whig* after March 19. Since the paper appeared from December 1837 through March 18, 1840, the clipping must come from the period 1838–1840 and is thus a later addition to the journal volume. The brackets appear in the clipping.

"INDIAN SERANADE. — Awake! flower of the forest — beautiful bird of the prairie.

Awake! awake! thou with the eyes of the fawn. When you look at me I am happy, like the flowers when they feel the dew.

The breath of thy mouth is as sweet as the fragrance of flowers in the morning — sweet as their fragrance at evening, in the moon of the fading leaf.

Does not the blood of my veins spring towards thee, like the bubbling springs to the sun, in the moon of the bright nights! [April.]

My heart sings to thee when thou art near, like the dancing branches to the wind, in the moon of strawberries! [June.]

When thou art not pleased, my beloved, my heart is darkened, like the shining river when shadows fall from above.

[109] What can be conceived so beautiful as actual Nature? I never see the dawn break or the sun set as last evening when from every grey or slate coloured cloud over the whole dome depended a wreath of roses or look down the river with its tree planted banks (from the bridge north of the house) absolutely *affecting* an elegancy, without a lively curiosity as to its reality & a ↑self↓ recollection that I am not in a dream. Well is this all superficial & is the earth itself unsightly? Look at a Narcissus or crocus or lily or petal or stamen or plumule, at any process of life and answer. What can be conceived so beautiful as an assemblage of bright & opake balls floating in space covered each with pretty races & each individual a counterpart & contemplator of the whole? [n]

> How many events shall shake the earth
> Lie packed in silence waiting for their birth [278]

Every thing to be appreciated must be seen from the point where its rays converge to a focus. This gorgeous landscape[,] these poetical clouds [—] what would they be if I should put my eye to the ground? a few pebbles: or into the cloud? a fog. So of human history, & of my own life. We cannot get far enough away from ourselves to integrate ⟨my⟩ ↑our↓ scraps of thought & action & so judge of ⟨my⟩ ↑our↓ tendency or ascend to ⟨my⟩ ↑our↓ idea. We ⟨cannot⟩ are in the battle, & cannot judge of its picturesque effect, nor ⟨at present of its⟩ how the day is going, nor at present of its consequences. The shepherd or the beggar in his red cloak little knows what a charm he

---

Thy smiles cause my troubled heart to be brightened, as the sun makes to look like gold the ripples which the cold wind has created.

Myself! behold me! blood of my beating heart.

The earth smiles — the waters smile — the heavens smile, but I — I lose the way of smiling, when thou art not here — awake! awake! my beloved."

[278] The couplet is in pencil, written between the lines of the ink entry above and below "Narcissus . . . stamen"; it was apparently written before the ink entry. The lines may be an unlocated quotation or perhaps Emerson's own poetic paraphrase of Shakespeare, *Othello*, I, 3, 377: "There are many events in the womb of time which will be delivered" (see p. 334 above). Five more lines of erased pencil writing, probably poetry, underlie the ink from "counterpart" to "history" below. Recovered words are as follows: under "counterpart" is "Tho"; under "rays converge" is "O noble friends"; under "poetical clouds what" is " ‖ . . . ‖ this ‖ . . . ‖ "; under "my eye to the ground? a few" is " ‖ . . . ‖ ⟨they⟩ oer arching sky" and under "cloud . . . history" is "still near ‖ . . . ‖ I pa ‖ . . . ‖ ".

gives to the wide landscape ⟨you⟩ that charms you on the mountain top & whereof he makes the most agreeable feature, & I no more the part my individuality plays in the All.[279]

[110] "As he was inferior however in cavalry & the liver of the victim appeared without a head he retired to Ephesus &c, &c." Plutarch Life of Agesilaus [vol. V] p. 42 [280]

To [281] an idle inquiry whether you are immortal, God maketh no answer. No argument of conviction can be found but do your duty, & you are already immortal: the taste[,] the fear of death has already vanished. We would study Greek & Astronomy if life were longer. Study them & life is already infinitely long.

1 December. Yesterday saw I at Waltham the eclipse of the Sun 10.45 digits. The fact that a prediction is fulfilled is the best part of it. Then the preternatural half night which falls upon the hills. & the violet shade which touches all the clouds. The fine fringes of the cloud made the best smoked glass thro' which to see the sun while the shadow encroached upon his face.

———

When the young philosopher forgets men's opinions nothing seems so worthy employment or rather life ⟨than⟩ as religious teaching. If I could persuade men to listen to their interior convictions[,] if I could express[,] embody their interior convictions[,] that were indeed life. It were to cease being a figure & to act the action of a man. But for that work he must be free & true. He must not seek to weld what he believes, to what he does not wish ↑publicly↓ to deny. Nothing can compensate for want of belief [—] no accomplishments no talents. A believing man in ⟨an⟩ ↑a↓ cause worthy of a Man

[279] "The shepherd . . . the All." has a penciled pointing hand and a note beside it in the margin, possibly by Emerson but more probably by Edward Emerson, referring to "Each and All," W, IX, 4. Emerson in the passage is perhaps recalling the North Italian peasants in their ornaments and scarlet cloaks as he described them on June 6, 1833. See p. 188 above. "Every thing to be. . . picturesque effect,": used in "English Literature: Introductory," Lectures, I, 225.

[280] Emerson is quoting, as he normally does for Plutarch's Lives, from the translation by John and William Langhorne, 8 vols. (Philadelphia, 1822), volumes 1–6 and 8 of which he had in his library.

[281] Centered under the ink entry of this paragraph and extending down in the next to "preternatural . . . which" is a pencil sketch of a male bust, left profile.

gives the mind a sense of stability & repose more than mountains. I could not help calling the attention [111] of my venerable neighbor to ⟨A Everett & J. Savage⟩ the different impression made by A Everett & J. Savage:[282] one, very accomplished, but inspires no confidence; for he is not much of a man; the other, tolerably well equipped, but is himself an upright singlehearted man pursuing his path by his own lights & incapable of fear or favor. Columbus did not affect to believe in a new continent & make dinner speeches about it (other than his egg speech) and George Fox & Emanuel Swedenborg never advise people to go to church for the sake of example.

———

It would give scope for many truths in experimental religion to preach from the text of "There shall be new heavens & a new earth."[283] Sometimes we perceive that God is wholly unknown in the world[,] that the church & the sermon & the priest & the alms are a profanation.

"We were early cast upon thy care," is a heathen expression.

<hr>

Compensation [284]

<hr>

Compensation. — Why should I keep holiday
                When other men have none
                Why but because when these are gay
                I sit & mourn alone

                And why when Mirth unseals all tongues [n]
                ⟨Should⟩ ↑Must↓ I ⟨alone sit⟩ ↑be ever↓ dumb
                Ah late I spoke to the ⟨listening⟩ ↑breathless↓
                    throng
                And now their hour is come.

[282] Alexander Everett (1790–1847), one of three well-known brothers, was a diplomat at The Hague and later in Spain as well as editor of *The North American Review*; James Savage (1784–1873) was one of the founders of the Boston Athenaeum, president of the Provident Institution for Savings, and editor of John Winthrop's *History of New England*.

[283] Cf. II Pet.3:13: "Nevertheless we . . . look for new heavens and a new earth, wherein dwelleth righteousness."

[284] The poem, an early variant of "Compensation" (see *W*, IX, 83), is in pencil, partly overwritten by the ink entry "priest . . . expression."

[112] December 2. Concord. The age of puberty is a crisis in the life of the man worth studying. It is the passage from the Unconscious to the Conscious; from the sleep of the Passions to their rage; from careless receiving to cunning providing; from beauty to use; from omnivorous curiosity to anxious stewardship; from faith to doubt; from ⟨peaceful⟩ ↑maternal↓ Reason to hard short-sighted Understanding; from Unity to disunion; the progressive influences of poetry, eloquence, love, regeneration, character, truth, sorrow, and of search for an Aim, & the contest for Property.

I look upon every sect as a Claude Lorraine glass through which I see the same sun & the same world & in the same relative places as through my own eyes but one makes them small, another large; one, green; another, blue; another, pink. I suppose that as ⟨|| ... ||⟩ an orthodox preacher's cry "⟨You are an⟩ ↑the natural man is an↓ enemy of God" only translates the philosopher's that "the instinct of the Understanding is to contradict the Reason"[;] [285] so Luther's Law & Gospel [286] (also St Paul's); Swedenborg's love of self & love of the Lord; William Penn's World & Spirit; the Court of Honor's Gentleman & Knave. The dualism is ever present through variously denominated[.]

The two conditions of Teaching are, 1. That none can teach more than he knows. 2. That none can teach ⟨more⟩ ↑faster↓ than the scholar can learn. Two conditions more: 1. He must say that they can understand. 2. But he must say that which is given to *him*.

[113] I have not so near access to Luther's mind through his works as through my own mind when I meditate upon his historical position.

[287] It is true undoubtedly that every preacher should strive to pay his debt to his fellowmen by making his communication intelligible to the common capacity. It is no less true that unto every mind is given one word to say & he should sacredly strive to utter that

---

[285] See p. 320 above.

[286] A further antithesis, "Devil & God", is written in the space below "Law & Gospel" and above "self & love of the Lord"; it is spaced somewhat closer to Luther's phrase than to Swedenborg's but might parallel either.

[287] The following paragraph is struck through with a wavy diagonal use mark in pencil.

word & not another man's word; ⟨but⟩ his own, without addition or abatement[.]

'John ↑Evang[elist]↓' says Luther, 'was simple & spake also simply but every word in John weigheth two Tons.' Table T[alk].[288]

When they jeered at the devil, Luther says, he went away. 'Quia est superbus spiritus & non potest ferre contemptum sui.' [289]

My own picture was ugly enough to me. I read that when his own picture was shown to Erasmus he said "look I like this picture? so am I the greatest knave that liveth," [n] which Luther relates with sharpness.[290]

If we will lie, let us do it roundly. Captain   of Providence affirmed that he had pumped the Atlantic Ocean three times through his Ship on the passage, and that it was very common to strike porpoises in the Ship's hold.

Francis comes to Doctor Ripley at breakfast to know if he shall drive the cow into the battle-field? [291]

A lockjaw which bended a man's head backward to his heels, and that beastly hydrophobia which makes him bark at his wife & children, — what explains these? [n]

[114] A real interest in your fellow creatures is of necessity reciprocal. For want of it how tragic is the solitude of the old man.[292] No prayer[,] no good wish out of the whole world follows him into his sick chamber. It is as frightful a solitude as that which cold produces round the traveller who has lost his way. This comes of management, of cunning, & of vanity. Never held he intercourse with any human being with thorough frankness, man to man but always with that imp-like second thought. And so hath no friend. Yet I

[288] Emerson is citing Henry Bell's translation of the *Colloquia Mensalia or . . . Divine Discourses . . .* , 1652, p. 368. The passage is used in "Martin Luther," *Lectures*, I, 121.

[289] "Because he is an arrogant spirit and cannot endure being scorned" (Ed.). *Ibid.*, p. 381.

[290] *Ibid.*, p. 433. Pp. 431–432 contain sharp censure of Erasmus with a marginal printed note on p. 431.: "sharp words."

[291] The battle of Concord Bridge where the "shot heard round the world" was fired took place in the pasture beside the Old Manse. See *J*, III, 378n.

[292] Dr. Ezra Ripley, Emerson's step-grandfather, with whom he and his mother were boarding during the winter of 1834–1835.

forget not his generosity[,] his tenderness to E[llen]. And his faults have not descended to his children. Blessed are the woods. In summer they shade the traveller from the sun[,] in Winter from the tooth of the wind. When there is snow it falls level: when it rains it does not blow in his face. There is no dust & a pleasing fear reigns in their shade. Blessed are the woods!

[293] I think the most devout persons be the freest of their tongues in speaking of the Deity, as Luther, Fuller, Herbert, ↑Milton↓ whose words are an offence to the pursed mouths which make formal prayers; & beyond the word, they are free thinkers also. "Melancthon discoursed with Luther touching the prophets who continually do boast in this sort & with these words 'Thus saith the Lord' &c — whether God spake in person with them or no? Then Luther said, They were very holy spiritual people which seriously did contemplate on holy & divine causes: therefore God spake with them in their consciences which the prophets held for sure Revelations." Table talk p. 362 folio ed. ↑So St. James he frankly called 'Epistola straminea.'↓ [294]

[115][295] Bring men near one another & love will follow. Once the men of distant countries were painted as of monstrous *bodies* without necks, with tails, &c. But commerce contradicted the report. Then they were described as having monstrous *minds*[:] thieves[,] sottish, promiscuously mixed, ⟨witho⟩ destitute of moral sentiments. But commerce has exposed that slander too, & shown that as face answereth to face in water so the heart of man to man.

A man is a very vulnerable creature. His manners & dignity are conventional. Leave him alone & he is a sorry sight.

---

[293] "I think . . . the Lord' " is struck through with a wavy diagonal use mark in pencil.

[294] "Epistle of straw." Luther's condemnation of St. James appears in almost all of Emerson's sources; the Latin version, however, has been found only in Pierre Bayle's *A General Dictionary, Historical and Critical*, trans. J. P. Bernard et al. (London, 1734–1741), II (1735), 940–941. The phrase is used in "Martin Luther," *Lectures*, I, 121.

[295] The paragraph is struck through with two vertical use marks, one in ink, one in pencil.

[296] It seems as if a simple manly character should never make an apology but always regard his past action with the same marble calmness as Phocion when he admitted that the event was happy yet regretted not his dissuasion from the action. This supposes of course that the act *was* genuine.

How sad how disgusting to see this Neidrig[niedrig] air on the face, a man whose words take hold on the upper world whilst one eye is eternally down cellar so that the best conversation has ever a slight savor of sausages & soapbarrels. Basest when the snout of this influence touches the education of young women & withers the blessed affection & hope of human nature by teaching that marriage is nothing but housekeeping & that Woman's life has no other aim. Even G. was capable of saying 'the worst marriage is better than none'. & S. made a similar stab at the sanity of his daughter.

[116] Concord 3 December. One morning Reason woke & exclaimed, "Demosthenes said well 'Whoso hath an evil cause the same hath no good fortune.'" "Not so Gammer," replied the Understanding, "The greater knave, the better luck."

The poor Irishman [—] a wheelbarrow is his country[.]

When I remember the twofold cord, then fourfold & go a little back a thousand & a millionfold cord ↑of↓ which my being & every man's being consists; that I am an aggregate of infinitesimal parts & that every minutest streamlet that has flowed to me is represented in that man which I am, so that if every one should claim his part in me I should be instantaneously diffused through the creation & individually decease, then I say if I am but an alms of All, & live but by the Charity of innumerable others, there is no peculiar propriety in wrapping my cloak about me & hiding the ray that my

---

[296] The paragraph is struck through with a wavy diagonal use mark in pencil. A further vertical use mark in pencil runs through both this paragraph and the next to the bottom of the page. "It seems as if . . . action.": used in "Heroism," *W*, II, 260. The anecdote concerning Phocion appears in "The Life of Phocion"; see Plutarch's *Lives*, 1822, VI, 26. Emerson probably took his version, however, from Montaigne's retelling of the story in the *Essays*, Bk. III, ch. 2 (1693, III, 42).

taper may emit. What is a man but a Congress of nations? [n] Just suppose for one moment to appear before him the whole host of his ancestors. All have vanished[;] he [—] the insulated result of all that character, activity, sympathy, antagonism working for ages in all corners of the earth — alone remains. Such is his origin[;] well was his nurture less compound. Who & what has not contributed something to make him that he is? Art, science, institutions, black men, white men, the vices & the virtues of all people, the gallows, the church, [117] the shop, poets, nature, joy, & fear, all help all teach him. Every fairy brings a gift.

Deliver us from that intensity of character which makes all its crows swans. So soon as I hear that my friend is engaged I perceive at once that a very ordinary person is henceforward adopted into that rose colored atmosphere which exhales from his self love & every trait, every trifle, every nothing about the new person is canonized by ⟨being⟩ identifying the same with the positive Virtue⟨s⟩ to which it is related ↑just as children refer the moon to the same ⟨sphere⟩ ↑region of heaven↓ with the stars↓. Talent becomes genius; inoffensiveness, benevolence; wilfulness, character, & even stupidity simplicity. Poor dear human nature; leave magnifying & caricaturing her. It frets & confuses us. More winning[,] more sociable & society-making is she as she stands[,] faults & virtues unpainted[,] confessed[;] then the fault even becomes piquant & is seen to prop & underpin some ↑excellent↓ virtue. Let us deal so with ourselves & call a spade a spade.[297]

6th Dec. Do you imagine that because I do not say Luther's creed all his works are an offence to me? Far otherwise. I can animate them all that they shall live to me. I can worship in that temple as well as in any other. I have only to translate a few of the leading phrases into their equivalent verities, to adjust his almanack to my meridian & all the conclusions[,] all the predictions shall be strictly true. Such is the everlasting advantage of truth. Let a man work after a pattern he really sees & every man shall be able to find a correspondence between these works & his own & to turn them to

<hr>

[297] Plutarch, "The Apophthegms of Kings and Great Commanders"; see the *Morals*, 1870, I, 196.

some account in Rome, London, or Japan, [118] from the first to the hundredth century.

———

On reading yesterday [298] P.M. to Aunt Mary Coleridge's defence of prayer against author of Nat. Hist Enthusiasm,[299] she ⁿ replied, "Yes, for our reason was so distinct from the Universal Reason that we could pray to it, & so united with it that we could have assurance we were heard."

8 December. The world looks poor & mean so long as I think only of its great men; most of them of spotted reputation. But when I remember how many obscure persons I myself have seen possessing gifts that excited wonder, speculation, & delight in me; when I remember that the very greatness of Homer, of Shakspeare, of Webster & Channing is the truth ⟨whic⟩ with which they reflect [300] the mind of all mankind[;] when ⁿ I consider that each fine genius that appears is already predicted in our constitution inasmuch as he only makes apparent shades of thought in us of which we hitherto knew not (or actualizes an idea,) and when I consider the absolute boundlessness of our capacity — no one of us but has the whole untried world of geometry, ⟨algebra⟩ fluxions, natural philosophy, ⟨Metaphysics⟩ Ethics, wide open before him [301]

When I ⟨think⟩ recollect the charms of certain women, what poems are many private lives, each of which ⟨will⟩ ↑can↓ fill our eye if we so will, (as the swan, the eagle, the cedar bird, the canary each seems the [119] [302] type of ⟨its⟩ ↑bird-↓kind whilst we gaze at it

[298] Faint traces of penciled writing underlie the ink entry from "yesterday" in the first paragraph through "boundlessness" in the second. Only the first line under "yesterday . . . Aunt Mary" is legible: "Let me save my ⟨live⟩ verse".

[299] In a note to sec. III of *On the Constitution of Church and State* entitled "Notes on Isaac Taylor's History of Enthusiasm"; see *Coleridge's Works*, 1854, III, 133–143.

[300] The following passage, "the mind . . . boundlessness", is struck through with a wavy diagonal use mark in pencil.

[301] The passage is left incomplete, perhaps because Emerson could not resolve his tangled syntax.

[302] Scattered penciled words appear on the page under the ink entry: "America" is written twice, once under "set down" and again under "heaven that" in the second paragraph; "Vespucci" is under "sorts of"; the entry below "Virtues & Powers" ("A fire . . . backlog.") is also in pencil.

alone,) and then remember how many millions I know not; then
I feel the riches of my inheritance in being set down in this world
gifted with organs of communication with this accomplished company.

———

Pray heaven that you may have a sympathy with all sorts of excellence even with those antipodal to your own. If any eye rest on
this page let him know that he who blotted it, could not go into
conversation with any person of good understanding without being
presently gravelled. The slightest question of ⟨t⟩his most familiar
proposition disconcerted him — eyes, face, & understanding, beyond
recovery. Yet did he not the less respect & rejoice in this daily gift of
vivacious common sense which was so formidable to him. May it
last as long as the World.

The application of Goethe's definition of genius "That power
which by working & doing gives laws & rules,"[303] to common life,
to the art of living, is obvious. Deacon Warren, Mr Turner, Mr
Crafts, and every new simple heart give us a new image of possible
Virtues & Powers[.]

A fire is made to burn yet we do not like to have coals run behind the backlog.

[120] If you ask me whether I will not be so good as to abstain
from ⟨any⟩ ↑all↓ use of ardent spirits for the sake of diminishing by
my pint per annum the demand & so stopping the distiller's pernicious pump, I answer, ⟨y⟩Yes, with all my heart. But will I signify
the same fact by putting my name to your paper? No. Be assured,
I shall always be found on your side in discouraging this use &
traffic. But I shall not deprive my example of all its value by ⟨taking⟩
abdicating my freedom on that point. It shall be always my example,
the spectacle to all whom it may concern of my spontaneous action
at the time.

Why, O diffuser of Useful K[nowledge]. do you not offer to
deliver a course of lectures on Aristotle & Plato or on Plato alone

[303] Emerson probably discovered the definition in "Goethe's Posthumous Works,"
Foreign Quarterly Review, XIV (Aug. 1834), 150 and 151 where, twice quoted, it
is assigned to the *Nachgelassene Werke* (1833), VIII.

or on him & Bacon & Coleridge? [n] Why not strengthen the hearts of the waiting lovers of the primal philosophy by an account of that fragmentary highest teaching which comes from the half ⟨poetic⟩ fabulous personages ↑Heraclitus↓, Hermes Trismegistus, & Giordano Bruno, & Vyasa, & Plotinus, & Swedenborg? [n] Curious now that first I collect their names they should look all so mythological.

[304] I rejoice in Time. I do not cross the common without a wild poetic delight notwithstanding the prose of my demeanour. Thank God I live in the country. Well said Bell that no hour[,] no state of the atmosphere but corresponded to some state of the mind; brightest day, grimmest night[.] [305]

[121] 9 December. The dear old Plutarch assures me that the lamp of Demosthenes never went out[,] that King Philip called his orations *soldiers,* & in a moment of enthusiasm on hearing the report of one of his speeches exclaimed "Had I been there I too should have declared war against myself." Flying before Antipater he wrote his own epitaph at Calabria [Calauria]. Ειχερ εισην ρωμην γνωμη Δημοσθενες εσχεσ Ουποτ' αν Ελληνων' ηρξεν Αρης Μακεδων. When Epicles twitted him ⟨with⟩ upon his exact preparation he said "I should be ashamed to speak what comes uppermost to so great an assembly." One day his voice failing him, he was hissed, & he cried unto the people, "Ye are to judge of players indeed by the clearness & tuneableness of their voice, but of orators, by the gravity & excellency of their sentences." Despising other orators, when Phocion arose, Demosthenes was wont to say, "⟨Hatchet⟩ pruning knife [n] of my orations, Arise!" [306]

---

[304] "I rejoice . . . my demeanour." is struck through with a wavy diagonal use mark in pencil: used in *Nature, W,* I, 9. Beneath "Bell . . . the atmosphere" in partially erased pencil writing is "Demosthenes orations soldiers"; the words are apparently a reference to or first note for the entry on Demosthenes on the following page.
[305] Possibly Emerson is here reworking Sir Charles Bell's *The Hand, . . . as evincing design,* 1833, p. 130: ". . . the perceptions or ideas arising in the mind, are in correspondence with the qualities of external matter."
[306] Emerson's sources for the anecdotes concerning Demosthenes are as follows: (a) "lamp of Demosthenes" — "Lives of the Ten Orators"; see the *Morals,* 1870, V, 53; (b) "King Philip . . . myself.'" — *ibid.;* see V, 46; (c) the epitaph of

Last night abed I recollected ⟨five⟩four names for ⟨five⟩four lectures; Luther, Michel Angelo, Milton, George Fox[;] then comes question of Epaminondas esteemed by the ancients ⁿ greatest of the Greeks; Demosthenes for the sake of his oratory & the related topics; Alfred for his human character. Sam Johnson for his genuineness. Phocion, More, & Socrates, for their three renowned deaths; Hampden for his Saxon soul, Muley Moloch; Reynolds; [307]

[122] But it seemed to me that a fit question to handle in a public lecture is the one involved in the claims & apologies made by people & orators in this New England raft of ours every day[.]

It is said that the people can look after their own interests, that "Common sense, tho' no science[,] is fairly worth the seven," [308] that a plain practical Man is better to the state than a scholar, &c.

He were a benefactor to his countrymen who would expose & pillory this stale sophism. We hold indeed that those reasons for a public action which are presented to us should be of that simple humane character as to be fully comprehensible by ⟨a⟩ every citizen of good capacity as well the uneducated as the educated. That is a good test & condition of such reasons. They should not be addressed to the imagination or to our literary associations but to the ⟨plain⟩ ear of plain men. Therefore are they such as plain men [—] farmers, mechanics, ↑teamsters,↓ seamen, or soldiers [—] might offer, if they would gravely, patiently, humbly reflect upon the matter. There is nothing in their want of book-learning to hinder. This doctrine affirms that there is imparted to every man the Divine light of reason sufficient not only to plant corn & grind wheat by but also to illuminate all his life his social, political, religious actions. Sufficient according to its faithful [123] use. Sufficient if faithfully used. The propositions

---

Demosthenes — "Hadst thou, Demosthenes, an outward force great as thy inward magnanimity, Greece should not wear the Macedonian yoke" — *ibid.*; see V, 50, and *JMN*, III, 164; (d) "When Epicles . . . sentences.' " — *ibid.*; see V, 52–53; (e) "Despising . . . Arise!' " — "Political Precepts," see the *Morals*, 1870, V, 109, or in a slightly different version, the life of Demosthenes (x,2). Some of the anecdotes are used in "Edmund Burke," *Lectures*, I, 198, 199.

[307] The list is left unfinished. See *The Spectator* No. 349, for comment on the heroic death of Muley Moloch (Abd el Malek), Sultan of Morocco.

[308] Pope, *Moral Essays*, "Epistle IV," 43–44, slightly misquoted.

are true to the end of the world with this inseparable condition. Every man's Reason is sufficient for his guidance, *if used*. But does it mean that because a farmer acting on deep conviction shall give a reason as good as Bacon could have given, that therefore the ordinary arguments of farmers are to be preferred to those of statesmen? that whatever crude remarks a circle of people talking in a bar room throw out, are entitled to equal weight with the sifted & chosen conclusions of experienced public men? And because God has made you capable of Reason therefore must I hear & accept all your ⟨low presumptuous⟩ selfish railing, your proven falsehoods, your unconsidered guesses as truth? No; I appeal from you to your Reason which with me condemns you ↑from Philip drunk to Philip sober↓.[309] It amounts to this; 'Every man's Reason can show him what is right. Therefore every man says what is right whether he use his Reason or no.' I hate this fallacy the more that it is, beside being dire nonsense, ⟨such⟩ ↑a↓ profanation of the dearest of truths. /Democracy/Freedom/ has its root in the Sacred truth that every man hath in him the divine Reason or that though few men ↑since the creation of the world↓ ⟨use⟩ live according to the dictates of Reason, yet all men are created capable of so doing. That is the equality & the only equality of all men. To this truth we look when we say, 'Reverence thyself. Be true to thyself.' Because every man has within [124] him somewhat really divine therefore is slavery the unpardonable outrage it is.

Dr Jarvis told me today that his brother Capt. J. had observed his ship to be covered sails & spars with a fine sand blown off the African coast (as he supposed) by the tradewinds when he was by his observation 1800 miles from Africa bound to S. America. And that when returning from the W. Indies he being confined below with sickness the mate sounded at ⟨short distances⟩ intervals & brought the lead down to him; he judged by the bottom brought up where they were & thinks he made no mistake. He ran ↑close↓ along the coral reefs of Florida himself assuming the helm, & putting two men on the bows to look over & cry Breakers; which, when they did, he put the ship off.

[309] Emerson was fond of this proverbial phrase from Valerius Maximus; see p. 15 and p. 319 above.

I would add to what should have been inserted p. 82, that It is not for nothing that one word makes such impression & the other none[;] it is not without preestablished harmony this sculpture in the memory. The eye was placed where that ray should fall, to the end that it might testify of that particular ray.[310]

There is great delight in learning a new language. When the day comes in the scholar's progress unawares when he reads pages without recurrence to his dictionary[,] he shuts up his book with that sort of fearful delight with which the bridegroom sits down in his own house with the bride, saying, 'I shall ⟨reside⟩ now live with you always.'

[125] [December] 21[11]. When the sick man came out of doors the stars seemed to shine through his eyes into his heart, & the blessed air that he inhaled seemed to lighten his frame from head to feet.

A little above I referred to one of my ⟨f⟩characters.[311] It might be added that if he made his forms a strait jacket to others, he wore the same himself all his years & so reanimated for his beholders the order of La Trappe. Tread softly Stranger on the dust of one who showed ever in his fireside discourse traits of that pertinency & judgment softening ever & anon into elegancy, which make the distinction of the scholar, & which, under better discipline, might have ripened into a Salmasius or Hedericus.[312] Sage & Savage strove harder in him than in any of my acquaintance, each getting the mastery by turns, & pretty sudden turns. "Save us" ↑he said in his prayer,↓

[310] Heavy double slash marks at the beginning and a single slash mark at the end of the paragraph set it off, probably to indicate its connection with the entry above, p. [82], to which Emerson refers. The following paragraph ("There is . . . always.'") is struck through with a wavy diagonal use mark in pencil.

[311] See pp. 338–339 above for the reference to Dr. Ezra Ripley. Within this paragraph "who showed . . . cold weather.'": used in "Ezra Ripley, D.D." W, X, 391–392. The earlier entry to which Emerson referred is also used in this essay; see *ibid.*, X, 387.

[312] Claude de Saumaise (1588–1653), noted scholar and professor at Leyden and then at the court of Christiana of Sweden. His *Defensio Regia pro Carolo I* brought forth Milton's more famous *Pro Populo Anglicano Defensio* (1650). Benjamin Hederich or Hedericus (1675–1748), scholar and linguist, was noted especially for his Greek Lexicon (1722).

"from the extremity of cold, & violent sudden changes." "The society will meet after the Lyceum, as it is difficult to bring the people together in the evening, & no moon, &c." "Mr N.F. is dead, & I expect to hear the death of Mr B. It is cruel to separate old people from their wives in this cold weather." Thus is one reminded of the children's prayers who in confessing their sins, say, "Yes, I did take the jumprope from Mary." Pleasantly said he at supper, "that his last cup was not potent in any way, neither in sugar, nor cream, nor souchong; it was so equally & universally defective that he thought it easier to make another, than to mend that."

[126] The Counsellor's fine simplicity & sweetness of character saved his speech the other evening from being distressful to the hearers. Charles is reminded by him of Edward. There are some points of resemblance. This for one, that neither was ever put out of countenance.

Concord.[313] 14 December. Yesterday I sealed & despatched my letter to Carlyle.[314] Today, riding to East Sudbury, I pleased myself with the beauties & terrors of the snow; the oak-leaf hurrying over the banks is fit ornament. Nature in the woods is very companionable. There, my Reason & my Understanding are sufficient company for each other. I have my glees as well as my glooms, alone. Confirm my faith (& when I write the word, Faith looks indignant.) pledge me the word of the Highest that I shall have my dead & my absent again, & I could be content & cheerful alone for a thousand years. I know no aisle so stately as the roads through the pine woods in Maine. Cold is the snowdrift topping itself with sand. How intense are our affinities: acids & alkalis. The moment we indulge our affections, the earth is metamorphosed; all its tragedies & ennuis

[313] Within the paragraph a wavy diagonal use mark in pencil strikes through from "Nature" above to "aisle" below. "How intense . . . persons." is struck through with a vertical use mark in pencil. "The moment . . . persons.": used in "Friendship," *W*, II, 193; "But then a person . . . Protestantism?": used in "Self-Reliance," *W*, II, 61.

[314] Probably Emerson's second letter to Carlyle, dated November 20, 1834, which he apparently kept unfinished on his desk for three weeks before sending it off. See *The Correspondence of Thomas Carlyle and Ralph Waldo Emerson, 1834–1872*, ed. Norton, 1884, I, 27–36.

vanish, all duties even, nothing remains to fill eternity with but two or three persons. But then a person is a *cause*. What is Luther but Protestantism? or Columbus but Columbia? And were I assured of meeting Ellen tomorrow would it be less than a world[,] a personal world? Death has no bitterness in the light of that thought[.]

[127] In Boston C[harles]. was witty with his philosophy of caoutchouc & his inspired ⟨apos⟩ address to Mr. Gannett.³¹⁵ Seize him Towzer! I cannot at all remember the instance I had alleged of false life where a man sees himself praised & exalted for that he is not; but C. said it was as if a man should see his shadow bowed [to] & honored & doing all for him.

And Hedge read me good things out of Schleiermacher concerning the twofold division of ⟨the⟩ study, 1. Physics, or that which is; 2. Ethics, or that which should be. Also his definition of *Science* & *Art*⟨as⟩ [—] the one, *All things brought into the mind*; the other, *the mind* going *into things*. Then the Ascetic or the discipline of life produced by the opinions.³¹⁶ Every man's system should appear in his ascetic. Scarce one man's does. I was reminded of Blanchard[,] that faithful man whose whole life & least part is conformed to his Reason[,] who upholds the Peace Society & works at the Bank Sundays & eschews the Communion & sweetens his tea with Canton sugar out of hatred to slavery & thinks Homer & Shakspeare to be the strongest War party.

House of Seem & house of Be. Coleridge's four classes of Readers. 1. the Hour glass sort[,] all in & all out; 2 the Sponge sort[,] giving it all out a little dirtier than it took in[;] 3 of the Jelly bag, keeping nothing but the refuse[;] 4 of the Golconda[,] sieves picking up the diamonds only.³¹⁷ Two sorts of diseases; those which kill &

---

³¹⁵ Charles Emerson wrote an extended essay on caoutchouc (rubber) from which Waldo copied eight pages in the notebook he devoted to his brother (see Charles C. Emerson, pp. [128]–[135]). Ezra Stiles Gannett was assistant pastor with Dr. Channing at New South Church and secretary of the American Unitarian Association.

³¹⁶ See *Die Sammtliche Werke*, 31 vols. (Berlin, 1835–1864), Pt. III, Philosophical, V, 32–37 and no. 26 in *Ideen, Reflexionen, und Betrachtungen aus Schleiermacher's Werken* (Berlin, 1854), pp. 13–14.

³¹⁷ See Thomas M. Raysor, *Coleridge's Shakesperean Criticism*, 2 vols. Cam-

those that don't. Wordsworth, "whose thoughts acquaint us with our own." Francis Osborn 11th Edition Miscel. Works. "Wishers & woulders were never [128] good householders." [318]

Dec. 17. If it has so pleased God it is very easy for you to surpass your fellows in genius; but surpass them in generosity of sentiment; see not their meanness, whilst your eyes are fixed on everlasting virtues; being royal, being divine, in your sentiments: this shall be 'another morn risen on mid noon.' [319] This shall be your own, — O no; — God forbid! not your own, but a vast accession of the Divinity into your trembling clay.

----

[320] Michel Angelo sent to Florence for Granacci & others to come & help him in painting in fresco the Sistine Chapel as he knew not the art.[n] But soon seeing that they wrought far enough from his desires, he shut himself up one morn in the chapel, & tore down all their work, & begun anew, nor would see them at his house. And they finding they could not get admission to him departed with mortification to Florence.[321] This crisis is most unpleasing surely, but is in the nature of things; how could it be avoided? And such occur in the history of genius every day.

----

bridge, Mass., 1930), I, 249–250 and II, 64. The two versions of Coleridge's classification are printed from unpublished notebooks and from Collier's report of the 1811–1812 lectures. The fourth class of readers is called the "Grand Mogul" rather than the "Golconda"; where Emerson found the supposedly unpublished material is not known.

[318] "Two sorts . . . don't." is unlocated. Though "whose thoughts . . . own." is connected with Goethe in Journal B, p. [148], the version here is a direct quotation ("Wordsworth, whose thoughts acquaint us with our own") from Ebenezer Elliott's "The Village Patriarch," IV, 32 (see *The Poetical Works of Ebenezer Elliott*, 3 vols., London, 1844, II, 50). The expanded title for Francis Osborn's work is *A Miscellany of Sundry Essays, Paradoxes, and Problematicall Discurses, Letters, and Characters* . . . , 2 vols., 11th ed. (London, 1722). For "Wishers . . . householders." see Ray, *English Proverbs*, 1817, p. 116, or Samuel Palmer, *Moral Essays on Proverbs* (London, 1710), p. 105.

[319] Milton, *Paradise Lost*, V, 310–311.

[320] The paragraph is struck through with both a wavy diagonal and a diagonal use mark in pencil. Each of the remaining two paragraphs on the page is also struck through with a wavy diagonal use mark in pencil.

[321] The anecdote is given in Richard Duppa, *The Life of Michael Angelo Buonarroti*, 2nd ed. (London, 1807), p. 52.

Every stroke of Michel Angelo's pencil moves the pencil in Raphael's hand.[322]

How many states of mind have I & those which are intense even in their mournful or practic⟨al⟩k influence, which refuse to be recorded. I can not more easily recall & describe the feeling I had yesterday of limited power, & the small worth to me of a day, than I could recall a fled dream. Only the impression is left; the self-evidence is flown.

[129] God has made nothing without a crack except Reason.

What can be better than this? — "quanto era proprio per far tutta la pompa del suo profondo sapere." Nota p. 162 *Vasari. Vita di M.A. Bonarroti.*[323]

Poets & painters ever walk abreast[.]

18 Dec. I am writing my Lecture on Michel Angelo clothed with a coat which was made for me in Florence, I would I were clothed with the ⟨beautiful⟩ spirit of beauty which breathed life into Italian art   Quello ch'apporta mane e lascia sera. Dante [*Paradiso*, XXVII, 138]

Solon said 'such as the speech such is the life of the man.' [324]

Loathsome lecture last eve. on precocity, & the dissection of the brain, & the distortion of the body, & genius, &c. A grim ⟨philosophy⟩ ↑compost↓ of blood & mud. Blessed, thought I, were those who, lost in their pursuits, never knew that they had a body or a mind.

19 Dec. He who makes a good sentence or a good verse exercises a power very strictly analogous to his who makes a fine statue,

---

[322] Cf. "The Life of Michael Angelo Buonaroti," *Lives of Eminent Persons*, 1833, p. 38. The sentence is used in *Lectures*, I, 109.

[323] Giorgio Vasari, *Vite de' Più Excellenti Pittori, Scultori, e Architetti*, 16 vols. (Milan, 1807–1811), XIV, 162; used in what is apparently Emerson's translation in *Lectures*, I, 104.

[324] According to Benham's *Book of Quotations*, 1907, p. 473, a common Greek proverb reads: "As the life is, so is the speech." Publius Syrus, *Sententiae*, no. 1073, phrases the idea as "Speech is the mirror of the soul; as a man speaks so is he." A similar passage appears in Cicero, *Tusculani Disputations*, V, 47. The proverb appears in connection with Solon only in Diogenes Laertius, *Lives of Eminent Philosophers*, I, 58, as "Speech is the mirror of action."

a beautiful cornice, a staircase like that in Oxford, or a noble head in painting.

One writes on air if he speaks, but no he writes on mind more durable than marble & is like him who begets a son, that is, originates a begetter of nations.

The maker of a sentence like the other artist launches out into the infinite & builds a road into Chaos & old Night [325] & is followed by those who hear him with something of wild creative delight.

[130] Dec. 20. I like well the doctrine 'that every great man, Napoleon himself, is an Idealist a poet with different degrees of Utterance'.[326] As the love of flowers contains the Science of Botany, so the innate love of novelty[,] enterprize like that which delighted me when a boy in Atkinson st. with climbing by help of a small ladder & (s)touching for the first time the shingles of the shed. Yes & makes every boy a poet (on) ↑when↓ a fine morning in spring seducingly shows him the uplands in the neighboring towns on his way to school. This ⁿ same desire of the untried, leads the young farmer in Maine to load his little wagon & rattle down the long hills on his way to Illinois.

A strictest correspondence ties all the arts. And it is as lawful and as becoming for the poet to seize upon felicitous expressions & lay them up for use as for Michel Angelo to store his (note b) sketchbook with hands, arms, triglyphs, & capitals to enrich his future Compositions. The wary artist in both kinds will tear down the scaffolding when the Work is finished & himself supply no clew to the curiosity that would know how he did the wonder.

———

↑Dec. 20.↓ The chickadees are very busy & happy in Caesar's woods between the spots of snow. I met them yesterday. What is the green leaf under the snow resembling a potentilla? [327]

[130ₐ][328] Unitarianism & all the rest are judged by the standing or

[325] Cf. Milton, *Paradise Lost*, II, 894–895 and 1025–1026.
[326] Emerson found the doctrine in Carlyle, "Luther's Psalm," *Fraser's Magazine*, II (Jan. 1831), 743.
[327] Potentilla is the cinquefoil or five-fingers.
[328] A sheet of paper measuring 16.3 x 22 cm is laid loose within the notebook

falling of their professors. ↑I refuse that test to this. It is true.↓ I see this to be true though I see it condemns my life & no man liveth by it. ↑They are truth itself[,] they are the measure of truth & can no more be affected by my falling away or all men's denial than the law of gravity is changed by my acting as if it were not.↓ Yet is it dangerous! It is very far from a system of negatives[;] it lowly earnestly sees & declares how its laws advance their reign forevermore into the Infinitude on all sides of us. Jesus was a setter up more than a puller down. Socrates was also. Both were spiritualists. ⟨W⟩ George Fox[,] Wm Penn were urgent doers[,] hard livers. But they were of wrath. I ⟨belong⟩ see the World & its Maker from another side. It seems to me beauty. He seems to me Love[.]

Spiritual Religion has no other evidence than its own intrinsic probability. It is probable because the Mind is so constituted as that they appear likely so to be.

It never scolds. It simply describes the laws ||of mora||l nature as the naturalist does physical ||laws & shows|| the surprizing beauties & terrors of human life. It never scolds & never sneers.

[130ᵇ] It is opposed to Calvinism in this respect that all spiritual truths are self evident but the doctrines of C. are not, & are not pretended to be by their understanding defenders. Mystery.

This is the only live religion. All others are dead or formal. This cannot be but in the new conviction of the mind. Others may.

This produces instant & infinite abuses. It is a two-edged sword because it condemns forms but supplies a better law only to the living[.] It leaves the dead to bury their dead. The popular religion is an excellent constable, the true religion is God himself to the believer & maketh him a perfect lover of the whole world; but it is only a cloak of licentiousness to the rest. It would dismiss all bad preachers & do great harm to society by taking off restraints. Th

Spiritual religion is one that cannot be harmed by the vices of its defenders[.]

---

between pp. [130] and [131]. Numbered in pencil "130a" and "130b" in a hand that seems to be neither Emerson's nor Edward Emerson's, the sheet contains also penciled directions for printing in Edward Emerson's hand. Though no clear evidence of its date exists, it is printed as a self-contained insert. The lower corner of the leaf is torn and the words are supplied from Edward Emerson's reading in *J*, III, 387–398, apparently made before the present mutilation.

[131] My Reason is well enough convinced of its immortality. It knows itself immortal. But it cannot persuade its downlooking brother the Understanding of the same. That fears for the cord that ties them lest it break. Hence Miss Rotch affirms undoubtingly "I shall live forever," and on the other hand does not much believe in her retaining her Personality.

21 Dec. Who says we are not chained? He lies. See how greedily you accept the verse of Homer or Shakspear; the outline of M. Angelo; the strain of Handel; ↑the word of Webster;↓ how thoroughly you understand and make them your own; & are well assured, too, that they are only units from an infinite store of the same kinds.ⁿ Well, now put out your own hands & take one more unit thence. I say you are chained.

———

M. Angelo was the Homer of Painting. Titian the Moore or better the Spenser. The difference is the same betwixt this stern Designer & the beautiful colorists that followed him, as between the severe Aristotle & the ornate Cicero[.]

Go show me ⟨how⟩ where to lay the first stone & I will build the chapel.[329]

[132] ⟨We have found out⟩ ↑Blessed is the day when the youth discovers↓ that Within and Above are synonyms.

That obscure experience which almost every person confesses that particular passages of conversation & action have occurred to him in the same order before, whether dreaming or waking — What of that, Bishop Bruno! [329a]

Actio agentis nihil aliud est quam extrahere rem de potentia ad actum. Aristotle [330]

⟨The artist is he whose hand obeys his mind.⟩ We can all put

[329] The preceding sentence is in pencil.

[329a] Bishop Bruno in Southey's ballad ("Bishop Bruno") awoke at midnight ·from a dream in which he had heard his own death knell. This dream he had twice; then during the day as he dined with the Emperor and danced at the ball he heard a mysterious voice repeat a warning of his doom, which came at the evening as he had dreamed.

[330] "The action of the mover is nothing other than the releasing of a thing from potentiality to motion" (Ed.). See *Physics*, III, 1, 201a, 10, 11, and 201a, 28, 29.

out our hands towards the desired truth but few can bring their hands to meet around it.

[331] He alone is an artist whose hands can perfectly execute what his mind has perfectly conceived.

"Solo a quello arriva

La man che obbedisce all'intelletto"

Michel Angelo [Sonnet I, ll. 3–4]

The domestic man loves no music so well as his kitchen clock and the airs which the logs sing to him as they burn ⟨upo⟩ ↑in↓ the fire-place[.]

The best means of mending a bad voice is to utter judicious remarks with it; the second best is to favor it by silence.

Translation of M. Angelo's Sonnet VII

"I know not if it is ⟨so that the imaginat⟩ ↑(it is)↓ the light↓ of its first Maker ⟨which⟩ ↑impressed on the imagination which↓ the soul perceives, or if from the memory, or from the mind, any other beauty shines through into the heart; or if in the soul yet ⟨shines⟩ ↑beams↓ & glows the bright ray of its primitive state, leaving of itself I know not what ⟨heat⟩ ↑burning↓ which is perhaps that which leads me to complain. [133] That which I feel, & that which I see, & that which guide me, is not with me, nor know I well where to find it in me; & it seems to me that another shows it to me. This, lady, happened to me when I first saw you, that a bittersweet, a yes and no, moved me; [Certainly it must be your eyes.]" [332]

---

[331] Each paragraph on the remainder of this page as well as the entry at the top of p. [133] through "independence of solitude." is struck through with a use mark in pencil. All are vertical use marks except for a wavy diagonal use mark through "The best means . . . silence." on p. [132]. "He alone . . . conceived.": used in "Michel Angelo Buonaroti," *Lectures*, I, 110. According to Cameron (*Emerson Society Quarterly*, III Q., 1960, Pt. II, p. 48) this sentence, canceled out immediately above in a simpler form, is paraphrased from Sir Joshua Reynolds's *Discourses* as quoted in "The Life of Michael Angelo Buonaroti," *Lives of Eminent Persons*, 1833, p. 38: ". . . he who knows that his hand can execute whatever his fancy can suggest, sports with more freedom in embodying the visionary forms of his own creation." Linked, however, as the sentence is with the lines from Michelangelo's first sonnet, which Emerson himself was later to translate in full (*W*, IX, 298), it is probably his own paraphrase of the verse which he was reading in the *Rime di Michelagnolo Buonarroti il vecchio* . . . ed. Giambattista Biagioli (Perugia, 1821), p. 1.

[332] The brackets around "Certainly . . . eyes." are in pencil. Emerson was

21 [22?] Dec. It is very easy in the world to live by the opinion of the world. It is very easy in solitude to be self-centered. But ⟨in⟩ the finished man is he who in the midst of the crowd ⟨and in⟩ ↑keeps with↓ perfect ⟨benevolence keeps the serenity &⟩ ↑sweetness↓ the ⟨total⟩ ↑⟨absolute⟩↓ independence of solitude.[333] I knew a man of simple habits & earnest character who never put out his hand nor opened his lips to court the public and having survived several rotten reputations of younger men, Honor came at last and sat down with him upon his private bench from which he had never stirred. I too can see the spark of Titan in that coarse clay.

↑Queisarte benigna↓ ⟨Quis⟩Et meliore [n] luto finxit praecordia Titan.[334] Wherever is life, wherever is God, there the Universe evolves itself as from a centre to its boundless irradiation. Whosoever therefore apprehends the infinite, and every man can, brings ⟨the⟩ all worth & significance into that spot of space where he stands though it be a ditch, a potato-field, a work-bench; or, more properly into that state of thought in which he is[,] whether it be the making a statue or designing a church like Michel Angelo or holding silent meetings like George Fox & Job Scott or fighting battles [134] like Leonidas, Washington, Lafayette; exploring the law⟨s⟩ of laws like Plotinus; or loving like Socrates, Petrarch, & Angelo; or prescribing the ethics of the Scholar like Schiller. Therefore is it in the option of every generous spirit to denominate that place in which he now is, his Rome, his World; his sunshine shall be Susa; his shade, Ecbatana; [335] & let him rest assured, if he invite them, not one deity will stay away from his feast. And therefore also is it that every good sentence seems to /recognize/imply/ all truth.

Truly exists that "quoddam vinculum commune" [336] between all the arts & knowledges of men. Vitruvius said that to understand architecture needed not only to draw well but also to ⟨study⟩ ↑understand↓ Music; and M. Angelo said of Architecture that he who did

reading the Italian of the sonnet in Biagioli's edition of the *Rime di Michelagnolo*, 1821, p. 7.
    [333] "It is very easy . . . solitude.": used in "Self-Reliance," *W*, II, 53–54.
    [334] "One whose soul the Titan has fashioned
       With kindlier skill and of finer clay." — Juvenal, *Satires*, XIV, 34.
    [335] See p. 304 above, and *JMN*, III, 319.
    [336] "certain common bond" (Ed.).

not understand something of the anatomy of the human body could know nothing of that subject.[337]

The philosophy of *Waiting* needs sometimes to be unfolded. Thus he who ⟨acts⟩ is qualified to act upon the Public, if he does not act on many, may yet act intensely on a few; if he does not act much upon any but from insulated condition & unfit companions seem[s] quite withdrawn into himself, still if he know & feel his obligations, he may be (unknown & unconsciously) hiving knowledge & concentrating powers to act well hereafter & a very remote hereafter. God is a rich proprietor [135] who though he may find use for sprouts & saplings of a year's growth finds his account also in leaving untouched the timber of a hundred years which hardens & seasons in the cold ↑&↓ in the sun. But a more lowly use (& yet with right feelings all parts of duty are alike lowly) is pleasing, that of serving an indirect good to your friends by being much to them, a reserve by which their sallies of virtue are fortified & they cordially cheered by the thoroughness of a mutual understanding. How has Edward served ↑us↓ most in these last ⟨s⟩years? by his figures & invoices? or through the healthful influence of his perfect moral health? How serves the Aunt M.? How but by bearing most intelligible testimony which is felt where it is not comprehended.

——

> "In Friendship too, observe my song,
> There is both equal, broad, & long;
> But this thou must not think to find
> With eyes of body but of mind."
> > *Empedocles.*

> "Love idle of himself takes up his rest
> And harbors only in a slothful breast."

> "Love into men poetic power infuses,
> Tho' ne'er before acquainted with the Muses."
> > *Euripides* [338]

[337] For the comment of Vitruvius, see p. 337 above. Michelangelo's remark appeared in a letter quoted in "The Life of Michael Angelo Buonaroti," *Lives of Eminent Persons*, 1833, p. 57, and in paraphrase on p. 56 with a cross reference to Duppa's *The Life of Michael Angelo Buonarroti*, 1807, p. 224. Emerson's version is also a paraphrase.

[338] Emerson quoted the verses from Plutarch, "Of Love," the *Morals*, 1718, IV,

[136] If I were more in love with life & as afraid of dying as you seem to insinuate I would go to a Jackson Caucus or to the Julien Hall & I doubt not the unmixed malignity, the withering selfishness, the impudent vulgarity that mark those meetings would speedily cure me of my appetite for longevity. In the hush of these woods I find no Jackson placards affixed to the trees.

⟨T⟩ We republicans do libel the monarchist. The monarchist of Europe for so many ages has really been pervaded by an Idea. He intellectually & affectionately views the king as the State. ⟨A crow⟩ And the monarch is pervaded by a correspondent idea & the worst of them has yet demeaned himself more or less faithfully as a State. A crown then is by no means 'a strip of velvet with jewels' nor is Louis XVI Mr Louis Capet, as we chuse to affirm. Certainly there is something that mightily tickles a human ear in being named a nation as Elizabeth of England, Mary of Scotland, Anne of Austria. V. p 145

[339] "His works do follow him," saith the blessed Revelation [14:13, misquoted], & the world echoes Amen. *What hath he done?* is the divine question which searches souls & transpierces the paper shield of every false reputation. A fop may sit in any chair of the world for his hour nor be distinguished from Homer or Washington, but there never can be doubt concerning the respective ability of human beings when we ⟨refuse to be trifled with &⟩ seek the truth. Pretension may sit still, but cannot act. Pretension [137] never feigned an ⟨Iliad⟩ act of real greatness. Pretension never wrote an Iliad nor drove back Xerxes nor Christianized the World nor ⟨abolished slave⟩ discovered America nor abolished Slavery. ↑"The light of the public square will best test its merit," said M. Angelo.↓[340] Mr Coleridge has thrown many new truths into circulation, Mr Southey never one.

272, 274, and 286; the ascriptions to Empedocles and Euripides appear in the source. In Goodwin's edition of the *Morals*, 1870, IV, 274 and 288, the Euripidean quotations are identified as from the *Danae*, Frag. 324, and the *Stheneboea*, Frag. 666.

[339] The paragraph and its conclusion on p. [137] are struck through with a vertical use mark in pencil. "*What hath* . . . abolished Slavery.": used in "Spiritual Laws," *W*, II, 158.

[340] "The Life of Michael Angelo Buonaroti," *Lives of Eminent Persons*, 1833, p. 72, slightly misquoted.

Yet falsehoods, superstitions, are the props the scaffolding on which how much of society stands. ⟨The⟩ Look at the relation betwixt the uneducated & the educated classes. 'One's afraid & t'other daresn't,' as the boys say. Each supposes much in the other which is not in him, & so the peace & place is kept. Accurately I suppose the graduate underestimates the grocer, whilst the grocer far overestimates the graduate, & so the strong hand is kept in submission to what should be the ⟨strong⟩ ↑wise↓ head. The reason why Mr Graduate's secret is kept & never any accident ⟨|| ... ||⟩discovers his bankruptcy & produces a permanent revolution, is, that there is a real object in Nature to which the grocer's reverence instinctively turns ↑viz. the intellectual man,↓ & though the scholar is ⟨th⟩not that object, he is its representative, & is, with more or less symptoms of distrust, honored for that which he ought to be. It is of primary importance to note that take out of the critic his professional Selfishness & you pluck out the splinter of offence from these facts. They may be stated in open day without sham apology or any ⟨injury⟩ ↑reluctance↓, because it is a manifest interest which comes home to my bosom & every man's bosom that there should be ⟨an⟩on every tower Watchers set

[continued on] p. 139 [341]

———

[138] Of the German Nation.

It is the only nation that addresses the Deity with the appellation Dear. Lieber Gott!

———

The Sun is the sole inconsumable fire
And God is the sole inexhaustible Giver.[342]

Dec. 23. A good chapter might be writ of *Optical Deceptions*. A sort of disappointment is felt by an ingenious man on hearing opinions & truths congenial to his own announced with effect ⟨from the pulpit or through the Press⟩ ↑in conversation↓. They are so near

---

[341] After the interruption the entry continues again on p. [139] with a repetition of "⟨should be⟩ Watchers set." The inadvertent repetition is omitted.

[342] Cameron (*EtE*, I, 251) calls the couplet Emerson's poetic version of the Swedenborgian concept of parallel suns.

to his own thought or expression, ⟨that⟩ ↑that he thinks↓ he ought to have spoken ⟨before⟩ first. That is an *optical deception* of the mind. If they had not been uttered ↑⟨any⟩ by this other,↓ he would not have uttered them. It is merely under the influence of this magnet that he becomes ⟨violently⟩ ↑intensely↓ magnetic. Take it away & this effect will subside in him. Perhaps I shall never write of Shakspear's sonnets; yet let any critic execute that work, & I should go to law with him for assault & battery.

Bottom in Shakspear is a philosopher of this kidney. He fathers ⟨the⟩ ↑each↓ new part, the moment it is named. It fills his whole horizon. He would be that alone. He mistakes his omnivolence for omnipotence. The only remedy is to present ↑still↓ a new thought to withdraw him from the last.

It results from the fact that every thought is one side of ⟨his⟩ Nature, & really has the whole world under it.

This exclusive prominence of one thought is that which Bacon indicated by idols of the cave[.] [343]

[139] "Time & patience change a mulberry leaf into satin." [344]
The disinterestedness of the truth-love is shown in this, that it only wants an intelligent ear. A good aunt is more to the young poet than a patron. Moliere had more happiness the year round from his old woman than from Louis[.] [345]

[from] ↑p. 137↓
to observe & report of every new ray of light in what quarter soever of heaven it should appear and their report should ↑be↓ eagerly & reverently received. There is no offence done certainly to the community in distinctly stating the claims of this office. It is not a coveted

[343] Emerson apparently filled out his thought later by adding "the cave" in pencil. For his reference, see *The Works of Francis Bacon*, 1860–1864, VIII, 77: "The Idols of the Cave are the idols of the individual man." Cf. also *ibid.*, VIII, 84, 86.
[344] Cf. "With Time and art, the mulberry leafs grow to be sattin," James Howell, *English Proverbs*, . . . (London, 1659), p. 3: used in "The American Scholar," *W*, I, 96.
[345] "The disinterestedness . . . Louis" is struck through with a wavy diagonal use mark in pencil.

office. It is open to all men. All see their interest in it yet very few feel any inclination to adopt it as their vocation. The blessed God has given to each his calling in his ruling love. Release by an act of law all men today from their contracts & all apprentices from their indentures & pay all labor with equal wages & tomorrow you should find the same contracts redrawn ⟨up anew⟩ for one ⟨from choice⟩ would ↑choose to↓ work in wood, ⟨&⟩ another in stone, and a third in iron; one would prefer a farm, ⟨&⟩ another the sea; one would ⟨draw⟩ paint, ⟨&⟩ another sing; ⟨and⟩ another survey land, ⟨&⟩ another deal in horses; & another project adventures. God has adapted the brain & the body of men to the work that is to be done in the world. Greenough has an invincible penchant ⁿ [140] to carve marble, & John Haskins ³⁴⁶ to fry caoutchouc. A small number of men meantime have a contemplative turn & voluntarily seek solitude & converse with themselves ↑a work↓ which to ⟨many⟩ most persons has a ⟨state prison savor⟩ ↑jail-smell↓. This needs a ⟨rare &⟩ peculiar constitution, a dormancy of some qualities & a harmonious action in all, that is rare. It has its own immunities and also its own painful taxes like the rest of human works. But where it is possessed, let it work free & honoured, in God's name. It is our interest as much in the economical way as that the pin or the chaise maker should be free & in a moral & intellectual view far far oh infinitely more. Every discovery he makes[,] every conclusion he announces is tidings to each of us from our own home. His office is to cheer our labor as with a song by highest hopes.

[141] Do, dear, when you come to write Lyceum lectures, remember that you are not to say, What must be said in a Lyceum? but what discoveries or stimulating thoughts have I to impart to a thousand persons? not what they will expect to hear but what is fit for me to say.

[142] "No matter where you begin. Read anything five hours a day & you will soon be knowing." said Johnson.³⁴⁷

³⁴⁶ Emerson's cousin, son of Thomas and Elizabeth Haskins of Roxbury.
³⁴⁷ Cf. ". . . I would not advise a rigid adherence to a particular plan of study . . . . A young man should read five hours in a day, and so may acquire a great deal of knowledge." See *Boswell's Life of Johnson*, ed. George B. Hill, 6 vols. (Oxford, 1887), I, 496.

Out of these fragmentary lobsided mortals shall the heaven unite Phidias, Demosthenes, Shakspear, Newton, Napoleon, Bacon, and St John in one person.

24 Dec.[348] Him I call rich[,] that soul I call endowed whether in man or woman, who by poverty or affliction or love has been driven home so far as to make acquaintance with the ⟨natural⟩ spiritual dominion of every human mind. Hence forward he is introduced into sublime society[;] henceforward he can wave the hand of adieu to all the things he coveted most. Henceforward he is ⟨beyond⟩ above compassion. He may it is true seldom look at his treasure[;] he may like one who has ⟨discovered a treasure in his own field⟩ ↑brought home his bride↓ go ⟨home⟩ ↑apart↓ & compose himself & only take furtive glances at his good with a fearful joy from the very assurance of confirmed bliss but him I leave within his heaven & all others I call miserably poor.

[143][349] A singular equality may be observed between the great men of the first & the last ages. The Astronomy, the arts, & the history of sixty centuries give Lafayette, Canning, Webster no advantage over Saladin, Scipio, or Agesilaus. The reason is, the Arts[,] the Sciences are in man, & the Spartan possessed & used the very talent in his war that Watt used for economical ends & the pride & selfsufficiency of the Ancient was founded on this very consciousness of infinitely versatile resources. The beggars of Sparta & of Rome hurled defiance with as proud a tone as if ⟨the Armada⟩ Lysander's fleet of tubs had been an Armada or the rude walls of Sparta had been the bastions of Gibraltar. The resources of the mechanic arts are merely costume. If Fabricius had been shown instead of Pyrrhus's elephants Napoleon's park of artillery, he would have displayed no more emotion; he would have found a counterbalance in himself; all the finites cannot outweigh one infinite. All the erudition of an

---

[348] The paragraph is struck through with a wavy diagonal use mark in pencil.

[349] The first paragraph is struck through with a vertical penciled use mark. "A singular . . . Parry.": used in "Self-Reliance," W, II, 85–86. "Hudson . . . Parry." is in lighter ink and separated from the rest of the entry by an irregular semicircular line, probably as a later illustrative addition.

University of doctors is not a match for the mother wit of one Æsop. Hudson, Behring, Parry.

———

Raphael's three manners of painting may be matched in the biography of every genius.

———

Nature keeps much on her table but more in her closet.

———

A few words writ by a trembling hand of old Isaiah or Homer become an immoveable palisado to guard their sense against change or loss through all the storms & revolutions of time.

[144] ↑Dec. 2⟨4⟩5↓ Where there is D E F there must be A B C saith Sancho's ⁿ aunt.[350] For heaven's sake [351] let me be alone to the end of the world unconsidered, unaided, rather than that my friend should affect an interest in me he does not feel or ⟨task himself⟩ ↑overstep↓ by so much as one word or one expression of countenance his real sympathy. It turns my stomach[,] it cuts my throat where I looked for a manly furtherance or at least a manly resistance to find a mush of concession. Better be a nettle in the side of your compan⟨y⟩ion than ⟨every man's⟩ ↑be his↓ echo. I lament with a contrition too deep for groaning every sacrifice of truth to fat good nature & not less those where Custom has insensibly produced a great alteration in a wellfounded opinion. I am thankful that I was permitted to write G[eorge].B.E[merson]. in his bereavement that I lacked sympathy with the character of his wife.[352] If I praise her virtues, he will now believe me. [December] 26. A good subject for book or lecture were it to read the riddle of the ancient Mythology; &

[350] Cf. "B is too often the mere shadow of A, and C of B, and Z of some or all the personages." Emerson may be paraphrasing J. W. Cunningham, *Sancho, or the Proverbialist* (London, 1819), p. 70. The volume gives Sancho, its hero, two aunts, one who repeats wise Bible verses, one who is "passionately addicted to proverbs."

[351] "For heaven's . . . alteration" is struck through with a wavy diagonal use mark in pencil. "For heaven's . . . echo.": used in "Friendship," *W*, II, 208.

[352] Emerson's second cousin, a noted scholar and teacher, had been married to Olivia Buckminister, whose epitaph Waldo had included in his journal (see p. 272 above). After her death in 1832 G. B. Emerson married another acquaintance of Waldo's, Mary Rotch of New Bedford. This second marriage occurred in November shortly before this entry.

show how far Minerva was only a fine word for wisdom. Bacon has done most & was fittest to do it. An obscure & slender thread of truth runs through all mythologies & this might lead often to highest regions of philosophy. Isis & Osiris. Eros & Anteros[.]

A singular correspondence is also to be remarked in the fables themselves. "Old Knurre Murre is dead" seems only a travestie of "The great god PAN is dead" in ⟨Isis & Osiris⟩ ?⟨EI⟩ Pythian oracles↓.³⁵³ Fit pendant such discourse might be to that [145] proposed on the First philosophers. v. p. 120

All pomps & ceremonies of courts do only flourish & idealize the simple facts in which that state begun, as the orders of architecture do in every ornament refer to some essential part of the building. "The pope performeth all ecclesiastical jurisdiction as in consistory among his cardinals which were originally but the parish priests of Rome." v. Milton [vol.] 1 p. 16[;] ³⁵⁴ so to the wise eye an etiquette is ↑a history↓[.]

A few persons, three or four perhaps[,] are to Burns what nations & races & long chronicles of annals are to Gibbon & often it may be suspected that Shakspeare tacks the name of Rome or France upon traits to which he had more truly given the name of Nicholas Bacon or John Sylvester.

---

³⁵³ Edward Emerson (*J*, III, 412n) identified "Knurre Murre" as a figure in a rhyme sung by an unknown voice to a homeward bound peasant:

"Hie home, Goodman Platt,
Tell thou the gib-cat,
That steals buttermilk out of the buttermilk vat,
That old Knurre Murre is dead."

The rhyme is a version of the "King of the cats" folktale, no. B342, in E. W. Baughman's classification (see *Comparative Study of the Folktales of England and America*, Ann Arbor University Microfilm Pub., no. 5855, 1953). The parallel phrase concerning Pan comes from Plutarch's "Why the Oracles Cease to Give Answers." See the *Morals*, 1870, IV, 23. As the canceled references to Isis, Osiris, and EI and the inserted reference to the Pythian oracles indicate, Emerson was probably thinking also of two other essays from Plutarch as examples of the permanent myths: "Of Isis and Osiris" and "Of the Word EI engraved over the Gate of Apollo's Temple at Delphi" (see the *Morals*, 1870, IV, 65–139 and 478–498).

³⁵⁴ Emerson cited "Of Reformation" from an edition he owned, *A Selection from the English Prose Works of John Milton*, ed. Jenks, 1826, I, 16–17.

How beautiful are the feet of him that bringeth good tidings that publisheth Salvation! Forever graceful in every unperverted eye are the acts of Jesus of Nazareth, the man who believed in moral nature & therefore spake, who came not in his own name[.] [355]

[146] There is no object in nature which intense light will not make beautiful.[356] & none which loses beauty by being nearer seen[.]

It is a thin partition that divides the housebreaker & the hero; him that ⟨bawls⟩ in the conventicle bawls Glory! & the philosopher who muses in amazement.

[357] 'Tis only an inventor that ⟨can appropriate⟩ knows how to borrow.

Knowledge transfers the censorship from the statehouse to the reason of every citizen & ⟨makes⟩ ↑compels↓ every man to mount guard over himself & puts shame & remorse for sargeants & maces.

27 Dec. We say every truth supposes or implies every other truth. Not less true is it that every great man does in all his nature point at & imply the existence & well being of all the institutions & orders of a state. He is full of reverence. He is by inclination (though far remote in position) the defender of the grammar school, the almshouse, the Christian Sabbath, the priest, the judge, the legislator, & the executive arm. Throughout his being is he loyal. Such was ⟨M⟩ Luther, Milton, Burke[;] each might be called an aristocrat though by position the champion of the people.

⟨The⟩ Bacon never mentions Shakspear nor Spenser though often very inferior Latin & Greek poets. Milton's praise of Shakspear is most unequal to the subject & Jonson's much more. Milton in his turn was not seen by his contemporaries & was valued most as a

---

[355] Cf. "How beautiful upon the mountains are the feet of him that bringeth good tidings, that publisheth peace; that bringeth good tidings of good, that publisheth salvation." Isa. 52:7. See also Nah. 1:15. For "who came . . . own name" see John 5:43.

[356] "There is . . . beautiful." is struck through with a wavy diagonal use mark in pencil: used in *Nature*, W, I, 15.

[357] " 'Tis only . . . maces." is struck through with three diagonal penciled use marks, two of which continue across "27 Dec . . . . people." The entry for this date is also struck through with one additional diagonal use mark in pencil. "Knowledge . . . maces." is written earlier in pencil under the ink.

scholar. Tasso, Dante, M. Angelo make no figure in Milton's estimate. ⟨& they⟩

[147] There are two kinds of blindness, one of incapacity to
see; the other, of preoccupied attention. The prophet, the bard, the
man of genius, absorbed with the Idea which haunts him ever, &
which he is appointed to utter, as he can, to his age, may easily ⟨send⟩
↑cast↓ such careless glances at other men's works, as not to detect
their superlative worth. A young man ⟨or maiden⟩ who falls in love
with a maiden can easily set at nought all the advantageous or glorious offers that others may make him & perform prodigious acts of
perseverance, courage, & self-denial in his quest. A [358] nation of men
unanimous & desperately bent on freedom or conquest can easily
confound all calculation of statists & in defiance of superior potentates accomplish wild & extravagant actions out of all proportion to
their numerical or fiscal strength," as the Greeks, ↑the Saracens,↓
the Swiss, the Americans, & the French did. Remember the 'Rostopchin' times & the 'last hoofs' of New England.[359]

Their eyes were holden that they should not see.[360]
Men of genius to be canonized after their death are disagreeable, sometimes hateful beggars in their lifetime. And when we see
them there is no beauty that we should desire them.

Snow & moonlight make all landscapes alike.
Every thing may be painted, every thing sung, but to be poetized
its feet must be just lifted from the ground[.]
The wind will go down with the sun[.]

[148] I believe the Christian religion to be profoundly true;

[358] The rest of the paragraph is struck through with two diagonal use marks in
pencil.
[359] Feodor Rostopchin (1760–1826) was governor of Moscow during the
Napoleonic invasion of 1812. He was accused of having set the city on fire, a charge
which he later denied in his book *Verité sur l'incendie de Moscow* (Paris, 1824). The
reference to the "last hoofs" has not been located.
[360] Emerson seems here to have blended two passages from the New Testament.
Cf. Rom. 11:10 — "Let their eyes be darkened that they may not see" — and
Luke 24:16 — "Their eyes were holden that they should not know him."

true to an extent that they who are styled its most orthodox defenders have never or but in rarest glimpses once or twice in a lifetime reached. I who seek to be a realist, to deny & put off every thing
that I do not heartily accept, do yet catch myself continually in a
practical unbelief of its deepest teachings. It taught, it teaches the
eternal opposition of the world to the truth,[n] & introduced the absolute authority of the spiritual law. Milton apprehended its nature
when he said "For who is there almost that measures wisdom by
simplicity, strength by suffering, dignity by lowliness?" [361] That do
I in my sane moments, & feel the ineffable peace, yea & the influx
of God that attend humility & love, and before the cock crows, I
deny him thrice.[362]

"There's nothing good or bad but thinking makes it so." [363]

A friend once told me that he never spent anything on himself
without deserving the praise of disinterested benevolence.[364]

[149] [blank]

[150] Saturday night [December 27]. There is in every man a
determination of character to a peculiar end, counteracted often by
unfavorable fortune, but more apparent the more he is left at liberty.
This ↑is↓ called his genius, or his nature, or his turn of mind. The
object of Education should be to remove all obstructions & let this
natural force have free play & exhibit its peculiar product. ⟨The⟩ It
seems to be true that no man in this is deluded. ⟨He⟩ This determination of his character is to something in nature; something real.
This object is called his Idea. It is that which rules his most advised
actions, those especially that are most his, & is most distinctly dis-
cerned by him in those days or moments when he derives the sin-
cerest satisfaction from his life. It can only be indicated by any action
not defined by any thing less than the aggregate of all his ⟨free⟩
↑genuine↓ actions; perhaps then only approximated. ↑Hence the

---

[361] *Reason of Church Government urged against Prelaty.* See *The Works of John Milton,* 1931–1940, III, Pt. I, 243.

[362] Cf. Matt. 26:75.

[363] Shakespeare, *Hamlet,* II, ii, 265–266.

[364] See p. 292 above for Emerson's earlier use of this anecdote and an identification of the "friend" as his brother Charles.

slowness of the ancients to judge of the life before death. "Expect the end."↓³⁶⁵ It is most accurately denoted by the ↑man's↓ name, ⟨of the individual,⟩ as when we say the Scipionism of Scipio; or "There spoke the soul of Caesar." The ancients seem to have expressed this spiritual superintendence by representing every human being as consigned to the charge of a Genius or Daemon by whose counsels he was guided in what he did best but whose counsels he might reject.

"Heathen philosophers taught that whosoever would but use his ear to listen might hear the voice of his guiding Genius ever before him, calling, &, as it were, pointing to that way which is his part to follow." *Milton* vol I p 251 ³⁶⁶

[151]³⁶⁷ [December] 28. Whenever I open my eyes I read that everything has expression, a mouth, a chin, a lock of hair, the lappel of a coat, the crimp or plait of a cap, a creampot, a tree, a stone. So much I concede to the physiognomist & craniologist. At the same time I see well enough how different is the expression of a pink ribbon upon one & upon another head. — But ah the pink ribbons of clouds that I saw last eve in the sunset modulated with tints of unspeakable softness and the air meantime had so much vivacity & sweetness that it was a pain to come in doors. C[harles]. saw the same ⟨clou⟩ flecks of cloud & likened them to gold fishes. Had they no expression? Is there no meaning in the ⟨all-living⟩ ↑live↓ repose which that amphitheatre of a valley behind Ball's hill ⟨gives⟩ ↑reflects↓ to my eye ↑&↓ which Homer or Shakspeare could not re-form for me in Words? ⁿ The ⟨dead⟩ ↑leafless↓ trees become ↑spires of↓ flame ⟨coloured⟩ in the sunset with the blue East for their back ground & ⟨every dead⟩ the stars of the dead calices of flowers & every withered stem & stubble

---

³⁶⁵ The concept is, of course, a classical commonplace. Cf. the Latin proverb "Respice finem" — "look to the end," or the saying attributed to Chilo of Sparta, "Remember the end," or the remark of Solon, "Keep thine eyes fixed upon the end of life."
³⁶⁶ Emerson cited "An Apology for Smectymnuus" from *A Selection from the English Prose Works of John Milton*, ed. Jenks, 1826.
³⁶⁷ Within the first paragraph "I saw . . . mute music." is struck through with three vertical use marks, two of them in pencil, one in ink. "But ah . . . music.": used in *Nature*, W, I, 17–18.

rimed with frost with all their forms & hues contribute something
to the mute music.

Rather let me be "a pagan suckled in a creed outworn" [368] than
cowardly deny or conceal one particle of my debt to Greek art or
poetry or virtue. Certainly I would my debt were more, but it is
my fault not theirs if 'tis little. But how pitiful if a mind enriched
& infused with the spirit [152] of their severe yet human Beauty
modulating the words they spake, the acts they did, the forms they
sculptured, every gesture, every fold of the robe; especially animating
the biography of their men with a wild wisdom and an elegance as
wild & handsome as sunshine; the brave anecdotes of Agesilaus,
Phocion, & Epaminondas; the death of Socrates, that holy martyr,
a death like that of Christ; the purple light of Plato which shines
yet into all ages & is a test of the sublimest intellects — to ⟨sh⟩ receive the influences however partial of all this, & to speak of it as if
it were nothing, or like a fool under praise it in a Sermon because
the worshippers ⟨were⟩are ignorant, & incapable of understanding that
there may be degrees & varieties of merit, & that the merit of Paul
shall not be less because that of Aristotle is genuine & great, — I
call that meanspirited, if it were Channing or Luther that did it. Be
it remembered of Milton who drank deeply of these fountains that
in an age & assembly of fierce fanatics he drew as freely from these
resources & with just acknowledgment, as from those known & honored by his party. "His soul was like a Star & dwelt apart." [369]

[153] I honor him who made himself of no reputation.[370] If I
were called upon to charge a young minister, I would say Beware of
Tradition: Tradition which embarrasses ⟨all⟩ life & falsifies all teaching. The sermons that I hear are all dead of that ail. The ⟨minister⟩
↑preacher↓ is betrayed by his ear. He begins to inveigh against
some real evil & falls unconsciously into formulas of speech which
have been said & sung in the church some ages & have lost all life.

---

[368] Wordsworth, "The world is too much with us," l. 10. Emerson marked the
whole sonnet in the margin in his personal copy of Wordsworth's poems. This single
line he used again in the Divinity School Address, *W*, I, 131.

[369] Wordsworth, "London, 1802," l. 9, with a misquotation of "His" for "Thy."
In Emerson's copy of Wordsworth's poems the sonnet is marked in the margin.

[370] Phil. 2:7. Emerson repeated the quotation again on the following page.

They never had any but when freshly & with special conviction applied. But *you* must never lose sight of the purpose of helping a particular person in every word you say. Thus my preacher summed the deaths of the past year & then reminded the bereaved that these were admonitions of God to them, &c. &c. Now all these words fell to the ground. They are Hamlet's "Many *As'es* of great charge"; [371] mere wind. He ought to have considered whether it were true as his ear has always heard to be sure without contradiction, that deaths *were* admonitions. By enumerating in his mind the persons that would be included in this address, he would quickly perceive that there was great disparity in the cases, ↑many had mourned but were not ↑now↓ mourners,↓ [372] that some of the deaths were to the survivors desireable[,] some quite indifferent, that some ↑of these survivors↓ were persons of that habitual elevation of religious view as to have just views of death & so were above this prose. Others were of such manifold business or preoccupation of [154] mind as that any death must occupy but a subordinate place in their thoughts & if any where the words might be spoken with strict propriety, they were yet so general as not to be likely to strike that ear. I am prolix on this instance yet the fault is obvious ↑to a discerning ear↓ in almost every sentence of the prayers & the sermons that are ordinarily heard in the Church. Not so with Edward Taylor that living Methodist[,] the Poet of the Church. Not so with the Swedenborgians if their pulpit resembles their book.

———

[December] 29. A critic pronounced that Wordsworth was a good man but no poet. "Ah!" said one present, "you know not how much poetry there is in goodness!"

———

C[harles]. says he has four stomachs like a camel & what law he reads in the morning he puts into the first stomach till evening; then it slides into the second.

Every truth is a full circle.[373]

[371] Shakespeare, *Hamlet*, V, ii, 43.

[372] The insertion of "many . . . mourners," differs in ink from the rest of the entry as does the further insertion "of these survivors" below. To the first insertion "now" is added in pencil, apparently by Emerson.

[373] Emerson's image for truth may have been influenced by Coleridge's quotation

'He made himself of no reputation.' The words have a divine sound.

To the music of the surly storm that thickens the darkness of the night abroad & rocks the walls & fans my cheek through the chinks & cracks[,] I would sing my strain though hoarse & small. Yet please God it shall be lowly, affectionate, & true. It were worth trial whether the distinction between a spiritual & a traditional religion could not be made [155] apparent to an ordinary congregation. There [374] are parts of faith so great so self-evident that when the mind rests in them the pretensions of the most illuminated[,] most pretending sect pass for nothing. When I rest in perfect humility[,] when I burn with pure love what ⟨are⟩ ⁿ ↑can↓ Calvin or Swedenborg ↑say↓ to me?

But to show men the nullity of churchgoing compared with a real exaltation of their being I think might ↑even promote parish objects &↓ draw them to church. To show the reality & infinite depth of spiritual laws[;] that all the maxims of Christ are true to the core of the world; that there is not, can't be, any cheating of nature, might be apprehended.

Every spiritual law I suppose would be a contradiction to common sense. Thus I should begin with my old saws that nothing ⟨was⟩ ↑can be↓ given; everything is sold; love compels love; hatred, hatred; action & reaction always are equal. No evil in society but has its check which coexists; the moral, the physical, the social world is a plenum & any /strain/flood/ in one place produces equal /yielding/ebb/ in another. Nothing is free but the will of man & that only to procure his own ⟨improvement⟩ ↑virtue↓: on every side but that one, he beats the air with his pompous action; that punishment not follows but accompanies crime. They have said in churches in this age "Mere Morality". O God they know thee not who speak contemptuously of

---

from Saint Augustine in *Aids to Reflection*, 1829, p. 304n, "God is a circle whose centre is every where and circumference is no where." In "Circles," however, Emerson cites this passage as from Saint Augustine (see *W*, II, 301). Or possibly Emerson may have recalled another aphorism of Coleridge's (*Biographia Literaria*, London, 1834, p. 278), "Truth and prudence might be imaged as concentric circles."

[374] "There are parts . . . to me?" is struck through with a wavy diagonal use mark in pencil. "When I rest . . . to me?" is further struck through with four heavy vertical use marks.

all that is grand. It is the distinction of Christianity, that it is moral. All that is personal in it is nought. When any one comes who speaks with [156] better insight into moral nature he will be the new gospel; miracle or not, inspired or uninspired, he will be the Christ. ⟨If I coul⟩ Persons are nothing. If I could tell you what you know not, could by my knowledge of the divine being ⟨make⟩ put that within your grasp which now you dimly apprehend, & make you feel the moral sublime, you would never think of denying my inspiration[.]

The whole power of Christianity resides in this fact, ↑that↓ it is more agreeable to the constitution of man than any other teaching. But from the constitution of man may be got better teaching still. See p. 71[.]

Morality [375] requires purity, but purity is not it; requires justice, but justice is not that; requires beneficence, but is something better. Indeed there is a kind of descent & accommodation felt when we leave speaking of Moral Nature to urge a virtue it enjoins. For ↑to↓ the Soul in her pure action all the virtues are natural & not painfully acquired. Excite the soul & it becomes suddenly virtuous. Touch the deep heart and all these listless stingy beefeating bystanders will see the dignity of a sentiment, will say This is good & all I have I will give for that. Excite the soul, & the weather & the town & your condition in the world all disappear, the world itself loses its solidity, nothing remains but the soul & the Divine Presence in which it lives. Youth & age are indifferent in this presence.

[157] Extremes meet. Misfortunes even may be so accumulated as to be ludicrous. To be shipwrecked is bad; to be shipwrecked on an iceberg is horrible; to be shipwrecked on an iceberg in a snowstorm, confounds us; to be shipwrecked on an iceberg in ↑a↓ ⟨snow⟩storm and to find a bear on the snow bank to dispute the sailor's landing which is not driven ⟨off but⟩ ↑away↓ till he has bitten off a sailor's arm, is rueful to laughter.

Some people smile spite of themselves in communicating the worst news.

---

[375] "Morality . . . virtuous.": used in "The Over-Soul," *W*, II, 275.

"Overturn, Overturn, and overturn," said our aged priest,[376] "until he whose right it is to reign, shall come into his kingdom."

The great willowtree over my roof is the trumpet & accompaniment of the storm & gives due importance to every caprice of the gale and the trees in the avenue announce the same facts with equal din to the front tenants. Hoarse concert: they roar like the rigging of a ship in a tempest.

The Unitarian preacher who sees that his orthodox hearer may with reason complain that the preaching is not serious, faithful, authoritative enough ⟨for him⟩ is by that admission judged. It is not an excuse that he can with clearness see the speculative error of his neighbor. But when a man speaks from deeper convictions than any party faith, ⟨he⟩ when he declares the simple truth he finds his relation to the Calvinist or Methodist or Infidel at once [158] changed in the most agreeable manner. He is of their faith, says each.

⟨The snow & moonlight make all landscapes alike.⟩ [377]

It is really a spiritual power which stopped the mouths of the regular priests in the presence of the fervent First Quaker [378] & his friends. If the⟨y⟩ dead-alive never learned before that they do not speak with authority from the Highest, they learn it then when a commissioned man comes who speaks, because he cannot ⟨forbear⟩ ↑hold back↓, the message that is in his heart.

Certainly I read a similar story respecting Luther; that the preacher's heart, stout enough before, misgave him when he perceived Luther was in the audience.

———

The height of virtue is only to act in a firm belief that moral laws hold. Jesus & St Paul & Socrates & Phocion believed ⟨that⟩ in

[376] Dr. Ezra Ripley, Emerson's step-grandfather, in whose house Waldo and his mother were living in the fall of 1834.

[377] See p. 377 above for an earlier and uncanceled version of this statement.

[378] The "fervent First Quaker" is, of course, George Fox. Emerson would have remembered either from his reading in Sewel's *The History of the . . . Quakers* or from Fox's own journal the frequent recurrence of regular priests who were silenced and abashed before Fox and the power of the Lord. Cf. "But the Lord's power was too hard for this opposing priest and stopped his mouth." *The Journal of George Fox*, Everyman ed. (London, 1924), p. 48 and the repetition of such phrases on pp. 42, 62, and 100.

spite of their senses that Moral law existed & reigned & so believing could not have acted otherwise. The sinner lets go his perception of these laws & then acts agreeably to the lower law of the senses. The logic of the sinner & of the saint is perfect. There is no flaw in either Epicureanism or Stoicism[.]

Does not Aristotle distinguish between Temperance for ends & Temperance for love of temperance? [379] Each of these virtues becomes dowdy in a sermon. They must be practised for their elegance. The virtuous man must be a poet ⟨in his⟩ & not a drudge of his virtues, to have them [159] perfect. If he *could by implication* perform all the virtues[,] that is not aim to be temperate nor aim to be honest nor aim to be liberal but in his lofty piety be all three without knowing it, then is he the good moralist. The Ecclesiastical dogma of 'Faith, not Works' [380] is based on this truth.

Jesus believed in moral nature and he did not come in his own name.[381] (When a preacher does not say he comes in his own name he generally looks it or speaks it plainer than by words.)

[160] [blank]

[161]–[162] [index material omitted]

[163]–[164] [382]

[165] [index material omitted] [383]

---

[379] Cf. *Nichomachean Ethics*, III, 10.

[380] This antinominian dogma rests particularly on such a passage as Gal. 2:16. See also Rom. 3:28, 5:1, and Gal. 3:24.

[381] See especially John 5:43 and n. 355 above.

[382] Following p. [162] nine leaves are cut from the journal. The first cut leaf was evidently once included in the pagination. On its verso is visible "26," "⟨y⟩" and "⟨I⟩". The other eight leaves were originally written in reverse and upside down, apparently in an exercise in penmanship. Only the beginnings of letters are visible on the stubs. See bibliographical note above for a description of the pagination break.

[383] The page is unnumbered but evidently included in the sequential pagination since p. [166] follows it. The entire ink entry on the page (an index) is canceled by four vertical lines as well as by horizontal markings through each entry line. The last two items in the index are in pencil; the final item is uncanceled, perhaps by oversight since it is also included in the rewritten index, p. [162].

[166][384] Charles M. Rider. Malone[,] Franklin Co[,] N. Y. C J
Rider [385]

[167]   "Were it the will of heaven an osier bough
         Were vessel safe enough the seas to plough"

                                              Homer [386]

[387] Every moment said Mr. Webster is eventful. I wish to make another remark; I wish to prepare the country for an *assault* on popular
prejudices. I think I understand it; I think I see the arms relied on to
carry on the warfare. I think I know the magazines from which the arms
are expected to be drawn. For aught I know, those arms may be such as
reason and justice, and the general good cannot resist. For aught I know,
every effort at resistance may prove feeble and powerless. I shall make an
effort, whether it prove successful or unsuccessful. I see in these vehicles
which communicate sentiments from high places, this sentiment every
where, — nay, I hear it boasted of as the unfailing security, the ground
not to be shaken, upon which these measures can stand, the natural hatred
of the poor to the rich! I know that under the shadow of the roof of this
Capitol, — among men sent here to devise means for the public good
and the public safety, that within the last twenty-four hours, *that* has
been referred to, to defend the Executive, and to support the late measures
to put down the Bank. The natural hatred of the poor to the rich! Sir,
it shall be the last moment of my existence; it shall be only when I am

---

[384] The entry here and the final written entry in the journal on p. [167], "Were
it . . . Homer", are in pencil.

[385] The persons represented in this penciled entry have not been identified; but
since Emerson lectured once in his life at Malone, Franklin County, New York, a
small town almost on the Canadian border, it may well be that the Riders were the
people with whom he made his arrangements for that lecture. If so, the entry is a
jotting put down in 1867. For Emerson's lecture in Malone on April 26, 1867, see
Charvat, *Emerson's American Lecture Engagements*, 1961, p. 43.

[386] Plutarch, "Why the Pythian Priestess Ceases her Oracles in Verse," comparing
the opinions of Homer with those of Pindar, the author of the quoted verses. See the
Morals, 1870, III, 93. On p. [185] of his notebook Transcript Emerson correctly
ascribes the line to Pindar.

[387] Pasted into the upper left corner of p. [167] and printed here in full is a
newspaper clipping, 1.9 x 15.8 cm. Its substance ("Every moment . . . . responded.")
is a version of Daniel Webster's speech in Congress on January 31, 1834, against Silas
Wright's resolution. Webster's speech, which Emerson noted and praised on February
10, 1834 (see pp. 261–262 above) was on the removal of the deposits from the United
States Bank and is sometimes referred to under the title "The Natural Hatred of the
Poor to the Rich." See *The Great Speeches and Orations of Daniel Webster* . . . (Boston, 1879), pp. 359–361.

driven to the verge of oblivion; when I shall cease to have affection for any thing on earth; that I will believe the people of the United States will submit to be trodden, beaten down, and cajoled on such a pretence. Sir, then would they show themselves unworthy of a free Government. Then would they be slaves — *already* slaves to their own passions — trodden down at the feet of the wooden idol erected by their own hands. The poor against the rich! A monied aristocracy!! a power as great as that which was resisted at the revolution!! Go back again to the Declaration of Independence!!! I am standing here to admonish the people. I wish to admonish every industrious man, every laboring man, and every man who has a dollar, or who hopes to earn a dollar, against the fallacy and fraud of such an argument, such a detestable and abominable argument. Sir, I say to you, and to your country, that the man who has the deepest interest in a sound currency, is that man who earns his daily bread by the sweat of his brow, — who sups at night upon the earnings of his daily labor, and who rises in the morning to labor for another supper. That, that is the man, who has a deep and vital interest in a sound currency. Your capitalists may defy you; your speculators, that hungry and overreaching race, who live on the earnings of the poor; they who wish to disturb your earnings, to speculate; they will defy, nay, they will thank you! They will tell you, that you are the government for them. Give them an opportunity of thus rising on the poor man's ruin, and they will tell you it is the happiest Government that God ever blessed.

"But the man who toils, drudges and sweats for his miserable pittance, and is paid at night in rags, filthy rags, instead of money, what will *he* think? Has the country secured him what it promised? Has it given him security for his labor? His labor is property — is money. There is no interest in this country so extensive, none so imperative in its demands, as the interests of labor! labor!! labor!!! We are a laboring community. We are a community, speaking generally, who have to earn our bread by our own industry; and it was for the protection of this, for this *great object, the Constitution was formed,* and has given us the power of protecting and regulating the currency. *If we are not true to this high trust, then are we recreant and deeply false to the Constitution under which we live.*"

No language that I can give will describe the effect of the burst so imperfectly recorded here. Every heart responded.

Maine

1834

This record is as Emerson called it a "fragment" describing in part a trip from Boston to Maine that began on July 3, 1834, and ended during the month, when Emerson was called back to the city to preach the funeral sermon for his friend George Sampson. The last dated entry is July 15, and no comment on the return trip from Maine to Boston is included.

For the bibliographical description, see p. 395 below in the headnote to the notebook France and England, within which the journal Maine is laid loose.

[front cover]

Fragment of Journal in Maine
1834.

[1] 1834.

July 3, Thursday 1 o'clock left Boston in the mail coach for Portland. Arrived at Portland at 6 o'clock Friday morning 112 miles. By night Wells & Kittery looked ill enough & Col. T. ⟨o⟩said 'they would show to more advantage if the driver would put out his lights.' Left Portland at 7 o'clock & arrived in Augusta at 3 P.M. Mr George Evans M.C. was in the stage[,] a very pleasant person. At Augusta Mr Lambard & Sybil ↑&↓⟨&⟩ 5 pretty children.[1] Mrs Eveleth[,] Mrs Moody. From Portland to Augusta   miles. Speculations on the character of the two women who rode from Newbury-

---

[1] George Evans (1797–1867) was a lawyer and politician in the House of Representatives, 1829–1841, and in the Senate, 1841–1847. Emerson's first cousin Sybil Farnham of Newburyport, married a Mr. Lambard (possibly Orville D.) of near Hallowell, Maine.

port to Portland — one a beautiful young mother, the other a chatty tailor's wife seeking her husband in Portland. A vulgar edition of M[ary].M[oody].E[merson].[,] wit & natural manners ⟨with⟩ demeaned by low associations. Beauty makes all men feel as if related to it. But Nox unfriendly covered up its brightest sparkle.
Saturday morng at 7 o'clock set out for Bangor. Fine ride to Vassalboro & China. China lies pleasantly along the banks of "12 mile pond." Unity. Dixmont. Arrived at Bangor at 6 o'clock; 68 miles.

[2] July 7. Rode up the river to the Mills. Noble sight is the saw mill of ten saws — the servitude of the river. It floats the timber down; then by the application of machinery the river hauls up the reluctant log into the mill as I have seen a halibut hauled into a ship; then the river saws the log into boards; then floats the raft into Bangor; then floats the brig or ship that receives the boards onward to the Ocean. The pride of the forest — White pines of four feet diameter which it cost a hundred years of sun & rain & cold to rear must end in a sawmill at last. Every body puts out a boom from his bank on the river, one man catches firewood. Another owns an eddy & catches logs & receives a fee for keeping them. ⟨&⟩
And all men are equally interested in the ⟨chance⟩ ↑event↓ of a ⟨freshet⟩ ↑full river↓. The lawyer, the physician, the bookseller all squint at the clouds & estimate the chance of a freshet.[2] ⟨& || ... ||⟩
[3] As we sailed down the river in the steamboat the Indians who have a camp at High Head came to the shore & looked down upon the show as if their Genius looked its last.
Further down the river I saw a large white headed eagle sitting upon the bough of a pine.

[4] [blank]

[5] 8 July. Walked in the ⟨unsunned⟩ forest but found there some old acquaintances [—] the Medeola, Ur⟨i⟩aspermum, a new Pyrola, the Linnaea, Diervilla, & some unknown plants. There grows the cedar & moosewood[.] [2a]

---

[2] "The lawyer . . . freshet." is struck through with a diagonal use mark.
[2a] All the plants, common to the Boston area, are described in Bigelow, *Florula Bostoniensis*, 1824. See pp. 141, 112, 173, 241, and 89.

[July] 10. Rode yesterday with Mr W[illiam]. Emerson[3] ↑of Bangor↓ to Stillwater & Oldtown. Visited the Indian town[,] wretched people — 300 in the tribe — Neptune, an able man. Boys shot at a cent. Women all squatting on the ground — listless & filthy yet good faces. They own all the islands in the Penobscot above Oldtown, & cultivate none. Manitou's skin.

Beautiful country. The islands picturesque in this broad stream. Every body looks most affectionately at the river, for it is the source of all the present, & prophet of all the future greatness of this great Country. Every ripple is a cupid. The ideas of the people are habitually enlarged by the activity of the Creation around them. ⟨No ma⟩ The farmer said at the 4 July dinner ⟨the other⟩ last week ⟨that⟩ in allusion to the two great fires lately [6] that the city of Bangor makes no more account of losing 20 houses than his wife would of spilling a ⟨milk⟩nice pan ↑of milk↓. A man goes out & puts up a frame of a house before breakfast as an ordinary morning's work. ⟨One of⟩ ↑Two of↓ my ⁿ neighbors are ↑(is)↓ making a street directly into the woods, & Mr E[merson]. says they shall have two dollars for every one they lay out. Already they have a charter for a rail road from B[angor]. to Oldtown, & a man in the tavern was projecting a railroad from an island in the St. John's to Bangor 200 miles. Canals, sluices, dams across rivers[,] bays almost, ⟨are as familiar⟩ the owning of ⟨s⟩five or six townships of land, & the purchase & sale of great territories which neither buyer nor seller ever saw, are ⟨as⟩ familiar transactions.

[7] Mr ↑Wm.↓E. fine natural character — takes a benevolent delight in the prosperity of the country to which for 30 years he has essentially contributed, in the growth of houses like grass on every field. They say of him that when the British plundered his store in the War he told them that they might do what they would, they would not hurt his creditors, for the goods were all paid for!

[July] 15. A bird sang ↑pe pe pillory pillory pe↓ he he hickery

---

[3] William Emerson may have been a distant relative. He was a merchant who had settled in Bangor before the War of 1812. Apparently he was a bachelor living with his brother-in-law, Colonel Cyrus Goss. See *L*, III, 353n, for Emerson's later acquaintance with this William Emerson.

hickery[.] Col. Carpenter. Passage down the river to Castine & Belfast. ⟨Then⟩ Beautiful view of Bucksport coming up. It is so fine that it seems as if the houses had been built with a design for that effect. The river is so narrow that when the frigate *John Adams* came up, the ⟨studdi⟩ they came so near shore that the studding sail boom swept the branches of the trees & the sailors amused themselves with their ship going to sea in the woods.

[8] Rode over to Exeter 23 miles to visit J.B. Hill, Esq.[4] There sat my old classmate in his office with a client, — himself without coat or ⟨wa⟩ vest or neckcloth, unshaved, &, as he said, fat & rusty. He kept his countenance wondrously, & talked as of yore, & what a pile of forehead! A magnanimous man altogether incapable of pettifogging & stout hearted as of ⟨yore⟩ old; a whig in the midst of town where the tories are 300 to 30. Fine farming town, noble forest.[n] You could drive a horse & chaise in the primitive forest of hard wood, ⟨No oak⟩ so free of underwoods. No oak within 20 miles.

Death of Mr Loomis. "This year thou shalt die" was the text, & he presently fell down in the pulpit.[5] He was carried home & put into a cold room, & proper means not used to restore him. On Tuesday noon a visiter found his stomach warm, & blood oozing from the arm and his head frozen.

[4] John Boynton Hill (1796–1886), one of the twins in Emerson's college class (see *JMN*, I, 57, n.59), was a lawyer.
[5] The Reverend Harvey Loomis, who had built a new church for the First Congregational Society of Bangor in 1823, fell in his pulpit in January 1825. His text was Jer. 28:19.

PART TWO

Miscellaneous Notebooks

France and England

1833

This volume was used sporadically as a miscellaneous notebook from the time of its probable purchase in Florence on May 8, 1833, until Emerson sailed from Liverpool on September 4. The book was physically designed for accounts, as its pattern of ruled perpendicular and vertical lines indicates. Emerson used it in Italy for language exercises, in France for first drafts of important entries concerning life on the Boulevards, his reactions to the Jardin des Plantes, and a visit to the famous cemetery of Père la Chaise. All these French entries appear in expanded and revised form in the journal Italy and France. Though this notebook overlaps in time with the journal Scotland and England, its entries are not repeated there. Loose within the notebook are two other brief records of Emerson's travels, the journal Sea 1833, kept on the trip home from England, and the journal Maine, a fragmentary report of a tour to Maine during July, 1834. Since each item is basically separate from the notebook France and England, though they are found within it, they are described bibliographically here but printed under individual headnotes.

Bluish-green marbled cardboard covers measuring 19.5 x 24.2 cm and attached now to the paper within at front and back by modern tape enclose a single gathering of 40 pages lined vertically and horizontally. Ten sheets are folded folio; the leaves measure 19.3 x 24.2 cm; the pages are numbered in pencil at the top inner folds, probably by Edward Emerson. A home-made label of white lined paper measuring 12.7 x 7.4 cm is pasted on the outside cover. According to the label, written in what appears to be the script of Emerson's later years, the notebook contains a record of visits to Maine, France, and England in 1833–1834. Actually the description is inaccurate and ignores the brief journal Sea 1833 found, like the journal Maine, loose within the covers of the notebook France and England.

The first of the two inserted records found loose between the pages of the larger notebook is the journal Maine, 8 pages made of 2 sheets of letter paper folded folio, one within the other and pinned together at the left margin fold. The 2 sheets were obviously cut from a single larger sheet; the resultant leaves measure 12.2 x 20.2 cm, somewhat unevenly folded. A loose brown-paper wrapper, 12.3 x 21.7 cm, bears a title written by Emerson in ink. At one time the journal Maine was attached elsewhere by a paper clip whose marks are still visible at the top of the wrapper. No indication of such a matching impression is evident on the notebook France and England. The 8 pages are unnumbered; pagination has been supplied by the editor.

The second loose insert found within the notebook France and England is a small, untitled fascicle made of two gatherings of letter paper. Sixteen pages are of paper marked "London Superfine Satin"; the 8 leaves, measuring 11.4 x 18.7 cm apiece, were originally folded quarto and then cut at the top edge. The fold between leaves 5 and 6 is still uncut and the inner pages (10–11) remain blank. This gathering is sewed at the inner fold and then sewed again into a second fascicle of 8 pages made from one large sheet folded quarto and cut at the top. The 4 leaves so made measure 12.2 x 20 cm apiece. The pages of the whole double gathering are unnumbered; the editor has supplied the pagination. Pages 20–22 are blank; the lower right corner of the final leaf (pages 23–24) was torn away before the entry was made.

[front cover]   Visits to Maine
                          France
                          England
                    1833 — 18⟨6⟩34

[front cover verso]
           Florence, 8 May, 1833 —

       alla dispensa della Gazzetta —

                40
               ⟨4⟩50   150
               10
               10

Dans un réduit obscur dont l'amour fait un Louvre,
Le doux objet qu'on aime efface les plus beaux;
Pour les indifferens s'il a quelques defauts,
L'Amour ne les voit pas, et l'Amitié les couvre.
     Au Dépôt de Gelée de pomme de Rouen, chez MIL-LEROT, confiseur, *passage des panoramas, no 3, en entrant par le boulevard.*[1]

[1] It is as good as the original

---

[1] A clipping, 7.2 x 2.4 cm, pasted to the lower left corner of the page, apparently from a French newspaper.

⟨C'⟩ e ⟨tanto⟩ buona ⟨che⟩ ↑come↓ l'originale
Bisogna sortire per paura che sarei tentato comprarla.
5 crazie

⟨Che⟩ ↑Quali↓ sono le ⟨piu⟩ miglior⟨e⟩i gallerie di Firenze

Ennui p. 89 [2]
A⟨l⟩ questo momento il pregiudizio na⟨t⟩zionale accresceva la
↑mia↓ preoccupazione contro ↑di↓ lui. Il Signor McLeod era non
solamente agente, ma Scozzese anche; ed io ⟨aveva il⟩ ↑era di↓ parere,
che tutti gli Scozzesi ⟨erano⟩ ↑fossero↓ astuti; perciò io conchiudeva
che la sua maniera Scortese, ⟨era⟩ ↑fosse↓ affettata, e la sua franchezza,
un modo di ⟨poli⟩ astuz⟨z⟩ia piu raffinata. ⟨Dopo⟩ ⟨l⟩La colazione
finita, egli mi rendeva ⟨ragione⟩ un ⟨risguardo⟩ ↑conto↓ generale dei
miei affari; egli mi sforzava fissar ⟨un⟩ ↑un↓ giorno ⟨pel⟩ ↑per l'↓
esame dei suoi conti, e poi, senza esprimere o mortificazione o dis-
piacere alla freddezza del mio portamento, o della mia repugnanza
alla sua pre⟨z⟩senza, egli con massima tranquillità, s↑u↓onava il⟨a⟩
campanello pel suo cavallo [2][3] mi ⟨voleva⟩ ↑augurava una↓ buona
mattina, e ⟨sorti⟩ usciva[.]
A questo tempo il cortile del mio castello era riempiuto d'una
calca d⟨e⟩i ⟨supplicanti⟩ ↑clienti↓ *vestiti co⟨v⟩↑n↓* ↑gran↓ *soprabiti* quali
i tutti [n] vennero a dimandare "se ↑si↓ puo vedere la ⟨sua⟩ ↑mia↓
Signoria" o "aspett⟨ivan⟩a↑v↓o ↑per↓ dire due parole alla mia eccellenza." Nelle molte attitudini oziose, appoggiandosi alle muraglie,
o ⟨camminando innanzi e indietro⟩ ↑aggirandosi↓ avanti ↑del↓la fines-

---

[2] "Ennui p. 89" through "non ⟨e⟩ ↑sia↓ nessuno." on p. [17] is an indication of
Emerson's diligent efforts to learn Italian. He is translating Maria Edgeworth's novel
Ennui, first published in 1809 and available in many editions. Perhaps in Vieusseux's
Public Reading Rooms, called by Mariana Starke (*Travels in Europe . . .* , 1828, p.
493) the best in Italy, he found Edgeworth's *The Tales of Fashionable Life*, 4th ed.,
6 vols. (London, 1813), from volume one of which he makes his translation. Though
he includes some page references as guides he leaves out more and does not follow the
text slavishly. Further page references have been supplied in brackets. There are, as
might be expected, a good many flaws in his Italian. For the sake of the reader who
wishes to follow the translation, the English original is supplied in an appendix
(see pp. 441–445 below).
[3] Scattered on the page, and apparently written before the entry, are 24 ornate
"R's" and two small areas of short, parallel wavy lines.

tra, per ⟨prender il mio occhio, eglino⟩ ↑farsi vedere da me↓ essi, con una pazienza superando la pazienza dei cortigiani aspettavano d'ora ⟨ad⟩ ↑in↓ ora, tutto il giorno ⟨pella loro volta o pel ⟨suo⟩ loro rischio⟩ ↑per avver a vicenda la probabilità↓ d'una audienza. Io m'⟨aveva⟩ ↑era↓ promesso il piacere di vedere il mio castello questo giorno, e di fare una girata nel mio terreno; ma questo era impossibile affatto. Non era più ⟨lungo⟩ ⟨il maestro⟩ ↑padrone↓ di me o del mio tempo.

[3] "Viva ⟨lungo⟩ molto tempo ↑per↓ regnare sopra ↑di↓ noi," era il segnal⟨ato⟩↑e↓ che pel futuro dovrei vivere ⟨come un⟩ ↑da↓ principe solamente pel servizio dei miei ⟨soggetti⟩ ↑sudditi↓. Come questi ⟨soggetti⟩ ↑sudditi↓ avevano ⟨saputi⟩ ↑potuto↓ esistere per tanti anni nella mia assenza, non poteva facilmente capire, perché, dal momento del mio arrivo, pareva evidente, che, senza me, non ⟨potrebbero⟩ ↑potessero↓ vivere.[4]

Uno aveva ⟨una⟩ moglie e sei fanciulli, e ⟨nullo⟩ ↑nessun↓ pezzo ⟨in tutta la terra⟩ ↑di terra, dove potesse↓ abitar↑e↓⟨si⟩, se la mia eccellenza non ↑gli↓ permetteva ⟨lo sotto⟩[n] vivere sotto ↑di↓ me ⟨nel alcuno⟩ ↑⟨chiunque⟩ in qualche↓ piccolo angolo del mio terrene che pote⟨va⟩sse pascolare una vacca.

Un altro aveva ↑un↓ fratello imprigionato e non poteva liberarsi senza ↑di↓ me.

---

p. 92]   I miei orecchi non furono mai tanto stanchi alcuno giorno della mia vita ⟨che sopra⟩ ↑quanto in↓ questo giorno. Non avrei potuto ⟨sostenerene⟩ ↑tollerarne↓ la fatica, se non ⟨era⟩ ↑fossi↓ stato sostenuto ⟨pella⟩ ↑per la↓ nozione piacevole della mia autorità e della mia consequenza — un potere, apparentemente, quasi despotico. Questo [4] ↑nuovo↓ impulso mi sosteneva per tre giorni in cui io era tenuto prigionero di ⟨rispetto⟩ ↑stato↓ nel mio castello, ⟨pelle⟩ ↑per le↓ calche che venivano par⟨e⟩ farmi omaggio ed ⟨per⟩ ↑a↓ dimandar la ⟨protezione⟩ mia bontà e la protezione. Vanamente ogni mattina il mio cavallo con sella e briglia era menato quà è là;

---

[4] Following this paragraph are four small designs below "senza me", apparently doodling only.

non era mai permesso montarlo. La quarta mattina quando mi credeva assicurato d'aver spedito ⟨i⟩ tutti, miei tormentatori, era riempiuto ⟨col⟩ ↑di↓ ⟨attonimente⟩ stupore e ⟨colla⟩ disperazione a vedere
la mia ⟨levata⟩ sala affollata ⟨per⟩ ↑da↓ un nuovo sciame di clienti.
Io comandava /↑ai miei servitori↓/alle mia gente/ ⟨a⟩ ↑di↓ dire che
dovrei ⟨sortire⟩ ↑uscire↓ e positivamente non potrei vedere nessuno.
Credeva che non potessero capire cio che i servitori Inglesi dissero,
per che non si mossero mai. Ad una seconda ambasciata, si confessa-
vano d'aver capis↑t↓o la prima, ma dicevano, che potrebbero aspettare
finche la mia eccellenza ⟨mi⟩ ritorn⟨erobbe⟩↑asse↓ [5] dalla mia ⟨girata.⟩
↑cavalcata.↓ Con difficoltà montai il cavallo e scappai ⟨dai ordini⟩
↑⟨dogli⟩ dalle schiere↓ serrate d⟨i⟩' miei persecutori. Alla notte comandava tenere le porte chiuse e proibiva al portiere d'ammettere alcuno
⟨a sua⟩ ↑sotto propria↓ pena. Quando mi alzava, ⟨mi⟩ godeva vedere il
campo aperto, ma il momento che usci⟨ssi⟩↑va↓, eccoli! fuori della
porta⟨l'eser[?]⟩ fu posto l'esercito degli assediatori, e nella mia pianura,
e lungo le strada, ed a traverso dei campi; mi seguivano; e quando io
⟨gli⟩ proibiva ↑loro↓ accostarmi quando andava a cavallo, il prossimo
giorno ⟨gli⟩ ↑ne↓ trovava le compagnie nella imboscata che m'aspettavano nel silenzio, levandosi i cappelli, chinandosi ⟨e chinandosi⟩ ↑sem-
pre↓ ⟨finche⟩ tanto chè non potessi astenermi ⟨di⟩ ↑dal↓ dir⟨gli⟩↑loro,↓
"Ebbene, miei amici, perchè state voi di la chinandovi?" Poi io era
fatto prigionero, e la mia briglia tenuta per una ora.

In breve io trovava che ⟨ora fossi⟩ ↑allora io era↓ posto in una
situazione in cui non poteva sperare nè la solitudine nè la comodità;
ma poteva goder⟨mi⟩ dei piaceri ⟨del potere⟩ ↑dell' autorità,↓ ⟨pel⟩ ↑per
la↓ quale la mia crescen⟨da⟩te inclinazione ⟨fosse⟩ ↑era↓ stata [6] estinta
certamente fra poco tempe ⟨senon⟩ per la mia indolenza abituale se
⟨non⟩ la mia gelosia del Signor McLeod non l'avesse tenutu in vita.

Un giorno quando ↑⟨che⟩↓ io aveva rifiutato ↑di↓ [94] sentire
un importuno fittuario e aveva dichiarato ⟨che⟩ ↑di ⟨non⟩ essere↓
⟨mai⟩ ⟨fosse *stato*⟩ ↑sempre↓ perseguito dai supplicanti ⟨dacchè⟩ ↑dopo↓
il mio arrivo, e che ⟨fossi⟩ ↑era↓ stanco a⟨l⟩ morte, l'uomo rispondeva,
"E vero, signore, e ho torto a faticarla cosi; e forse dovrei andare
dal Signor McLeod; certamente l'agente farà ⟨quanto⟩ ↑altra tanto↓
bene, e dire piu non bisogna. Signor McLeod fara tutto, come ⟨e'⟩ [n]
↑al↓ solito."

"Il Signor McLeod fara tutto!" dissi, io, "Non; in nessuno conto."

p. 94   "A chi parleremo dunque?" disse l'uomo. "A me stesso," dissi io, con un ⟨aria⟩ ↑tuono↓ tanto altiero quanto quello di Luigi XIV quando egli annunziava alla sua corte la sua risoluzione d'essere ministro, da se. Dopo questa intrepida dichiarazione, non poteva [7] ⟨indulgermi nella⟩ ↑piu favorire e↓ mia indolenza abituale. Tanto il mio amore proprio era stato offeso ⟨ed⟩ ↑ed ⟨gli⟩ anche gli↓ altri sentimenti ⟨anche⟩, per la condotta del Capitano Crawley, ⟨quanto⟩ che io pren⟨dessi⟩↑si↓ la risoluzione ↑di↓ mostrare a chichessia, che io non dove⟨ssi⟩↑va↓ esser ingannato la seconda volta ⟨per⟩ ↑da↓ un agente.

Quando, al giorno fissato, il Signor McLeod veniva per saldare i suvi conti ↑⟨la⟩ ⟨ragioni⟩↓, io, con un'aria d'importanza propria, quasi ⟨io⟩ fossi solito tutta la mia vita a esaminare i miei affari, mi sedeva a vedere le carte, e dubit⟨a⟩↑i↓ chi vuole, spediva il tutto ad una sessione, senza un solo sbadiglio; ⟨amento;⟩ [n] e per un uomo che non mai avanti aveva veduto un conto, capiva la ragione di creditore e di debitore ↑a↓ mara⟨vi⟩vigli↑a↓ ⟨osamente bene⟩: ma, col mio estremo desiderio d'esibir la mia scienza aritmetica non poteva scoprir il minimo errore [n] [8] ⟨nelli ‖ . . . ‖ conti⟩ ⟨nelli⟩ ↑nei↓ conti; ed era chiaro che il Signor McLeod non era il Capitano Crawley; però prima di creder⟨lo⟩↑e↓ ⟨che⟩ ↑ch'egli ⟨po⟩ potesse↓ essere ⟨potuto tutti e due⟩ ↑ad un tempo↓ ↑ed↓ agente e ⟨onesto⟩ ↑galantico↓ uomo, io conchiudeva che se ↑egli↓ non mi ⟨d'ingannava⟩ [n] ↓defraudava↑ del mio danaro, era ⟨il⟩ suo disegno ⟨d'ingannarmi⟩ ↑il privarmi↓ del mio potere; e credendo che egli vole⟨va⟩sse essere uomo d'autorita e di consequenza nel paese, gli trasferiva istantemente i pensieri che trapassavano nel mio animo, e ⟨l⟩ considerava ↑come↓ stabilito, che questo uomo ⟨era⟩ ↑fosse↓ spronato ⟨per l'⟩ ↑dall'↓ amore del potere in tutto ↑quel↓ che faceva per ↑l↓ mio servizio.

p. 96   ⟨Fra⟩ ↑Verso↓ questo tempo mi ricordo d'essere stato turbato nel mio animo da una lettera che il Signor McLeod riceveva ⟨nelle⟩ ↑in↓ mia presenza, e /di cui/della quale/ leggeva a me solamente una porzione. Io non riposai mai [n] finchè ⟨avessi⟩ ↑non ⟨l'⟩ebbi↓ veduta ⟨la⟩ tutta. L'epistola merito bene [n] la fatica di decifrarla, apparteneva al lastricare del mio cortile da poll⟨astri⟩↑i↓. Come il Re di Prussia, ⟨chi era detto⟩ ↑del quale si diceva↓ ⟨d'esser⟩ [9] ↑che fosse↓ stato tanto geloso del potere, che voleva regolare tutti le trappole nel suo regno, io subito intreprendeva da me la condotta d'una perplessa⟨nte⟩ moltiplicità delle ⟨particolarità⟩ piccole ed inutili particolarità. Oimè! Scopriva a⟨l⟩ mio costo che l⟨a⟩' ⟨fatica⟩ ↑incomodo↓ e compagn⟨a⟩o inseparabile dell'autorità, e spesse volte nei primi dieci giorni del mio regno era pronto ⟨rendere⟩ ↑a deporre↓ la mia dignità ⟨dalla'⟩ ↑per↓ estrema stanchezza.

Una mattina di buon' ora, dopo una notte [97] febbricitante,[n] e essendo stato tormentato nei sogni dalle voci e faccie della gente che m'aveva circondato il giorno precedente, mi svegliava al suono di qualcheduno che accendeva il mio fuoco. Credeva che ⟨era⟩ ↑fosse↓ Ellinor e l'idea dell'affezione disinteressata de⟨lla⟩ questa povera riempiva il mio animo, ↑in↓ contrast⟨andosi⟩↑o↓ ⟨alla⟩ ↑con quella della gente↓ interessata ed ⟨‖ … ‖⟩ ↑avida↓ ⟨usurpante⟩ dalla quale era stato recentemente ⟨infestato.⟩ molestato.

[10] "Come sta? mia buona Ellinor" dissi io "Non ⟨vene⟩ ho veduto ⟨niente⟩ ↑da, ⟨per⟩↓ una settimána" in qua, ⟨or⟩ in poi.

Noncé Ellinor *affatto*, mio Signore, disse una nuova voce.

E perchè? Perche non accende Ellinor il mio fuoco?

Io non so, Signore mio,

Andate ⟨mandarla⟩ ↑a cercarla↓ adesso.

È ritornata nella sua casa, sono tre giorni, mio signore,

E ritornata ⟨?⟩! E'ammalata?

Io non so, mio signore; non so cosa aveva, ⟨fuorchè avesse⟩ ↑eccettuato che aveva↓ gelosia di me ⟨che⟩ ↑perchè↓ accendeva il fuoco. Ma non posso dire cosa aveva, poichè partiva senza ⟨parola, o buona o⟩ ↑dir niente ne'in bene ne'in↓ male, quando mi vedeva accender questo fuoco, il ⟨quale⟩ ↑che io↓ faceva ⟨al comando⟩ ↑per ordine↓ della casiera.

⟨A⟩Ed ora mi ricordava della richiesta ⟨di⟩ ↑della↓ povera Ellinor e m'accusava d'aver negletto ⟨a⟩ ↑di non↓ tenere la mia parola ↑in↓ ⟨da⟩ ↑⟨in⟩↓ una cosa che, ⟨da se⟩ ↑⟨per⟩↓ ↑quantunque in se↓ affare di nulla, era però [n] molto interessante [11] ⟨ad essa.⟩ per lei.

---

p. 138 ⟨Io era⟩ ↑Mi dispiaceva↓ sempre ⟨dispiacuto⟩ ↑d'↓ esser invitato a dare attenzione a qualunque ⟨cosa⟩ oggetto, pero, entrando⟨si⟩ la ⟨signorina⟩ ↑⟨damigella⟩ la dama↓ Geraldina, le⟨i⟩ dava uno sguardo involontario di⟨della⟩ curiosità. Vedeva una ⟨alta⟩ donna alta, ben formata che aveva l'aria ⟨comandante⟩ ↑imperiosa↓ d'una ⟨donna⟩ ↑dama↓ di ⟨bel grado⟩ ↑distingione↓. Ella si mosse graziosamente non colla timidità femminile ma con ↑⟨la⟩↓ facilità ⟨la⟩ prontezza e ⟨la⟩decisione. ⟨Ella⟩ Aveva be⟨gli⟩lli occhi e bella ⟨complessione⟩ ↑carnagione↓, pero ⟨nulla⟩ ↑nessuna↓ regolarità nelle fatezze. Una cosa solamente mi pareva straordinaria, la sua freddezza quando io ↑le↓ era introdotto. Ognuno appariva d'aver molto desiderio che io ved⟨rei⟩↑essi↓ la sua Signoria e che la sua Signoria ved⟨rebbe⟩↑esse↓ me; ed io era un poco sorpreso alla sua aria indifferente. Questa mi piccava e fissava la mia attenzione. Ella ↑si↓ voltava da me e cominci-ava ↑a↓ conversare con altri. La sua voce era piacevole benchè un poco forte. Non parlava coll'accento ⟨Hibernian⟩ Irlandese, ma quando ↑io↓ ascoltava maliziosamente, scopriva certo[n] [139] inflessioni[n] Hibernic⟨e⟩↑he↓; niente del volgare idioma Irlandese ma qualche cosa piu [12] d'interrogazione d'esclamazione e forse di ↑⟨della⟩↓ re↑t↓-torica che ↑non↓ trovasi nel comune discorso delle signore Inglesi, e accompagnato dalla ⟨gran'd anim⟩ molta animazione dell'aspetto e dal gesto significante; ciò che mi sembrava singolare e insolito, ma non affettato. Aveva un straordinaria eloquenza, e però le sue parole non bastavano ad esprimere i suoi pensieri, senza il anche gesto[n] ↑⟨atto⟩↓. La sua maniera era forestiera, ma non interamente Francese. Se io fossi stato ⟨compulsato⟩ ↑costretto a↓ deciderne, l'avrei chiamata piu Franc⟨h⟩ese che Inglese. Per determinar⟨la⟩↑e↓ che ↑cosa↓ fosse, io stava considerando la sua signoria con piu grande attenzione che ↑non↓ aveva mai dato ↑finqui↓, ⟨prima⟩ ↑⟨avanti⟩↓ a nessuna. Le parole "percuotente," "fascina⟨t⟩zione," "ammaliante," m'occorrevano come io la riguardava e la sentiva parlare. Risolveva ⟨avertere⟩ ↑volgere altrove↓ i miei occhi e chiudere i miei orecchi; perchè era assolu-tamente determinato di non amarla tanto paura aveva io d'un secondo matrimonio. Mi ritirava all⟨a⟩' ultima finestra, e mirava con molto serietà un fangoso vivaio. Il pranzo era annunziato.

[13] Io osservava che la dama K. aveva l intenzione di mettermi ⟨appresso la⟩ ↑accanto alla↓ sua figlia, la [140] dama Geraldina, a⟨lla⟩ tavola ↑a mensa↓; ma ↑la↓ Signora Geraldina ⟨contramminava⟩ ↑fras-tornava↓ questo movimento. Era ancora sorpreso e piccato. La sedia invidiata concessa ad ↑un'↓ altra Signora, ↑io↓ sentiva la dama Ger-aldina bisbigliar alla sua prossima, "Sconcertata, mamma!"

Era per me una cosa straordinaria, ↑il↓ sentire una picca⟨ta⟩ perchè una giovane non voleva sedersi vicino a me. Dopo pranzo ↑io↓ lasciava i signor⟨e⟩i ⟨il⟩ ↑al↓ piu presto ⟨che era⟩ possibile, perchè la loro conversazione mi faticava. Milord K. l'oratore principale era ⟨un⟩ cortigiano e non poteva parlare d'altro che ⟨il⟩ ↑del↓ Castello di Dublin e delle levate di Milord il luogotenente, cose di cui ancora ↑io↓ non sapeva niente.

Al momento che mi mostrava alle signore, era arrestato dalla officiosa ⁿ Signora Bland che non parlava d'altro che della dama Geraldina, la quale sedeva tanto distante da noi, ↑e↓ ⟨ed⟩ ↑⟨della stesso⟩↓ discorreva ↑ella stessa↓ con tanto ⁿ ⟨animazione⟩ ↑spirito↓ che non poteva udire ⟨la sua adulatorose la⟩ il ↑rac↓cont⟨ar⟩o della sua adulat⟨ose⟩↑rice↓, Signora B.

[14] Costei m'informava che la sua amica la dama G. era una donna d'abilità; veramente di tanta abilità che molte persone ↑la temevano↓ *avevano paura di essa* ma che non ↑ve↓ n⟨e⟩'era ↑⟨nulla⟩↓ occasione perchè ⟨a⟩ chiunque ⟨la⟩ ↑le↓ piaceva ⟨ella[?]⟩ nessuna sapeva meglio farsi affabile ⟨è⟩ e convenevole. Questa amica giudiziosa un momento piu tard⟨i⟩o mi diceva ⟨come un⟩ ↑in↓ gran segretezza che la dama G. ⟨fa⟩era una mima ammirabile; che sapeva fare le caricature per delineamento o per voce; e che aveva un maraviglioso talento per inventare i cognomi ⟨ed i⟩ ⟨e gli⟩ ↑ed i↓ ⟨ag⟩nomi che s'adattavano cosi ⟨applicabil⟨i⟩mente⟩ ↑esattamente↓ alle persone che non appena potevano esser ob⟨b⟩liati o perdonati. ⟨Io aveva un poco ansioso informarmi⟩ Io aveva un poco d'ansieta d'esser informato se la sua signoria ⟨m'⟩ ↑⟨m'⟩↓ onor↑er↓eb⟨b⟩e ⟨me stesso con un⟩ ↑anche me d' un↓ ⟨ag⟩nome; ⟨Non poteva imparare⟩ il che non poteva ⟨imparare⟩ ↑sapere↓ dalla Signora Bland ed aveva troppo ↑di↓ prudenza di scoprire la mia curiosità.

[15] *p. 141* Un poco di paura dei talenti della dama Geraldina ⟨faceva svegliarsi⟩ ↑teneva svegliata↓ la mia attenzione. ⟨Fra la⟩ ↑Nel corso della↓ serata la Dama K. chiamava la sua figlia ⟨alla⟩ sala di musica e m'invitava a venire a sentire un can⟨to⟩zone Irlandese. Io mi sforzava d'abzarmi e sequirla al momento; ma la dama Geraldina, benchè ⟨citata⟩ ↑⟨tra⟩↓ ↑fosse invitata↓, non ⟨s'⟩appariva. La Signora Bland accordava l'arpa ed apriva i libri di musica sul piano forte, ma non veniva la dama G. La Signora Bland era mandata indietro ed innanzi coi messag⟨i⟩gi, ma fu *l'ultimatum* della dama G. "che non

poteva cantare dalla paura del mal di denti." Mentro, Iddio sa, che la sua bocca non era stata chiusa ⟨la⟩ tutta ↑la↓ sera. "Ebbene" disse la dama K. "ma essa ↑⟨ei⟩↓ puo suonar⟨e⟩↑i↓ ↑per noi↓, non ⟨si puo?⟩ ↑è vero?↓" Non, la sua signoria temeva il freddo della sala di musica. "La prego, Milord Glenthorn, vada a dire ↑al↓la cara capriciosa che ↑qui↓ abbiamo molto caldo."

/Di mala vo⟨l⟩glia/Con gran ripugnanza/ io ↑l'↓obbediva.

[16] La dama G m'ascoltava e mi rispondeva con l'aria d'una principessa.

"Far⟨'⟩l⟨a⟩e l'onore ⟨a⟩ ↑di↓ suonare ↑per lei↓ milord! ↑Mi↓ scusa [n] ⟨mi⟩; non sono professore; — io suono tanto male che ⟨l'⟩ho per ⟨una⟩ regola di non suonare mai eccetto chè pe⟨l⟩r mio divertimento. Se vuole musica ecco la Signora Bland; essa suona a maraviglia, ed oso dire si ⟨contera⟩ ↑stimerà↓ felice d'obbligare vossignoria." Mai ⟨non⟩ non mi sentiva tanto semplice nè tanto vergognoso ⟨che a⟩ ↑quanto in↓ questo momento. "Ecco ⟨il che⟩ ↑quel che ne↓ viene", pensava ⟨da⟩ fra me, "dall'agir⟨si⟩ ⟨non da se ma dagli altri⟩ ↑fuori di carattere↓. Che m'ammaliava a sforzarmi ad invitare una donna a suonare? io, che ⟨sono stato pronto a morire di fatica⟩ ↑mi sono annojato a morte↓ della musica. Perchè mi lasciai ↑⟨feci⟩↓ ⟨esser messo⟩ ↑mandare↓ quando non ebbi ⟨nulla⟩ ↑nessun⟨à⟩↓ interesse nell'ambasciata.

Per convincerme ed altri della mia indifferenza, mi gettava sopra il⟨a⟩ sofà ⟨&⟩ e non mai mi moveva né parlava per tutto il resto della sera.

[17] Credo che ⟨appariva⟩ ↑sembrassi↓ dormire profondamente; altrimenti la dama G. non avrebbe detto ⟨in mio udito⟩ ↑a portata↓ delle mie orecchie,

"la Mamma vuole che io ⟨prenda⟩ ↑⟨leghi⟩↓ ↑cacci↓ alcuno ⟨ed essere prosa⟩ ↑e sia cacciata ⟨legata⟩↓ d↑a↓⟨'⟩alcuno; ma non ⟨fara cosi;⟩ ↑si potrà,↓ perchè, capisce, io credo che alcuno ⟨e nes⟩ non ⟨e⟩ ↑sia↓ nessuno."

[18] [5]Mezzeria or system of metayer universal in Tuscany. Much distress. Potato very recently introduced into general use

---

[5] "Mezzeria . . . francesconi." is struck through with a slightly broken X mark that may indicate its cancellation. The passage is revised and expanded in the journal Italy and France; see p. 180 above.

which is very advantageous. Straw hats. The straw is the common wheat but planted only for straw. ⟨One⟩A woman makes a hat in a week[,] Miles a thousand hats a week. An ox entering Florence pays 11 francesconi.

[19]   Paris[6]

       malatiffer
       endimancher
       malchausser
       s'orienter

[7]*Paris.* Saturday.

    13 July. Cabinet of natural history in the garden of plants. How much finer things are in composition than alone. When I got into the ornithological chambers I wished I had come ↑only↓ there ⟨alone⟩. The ⟨coloured⟩ fancy coloured vests of those elegant beings make me as pensive as the hues & forms of a cabinet of shells formerly. It is a beautiful collection & makes ⟨you⟩ ↑one↓ as calm & genial as a bridegroom. The limits of the possible are enlarged & the ⟨tr⟩ real is stranger than the imaginary. Some of the birds have a fabulous beauty. One parrot of a fellow, called Psittacus erythropterus, from New Holland, deserves as especial mention as a picture of Raphael in a Gallery. He is the beau of all birds. Then the ⟨Trochili⟩ hummingbirds how little & how gay; the least of all is the Trochilus niger. I have seen beetles larger. The Trochilus pella hath such a neck [20] of gold & silver & fire! The Trochilus Delalandi from Brazil is a glorious little tot.   ⟨mouche magnifique⟩ Then I marked among the birds of Paradise the Manucode or Paradisaea regia from New Guinea
the Paradisaea Apoda
& the Paradisaea rubra
Forget not the Veuve à epaulettes or Emberiza longicauda, ↑black↓ with its fine shoulder ornaments

[6] "Paris malatiffer . . . s'orienter" is in pencil.
[7] "*Paris* . . . naturalist.' " on pp. [19]–[21] is struck through with an X mark, which may mean cancellation in view of the reworking and use of the passage in the journal Italy and France; see pp. 198–199 above. The material forms the basis for part of "The Uses of Natural History," *Lectures,* I, 8–10.

nor the Ampelis Cotinga
nor the Phasianus Argus a peacock looking pheasant
nor the Trogon pavoninus called also Couroncou pavonin.

I saw black swans, & white peacocks, the *ibis*[,] the sacred & the rosy, the Flamingo with a neck like a snake, the Toucan rightly called rhinoceros, & a vulture that would make your flesh quiver to meet in a wilderness. He looked like an executioner.

[21]   Le moment ou je parle est deja loin de moi[.] [8]

Cabinet of Anatomy
The skeleton of the Balena looks like the frame of a schooner turned upside ⟨n⟩down.

amber [n] with musquitoes within, ⟨pieces of quartz⟩ grand blocks of quartz. ⟨gold⟩ native gold in all its forms of crystallization & combination[,] threads, plates, crystals, dust; & silver black as from fire. Ah this is benevolence, this is philanthropy, this is wisdom, this is taste to form a cabinet of natural history. ⟨A s⟩ Many students were there & a class of boys with their books, & tutor.

You are impressed with the inexhaustible gigantic riches of nature. The Universe is a more amazing puzzle than ever, as you look along this bewildering series of animated forms [—] the hazy butterflies, the carved shells, the birds, beasts, insects, fishes, snakes, & the upheaving principle of life every where incipient in the very rock aping organized forms. Not a form so grotesque, so savage, nor so beautiful but is an expression of some thing in man the observer. An occult relation between the very scorpions & man. I am moved by strange sympathies. I say continually, 'I will be a naturalist.'

[22] "M. Andrieux se faisait entendre à force de se faire écouter." [9] —

[July][10] Walk along the Boulevards here & see how men live. One man has live snakes crawling round him & sells soap & essences.

---

[8] See *Œuvres complètes de Boileau*, 1872, II, 163, Épitre III, à M. Arnauld . . . . See p. 199, n.74, above.

[9] Apparently a well-known comment since it is included by the *Nouvelle Biographie générale* (Paris, 1859), II, 607, in its article on Andrieux, explaining his ability to make his feeble voice heard.

[10] "Walk along . . . four legs" is struck through with a single diagonal use mark. The passage is reworked in the journal Italy and France; see pp. 197–198 above.

Another man has books lying on the ground for sale. Another carries watchchains. Half a dozen beseige me every day with ⟨canes to sell⟩ an armful of canes. A little further on one man sells cane tassels at 5 sous. Next sits Boots brandishing his brush at every dirty shoe that walks by. Then several great tubs of gold fish. Another sits at his table cleaning gold & silver spoons with emery & descanting ⟨aloud & always⟩ upon its merits. Another has a little table of card puppets which he makes crawl. Then a hand organ. Then a wooden figure which can put an apple in its mouth whenever a child buys an almond. Then a flower merchant. Then a ⁿ ⟨aviary⟩ ↑birdshop↓ with perhaps twenty parrots, four swans, hawks, & nightingales. Then the exhibition of the boy with four legs[.]

[23] Sunday, 28 July. I attended service this morng in Westminster [11] Abbey & heard the bishop of Gloucester preach. Under my feet was writ on the pavement R[ober]t. South 1716, Music[.] [12] P.M. Went to St James' Church. On ⟨the⟩ ↑a↓ gravestone in the yard I read the names of Susanna Shakespear & John Shakespear dead in 1815 & 1823.

31 July — At ⟨M⟩Dr Bowring's — Milton's house — inscription on the wall, "Sacred to Milton, the Prince of Poets." Talleyrand said of Bentham, Pillé par tout le monde il reste toujours riche or something like it.[13] Mackintosh, Brougham, Stanley, Althorp[.] [14]

5 Aug.[15] This morn I went to Highgate & called at Dr Gillman's

[11] Emerson has later overwritten the very faint "in" of "Westminster" in heavier black ink. The entry is in very faint, almost illegible light ink.

[12] Dr. James Henry Monk (1784–1856), made Bishop of Gloucester in 1830, and Robert South (1634–1716), notable controversialist and preacher, who is apparently being remembered for his youthful publication *Musica Incantans* (1655).

[13] See Dr. John Bowring, ed., *The Works of Jeremy Bentham*, 11 vols. (Edinburgh, 1843), XI, 75 for the anecdote. Volume XI, separately entitled *Memoirs of Bentham*, is a life by Bowring, who was Bentham's literary executor.

[14] Though Emerson knew Mackintosh and Henry, Lord Brougham, best by their writing, the listing here is apparently of political figures, since it includes Edward John Stanley of Alderly (1802–1869), an English liberal who had entered Parliament in 1831, and John Charles Spencer Althorp (1782–1845), chancellor of the Exchequer in the Whig government in 1830.

[15] The entry for August 5 on the visit to Coleridge is used in detail in *English Traits*, W, V, 10–14, but no use mark appears on this page of the entry.

& sent up a note to Mr Coleridge requesting leave to see him. He sent me word that he was in bed but if I would call after 12 o'clock he would see me. I named one o'clock. At one I called & he appeared, a short thick old man with bright blue eyes, ↑black suit & cane,↓ & any thing but what I had imagined[,] a clear clean face with fine complexion — a great snuff taker which presently soiled his cravat & neat black suit. He asked me if I knew Allston [16] & then launched into a discourse upon his merits & doings when he knew him in Rome[,] ↑how Titianesque he was, &c.↓ Then upon Dr Channing & what an unspeakable misfortune to him it was that he should have turned out an Unitarian after all. Thence he burst into a long & indignant declamation upon the folly & ignorance of Unitarianism[,] its high unreasonableness   (*turn over two pages*) [17]

[24] Size of Paris   population
rents
Abbe Chatel 40,000 fr.   pathetic circumst. of a new Ch.[18]
Cafés

[July] 15.[19] Pere le Chaise. It well deserves a visit & does honour to the French. But they are a vain nation. The tombstones have a beseeching importunate vanity. They remind you of advertisements. But many are affecting. One which was of dark slate stone had only this inscription; *Mon Pere*. I prefer the "Ci git" to the "⟨i⟩Ici repose" but I thought the *classics* rather carried the day[,] take the cemetery through. One inscription was singular enough. "Ici repose Auguste Charles Collignon, mort plein de confiance dans la bonté de Dieu, à l'age de 68 ans et 4 mois, le 15 Avril, 1830. Il aima et chercha ⟨d⟩ à faire du bien, et mena une vie douce et heureuse en suivant, autant qu'il

---

[16] Coleridge had known and admired the American painter Washington Allston, who was in Rome, 1805–1808. Allston had said of the friendship, "To no other man do I owe as much intellectually as to Mr. Coleridge . . . ."

[17] The entry is continued on p. [26].

[18] "pathetic . . . Ch." is enclosed at the left by an irregular bracket. Abbé Chatel, the founder of a new church, "L'Église Catholique Française," paid an annual rent of 40,000 francs for his Chapel in the Rue St. Honoré; see p. 203 above.

[19] "Pere le Chaise" through "de ton semblable." on p. [25] is struck through with diagonal use marks, perhaps to indicate its assimilation and reworking in the journal Italy and France. See pp. 200–201 above.

put, la morale et les lecons des essais de Montaigne, et des Fables de la Fontaine."

Every where the French write as in the above '*Here lies Augustus*' &c. & we write '*Here lies the body of*' &c[,] a more important distinction than *roi de France* & *roi des Francais*.

[25] On one tomb was writ, L'Ange de la mort veille dans cette enceinte,

Mortel, respect le dernier azile [asile] de ton semblable.

There are many magnificent monuments. ⟨General Foy's⟩ That erected to General Foy by his fellow citizens is conspicuous. I saw the tomb of Benjamin Constant, & those of several of Buonaparte's Marshals; Suchet[,] Lefeb[v]re[.]

> "When one by one those ties are torn
>   And friend from friend is snatched forlorn
> And man is left alone to mourn
>   Ah! then how easy 'tis to die." [20]

[26][21] & took up B[isho]p Waterland [22] which lay (laid there I think for the occasion) upon the table & read me with great vehemence two or three pages of manuscript notes writ by him in the fly leaves, passages too which I believe are in the Aids to Reflexion.

As soon as he stopped a second to take breath, I remarked to him that it would be cowardly in me, after this, not to inform him that I was an Unitarian, though much interested in his explanations. Yes, he said, I supposed so[,] & continued as before. He spoke of the wonder that after so many ages of unquestioning acquiescence in the doctrine of St Paul[,] the doctrine [of] the Trinity[,] which was also

---

[20] Mrs. Barbauld, "A Thought on Death," ll. 9–12. Emerson had given *The Works of Anna Laetitia Barbauld with a Memoir by Lucy Aiken* [ed. J. P. Dabney], 3 vols. (Boston, 1826) to his mother. The volumes are still in his library.

[21] The material on pp. [26]–[31], the continuation of the report on the visit to Coleridge, is struck through with heavy vertical use marks in pencil: used in *English Traits, W*, V, 10.

[22] Daniel Waterland (1683–1740) was the author of treatises against Arianism and Deism and, as a champion of Trinitarianism against the heresies of Dr. Samuel Clarke, the author of *A Vindication of Christ's Divinity*, 2nd ed. (Cambridge, 1719). Coleridge wrote on him in what were then, as Emerson remarks, manuscript notes — "Notes on Waterland." See *The Complete Works of Samuel Taylor Coleridge*, ed. Shedd, 1853, V, 404–426.

according to Philo Judaeus the doctrine of the Jews before Christ —
this handful of Priestleians should take upon themselves to deny it
&c. Very sorry that Dr Channing a man to whom he looked up —
no,[n] to say he looked up to him, would be to speak falsely, — but
a man whom he looked *at* with so much interest should embrace such
views. But when he saw Dr C he hinted to him that he was afraid
he loved Christianity for what was lovely & excellent [—] he [27]
loved the good in it & not the true. And I tell you sir that I have
known many persons who loved the good, for one person who loved
the true. But it is a far greater virtue to love the true for itself alone
than to love the good for itself alone. He knew all this about Unitarianism perfectly well because he had once been an Unitarian & knew
what quackery it was. He ⟨was⟩ ↑had been↓ called the rising Star of
Unitarianism. Then he expatia⟨ta⟩ted upon the Trinitarian doctrine
of the Deity as being Realism [n] &c &c, upon the idea of God not
being essential but super essential &c, upon trinism & tetrakism, upon
the *will* [n] being that by which a person is a person because if he
should push me in the street & so I should force ⟨a⟩the man next me
into the kennel I should at once exclaim to the sufferer 'I did not do
it sir,' meaning it was not done with my will. &c &c — I insisted that
many Unitarians read Mr Coleridge's books with pleasure & profit
who did not subscribe to his theology[.]

[28] He told me that if I should insist on my faith here in
England & he should insist on his, his would be the hotter side of
the fagot.

I asked about the ⟨passage⟩ ↑extract↓ in the Friend; [n] he said it was
from a pamphlet in his possession entitled the Protest ⟨as⟩of one of
the Independents [23] or something to that effect. I said how good it
was. Yes, he said, the man was a chaos of truths, but lacked the knowledge that God was a God of Order. But the passage no doubt would
strike me more in the quotation than in the original for he had filtered
it. I rose to depart & he said, I do not know whether you care about
poetry but I will mention some verses I lately made upon my baptismal anniversary & he recited with great emphasis, standing, ten

[23] The passage in *The Friend*, 1818, III, 70–77, is cross referenced on the back
cover recto of Emerson's copy with the entry "English Independent's Tract, p. 70" and
is repeatedly marked in the margin.

or twelve lines that were very interesting.[24] Then he alluded to my ⟨journ⟩ visit to Malta & to Sicily & compared one place with the other repeating what he said to the Bp of London when he returned from that country[:]

[29] That Sicily was an excellent place to study political economy; for in any town there, it was only necessary to ask what the government enacted & reverse that to know what ought to be done. It was the most felicitously opposite course to every thing good & wise. There were only three things which the govt brought on that garden of delights, viz. ⟨i⟩Itch, Pox, & Famine. Whereas in Malta the force of law & mind was seen in making that barren rock of Semi Saracen inhabitants, the seat of population & plenty. Going out, he showed me in the parlour Alston's picture, & told ⟨tha⟩me that Montagu the famous picture dealer once came to see him & the moment he laid eyes upon this said "Well you have got a picture" thinking it a Titian or a Paul Veronese. Afterward as he talked with his back to the picture the said Montagu put up his hand & touched it & exclaimed "By —— this picture is not ten years old!" so intensely delicate & skilful was that man's touch.

[30] I asked if he had had any correspondence with Marsh[;] [25] he said No for he had received his book or letter at a time when he was incapable of any effort & soon should send him some new books [n] & asked if I had seen his Church & State. He begged me to call upon Mr Alston from him & present him his regards. And so I left him wishing him renewed health.

But I have put down the least part of the conversation or rather discourse of Mr C. I was in the room an hour & much of the discourse was like so many printed paragraphs in his book, perhaps the same; not to be easily followed.

[31] Almost nobody in Highgate knew his name. I asked sev-

[24] Emerson expanded this memory somewhat in *English Traits, W,* V, 13, adding a report of the first line of the baptismal verses, "Born unto God in Christ — "; Coleridge first printed the sonnet in 1834 in *Friendship's Offering* under the title "My Baptismal Birthday." The first line of the poem then read, "Born unto God in Christ — in Christ, my All!"

[25] James Marsh, president of the University of Vermont and American editor of Coleridge's *Aids to Reflection*, 1829. Emerson knew the long "Preliminary Essay" to that volume well.

eral persons in vain[;] at last a porter wished to know if I meant an elderly gentleman with white hair? 'Yes, the same' — Why he lives with Mr Gillman. Ah yes that is he. So he showed me the way.

Dr Bowring says that Wilson & Hogg [26] went to see Wordsworth & the morning was fine & then there was a rainbow & altogether it was genial. So Hogg said to Wordsworth this is a fit spot for poets to meet in. Wordsworth drew himself up with ineffable disdain saying *"Poets* indeed!"

Mr Highmore

"Her was not corked yesterday"

[32]Matlock; Tuesday ev.g 9 o'clock Aug. 13.

Beautiful valley! esteemed the most romantic dell in England. Here sit I ⟨aga⟩ close by the Derwent, & under the eaves of the caverns of ⟨the⟩ the Peak of Derbyshire. — But it will not do, to visit even these fine things alone. I think I must not stay to visit even Haddon Hall & Chatsworth[.]

Pleasant it was to me to spend yesterday with Mr Dewey [27] in such a visit. How reared himself old Kenilworth into the English morning sky. The ruin is as lordly as was the perfect state. I thought if I had a boy to educate I would carry him by moonlight into the inner floor of the Lancaster building. It would doom him a poet. The smell of the fresh ground, the cellar smell in a hall so princely as Leicester's was tragical. "The hall of Cyndyllan is gloomy this night   Wanting fire wanting candle." I will weep awhile & then be silent.[28]

[26] John Wilson (1785–1854), who as "Christopher North" was a well-known Scottish critic and poet. For years (1822–1835) he had furnished the "Noctes Ambrosianae" to *Blackwood's Magazine*. James Hogg (1772–1835), known as the "Ettrick Shepherd," was a poet of rural scenes and people.

[27] Orville Dewey, Emerson's kinsman, who was pastor at New Bedford and in whose church Emerson had often preached.

[28] William Owen, trans. "Elegy on Cynddalan ap Cyndrwyn," *The Heroic Elegies and other Pieces of Llywarç Hen* . . . (London, 1792), pp. 77–78, st. 18, slightly misquoted. The final line of the stanza may be an afterthought since it is not included within the quotation marks. The stanza actually reads:

"The hall of Cynddylan is gloomy this night,
Without fire, without bed —
I must weep a while, and then be silent!"

The passage is used in "Traits of the National Genius," *Lectures*, I, 240. Emerson

↑The visit to↓ Warwick Castle is a proper appendix to the visit to Kenilworth for Warwick is what Kenilworth was. It overhangs the Avon.

In the interim betwixt these two visits we went to St Mary's Church & saw "our Lady's Chapel"[.]

[33] In this day's ride I marked that the botany of England & America are alike. The clematis, the mints, the golden rods, the gerardias, the wild geranium, the wild parsley, & twenty more better known to my eye than to my ear [—] I saw & recognized them all. I passed through Tamworth & saw the tower & the town & thought up the old jingle of my school days

> "Largess Largess Lord Marmion
> They hailed him Lord of Fontenaye
> of Lutterworth & [Scrivel] bay
> of Tamworth tower & town." [29]

We passed through Ashby de la Zouch & I saw the ruin of the old Castle. We crossed the Trent[;] we came to Derby. We see throughout Europe the counterparts of the Americans. I passed Sir Robert Peel's place, then Sir Richard Arkwright's. ⟨It can scarcely be felt what are the emotion.⟩ ⟨It can not be known how deeply the hour of that thought ‖ . . . ‖ the hours of what ‖ . . . ‖⟩ [30]

[34] 21 July.[31] Sunday. Arrived in London & landed at the Tower Stairs. Took lodgings immediately at Mrs Fowler's[,] 63 Russel Square. Went into St Paul's where service was saying. Poor Church.

> Westminster Abbey
> St Stephen's
> Haymarket

---

may well have run across this passage not in Owen but in Scott's *Rokeby* (1830), which as note LIV printed this stanza among the twelve there included.

[29] Sir Walter Scott, *Marmion*, I, 11. The arrangement within the stanza is modified. Emerson is actually quoting l. 13 first and then ll. 7–9.

[30] From "be known" to the end of the cancellation, not only simple cancellation but very elaborate circular overwriting in an attempt at concealment is evident.

[31] The entry overlaps a similar one in the journal Italy and France, pp. 204–205 above, which also describes Emerson's arrival in London on Sunday, July 31, 1833.

Mr Irving's Chapel [32]
Gallery of Practical Science
London University
Zoological Gardens
Regent St
Atheneum
Westminster Church. St James
⟨St Jo⟩ Mr Fox's Chapel [33]
Wilberforce's funeral [34]
Regent's Park
Immense city. Very dull city.
British Museum
Mr Coleridge
Dr Bowring

[35] Left London on Friday Morng 9 July [August] for Oxford.
    [August] 10. Birmingham
       Sunday 11.
             12. Kenilworth & Warwick
             13. Matlock
             14. Haddon Hall, Bakewell, Sheffield
             15. York
             16. Newcastle, Berwick, Edinburgh
             17.
      S. 18.
             19.
             20.
             21. Leith, Stirling, Doun, Callender

[32] The Reverend Edward Irving (1792–1834) was a celebrated preacher and a friend of Carlyle. He was ejected from his church in Regent Square by his presbytery in 1832 but he continued to preach in his chapel in Newman Street, often in "tongues," like the early Christians at Pentecost.

[33] The Reverend William J. Fox (1786–1864), noted Unitarian preacher, radical political figure, and owner of *The Monthly Repository* after 1831. He preached at the South Place Chapel.

[34] William Wilberforce (1759–1833), philanthropist and Parliamentary member from Hull who was famed for his labors toward the abolition of the slave trade. His funeral in July, 1833, was attended by a vast crowd.

    22. Loch Katrine, Loch Lomond, Inversnaid, Glasgow
    23.
    24. Dumfries
S. 25.
    26. Carlisle
    27. Penrith, Keswick, Ambleside
    28. Kendal
    29. Lancaster, Burton, Manchester, Liverpool
    30.
    31.
S. [September] 1.
    2.
    3.
    4. Sailed for New York

[36]³⁵ I don't think that we are yet masters of all the reasons why we should cultivate it. Nat. Magic good for society, a diffused taste in Nat. science good in a higher degree to the cultivators[:]

    1. in the knowledge it communicates ↑pump. nat. steam engine. ship. boundaries↓

    ⟨2 in the effect upon the character⟩

  ⟨3⟩2. in the explanation it gives of moral truth
       ↑shells. symbols.↓

    3. in the effect upon the character
       It makes the intellect exact[.]   brazier ³⁶
       It makes the manners simple. makes all boys.
       It generates enthusiasm[.]

↑4↓ ³⁷ Salutary to the body. Antaeus.
    Higher questions. Beauty. How old is the pebble[?]
    "Is it true?"
    Nat. hist. of Water. of Coal.

---

³⁵ Probably the entry comes after Emerson's return to Boston where he is beginning to work out lectures on Water, Natural History, and the relation of the human being to science. The notes are connected especially with the matter in "The Uses of Natural History," *Lectures*, I, 5–26.

³⁶ "brazier" is circled.

³⁷ The "4" is inserted in pencil, possibly by Edward Emerson.

It makes every natural event a scientific experiment as a snow-storm[.]

Compare an orrery with the solar system to see how beautiful is nature. Her ropes never entangle nor crack nor wear nor weigh. They are invisible[.] So the magnet.[38] Simplicity of the means. Bees fanning themselves, *earth-worms*[.]

Good for the body
Good for the knowledge it communicates
Good in its effect upon the mind & character
Explains moral truth

[37] *The Saxons.* "The infant state of this people when the Romans first observed them exhibited nothing from which human sagacity would have predicted greatness. A territory on the neck of the Cimbric Chersonesus & three small islands contained those whose descendants occupy the circle of Westphalia, the Electorate of Saxony, the British Islands, the United States of ↑N↓ America, & the British Colonies in the two Indies." *Turner* [39]

Elementary ⟨construction⟩ forms of bodies revealed by polarization of light[.]
Elective affinities
Polarity of matter. light. electricity. ⟨heat.⟩ galvinism. magnetism

[40][40] ⟨Non⟩ avrei dovuto visitar[.]
Io ⟨doveva aver visitate⟩ parecchii amici, ma non l'ho fatto[.]
Io dovrei visitar i parecchi[.]
Io dovrei ⟨pagare⟩ ↑far↓ ⟨le⟩ parecchie visite che non ho fatto.

Mi ⟨a⟩farebbe molto piacere vederla spesso[.]

Venite ↑a↓ vedermi ⟨tanto⟩ ↑⟨piu⟩↓ spesso ⟨che⟩ ↑quanto↓ potete[.]

[38] Following "magnet" is an undeciphered word which appears to be of four letters in a strange combination of Gothic printing and script.

[39] Sharon Turner, *The History of the Anglo-Saxons*, 2nd ed., 2 vols. (London, 1807), I, 39.

[40] The last three pages, [40]–[38], are written as Italian exercises from the back forward. They are therefore upside down and in reverse order and are printed in the order of composition, reading from p. [40] through p. [38].

Si venga a vedermi ⟨quanto⟩. spesso quanto ⟨pu⟩si puo.

Il mio amico vuol copiare questa pittura. Che gli bisogna fare per ottenere la permissione?

Yes, I thought as much[.]
Si, ⟨l'aveva creduto⟩ credeva altrettanto. ↑Io↓ Aveva cosi creduto[.]

Ci sono molte facilità ⟨pelli⟩ ↑per gli↓ artiste di qui[.]

By & by. One of these days — in a little while in breve; un di questi giorni — fra poco tempo [39] Tutti e due

---

↑Il↓ Principe ⟨dei⟩ Corsini
⟨c⟩to *board*, stare a dojjina   ire
Speak out, speak plainly, don't mutter so
Parlate chiaro, parlate distintamente, non brontolate cosi

Posso capirla se parla ⟨piu⟩ un poco piu ⟨lentamente⟩ ↑adagio↓.

> God does with us, as we with torches do,
> Not light them for themselves[.] [41]

Era trattenuto ⟨lun⟩ piu a lungo che non m'aspettava.
Non ⟨vieni⟩ ↑venni↓ fuori si presto ⟨quare⟩ come m'aspettava[.]
Mi piace molto Firenze   Come posso io partire
When you are at leisure
Quando è in comodo   Sta bene qui

[38] "Lo prega, è vero, di non dir nulla a nessuno."
             I promessi sposi [1827] vol 1 p 273

L'imperatore Carlo V ha detto che quante piu lingue parla un uomo, tanto piu e uomo.[42]

---

[41] To the left and below the couplet, half-surrounding "Not" is an ink scribbling in a semi-rectangle formed of small straight lines. The verse is from Shakespeare, *Measure for Measure*, I, i, 33–34 with "God" in place of "Heaven."
[42] This saying, usually attributed to the Emperor Charles V, is normally given

Il canto degli angelli.

bramo molto il [43] sentire ↑cantare↓ il ros⟨s⟩ignol⟨e⟩o ⟨cantare⟩

persiane

imposte

di gran lunga la maggior parte dei ⟨cr‖ . . . ‖citori⟩ dotti Inglesi ↑⟨send[?]⟩↓ non capiscono a fondo la loro lingua.

ha spiegato carattere

Quando vuol darmi una seduta pel suo ritratto?

How do you like Florence[?]

Come le⟨i⟩ piace Firenze?

It is cold. Fa freddo.   ⟨egli⟩ fa ↑egli↓ freddo

Have you a cheaper edition   a cheaper sort

fluently

    Vorrei una specie di scarpi di minore valore a miglior⟨e⟩ mercato

[inside back cover] [44]

Florence	Triviglio
Fontebuona	Castano
Monte Carelli	Cascina de Pecchi
Pietra mala	Milan
Filigare	Ro
	Cascina d Corde
	Sesto Calende
Bologna	Arona
	Baveno
Tedo	Vogogna
Capo d'Argine	Domo d'Ossola
Malalbergo	Isella
Ferrara	Villagio del Sempione

---

as "Quot linguas calles, tot homines vales." — "You are worth as many men as you know languages." Emerson cites it in English in Journal A, p. 304 above.

[43] The word is half-covered by an ink blot, apparently an inadvertence rather than a cancellation.

[44] Written vertically between the two columns and extending from the line beginning "Ponte di Lago Scuro" to "Padua" below is the name "Emerson", written twice, and "Em", twice. The writing is scrawled clumsily in heavy ink as though inscribed with the left hand.

Ponte di Lago Scuro	Briga
Polesella	⟨S Maurice⟩
Arqua	⟨Ai⟩
Battaglia	Sion
Rovigo	
Monselice	Martigny
Padova	
Dolo	S Maurice
Mestre	
Venezia	Aigle
Mestre	Villeneuve
Dolo	Vevay
Padua	Lausanne
Slesega	
Vicenza	Geneva [45]
Montebello	
Caldiero	
Verona	
Castelnuovo	
Desenzano	
Ponte San Marco	
Brescia	
Ospitaletto	
Chiari	
Antignate	
Caravaggio	

[45] The list of names is the itinerary of Emerson's post stops from Italy to France arranged in double columns, each column to be read from top to bottom.

Pocket Diary 2

1 8 3 3

This pocket memoranda and date book was purchased in London during the summer of 1833 and kept sporadically from July 21 until October 5 to record appointments, addresses, accounts, and miscellaneous notes.

Bound into a red leather cover with a tab end that fits into a slot, the notebook was printed in London as one of "Ruffey's Improved Series of Pocket Books" and is titled "The Polite Repository for 1833." The face of the outer cover measures 8 x 11.8 cm. A brown paper label inscribed "1833. x" is pasted to the spine. The inner notebook was originally glued to the leather cover; it is now loose within the enclosing wallet. Paste-down end-papers in front and back have come loose from both the cover and the notebook. They are used for entries as is the recto of the engraved frontispiece. Following the frontispiece is a title page with a blank verso, a table of contents with a printer's notice on the verso, both unnumbered but included in the sequence of pagination, and on pages 3–15 a printed selection of essays, poems, and information as follows: an essay, "Margaret of Anjou at the Tomb of Duke Humphrey," pages 3–6; a poem, "The World we have not seen," page 7; descriptions: "Berry-Pomeroy Castle, Devonshire," page 8; and "Thurlmere Lake, Cumberland," page 9; poems: "Music: a Fragment," pages 10–11; "The Mother to her Infant," page 11; "May," page 12; essays: "On Chemical Attraction," pages 13–14 and "The Mocking Bird," pages 14–15; "A List of Bankers," pages 16–31; "Holidays Kept at Public Offices," page 31; colleges and officers of the universities of Oxford and Cambridge, page 32. Pages 33–57 are unnumbered but included in the sequence of printed pagination. Page 33 is a lined page for "Memorandums." Pages 34–57 are lined and dated for daily entries throughout the calendar year. Dates in the text followed by the abbreviations for a day are printed calendar dates rather than dates in Emerson's hand. Pages 58–70 are unnumbered and designed for monthly and total account entries; pages 71–81 are headed "Memorandums"; pages 82–135 are numbered and contain the following useful information for the traveler: a list of the names of members of the Parliament; a list of officers of the departments of government; an abstract of the voting laws; a list of the baronets of England; international exchange tables; tax information; a brief London directory; regulations for hackneys and fares; tide and water transportation tables; a list of London bankers and stocks; university dates; tables for reckoning interest and commercial stamps; information on English and European royalty; tables of weights, measures, and astronomical data. Pages 137–

139 are end-papers, used for entries. Emerson uses only 22 pages in the volume for his entries. Material in the notebook is normally written in columnar form because of the size of the page. It is printed here in running order unless the column is useful to clarify Emerson's meaning. Pages are listed as blank if they carry no entry by Emerson.

[inside front cover]¹ 3/.6 — Richd Dawson, Rebecca Dawson, Ann Thomas, J. H. Henley, Jno Hudson, Robt Johnston, F H Pattison, C S Malet, Edwd H. Greathed, E Robbins, W Ward, Peter Richd Kenrick

[frontispiece recto]²   R. W. Emerson

     74.01
     71.30 at 3 p.m. 5 Oct.
     ————
     2.31
         30 25
         30 30
         30 35

Ἀνδρῶν τε παντων Σοκρατες σοφωτατος³

[1]–[46] [blank]

¹ The entry for the page is in pencil. "3/.6" is apparently the bookseller's price mark in his hand; the list of names in columnar form is Emerson's record of his fellow passengers aboard the *New York*, Captain Hoxie, which sailed from Liverpool on September 4 and docked in New York on October 7. The full passenger list given by *The New-York Commercial Advertiser*, October 8, 1833, p. 2, col. 6 is: "Rev. P.R. Kenrick, of Dublin; Rev. R. W. Emerson, Boston, Mass.; Capt. C.S. Malet, 8th Reg. Br. army; Lt. Edw. H. Greathed, do.; R. Dawson and Lady, Ireland; Mrs. Ann Thomas, Doncaster, Eng.; J.H. Henley, Esq. Dublin; John Hudson, New York; R. Johnston, Augusta, Ga.; F.H. Pattison, Glasgow; E. Robbins, Charleston, S.C.; W. Ward, New York — and 15 in the steerage."

² Beneath what is evidently a calculation for the latitude and longitude on October 5 and the Greek quotation is a sum "46 x 2 = 92"; upside down under a heavy cross line is "à Monsieur Frumfredèvi[?], vestvenipoel Londres". All entries on the page are in pencil except for Emerson's signature. The French address is not in Emerson's hand.

³ "Of all men living Socrates most wise," the oracle of the Pythian priestess concerning Socrates. See Diogenes Laertius, *Lives of Eminent Philosophers*, II, 37.

[47][4] 21 July Su At Mrs F[owler]'s Russel[l] Square
          22 July M Rec'd letters
          23 July T Mr John Stuart Mill
          24 July W Mr Wiggin [5]
          25 July Th Westminster Abbey & House of Commons
          26 July F St Paul's
          27 July S Court of Chancery
          28 July Su Westminster Abbey
[48]   11 August Su Birmingham
          12 August M Kenilworth Warwick Castle
          13 August T Matlock
          14 August W Haddon Hall
          15 August Th York Minster
[49]   23 August F Glasgow
          24 August S Mosgill, Nithsdale, Buccleugh Ben [?]
          29 August Th To Liverpool from Manch[ester] 90 m[inutes]
in 1 hour 21 miles: 31 [miles], 1 hour 25′

[50]–[57] [blank]

[58] Mr E requests the privilege of waiting on Mr W. at such hour
as Mr W may find most convenient to thank him for [6]

[59] ⟨Matthews & Polly Middle Row Holborn⟩
Mrs Wiggin, Mr Mill, Zoological Gardens, Lloyd's, British Museum
Tuesday Ev.g
          Dr Bowring Queen St
          T. M Brewer
          E S Gannett [7]

---

[4] The dates here and on the following page are not in Emerson's hand but are
printed in column under the month. The entries are penciled on the line beside each
date. The itinerary is incomplete; for the full list of Emerson's travels between London and Liverpool see L, I, 393–394.
  [5] Mr. Wiggin was apparently a friend of the Emerson family in London, for
Edward Emerson in a letter of August 16, 1833, recalls to Waldo that he had dined
with Mr. Wiggin in 1826 and been hospitably treated.
  [6] The incompleted entry is in pencil, as are the cancellation and list of names
written in column. The appointments are apparently for Tuesday, July 23.
  [7] Ezra Stiles Gannett (1801–1871) was an early member with Emerson in the

[60]–[62] [blank]

[63] Mr Wood desires copies of "Sunday School Addresses" [8] &
"Bible Stories"[.]

[64] [accounts omitted]

[65]–[70] [blank]

[71] 29 [July] ⟨Zoological Gardens.⟩ Coliseum
       Mr Saxton, Mr Carpenter [9]
       Mrs Brown 267 Regent
       ⟨Mr Wiggin⟩
       ⟨Mr Mill.⟩
       Longman, Rees, Hurst [10]
       The tailor

30 [July] Tomorrow Dr Bowring, British Museum, Mrs Brown

[72]   Lumley Chancery Lane
    Ben Johnson 6 vols 15/

---

club without a name at Harvard, later colleague pastor of Dr. Channing at the New
South Church (Federal Street Church). He organized the American Unitarian Society
in 1824.
   [8] On November 10, 1830, Emerson spoke of Francis Wayland's excellent sermon
on Sunday schools, "Encouragements to religious effort: a sermon delivered at the request of the American Sunday School Union, May 25, 1830" and later included in
Anniversary Sermons delivered at the request of the American Sunday-School Union
(Philadelphia, n.d.) pp. 3–36 (see *JMN*, III, 208). Other so-called Sunday school
addresses with which he may have been familiar are: (a) N. Parker, "Address, May,
1820 to the teachers of the South Parish S.S. Portsmouth" [1820]; (b) B.B. Wisner,
"Benefits and Claims of Sabbath Schools," sermon of January 17, 1830, Boston; (c)
E.S. Gannett, "Address before the Boston Sunday School Society on their 50th
Anniversary, Sept. 14, Boston, 1831."
   [9] Dr. Lant Carpenter (1780–1840), a prolific writer and noted Unitarian minister, was for many years pastor at Exeter and then at Bristol. Bowring wrote of him:
"for many a year I deemed him the wisest and greatest of men" (*Autobiographical
Recollections of Sir John Bowring*, London, 1827, p. 43).
   [10] The English publishing firm which in 1826 had taken over sole ownership of
The Edinburgh Review. Thomas Norton (1771–1842) took Owen Rees into partner-
ship and then in the 1820's, with new partners, the firm became actually Longman,
Rees, Hurst, Orme, Brown, and Green.

Wotton		4/6
Plutarch's Morals		
Mackintosh		
Alcoran		2/6
Cicero	10	20/ [11]

[73]–[75] [accounts omitted] [12]

[76] A[lexander] Ireland. [13] No 37 South Bridge St Edinburgh.

Perkin's experiment on air in Trans. of Royal Soc. 1826 [14]

[77] 2 Oct. At noon Lat. 41.13
         Long. 63.36

         Going alway
         By night & by day
         Under starlight under clouds
         With swimming deck & singing shrouds

[11] The books purchased in London were probably:
(a) *The Works of Ben Johnson*, 6 vols. (London, 1716); only 5 volumes remain in Emerson's library. Volume 2 is missing.
(b) *Reliquiae Wottonianae or a Collection of Lives, Letters, Poems*, 4th ed. (London, 1685).
(c) *Plutarch's Morals*, 5 volumes of the "Several Hands" edition (London, 1718), still in Emerson's library.
(d) Sir James Mackintosh: probably *England*, vol. 1 (Cabinet Cyclopaedia of Dionysius Lardner), London, 1830–1832.
(e) Alcoran. No edition of the Koran is listed in the record of Emerson's library.
(f) Cicero — there are several editions of Cicero in Emerson's library. Perhaps the one involved here is *The Familiar Epistles of M. T. Cicero* . . . (London, 1640).
[12] The omitted petty cash accounts cover traveling expenses from Matlock, August 14, through Bakewell, Sheffield, York, Newcastle, to Edinburgh. On p. [74] the accounts continue for August 16–22 from Berwick through Loch Lomond. On p. [75] the accounts are carried through August 30 and the arrival at Liverpool.
[13] Alexander Ireland, staunch friend and biographer, author of *Ralph Waldo Emerson. A Biographical Sketch* (London, 1882), served as Emerson's guide in Edinburgh during his visit there, August 16–21.
[14] Volume 116, Pt. III, pp. 541–548: "On the progressive compression of water by high degrees of force . . . ."

[78]–[79] [blank]

[80] Indicio Pylium, Genio Socratem, Arte Maronem, Terre tegit,
Populus moeret, Olympus habet Populus.[15]

Stay passenger, why goest thou by so fast?
Read if thou canst whom envious death has placed
Within this monument; Shakespear, with whom
Quick Nature died; whose name doth deck this tombe
Far more than cost; sith all that he hath writ
Leaves living art but page to serve his wit
    Ob.t A. D. 1616, aet 53 [16]

[81] Rev. W. J. Fox, West Stamford Grove
      Upper Clapton [17]

[82][18]–[136] [blank]

[137] [...] [19]

[138] Dumfries, 24 Aug[us]t. ⟨As I stopped⟩ As ⁿ the coach stopped
at the King's Arms the guard pointed out to me a man standing on
the doorstep who was Robert Burns[,] the son of Robert Burns.
There ⁿ was nothing striking in his appearance & yet I perceived
some resemblance to the points of his father's head. I bid the waiter
after dinner conduct me to the monument of Burns. We passed the
house in which his widow, now 80 years old, lives; quite a small
tenement. On his tomb is no inscription but his name. I asked the
sexton's boy who ⟨attended⟩ ↑admitted↓ me,ⁿ Who Burns was? "A

---

[15] "By title Nestor, by genius Socrates, by skill Virgil — earth protects these, the
people mourn these, Olympus holds these" (Ed.).

[16] The noted inscription, slightly misquoted, from Shakespeare's monument on
the north chancel wall of the parish church at Stratford.

[17] See p. 414, n.33, above.

[18] Page [82] contains a printed listing of the House of Peers. Beside the printed
material Emerson has penciled "424", apparently his count of the number in the
House. On p. [90] is printed the list of members of the House of Commons. Here at
the top of the page is the penciled note: "Am. H. R. 215. 30 000 send 1 representative" and a half-bracketed count of the number in the House of Commons, "658".

[19] Omitted is a penciled division of the House of Peers giving the number of
royal dukes, archbishops, dukes, marquises, earls, viscounts, and barons.

ploughman." & what else? "A maker of poems." Did he ever hear any of his songs? "Ay"

This was all I could get.

[inside back cover] [20] Carlyle said, to see her was like looking at King Agamemnon.

N.Y. to Prov[idence]. 220 miles. Shortest passage made by the steamboat Providence thirteen hours.

Shortest of the Boston 14 h 28′

[20] The entry is in pencil. Between "Agamemnon" and "N.Y." is a note on laundry or clothes purchase, a multiplication of 9 x 18, and running down the center through and under the final entry a column of addition coming to 424, which is another set of figures on the composition of the House of Peers, including the count as given on p. [137] and adding the number of Bishops (24), of Peers of Scotland (16), and of Peers of Ireland (24).

Composition

1 8 3 2 ?

A topical rather than a miscellaneous notebook, this fragmentary compilation is culled largely from two journals, Blotting Book III (see *JMN*, III) and Q. The passages from 1831 to 1832 listed under rhetoric and laws of composition in the index which Emerson appended to Blotting Book III are all entered in this notebook, ranging in date from July 8, 1831, to January 7, 1832. Besides these fourteen passages Emerson lifted seven or possibly eight entries from Journal Q. These passages were originally entered in the journal between March 30 and mid-December, 1832. Since this notebook includes none of the extensive remarks on rhetoric entered in Journal A in April, 1834, and apparently nothing from the portion of Journal Q written after the European travels, it seems probable that Emerson compiled these notes on rhetoric late in 1832, though his citation from a volume of Ben Jonson, apparently one purchased in London, may tend to shift the date of compilation to the fall of 1833.

The uncovered, home-made notebook is composed of 12 sheets folded folio into a single gathering sewed from the outside into the middle fold between pages 24 and 25. Of the original 24 leaves, one (leaf 7 composing pages 13–14) has been roughly torn out, leaving only a narrow stub; five other leaves are partially mutilated or torn away; of these ten mutilated pages, 2 are blank, 8 have partial entries. Pages within the notebook measure 16.3 x 19.9 cm. Perhaps because no protective cover exists, the outer sheet of the volume is torn so that the front and back leaves are no longer conjugate. Pagination exists in ink only for pages 2, 3, 6, 7, 8, 10, and 11. Further pagination has been added by the editor.

[1]   Contra
Dt ¹   ⟨|| . . . ||⟩   Cr.

Laws of Composition
    Crystallization   Jan. 7, 1832.²
    Secrecy   Goethe ³
    No choice. Self abandonment to the truth ⟨of things⟩ makes
words things[.] ⁴
    ↑all the length of all the veins It shall be given thee in that
hour what to say[.]↓⁵

    Method of Shakspear ⁶

    Heat   fusion of thought. perfect flexibility ⁷
    When rhymes cease to be rudders & become perfect rhymes and
perfect sense ⁸   every thought is myriad faced. The best thoughts
have been best expressed. The ⟨reign⟩ ↑age↓ of Words

   ¹ The page is ruled in ink into columns, apparently for debit and credit accounts.
   ² In an entry dated January 7, 1832, in Blotting Book III (*JMN*, III, 316)
Emerson developed an extensive analogy between the process of crystallization within
the mind and the same process within minerals.
   ³ Emerson is later to link Goethe often to the idea of secrecy, especially in the
phrase "the open secret" of the universe which he drew from Carlyle (see p. 87
above) and which he had read in five essays from Carlyle's pen by the end of 1832.
   ⁴ Cf. *JMN*, III, 270–271 for the entry of July 8, 1831, and the note inserted
on October 27 on the earlier entry: "No man can write well who thinks there is any
choice of words for him." "In good writing words become one with things." The
jotted note is expanded, pp. 431–432 below.
   ⁵ This inserted passage has not been located in any earlier journal. For "It shall
be . . . to say." see Matt. 10:19, slightly misquoted.
   ⁶ Cf. Blotting Book III, October 27, 1831: "His poetry never halts, but has what
Coleridge defines Method, viz. progressive arrangement." See *JMN*, III, 299.
   ⁷ The phrases are notes on Herbert's style which are developed below (see p. 432).
The material, originally drawn from Blotting Book III (*JMN*, III, 284–285), was
later used in "Ben Jonson, Herrick, Herbert, Wotton," *Lectures*, I, 350.
   ⁸ Cf. Butler's *Hudibras*, I, i:
        "Rhyme the rudder is of verses
        With which like ships they steer their courses."
Emerson had cited the couplet in Blotting Book Psi, February 28, 1830. See *JMN*,
III, 182.

Examples of the moral sublime [9]
Each man's subject [10]

"Action comes less near to vital truth than description" Plato [11]

[2]

Bonus orator bonus vir [12]

Who would write heroic poems should make his life a heroic poem. [13]

The blundering rhetorician seeks in the ⟨tones⟩ rising & falling inflexions, or in the gestures of Cha||tham|| or Adams, or in the circumstances of the par||ties|| present or concerned, the electricity that lay only in the breast of Chatham & Adams, *Pectus est disertum et vis mentis.* [14]

Patrick Henry's speech full of religion [15]

"The Prometheus is the grandest poetical conception that ever entered into the heart of man. Critics talk most about the visible in sublimity, the Jupiter, the Neptune. Magnitude & power are sublime but in the second degree, managed as they may be. When the heart is not shaken, the gods thunder & stride in vain. True sublimity is the perfection of the pathetic

---

[9] The jotting refers to an entry for July 21, 1831, in Blotting Book III (*JMN*, III, 274–275) which lists examples of the moral sublime from Young, Shakespeare, and Bacon.

[10] The note is apparently a reference to an entry in Blotting Book III, November 3, 1831 (*JMN*, III, 303) on finding the subject for each hour or for life.

[11] See *JMN*, III, 314, for Emerson's first citation of this comment from Plato's *Republic*, V, 473. See p. 261, n.39, above for the history of his use of the quotation.

[12] "A good orator, a good man" (Ed.). The Latin tag appeared in Journal Q, May 23, 1832; see p. 25 above.

[13] From an entry in Journal Q for October 28, 1832, Emerson is quoting a paraphrase by Carlyle of a passage in Milton's "Apology for Smectymnuus"; see p. 54 above.

[14] A shortened version of a passage from Quintilian's *Institutio Oratoria*, X, vii, 15, "Pectus est enim, quod disertos fecit, et vis mentis" — "For it is feeling and force of imagination that makes us eloquent." Emerson had cited the quotation twice in Journal Q. See pp. 10 and 16 above. The whole passage ("The blundering . . . mentis.") is lifted and slightly paraphrased from its earlier appearance in the entry for April 2, 1832, p. 10 above.

[15] See the entry for August 11, 1832, in Journal Q, p. 34 above.

which has other sources than pity, — generosity, for instance, & self-devotion." Landor Vol 3. p 205 [16]

[3] [17]Do you say that a mechanic must attend to language & composition? [n] You are looking the wrong way & seeking the source in the river. Strong thinking makes strong language. Correct thinking correct speech.

Write always to yourself, & you write to an eternal public.

[18] I never read Wordsworth without chagrin [—] a man of such ⟨great⟩ powers & equal ambition, so near to the Dii Majores, — to fail so meanly in every attempt. A genius that hath epilepsy — a deranged archangel. The ode to Duty, conceived & expressed in a certain high severe style, does yet miss of greatness, & of all effect, by such falsities or falses, as, "And the most ancient Heavens through thee are fresh & strong," — which is throwing dust in your eyes, because they have no more to do with duty than a dung cart has: so that fine promising passage about the Mountain winds being free to blow upon thee, flats out into "me & my benedictions." [4] If he had cut in the dictionary for words he could hardly have done worse.

[19] 'Rob Roy' excellent, much happier diction than ordinary. Poet's epitaph, fine account of him;

[16] The quotation from "Duke de Richelieu, Sir Fire Coats and Lady Glengrin," in Landor's *Imaginary Conversations*, 1st ser., 1828, was lifted from the entry for September 17, 1832, in Journal Q. See p. 44 above.

[17] The paragraph, struck through with a wavy diagonal use mark, is copied verbatim from the entry of October 14, 1832, in Journal Q (see p. 51 above) and is repeated and struck through with a use mark in pencil on p. [11] of this compilation. There, however, it is not printed.

[18] The following paragraph is drawn with very slight variations from the entry of December 1, 1832, in Journal Q. See p. 63 above.

[19] The following passage on Wordsworth through "by being pondered." on p. [5] is drawn with slight variations and omissions from the entry of November 18, 1831, in Blotting Book III. See *JMN*, III, 305–307. Coleridge's tribute to Wordsworth in *The Friend* (see *The Complete Works*, 1884, II, 169) Emerson quoted not only in the entry above but partially in the entry for July 21, 1831, which he drew upon earlier for examples of the "moral sublime." See above, p. 429. The passage may be translated, "whom, as often as I read, I seem to hear, not words, but thunder" (Ed.).

'You must love him ere to you
He will seem worthy of your love'

'Content to enjoy
The things which others understand.'

but miserable is this last verse. Sublime is the severe eternal strain of "Dion." What they say of Laodamia were better said of this that it might be read to heroes & demigods in Elysium. 'The Happy Warrior.' Almost I can repeat Coleridge's compliment 'quem quoties lego non verba mihi videor sed tonitrua audire'. His noble distinction is that he seeks the truth & shuns with brave self denial every image & word that is from the purpose; means to stick close by his own thought, & give it in naked simplicity, & so make it ⟨g⟩God's affair, not his own, whether he shall succeed. But he fails of executing this purpose fifty times for the sorry purpose of executing a rhyme, in which he has no skill; or from imbecility losing sight of his thought, or from succumbing to custom in poetic diction, e.g. the inconsistency with his own principles in the two lines about the Thunderer's eye & the Cestus[.] Vol 3 p 27

[5]²⁰ Almost every moral line in his book might be framed like a picture, or graven on a temple porch, & would gain & not lose by being pondered.

[6] ↑8 July↓

No man can write well who thinks there is any choice of words for him. The laws of composition are as str⟨ai⟩ict as those of sculpture and architecture. Th‖msm‖ [7] as well as for the bard. Then I may freely apply the words beautiful, grand, sweet[,] for whatever is true

---

²⁰ The leaf for pp. [5]–[6] is torn out except for a narrow stub on the inner margin and a strip about two inches wide at the top of the leaf. On p. [5] the entry, a continuation of the comment on Wordsworth, seems to be complete and no remnants of any writing appear on the stub; but the entry for p. [6] is apparently mutilated by the tear since letters are visible on the stub. The remnant of the entry for p. [6] is struck through with a use mark and was drawn verbatim from Blotting Book III (see *JMN*, III, 270–271). Since p. [7] carries on an approximation of the same entry — the insertion of October 27–28, 1831 — one may conjecture that the missing material might be supplied from Blotting Book III.

of thought is true of the poem. It is adamant. Its reputation will be slow but sure from every caprice of taste. No critic can hurt it; he will only hurt himself by tilting against it. This is the confidence we feel concerning Shakspear. We know that his record is true. This is the ordeal which the new aspirant Wordsworth must undergo. He has writ lines that are like outward nature [—] so fresh, so simple, so durable [—] but whether all or half his texture is ⟨so durable⟩ as firm I doubt[.] [21]

Every composition in prose or verse should contain in itself the reason of its appearance. So should every sentence. It should be born alive — a lively oracle that will preserve its own memory in the world until actions express it better. But thousands of volumes have been [8] written & glitter in libraries of which this reason is yet to seek — does not appear. Then comes Adam Smith, Bacon, Burke, Milton[,] then comes any good sentence & its apology is its own worth. It makes its own pertinences.

Thomas Campbell's ↑new↓ verses about the Poles are alive. Most of the Pleasures of Hope has no life.[22]

Herbert's thought has so much heat as actually to fuse the words so that language is wholly flexible in his hands, & his rhyme never stops the progress of the sense. And in general according to the elevation of the soul will the power over language always be, & lively thoughts will ⟨break out into⟩ ↑enforce for themselves↓ spritely verse. No metre so difficult but will be tractable so that you only raise the temperature of the thought. To this point I quote [9] gladly my old gossip Montaigne "For my part I hold & Socrates is positive in it That whoever has in his mind a spritely & clear imagination he

[21] The preceding entry, probably a continuation of material from mutilated p. [6], is struck through with a vertical use mark. The passage is drawn with slight variations from the entry of October 28, 1831, in Blotting Book III. See *JMN*, III, 271.

[22] Except for "So should . . . better." the material in the two preceding paragraphs is drawn with only slight variations from the entry of August 16, 1831, in Blotting Book III. See *JMN*, III, 280. "Then comes any good sentence . . . worth.": used in "Ben Jonson, Herrick, Herbert, Wotton," *Lectures*, I, 349.

will express it well enough in one kind or another & though he were dumb by signs." Verba quae praevisam rem non invita sequentur. (Horace) Cum Res animum occupavere verba ambiunt. Seneca. Ipsae res verba rapiunt. Cicero

> "Prose Poets like blank verse;
> Good workmen never quarrel with their tools."
> > Byron [*Don Juan,* I, cci]

> "O how that name inspires my style
> The words come skelpin rank & file
> > Amaist before I ken!"
> > > *Burns* ["Epistle to Davie," ll. 141–143] [23]

A man's style is his mind's voice. Wooden minds have wooden voices.[23a] Truth is shrill as a fife[,] various as a panharmonicon.

[10][24] Therefore it is some presumption in favor of the argument which is couched in a manly & rich expression. The best patriots in Congress are the best speakers. *transferred*

'When you sit down to write, the main thing is to say what you have to say.' *Guesses at Truth* [1827, I, 248]

Indignatio facit versus. *transferred* [25]

---

[23] The preceding paragraph from "Herbert's thought" and the two quotations from English verse are struck through with vertical use marks in pencil. The use-marked material is drawn, almost verbatim, from the entry for September 15, 1831, in Blotting Book III (see *JMN,* III, 284–285); the Latin citations are all in Montaigne, on the same page of Emerson's copy of *The Essays,* 1693 (I, 261). Cotton's English for the passages is as follows: Horace — "When once a thing conceiv'd is in the Wit,/ Words soon present themselves to utter it." Marcus Annaeus Seneca — "When things are once form'd in the Fancy, Words offer themselves in muster." Cicero — "The things themselves force Words to express them."

[23a] "Wooden minds . . . voices." is paraphrased from the entry for June 2, 1832, in Journal Q, p. 27 above.

[24] Except for the final entry on the page, the quotation from Sidney which is written, perhaps as an addition, in ink differing in color from the other entries, each entry is struck through with a short diagonal use mark in pencil. The word "transferred" which is starred after the first and third entries is in pencil. The citation from *Guesses at Truth* is copied from the entry of October 28, 1831, in Blotting Book III. See *JMN,* III, 271 and for a slightly shortened version, p. 315.

[25] The actual Latin from Juvenal's *Satires,* I, 79, is "facit indignatio versum" — "indignation will prompt my verse." Emerson had cited this passage, probably earlier than in this entry, in Blotting Book II, p. [7] and Encyclopedia, p. [81].

"Look in thy heart & write" Sir P. Sidney.

["Astrophel and Stella," Sonnet 1, l. 14]

[11] [...] [26]

People sometimes wonder that persons wholly uneducated to write, yet eminent in some other ↑sort of↓ ability should be able to write language with so much purity & force. But it is not wonderful. The manner of using language is surely the most decisive test of intellectual power & he who has intellectual force of any kind can scarcely conceal it there. For that is the ↑first &↓ simplest vehicle of mind, is of all things next to the mind, & the vigorous Saxon that uses it well is of the same block 'adamas ex vetere rupe' [27] as the vigorous Saxon that formed it & works after the same manner.

[12] [blank]

[13]–[14] [torn out] [28]

[15] One is daunted by every one of a multitude of rules which he reads in books of criticism but when we speak or write unconsciously, we are carried through them all safely, without offending or perceiving one.

[16] I have nothing to do now with that other class of wretched speakers who frequent pulpits. The proper rhetoric for them would be to join a spelling class and not call 'Providence' *Pravilence* nor

[26] The whole page is struck through with a vertical use mark in pencil. Omitted from the text are four sentences written above on p. [3] and copied a second time here. The rest of the entry is drawn with slight variations from the entry for January 11, 1832, in Blotting Book III. See *JMN*, III, 319.

[27] Emerson apparently remembered this quotation from Sir Thomas Browne's *Hydriotaphia* rather than looking it up either in Blotting Book Psi (see *JMN*, III, 219) where he had entered it on December 29, 1830, or in Browne's *Tracts* (London, 1822), from which he had originally quoted it. The version he had entered in Blotting Book Psi read, "Adamas de rupe veteri praestantissimus" — "a most excellent gem of the old rock" (Ed.).

[28] All pagination after p. [12] is supplied by the editor. The leaf on which pp. [13]–[14] should be carried is torn out leaving only a narrow stub in the inner margin. A few beginning strokes of letters are visible on the stub of p. [13]; p. [14] was apparently blank.

'God' *Gard* nor 'merciful' *massiful*. There must be the presence of
the soul to every ⟨a⟩ word: especially in this act. & mispronunciation
& these ⟨horrid⟩ outrages upon common euphony intimate the absence
of the soul.

———————

Only once or twice in a lifetime can a man want the words "dire"
or "tremendous."
The forms of strengthening a statement are commonly weakening it.
Vehemence is feminine.

Men know what a dead ninepin or a spent ball is but a dead word
they confound with a true one.
Thus, "to perpetrate a poem," or to speak of a "scathing rebuke,"
or "a scorching rebuke," each of these was good once, but have been
used up long ago[.]

[17]²⁹ In poetry, do not use the compounds of "less" if they
be verbs; as, 'tireless,' 'fadeless,' 'swerveless.'

[18] Still the objection to these speculations remains that the
most important part of Rhetoric is that which cannot be taught[,]
which every one must learn ↑by↓ himself, & which cannot part from
his consciousness. Certain moods of mind arise in me which lead me
at once to my pen & paper, but which are quite indescribable: and
these attend me through every sentence of my writing, & determine
the form of every clause, yet are these muses quite too subtle &
evanescent to sit for their portraits.

[19]³⁰ a||msm||
pres||msm||
do just||msm||
to his own, ||msm||
would serve Go||msm||

²⁹ The entry on this page ("In poetry . . . swerveless.' ") is struck through with
a diagonal use mark.
³⁰ The leaves for pp. [19]–[22] are mutilated by being torn off from the upper
inner margin to the middle of the outer edge. Page [19] bears the beginnings of five
lines of writing; p. [20] is blank except for "ded" (not reproduced), the apparent
end of a word in the upper inner margin; p. [21] has the beginnings of five lines of
comment; p. [22] is blank.

[20] [torn]

[21] Theobald rea||msm||
To write *soul*||msm||
base blank vers||msm||
Johnson's Irene, ||msm||
just criticism in ||msm||

[22] [torn and blank]

[23]-[33] [blank]

[34]

————————

Orators magnify & micrify.

————————

————

The ocean overpeering of his *list*
Eats not the flats with more impetuous haste
Hamlet [V, v, 99-100]

————

"O God I could be bounded ⟨by⟩ ↑in↓ a nutshell & count myself a
king of infinite space; were it not that I have bad dreams."
Hamlet [II, ii, 260-262]

————

trade & navigation of Roxbury Ditch [31]

so that my arrows
Too slightly *timbered* for so loud a wind
[*Hamlet*, IV, vii, 21-22]

————

his guilt unkennel in one speech
[*Hamlet*, III, ii, 85-86, misquoted]

————

Montague said Commend &c

[31] Cf. the anecdote which Emerson tells in full in "Art and Criticism," *W*, XII,
301: "When Samuel Dexter, long since, argued the claims of South Boston Bridge,
he had to meet loud complaints of the shutting out of the coasting-trade by the proposed improvements. 'Now,' said he, 'I come to the grand charge that we have
obstructed the commerce and navigation of Roxbury Ditch.'" The story is told to
show that all things have two sides, or two handles.

And more he would have said; & more he spoke
which sounded like a cannon in a vault, ⟨that⟩
That might not be distinguished
　　　　　　Hen VI Pt III [V, ii, 40–45, misquoted]

[35]–[38] [blank]

[39] [torn and blank]

[40] ‖msm‖oth.
‖msm‖, yet cannot
‖msm‖age,

[41] [blank]

　　[42] There is a kind of negligent grandeur in some old English
verses, often translated verses, that much takes me. Let me set down
some specimens[;]
　　"This mighty power of mind he dying had."
Lucan lib 8[636]
ap[ud] Montaigne [32]

　　　　　　　　　　Where the Athenian Youth
　　　The famed foundations of their freedom laid [33]

　　　Tho' blind a mighty boldness in his looks
　　　　　　　　　　　Pope & M M E [34]

<hr />

　　[32] What seems to be a bracket or a half parenthesis is in the left margin beside the
citation. In Emerson's copy of *The Essays*, 1700, II, 64, the Latin — "Jus hoc animi
morientis habebat" — is given first and then the translation is quoted in a note.
　　[33] Plutarch used the lines, originally from Pindar, both in the *Lives* and in the
Morals. Emerson may have known the Langhorne version in the "Life of Themistocles":
　　　　　　" 'Twas then that Athens the foundation laid
　　　　　　Of liberty's fair structure."
See *Lives*, 1811, II, 13. But here as elsewhere he found the Several Hands translation
of the *Morals* to his taste. He is quoting here from "Concerning Such Whom God is
Slow to Punish"; see the *Morals*, 1870, IV, 150.
　　[34] The line of Pope's "The Temple of Fame" (l. 186), which Mary Moody
Emerson had revised, originally read, describing Homer, "Tho' blind, a boldness in
his looks appears."

[43]-[44] [blank]

[45] "It was requisite, said Gen. Jackson, to frame a law coextensive with the embarrassments which it recognizes." [35]

False use of the words

                  Graphic (right use B. Jonson Vol. 1, p. 9) [36]
                  Moiety
                  terrible

Vulgar confounding of set & sit
                      lie & lay
                      shall & will
He don't for he does n't

[46]   *Choice of Words.*
            man that can so much command
         His *blood* & his affection   B. Jonson [37]

Behaviour Behaved

[47] [blank]

[48] [38] ||msm||, know
||msm|| ⟨tory of England vol. 1 p.⟩

---

[35] The unlocated quotation is used again later in Journal B.

[36] In *The Works of Ben Johnson in Six Volumes* (London, 1716), a set of which Emerson bought in London and brought back with him in 1833, the word *graphic* in "Upon Sejanus," I, 9, is used as follows: "And through thy Subject woven her graphick Thred." In "Art and Criticism," *W*, XII, 293, Emerson gives his own definition of the word: "the adjective *graphic*, which means *what* is *written*, graphic arts and oral arts, arts of writing, and arts of speech and song, — but is used as if it meant *descriptive*: 'Minerva's graphic thread.' "

[37] Cf. *Every Man out of his Humour*, I, i, 2–4:
    ". . . but, Stoic, where, in the vast world,
    Doth that man breathe, that can so much command
    His blood and his affection?"

[38] On the final leaf an inch and a half is torn away at the top. The remnant of the mutilated entry is struck through with a use mark. An irregular brace half encloses the partial and canceled bibliographical note, which is possibly a reference to Hume's *History of England*, a work which Emerson had known since borrowing it from the Boston Library Society in September 1822.

Appendix

Textual Notes

Index

Appendix

Excerpt from Maria Edgeworth's novel, *Ennui*, which was translated into Italian by Ralph Waldo Emerson in his notebook France and England. The edition used was *The Tales of Fashionable Life*, 4th ed., 6 vols. (London, 1813). The excerpt begins on page 89.

Upon this occasion, national prejudice heightened the prepossession, which circumstances had raised. Mr. M'Leod was not only an agent, but a Scotchman; and I had a notion that all Scotchmen were crafty: therefore I concluded, that his blunt manner was assumed, and his plain-dealing but a more refined species of policy.

After breakfast, he laid before me a general statement of my affairs; obliged me to name a day for the examination of his accounts; and then, without expressing either mortification or displeasure at the coldness [90] of my behaviour, or at my evident impatience of his presence, he, unmoved of spirit, rang for his horse, wished me a good morning, and departed.

By this time my castle-yard was filled with a crowd of "great-coated suitors," who were all *come to see — could they see my lordship?* or *waiting just to say two words to my honour.* In various lounging attitudes, leaning against the walls, or pacing backwards and forwards before the window, to catch my eye, they, with a patience passing the patience of courtiers, waited, hour after hour, the live-long day, for their turn, or their chance, of an audience. I had promised myself the pleasure of viewing my castle this day, and of taking a ride through my demesne; but that was totally out of the question. I was no longer a man with a will of my own, or with time at my own disposal.

"Long may you live to reign over us!" was the signal, that I was now to live, like a prince, only for the service of my subjects. How these subjects of mine had contrived to go on for so many years in my absence, I was at a loss to conceive; for, the moment [91] I was present, it seemed evident that they could not exist without me.

One had a wife and six *childer*, and not a spot in the wide world to live in, if my honour did not let him live under me, in any bit of a skirt of the estate that would feed a cow.

Another had a brother in jail who could not be *got out* without me . . . .

[p. 92] Never were my ears so weary any day of my life as they were this day. I could not have endured the fatigue, if I had not been supported by the agreeable idea of my own power and consequence; a power seemingly next to despotic. This new stimulus sustained me for three days that I was kept a state-prisoner in my own castle, by the crowds who came to do me homage, and to claim my favour and protection. In vain every morning was my horse led about saddled and bridled: I never was permitted to mount. On the fourth morning, when I felt sure of having dispatched all my tormentors, I was in astonishment and despair on seeing my levee crowded with a fresh succession of petitioners. I gave orders to my people to say that I was going out, and absolutely could see nobody. I supposed that they did not understand what my English servants said, for they never stirred from their posts. On receiving a second message, they acknowledged that they understood the first; but replied, that they could wait there [93] till my honour came back from my ride. With difficulty I mounted my horse, and escaped from the closing ranks of my persecutors. At night I gave directions to have the gates kept shut, and ordered the porter not to admit any body at his peril. When I got up, I was delighted to see the coast clear: but the moment I went out, lo! at the outside of the gate, the host of besiegers were posted, and in my lawn, and along the road, and through the fields; they pursued me when I was on horseback; the next day I found parties in ambuscade, who laid wait for me in silence, with their hats off, bowing and bowing, till I could not refrain from saying, "Well, my good friend, what do you stand bowing there for?" Then I was fairly prisoner, and held by the bridle for an hour.

In short, I found that I was now placed in a situation where I could hope neither for privacy nor leisure; but I had the joys of power: my rising passion for which would certainly have been extinguished in a short time by my habitual indolence, if it had not been kept alive by jealousy of Mr. M'Leod.

[94] One day, when I refused to hear an importunate tenant, and declared that I had been persecuted with petitioners ever since my arrival, and that I was absolutely tired to death, the man answered, "True, *for ye,* my lard; and it's a shame to be troubling you this way. Then, may be it's to Mr. M'Leod I'll go? Sure the agent will do as well, and no more about it. Mr. M'Leod will do every thing the same way as usual."

"Mr. M'Leod will do every thing!" said I hastily: "No, by no means."

"Who will we speak to then?" said the man.

"To myself," said I, with as haughty a tone as Lewis XIV. could have assumed, when he announced to his court his resolution to be his own minister. After this intrepid declaration to act for myself, I could not yield to my habitual laziness. So much had my pride been hurt, as well as my other feelings, by Captain Crawley's conduct, that I was determined to show the world I was not to be duped a second time by an agent.

When, on the day appointed, Mr. M'Leod came to settle accounts with me, I, with an [95] air of self-important capability, as if I had been all my life used to look into my own affairs, sat down to inspect the papers; and, incredible as it may appear, I went through the whole at a sitting, without a single yawn; and, for a man who had never before looked into an account, I understood the nature of debtor and creditor wonderfully well: but, with my utmost desire to evince my arithmetical sagacity, I could not detect the slightest errour in the accounts; and it was evident, that Mr. M'Leod was not Captain Crawley; yet, rather than believe that he could be both an agent and an honest man, I concluded, that if he did not cheat me out of my money, his aim was to cheat me out of power; and fancying that he wished to be a man of influence and consequence in the county, I transferred to him instantly the feelings that were passing in my own mind, and took it for granted, that he must be actuated by a love of power in every thing that he did apparently for my service.

96 [95] About this time I remember being much disturbed in my mind, by a letter which Mr. M'Leod received in my presence, and [96] of which he read to me only a part: I never rested till I saw the whole. The epistle proved well worth the trouble of deciphering: it related merely to the paving of my chicken-yard. Like the King of Prussia *, [Edgeworth's note: * "Mirabeau — Secret Memoirs."] who was

said to be so jealous of power, that he wanted to regulate all the mouse-traps in his dominions, I soon engrossed the management of a perplexing multiplicity of minute insignificant details. Alas! I discovered, to my cost, that trouble is the inseparable attendant upon power; and many times, in the course of the first ten days of my reign, I was ready to give up my dignity from excessive fatigue.

[97] Early one morning, after having passed a feverish night, tortured in my dreams by the voices and faces of the people who had surrounded me the preceding day, I was wakened by the noise of somebody lighting my fire. I thought it was Ellinor; and the idea of the disinterested affection of this poor woman came full into my mind, contrasted in the strongest manner with the recollection of the selfish encroaching people by whom, of late, I had been worried.

"How do you do, my good Ellinor?" said I: "I have not seen any thing of you this week past."

"It's not Ellinor at all, my lard," said a new voice.

"And why so? Why does not Ellinor light my fire?"

"Myself does not know, my lard."

"Go for her directly."

[98] "She's gone home these three days, my lard."

"Gone! is she sick?"

"Not as I know *on,* my lard. Myself does not know what ailed her, except she would be jealous of my lighting the fire. But I can't say what ailed her; for she went away without a word good or bad, when she seen me lighting this fire, which I did by the housekeeper's orders."

I now recollected poor Ellinor's request, and reproached myself for having neglected to fulfil my promise, upon an affair which, however trifling in itself, appeared of consequence to her . . . .

[138] I was always rather displeased to be called upon to attend to any thing or any body, yet as Lady Geraldine entered, I gave one involuntary glance of curiosity. I saw a tall, finely shaped woman, with the commanding air of a woman of rank: she moved well; not with feminine timidity, but with ease, promptitude, and decision. She had fine eyes and a fine complexion, yet no regularity of feature. The only thing that struck me as really extraordinary was her indifference when I was introduced to her. Every body had seemed extremely desirous that I should see her ladyship, and that her ladyship should see me; and I was rather surprised by her unconcerned air. This piqued me, and fixed my attention. She turned from me, and began to converse with others. Her voice was agreeable, though rather loud: she did not speak with the Irish accent; but, when I listened maliciously, I detected certain Hibernian inflec-[139]tions; nothing of the vulgar Irish idiom, but something that was more interrogative, more exclamatory, and perhaps more rhetorical, than the common language of English ladies, accompanied with much animation of countenance and demonstrative gesture. This appeared to me peculiar and unusual, but not affected. She was uncommonly eloquent, and yet, without action, her words were not sufficiently rapid to express her ideas. Her manner appeared foreign, yet it was not quite French. If I had been obliged to decide, I should, however, have pronounced it rather more French than English. To determine which it was, or whether I had ever seen any thing similar, I stood considering her ladyship with more attention than I had ever bestowed on any other woman. The words *striking — fascinating — bewitching,* occurred to me as I looked at her and heard her speak. I resolved to turn my eyes away, and shut my ears; for I was positively determined not to like her; I dreaded so much

the idea of a second Hymen. I retreated to the farthest window, and looked out very soberly upon a dirty fish-pond. Dinner was [140] announced. I observed Lady Kildangan manoeuvering to place me beside her daughter Geraldine, but Lady Geraldine counteracted this movement. I was again surprised and piqued. After yielding the envied position to one of the Swadlinbar Graces, I heard Lady Geraldine whisper to her next neighbor, "Baffled, mamma!"

It was strange to me to feel piqued by a young lady's not choosing to sit beside me. After dinner, I left the gentlemen as soon as possible, because the conversation wearied me. Lord Kilrush, the chief orator, was a courtier, and could talk of nothing but Dublin Castle, and my lord lieutenant's levees, things of which I, as yet, knew nothing. The moment that I went to the ladies, I was seized upon by the officious Miss Bland: she could not speak of anything but Lady Geraldine, who sat at so great a distance, and who was conversing with such animation herself, that she could not hear her *prôneuse*, Miss Bland, inform me that "her friend, Lady Geraldine, was extremely clever: so clever, that many people were at first a little afraid of her; but that there was not the least occasion; [141] for that, where she liked, nobody could be more affable and engaging." This judicious friend, a minute afterwards, told me, as a very great secret, that Lady Geraldine was an admirable mimic; that she could draw or *speak* caricatures; that she was also wonderfully happy in the invention of agnomens and cognomens, so applicable to the persons, that they could scarcely be forgotten or forgiven. I was a little anxious to know whether her ladyship would honour me with an agnomen. I could not learn this from Miss Bland, and I was too prudent to betray my curiosity . . . . A slight degree of fear of Lady Geraldine's powers kept my attention alert. In the course of the evening, Lady Kildangan summoned her daughter to the music-room, and asked me to come and hear an Irish song. I exerted myself as far as to follow immediately; but though summoned, Lady [142] Geraldine did not obey. Miss Bland tuned the harp, and opened the music-books on the piano; but no Lady Geraldine appeared. Miss Bland was sent backwards and forwards with messages; but Lady Geraldine's ultimatum was, that she could not possibly sing, because she was afraid of the tooth-ache. God knows, her mouth had never been shut all the evening. "Well, but," said Lady Kildangan, "she can play for us, cannot she?" No, her ladyship was afraid of the cold in the music-room. "Do, my Lord Glenthorn, go and tell the dear capricious creature, that we are very warm here."

Very reluctantly I obeyed. The Lady Geraldine, with her circle round her, heard and answered me with the air of a princess.

"Do you the honour to play for you, my lord! Excuse me: I am no professor — I play so ill, that I make it a rule never to play but for my own amusement. If you wish for music, there is Miss Bland; she plays incomparably; and I dare say, will think herself happy to oblige your lordship." I never felt so silly, or so much abashed, as at this instant. "This comes," [143] thought I, "of acting out of character. What possessed me to exert myself to ask a lady to play; I that have been tired to death of music! Why did I let myself be sent ambassador, when I had no interest in the embassy?"

To convince myself and others of my apathy, I threw myself on a sofa, and never stirred or spoke the remainder of the night. I presume I appeared fast asleep, else Lady Geraldine would not have said, within my hearing,

"Mamma wants me to catch somebody, and to be caught by somebody; but that will not be; for, do you know, I think somebody is nobody."

444

Textual Notes

Q

5 περι πατρης₂ αμυνεσθαι₁ [indication of order in pencil] 14 & ⟨there 16 manners. . . . civilization. 18 know. 21 upon. 22 magnanimous. | world. 24 Somerville. 27 minds. 30 of of 32 men. 33 amazed. 35 Marvell. 40 itself. 41 death. 42 They 46 He 47 We 49 *way*. 50 Shakspear. | Newton. | Lafayette. 51 composition. | One 52 meditation. 59 *called* | practical. | 61 proverb, 64 is ⟨passed 65 places, 68 debtors. 69 consider[100]ations 71 have ha⟨ve⟩s 72 duty. | intervene. | *expressed* | un*derstood* | opera. 74 can; 80 improvements. | myself. 83 sun 87 cabin. 88 truths. | conversation, It | constellation. 90 Caesar a part 92 world. 94 experiments | or a ⟨word⟩ an | made. | the ⟨obt⟩ 95 testified.

Sicily

103 consola[3]tion 104 ex[4]press 105 insignificance. 106 will. 111 ⟨an⟩↑an↓alysis 112 tablets. 113 Atlas. 115 dif[25]ference 116 beg[27]gars. 117 All 120 invitat⟨at⟩ion 122 here. | A 124 ,& ⟨a few | years. | ⟨practice⟩[*"practice"* is written in pencil above the cancellation, probably by Edward Emerson] 127 inscription. 128 miles. | flowers. 131 Benedictines.

Italy

138 1250; 139 Sicily; 140 unsuccess[18]ful 142 born. 144 piles. 146 are 148 sup[36]posed 151 Lateran,'⟨s⟩ | an[43]cient 152 to[44]morrow 154 hope. 155 eum". | word. 156 representations. | They 160 grace. | A

Italy and France

172 gar[21]den. 174 Caesar. 178 Florence, And 181 Marsilius. 182 others. 183 Pi[46]azza 184 exe*cution* | 300. 185 lookout. 186 gon[53]dola 190 com[63]pleted 191 &c, 192 name. | moun[71]tains 196 fences. | fac[81]-tion 198 when[85]ever 199 Apoda. 200 *ground*. 201 *of*," &c | mag [93]nificence 202 Twenty 203 re[97]lieved

Scotland and England

217 Highlands. | way, | When 218 in | the lake. ↑and↓ ⟨We⟩got | the | impracticable & | there | no | cataract, 219 the | swel[17₈]tered | courage & ⟨had 222 politics. 225 know[29]ledge 226 ⟨to⟩

Sea *1833*

237 not. 241 The | Without 242 Man 243 ⟨in⟩ | The 245 p⟨lay⟩iece | draw | *well*.

A

250 "May I "consult 256 biography. | conscious. | solitude. 257 it. | graceful. | cloister; 260 civilization. | young. 264 cho*ice* . . . obed*ience* 270 direc[24₂]-tion | true. | philanthropical₂ . . . political₁ 274 vain. | wisdom. | us. 275 assem-

445

bly. **276** boot. **281** images. **282** b*o*dy **283** contemplations. | himself. **286** late. | poet. **288** thought. **290** tendency, | animals. **295** let . . . go &$_2$ hang . . . letter.$_1$ | It$_2$ is yet$_1$ | friend. **296** Word **298** all-sided, — gifted, | apo⟨thegm⟩ph-thegm **299** house. | tone, If **304** mens' **306** woman; **308** says. | not. **309** source. | Gods. | God. **310** times. **311** style, **312** Masters' **313** impertinent. | not. | Monday. | himself. | religion. **314** 'blood$_2$ atoning'$_1$ | print. **316** satisfy. | hours. **318** unconsciously. . . . childhood. **319** inclination. **320** goes; **326** safe. That **327** America. **329** description. **330** apostles. **331** phenomenal. | a ⟨walk.⟩ an | Never **333** boot. **335** Don⟨t⟩ot | ⟦You . . . dupe.$_2$ It . . . life.$_1$⟧ **336** other. **338** death. **339** Revelations. **342** benevolence. | why | circumstances. **345** whole. **347** all tongues$_2$ unseals$_1$ **349** liveth." | these. **352** nations. **353** Enthusiasm; She | When **355** Coleridge. | Swedenborg. | ⟨Hatchet ⟨or⟩ pruning knife⟨⟩⟩ **356** ancients ["s" is added in pencil, probably by Edward Emerson] **361** art; But **363** school, this **365** kinds; Well **367** melior↑e↓ ["e" is added in pencil, probably by Edward Emerson] **372** pen[140]chant **374** sancho's **377** strength. **378** truth. **379** Words. **382** are ↑can↓

Maine

390 My neighbors ⟨are⟩ **391** forest, You

France and England

397 tutti$_2$ i quali$_1$ **398** ⟨lo⟩ sotto **399** ⟨come e'⟩ **400** sbadiglio↑;↓ ⟨amento;⟩ | er[8]rore | m↑i↓⟨'⟩d⟨'ingannava⟩ | mai$_2$ riposai$_1$ | bene$_2$ merito$_1$ **401** febbri[97]-citante | pero$_2$ era$_1$ **402** certe⟨e⟩↑o↓ | infless[139]ioni | gesto$_2$ anche$_1$ **403** ⟨n⟩↑o↓ffi-⟨z⟩↑c↓iosa | tant⟨a⟩↑o↓ **404** scus⟨a⟩i **406** amber, [capitalized in pencil, by Edward Emerson?] **407** an ⟨aviary⟩ **410** No | Realism. &c | wi*l*l | Friend, **411** books.

Pocket Diary 2

425 as | THere | me.

Composition

430 composition.

446

Index

This Index includes Emerson's own index material omitted from the text. His index topics, restricted to Journals Q and A, are listed under "Emerson, Ralph Waldo: INDEX TOPICS." If Emerson did not specify a manuscript page or a date to which his index topic referred, the editor has chosen the most probable passage(s) and added "(?)" to the printed page number(s). If Emerson's own specified manuscript page number is an obvious error, it has been silently corrected.

References under "Emerson, Ralph Waldo, POEMS:" are to the drafts of poems written into these journals. Cross references to later printed versions both of the Poems and the Discussions are included under the heading "Emerson, Ralph Waldo: WORKS."

Abbeville, 204
Abela, Giovanni Francesco, *Malta Illustrata,* 118, 120
Abernethy, John, *Physiological Lectures . . . ,* 9, 11, 25, 233, 322
Académie Royale de la Musique, 202
Acherontian Marsh, 146
Achray, Loch, 217
Acradina, 124
Action(s), reasons for, 265–266
Adam, 109, 141, 190; 200, 221, 240
Adams, Abby Larkin, 62n, 252
Adams, Abel, 252n
Adams, Daniel, *The Scholars' Arithmetic,* 118
Adams, John, 10, 21, 35, 257, 329, 429
Adda River, 192
Addison, Joseph, 242
Adige River, 182, 187
Adorno, Padre Anselmo, 131
Adriatic Sea, 180, 185
Advertising, 221, 236, 408
Aesop, 66, 120, 374. *See also* Stag, fable of
Affections, the, 93, 224 280, 288, 319, 342, 359
Africa, 91, 104, 113, 357
African, the, 276
Agamemnon, 426
Agesilaus, 50n, 51n, 373, 380
Agnana, Lake of, 143
Agriculture, 60, 180, 230, 404–405
Aimer, pleurer, mourir, 76
Alaric, 308
Alcoran, *see* Koran

Alessandro, Signore(?), 204
Alexander, Francis, 155, 156n
Alexander, Mr. (?), 272
Alexander the Great, 9, 173, 253, 299, 306, 337
Alexandria, Va., 96n
Alfieri, Conte Vittorio, 169, 230
Alfred the Great, 4, 35, 50, 109, 260, 315, 356
Alison, Archibald, *Essays on . . . Taste,* 340n
Allah, 314
Allen, William, 208
Alloa, Scotland, 217
Allston, Washington, 408, 411
Alps, the, 113, 190, 192, 194, 196, 283
Althorp, John Charles Spencer, 407
Ambleside, England, 222
Ambrosian Library and Museum, Milan, 191
America, 77, 81, 85, 103, 104, 113, 115, 131, 156, 161, 166, 171, 191, 192, 203, 222, 225, 240, 282, 298, 301, 315, 317, 327, 334, 353n, 369
American(s), 81, 103, 109, 158, 191, 198, 224, 241, 305, 377, 413
American Almanac . . . , 67
American Encyclopedia, The, 24, 338n
American genius, 296
American literature, 297
American Quarterly Review, 271
American Sunday-School Union, 423n
American Unitarian Association, 31n, 251, 261n, 309, 360n, 423n
Amici, Giovanni Battista, 170, 230

447

Anakim, 260

Anapus River, 126, 127

Andalusia, 113

Andes, the, 329

Andrieux, François J. G. S., 406

Angrisani, Signor(?), 149, 216

Animals, 9, 25, 199–200, 221, 289, 290, 296–297, 324

Annales de Chemie et de Physique, 204n

Annandale, Scotland, 220

Anne of Austria, 369

Antaeus, 415

Anteros, 375

Antimasonry, 342, 343

Antinous, the (statue), 150

Antipater, 355

Apennines, the, 158, 159, 176

Apollo, 293

Apollo (statue), 74, 150, 168

Appleton, Mr.(?), 284

Appleton, Thomas Gold, 63

Appleton, William Channing, 63

Aquila, Signor(?), 147

Arabic language, 116, 118

Aracoeli, Church of, Rome, 160–161

Arago, Domenique-François, 204

Arbuthnot, John, 310n

Archimedes, 63–64, 122, 124

Architecture, 60, 75, 119–120, 131, 182, 189, 337, 367, 375

Architecture, divine, 60, 107

Arethusa, Fountain of, Syracuse, 122, 124–125

Arezzo, 167, 179

Arianism, 409n

Ariosto, Lodovico, 181

Aristides, 50, 142, 296

Aristotle, 7, 175, 329, 337, 354, 365, 380, 385; *Nichomachean Ethics*, 385n; *Physics*, 365n; *Poetics*, 55, 56n, 261n

Aristotle's Ethics and Politics (tr. J. Gillies), 7n

Arkwright, Sir Richard, 413

Armenian language, 118, 156

Armenian people, 118

Armstrong, Dr. Francis, 334

Arno River, 169, 170

Arno, Val d', 167

Arona, 192

Arqua, 182

Art(s), 38, 45, 47, 63, 65, 104, 139, 142, 159, 321, 360, 363, 367, 373, 431

Artist(s), 153, 301, 363, 365, 366

Ascension, Feast of, 173–174

Ashby de la Zouch, England, 413

Asia, 91, 116

Askew, Mr.(?), 172

Assisi, 167

Astronomy, 25, 26, 60, 83, 107, 238, 346, 373

Atheist, 24, 281

Athenaeum (Club), London, 414

Athens, Greece, 282

Atlantic Ocean, 86, 113, 243, 349

Atlantis, 282

Atlas, Mount, 113

Attila, 308

Auber, Daniel F. E., "Gustave III," 202

Audubon, John J., *Ornithological Biography*, 62

Augusta, Me., 388

Augustine, Saint, 382n

Aunt Mary, *see* Emerson, Mary Moody

Austin, Sarah, *Characteristics of Goethe*, 255n, 258n, 265n, 266n, 267n, 275n, 279n, 289n, 301n, 302n

Austria, Emperor of, 154, 170

Austrians, the, 185, 191, 205

Aventine Hill, 166

Avernus, Lake, 145, 146

Avon River, 413

Azores, 108

Baber, Zehir-ed-Din, *Memoirs . . .* , 233

Bacon, Francis, 30n, 35, 36, 50, 174, 325, 330, 337, 355, 357, 371, 373, 375, 376, 429n, 432; *The Advancement of Learning*, 13n, 212n, 253n, 254n; *De Augmentis*, 338n; "Of Expense," 4; *Instauratio Magna*, 95; *Works*, 371n

Bacon, Roger, 283

Bacon, Sir Nicholas, 375

Baiae, 141, 145, 146

Bailey, Samuel, *Essays on the Pursuit of Truth . . .* , 99

Baker, Mr.(?), 126

"Ballads of the Reformation," 340. *See also* Luther, Martin

Ballet, 171

Balloch, Scotland, 219

Baltimore, Md., 237

Bangor, Me., 306, 307n, 308, 310n, 389, 390

Bannockburn, Scotland, 217

Baptistery of Constantine, Rome, 151

Barbary Coast, 113

Barbauld, Anna Letitia, ["The Brook"], 316; "A Thought on Death," 409; *Works . . .*, 409n
Barberini Palace, Rome, 151
Barbour, John, *The Bruce*, 269
Barclay, Mr.(?), 140
Bardi, Giovanni, 230
Bates, Rev. James, 91
Bath of Caracalla, 142
Battaglia, 182
Battle of Concord Bridge, 349n
Bayle, Pierre, *A General Dictionary . . .*, 350n
Beaujolais, Louis Charles d'Orléans, Comte de, 85
Beaumont, Francis, 73, 174
Beauty, 13, 16, 43, 69–70, 77, 95, 120, 130, 150, 161, 165, 168, 188, 230, 260, 278, 288, 311, 314, 319, 321, 359, 362, 364, 376, 377, 379, 380, 389, 415
Beauvais, 204
Bee, homing instinct of, 217
Beecher, Edward or Lyman (?), 319
Beethoven, Ludwig van, 162, 195
Beggar(s), 117, 124, 131, 138, 143, 144, 145, 146, 168, 171, 186, 187, 191, 277, 317, 345, 373, 377
Belfast, Me., 391
Bell, Henry, tr., *Colloquia Mensalia . . .*, 251n, 349n
Bell, Sir Charles, *Animal Mechanics . . .*, 99, 100n; *The Hand . . .*, 254, 355
Bellini, Vicenzo, "La Straniera," 72, 171, 318
Bello Sguardo, Florence, 177
Beloe, William, tr., *The History of Herodotus*, 259
Ben An, 218
Ben Lomond, 217
Ben Venue, 218
Benedictines, 131
Benedictine Convent, Palermo, 140
Bennett, Rev. Mr.(?), 148
Bentham, Jeremy, 33, 326, 407
Benthamism, 221
Béranger, Pierre Jean de, 301
Berber, the, 122
Bering, Vitus, 374
Bernard, Saint, 86, 210
Bernardin de Saint-Pierre, James-Henry, 92; *Studies of Nature*, 92n, 340n; *A Voyage to the Isle of France*, 92n
Berni, Francesco, 259

Berri, Duc de, 247
Bewick, Thomas, 25
Biagioli, Giambattista, ed., *Rime di Michelagnolo . . .*, 366n, 367n
Bias of Priene, 110, 253
Biber, Edward, *Henry Pestalozzi . . .*, 6, 12n, 20n
Bible, 118; Sacred Scriptures, 31, 53, 93, 94, 119; *Apocrypha*: Wisdom of Solomon, 311; *OT*: 120; Chronicles, 36; Daniel, 297n; Ecclesiastes, 4, 36, 325n; Esther, 111n; Genesis, 10n, 19n; Isaiah, 36, 251, 291n, 376n; Jeremiah, 36, 391n; Kings, 278n; Nahum, 376n; Proverbs, 36; Psalms, 36, 50n; Samuel, 326n, 339n; *NT*: 39, 308n, 377n; Acts, 111n, 117; Corinthians, 295n; Galatians, 250n, 385n; Hebrews, 18n, 66; James, 350; John, 35n, 44n, 88n, 282n, 291n, 322, 376n, 385n; Luke, 20n, 36, 63n, 295n, 308n, 333n, 377n; Mark, 155n, 307n, 308n; Matthew, 12n, 39n, 63n, 89n, 90, 91n, 155n, 295n, 308n, 378n, 428n; Peter, 34n, 80n, 237n, 296n, 347n; Philippians, 15n, 380n; Revelation, 18n, 339, 369; Romans, 85n, 377n, 385n; Sermon on the Mount, 26; St. Paul's Epistles, 26; Thessalonians, 89; Timothy, 283n
Bibliographie de la France, 76n
Bigelow, Andrew, *Travels in Malta and Sicily . . . in 1827*, 106, 136n
Bigelow, Jacob, *Florula Bostoniensis*, 282n, 283n, 300n, 389n
Biography, 54, 256
Biot, Jean Baptiste, 204, 235
Biscari, Prince of, 131, 132
Black, Joseph, *Lectures on . . . Chemistry*, 62n
Blackwood's Magazine, 220n, 412n
Blagden, George Washington, 318, 319–320
Blanc, Mont, 193, 194, 196
Blanchard, Joshua P., 30, 31n, 92, 360
Blindness, 377
Board blanket, anecdote about, 243
Boboli Gardens, 176
Boccaccio, Giovanni, 89, 230
Boileau-Despréaux, Nicolas, *Oeuvres . . .*, 199n, 406n
Bologna, 180–181, 182, 205; Academy, 181; Cathedral, 181
Bologne, Jean, 173; Father Apennine (statue), 180; Neptune (statue), 181
Bombay, 283

Bonaparte, Jerome, 170

Bonaparte, Louis, 170

Bonaparte, Napoleon, 50, 170, 186, 189, 191, 192, 235, 256, 257, 304, 306, 343, 363, 373, 409

Bond, George (?), 261

Bonifazio Veronese, 184

Bootblack, anecdote about, 222

Bora, Katherina von, 337, 340

Bordeaux, Duc de, 247

Borghese Palace, Rome, 151, 158

Borromeo, Saint Carlo, 77, 190, 192

Bossuet, Jacques Benigne, *Discours sur l'histoire universelle*, 67

Boston, Mass., 4, 53, 91, 102, 115, 121, 123, 176, 210, 226, 229, 230, 236, 239, 241, 252, 253n, 265, 272, 277, 306, 308, 320, 325, 360, 388, 415n

Boston Athenaeum, 25n, 59, 232, 256n, 265n, 300n, 347n

Boston Daily Advertiser, The, 53n

Boston Library Society, 260n, 438n

Boston Mercantile Journal, 258

Boston Public Library, 232n

Boston (steamboat), 426

Boswell, James, *The Life of Samuel Johnson*, 99, 106n, 372n

Boswellism, 320

Botany Bay, 332

Boulevards of Paris, 197–198

Boulogne, 78, 204

Bower, Alexander, *The Life of Luther . . .* , 339n

Bowring, Sir John, 412, 414, 422, 423; *Autobiographical Recollections . . .* , 423n; ed., *The Works of Jeremy Bentham*, 407

Bradford, Dr. Gamaliel, 256

Bradford, George P., 265, 266, 285

Brayton, Mrs. Deborah, 97n, 263n

Brenta River, 183

Brera, Palazzo di, Milan, 191

Brescia, 187–188, 189

Brewer, T. M., 422

Brewster, Sir David, *The Life of Sir Isaac Newton*, 87n; "Optics," 254n

Bridge of Sighs, 183, 185

Bridgen, Anna, and sister, 158, 172, 177, 192, 195, 206

Bridgewater, John Egerton, 1st Earl of, 89n

Bridgewater, Mass., 320

Bridgewater Treatises, 254n

Briga, 193, 206

British Museum, 414, 422, 423

British Plutarch, 35n

Brooks, Peter Chardon, 234n

Brougham, Henry Peter, Baron Brougham and Vaux, 21, 317, 327, 407; *Natural Philosophy*, 253n, 254n

Brown, Dr. John, 292

Brown, Mrs.(?), 423

Brown, Thomas, 7n; *Lectures on the Philosophy of the Human Mind*, 284n

Browne, Sir Thomas, *Hydriotaphia*, 434n; *Tracts*, 434n

Bruno, Giordano, 355

Brutus, Marcus Junius, 276

Bryant, Ann H., 6

Bryant, Frances G., 6

Bryant, John, 23n

Bryant, William Cullen, "The Old Man's Funeral," 210n

B. S., 262

Bucentaur, 185

Bucksport, Me., 391

Buenos Aryean, 58

Buffon, Georges Louis Leclerc, Comte de, 311

Bull, John, 110

Bunker Hill, 233, 234n

Burke, Edmund, 36, 43, 174, 332, 376, 432; "Speech on American Taxation," 114n; "Speech on . . . A Plan . . . for the Economical Reformation of the Civil and Other Establishments," 307n

Burns, Robert, 16, 54n, 221, 375, 425; "The Brigs of Ayr," 10; "Epistle to Davie," 433

Burns, Robert, son(s) of, 226, 425

Burton, Robert (?), 58, 322

Bush, George, *The Life of Mohammed*, 341n

Butler, Charles, *The Life of Erasmus . . .* , 233

Butler, Joseph, 7n, 84, 89

Butler, Samuel, *Hudibras*, 428n; *The Tale of the Cobbler and the Vicar of Bray*, 189n

Buttera, Prince of, 139

Byron, George Gordon, Lord, 159, 169, 174, 181, 185, 194, 279, 315; *Childe Harold's Pilgrimage*, 28n, 149n, 152n, 153n, 164n, 165, 167n, 168n, 185n; *Don Juan*, 24n, 51n, 433; *Mazeppa*, 86; *Marino Faliero, Doge of Venice*, 184n; statue of (Thorwaldsen), 151

C C E, *see* Emerson, Charles Chauncy

Cade, Jack, 285

Caesar, Julius, 36, 38, 90, 153, 174, 262, 379
Caesars, 150; Palace of the, Rome, 151
Cairo, 304
Calabria [Calauria], 355
Calcio, 189
Caldani, Professor (?), 183
Calderon de la Barco, Pedro, 87n
Calhoun, John, 257
Callender, Scotland, 217
Calvin, John, 194, 382; portrait of (Titian), 151
Calvinism, 26, 41, 80, 309, 342, 364
Calvinist, 9, 24, 91, 195, 384
Camaldoli, 142
Cambridge, Mass., 234, 272
Cambus Kenneth, Abbey of, 217
Campagna di Roma, 159, 165
Campbell, Thomas, 8; *The Pleasures of Hope*, 432; *Poland; a Poem* . . . , 432
Campo Santo, Ferrara, 181–182; Syracuse, 126
Canning, George, 42, 306, 317, 373
Canova, Antonio, 150, 182, 184, 188; Mme Bonaparte (statue), 184; Hercules (statue), 184; Perseus (statue), 150
Canterbury, Roxbury, Mass., 242
Canton, China (?), 234
Canton, Mass., 210
Caoutchouc (rubber), 360, 372
Cape Clear, 238
Cape Cod, 320
Cape Spartel, 113
Cape Trafalgar, 113
Cape Verde Islands, 53
Capet, Louis (Louis XVI, of France), 369
Capitoline Hill, 150, 151, 166
Capitoline Museum, 150, 165
Capri, 146
Capuchins, 125–126, 128, 138, 214
Carbery, Alice Egerton, Countess of, 88, 89n
Carbery, Frances, Countess of, 88, 89n
Carbery, Richard Vaughan, 2nd Earl of, 89n
Carlisle, England, 219
Carlyle, Jane Welsh, 220–222
Carlyle, Thomas, 52, 60, 77, 78, 79, 80, 82, 83, 173, 219–222, 223, 234, 236, 273, 274, 275, 288n, 292, 300, 302, 319, 326, 359, 414n, 426, 428n, 429n; "Biography," 87n; "Characteristics," 15n, 18n, 271n, 289; "Corn Law Rhymes," 28n, 45n; "The Death of Goethe," 87n; "German Literature in the 14th and 15th Century,"

67n; "Goethe," 87n, 303n; "Goethe's Portrait," 40n; "Goethe's Works," 53n, 59n, 220n, 302n; "Jean Paul Friedrich Richter," 54n, 271n; "Jean Paul Friedrich Richter Again," 54n, 87n, 340n; *Life of Friedrich Schiller*, 54, 55, 240n; "Life of Robert Burns," 54n, 221; "Luther's Psalm," 53n, 340n, 363n; "Novalis," 302n, 320n; *Sartor Resartus*, 220n, 271n, 292n, 308n, 319n; "The State of German Literature," 87n; tr., Goethe's *Wilhelm Meister's Apprenticeship*, 40n, 171n, 271n; *Wilhelm Meister's Travels*, 75n
Carmeliti, Chiesa dei, Naples, 184
Carolina (state), 331
Caroldstadt, 339
Carpenter, Col. (?), 391
Carpenter, Dr. Lant, 423
Carracci, Annibale, 157, 181
Carrara, Francesco da, 186
Carrara Mountains, 177
Carthaginians, 127
Casal, Marquis di, 126, 214
Cascade of Pissevache, 193
Cascade of Velino, 166
Cascina, Florence, 169, 170, 173, 176
Cassière, John de la, 118
Castine, Me., 391
Catania, 128–129, 130, 132, 133, 210, 213, 214
Catholic Church, 152
Catiline, 151n
Cato (the Elder?), 90
Catullus, 165
Cause and effect, 335
Cavendish, Thomas, 100
Céard, Nicholas, 192
Cellérier, Jean Israel Samuel, 195
Center, Mr. (?), 251
Cervantes Saavedra, Miguel de, 89, 235
Cethegus, 151
Ceuta, 113
Chain of Being, 283, 365
Chamberlain, John, 252
Chambers's Edinburgh Journal, 239
Channing, William Ellery, 21, 84, 225–226, 251, 279, 314, 326, 353, 360n, 380, 408, 410, 422n
Character, 21, 43, 54, 71, 256, 262, 306, 351, 378, 415, 416
Charity, 53
Charles V, Holy Roman Emperor, 117, 136, 304, 417

Charleston, S.C., 152n, 236, 242
Charlestown, Mass., 57n
Charron, Pierre, 173
Charybdis, 138
Chatêl, Abbé Toussaint François, 203, 408
Chatham, Earl of, see Pitt, William
Chatsworth Mansion, 412
Chelmsford, Mass., 79n
Chemistry, 60, 197n
Chenevière, Jean Jacques, 195
Chesterfield, Philip Dormer Stanhope, 4th Earl of, 174; The Letters . . . , 73
Chiesa Nuova, Rome, 153
Chiffinch, William, 22
Chigi Palace, Rome, 157
Child, the, 84, 292, 309–310, 314, 338
Child, Mrs. Lydia Maria Francis, The Biographies of Madame de Staël and Madame Roland, 40n
Childhood, 318
Children's Drama Theatre, Paris, 202
Chillon, Castle of, 193
Chilo of Sparta, 379n
Chilon, 111n, 253n
China, Me., 389
Chinese, 112
Cholera, 37, 62
Christian III, of Denmark, 339
Christian Examiner, The, 57n, 64n, 195n
Christian Messenger, The, 281n
Christian Register, The, 31n
Christiana of Sweden, 358n
Christianity, 8, 26, 40, 45, 77, 92, 124, 128, 282, 309, 377, 383, 410
Christmas, 227
Churches, 75, 117, 131, 169, 184, 190–191, 225
Cicero, 30n, 36, 90, 124, 128, 142, 143, 152n, 242, 257, 365, 424, 433; Against Verres, 122, 124, 125; Familiar Epistles . . . , 424n; In Catilinam, 96n; Tusculan Disputations, 122, 362n
Circle(s), 337, 381
Civita Castellana, 166, 179
Clarendon, Edward Hyde, 1st Earl of, 239
Clarens, Switzerland, 193
Clarke, Samuel, 89; A Vindication of Christ's Divinity, 409n
Clay, Henry, 257
Clematis (ship), 234
Clitumnus, Temple of, 167
Cloud(s), 28, 95, 104, 273, 345, 379
Clyde River, 219

Cobham, Lord, see Oldcastle, Sir John
Cochrane, Grizel, 239
Coelian Hill, 166
Colburn and Bentley, publishers, 221, 236
Coleridge, Samuel Taylor, 78, 220, 223, 312, 325, 326, 335, 340, 353, 355, 360, 369, 381n, 407–408, 409–412, 414, 428n, 431; Aids to Reflection, 327n, 332n, 353n, 382n, 411n; Biographia Literaria, 382n; On the Constitution of Church and State, 297n, 326n, 328n, 339n, 344n, 353n, 411; The Friend, 233n, 290, 291n, 340n, 410, 430n; "Notes on Waterland," MS Notes for, 409n; tr., The Piccolomini; or, the First Part of Wallenstein (Schiller), 265, 325n; The Statesman's Manual, 329n
Coliseum, 149, 156, 157
Collège du Droit, Paris, 197
Collège Royale de France, 197
Collier, John Payne, 361n
Collignon, Auguste Charles, 201, 408
Colonna Palace, Rome, 151
Colton, Charles G., Lacon, or Many Thoughts in Few Words, 10n
Columbian Centinel, The, 239n
Columbus, Christopher, 76, 107, 109, 347, 360
Commodia, Andrea, 190, 205
Communication, 350, 354, 383
Communion (The Lord's Supper), 27n, 30, 227, 360
Companion to the British Almanac for 1830, The, 67n
Compensation, 66, 84, 86, 260, 281, 313–314, 322, 346, 382
Composition (environmental), 288, 291, 345–346, 405
Composition (rhetorical), 51, 273, 275, 276, 304, 315, 324, 336, 362–363, 428–438
Concord, Mass., 234, 335, 348, 351, 359
Concord, N.H., 229, 251
Conder, Josiah, Italy, 135n, 137, 161n, 193n
Confucius, Shi King, 300
Congress (U.S.), 433
Congreve, William, 175
Connecticut, 196
Connecticut River, 182, 241
Conscience, 7, 37, 53, 56, 91, 318, 326, 348
Conscious, the, 348
Constance of Sicily, 138
Constant, Benjamin, 409
Contini (Contino, Antino?), 131
Conway, N.H., 27, 229

Cook, John (?), 22
Cook, Mrs. (?), 22, 96
Copenhagen, 283
Copernican astronomy, 26
Copernicus, Nicolaus, 235
Coppet, 194
Cordis, Mr. (?), 195
Corn Law Rhymes, see Elliott, Ebenezer
Cornaro, Luigi, 210, 211n
Corpus Christi, Feast of, 187
Correggio, 142
Correspondence, doctrine of, 11, 14, 53, 75, 84, 95, 112, 119, 199–200, 216, 230, 288, 331, 352, 355, 363, 406
Corsini, Prince of, 170, 417
Corsini Palace, Rome, 157
Cortona, 167, 193
Cosmos, 16. *See also* Universe
Cotton, Charles, 239; tr., *Essays of . . . Montaigne*, 36n, 433n
Council of Lateran, 227
Council of Trent, 227
Court of Chancery, London, 422
Court of Honor, 348
Cousin, Victor, 58, 225; *Introduction to the History of Philosophy*, 318; trans. from Tennemann, *Manuel de l'histoire de la philosophie*, 99, 100n
Crabbe, George, 8
Crafts, Mr.(?), 354
Cranch, Christopher Pearse, 155n
Cranch, John, 77, 155, 156, 157, 158, 159, 164
Cranmer, Thomas, 15
Crassus, Dives, 153n
Crawford, Ethan Allan, 27, 228, 229
Crawford, T[homas?], 229
Criffel, Mount, 220
Croker, John Wilson, 99
Crombie, Alexander, 31
Cromek, Robert Hartley, *Reliques of Robert Burns*, 16n
Crusades, the, 308
Crystallization, 428
Cuba, 65
Cumaeans, 143
Cumberland, England, 219
Cumbre de Mulahacin, 114
Cunningham, Allan, 220
Cunningham, Francis, 162
Cunningham, J. W., *Sancho, or the Proverbialist*, 374n
Currency conversion data, 134–135, 136, 213

Currie, James, 292
Cushing, Caleb (?), 294
Custom, 374
Cuvier, Georges L.C.F.D., Baron, 33, 89, 279, 344; *Discourse on the Revolutions of the . . . Globe*, 255
Cyane, Fountain of, Syracuse, 127

D. P., 294
D., Mme, 202
D., Mr., 322
[Dabney, J. P.], ed., *The Works of Anna Laetitia Barbauld . . .* , 409n
Daggett, Herman, ed., *An Abridgment of the Writings of Lewis Cornaro . . .* , 211n
Dalton, John, atomic theory of, 224
Dampier, William, 98, 245, 246n
Daniell, John F., *Meteorological Essays and Observations*, 62n, 67n
Dante Alighieri, 89, 162, 169, 172, 230, 377; *Paradiso*, 250, 258, 259n, 362
Darwin, Erasmus, *Zoonomia . . .* , 292
Davis, Mr. (?), 19
Davis, Mrs. (?), 251
Davy, Dr. John, 120, *Notes and Observations on the Ionian Islands*, 120n
Davy, Mrs. John (Margaret Fletcher), 118, 120
Davy, Sir Humphrey, 25, 120, 174
Death, 37, 41, 57, 60, 64, 72, 259–260, 325, 360, 381, 409
Defoe, Daniel, *Robinson Crusoe*, 220
Deism, 409n
Delavigne, Casimir, *Les Enfants d'Édouard*, 202
Delaware Bay, 96n
DeLolme, John Louis, 224; *The Constitution of England . . .* , 225n
Delsere, Signora (?), 171, 176
Democracy, 342, 357
Demosthenes, 45, 56, 351, 355, 356, 373
Deptford, England, 205
Derby, England, 413
Derbyshire, Peak of, 412
Derwent River, 412
Desenzano, 187
Design, 69, 130, 358
Devil(s), 58, 68, 330, 337, 349
Dewey, Orville, 97n, 268n, 412
Dexter, Samuel, 436n
Dicearchia, 143
Diet, 210, 211
Dilettantism, 297

Dimeck, Sigismundo, 120–121
Diodati, Charles, 87, 240n
Diogenes, 20n, 304
Diogenes Laertius, "Bias," 111n; "Chilon," 111n, 253n; *Lives of Eminent Philosophers*, 362n, 421n
Dion, 124
Dionysius' Ear, 122, 214
Dionysius the Elder, 127
Dis, 127
D'Israeli, Isaac, *Curiosities of Literature*, 17n, 264n
Dix, Mrs. (?), 22
Dixmont, Me., 389
Dodsley, Robert, *Select Fables of Esop . . .* , 66n, 270n
Dolci, Carlo, 170
Dolland, John, 254
Domenichino, Il, 139
Dominic, Saint, 181
Domo d'Ossola, 192, 205, 206
Donatus, Aelius, 174
Donatus, the Monk, 131
Donne, John, "An Anatomy of the World," 337; "Eclogue of Dec. 26, 1613," 291n
Doria Palace, Rome, 154
Doune, Scotland, 217
Dover, Inverness, 235
Downes, Commodore John, 53
Dracopoli, Signor (?), 166
Dreams, 71, 289, 296
Drummond, James L., *Letters to a Young Naturalist*, 25n
Ducal Palace, Venice, 184
Dumbarton, Scotland, 219
Dumfries, Scotland, 219, 226n, 425
Dumont, Pierre Étienne, 285
Dunscore, Scotland, 219
Duppa, Richard, *The Life of Michael Angelo Buonarroti*, 361n, 368n
Durante, Mr. (?), 144
Duty, 40, 75, 88
Dying Gladiator, the (statue), 150, 165

E B E, *see* Emerson, Edward Bliss
Early English Navigators, *see Lives and Voyages . . .*
Earth, 65
Easter, 156, 227
Eastport, Me., 306
East Sudbury, Mass., 359
Ecbatana, 304, 367
Ecce Homo, Il Santissimo (ship), 121

Eclipse of the sun, 346
Edgeworth, Maria, *Ennui*: Emerson's translation into Italian, 397–404. *See also* Appendix, 441–445
Eddystone lighthouse, 253
Edinburgh, 77, 217, 424
Edinburgh Review, The, 11n, 15n, 16n, 18n, 23, 24n, 28, 41n, 45, 54n, 99, 100n, 148n, 221n, 233n, 271n, 423n
Education, 24, 47, 222, 262, 263, 276, 286, 322, 327, 351, 378
Edwards, Jonathan, *Freedom of the Will*, 257
Église Catholique Française, 203, 408n
EI, 375
Elgin marbles, 160
Elizabeth I, of England, 230n, 369
Ellen's Isle (Helen's Island), 218
Elliott, Ebenezer, *The Corn Law Rhymes*, 28n, 45; "The Village Patriarch," 361n
Ellis, Capt. Cornelius, 102, 103, 111, 114, 115, 213
Emerald (ship), 239n
Emerson, Charles Chauncy (brother), 4n, 13, 14, 20, 21n, 31n, 72, 96, 149n, 228, 252n, 253n, 254, 255n, 262, 272, 286, 292, 294, 315, 319, 343(?), 359, 360, 378n, 379, 381
Emerson, Edward Bliss (brother), 4, 36, 92, 151n, 166, 243, 244n, 272, 325–326, 330, 334n, 344, 359, 368, 422n; Master's Oration, 312
Emerson, Edward Waldo (son), 16n, 27n, 36n, 63n, 110n, 112n, 117n, 174n, 212n, 217n, 243n, 329n, 331n, 335n, 336n, 346n, 364n, 375n, 415n
Emerson, Ellen Tucker (first wife), 7, 60, 70, 72, 210n, 251n, 263, 300, 325n, 350, 360
Emerson, George Barrell, 197n, 272n, 374n
Emerson, Joseph, of Malden, 212n
Emerson, Mary Moody (aunt), 9n, 53, 72n, 76, 228, 229, 268n, 275, 277, 300, 323, 353, 368, 371, 389, 437
Emerson, Olivia Buckminster, 272, 374n
Emerson, Ralph, 197, 305
Emerson, Ralph Waldo, Account Book, 1828–1835, 31n, 252n; Blotting Book Psi, 428n, 434n; Blotting Book II, 433n; Blotting Book III, 21n, 428n, 429n, 430n, 431n, 432n, 433n, 434n; Blotting Book IV, 97n; Catalogue of Books Read, 35n; cipher, 234–235; Encyclopedia, 10n, 12n, 52n, 59n, 76n, 255n, 433n; Journal B, 361n;

454

Phi Beta Kappa Poem, 315; School and Preaching Record, 252n; Notebook T, 386n. *See also* "Chronology," xvii–xx, *and* "self," *under* DISCUSSIONS below

DISCUSSIONS: acknowledgment of God, 103–104; the artist, 153–154; astronomy and theology, 24–27; beauty of nature, 321–322; 345–346; biography, 35–36, 256, 331; "Blessed are the woods," 350; blindness of love, 352; boundless ability of mankind, 353–354; Byron and Italy, 165; capacities of men, 310; character acquired by effort, 20–22; the choice of goodness, 13; Christianity, truth of, 92–94, 377–378; classification and the idea, 286–291; Communion (The Lord's Supper), 29–30, 227; comparative anatomy, 25; compensation, 15, 21–22, 33–35, 294–295, 302–303; the connection of good and evil, 281; the conscience, 7; conventionality of pomp and ceremony, 153, 155; conversation on weather, 104–105; creation and the general law, 284–285; a day and the wise man, 283–284; dead tradition and the preacher, 380–381; death and grief, 57; deism and atheism, effects of, 280–281; design in nature, 253–254; divine light of reason, 356–357; each man's calling, 370, 371–372; education, 63–64; envy, 19–20; Erminia, the flower girl, 175–176, 300(?); experience and good judgment, 256; Ezra Ripley, 338–339, 358–359; faith, 88; friendship, 270–271; George Fox, 31–33; genealogy of thoughts, 337; God and the soul, 33; God's mnemonics, 88–89; Goethe, 298, 300–302; Goethe's jubilee, 258; imitation in American literature, 297–298; immortality, 41–42; individuality of the genuine man, 378–379; influence of the Greeks, 380; Italy, American traveller in, 78; Ben Jonson, 245; visit to Walter Savage Landor, 172–173, 174–175; value of life, 40–41; locomotives, 82–83; Luther's place in history, 339–341; the machinery of society, 276–277; the genuine man, 37–38, 49–50; man as the interpreter of nature, 95; man the dwarf of himself, 274–275; Man a part of the whole, 351–352; men of genius, 78–79; Michelangelo, 258–260; the *Miserere*, 154–155; moral law and religion, 83–84; moral nature, 86–88; nature's revelations, 267–268; the oneness of

truth, 352–353; on learning French, 304–305; opera, 140; *"Optical Deceptions,"* 370–371; Order of Misericordia, 172; Palm Sunday ceremonies in Rome, 152–153; definition of a passenger, 123; the passions, 7–8; the philosophy of waiting, 368; politics, 325–326, 327–328, 332–335; practical and contemplative men, 59, 327; proverbs on idleness, 10; providence, 264–265; the Quaker inner voice, 263–264, 318; Raphael's "Transfiguration," 150; religious forms, 313–314; reputation, 316–318; reverence for man's soul, 38–40; the sailor, 106, 107, 109–110; self, 6, 7, 27, 29–30, 33, 34, 35, 40, 54, 67, 68, 72, 73, 74–75, 76–77, 77–78, 79, 80–81 (concluded, 83), 81–82, 87, 91, 102–103, 105, 106–107, 110–111, 112, 126, 129, 132, 133, 138, 139, 141, 143–144, 149, 150, 151, 152, 157, 158, 161–162, 165, 168, 169, 171, 178, 186, 187, 189, 193, 200, 201, 202, 203, 211, 217, 219, 226, 237–238, 239, 240, 242, 253, 255, 256, 263, 264, 267, 272, 273, 274, 275, 278, 280, 290, 292, 296, 300, 304, 306, 309, 314, 315, 315–316, 318, 320, 324, 325, 329, 334, 335, 336, 342, 344, 346, 349, 354, 355, 359, 362, 363, 364, 371, 372, 374, 380, 382, 435; the self and the universal man, 67–68; self-education, 50–52; self-expression, 108–109; self-reliance, 50–51, 269–270; Shakespeare, 18–19, 311, 312; Shakespeare's sonnets, 286; society and solitude, 66–67, 367; the soul, 28–29; spiritual religion, 364; a spring day, 272–273; Swedenborgian doctrine of "Affections Clothed," 342–343; temperance, 4–6; travel, futility of, 320; terror of freedom, 45–46; true wealth, 373; truth in relationship to Christianity, 45; truth, trust in, 42–44, 46–47; value of the man of action, 114–115; Venice, 186; the will, 256–257, 260; "The Winter's Day," 60–61, 62, 65; "On the Wisdom of Ignorance in Poets," 312–313; Wordsworth, 63, 430–431; the art of writing, 314–315, 362–363; universal truth, 367–368; Zoroastrism, 11–12

INDEX TOPICS: "Actions betray themselves," 21–22(?); "Affections," 359–360; "Analogy of Matter & Mind," 254–255, 367–368; "Anschauung," 266, 267, 277, 321, 331, 355, 377; "Antagonisms,"

295; "Autobiography," 269, 315–316, 325, 363; "Beauty of Nature," 341–342, 345–346, 359, 379–380; "Being & Seeming," 268, 275–276, 293, 307, 310, 326–327, 328, 329, 344, 369; "Best persons freest speakers," 282, 350; "Bias," 378–379; "Biography," 35(?); "Biographical heads," 4; "Blagden, [G.W.]," 318–319; "Boston," 306–307; "Boy," 363; "Bradford, G. P.," 265, 266; "Canning, [George]," 306; "Carlyle," 300–301, 302, 319, 359; "Cause & Effect," 284–285; "Character," 338–339, 349–350, 357, 358–359; "Christianity," 309, 377–378, 382, 383, 385; "Coleridge," 290; "Compensation," 302–303, 306, 322, 324, 329, 368; "Composition," 284–285, 291; "Consciousness vicious," 314–315; "Death of Miss Margaret Tucker," 64–65; "Death of Mrs. Tucker," 72; "Disagreeable becomes agreeable," 298, 311, 322–323; "Dreams," 296–297; "Eclipse," 346; "Education," 378; "Emerson, C. C.," 294, 296, 359, 360, 381; "Edward Bliss Emerson," 325, 330; "E[llen]. T[ucker]. E[merson].," 300; "Emerson, M[ary]. M[oody].," 277; "Emerson, Mrs. Ruth," 272; "Experience," 256, 261; "First thoughts," 308–309, 317–318; "Friendship," 299, 320, 359–360, 368, 374; "Genealogy of Thoughts," 337, 367–368; "Gentlemen," 292, 293, 294, 320, 326; "Genuineness," 283, 294, 299, 309, 312, 314, 316–317, 324, 335, 351; "Goethe," 298, 300–301; "Indians," 303, 305–306; "Influence," 362; "Language," 293, 304–305, 358; "Life, Value of," 369; "Love," 368; "Man, practical," 327; "Manners," 284, 299; "Means & ends," 284; "Milton," 312, 378, 379, 380; "Mind, states of," 362; "Montaigne," 273; "Moral," 309, 377–378, 382–383, 385; "Naturalist," 286, 290, 311, 331; "Optical deceptions," 370–371; "Order of Wonder," 284; "Over refiners," 30(?); "Pepperell, Sir William," 306(?), 323(?); "Perseverance," 295–296, 306–307; "Plastic idea," 287–288, 290; "Practical man," 59; "Present becoming Past," 21–22(?); "Progress," 320–321, 324, 327; "Public, true," 292–293, 344; "Railroad," 296; "Religious forms," 313–314; "Repairs," 34(?); "Reputation cumulative," 21–22; "Rhetoric," 290; "Ripley, Dr. Ezra," 338–339, 349, 358–359, 384; "Rotch, Mary," 263–264, 267–268; "Sampson, George A.," 267, 307; "Shakspear," 18–19, 286, 311–312; "Snakes," 321; "Solitude," 329, 359–360; "Solitude & Society," 66–67; "Speak to the public as to Self," 44(?), 52(?); "Stars," 267; "Swedenborgian can't explain," 49(?); "Teaching," 348–349; "Theoptics [Vision of God]," 28, 274, 275, 320, 321, 342, 373, 382–383; "Theory of Nature," 287, 288, 289–290; "Travelling," 303–304, 320; "Truth a horse for Christianity," 45(?); "Turns," 310; "Virtue," 384–385; "Voice," 366; "Waiting," 261, 368; "Wave," 287; "We dismiss our thought because 'tis ours," 50(?); "Webster, D.," 261–262, 386–387; "Which Schiller?," 54(?); "Williamson, [W. D.]," 303, 306, 307; "Woman," 257, 293–294, 299–300, 351; "Wonder," 284–285; "Wordsworth," 63; "Writers," 372

LECTURES: "Ben Jonson, Herrick, Herbert, Wotton," 255n, 428n, 432n; "Chaucer," 300n; "Edmund Burke," 356n; "English Literature: Introductory," 346n; "Martin Luther," 328n, 330n, 339n, 341n, 349n, 350n; "Michel Angelo Buonaroti," 258n, 362n, 366n; "John Milton," 328n; "The Naturalist," 255n, 282n; "The Relation of Man to the Globe," 267n; "The Study of Natural History," 311n; "Traits of the National Genius," 412n; "The Uses of Natural History," 25n, 92n, 198n, 255n, 405n, 415n; "Water," 254n

POEMS: "Always day and night . . . ," 227; "America, my country . . . ," 240–242; "The bee upsprings," 62; "Compensation," 347; "Dear brother would you know," 243–245; "Going alway," 424; "The golden days of youth are gone," 28; "Hard is it to persuade the public mind," 56; "The heart must have the heart," 94; "How many events shall shake the earth," 345; "Hymn for the Ordination of Chandler Robbins," 97–98; "I will not hesitate to speak the word," 89–90; "I will not live out of me," 47–48; "None spares another," 65; "O what is Heaven but the fellowship," 341; "On bravely thro' the sunshine," 73; "The Sun is the sole inconsumable fire," 370; "We are what we are made," 129n, 130; "What is it to sail," 70; "Written at Naples," 69–70; "Written at Rome," 71

SERMONS: 52, 39n; 54, 325; 104, 294n; 147, 5; 151, 11n; 152, 9; 156, 10n, 19n, 22n; 157, 24n; 161, 10n; 162, "The Lord's Supper," 30n; 163, 40n, 42n; 164, 38n, 39n, 212n, 294n, 314n

WORKS: "Address to Kossuth, at Concord, May 11, 1862," 47n; "The American Scholar," 20n, 371n; "Art," 150n, 253n; "Art and Criticism," 436n; "Circles," 382n; "Compensation," 66n, 92n, 329n, 347n; "The Conservative," 259n; "Considerations by the Way," 286n; "Country Life," 268n; "Day by Day Returns," 309n; Divinity School Address, 380n; "Each and All," 291n, 304n, 346n; "English Reformers," 240n; English Traits, 173n, 174n, 219n, 220n, 222n, 407n, 409n; "Ezra Ripley, D. D.," 338n, 358n; "Friendship," 314n, 374n; "Goethe; or, the Writer," 285n; "Heroism," 255n, 311n, 325n, 351n; "History," 304n, 323n; "The Man of Letters," 73n; "May Day," 272n; "Milton," 8n, 240n; "Natural Religion," 39n; Nature, 33n, 92n, 96n, 216n, 237, 254n, 255n, 266n, 277n, 293n, 311n, 326n, 332n, 338n, 376n, 379n; "Ode to Beauty," 260n; "The Over-Soul," 342n, 383n; Parnassus, 89n, 300n; "The Preacher," 280n; "Politics," 333n; "Self-Reliance," 21n, 48n, 50n, 109n, 266n, 275n, 283n, 287n, 324n, 359n, 367n, 373n; "Spiritual Laws," 21n, 338n, 369n

Emerson, Robert Bulkeley (brother), 252n
Emerson, Ruth Haskins (mother), 230, 330, 344, 409n; portrait of, 272
Emerson, William (brother), 166n, 334n
Emerson, William (grandfather), 212n
Emerson, William, of Bangor, 390
Empedocles, 368, 369n
Enfantin, Barthélemy Prosper (?), 203
Enfield, William, Institutes of Natural Philosophy . . . , 255n; ed., The Speaker: or Miscellaneous Pieces, 14n
England, 52, 67, 78–80, 81, 135, 136, 156, 168, 222–226, 234, 236, 263, 297, 304, 317, 334, 340, 396, 407–408, 409–415
England, Bishop John, 152
English Channel, 238
English Chapel, Naples, 148; Rome, 159
English language, 90, 116, 126, 128, 139, 157, 192, 195, 205, 238, 247
English people, 116, 118, 119, 126, 138, 139, 140–141, 149, 159, 176, 200, 241

English Reading Room, Paris, 202
English ship, 110
Epaminondas, 356, 380
Epictetus, 321
Epicureanism, 385
Erasmus, 349
Eros, 375
Erskine, William, 233n
Esaus, 105
Esquiline Hill, 166
Esquimaux, 98
Essex (ship), 265
Este, 182
Estrées, Jean, Comte d', 246
Ethics, 309
Etna, Mount, 119, 125, 128, 129, 132, 140
Euclid, 329
Euler, Leonhard, 327, 332
Euripides, 125, 368; Danae, 369n; Stheneboea, 369n
Europe, 74, 78, 81, 84, 85, 103, 104, 109, 113, 115, 116, 139, 210, 241, 339, 369, 413
Evans, George, 388
Eveleth, Mrs.(?), 388
Evelyn, John, 88
Everett, Alexander, 347
Everett, Edward, 42, 56, 257(?), 317; Orations and Speeches, 180n
Evil(s), 8, 18, 34, 36, 281, 330, 334, 335, 349, 380, 382
Example(s), 49, 52, 56, 59, 68–69, 240, 347, 354
Excellence, 58, 82, 354
Exeter, Me., 391
Experience, 256, 261
"External Restraint," 46
Extremes, meeting of, 383
Eynaud, Paul, 115n, 116, 120, 123n, 213

Fabius (Quintus Fabius Pictor), 16
Fabricius (Gaius Fabricius Lusinus), 373
Faith, 54, 83, 98, 225, 359, 382
Faliero, Marino, 184
Falkirk, Scotland, 217
Falkland, Lucius Cary, Viscount, 35, 50, 328
Falmouth, Mass., 307
Faneuil Hall, Boston, 230, 277
Faraday, Michael, 94
Farnese Palace, Rome, 157
Farnesina Palace, Rome, 153
Farnham, Sybil, 388n
Farrar, Eliza Rotch, 263

Farrar, John, 263, 392; *Elements of Electricity, Magnetism* . . . , 251

Fenélon, François de Salignac de la Mothe–, 84, 301, 315

Ferney, 194

Ferrara, 181–182; Cathedral, 181

Ferrara, Abate, 139

Festus, Sextus Pompeius, *De Verborum Significatu*, 152n

Fichte, Johann Gottlieb, 264

Fielding, Thomas, *Select Proverbs* . . . , 6n, 9n, 17n, 212n, 264n

Fiesole, 179

Figline, 167

Fingal's Cave, 223

Fire, 114, 354, 370

First and third thoughts, 292

First Cause, 29

First Church, Boston, 278n

First Parish Church, Newton, 91n

First philosophy, 20, 79, 355, 375

First questions, 18, 25–26, 58, 227, 298, 325, 369

First thoughts, 308, 317

Flaminius, Gaius, 167

Flatterers, 79

Fletcher, John, 73, 174

Florence, 72, 89, 164, 166–180, 184, 208, 230, 361, 362, 396, 405, 418; Baptistery, 168; Campanile, 168, 172, 185; Cathedral, 168

Florida, 357

Flowers, 69, 75, 126, 129, 130, 165, 167, 188, 218, 223, 273, 300, 321, 363

Foligno, 166, 167

Fondi, 149

Fontenelle, Bernard le Bovier de, 13, 14n, 252, 253n, 284

Foreign Quarterly Review, 53n, 59n, 67n, 220n, 343n, 354n

Foreign Review, 54n, 271n, 302n, 303n, 320n, 340n

Forms, 40, 153

Fornarina (statue), 169

Forsyth, Joseph, *Remarks on Antiquities . . . in Italy* . . . , 137, 193n

Forth, Firth of, 217

Forum, the, 149

Foster, Deacon (?), 22

Fourier, Jean Baptiste Joseph, *Mémoires de l'institut*, 255n

Fowler, Mrs. (?), 205, 207, 413, 422

Fox, George, 4, 31–33, 35, 37, 38n, 43, 50, 59, 92, 315, 319, 328, 337, 347, 356, 364, 367, 384; *The Journal* . . . , 384n

Fox, Capt. Philip, 239

Fox, Rev. William J., 414, 425

Foy, Gen. Maximilien S., 409

France, 78, 136, 156, 169, 193, 194, 195, 196–204, 205, 287, 298, 320, 375, 396

Francis (?), 349

Franklin, Benjamin, 36, 50, 194, 315, 338; "The Whistle," 132n

Frascati's gambling house, Paris, 203–204

Fraser's Magazine, 40n, 52n, 53, 220n, 239, 340n, 363n

Frederick II, Holy Roman Emperor, 138

Frederick the Great, grandmother of, *see* Sophia Charlotte

Freedom, 46, 201, 283, 312, 354, 357

Freethinker(s), 282, 350

French language, 90, 139, 193, 305

French people, 58, 185, 192, 196, 200, 201, 203, 246, 271, 377, 408

Fresh Pond, 272

Friendship, 19, 56, 270, 271, 295, 299

Friendship (ship), 53n

Frog Pond, 146

Frothingham, Nathaniel, 277–278

Fryeburg, Me., 228

Fuller, Thomas, 350; *The History of the Worthies of England*, 189n

Füssli, Johann Heinrich ("Fuseli"), 23

Future, 34, 41, 52, 58, 67, 84, 87, 276, 278–279, 301

G., 351

Gaelic language, 218

Galen, 10, 11, 25, 329

Galignani, John and William, 202n

Galignani's reading room, Paris, 202

Galileo, 10, 89, 168, 175, 179, 230, 235n

Gannett, Rev. Ezra Stiles, 360, 422; "Address before the Boston Sunday School Society . . . ," 423n

Gardner, Mr. (?), 139

Garofalo, Benvenuto da, 158, 182

Garofalo, Italy, 320

Gaussen, Louis, 195

Gay-Lussac, Joseph-Louis, 197, 204, 329

Gelo, 127

General and particular, 60, 285, 286–287, 288–289, 322, 345, 363

Geneva, 193, 194–195

Genius, 15, 19, 20, 52, 73, 225, 258, 260, 297, 300, 311, 318, 319, 325, 334, 353, 354, 361, 362, 374, 378, 379, 389. *See also* man of genius

Gentlemen, 159, 222, 262, 292, 317, 326
George, Duke of Saxony, 339, 340, 341n
George IV, of England, 72, 120, 220n
George, Lake, 125
Gérando, Marie Joseph de, 326; *Histoire comparée des systèmes de philosophie*, 173, 298n
Gerard, Dr. Alexander, 329
German language, 220, 293, 370
Germans, 116, 156, 370
Gesuiti, Chiesa dei, Venice, 184
Gesu Nuovo, Church of, Naples, 144
Giardini, Italy, 133
Giarre, village, Sicily, 132
Gibbon, Edward, 160, 194, 221, 227, 232, 375; *Autobiography*, 161n
Gibbons, Mr.(?), 344
Gibraltar, 86, 108, 113, 373
"Gigman," 220
Gillies, John, tr., *Aristotle's Ethics and Politics*, 7n
Gillman, Dr. James, 407, 412
Giorgine, Il, 186
Giotto, 172, 173, 185
Giovanni da S. Giovanni, 177
Girard, Stephen, 37
Gissot, M. (?), 195
Glasgow, 217, 218, 219; Cathedral, 219
Glauber, Johann Rudolf, 255
Gloucester, Bishop of (Dr. James Henry Monk), 78, 407
God, 8, 14, 24, 26, 29, 33, 34, 39, 40, 46, 47, 48, 53, 60, 66, 68, 69, 77, 86, 87, 90, 91, 97, 103–104, 108, 111, 130, 211, 220, 237, 240, 242, 255, 266, 267, 269, 275, 278, 280, 281, 285, 292, 295, 300, 301, 303, 308, 309, 313, 319, 320, 324, 329, 333, 335, 342, 346, 347, 350, 357, 359–361, 362, 364, 367, 368, 370, 372, 378, 381, 382, 383, 384, 410, 417
God within man, 28, 39, 40, 45, 56, 84, 92, 109, 278, 281, 309, 313, 356, 357, 361, 365
Goethe, Johann Wolfgang von, 33, 52, 58, 142, 145, 171, 178, 221, 227, 255, 258, 259, 260, 266, 267, 275, 279, 282, 285n, 288, 289, 292, 298, 300, 301, 302, 337, 343, 344, 354, 361n, 428; *Italienische Reise*, 137n, 178n; *Maximen und Reflexionen*, 87n; *Nachgelassene Werke*, 343n, 354n; *Reinecke Fuchs*, 60n; *Die Römische Elegien*, 301n; *Tag-und-Jahres Hefte*, 178n, 275n, 279n, 298, 301; *Werke*, 145n; *West-Östlicher Divan*, 271n;

Wilhelm Meister's Apprenticeship, 15n, 40n, 88n, 171n, 223, 298, 299n, 303n, 317n; *Wilhelm Meister's Travels*, 75n, 294n, 301n; *Zahme Xenien*, 59n
Golden mean, 237, 245–246
Goldoni, Carlo, 105, 106; *Scelta di alcune commedie . . .* , 105n
Good cause, a, 34, 40, 252, 333, 340
Good ear, the, 278
Good Friday, 156
Goodness, 22, 34, 36, 41, 52, 252, 266, 275, 280, 281, 381
Goodrich, Samuel G., *A System of School Geography*, 118; *A System of Universal Geography*, 137n, 138n
Goss, Col. Cyrus, 390n
Gozzi, Gasparo, 87n
Grace, 337
Grafton, Rev. Joseph, 309
Granacci, Francesco, 361
Grand Canal, 183
Grant, Patrick (?), 149, 151, 158
Grasmere, 226n
Gratian, 227
Gray, Thomas, Ode IX, 323n
Greece, 138, 140, 245
Greek language, 118, 197n, 346
Greek Mass, 156
Greeks, the, 116, 173, 377, 380
Greek sculpture, 173, 322
Greene, Robert, *A Groatsworth of Wit*, 6n
Greenland, 65
Greenough, Horatio, 173n, 174, 372
Greenwich, 204
Greenwood, Francis W. P., *A Collection of Psalms and Hymns for Christian Worship*, 42n
Grenada, mountains of, 113
Grey, Dr. R., *Memoria Technica*, 234n
Griswold, Rufus Wilmot, *The Prose Writers of America*, 39n
Grotto del Cane (near Naples), 143
Grotto of Egeria, Rome, 153
Guarda, Lago di, 187
Guelph, William and Adelaide, 220n, 221
Guercino, 181, 182
Guicciardini, Francesco, *The History of Italy . . .* , 177
Guido, *see* Reni, Guido
Gulliver, Deacon (?), 344
Gustave III, ou le bal masqué, 202

Haddon Hall, 412

Hallam, Henry (?), 231; *View of the State of Europe* . . . , 231n
Halleck, Mr. (?), 118
Hallowell, Me., 388n
Hamel, Jean-Pierre-François Guillot du, 254
Hamilton, Col. (?), 225
Hamlin, R. E., 252
Hammett, Alexander, 216
Hampden, John, 35, 296, 328, 356
Handel, George Frederick, 365
Hannibal, 167, 179
Hanover Street Church, Boston, 319n
Hardenberg, Friedrich, Baron von (pseud. Novalis), 300, 302; *Die Schriften*, 15n
Hare, Julius Charles, 175; *Guesses at Truth*, 173, 273n, 276n, 433
Hartford, Conn., 182
Hartley, David, 99; *Observations on Man*, 7, 100n; *Theory of the Human Mind*, 100n
Harvard College, 58n, 63n, 149n, 151n, 170n, 256n, 263n, 276, 422n
Harvard College Library, 233
Haskins, Hannah, 31
Haskins, John, 212n, 372
Haskins, Phebe Ripley, 252n
Haskins, Thomas and Elizabeth, 372n
Hatchett, Charles, 232
Hat manufacture, Tuscany, 180, 405
Hawk, 281
Hayden, Miss (?), 251
Hazlitt, William, 220; *Essays on the Principles of Human Action* . . . , 99
Heari, Professor (?), 201
Heart, the, 45, 48, 49, 52, 58, 65, 87, 90, 92, 94, 97, 250, 257, 278, 292, 341, 350, 383
Heaven, 41, 42, 66, 260, 280, 299, 303, 326, 341, 373
Heber, Reginald, 283
Hederich, Benjamin (Hedericus), 358
Hedge, Barnabas, 261
Hedge, Frederic H., 360; "The Progress of Society," 64n
Hedge, Levi, 292
Hegel, Georg Wilhelm Friedrich, 33
Helen's Island, *see* Ellen's Isle
Hell, 42, 146, 296
Hemans, Felicia, 11n; "To Corinna at the Capitol," 300n; "The Voice of Music," 343n
Henley, J. H., 247n, 421
Henry IV, of France, 188–189, 196
Henry VI, Holy Roman Emperor, 138
Henry VIII, of England, 340

Henry, Patrick, 34, 429
Heraclitus, 355
Herbert, George, 350, 428n, 432–433; "Affliction," 255, 258; *Jacula Prudentum, or Outlandish Proverbs*, 9n; "The Pulley," 89; "The Search," 7; "The Size," 210n; "Virtue," 61n
Herculaneum, 142, 146
Hercules, Pillars of, 113
Hercules, Temple of, Brescia, 188
Hercules, Torso of (statue), 150
Herder, Johann Gottfried von, 289n, 301
Hero, *see* Man, great, *and* Man of genius
Herodotus, 329; *History*, 51n, 127n, 259n
Herrick, Robert, 333; "The Way," 343n
Herschel, Sir John F. W., 24 (?), 170, 174, 237, 238; *A Preliminary Discourse on . . . Natural Philosophy*, 174n; *A Treatise on Astronomy*, 174n, 237n
Herschel (planet, Uranus), 26
Hiero, 122
High Head, Me., 389
Highlands of Scotland, 217
Highmore, Mr. (?), 412
Hill, John Boynton, 391
Hillman, Mr. (?), 263
Himalaya, the, 329
Hincks, William, 79, 80n
Hindu, the, 276
Hiram, 184
Histoire de l'Académie des Inscriptions . . . , 12
History, 92, 104, 197, 285, 311, 336, 339, 345, 373, 375
Hobart, Nathaniel, "Life of Swedenborg," 38n
Hobbes, Thomas, *Tripos in Three Discourses*, 99; *Humane Nature* . . . , 99
Hogg, James, 412
Holbrook, Mrs. Silas P., 128n, 236
Holbrook, Silas P., 117, 128n, 179–180, 213, 214, 215, 216
Holroyd, J. B., Lord Sheffield, ed., *The Miscellaneous Works of Edward Gibbon* . . . , 232
Holyhead, 236
Home, Sir Everard, "On the Egg," 232
Homer, 44, 260, 285, 312, 353, 360, 365, 369, 374, 379, 386, 437n; *The Iliad*, 5n, 112n, 369; *The Odyssey*, 323n
Homer, Dr. Jonathan, 31n, 91n
Homer, Mrs. Jonathan, 31
Hone, Philip, 328, 333
Hope, 251, 253, 280, 326, 327, 330, 339

Hopkinton Springs, Mass., 230
Horace, 165, 433; *Epistles*, 7; *Satires*, 14n, 101n; *Sermones*, 41
House of Commons, 422, 425n
House of Peers, 425n, 426n
House of Representatives (U.S.), 425n
Howard, Eleazar, 22
Howard, John, 315
Howe, Mrs. (?), 22
Howell, James, *English Proverbs*, 371n
Hoxie, Capt. (?), 238, 239, 247
Hudson, Henry, 374
Hudson, John, 247n, 421
Humboldt, Friedrich, Baron von, 245n, 279, 329; *Personal Narrative of Travels* . . . , 331
Hume, David, 89; *Essays and Treatises on Several Subjects*, 99; *The History of England*, 15n, 438n; *Treatise on Human Nature*, 100n
Hunt, Benjamin Peter, 79, 80
Hunter, John, 11
Hunterian Museum, Glasgow, 219
Hussey, Mr. (?), 140
Hutcheson, Francis, 7n
Hydrostatics, 60
Hypocrisy, 38, 258, 314, 318, 351, 369

Iamblichus, *Protrepticus*, 66n
Idea(s), 11, 18, 287, 288, 289, 329, 340, 342, 353, 369, 377, 378
Ignorance, 18, 42, 67, 107, 111, 227, 282, 312
Illinois, 363
Imitation, 50, 75
Immortality, 41, 87–88, 221, 346, 365
Imperial Magazine, The, 238n
Incisa, 167
India, 283
Indian(s), American, 153, 303, 389, 390
Instincts, 91, 270, 292, 335
Institut de France, 204
Intuition, 263–264, 277, 318
Inversnaid, 218
Invisible law(s), 85, 96, 285–286, 326. See also Spiritual law(s)
Ipswich, Mass., 320
Iran, 11
Ireland, 236, 237, 240
Ireland, Alexander, 424
Irishmen, 221, 245, 333, 351
Irving, Rev. Edward, 414
Isaiah, 92, 374
Isis, 103, 375

Italian language, 90, 116, 118, 133, 139, 176, 193, 397–404, 416–418; translation from by RWE, 366
Italians, 154, 176, 192, 196
Italy, 68, 78, 135, 141–188, 189–192, 197, 205, 241, 245, 320
Itellario (priest in Messina), 133
Itinerary, Florence-Geneva, 418–419; London-Glasgow-Liverpool, 414–415, 422

Jackson, Andrew, 57, 281, 342, 438
Jacksonianism, 20, 287, 297, 326, 328, 332, 369
Jacobi, Friedrich Heinrich, 320n
James I, of England, 19, 220
James, Saint, 350
Janiculum, Mons, 157
Januarius, Saint, 144
Japan, 353
Jardin des Plantes, Paris, 11n, 197, 198–200, 405–406
Jarvis, Capt. (?), 357
Jarvis, Dr. Edward, 170, 357
Jasper (ship), 102, 213n
Jefferson, Thomas, 338
Jeffrey, Francis, 11, 16n, 233n, 256
Jenks, Francis, ed., *A Selection . . . of John Milton . . .* , 57n, 375n, 379n
Jesus Christ, 14, 23, 30, 32, 35, 36, 39, 43, 45, 92, 93, 153, 154, 220, 268, 286, 295, 309, 315, 330, 364, 376, 380, 382, 383, 384, 385; paintings of, 150, 183, 191
Jew, baptism of, 156
Jewish Law, 8, 165
Jews, the, 6, 282, 410
Jews' quarter, Ferrara, 181–182
John Adams (ship), 391
John of Bologna, *see* Bologne, Jean
Johnson, Samuel, 80 (?), 104, 336, 356, 372; *The Idler*, 104; *Irene*, 436; *Life of Pope*, 57n; "Lines added to Goldsmith's 'The Traveller,'" 72
John the Evangelist, 282, 349, 373 (?)
Jonson, Ben, 244–245, 376, 423; *Every Man out of his Humour*, 438n; *The Sad Shepherd*, 13n; *Sejanus*, 330n; *Timber*, 168n; "Upon Sejanus," 438; *Works*, 424n, 438n
Jortin, John, 23
Jouffroy, Théodore, 197, 204
Journal des Débats, 202
Jove, 160, 161, 293
Jove, Temple of Olympian, Syracuse, 127
Judas Iscariot, 154

Judgment, 256
Julien Hall, Boston, 326, 369
Juliet's Tomb, Verona, 187
Jung-Stilling, Johann Heinrich, 52
Jupiter, 12, 39
Jupiter Capitolinus, Temple of, Rome, 160
Jupiter (planet), 26, 119
Jura, Mount, 194, 196
Jussieu, Adrien L. H. de, 200
Jussieu, Antoine Laurent de, 200n
Jussieu, Bernard, 11
Justification, 337
Juvenal, *Satires*, 367n, 433n

Kant, Immanuel, 58, 235
Katrine, Loch, 217, 218
Keble, John, *The Christian Year*, 89n;
    "Morning," 35
Kendal, England, 226
Kenilworth Castle, 412, 413
Kent, Margaret Tucker, 60n, 72
Kentucky, 155
Kepler, Johannes, 235
Kettell, Samuel, 67(?), 114–115(?), 128,
    213, 214, 215, 216
Kidd, John, *On the Adaptation of External
    Nature* . . . , 254n, 304n
Kindness, 13, 49, 90, 300
Kingdom, 58
Kingston, Mr. (?), 149
Kirkcudbrightshire, 220n
Kittery, Me., 388
Kneeland, Abner, 281, 326n
Knights Hospitalers, 67, 117, 120, 136
Knights of St. John, *see* Knights Hospitalers
Knowledge, 18, 19, 24, 50, 51, 114–115,
    270, 282, 291, 367, 376, 415, 416
Knowles, John, *The Life and Writings of
    Henry Fuseli*, 24n
Knox, John, 219, 220
Knox, Vicesimus, *Elegant Extracts* . . .
    in Prose, 9n, 10n, 12n, 14n, 15n, 16n,
    20n, 21n, 85n, 212n, 284n
Knurre-Murre, 375
Koran, 424

Lacca, 180
Ladd, Hannah, 30
Ladd, William and Mary Haskins, 31n
Lafayette, Marquis de, 50, 76, 198, 298–299,
    328, 329, 367, 373
La Fontaine, Jean de, *Fables*, 201, 409
Lambacari, Palazzo, Bologna, 181
Lambard, Orville D. (?), 388

Lancaster, England, 226
Landor, Walter Savage, 51, 52, 73, 77, 78,
    172–175, 176, 179, 221, 231, 341, 430;
    "Barrow and Newton," 47n, 48; "Duke
    de Richelieu, Sir Fire Coats, and Lady
    Glengrin," 44, 341n, 430; "Epicurus,
    Leontion, and Ternissa," 46, 49; *Im-
    aginary Conversations*, 53; "William
    Penn and Lord Peterborough," 48
Langhorne, John and William, tr., *Plu-
    tarch's Lives*, 212n, 346n, 437n
Language(s), 14, 51, 67, 90, 106, 133, 139,
    140, 161, 245, 293, 304, 358, 434
Laocoön (statue), 150, 168
Laplace, Pierre Simon, Marquis de, 26
Lardner, Dionysius, *Cabinet History of Eng-
    land* . . . , 234n, 424n
Latin language, 133, 225
La Trappe, Order of, 358
Lausanne, 193–194, 207
La Valetta, 84, 115n, 116–121
La Valetta (Grand Master of Malta), *see*
    Valetta
Lavater, Johann Kaspar, 343
Law, *see* Moral, Natural, Invisible, Spiritual
    law
Lefebvre, François Joseph, 409
Leghorn, 208, 241
Leibnitz, Gottfried Wilhelm, Baron von,
    23, 327
Leicester, Robert Dudley, 1st Earl of, 412
Leighton, Robert, 18n; *Select Works*, 5n
Leipzig, 339
Leman, Lake, 193, 194
Lentulus, 151
Leonardo da Vinci, 197; Madonna, 160;
    Modesty and Vanity, 158; Last Supper,
    191
Leonidas I, of Sparta, 367
Leonidas (ship), 240
Leopold, 231
Leslie, John, et al., *Narrative of . . . the
    Polar Seas* . . . , 62n
Levane, 167
Levi, Lt. (?), 198
Library of Useful Knowledge, The, 258
Life, 29, 35, 37, 41, 67, 88, 94, 96, 148,
    276, 278–279, 369
Lighthouse keeper, anecdote about, 238
Lilliput, 104
Lilliputians, 142
Limitation(s), human, 74, 79, 82, 260, 274–
    275, 280, 314–315, 323, 340

Linberg, Henning Gotfried, 318
Lincoln, England, 303, 304, 320; Cathedral, 303n, 304
Lincoln, Mass., 234
Lincoln, Miss (?), 251
Linnaeus, Carolus, 282, 283, 311
Lipari Islands, 138
L'Isle d'Adam, Philippe de Villiers de, 117, 136
Literalness, 295
Liverpool, 78–81, 85, 220, 221, 226, 236, 237, 238, 239, 247, 333
Lives and Voyages of Drake, Cavendish, and Dampier . . . , 98n, 100n, 101n, 230n, 245, 246n
Lives of Eminent Persons, 258n, 259n, 341n, 362n, 366n, 368n, 369n
Lombardy, 189, 191, 192, 205, 230
Lomond, Loch, 217, 218
London, 34, 65, 78, 80n, 170, 204–205, 207, 220, 221, 245, 353, 407–408, 413–414; University of, 414
London, Bishop of, 34, 411
London Literary Gazette, The, 335
Longinus, 340
Longman, Rees, Hurst, publishers, 423
Lonsdale, Earl of, 220
Loomis, Rev. Harvey, 391
Loring, Sarah S., 6
Lorraine, Claude, 154, 348
Louis XIV, of France, 371
Louis XVI, of France, 369
Louis XVIII, of France, 247
Louis Philippe, of France, 85n, 196
Louvre, the, 189, 197, 241
Love, 13, 20, 90, 93, 98, 260, 282, 309, 315, 350, 363, 364, 367, 382
Lowell, Mass., 229
Lowndes, William, 38n, 39n, 44n, 212n
Lucan, 437
Lucas, Richard, *An Enquiry after Happiness*, 44, 173; *Practical Christianity, or an Account of the Holiness . . .* , 44, 173
Lucretius, 225
Lucrine Lake, 145, 146
Luculli, 160
Luther, Martin, 4, 23, 35, 43, 53, 59, 74, 151, 256, 257, 328, 329, 330, 333, 336, 337, 339–340, 341, 348, 349, 350, 352, 356, 360, 376, 380, 384; *Colloquia Mensalia . . .* , 251n, 349, 350; *Geistliche Lieder*, 53n; portrait of (Titian), 151
Lutzen, Battle of, 235
Lyceum Lectures, 372

Lynn, Mass., 129
Lysander, 373

Macaulay, Thomas Babington, Review of Boswell's *Life of Johnson*, 99n
Mac Gillivray, William, *Travels . . . of von Humboldt*, 245n
Machiavelli, Niccolò, 168, 230, 297
Mackintosh, Sir James, 21, 33, 58, 89, 173, 233n, 235, 340, 407; *A General View of . . . Ethical Philosophy*, 7, 13, 94, 99n, 173n; *History of England*, 234n, 424n
Madonna dei Miracoli, Church of, Brescia, 188
Madonna della Guardia, Church of, Bologna, 181
Maecenas, 165
Maffei, Francesco Scipione, Marchese di, 187
Maggiore, Lago, 192, 206
Magnetism, 94
Maine, 303, 359, 363, 388–391, 396
Malaga, 113
Malan, Henri-Abraham César, 195n
Malay, the, 58, 247
Malone, N.Y., 386
Malta, 65, 67, 68, 78, 84, 85n, 102, 115–121, 213, 214, 219, 236, 411
Maltby, John, 307n
Malte-Brun, Conrad, *Universal Geography . . .* , 135, 136n, 137n, 138n
Maltese language, 118, 119
Maltese people, 116, 119
Malthus, Thomas Robert, 20
Mälzel, Johann Nepomuc, 312
Mamertine Prison, 151
Man, 29, 34, 36, 42, 49, 51, 56, 57, 90, 91, 119, 200, 221, 227, 278, 285, 298, 301, 309, 322, 327, 329, 331, 333, 335, 336, 337, 339, 340, 341, 346, 350, 352, 376, 378. *See also* Men
Man (men), of action, 43, 115, 273, 327, 333. *See also* Man, practical
Man (men), artificial, 43, 307, 310
Man (men), of genius, 26, 79, 82, 266, 328, 377. *See also* Man, great
Man (men), genuine (true), 43, 44, 54, 56, 212, 240, 294, 306, 307, 308, 309, 310, 314, 317, 321, 322, 326, 328, 346, 351, 367, 369, 373, 384
Man (men), great, 21, 42, 43, 50, 69, 77, 79, 80, 84, 88, 109, 142, 173, 174, 183, 260, 279, 315, 328, 331, 336, 353, 357, 363, 369, 373, 376. *See also* Man of genius, Universal Man

Man (men), practical, 59, 327, 356. *See also* Man of action

Man, reverence for, 38, 342, 357, 370

Man (men), wise, 86, 90, 253, 268, 279, 281, 283, 284, 316, 327

Man (men), young, 49, 76, 157, 201, 262, 278, 286, 293; 321, 322, 377

Manchester, England, 226, 247

Manfrini Palace, Venice, 186

Manners, 15, 51, 81, 89, 132, 141, 154, 262, 322, 341, 350, 415

Manzoni, Alessandro, *I Promessi Sposi*, 73, 74n, 175n, 176n, 177, 190, 259, 322, 417

Marcellus, Marcus Claudius, 128

Mariner's Society, 251

Marmoreus, 124

Mars, Mlle, 202

Marsa Muscette, Malta, 67, 115

"Marseillaise," 340

Marsh, James, ed., S. T. Coleridge's *Aids to Reflection*, 327n, 411

Marsigli, Luigi Ferdinando, 181

Martial, *Epigrams*, 61n

Martigny, 193

Martineau, James, 79, 80n

Marvell, Andrew, 35; "An Horatian Ode . . . ," 259n

Mary, Queen of Scots, 369

Mason, Sidney, 334

Masonic Hall, New York City, 334

Masons, 287

Massachusetts, 331

Massachusetts Peace Society, The, 31n, 360

Massinger, Philip, 73, 174

Matthews & Polly, firm of (?), 422

Maxwell, Hugh(?), 334

Mayer, Brantz, 166

Mazarine Library, Paris, 204

Medici, 230

Mediterranean Sea, 103, 113, 118–119, 124

Melanchthon, 350

Mela River, 189

Mellili, Sicily, 129

Mémoires de l'Académie de la Littérature, 233

Memory, 111, 119, 234, 299

Men, 47, 54, 129–130, 139, 142, 197, 226, 257, 324, 377, 406. *See also* Man

Mendelssohn, Moses, *Phédon*, 211

Mercury, Temple of, Baiae, 145

Meredith Bridge, N.H., 229

Messina, 132–133, 136, 138, 139, 188, 215, 231

Mestre, 183, 186

Metella, Cecilia, 149, 153

Metellus Creticus, 153n

Methodist(s), 282, 381, 384

Mezzeria, system of, 180, 230, 404

Michelangelo Buonarroti, 155, 157n, 160, 166n, 168, 169, 173, 178, 230, 258, 260, 328, 356, 361, 362, 363, 365, 367, 369, 377; David, 168; Last Judgment, 153, 170; Moses, 165; Self-portrait, 165; Sonnets I, VII, 366; Sonnet VI, 305; bust of, 175

Michelozzi Villa, near Florence, 177

Microscopes, 170, 268, 286

Milan, 75, 189–192, 205, 206; Cathedral, 75, 189–190, 205

Miles, Henry, 170, 405

Miles family of Concord, Mass., 338–339

Mill, John Stuart, 221, 422, 423

Milner, Joseph and Isaac, *The History of the Church of Christ*, 341n

Milton, John, 35, 43, 80, 88, 89, 92, 235, 240, 274, 282, 312, 313, 328, 337, 340, 344, 350, 356, 375, 376, 377, 378, 380, 407, 432; *An Apology for Smectymnuus*, 54n, 57, 379, 429n; *Comus*, 5, 89; "Considerations touching . . . means to remove hirelings . . . ," 340n; "The Doctrine and Discipline of Divorce," 282n; Letter VII, 87, 240n; *Lycidas*, 103, 111; *Paradise Lost*, 24, 61n, 313n, 332n, 361n, 363; *Paradise Regained*, 328; *Pro Populo Anglicano Defensio*, 358n; *Reason of Church Government*, 378n

Mincio River, 187

Minerva, 299, 375

Minerva (statue), 124

Minerva, Temple of, Syracuse, 122, 123, 124

Ministry, the, 27, 91, 96, 307, 308, 348–349, 380, 384, 434–435. *See also* Preaching, Sermons

Mirabeau, Victor Riqueti, Marquis de, 80, 285

Miseno, 141

Miserere, 154, 155

Misericordia, Order of, 172

Modena, 230

Modena, Duke of, 165

Mohammed, 341

Moiselles, 204

Molière, 371

Molo di Gaeta, 149

Monarchists, 369

Monselice, 182

Montague, Basil (?), 411

Montaigne, Michel Eyquem de, 38, 68, 173, 239, 273, 315, 409, 432, 437; "Cowardice . . . ," 210n; "Of the Education of Children," 309n; *Essays*, 36, 68n, 201, 210n, 351n, 433n, 437n; "Of Friendship," 270; "Of Physiognomy," 39n; "Of Vanity," 85n, 252n

Monte Nuovo, 146

Monte Reale, 140, 149

Montesquieu, Charles de Secondat, Baron de, *Lettres Persanes*, 26n

Montgomery, James, 42n

Monthly Repository, The, 414n

Montreuil, 204

Moody, Mrs. (?), 388

Moore, Thomas, 365; "Verses to the Poet Crabbe's Inkstand," 8

Moors, 116

Moral(s), 39, 157, 224

Moral beauty, 77, 120, 240

Moral education, 326, 327

Moral law(s), 26, 83, 84, 254, 322, 364, 384, 385

Moral nature, 43, 45, 83, 84, 86, 93, 120, 313–314, 376, 383, 385

Moral reformation, 341

Moral sublime, 39, 255, 383, 429

Moralist, the good, 385

More, Miss (?), 22

More, Sir Thomas, 4, 35, 43, 50, 356

Morocco, 113

Moscow, 377

Moses, 92

Mother Carey's chickens, 244

Mount Auburn Cemetery, 272–273

Mozart, Wolfgang Amadeus, 154

Mugnone River, 176

Muley Molak (Abd el Malek), 50, 356

Murat, Achille, 242

Murillo, Bartolomé Estaban, 197

Museum of Natural History, Florence, 175

Music, 112, 114, 118, 131, 153, 170, 202, 300, 343, 367, 380. *See also* Opera

Mussulman, the, 314

Mystery of the Tre Ore, 156

Mythology, 374, 375

Nahant, Mass., 146

Naples, 68, 129, 138, 140, 141–149, 151, 167, 170, 189, 215, 216, 320

Nash, Paulina Tucker, 60

Natural character, 114

Natural history, 199, 282, 290, 311, 405, 415

Naturalist, 25, 94, 200, 406

Natural law(s), 12, 86, 95, 254, 284, 322, 364

Natural science, 322, 415

Nature, 60, 69–70, 92, 95, 112, 167, 175, 199, 237, 267–268, 273, 282, 288, 289, 296, 343, 359, 374, 376, 378, 382, 406, 416

Nature as language, 60, 95, 267–268, 406

Neapoli (suburb of Syracuse), 124

Negro, the, 297

Nemesis, 308

Neptune (Indian in Maine), 390

Nereidos, Lady, 127

Nero, 127, 221

Nestor (*Iliad*), 425n

New Bedford, Mass., 96, 97n, 157n, 252, 261, 263, 265, 267, 268, 269, 321, 412n

New England, 114, 117, 179, 356, 377

New Jerusalem Magazine, 18, 33, 38n, 45, 46n, 56, 336n

New Smyrna, 166

New South Church, Boston, 360n

New York City, 62, 183, 197, 210, 238, 241, 325, 327, 328n, 334, 415, 426

New York Commercial Advertiser, The, 247n

New York Daily Whig, 344n

New York (ship), 236; passenger list of, 421

Newburyport, Mass., 228, 388–389

Newgate Calendar, The, 54

Newhall, Mary, 268

Newspaper(s), 221, 225, 315, 332, 342, 343, 396

Newton, Mass., 31n, 91, 93, 280, 287, 308, 309n, 316

Newton, Sir Isaac, 25, 26, 35, 50, 87n, 89, 174, 227, 235, 255, 256, 287, 373

Newtonian theory, 224

Niagara, 304

Nicolini, Signor (?), 126, 128

Nicolosi, Francesco, 133

Nicosia, Signor, *see* Nicolini

Niederer, Johannes, 6, 11

Nile, the, 104

Niles' Weekly Register, 53n

Noah, 200

"Noodle's Oration," 148

North, Christopher, pseud. of Wilson, John

North, Roger, *Examen . . .* , 233

North American Review, The, 347n

Northcote, James, 24

Northerners, 262

Norton, Andrews, *A Statement of Reasons for not believing the Doctrines of Trinitarians . . .* , 80

Norton, Thomas, 423n
"No" sayers, 73
Notre Dame, Church of, Paris, 201
Novalis, pseud. of Hardenberg, Baron Friedrich von

Oberlin, Jérémie Jacques, 283
Odescalchi Palace, Rome, 152
Odin's Prophetess, 323
O'Flanagan, Rev. Fr. (?), 166
Ohio, 331
Oldcastle, Sir John (Lord Cobham), 35
Old Manse, Concord, Mass., 349n
Old South Church, Boston, 277n, 319n
Oldtown, Me., 390
Oliver, Nathaniel K. G., 53
Opera, 132, 140, 170, 202, 230. See also Music
Optics, 60, 94, 170, 254n
Optimism, 77, 253
Organic form, 36–37, 199–200
Ornithological Chambers, Jardin des Plantes, 198–199, 405–406
Orthodoxy, 342, 343
Ortygia, 123
Osborn, Francis, 361; A Miscellany of Sundry Essays . . . , 361n
Osiris, 103, 375
Ospitale dei Frati Fatebenefratelli, Milan, 191
Ospitale Grande, Milan, 191
Ossipee, N.H., 229
Otanes the Persian, 259n
Over refiners, 30, 113
Ovid, 44; Fasti, 29n; The Heroides, 5n; The Metamorphoses, 127
Owen, Robert, 326
Owen, William, tr., "Elegy on Cynddalan ap Cynddrwyn," 412n
Oxford, England, 283, 414

Pachomius, Saint, 76
Pacini, Giovanni, "Ivanhoe," 176n
Padua, 89, 182–183, 184, 186; Cathedral, 182; University of, 183
Paganism, 124
Painter(s), 168, 177, 183, 362, 365
Palais Royal, 201
Palatine Hill, 166
Palermo, 137, 138–140, 149, 215, 231
Paley, William, 55; The Principles of Moral and Political Philosophy, 99, 100n
Palgrave, Sir Francis, History of England, 34; Rise and Progress of the English Commonwealth, 41n

Palladio, Andrea, 183, 186
Palma Giovano, 184
Palma Vecchio, 184
Palmer, Samuel, Moral Essays on Proverbs, 361n
Palm Sunday, 152
Pan, 375
Panharmonicon, the, 312n
Pantheon, Rome, 151
Papyrus, 127
Paradise Street Chapel, London, 80n
Paris, 69, 76, 77, 130, 188–189, 191, 195, 196–204, 305, 405, 406–407, 408–409
Parker, N., "Address . . . to the Teachers of the South Parish S. S. . . . ," 423n
Parkman, Rev. Francis, An Offering of Sympathy, 251
Park Street Church, Boston, 319n
Parry, Sir William Edward, 65, 374
Passage aux Panorames, Paris, 201
Passignano, 167, 179
Passion(s), 40, 95, 319, 348
Past, 21, 22, 69, 275
Patrick, Bishop Simon, The Parable of a Pilgrim . . . , 44n
Patriotism, 327
Paul, Saint, 111, 151, 309, 315, 329, 348, 380, 384, 409
Payson, John L., 215
Payta Head, 265
Peabody, Ephraim (?), 96
Peel, Sir Robert, 413
Pelletier, James, 253
Penn, William, 14, 84, 348, 364; The Christian Quaker, 253n
Penny Magazine, The, 372
Penobscot River, 389, 390, 391
Pepperell, Sir William, 303n, 306, 323
Père Lachaise Cemetery, 200–201, 408–409
Pergola Theatre, Florence, 171
Perkins, Jacob, 80, 82, 83, 226, 424
Perrin, John, The Elements of French and English Conversation, 106
Persian, the, 51, 258, 259n
Persius, Satire I, 318n; Satire V, 199n
Perspective, 9, 22, 52, 92, 255, 257, 274, 277, 323, 345, 348, 352, 364, 378, 379
Perugia, 167, 179
Perugino, Il, 173
Pestalozzi, Johann Heinrich, 6, 11, 19–20, 326, 327; Leonard and Gertrude, 20n
Peter, Saint, 151
Petrarch, Francesco, 89, 132, 167, 179, 182, 191, 259, 367

Phidias, 373

Philadelphia, Pa., 37, 237

Philip of Macedon, 10n, 15, 173, 355, 357

Philistidos, Lady, 127

Philistus, 127

Phillips, Samuel (?), 59

Philo Judaeus, 410

Philosopher(s), 52, 84, 298, 310, 346, 371, 375

Philosophical Transactions, 232

Philosophy, 47, 48, 52, 197n, 254, 277, 296, 302, 333, 335, 375

Phocion, 4, 43, 50, 174, 296, 321, 351, 355, 356, 380, 384

Pincian Hill, 166n

Pindar, 386n

Pious Minstrel, The, 89

Pitt, William, Earl of Chatham, 10, 36, 257, 429

Pitti Palace, 168, 241

Plants, 229–230, 282, 283, 290, 321, 389, 413. *See also* Flowers

Plato, 4, 11, 38, 261, 282, 289, 354, 380, 429; *The Republic*, 43n, 261n, 329n, 429n; *The Symposium*, 43n

Platonism, 260

Plautus, Titus Maccius, *Miles Gloriosus*, 87n

Playfair, John, 256, 267; *Illustrations of the Huttonian Theory* . . . , 267n

Pliny, *Natural History*, 152n, 175n

Plotinus, 355, 367

Plutarch, 274, 325, 355; *Lives*, 284; life of: Agesilaus, 51n, 342n, 346; Alexander, 337n; Demosthenes, 356n; Phocion, 351n; Pompey, 212n, 227n; Themistocles, 437n; *Morals*: "Apophthegms of Kings and Great Commanders," 51n, 262n, 352n; "Concerning Such Whom God is Slow to Punish," 437n; "Of Curiosity," 10n; "How a Man may be sensible of his Progress in Virtue," 51n; "How a Man may Praise himself without being Envied," 51n, 96n; "How to Profit by our Enemies," 20n; "Of the Fortune or Virtue of Alexander the Great," 253n; "Of Isis and Osiris," 103n, 375n; "Lives of the Ten Orators," 355n; "Of Love," 368; "Political Precepts," 356n; "Of Proceedings in Virtue," 340n; "Of the Tranquillity of the Mind," 315n; "The Symposiacs," 114n; "Why the Oracles Cease to Give Answers," 375n; "Why the Pythian Priestess Ceases her Oracles in Verse," 386n; "Of the Word

EI engraved over the Gate of Apollo's Temple at Delphi," 375n

Plutarch's Lives (tr. John and William Langhorne), 212n, 346n, 437n

Plutarch's Morals, Several Hands Edition, 10n, 20n, 424, 437n

Plymouth, England, 100

Plymouth, Mass., 252, 261, 265, 267

Poet(s), 70, 227, 298, 312, 316, 323, 330, 362, 363, 376, 377, 381, 385, 412, 432

Polarity of matter, 416

Polehampton, Edward T. W. and John M. Good, *The Gallery of Nature and Art* . . . , 61n, 62

Pomeranus, Cardinal (Johann Bugenhaften), 23

Pompeii, 139, 142, 146–147

Pompey the Great, statue of, 153

Ponsonby, Sir Frederick, 120

Pont Neuf, Paris, 188, 196

Ponte Trinità, Florence, 176

Pope, the, 182, 339, 375

Pope Gregory XVI, 152, 154, 155, 156–157

Pope, Alexander, 56–57, 174; *The Dunciad*, 57n; *Moral Essays*, 356n; "Song of a Person of Quality," 148n; "The Temple of Fame," 437n; "The Universal Prayer," 26

Popery, 339

Population data, 136, 137, 138, 162

Po River, 182

Porta, Fra Guglielmo della, 160

Porta di Fuga, Spoleto, 167

Portici, 146

Portland, Me., 228, 240, 388, 389

Porto Maggiore, Syracuse, 126, 127

Portsmouth, N.H., 228

Posilippo, 141; Grotto of, 142

Potowmac (ship), 53

Poverty, 10, 16, 221, 261n, 321, 373

Pozzuoli, 143, 146

Prato Gate, Florence, 170

Pratolino, 180

Pratt, William, 151

Prayer, 86, 97, 104, 211, 278, 280, 299, 350, 353, 381

Preaching, 44, 91, 159, 275, 278, 281, 294, 309, 313, 314, 319, 348–349, 384, 385. *See also* Ministry, Sermons

Preleveque, 207

Present, 21, 22, 41, 84, 266, 275

Preti, Mattia, 118

Privy, 307

Procida, 141

Procreation, 257
Progress, 253
Prometheus, 12
Proserpine, 127
Protestantism, 360
Proteus, 323
Proverbs, 9, 12, 14, 15, 16–18, 52n, 58, 59n, 68n, 85, 210, 212, 264, 278, 284, 304, 322, 361, 374
Providence, 37, 132, 264
Providence, R.I., 210, 349, 426
Providence (steamboat), 426
Provident Institution for Savings, The, Boston, 347n
Ptolemaism, 26
Puberty, age of, 348
Public lectures, 335, 362
Publius Syrus, 330n; *Sententiae,* 362n
Puerto Rico, 14, 325, 334n
Puritan Conventicles, The, 308
Putnam, Israel, 252n
Putnam, Joan, 251, 252n
Pyrrhonism, 310
Pyrrhus, 373
Pythagoras, 66, 288
Pythian oracle, 375, 421n

Quaker(s), 87, 97, 263, 268
Quarantine, 115–116
Quarterly Review, The, 328
Queensberry, Duchess of, 220
Quintilian, *Institutio Oratoria,* 11n, 16n, 429n
Quirinal Hill, 166

Radicalism, 285
Radici, Signor, "Review of the *Rime,*" 258, 259n
Railroad(s), 82–83, 226, 277, 293, 296
Raimondo (last name unknown), 140
Rammohun Roy, Raja, 283
Randolph, Thomas, "An Answer to . . . Ben. Jonson's Ode . . . ," 316n
Ranz des Vaches, 340
Raphael Sanzio, 121, 142, 149, 173, 183, 199, 230, 362, 374, 405; Caesar Borgia, 151; Fornarina, 151; Frescoes, 153; Self-portrait, 158; Transfiguration, 150, 183
Ravenna, 89, 169
Ray, John, *A Complete Collection of English Proverbs,* 9n, 17n, 212n, 322n, 361n
Raymond, Me., 228
Reason, 44, 49, 53, 297, 298, 299, 313, 319, 320, 336, 339, 348, 351, 353, 356, 357, 359, 360, 362, 365, 376

Réaumur, René Antoine Ferchault de, 9n, 253
Reed, David, 31
Reed, Sampson, 44, 335, 336n; "Sleep," 56n
Rees, Owen, 423n
Re Ferdinando (ship), 140
Regent's Park, London, 414
Regulus, Marcus Attilius, 90, 296
Religion, 27, 38, 40, 80, 282, 313, 335, 347, 364–365, 382
Religion of forms (ritualistic), 27, 30, 31, 40, 81, 282, 313, 364
Religion, Saxon, 34
Rembrandt van Rijn, self-portrait, 170
Reni, Guido, 142, 181; Beatrice Cenci, 151; Magdalen, 158; Martyrdom of St. Sebastian, 151; Paradise (fresco), 181
Renunciation, 301–302, 308
Republic, 58
Republicans, 313, 369
Reputation, 22, 43, 46, 369, 380, 382
Resina, 146, 148
Retribution, 46
Retrospective Review, 258, 259n
Reynolds, Dr. Edward, 251
Reynolds, Richard, 252, 352(?)
Reynolds, Sir Joshua, *Discourses,* 366n
Rhodes, 117, 136
Rhône River, 194
Rhyme(s), 428
Rialto Bridge, 183
Ricciardi, Signor Guiseppe, 126, 128, 131
Richmond, Legh, *The Dairyman's Daughter,* 118
Richter, Jean Paul Friedrich, *Vorschule der Aesthetik,* 54n
Rider, C. J., 386
Rider, Charles M., 386
Rienzi, Cola di, 149
Rinaldi (?), (Roman artist), Mosaic of Paestum, 159
Ripley, Dr. Ezra (stepgrandfather of RWE), 31, 212n, 338–339, 344n, 349–350, 358–359, 384
Ripley, Ezra (grandson of Dr. Ezra Ripley), 344
Ripley, Phebe Bliss Emerson (grandmother of RWE), 338
Ripley, Samuel, 234, 344n
Ripley, Sara Alden Bradford, 162(?), 300
Ritchie, Mr. (?), 169
Robbins, Rev. Chandler, 97
Robertson, William, *History of America,* 220
Rochester, Henry Wilmot, Earl of, 301
Rodman, Benjamin, 263

468

Rodman, Elizabeth, 268
Roger I, of Sicily, 138
Rogers, Mr. (?), 143
Roland, Mme Jeanne Manon, 40
Roman daughter, the, 151, 152n
Roman Gate, Florence, 177, 179
Roman Senators, 146
Rome, 69, 72n, 76, 90, 106, 122, 130, 140, 149–162, 164–166, 167, 168, 172, 179, 184, 216, 259, 283, 285, 301, 353, 367, 373, 375, 408
Romilly, Sir Samuel, "Bentham on Codification," 99, 100n
Rosa, Monte, 194
Rosa, Salvator, 170
Roscoe, Thomas, "The Life of Michael Angelo Buonaroti," 258n, 259n; tr., Sismondi's *Historical Views of the Literature of the South of Europe*, 105n
Roscoe, William (?), 132
Rossini, Giacchino Antonio, "Ivanhoe," 176n
Rostopchin, Feodor, 377n; *Verité sur l'incendie de Moscow*, 377n
Rotch, Mary, 263–264, 267, 268, 365, 374n
Rousseau, Jean Jacques, 194; *Confessions*, 220
Rovigo, 182
Roxbury Ditch, 436
Roxbury, Mass., 273, 372n
Rubens, Peter Paul, 139
Rush, Dr. Benjamin, 37
Rydal, Mount, 222

S., 51, 351
Sabina, 167
Sacchi, Andrea, Vision of St. Romoaldo, 159
Sacy, M. Silvestre de, 233n
Sailor(s), 103, 106, 107, 109–110, 112
St. Agatha, Church of, Syracuse, 131
St. Angelo, Bridge of, Rome, 157
St. Augustine, Fla., 242
St. Cloud, Paris, 204
St. Denis, France, 204
St. Elmo's Light, Malta, 115
St. Gaetano, Church of, Naples, 144
St. George's Channel, 237
St. Iago, Church of, Messina, 133
St. James's Church, London, 407, 414
St. John, Church of, Syracuse, 128
St. John, Gate of, Rome, 149
St. John Lateran, Basilica, Rome, 151
St. John's Church, La Valetta, 84, 85n, 116, 117, 169, 211, 213, 214,
St. John's River, 390

St. Laurentio, Church of, Naples, 144
St. Mark's Church, Venice, 183
St. Mark's Piazza, Venice, 74, 183, 185, 186
St. Martin's Church, Naples, 141
St. Mary's, Azores, 108
St. Mary's Church, Warwick, 413
St. Maurice, Switzerland, 193, 206, 207
St. Onofrio, Church of, Rome, 160
St. Paul's Bay, Malta, 115
St. Paul's Cathedral, London, 205, 413, 422
St. Peter's Church, Rome, 75, 78, 116, 131, 149, 151, 153, 155, 156, 157, 158–159, 160, 169, 190, 241, 258, 284
St. Popilius, Church of, La Valetta, 117
St. Simon's Church, Palermo, 140
St. Stephen's Church, London, 413
St. Thomas, Church of, La Valetta, 117
Sais, 296
Sala di Giustizia, Padua, 182
Saladin, 373
Salem Street Church, Boston, 318n
Salmasius, see Saumaise, Claude de
Saltmarket, Glasgow, 219
Salute, Chiesa della, Venice, 184
Salvatore, Signore (?), 216
Samer, France, 204
Sampson, Albert, 310
Sampson, George A., 66, 178, 262, 267, 307, 310n, 325
San Antonio, Church of, Padua, 182
San Clementi, Duke of, 169
San Domenico, Church of, Bologna, 181; Milan, 191
San Domenico di Fiesole, 172–173, 179
San Giorgio, Church of, Verona, 187
San Justin, Church of, Padua, 182
San Pietro in Vinculo, Church of, Rome, 165
San Zenobia, Bishop of Florence, 178
Sandwich Islands (Hawaiian Islands), 23
Sanguinetto River, 167
Santa Clara, Church of, Naples, 144
Santa Croce, Church of, Florence, 74, 168, 175, 230
Santa Maria Maggiore, Church of, Rome, 154
Santa Maria Novella, Church of, Florence, 169
Santo Geronimo, Church of, Naples, 144
Saracens, the, 377
Sarto, Andrea del, 151
Sass, Henry, *A Journey to Rome and Naples . . .* , 137n
Saturnalia, 173
Saturn (planet), 26

Saul, King, 326

Saumaise, Claude de (Salmasius), 358; *Defensio Regia pro Carlo I*, 358n

Saunders, J. M., 251

Saurin, Jacques, 9n

Saussure, Horace Bénédict de, 196; *Voyages dans les Alpes*, 196n

Savage, James, 347

Savile, John T., 252

"Savings Bank," 250

Saxon(s), 287, 416, 434

Saxony, 339

Saxton, Mr. (?), 423

Scauri, 160

Schiller, Johann Christoph Friedrich von, 15n, 18n, 52n, 53, 54, 55, 87n, 325n, 337, 367; "Archimedes und der Schüler," 64n; *Don Carlos*, 338n; *The Robbers*, 55

Schlegel (August Wilhelm von? Karl Wilhelm Friedrich von?), 273

Schleiermacher, Friedrich E. D., 360; *Ideen, Reflexionen, . . .* , 360n; *Die Sammtliche Werke*, 360n

Scholar, the, 297, 348, 358, 367, 370

Sciarra Palace, Rome, 158

Science, 38, 286, 360, 373

Scipio (Africanus?), 36, 50, 90, 153, 252, 373, 379; bust of, 132

Scipios (statues), 150

Scotland, 78, 217–222

Scott, John, *Luther and the Lutheran Reformation*, 330n, 341n

Scott (of Amwell), John (?) (Job), 367

Scott, Sir Walter, 35, 89, 220, 235, 279, 311, 312, 317; *The Bride of Lammermoor*, 193n; *The Fortunes of Nigel*, 144; *Guy Mannering*, 144; *The Heart of Midlothian*, 219; *Kenilworth*, 9n; *The Lady of the Lake*, 21n, 218; *Marmion*, 413; *Rob Roy*, 219; *Rokeby*, 413n; *Tales of a Grandfather*, 17n

Scott, Thomas, *The Force of Truth*, 118

Scottish language, 219, 220

Scougal, Henry P., *The Life of God in the Soul of Man*, 118

Scudder, Horace, 97n

Scylla, 138

Sea, 70, 103, 106, 108, 112, 133, 231, 239, 242

Search, Edward, pseud. of Tucker, Abraham

Seasickness, 102–103, 105, 238

Seckendorf, Veit Ludwig von, *Commentarius Historicus . . .* , 339

Second Church of Boston, 54, 97n, 162n, 178n, 228n, 325

Second Unitarian Church, New York City, 328n

Secrecy, 42, 85, 337, 428

Sect(s), religious, 49, 83, 348, 382

Seine River, 188, 196

Selborne, England, 283

Self-education, 50, 58, 68, 84, 277, 301

Self-knowledge, 6, 68, 319

Self-reliance, 47–48, 49, 50, 90, 140, 141, 269, 274, 275, 279, 283, 284, 292, 304, 317–318, 319, 324, 335, 342, 346–347

Sempione, 191, 192, 193

Seneca, Marcus Annaeus, 5n, 18n, 21n, 22, 142, 422; *Ad Lucilium Epistulae Morales*, 39

Serapis, Temple of, Pozzuoli, 143

Sermon(s), 9, 14, 16, 49, 80, 89, 148, 252, 277, 278, 279, 294, 309, 319, 325, 380, 381

Sesto Calendo, 192

Severini family, 144

Sewel, William, *The History of the . . . Quakers*, 31n, 32, 38n, 275n, 384n

Shaftesbury, Anthony Ashley Cooper, 3rd Earl of, 55; *Characteristics*, 99, 100n, 210n

Shakespear, John, 407

Shakespear, Susanna, 407

Shakespeare, William, 18–19, 20, 35, 36, 43, 50, 55, 73, 80, 89, 96, 168n, 235, 244, 245, 274, 279, 284, 312, 315, 353, 360, 365, 373, 375, 376, 379, 425, 428, 429n, 432; *Antony and Cleopatra*, 18, 311, 315; *As You Like It*, 132n; *Cymbeline*, 22; *Hamlet*, 19, 264, 275n, 311, 378n, 381, 436; *I Henry IV*, 54n, 219n, 244; *II Henry IV*, 311; *Henry VI, Pt. I*, 437; *King Lear*, 47n, 244, 311, 312; *Macbeth*, 23, 240n, 311; *Measure for Measure*, 417n; *Midsummer Night's Dream*, 297, 371; *Much Ado about Nothing*, 24n, 34n; *Othello*, 311, 334n, 345n; *Pericles*, 248n; *Sonnets*, 371; *Tempest*, 19; *Twelfth Night*, 266n

Shells, 75, 129, 139, 282, 291, 405, 415

Shirley, James, *The Contention of Ajax and Ulysses*, 24

Sicilian(s), 103, 116, 124, 133, 139

Sicily, 78, 121–133, 138, 147, 214, 411

Siculi, 132

Sidney, Sir Philip, "Astrophel and Stella," 434

Sierra Nevada, 113, 114

Silenus, 323

Silkworms, 188

Simaethus River, 129

Simplon Road, 191, 192, 206, 207

Sin, 222

Sion, Switzerland, 193, 207

Sismondi, J.C.L. Simonde de, 178; *Historical Views of the Literature of the South of Europe*, 105; *Nouveaux Principes d'économie politique*, 180n

Sistine Chapel, 152, 153, 154, 155, 361

Slavery, 29, 92, 306, 357, 360, 369

Sleep, 56

Small's Rocks Lighthouse, 238

Smeaton, John, 253, 254n

Smith, Adam, 432

Smith, Mr. (?), 164

Smith, Sydney, 55; "The Book of Fallacies . . . ," 148n

Snow, 61, 359, 377, 384

Society, 30, 47, 93, 178, 222, 224, 237, 238, 256, 262, 270–271, 274, 276, 278, 283, 294, 299, 308, 310, 316, 330, 341, 342, 370, 382

Socrates, 4, 12, 35, 38, 39n, 43, 73, 80, 84, 109, 174, 211, 227, 264, 298, 301, 309, 315, 319, 320, 321, 330, 336, 337, 356, 364, 367, 380, 384, 421, 425, 432

Solitude, 29, 92, 104, 157, 158, 237, 256, 259, 266, 280, 290, 296, 308, 314, 329, 347, 349–350, 359, 367, 372

Solomon, 184, 313

Solon, 362, 379n

Somerville, Mary, 24

Sophia Charlotte, of Prussia, 23

Soracte, Mount, 158

Sorbonne, the, 197

Soul(s), 15, 29, 33, 39, 40, 41, 42, 55, 57, 82, 84, 87, 88, 90, 91, 93, 95, 104, 109, 260, 264, 266, 274, 278, 279, 280, 285, 295, 310, 383

South, Robert, *Musica Incantans*, 407

South America, 247, 357

Southerners, 262, 287

Southey, Robert, 173, 369; "Bishop Bruno," 365n

Spada Palace, Rome, 153

Spagnoletto, Lo, 141; *Dead Christ*, 141

Spain, 63, 113

Spalatin, Georg, 339

Spaniard, the, 113

Spanish language, 139

Sparta, 373

Spectator, The, 356n

Spedale dei Pazzi, Messina, 139

Spenser, Edmund, 286, 365, 376

Spiritual law(s), 28, 83, 86, 378, 382

Spoleto, 167, 179

Spurzheim, Johann Kaspar, 326

Stabler, Edward (?), 96

Stackpole, Joseph Lewis, 151

Staël, Madame de (Anne Louise Germaine, Baronne de Staël-Holstein), 194, 325, 337; *Corinne*, 40, 75n, 260–261; *Germany*, 13n, 253n, 289n, 296n, 326, 338n

Staffa, England, 223

Stag, fable of, 270, 329

Stanhope, George, tr., *Pious Breathings* . . . , 86n, 210n

Stanley, Edward George, Lord, 257

Stanley, Edward John, Baron of Alderly, 407

Starke, Mariana, *Travels in Europe . . . 1824 . . . 1828*, 127n, 168n, 183n, 216n, 397

Steam engines, 80, 82–83, 226, 237, 415

Stearns, Samuel H., 277

Stebbins, Dr. Artemas, 269

Sterne, Laurence, 174; *Tristram Shandy*, 220

Stewardson, Thomas, 179n, 182, 187, 192, 195

Stewart, Dugald, 7n

Stillwater, Me., 390

Stirling, Scotland, 217; Castle, 217

Stoic, the, 4

Stoicism, 385

Stratford-on-Avon, 425n

Stromboli, Mount, 138

Stuart, Gilbert, 234

Stuart, Sir James, *Three Years in North America*, 222

Sturgis, William, 23

Sublime, the, 39, 44, 83, 148, 157, 174, 258, 333, 341, 429

Suchet, Louis Gabriel, 409

Suetonius, *De Vita Caesarum*, 221n

Sunday School, 93; idea for lesson (?), 216–217

Superstition, 117

Susa, 304, 367

Swain, William W., 265, 284

Swammerdam, Jan, 288

Swedenborg, Emmanuel, 33, 37, 38n, 84, 92, 235, 292, 317, 318, 347, 348, 355, 382; *The Apocalypse Revealed*, 343n

Swedenborgianism, 11, 44n, 269, 288, 342, 370n
Swedenborgians, 381
Swift, Jonathan, 148n, 310n
Swiss, the, 377
Switzerland, 78, 139, 193–195
Sylvester, John (Joshua?), 375
Symbolism, see Correspondence, doctrine of
Syracusan, 63
Syracuse, Sicily, 122–128, 129, 131, 213, 214; Catacombs, 122; trip to, 121–122

T., Col., 388
Tacitus, 167, 179; *Annals*, 13n
Talleyrand-Périgord, Charles Maurice de, 407
Talma, François Joseph, 202
Tamworth, England, 413
Tangiers, 113
Taormina, Sicily, 133
Tar, Jack, 110
Tarifa Light, 113
Tarpeian Rock, 150
Tasso, Torquato, 160, 181, 377
Taunton, Mass., 320
Tavassi, Signore (?), 145, 161
Taylor, Edward T., 59, 251, 381
Taylor, Emily, *Sabbath Recreations . . .*, 210n
Taylor, Isaac, *Fanaticism*, 330, 333; *The Natural History of Enthusiasm*, 330n, 353
Taylor, Jeremy, 42n, 59, 88; *The Great Exemplar*, dedication of, 89n; *Holy Dying*, Epistle Dedicatory, 89n
Teacher(s), 45, 46, 50, 67, 83, 93–94, 278, 279, 297
Teaching, 91, 93, 348, 355. See also Self-education
Telegraph, 236
Telescope, 170, 254, 286
Temperance, 68, 88, 90, 343, 354, 385
Temple, Mr. (?), 118, 119
Templier, Le, 203
Temptation, 69, 71
Tennemann, William Gottlieb, *Geschichte der Philosophie*, 100n
Tennyson, Alfred, Lord, "The Dirge," 325
Terni, 166, 167, 179, 320
Thames River, 204
Thayer, Sylvanus (?), 201
Théâtre Français, 202
Theism, 81
Themistocles, 50
Thénard, Louis Jacques, 197
Theobald, Lewis (?), 436
Theologia Thomae ex Charmes, 126

Theology, 24, 26, 40, 82
Thinker, the, 291
Thinking, 51, 58, 242, 262
Thomas a Kempis, 84
Thomson, James, *The Seasons*, 168n
Thorwaldsen, Bertel, 151
Thought(s), 14, 18, 27, 28, 49, 52, 53, 57–58, 76, 77, 95, 260, 274, 301, 304, 325, 334, 337, 371, 428
Thrasimene, Lake of, 167, 179
Three Days, the (of July Revolution, 1830), 203
Tiber River, 149, 157, 159
Timbuctoo, 129
Time, 27, 67, 73, 92, 221, 250, 252, 355, 371
Timoleon, 124, 174
Tintoretto, Il, 184; Paradise, 184
Titan, the, 367
Titian, 142, 158, 184, 230, 365, 411; Assumption of the Madonna (Venice), 183; Assumption of the Madonna (Verona), 187; Portrait of Calvin, 151; of Luther, 151; of Machiavelli, 154; of his Mistress, 158; Presentation of the Virgin, 183
Tivoli, 164, 167
Tooke, Horne, 174
Tories, 333, 339, 391
Torlonia Palace, Rome, 184
Tower of London, 120, 204, 205n, 413
Townsend, Deborah, 6
Tradition, 380
Trajan, 187
Transactions of the Royal Society, 232n, 424
Trapp, Mr. (?), 216
"Trap Rocks," 24
Travel expenses, accounts of, 205–207, 213–216, 228–229, 230, 231–232, 396
Travel, limitations of, 85, 320
Trent River, 413
Trevi, 179
Tribune, Florence, 168
Trieste, 135
Trinità dei Monti, Church of, Rome, 71
Trinitarianism, 409n
Trinity, doctrine of, 23, 409, 410
Trismegistus, Hermes, 355
Trosachs, the, 217–218
Troy, 132
Truth(s), 18, 24, 27, 33, 41, 44, 45, 46, 47, 48, 51, 52, 59, 77, 80, 83, 88, 91, 93, 95, 96, 159, 221, 266, 274, 277, 294, 309, 311, 313, 319, 329, 352, 353, 364, 367, 369, 371, 374, 375, 376, 378, 381, 415, 416, 428, 431, 433

Tucker, Abraham (pseud. Edward Search), *The Light of Nature Pursued*, 99, 100n
Tucker, Elizabeth, 62n, 118n
Tucker, Margaret, 60, 61n, 62, 64–65
Tucker, Mrs. (?), 31
Tuileries, 189, 202
Turk(s), 90, 116, 117, 136, 337
Turkish language, 118
Turner, Edward, *Elements of Chemistry*, 99, 110n, 233
Turner, Mr. (?), 354
Turner, Sharon, *The History of the Anglo-Saxons*, 416n
Tuscan taxation, 180
Tuscany, 180, 241, 404
Tycha (suburb of Syracuse), 124
Tyrant's Chamber, Syracuse, 123

Umbria, 167, 179
Unconscious, the, 309–310, 348
Understanding, the, 40, 299, 313, 320, 348, 351, 359, 365
Unitarian(s), 26, 83, 195, 203, 384, 408, 409
Unitarianism, 83, 237n, 363, 408, 410
Unity, Me., 389
Universalists, 281
Universal Man, 68
Universe, the, 39, 60, 88, 90, 96, 104, 199, 223, 255, 275, 280, 285, 297, 309, 328, 367; Idea of, 287
Upham, Charles W., *Letters on the Logos*, 233

Valerius Maximus, 15n, 319n, 357n
Valetta, Jean Parisot de la, 117
Vandyke, Sir Anthony, 139
Vane, Sir Harry, 35
Varens, Mount, 194
Varus, Quintilius, 165
Vasari, Giorgio, *Vite de' Più Excellenti Pittori*, 168n, 362; Last Supper, 175
Vases, 121
Vassalboro, Me., 389
Vatican, 150, 153, 158, 159, 160
Veii, 179
Vene, 167
Venetian government, 185
Venice, 74, 182, 183–186; Campanile, 185
Vennacher, Loch, 217
Venus, 74
Venus, Temple of, Baiae, 145, 146; Pompeii, 147
Venus de' Medici (statue), 168, 169, 173

Venus Kallipyge (statue), 127
Venus (planet), 26, 119
Venus (statue), 150
Verme, Conte del, 190–191
Verona, 187; Amphitheatre of, 187; Cathedral, 187
Veronese, Paolo, 184, 187, 411; Laura, 157
Vespucci, Amerigo, 230, 353n
Vesta, 160
Vesta, Temple of, Florence, 164; Rome, 149
Vesuvius, 141, 147, 148
Vevey, 193
Vicar of Bray (Rev. Symon Aleyn), 189
Vice(s), 46, 58, 364
Vicenza, 186–187; Cathedral, 187
Victory (statue), 188
Vienna, 154
Villa d'Este, 165
Villa Imperiale (near Venice), 183
Villa Reale, Naples, 141, 142
Viminal Hill, 166
Virgil, 142, 191, 225, 425; *Eclogue VI*, 323n
Virtue(s), 21, 41, 43, 55, 68, 69, 88, 252, 276, 307, 322, 341, 352, 354, 374, 382, 383, 384, 385
Vitruvius Pollio, Marcus, 187, 337, 367, 368n; *Of Architecture*, 338n
Volta, Count Alessandro, 94
Voltaire, 173, 175, 194
Vyasa (Krishna Dwapayana), 355

Wakefield, Gilbert, 23
Walker, Rev. James, 57
Wall, William Allen, 157, 164, 166, 176, 179–180(?), 182, 186, 187, 192, 193, 205, 292(?)
Walsh, Robert M., 166
Waltham, Mass., 21n, 234, 294, 346
War of 1812, 390
Warden, David Bailie, 198, 204
Wardlaw, Ralph, 237; *Discourses on the Principal Parts of the Socinian Controversy*, 80
Ware, Henry, Sr., 292
Warren, Deacon (?), 354
Warren, James Sullivan (?), 149, 151
Warwick Castle, 413
Washburn, Abdiel(?), 325
Washington, George, 21, 38, 50, 56, 173, 174, 194, 235, 260, 283, 315, 326, 337, 367, 369; statue of, 234; portrait, with wife (Stuart), 234
Washington, Mount, 228
Watch-watch, The, 21

Waterford, Me., 228

Waterland, Bishop Daniel, 409

Watertown, Mass., 234, 294

Watt, James, 373

Watts, Isaac, 118, 313; *Hymns and Spiritual Songs*, 340

Wave, the, 287

Wayland, Francis, "Encouragements to religious effort . . . ," 423n

Wealth, 261n, 262–263, 283, 321, 322, 373

Webb, John (?), 207, 208

Webster, Daniel, 21, 235, 257, 261, 284, 287, 297–298, 312n, 315, 317, 321, 353, 365, 373, 386–387; "The Natural Hatred of the Poor to the Rich," 386n

Webster, Noah, *An American Selection of Lessons in Reading . . .* , 14n, 20n

Weimar, 221

Weld, Cardinal Thomas, 152

Wells, Me., 388

Welsh, Jane Baillie, 220

Welsh, John, 220

Westboro, Mass., 230

West Indies, 357

Westminster Abbey, 78, 168, 407, 413, 422

Westminster Church, 414

Whale, white, 265

Wheelock, Mrs. (?), 22, 30, 31n

Whig(s), 328n, 332, 333, 334, 391

White, Gilbert, 283

Whitehaven, England, 220

White Mountains, 27, 29, 228n, 229n

Whitsuntide, 227

Wicklow Mountains, 236

Wigan, England, 247

Wiggin, Mr. and Mrs. (?), 422, 423

Wilberforce, William, 315, 414

Wilde, Richard Henry, 38n, 44n, 212n

Wiles, George, and Co., 208

Will, the, 46, 56, 257, 263, 300, 341, 382, 410

Willard, Emma, *Journal and Letters from France and Great Britain*, 271n

William IV, of England, 220

William (ship), 242

Williamson, William D., *The History of . . . Maine . . .* , 303, 305, 306, 307, 323n

Wilson, John, 412; "On Reading Mr. Clarkson's History of the Abolition of the Slave Trade," 47n

Windsor Castle, 72

Winslow (ship), 265

Winthrop, John, *History of New England*, 347n

Wisdom, 43, 48, 50, 72, 279, 312, 375

Wisner, Benjamin, 278n, 319n; "Benefits and Claims of Sabbath Schools," 423n

Witherlee, Brother (?), 96

Wittenberg, 339

Wolf, Mr. (?), 195

Woman, 72, 161, 256–257, 260, 293, 299, 300, 351

Wood, Mr. (?), 423

Worcester's *Dictionary*, 337

Wordsworth, William, 63, 78, 80, 109, 174, 220, 222–226, 312, 315, 317, 326, 337, 361, 381, 412, 422(?), 428, 430–431, 432; "Alas! What Boots the Long Laborious Quest," 291n; "Character of the Happy Warrior," 338n, 431; "Dion," 431; *The Excursion*, 87, 104n, 224, 274n; "Indignation of a High-Minded Spaniard," 224; "Itinerary Poems," 223–224; "Laodamia," 39n, 431; "Lines Composed . . . above Tintern Abbey," 92n, 224; "London, 1802," 380n; "Not 'mid the World's vain Objects," 250n; "Ode to Duty," 63, 430; "Peter Bell," 304n; *Poems dedicated to National Independence . . .* ," 251n, 326n; "The Poet's Epitaph," 430–431; "Rob Roy," 430; "To a Skylark," 224; "These Times Strike . . . ," 251; "Thoughts of a Briton on the Subjugation of Switzerland," 224; "The World is Too Much with Us," 380n

World, the, 9. *See also* Cosmos, Universe

Worms, Germany, 53

Worsley, Thomas, 173

Wotton, Sir Henry, 89; *Reliquiae Wottonianae . . .* , 424n

Wrangham, Francis, *British Plutarch*, 35n

Wright, Mrs. (?), 207

Wright, Silas, 261, 386n

Xenophanes, 298n

Xenophon, *Memorabilia*, 212n

Xerxes, 369

Yates, Rev. James, 79–80, 236–237; *Vindicating Unitarianism*, 80n

York, Duke of, 245

York, England, 80n

Young, Edward, 429n; *Night Thoughts*, 25n, 341n

Zeno, 337

Zoological Gardens, London, 414, 422

Zoroaster, 11

Zoroastrism, 11–12